# the Damron Women's Traveller

**C0-ASJ-126**

## is produced by

| | |
|---|---|
| Publisher | **Damron Company** |
| President & Editor-in-Chief | **Gina M. Gatta** |
| Managing Editor | **Ian Philips** |
| Editors | **Drew Campbell** **Erika O'Connor** |
| Director of Sales | **David Howley** |
| Art Direction & Graphic Design | **Kathleen Pratt & Beth Rabena Carr** |

## Board of Directors

| | |
|---|---|
| Executive Director | **Edward Gatta, Jr.** |
| Chairman | **Mikal Shively** |
| Secretary & Comptroller | **Louise Mock** |

## How to Contact Us

| | |
|---|---|
| Mail: | PO Box 422458 San Francisco, CA 94142-2458 |
| Email: | damron@damron.com |
| Web: | http://www.damron.com/ |
| Fax: | (415) 703-9049 |
| Phone: | (415) 255-0404 |

Copyright ©1998 Damron Company Inc. • Printed in Hong Kong

All rights reserved. Reproduction of the Damron Women's Traveller in whole or in part without written permission from the Damron Company is prohibited.

# Curve

*America's Best-Selling*
## LESBIAN MAGAZINE

DIANE BUTLER

*To Subscribe Call*
**(800) 705-0070**
*or*
**(415) 863-6538**

**Just**
**$17.95**
**per year!**

*1 Haight Street, Suite B, San Francisco, CA 94102*

# The Highlands Inn

## A LESBIAN PARADISE

*Secluded, romantic mountain hideaway on 100 scenic acres, centrally located between Boston, Montreal & the Maine coast. Close to Provincetown.*

*Experience the warm hospitality of a New England country inn YOUR way... a lesbian paradise!*

## THE HIGHLANDS INN
**PO BOX 118WT**
**VALLEY VIEW LANE**
**BETHLEHEM, NEW HAMPSHIRE 03574**
**603 • 869 • 3978**
*See Our Listing Under New Hampshire*

BLUE SCREW

Pour two ounces of Skyy vodka over ice and add three and a half ounces of orange juice. Also known as a Screwdriver, Skyydriver, Skyy Orange Juice. For exceptionally clean, clear vodka produced by four-column distillation and triple filtration, always reach for the Skyy.

DISTILLED IN AMERICA FROM AMERICAN GRAIN. 40% ALC/VOL (80 PROOF) 100% GRAIN NEUTRAL SPIRITS.
©1997 SKYY SPIRITS, INC. SAN FRANCISCO, CALIFORNIA

## Olivia Cruises & Resorts *Vacations for Women*
# Call 800-631-6277

**1997**
Hawaii Cruise, December

**1998**
Costa Rica Windstar Cruise, February
Eastern Caribbean Cruise, April
Alaska Cruise, August
Mexico Resort, October
Panama Canal Cruise, November

**1999**
Bali/Singapore Windstar Cruise, February

*Call for our free catalog!*

4400 Market, Oakland, CA 94608
Phone:510-655-0364
Fax: 510.655.4334
email: info@oliviatravel.com
Web: http://www.oliviatravel.com

**AmericanAirlines** Official Airline of Olivia Cruises and Resorts
800-433-1790 · Star Reference #S9900

# Have you
## seen your
# Girlfriends MAGAZINE
## lately?

# 800-GRL-FRND

# There's a unique place in the world ...

**Where You Can
Hold Her Hand on the
Street or Kiss Her on the
Street. Where Sun, Sea and
Freedom Meet.**

# Provincetown

**Discover Freedom.
Discover Provincetown.**

**(800) 933-1963
www.provincetown.com/wip**

# The Women Innkeepers

# A New Direction In Travel

## DIFFERENT ROADS Travel

**Full Service...Leisure & Corporate**

---

## 1998 Exclusives

---

QUANTAS VACATIONS'
**PRISCILLA TOUR**
SYDNEY TO ALICE SPRINGS
MARCH 26 - APRIL 12
BRING YOUR OWN HEELS

WINTER PARTY '98
SOUTH BEACH, MIAMI
MARCH 5-MARCH 9
TROPICAL FANTASY

GAY GAMES
AMSTERDAM
31 JULY - 09 AUG
DELUXE W/AIR

Exclusively Gay & Lesbian

# 1-888-ROADS-55
# e-mail robw@tzell.com

# club Skirts
San Francisco

## The 3rd Annual Club Skirts
# Labor Day In Monterey
# Women's Weekend

## September 4th-7th, 1998

At the private Monterey Hyatt Regency
Call (408) 372-1234 for reservations.
(Mentions Club Skirts for special room rates)

## Huge Dance Parties

Go-Go Dancers • Pool Parties
with Live Bands • Sailing •
Kayaking • Cycling •
Celebrity Golf
Tournament

Call for a detailed
brochure or to receive
reduced airline fare:
1-415-337-4962
or visit our website:
www.girlspot.com

Sponsored by
Absolut Vodka

# THE POWER OF
## *REMEMBRANCE*

Ten years after the first panel
was sewn, the NAMES Project
AIDS Memorial Quilt
continues to unleash its
power thousands of times
each year as it is displayed
in communities across
the country and around
the world.

Whether you want
to memorialize a
loved one with a
panel, use the
Quilt for HIV
prevention
education, or
support the NAMES
Project in other ways, we
need your help.
AIDS is not over.

For more information about how you
can get involved with the NAMES Project,
please call your local chapter or
(415) 882-5500, or visit the
NAMES Project online at
http://www.aidsquilt.org.

THE NAMES
PROJECT
FOUNDATION
1987-1997

THE NAMES PROJECT IS GRATEFUL TO ITS TENTH YEAR SPONSORS:

MAJOR SPONSORS                    SUPPORTING SPONSORS

AMERICAN EXPRESS    Stadtlander.s    /// UNITED AIRLINES    theAdvocate
                    Pharmacy

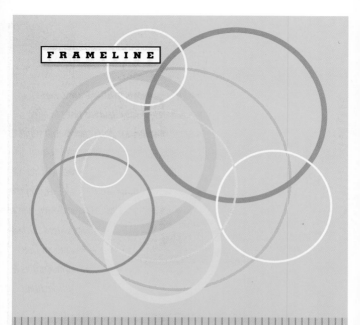

# 22nd San Francisco International Lesbian & Gay Film Festival

June 19 - 28, 1998

Castro Roxie Victoria

346 Ninth Street San Francisco, CA 94103 ph: [415] 703-8650 fax: [415] 861-1404
e-mail Frameline@AOL.com website: www.frameline.org

# Somewhere Over the Rainbow...

...You'll find easy access to all the excitement and activities the Hawaiian Islands have to offer. Discover spectacular gay beaches and night-life, and experience the natural beauty of the tropics from our convenient, ocean-front locations. With our exclusive Rest Assured Policy, you're guaranteed the best value in fine accommodations & complete satisfaction.

**ROYAL KONA RESORT** on the "Big Island"
**ROYAL LAHAINA RESORT** on Kaanapali, Maui
**KAUAI COCONUT BEACH RESORT** on Kauai
**KAHANA BEACH CONDO HOTEL** on Maui

*www.hawaiihotels.com*
*hhr@hawaiianhotels.com*

## 800·774·6641

805-494-4323

Reservations Fax:
800-774-6641

**HAWAIIAN** HOTELS & RESORTS

*Oceanfront...Affordable...
Outstanding!*

# Subscribe Today!

# The Lesbian News

## The Longest-Running National Lesbian Publication

**Subscriptions or Advertising**

**800. 458. 9888**

E-mail: TheLN@earthlink.net • P.O. Box 55 Torrance, CA 90507
Visit us at: www.LesbianNews.com

# DINAH
# SHORE
## WEEKEND
### PALM SPRINGS

**MARCH 26-29, 1998**

Produced by JOANI WEIR PRODUCTIONS
POM POM PRODUCTIONS
KLUB BANSHEE

Photos by LINVIL

LIVE CELEBRITY ENTERTAINMENT • COMEDY SHOW

POOL PARTIES • DANCE PARTIES

TENNIS COURTS • VOLLEYBALL • GOLF PACKAGES

CASUAL AND FINE DINING • SHOPPING

CONTESTS WITH AMAZING GIVEAWAYS

## The Ultimate Hotel & Entertainment Package at the All Inclusive

# DOUBLE TREE RESORT

Book today to ensure availability
For hotel and party ticket Information Call

## 310.281.7358

GREAT VACATION FOR COUPLES AS WELL AS SINGLES

EVERYTHING YOU WILL NEED OR WANT CAN BE FOUND AT THIS RESORT...JUST FLY IN...THEN PARK AND PLAY

TRULY A SPRING GETAWAY WEEKEND TO GET THE WINTER BLOOD FLOWING

For Airline reservations call 1-800 433-1790

club **Skirts**®
San Francisco

&

**Girl Bar**®
Los Angeles

Bring You

The
**1998**
**Dinah Shore**
**Weekend**
Palm Springs
California

**March 26-29**

**FOR REDUCED AIRLINE FARES**
**CALL AMERICAN AIRLINES**
**1 (800) 433-1790**
**MENTION STAR # A0738UD**

Our Proud Sponsors:

# IT ALL HAPPENS HERE. . .

Stay at the luxurious Wyndham Hotel
### exclusively ours for the weekend.

FOR HOTEL RESERVATIONS CALL 1 (760) 322-6000
be sure to mention the Dinah Shore weekend

PARTY & PLAY with 15,000 of the
HOTTEST WOMEN from across the planet.

Attend the WORLD FAMOUS PARTIES you keep hearing about.

Our Weekend features, National Recording artists,
The hottest names in Lesbian comedy, Huge pool parties,
Live Bands, BBQ'S, Golf, Tennis, and more!

This year promises to be our BEST event yet.

## BOOK TODAY BEFORE IT'S TOO LATE!
Our Hotel reservations are held with a $75 deposit.
We enforce a two week cancellation policy.

## FOR TICKET INFORMATION
## AND TO RECEIVE A FREE BROCHURE CALL
# 1 (888) 44 DINAH
[ 3 4 6 2 4 ]

Get a free issue of Tzabaco, America's premier catalog for gays, lesbians, our friends and families.

**TZABACOWEAR**

**SPA TREATMENT**

**AUTHENTIC TZABACO**

**TZABACO AT HOME**

**COMMUNITY PARTNERS**

**CAMP TZABACO**

# TZABACO™
*The "T" is silent; the quality is loud and clear.*

GET A
# $5
GIFT
CERTIFICATE
WHEN YOU
REQUEST
YOUR
FREE
ISSUE

Please send a catalog to:

Name

Address

City                    State        Zip

e-mail address

# 1-800-856-1667

visit us at www.tzabaco.com          ☎ 601A

Subscribe to
America's
Award-winning
Gay & Lesbian
Newsmagazine

One year
(26 Informative issues)
for $39.97

**theAdvocate**

# 1-800-827-0561

6922 Hollywood Blvd., Los Angeles, CA 90028
Visit our Web site: www.advocate.com

# damron

## WORLD

all-inclusive holidays

great rates on airfare

a full-service travel agency

gay-owned & operated

offices nationwide

# atlas
## TRAVEL

| usa tollfree | **888•907•9771** |
| san jose, ca | **888•280•7233** |
| charlotte, nc | **800•243•3477** |
| os angeles, ca | **310•670•6991** |

**web** http://www.damronatlas.com
**email** travel@damronatlas.com

iglta • asta • clia • iata

# Damron
# Accommodations

Now you'll always have a home away from home! The

first and only **full-color guide** to gay-friendly B&Bs, inns, hotels and other accommodations in North America, Europe and Australia. Most listings include **color photographs** (not even straight B&B guides do this!) and a comprehensive description. Sophisticated travellers will appreciate the handy multiple **cross-referenced index**. Over 400 pages.    Only **$18.95**

# Damron Road Atlas

The only lesbian & gay atlas is the perfect travelling companion to the **Address Book** and the **Women's Traveller**! This attractive full-color guide features **more than 125 maps** with color-coded dots that pinpoint lesbian & gay bars, accommodations and bookstores in **over 65 cities** and resorts worldwide. Unmapped listings cover restaurants, cafés, gyms, travel agencies, publications and more. "Info boxes" detail major annual gay events, local tourist attractions, transit, weather, best views of the city, and directions from the airport. New cities this edition: London, Paris, Berlin, Amsterdam, Albuquerque, Raleigh/Durham, and San Juan, Puerto Rico. 345 pages.                          Only **$15.95**

# Damron
# Amsterdam

## Finally, Damron does Europe!

Our first city guide has been designed to be the sleekest, most useful – and *only!* – guide you'll need. The perfect marriage of typical tourist's info and gay/lesbian listings, **Damron Amsterdam** slips in your pocket at only 4" x 5.5", with *no advertising*! It's easy-to-use when on the run, with quick-read listings and advice, a handy index, and color maps. Plus a full section on the **Gay Games 1998**. You won't need anything else but your suitcase! Only **$9.95**

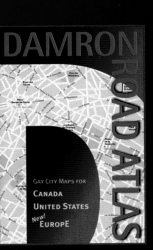

To order, ca

(800) 462-665

Ask for a FRE

DAMRON CATALO

of internation

lesbian & g

travel guide

# Damron Mail Order

| | |
|---|---|
| Women's Traveller | $12.95 |
| Women's Traveller T-Shirt  M-L-XL (size_____) | $14.00 |
| (XXL_____) | $20.00 |
| Damron Tank Top    M-L-XL      (size_____) | $14.00 |
| Damron Accommodations | $18.95 |
| Damron Address Book | $15.95 |
| Damron Road Atlas | $15.95 |
| Damron Amsterdam | $9.95 |
| Betty & Pansy's  Review  (New York) | $10.95 |
| (San Francisco) | $10.95 |
| Hot! Int'l Phrasebook (Lesbian) | $12.95 |
| The Packing Book | $8.95 |
| Everywoman's Travel Journal | $9.95 |
| Damron Mail Order Catalog | Free |

Subtotal ........................

CA Residents add 8.25%  sales tax ........................

Postage & handling -$5 + $1 per each additional item ........................

Overnight delivery add $15.00

Total ........................

**Payment:** (Send no cash or postage stamps. No C.O.D. orders.)

☐ Check/Money Order      ☐ Mastercard
   payable to **Damron Company**    ☐ Visa      ☐ Amex

Card #_____Exp: _____

Signature _____

Name_____

Address _____

City _____

State/Zip _____

Phone #_____

## Call: 1-800-462-6654 or 415-255-0404
Or Send Check or Money Order To:
Damron Company
PO Box 422458 • San Francisco, CA 94142-2458
Packaged discreetly
Please allow 4-6 weeks for check clearing and delivery.

VIN!

**NIGHTS**

COMMODATIONS

R TWO ON

E BIG
LAND OF
AWAII

Experience the exotic charm of

# THE RAINBOW'S INN

(SEE AD ON PAGE 204)

## Sweepstakes Rules

**Responsibility:** Damron Company assumes no responsibility for any delay, loss or accident caused by fault or negligence of any hotel, transportation company or local operator rendering any part of tour services, nor for any damage or inconvenience caused by late air travel. Damron Company shall not be responsible for any expense caused by loss or damage of personal items including but not limited to luggage and its contents.

**Deadline**: Entries must be received by June 15, 1998

**Prize**: 4 nights lodging in Pahoa, Hawaii. Airfare and/or transportation not included.

**Drawing**: Prize Winner will be determined by random drawing on June 20, 1998 from all entries received. Prize winners will be notified by mail and/or phone.

**Eligibility:** Open to anyone over 18 years of age, except employees of Damron Company, their affiliates and agencies or employees and agents for the resorts participating in these sweepstakes. Void where prohibited or restricted by law. All federal, state and local laws apply.

No purchase necessary. One entry per person. Complete entry form and mail to the Damron Company.

# Traveller Sweepstakes

## Clip-and-mail this coupon

*Entries received after June 15, 1998, will be entered in the 1999 Sweepstakes.*

☐ I'd be happy to accept a **FREE Damron catalog**

Name _____

Address _____

City _____

State/Zip _____

Phone _____

I hereby certify that I am 18 years of age or older, and I have read the rules and regulations governing this sweepstakes and comply.

Signature _____

complete and mail to: **Women's Traveller Sweepstakes '98**, PO Box 422458, San Francisco, CA 94142-2458

# National Resources

## AIDS/HIV

| | |
|---|---|
| **National AIDS/HIV Hotlines** | [800] 342-2437 |
| | *TTY:* [800] 243-7889 |
| | *en español:* [800] 344-7432 |
| **Sexual Health Information Line** (Canada) | [613] 563-2437 |

## HATE CRIMES

| | |
|---|---|
| **National Hate Crimes Hotline** | [800] 347-4283 |

## LEGAL RIGHTS

| | |
|---|---|
| **Lambda Legal Defense Fund** (New York City, NY) | [212] 995-8585 |
| **National Gay/Lesbian Task Force** (Washington, DC) | [202] 332-6483 |
| | *TTY:* [202] 332-6219 |

## YOUTH SERVICES

| | |
|---|---|
| **Hetrick-Martin Institute** (New York City, NY) | *voice/TTY:* [212] 674-2400 |
| **LYRIC – Lavendar Youth Recreation/ Information Center** (San Francisco, CA) | [800] 246-7743 |
| | [415] 863-3636 |

## CHEMICAL DEPENDENCY

| | |
|---|---|
| **Pride Institute** | [800] 547-7433 |

## GAY TRAVEL

| | |
|---|---|
| **International Gay/Lesbian Travel Association (IGLTA)** | [800] 448-8550 |
| **National Association of Lesbian & Gay Community Centers** (New York City, NY) | [212] 620-7310 |
| **Caritas Worldwide Homeshares** | [800] 227-4827 |
| **Box Office Tickets** | [800] 494-8497 |
| **Damron Atlas World Travel Agency** | [888] 907-9771 |
| **Damron Website & Database** | http://www.damron.com |

# Traveller Codes

Most of the codes used in this book are self-explanatory. Here are the few, however, which aren't.

▲—This symbol means an advertiser. Please look for their display ad near this listing, and be sure to tell them you saw their ad in the *Damron Women's Traveller*.

**Popular**—So we've heard from the business and/or a reader.

**Mostly Women**—80-90% lesbian crowd.

**Mostly Gay Men**—Women welcome.

**Lesbians/Gay Men**—60%(L)/40%(G) to a 40%(L)/60%(G) mix.

**Lesbigaytrans**—Lesbian, Bisexual, Gay, and Transgendered.

**Gay-friendly**—Lesbigaytrans folk are definitely welcome but are rarely the ones hosting the party.

**Neighborhood bar**—Regulars and a local flavor, often has a pool table.

**Dancing/DJ**—Usually has a DJ at least Fri & Sat nights.

**Transgender-friendly**—Transsexuals, cross-dressers, & other transgendered people welcome.

**Live Shows**—From a piano bar to drag queens and dancers.

**Multi-racial**—A good mix of women of color & their friends.

**Beer/Wine**—Beer and/or wine. No hard liquor.

**Smokefree**—No smoking anywhere inside premises.

**Private Club**—Found mainly in the US South where it's the only way to keep a liquor license. Call the bar before you go out and tell them you're visiting. They will advise you of their policy regarding membership. Usually have set-ups so can BYOB.

**Wheelchair Access**—Includes restrooms.

**IGLTA**—Member of International Gay and Lesbian Travel Association (please support our industry).

# Table of Contents

| | |
|---|---|
| Alabama | 32 |
| Alaska | 34 |
| Arizona | 36 |
| Arkansas | 46 |
| California | 50 |
| Colorado | 138 |
| Connecticut | 144 |
| Delaware | 148 |
| District of Columbia | 152 |
| Florida | 161 |
| Georgia | 192 |
| Hawaii | 202 |
| Idaho | 215 |
| Illinois | 216 |
| Indiana | 228 |
| Iowa | 232 |
| Kansas | 234 |
| Kentucky | 237 |
| Louisiana | 239 |
| Maine | 250 |
| Maryland | 258 |
| Massachusetts | 261 |
| Michigan | 296 |
| Minnesota | 306 |
| Mississippi | 310 |
| Missouri | 312 |
| Montana | 317 |
| Nebraska | 320 |
| Nevada | 321 |
| New Hampshire | 324 |
| New Jersey | 327 |
| New Mexico | 332 |
| New York | 337 |
| North Carolina | 362 |
| North Dakota | 369 |

# Table of Conter

Ohio                              370
Oklahoma                          381
Oregon                            385
Pennsylvania                      394
Rhode Island                      407
South Carolina                    409
South Dakota                      411
Tennessee                         412
Texas                             413
Utah                              436
Vermont                           438
Virginia                          441
Washington                        445
West Virginia                     456
Wisconsin                         457
Wyoming                           465

## International

Canada                            468
Caribbean                         496
Mexico                            501
Costa Rica                        509
France • Paris                    511
United Kingdom • London           515
Germany • Berlin                  520
The Netherlands • Amsterdam       522
Spain                             526

## Calendar of Tours & Events

Camping & RV                      530
1998 Tours & Tour Operators       534
Events Calendar                   551
Mail Order                        564

## ALABAMA

### Anniston (205)

BOOKSTORES & RETAIL SHOPS
**Rainbow Quick Stop** 2110 W. 10th St.
**235-2527** 6am-10pm • convenience store
• deli • tanning • gay-owned

### Birmingham (205)

INFO LINES & SERVICES
**Birmingham Gay & Lesbian Info Line**
205 32nd St. S. **326-8600** 7pm-10pm
Mon-Fri
**Common Ground** 5117 1st Ave. N.
(Covenant MCC) **599-3363/836-0300**
coffeehouse for youthful gays & lesbians

BARS & NIGHTCLUBS
**22nd Street Jazz Cafe** 710 22nd St. S.
**252-0407** clsd Sun-Tue • gay-friendly •
call for events • alternative night Wed •
live shows • food served
**Bill's Club** 208 N. 23rd St. **254-8634**
6pm-4am Wed-Sat, from 5pm Sun, clsd
Mon-Tue • mostly women • dancing/DJ •
live shows • karaoke • wheelchair access
**Club 21** 117-1/2 21st St. N. **322-0469**
10pm-4am Th-Sat • gay-friendly • danc-
ing/DJ • mostly African-American • live
shows
**Mikatam** 3719 3rd Ave. S. **592-0790**
3pm-? • mostly men • dancing/DJ •
wheelchair access • patio
**Misconceptions Tavern** 600 32nd St. S.
**322-1210** mostly gay men • food served
• videos
**The Quest Club** 416 24th St. S. **251-
4313** 24hrs • lesbians/gay men • DJ Tue-
Sun • patio • wheelchair access
**Southside Pub** 2830 7th Ave. S. **324-
0997** 3pm-midnight Sun-Wed, til 2am
Th, til 3am Fri-Sat • gay-friendly • also
restaurant
**Tool Box** 5120 5th Ave. S. **595-5120** les-
bians/gay men • neighborhood bar •
dancing/DJ • country/western

CAFES
**Bottega Cafe & Restaurant** 2240
Highland Ave. **939-1000** 11am-10pm,
clsd Sun

RESTAURANTS
**Anthony's** 2131 7th Ave. S. **324-1215**
lunch 11am-2:30pm weekdays, dinner
5pm-11pm Mon-Sat, clsd Sun • les-
bians/gay men • some veggie • full bar •
wheelchair access • $6-15

**Highlands Bar & Grill** 2011 11th Ave. S.
**939-1400** 6pm-10:30pm, bar from 4pm,
clsd Sun-Mon
**John's** 112 21st St. **322-6014** 11am-
10pm, clsd Sun
**Sarvac's** 401 18th St. S. **251-0347**
10:30am-3pm, clsd Sat

BOOKSTORES & RETAIL SHOPS
**Lodestar Books** 2020-B 11th Ave. S.
**939-3356** 10am-6pm, 1pm-5pm Sun •
lesbigay/feminist • wheelchair access
**Planet Muzica** 731 29th St. S. **254-9303**
noon-8pm, til 9pm Fri-Sat, 1pm-6pm Sun
• lesbigay gifts • videos • magazines

PUBLICATIONS
**Alabama Forum** 328-9228 statewide
paper
**The Rainbow Pages** 425-2286/985-
5609 annual business & organization
guide

TRAVEL AGENTS
**A World of Travel** 2101 Civic Center
Blvd. **458-8888/(800) 458-3597** 8am-
8pm, til 5pm Fri, 1pm-5pm Sun, clsd Sat
**Exotic Travel** 1406 17th St. S. **930-
0911/(800) 414-7015** IGLTA
**Village Travel** 1929 Cahaba Rd. **870-
4866/(800) 999-2899** IGLTA

SPIRITUAL GROUPS
**Covenant MCC** 5117 1st Ave. N. **599-
3363** 11am & 7pm Sun

EROTICA
**Alabama Adult Books** 901 5th Ave. N.
**322-7323** 24hrs
**Birmingham Adult Books** 7610 1st Ave.
N. **836-1580** 24hrs
**The Downtown Bookstore** 2731 8th Ave.
N. **328-5525**

### Decatur (205)

ACCOMMODATIONS
**Days Inn** 810 6th Ave. NE **355-
3520/(800) DAYS-INN** gay-friendly

### Dothan (334)

BARS & NIGHTCLUBS
**Chuckie Bee's** 137 N. St. Andrews St.
**794-0230** 9pm-6am Th-Sun •
lesbians/gay men • dancing/DJ • live
shows

TRAVEL AGENTS
**Accent on Travel** 802 Selkirk Dr. **793-
3984**

## Heflin (205)

### BOOKSTORES & RETAIL SHOPS
**Rainbow Quick Stop II** 2203 Hwy. 46 E. **463-7222** 24hrs • convenience store • deli • tanning • gay-owned

## Huntsville (205)

### INFO LINES & SERVICES
**Pink Triangle Alliance** 539-4235 9am-9pm • resource & info line

### BARS & NIGHTCLUBS
**Upscale** 4420 University Dr. **837-3252** 8pm-2am Fri-Sat, 6pm-2am Sun • lesbians/gay men • dancing/DJ • call for events • patio • 'Alabama's largest gay dance complex' • wheelchair access
**Vieux Carre** 1204 Posey **534-5970** 7pm-2am, from 4pm Sun • lesbians/gay men • neighborhood bar • DJ Fri-Sat • shows Sun • patio • wheelchair access

### CAFES
**La Boheme** 511 Pratt Ave. **539-5282** hours vary, clsd Mon • cafe • live shows • patio

### BOOKSTORES & RETAIL SHOPS
**Rainbow's Ltd.** 1009 Henderson Rd. #400-B **722-9220** 11am-9pm Mon-Sat, 1pm-6pm Sun, clsd Mon-Tue • lesbigay • wheelchair access

### TRAVEL AGENTS
**Ustravel Sterling Travel Agency** 720 Madison St. **533-1301**/**(800) 621-5299** IGLTA

### SPIRITUAL GROUPS
**MCC** 3015 Sparkman Dr. NW **851-6914** 11am & 6:30pm Sun, 7pm Wed

## Mobile (334)

### INFO LINES & SERVICES
**Pink Triangle AA Group** 2500 Dauphin St. **438-1679** 7pm Tue & 8pm Sat

### BARS & NIGHTCLUBS
**B-Bob's** 6157 Airport Blvd. #201 **341-0102** 5pm-? • lesbians/gay men • dancing/DJ • private club • also lesbigay gift-shop • wheelchair access
**Gabriel's Downtown** 55 S. Joachim St. **432-4900** 5pm-?, from 3pm Sun • lesbians/gay men • videos • private club
**Golden Rod** 219 Conti **433-9175** 9am-?, 24hrs wknds • lesbians/gay men • private club

### On The Roxx
**On The Roxx** 20 S. Conception **432-9056** 5pm-close, clsd Mon-Tue • mostly women • dancing/DJ • live shows • women-owned/operated
**Society Lounge** 51 S. Conception **433-9141** noon-? • popular • lesbians/gay men • dancing/DJ • live shows • private club • wheelchair access
**Zippers** 215 Conti St. **433-7436** 4pm-? • mostly gay men • neighborhood bar • private club

### SPIRITUAL GROUPS
**Cornerstone MCC** 2201 Government St. **476-4621** 11:30am & 7pm Sun

## Montgomery (334)

### INFO LINES & SERVICES
**Alabama Bureau of Tourism & Travel** 242-4169/**(800) 252-2262**
**Montgomery Institute** 514-1822 transgender info line • contact Christine Marshall

### ACCOMMODATIONS
**Lattice Inn B&B** 1414 S. Hull St. **832-9931** gay-friendly • full brkfst • swimming • hot tub • $60-80

### BARS & NIGHTCLUBS
**Jimmy Mac's** 211 Lee St. **264-5933** 7pm-2am • lesbians/gay men • dancing/DJ • private club
**The Plex** 121 Coosa St. **269-9672** 8pm-?, til 2am Sat, clsd Tue • popular • lesbians/gay men • dancing/DJ • live shows • private club

### SPIRITUAL GROUPS
**MCC** 5280 Vaughn (Unitarian Church) **279-7894** 5:30pm Sun

## Tuscaloosa (205)

### INFO LINES & SERVICES
**Gay/Lesbian/Bisexual Alliance** UA Ferguson Student Center, 3rd flr. **348-7210** self-help/rap groups
**Tuscaloosa Lesbian Coalition** 333-8227 meets 1st Sat 8pm • call for location

### BARS & NIGHTCLUBS
**Michael's** 2201 6th St. **758-9223** 6:30pm-?, clsd Sun • lesbians/gay men • dancing/DJ • live shows
**Michelle's** 2201 6th St. **758-9223** clsd Sun • mostly women • dancing/DJ

### SPIRITUAL GROUPS
**MCC** 1209 21st Ave. E. (Unity Church) **345-2044** 7pm Sun

## ALASKA

### Anchorage (907)

#### INFO LINES & SERVICES
**AA Gay/Lesbian** 1231 W. 27th Ave. **272-2312** 7pm Mon, Th & Sun

**Anchorage Gay/Lesbian Helpline 258-4777** 6pm-11pm

**I.M.R.U.2** 1057 W. Fireweed Ln. #102 **566-4678** 5:30pm-7:30pm Wed • lesbigay youth group

**Women's Resource Center** 111 W. 9th St. **276-0528** 8:30am-5pm, clsd wknds • one-on-one counseling & referrals

#### ACCOMMODATIONS
**Arctic Feather B&B** 211 W. Cook **277-3862** lesbians/gay men • 5 min. to downtown • nice view

**Aurora Winds Resort B&B** 7501 Upper O'Malley **346-2533** lesbians/gay men • on a hillside above Anchorage

**Cheney Lake B&B** 6333 Colgate Dr. **337-4391/(888) 337-4391** gay-friendly • smokefree • lesbian-run • $65-85

**Gallery B&B** 1229 'G' St. **274-2567** full brkfst • $35-75

**Rose-Beth's B&B 337-6779** mostly women • unconfirmed

#### BARS & NIGHTCLUBS
**O'Brady's Burgers & Brew** 6901 E. Tudor Rd. **338-1080** 10am-midnight • gay-friendly • some veggie

**Raven** 618 Gambell **276-9672** 11am-2:30am • lesbians/gay men • neighborhood bar • wheelchair access

▲ **The Wave** 3103 Spenard Rd. **561-9283** 6pm-2:30am, clsd Sun-Tue (seasonal) • lesbians/gay men • dancing/DJ • live shows • theme nights • videos • espresso bar upstairs (year-round) • wheelchair access

#### RESTAURANTS
**China Lights** 12110 Business Blvd., Eagle River **694-8080** 10:30am-10pm

**Garcia's** Business Blvd. (next to Safeway), Eagle River **694-8600** Mexican • $9-15

**Simon & Seafort's** 420 'L' St. **274-3502** lunch & dinner, seafood & prime rib

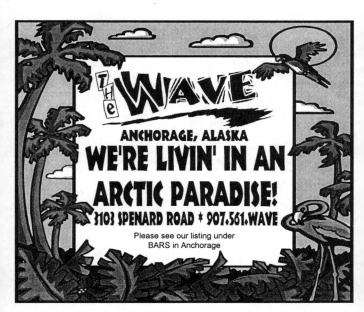

BOOKSTORES & RETAIL SHOPS
**Cyrano's Bookstore & Cafe** 413 'D' St. **274-2599** 10am-6pm • live shows • food served • beer/wine • wheelchair access

PUBLICATIONS
**Anchorage Press 561-7737** alternative paper • arts & entertainment listings
**Identity Northview 258-4777** also sponsors 4th Fri potluck

TRAVEL AGENTS
**Apollo** 1207 W. 47th Ave. **561-0661**/(800) 770-0661 IGLTA

SPIRITUAL GROUPS
**Lamb of God MCC** 417 Barrow St. **258-5266** 11am Sun & 7pm Wed
**Unitarian Universalist Fellowship** 3201 Turnagain St. **248-3737/248-0715** 9am & 10:30am Sun

EROTICA
**Ace's** 305 W. Dimond Blvd. **522-1987** 24hrs

## Fairbanks (907)

INFO LINES & SERVICES
**Lesbian/Gay Info Line** 458-8288 8pm-10pm Tue & Th

ACCOMMODATIONS
**Alta's B&B 389-2582/457-0246** lesbians/gay men • log home above the Chatanika River • full brkfst • $50-100
**Billie's Backpackers Hostel** 2895 Mack Rd. **457-2034** gay-friendly • hostel & campsites • kids ok • food served • women-run • $15-20
**Crabtree Guest House 451-6501** mostly gay men • shared baths • kitchens • kids ok
▲ **Fairbanks Hotel 456-6411**/(888) 329-4685 gay-friendly • $55-95

BARS & NIGHTCLUBS
**Palace Saloon** Alaskaland 456-5960 7pm-10pm, til 3am Fri-Sat (seasonal) • gay-friendly • dancing/DJ • live shows • gay after 11pm Fri-Sat only

## Homer (907)

ACCOMMODATIONS
**Island Watch B&B** 235-2265 gay-friendly • also cabins • full brkfst • kitchens • smokefree • kids/pets ok • wheelchair access • women-owned/run • $80-110/double

❖

THE
FAIRBANKS
HOTEL

517 THIRD AVENUE
FAIRBANKS, AK 99701

❖ 24 HR SERVICE
❖ (907) 456-6411
❖ FAX (907) 456-1792
❖ TOLL FREE
   (888) FBX-HOTL
   (888) 329-4685

❖ NEWLY RESTORED
❖ THE OLDEST HOTEL
   IN FAIRBANKS
❖ REASONABLE
   RATES
❖ ART DECO STYLE
❖ FREE AIRPORT &
   TRAIN SHUTTLE
   SERVICE WITH
   RESERVATIONS

*Serving guests since World War II. Stay at the newly restored, historic, Fairbanks Hotel in the heart of the Golden Heart City!*

www.alaska.net/~fbxhotl
fbxhotl@alaska.net

ENTERTAINMENT & RECREATION
**Alaska Fantastic Fishing Charters**
**(800) 478-7777** deluxe cabin cruiser for big-game fishing (halibut)

## Juneau (907)

INFO LINES & SERVICES
**Alaska Tourism Marketing Council**
465-2010 ask for vacation planner
**SEAGLA Helpline** 586-4297

ACCOMMODATIONS
**Pearson's Pond Luxury Inn** 4541 Sawa Cir. **789-3772** gay-friendly • hot tub • $79-169

RESTAURANTS
**Inn at the Summit Waterfront Cafe** 455 S. Franklin St. **586-2050** 5pm-10pm • full bar • $15-38

ENTERTAINMENT & RECREATION
**Women's Prerogative** KTO (104.3 & 103.1 FM) **586-1670** 9pm Wed • women's music

## Ketchikan (907)

ACCOMMODATIONS
**Millar Street House** 225-1258/(800) 287-1607 gay-friendly • also kayak tours

## Kodiak (907)

SPIRITUAL GROUPS
**St. James the Fisherman Episcopal Church** 421 Thorsheim **486-5276** 7:30am, 10am & 7pm Sun

## Seward (907)

ACCOMMODATIONS
**Sauerdough Lodging** 224-8946 gay-friendly • $125-210

## Sitka (907)

ACCOMMODATIONS
**Crescent Harbor Hideaway** 709 Lincoln St. **747-4900** gay-friendly • also marine tours • $79-105

# ARIZONA

## Bisbee (520)

BARS & NIGHTCLUBS
**St. Elmo's** 36 Brewery Gulch Ave. **432-5578** 10am-1am • gay-friendly • live bands Fri-Sat

## Bullhead City (520)

*(includes Laughlin, Nevada)*

BARS & NIGHTCLUBS
**The Bandstand** 1119 Hwy. 95 **754-2414** 9am-1am • lesbians/gay men • neighborhood bar • live shows • karaoke Tue-Wed • dancing/DJ Fri-Sun

## Chandler (602)

TRAVEL AGENTS
**Adventure Bound Travel** 2100 W. Chandler Blvd. #38 **963-2506** IGLTA

## Flagstaff (520)

ACCOMMODATIONS
▲ **Hotel Monte Vista** 100 N. San Francisco St. **779-6971/(800) 545-3068** gay-friendly • historic lodging circa 1927 • food served • full bar • cafe • $25-120
**Piñon Country Cottage** 5339 Parsons Ranch Rd. **526-4797** mostly women • cabin • $65

BARS & NIGHTCLUBS
**Charlie's** 23 N. Leroux **779-1919** 11am-1am, Sun brunch • gay-friendly • food served • some veggie • patio • wheelchair access • $7-14
**Monte Vista Lounge** 100 N. San Francisco St. **779-6971** 10am-1am, cafe from 6am • gay-friendly • live shows • some veggie

CAFES
**Cafe Olé** 119 S. San Francisco **774-8272** til 8pm

RESTAURANTS
**Pasto** 19 E. Aspen **779-1937** 5pm-9:30pm, til 10pm Fri-Sat • Italian • $7-15

BOOKSTORES & RETAIL SHOPS
**Aradia Books** 116 W. Cottage **779-3817** 10:30am-5:30pm, clsd Sun • lesbian/feminist • wheelchair access • women-owned/run

## Jerome (520)

ACCOMMODATIONS
**The Cottage Inn Jerome** 634-0701 kids ok • pets ok

## Kingman (520)

ACCOMMODATIONS
**Kings Inn Best Western** 2930 E. Andy Devine **753-6101/(800) 528-1234** gay-friendly • swimming • non-smoking rms. avail. • food served • bakery on premises

## Lake Havasu City (520)

TRAVEL AGENTS
**Sun Kachina Travel** 1987 McCullich #108 **855-0066** IGLTA

EROTICA
**Adult World Bookstore** 3596 N. London Bridge Rd. **764-3066**

## Mesa (602)

EROTICA
**Castle Superstore** 8315 E. Apache Trail **986-6114** 24hrs

## Phoenix (602)

*(see also Scottsdale & Tempe)*

INFO LINES & SERVICES
**AA Lambda Club** 2622 N. 16th St. **264-1341** 6pm & 8pm
**Arizona Office of Tourism** 230-7733/(800) 842-8257
**Lesbian Resource Project** 3136 N. 3rd Ave. **266-5542/266-5797 (TDD)** call for events • social/educational groups
**Lesbian/Gay Community Switchboard** 3136 N. 3rd Ave. **234-2752 (ALSO TDD)** 10am-10pm (volunteers permitting)
**Valley of the Sun Gay/Lesbian Center** 3136 N. 3rd Ave. **265-7283**

# Enjoy historic downtown Flagstaff at the charming <u>Hotel Monte Vista</u>.

*Northern Arizona's oldest, nicest historic hotel.*

We're as nice as we look!

Did you know that Barbara Stanwyck slept here?

- Restaurant, bar & lounge; live entertainment nightly
- Inexpensive suites, double and single rooms
- Convenient to Sedona, the Grand Canyon and Oak Creek Canyon
- Grand Canyon access by auto, train, plane and bus

*Hotel Monte Vista*
*100 N. San Francisco St.*
*Flagstaff, AZ 86001*
*(520) 779-6971 Fax: 779-2904*

**For reservations, call toll free at 800-545-3068.**

## Phoenix

*C*an't stand another cloudy day? Sick of spending your summers in a fog bank and your winters in a snowdrift? Try Phoenix, a sun-worshiper's paradise. Here the winters are warm and the summers sizzle. And each day ends with a dramatic desert sunset.

The people of Phoenix have perfected many ways to soak up the incredible sunshine. Some do it as they hike or horseback ride along the many trails along Squaw Peak (off Lincoln Dr.) or Camelback Mountain. Some do it by the pool or on the golf course or tennis court. Some do it as they hover over the valley in a hot air balloon.

Some do it between galleries as they enjoy the popular Thursday night Art Walk along Main St., Marshall Way and 5th Ave. in Scottsdale. Others do it dashing from the car to the Scottsdale Galleria or Fashion Square. Still others get sun on the half-hour trip north to Rawhide (563-1880), Arizona's real live western town and Native American village, complete with gunfights and hayrides.*

What do lesbians do in Phoenix? Pretty much the same things, but usually in couples. Couples will feel free to enjoy themselves at **Be My Guest B&B** or **Mom's,** the women-only B&Bs in town. The single lesbian traveller searching for someone to share her journeys should try one of the friendly women's bars in town: **Desert Rose** or **Incognito Lounge.** Phoenix also has a large sober women's community and its own AA club house. And many lesbians just like to get away from it all on camping, fishing, or hiking trips.

*Driving in the Arizona desert during the summer can be dangerous. Always carry a few gallons of water in your vehicle, and check all fluids in your car both before you leave and frequently during your trip.

## Phoenix (602)

**Where the Girls Are:** Everywhere. Phoenix doesn't have one section of town where lesbians hang out, but the area between 5th Ave.-32nd St., and Camelback-Thomas streets does contain most of the women's bars.

**Lesbigay Pride:** June: 352-7165.

**Annual Events:**

August - **Dog Days of Summer**: 266-5542. 3-day lesbian extravaganza.

September - **Women's Music Festival**: 266-5542.

October - **AIDS Walk**: 265-3300.

**City Info:** 254-6500. Arizona Office of Tourism: 230-7733, 800/842-8257.

**Attractions:** Castles & Coasters Park on Black Canyon Fwy & Peoria. Phoenix Zoo & Desert Botanical Garden in Papago Park.

**Best View:** South Mountain Park at sunset, watching the city lights come on.

**Weather:** Beautifully mild and comfortable (60°s-80°s) October through March or April. Hot (90°s-100°s) in summer. August brings the rainy season (severe monsoon storms) with flash flooding.

**Transit:** Yellow Cab: 252-5252. Super Shuttle: 244-9000. Phoenix Transit: 253-5000.

# DINAH SHORE
## PALM SPRINGS WEEKEND
### MARCH 26-29, 1998

The Ultimate Hotel & Entertainment Package at the All Inclusive

**DOUBLE TREE RESORT**

Book today to ensure availability. For hotel and party ticket Info Call

# 310.281.7358

For Airline reservations call
1•800•433•1790

Produced by JOANI WEIR PRODUCTIONS • POM POM PRODUCTIONS • KLUB BANSHEE

**Valley One In Ten** 3136 N. 3rd Ave. **264-5437** 7pm Wed • youth group • HIV peer education

### ACCOMMODATIONS

**Arrowzona 'Private' Casitas** 561-1200/(800) 266-7829 lesbians/gay men • 2-rm B&B in private home • hot tub • IGLTA • $69-199

**Be My Guest B&B** 893-6663 women only • swimming • great location

**Bed & Breakfast Inn Arizona** 561-0335/(800) 266-7829 gay-friendly• $45-295

**Larry's B&B** 502 W. Claremont Ave. **249-2974** mostly gay men • B&B-private home • full brkfst • swimming • hot tub • nudity • $45-65

**Mom's B&B** 5903 W. Cortez, Glendale 979-2869 women only • swimming • available for outdoor weddings/commitment ceremonies • wheelchair access • women-owned/run

**Stewart's B&B** 1319 E. Hayward 861-2500 mostly gay men • leather-friendly • nudity • wheelchair access • $55-75

**Westways Resort** 488-1110 gay-friendly • swimming • IGLTA

**Windsor Cottage B&B** 62 W. Windsor 264-6309 lesbians/gay men • 2 English Tudor-style cottages • swimming • nudity • patio • gay-owned/run • $65-115

### BARS & NIGHTCLUBS

**307 Lounge** 222 E. Roosevelt **252-0001** 6am-1am • mostly gay men • neighborhood bar • transgender-friendly • live shows • food served • Sun brunch from 10am • wheelchair access

**Ain't Nobody's Bizness** 3031 E. Indian School #7 **224-9977** 2pm-1am • lesbians/gay men • dancing/DJ • complimentary food Fri-Sat • wheelchair access

**Apollos** 5749 N. 7th St. **277-9373** 8am-1am, from 10am Sun • mostly gay men • neighborhood bar • karaoke • darts

**Cash Inn** 2140 E. McDowell Rd. **244-9943** 6pm-1am, from 3pm Sun, clsd Mon-Tue • lesbians/gay men • dancing/DJ • country/western • wheelchair access

**Country Club Bar & Grill** 4428 N. 7th Ave. **264-4553** 11am-1am • lesbians/gay men • dancing/DJ • country/western • karaoke • food served • patio • wheelchair access

**Desert Rose** 4301 N. 7th Ave. **265-3233** 11am-1am • women only • country/western • live shows • food served • wheelchair access • women-owned/run

**Foster's** 4343 N. 7th Ave. **263-8313** 4pm-1am • lesbians/gay men • dancing/DJ • 'Trash Disco' Sun • leather-friendly • wheelchair access

**Harley's 155** 155 W. Camelback Rd. **274-8505** noon-1am • lesbians/gay men • dancing/DJ • also 'The Cell' in back • mostly gay men • leather

**Incognito Lounge** 2424 E. Thomas Rd. **955-9805** 2pm-1am, til 3am Fri-Sat, clsd Mon • popular • mostly women • dancing/DJ • live bands • wheelchair access

**J.C.'s Fun One Lounge** 5542 N. 43rd Ave., Glendale **939-0528** 11am-1am • lesbians/gay men • dancing/DJ • live shows • wheelchair access

**Marlys'** 15615 N. Cave Creek Rd. **867-2463** 3pm-1am • lesbians/gay men • neighborhood bar • live bands • food served

**The Metro/Detour** 4102 E. Thomas Rd. **224-9471/224-9457** mostly gay men • women's night Wed at 'Cat Walk' • 3-level dance floor • dancing/DJ • leather • live shows • patio • wheelchair access

**Nasty Habits** 3108 E. McDowell Rd. **231-9427** noon-1am • lesbians/gay men • sports bar • dancing/DJ • karaoke Fri • videos

**Pookie's Cafe** 4540 N. 7th St. **277-2121** 11am-midnight • lesbians/gay men • Sun brunch • live shows • $5-7

**The Roscoe's on 7th** 4531 N. 7th St. **285-0833** 3pm-1am, from 1pm Sun • mostly gay men • pub appetizers • sports bar

**Trax** 1724 E. McDowell **254-0231** 6am-1am, til 3am Fri-Sat • popular • mostly men • dancing/DJ • alternative • leather • wheelchair access

**Winks** 5707 N. 7th St. **265-9002** 11am-1am • popular • lesbians/gay men • live shows • piano bar • lunch & Sun brunch served • wheelchair access • $5-9

### RESTAURANTS

**Alexi's** 3550 N. Central **279-0982** clsd Sun • intercont'l • full bar • patio • $6-9

**Azz Jazz** 1906 E. Camelback Rd. **263-8482** 5pm-10pm, til 1am wknds, clsd Mon • Argentinian • live shows • full bar • wheelchair access • $10-15

**Eddie's Grill** 4747 N. 7th St. **241-1188**
lunch & dinner, clsd Sun • full bar •
some veggie • patio • wheelchair access
• $10-18

**Katz's Deli** 5144 N. Central **277-8814**
7am-3pm, til 7:30pm Tue-Fri • some
veggie • $5

**Los Dos Molinos** 8646 S. Central Ave.
**243-9113** 11am-9pm Tue-Sun • robust
home cooking

**Vincent Guerithault on Camelback**
3930 E. Camelback Rd. **224-0225**
Southwestern fare w/touch of French
chic • $19.75 à la carte

## BOOKSTORES & RETAIL SHOPS

▲ **Obelisk the Bookstore** 24 W.
Camelback #A **266-2665** 10am-10pm,
noon-8pm Sun • lesbigay • wheelchair
access

**Sexy Styles** 2104 W. Camelback Rd. **242-
2886** 11am-7pm, til 6pm Fri-Sat, clsd
Sun • wigs • leather • lingerie • shoes
up to size 14

**Unique on Central** 4700 N. Central Ave.
#105 **279-9691/(800) 269-4840** 10am-
9pm, til 6pm Sun • cards, gifts & more •
wheelchair access

## PUBLICATIONS
**Echo Magazine** 266-0550

## TRAVEL AGENTS
**All About Destinations** Gallery Three
Plaza, 3819 N. 3rd St. **277-2703/(800)
375-2703** IGLTA

**Artemis Travel & Trading Co.** 12235 N.
Cave Creek Rd. #6-341 **493-8382** IGLTA

**Casablanca Travel** 3030 N. Central
#106 **631-9050** IGLTA

**FirsTravel Ltd.** 4700 N. Central Ave.
#205 **265-0666/(800) 669-8885** IGLTA

**TGI Travel Agency** 5540 W. Glendale
Ave. #A-102, Glendale **939-1445/(800)
289-2172** IGLTA

**Travel Easy** 1133 E. Glendale Ave. **954-
4060** IGLTA

## SPIRITUAL GROUPS
**Augustana Lutheran Church** 2604 N.
14th St. **265-8400** 10:30am Sun

**Casa de Cristo Evangelical Church**
1029 E. Turney **265-2831** 10am &
6:30pm Sun

*largest selection
of womens titles in
San Diego & Phoenix*

# obelisk
**A source like no other**

1029 University Ave
San Diego, CA 92103
**619-297-4171**

24 W. Camelback #A
Phoenix, AZ 85013
**602-266-2665**

Community Church of Hope 440 N. Central **234-2180** 10am Sun • independent Christian church & counseling center

Dignity/Integrity Phoenix 2222 S. Price Rd. **222-8664** weekly services in Phoenix & Tempe • call for info

Gentle Shepherd MCC 2nd & Osborne **285-9020** 10am Sun

### GYMS & HEALTH CLUBS

Beauvais Fitness Center 1301 E. University **921-9551** gay-friendly

### EROTICA

The Barn 5021 W. Indian School Rd. **245-3008** 24hrs

Castle Superstore 300 E. Camelback **266-3348** 24hrs • also 5501 E. Washington 231-9837 • 8802 N. Black Canyon Fwy. 995-1641 • 8315 E. Apache Trl. 986-6114

International Bookstore 3640 E. Thomas Rd. **955-2000** 24hrs

Tuff Stuff 1714 E. McDowell Rd. **254-9651** 10am-6pm, til 3pm Sat, clsd Sun-Mon • leather shop

## Scottsdale                    (602)

### BARS & NIGHTCLUBS

B.S. West 7125 5th Ave. (pedestrian mall) **945-9028** 1pm-1am • lesbians/gay men • dancing/DJ • videos • Sun BBQ • wheelchair access

The Works 7223 E. 2nd St. **946-4141** 10pm-3am Th-Sun • popular • mostly gay men • dancing/DJ • alternative • live shows • videos • call for events • wheelchair access

### RESTAURANTS

AZ-88 7535 E. Scottsdale Mall **994-5576** 11am-midnight • upscale American • some veggie • $8-15

Malee's 7131 E. Main **947-6042** lunch & dinner • Thai • plenty veggie • $12-20

### TRAVEL AGENTS

Dolphin Travel Services 10632-B N. Scottsdale Rd. **998-9191**/**(800) 847-2835** IGLTA

### EROTICA

Zorba's Adult Book Shop 2924 N. Scottsdale Rd. **941-9891** 24hrs

## Sedona                    (520)

### ACCOMMODATIONS

Huff & Puff, A Straw Bale Inn 567-9066 gay-friendly • kids ok • pets by arr. • tours avail. • near Montezuma's Well • solar powered • wheelchair access • lesbian-owned/run • $50-70

Iris Garden Inn 390 Jordan Rd. **282-2552/(800) 321-8988** gay-friendly • motel • smokefree • $55-119

Mustang B&B 4257 Mustang Dr., Cottonwood **646-5929** lesbians/gay men • full brkfst • 25 min. from Sedona • smokefree • 1 RV hookup • movie theater • $45-65

Paradise Ranch Guesthouse 135 Kachina Dr. **282-9769** women only • smokefree • kitchens • lesbian-owned/run • $85-125

### RESTAURANTS

Judi's 40 Soldier Pass Rd 282-4449 $11-21

Shugrue's West 2250 W. Hwy. 89-A **282-2943**

## Tempe                    (602)

### BOOKSTORES & RETAIL SHOPS

Changing Hands 414 S. Mill **966-0203** 10am-9pm, til 10pm Fri-Sat, noon-5pm Sun • general • lesbigay section

### EROTICA

Modern World 1812 E. Apache **967-9052** 24hrs

## Tucson                    (520)

### INFO LINES & SERVICES

AA Gay/Lesbian 624-4183 many mtgs. • call for schedule

Wingspan Community Center 422 N. 4th Ave. **624-1779** lesbigay & youth info • lesbigay AA • library • call for events

### ACCOMMODATIONS

Casa Alegre B&B Inn 316 E. Speedway Blvd. **628-1800/628-5654** gay-friendly • 1915 craftsman-style bungalow • full brkfst • hot tub • swimming • smokefree • kids ok by arr. • $70-105

Casa Tierra Adobe B&B Inn 11155 W. Calle Pima **578-3058** gay-friendly • full brkfst • hot tub • smokefree • kids age 3+ ok • patio • 30 min. outside Tucson • $75-95

# *Tucson*

**M**ention Tucson's torrid weather, and you're likely to hear, "Yeah, but it's dry heat!"

Whether you believe that or know better, you can make the most of Tucson's sunshine. Leave your overcoat at home, pack your SPF 160 sun lotion and a good pair of shades, and prepare for a great time.

You'll see the rainbow everywhere, but mainly around shops on 4th Ave., the downtown Arts District, and residences in the Armory Park Historic neighborhood. (The annual homes tour might as well be called the 'who's who of home-owning homos'!)

Downtown is where you'll find such gay-friendly establishments as **Cafe Magritte, Rainbow Planet Coffee House, the Grill on Congress, Cafe Quebec,** and **Hydra,** purveyor of fine BDSM gear. At night, grab a beer in the **Tap Room** at **Hotel Congress** or pay a visit to one of the better-known bars like **Ain't Nobody's Bizness.**

Just a few blocks notheast is 4th Ave., where you'll find queer businesses standing strong between sports bars. In addition to gay-owned hair and skin care salons, real estate offices, restaurants, and retail stores, you'll find **Wingspan,** the lesbigay community center, and **Antigone Books,** one of the best women's bookstore in the Southwest. Also check out the très lavender women's bookstore in N. Oracle, **Girlfriends;** they also feature acoustic music now and then.

West of Tucson, near the famed Desert Museum, is a women's community called Adobe Land. For general outdoor hilarity, Tucson's gay softball league can't be beat.

Lesbigay spirituality and healing groups abound, as do Latina, discussion, writers, and readers groups. For films, try the Loft or Catalina theaters and The Screening Room or one of the three film festivals.

When you're done with the entertainment, and the temperature at midnight has dropped its usual 30 or 40 degrees, settle in at one or the many gay-owned or gay-friendly B&B's in town.

*– By reader Karen Falkenstrom. Updated by Damron editors.*

**Catalina Park Inn** 309 E. 1st St. **792-4541**/**(800) 792-4885** gay-friendly • full brkfst • smokefree • kids 10+ okay • $50-115

**Elysian Grove Market B&B** 400 W. Simpson **628-1522** gay-friendly • renovated historic adobe building w/garden • full brkfst • smokefree • kitchen in suite • women-owned/run • $75

**Gateway Villas B&B** 228 N. 4th Ave. **740-0767** gay-friendly • swimming • rms & suites

**Hacienda del Sol Guest Ranch Resort** 5601 N. Hacienda del Sol Rd. **299-1501**/**(800) 728-6514** gay-friendly • rms & casitas • food served • massage avail.

**Hotel Congress** 311 E. Congress **622-8848**/**(800) 722-8848** gay-friendly • food served • $29-55

**Montecito House** 795-7592 gay-friendly • smokefree • kids ok by arr. • lesbian-owned/run • $30-40

**Natural B&B** 3150 E. Presidio Rd. **881-4582** lesbians/gay men • full brkfst • smokefree • private/shared baths • kids ok • massage avail. • $55-65

**Santuario Inn Tucson** 519-0390 lesbians/gay men • relaxation retreat

**Suncatcher B&B** 105 N. Avenida Javelina **(800) 835-8012** gay-friendly • full brkfst • hot tub • swimming • smokefree • kids ok • on 4 acres • wheelchair access

▲ **Tortuga Roja B&B** 2800 E. River Rd. **577-6822**/**(800) 467-6822** lesbians/gay men • hot tub • swimming • nudity • smokefree • kids ok in cottage • wheelchair access • IGLTA • $50-95

### BARS & NIGHTCLUBS

**Ain't Nobody's Bizness** 2900 E. Broadway #118 **318-4838** 2pm-1am • mostly women • dancing/DJ • wheelchair access

**Congress Tap Room** 311 E. Congress (at Hotel Congress) **622-8848** 11am-1am • dance club from 9pm • gay-friendly • alternative • live bands • theme nights

# TORTUGA ROJA
## BED & BREAKFAST

**2800 EAST RIVER ROAD
TUCSON, ARIZONA 85718
(520) 577-6822 • (800) 467-6822**

**The Fineline** 101 W. Drachman **882-4953** 6pm-1am, til 4am Fri-Sat, clsd Sun • gay-friendly • dancing/DJ • 18+

**Hours** 3455 E. Grant **327-3390** noon-1am • popular • lesbians/gay men • neighborhood bar • dancing/DJ • country/western (Wed-Sun) • patio • wheelchair access

**IBT's (It's About Time)** 616 N. 4th Ave. **882-3053** noon-1am • lesbians/gay men • dancing/DJ • live shows • wheelchair access

**Stonewall Eagle** 2921 N. 1st Ave. **624-8805** noon-1am • 'Stonewall' from 9pm • dancing/DJ • leather • patio • wheelchair access

## CAFES

**Cafe Magritte** 254 E. Congress **884-8004**

**Cafe Quebec** 121 E. Broadway **798-3552**

**Rainbow Planet Coffee House** 606 N. 4th Ave. **620-1770** 9am-10pm

**Stacia's Bakery Cafe** 3022 E. Broadway **325-5549** 7am-5:30pm, 8am-4:30pm Sat, clsd Sun • low-fat baked goods • gourmet lunch menu • gay-owned/run

## RESTAURANTS

**Blue Willow** 2616 N. Campbell **795-8736** brkfst served all day • $5-8

**Cafe Sweetwater** 340 E. 6th St. **622-6464** lunch & dinner • $5-15

**Cafe Terra Cotta** 4310 N. Campbell Ave. **577-8100** dinner til 10:30pm • $6-20

**The Grill on Congress** 100 E. Congress **623-7621**

## BOOKSTORES & RETAIL SHOPS

**Antigone Books** 411 N. 4th Ave. **792-3715** 10am-6pm, til 5pm Sat, noon-5pm Sun • lesbigay/feminist • wheelchair access

**Girlfriends** 3540 N. Oracle Rd #126 **888-4475** noon-11pm, til 9pm Sun, clsd Mon • lesbian bookstore & cafe • occasional acoustic music • wheelchair access

## PUBLICATIONS

**The Observer** 622-7176

## TRAVEL AGENTS

**Arizona Travel Center** 2502 E. Grant Rd. **323-3250/(800) 553-5471** IGLTA

**PSI Travel** 2100 N. Wilmot #203 **296-3788** IGLTA

## SPIRITUAL GROUPS

**Cornerstone Fellowship** 2902 N. Geronimo **622-4626** 10:30am Sun • 7pm Wed Bible study

**Water of Life MCC** 3269 N. Mountain Ave. **292-9151** 10:45am Sun

## EROTICA

**The Bookstore Southwest** 5754 E. Speedway Blvd. **790-1550**

**Caesar's Bookstore** 2540 N. Oracle Rd. **622-9479**

**Hydra** 145 E. Congress **791-3711** SM gear

# Yuma (520)

## EROTICA

**Bargain Box** 408 E. 16th St. **782-6742** 24hrs

## ARKANSAS

### Crossett (501)

CAFES

**Pig Trail Cafe** Rte. 16, east of Elkins 643-3307 6am-9pm • popular • American/Mexican • under $5

### Eureka Springs (501)

ACCOMMODATIONS

**Arbour Glen Victorian Inn B&B** 7 Lema 253-9010/(800) 515-4536 gay-friendly • historic Victorian home • full brkfst • jacuzzis • fireplaces • $75-125

**Cedarberry Cottage B&B** 3 Kings Hwy. 253-6115/(800) 590-2424 gay-friendly • full brkfst • kids ok • $69-89

▲ **The Chili Pepper B&B** 110 Wall St. 253-7373 gay-friendly • full brkfst • hot tub • smokefree • women-owned

**Cliff Cottage B&B Inn** 42 Armstrong St. 253-7409/(800) 799-7409 gay-friendly • suites & guestrooms in 1892 'Painted Lady' • full brkfst • Victorian picnic lunches • smokefree • cruises • massage • women-owned/run • $99-140

**Crescent Dragonwagon's Dairy Hollow House B&B** 516 Spring St. 253-7444/(800) 562-8650 gay-friendly • full brkfst • hot tub • special occasion dining • call for dates

**The Gardener's Cottage** 253-9111/(800) 833-3394 gay-friendly • seasonal • private cottage on wooded site • jacuzzi • smokefree • kitchens • kids ok • women-owned/run • $95-115

**Golden Gate Cottage B&B** 253-5291 women only • on the lake • hot tub • swimming • kitchens • women-owned/run • $35-50

**Greenwood Hollow Ridge B&B** 253-5283 exclusively lesbigay • on 5 quiet acres • full brkfst • near outdoor recreation • shared/private baths • kitchens • pets ok • RV hookups • lesbian-owned/run • $45-65

**Heart of the Hills B&B** 5 Summit 253-7468/(800) 253-7468 gay-friendly • full brkfst • kids/pets ok • evening desserts • patio

**Maple Leaf Inn** 6 Kings Hwy. 253-6876/(800) 372-6542 gay-friendly • restored Victorian • full brkfst • hot tub • kids ok • gay-owned/run • $85-105

# The Chili Pepper
# Bed & Breakfast

Enjoy personal hospitality in the beautiful Ozarks. Near to the fabulous shopping of Eureka Springs and less than an hour from Branson, MO

 Full Breakfast

 Evening refreshments

Serenity garden

Call for a brochure and reservations

110 Wall Street

Eureka Springs, AR 72632

(501) 253-7373

**Morningstar Retreat** 253-5995/(800) 298-5995 gay-friendly • cabins • $75-95/double • $10/each add'l person

**Palace Hotel & Bath House** 135 Spring St. **253-7474** gay-friendly • bath house open to all • wheelchair access

**Pond Mountain Lodge & Resort** 253-5877/(800) 583-8043 gay-friendly • mountain-top inn on 159 acres • cabins • full brkfst • swimming • smokefree • kids ok • wheelchair access • lesbian-owned/run • $60-140

**Rock Cottage Gardens** 10 Eugenia St. 253-8659/(800) 624-6646 gay-friendly • cottages • full brkfst • hot tub • gay-owned/run • $95-110

**Singleton House B&B** 11 Singleton 253-9111/(800) 833-3394 gay-friendly • full brkfst • kids ok • restored 1890s country Victorian home • near shops • women-owned/run • $65-95

**The Woods** 50 Wall St. 253-8281 gay-friendly • cottages • jacuzzis • kitchens • smokefree • $99-139

### BARS & NIGHTCLUBS

**Celebrity Club** 75 Prospect (Crescent Hotel) **253-9766** gay-friendly • 6pm-1am Fri-Sat • grill • under $5 • also sports bar • karaoke on wknds

**Center Street Bar & Grille** 10 Center St. **253-8102** 6pm-2am • kitchen open til 10pm Th-Mon, clsd Sun • Mexican • plenty veggie

**Chelsea's Corner Cafe** 10 Mountain St. 253-6723 11am-2am, clsd Sun • gay-friendly • patio • also restaurant • plenty veggie • women-owned/run • $5-8

### RESTAURANTS

**Autumn Breeze** Hwy. 23 S. **253-7734** 5pm-9pm • cont'l • $9-18

**Cottage Inn** Hwy. 62 W. **253-5282** seasonal • lunch & dinner, clsd Mon • Mediterranean • $8-19

**Ermilio's** 26 White **253-8806** 5pm-8:30pm, clsd Th • Italian • plenty veggie • $8-17

**Jim & Brent's Bistro** 173 S. Main **253-7457** 5pm-11pm, clsd Th

**The Plaza** 55 S. Main **253-8866** lunch & dinner • French • $9-19

### BOOKSTORES & RETAIL SHOPS

**The Emerald Rainbow** 45-1/2 Spring St. **253-5445** 10:30am-5:30pm

### SPIRITUAL GROUPS

**MCC of the Living Spring** 17 Elk St. (Unitarian Church) **253-9337** 7pm Sun

## Fayetteville (501)

### INFO LINES & SERVICES

**AA Gay/Lesbian** 443-6366

### BOOKSTORES & RETAIL SHOPS

**Passages** 200 W. Dickson **442-5845** 10am-6pm, til 8pm Fri, 1pm-6pm Sun • new age/metaphysical

### TRAVEL AGENTS

**World Wide Travel** 3810 Front St. #8 **521-3440** IGLTA

## Fort Smith (501)

### BARS & NIGHTCLUBS

**Burnzee's on the Hill** 1217 South W. **494-7300** popular • lesbians/gay men • 6pm-2am, clsd Mon • dancing/DJ • live shows • private club

### BOOKSTORES & RETAIL SHOPS

**Reflection of Women** 115 N. 10th St. #105-B **782-8252** 10am-6pm, clsd Sun

## Helena (501)

### ACCOMMODATIONS

**Foxglove B&B** 229 Beech **338-9391**/(800) **863-1926** gay-friendly • $59-70

## Hot Springs (501)

### BARS & NIGHTCLUBS

**Our House Lounge & Restaurant** 660 E. Grand Ave. **624-6868** 7pm-3am • popular • lesbians/gay men • dancing/DJ • shows monthly • wheelchair access

## Little Rock (501)

### INFO LINES & SERVICES

**AA Gay/Lesbian** 3rd & Pulaski (Capitol View Methodist) **664-7303** 8pm Wed & 6pm Sun

**Arkansas Department of Tourism** (800) **628-8725**

**Gay/Lesbian Task Force Switchboard** **375-5504**/(800) **448-8305** (IN AR) 6:30pm-10:30pm • statewide crisis line & referrals

# Little Rock

*I*f you want a city with a pace of life all its own, a city whose history reflects the dramatic changes within the South, and a city surrounded by natural beauty, you've made the right choice to visit Little Rock.

Here you can enjoy relaxing summer days in the shade beside the slow-moving Arkansas River that winds through town. Or you can take off to the nearby lakes and national forests to camp, rock climb, or water-ski. Stay in town and you can spend your days exploring the State Capitol, touring the historic homes of the Quapaw Quarter district, or browsing in Little Rock's many shops. Rumor has it that Bill Clinton's boyhood home is owned by a friendly lesbian couple.

At night, you can make an evening of it with dinner, a program at the Arkansas Arts Center, and a visit to Little Rock's lesbian bar, the **Silver Dollar.** If you're in town at the right time of the month, cruise by the monthly women's coffeehouse at **Vino's Pizza**—call the **Women's Project** to find out when.

Of course, if that isn't enough excitement, you can always head out for the northwest corner of the state. We've heard there are many lesbian landowners, living alone and in groups, throughout this region. And while you're out there, be sure to visit the funky Ozark Mountain resort town of Eureka Springs. There are loads of gay-friendly B&B's in this quaint, old-fashioned town, as well as a popular Passion Play. **Golden Gate Cottage** is women-only B&B, **Greenwood Hollow Ridge B&B** offers exclusively lesbigay accommodations, and **Center Street Bar & Grille** is the casual place to dance.

**Women's Project** 2224 Main St. **372-5113** 10am-5pm Mon-Fri • library open Sat • educational group • lesbian support group 7pm 2nd & 4th Tue • bookstore

## ACCOMMODATIONS

**Little Rock Inn** 601 Center St. **376-8301** gay-friendly • swimming • kids/pets ok • full bar • wheelchair access • $30

## BARS & NIGHTCLUBS

**Backstreet** 1021 Jessie Rd. #Q **664-2744** 9pm-? • lesbians/gay men • dancing/DJ • live shows • private club • wheelchair access

**Discovery III** 1021 Jessie Rd. **664-4784** from 9pm, clsd Sun-Wed • popular • gay-friendly • dancing/DJ • transgender-friendly • live shows • private club • wheelchair access

**Plumtastics Lounge** 601 Center St. (at Little Rock Inn) **376-8301** 9pm-2am, 4pm-10pm Sun • lesbians/gay men • dancing/DJ • live shows • wheelchair access

**Silver Dollar** 2710 Asher Ave. **663-9886** 4pm-1am, til midnight Sat, clsd Sun • mostly women • dancing/DJ • beer/wine • women-owned/run

## RESTAURANTS

**Vino's Pizza** 923 W. 7th St. **375-8466** beer/wine • inquire about monthly women's coffeehouse

## BOOKSTORES & RETAIL SHOPS

**Twisted Entertainment** 7201 Asher Ave. **568-4262** 11am-10pm, clsd Tue • gift shop

**Wild Card** 400 N. Bowman **223-9071** 10am-8pm, 1pm-5pm Sun • novelties & gifts

## PUBLICATIONS

**Lesbian/Gay News Telegraph (314) 664-6411/(800) 301-5468** some AR coverage

**Triangle Journal News (901) 454-1411** some AR coverage

**Triangle Rising** 568-4606

▲ **Womyn to Womyn** 325-7006 nat'l magazine w/ correspondence club for lesbian/bi-women (see ad in back mail order section)

## SPIRITUAL GROUPS

**MCC of the Rock** 2017 Chandler, N. Little Rock **753-7075** 11am Sun, 7pm Wed

**Unitarian Universalist Church** 1818 Reservoir Rd. **225-1503** 11am Sun • child care avail. • wheelchair access

# Little Rock    (501)

**Where the Girls Are:** Scattered. Popular hangouts are the Women's Project, local bookstores, and the monthly women's coffeehouse at Vino's Pizza.

**Lesbigay Pride:** June.

**Annual Events:** October: State Fair.

**City Info:** Arkansas Dept. of Tourism: 800/628-8725.

**Attractions:** Check out Bill & Hillary's old digs at 18th & Center Sts. Decorative Arts Museum: 372-4000. Quapaw Quarter Historic District: 371-0075 (walking tour).

**Best View:** Quapaw Quarter (in the heart of the city).

**Weather:** When it comes to natural precipitation, Arkansas is far from being a dry state. Be prepared for the occasional severe thunderstorm or ice storm. Summers are hot and humid (mid 90°s). Winters can be cold (30°s) with some snow and ice. Spring and fall are the best times to come and be awed by the colorful beauty of Mother Nature.

**Transit:** Black & White Cab: 374-0333.

## CALIFORNIA

### Alameda (510)

TRAVEL AGENTS
**Uniglobe Total Travel** 2150 Mariner Sq.
Dr. #100 **523-9796/(800) 544-3076**
IGLTA

### Anaheim (714)

INFO LINES & SERVICES
**Gay/Lesbian Community Services
Center** 12832 Garden Grove Blvd. #A
**534-0862** 10am-10pm

ACCOMMODATIONS
**Country Comfort B&B** 5104 E. Valencia
Dr., Orange **532-2802** lesbians/gay men
• full brkfst • hot tub • swimming •
inquire about kids & pets • 7 mi. from
Disneyland • wheelchair access •
women-owned/run • $65-70

TRAVEL AGENTS
**All Destinations Travel** 2500 E. Imperial
Hwy. # 102, Brea **529-4400** IGLTA
**Bon Voyage Travel** 5955 Ball Rd.,
Cypress **236-9094/(800) 477-6025**
IGLTA

SPIRITUAL GROUPS
**Calvary Open Door Center** 514 W.
Katella (Metro Court Business
Complex), Orange **284-5775** 10am Sun

### Apple Valley (760)

BARS & NIGHTCLUBS
**Victor Victoria's** 22581 Outer Hwy.18
**240-8018** 4pm-2am • lesbians/gay men
• dancing/DJ • patio

### Bakersfield (805)

INFO LINES & SERVICES
**Friends 323-7311** 6:30pm-11pm • info •
support groups & community outreach

BARS & NIGHTCLUBS
**Casablanca Club** 1030 20th St. **324-
1384** 7pm-2am, clsd Mon • lesbians/gay
men • neighborhood bar • dancing/DJ
**The Cellar** 1927 'K' St. **324-7711** 5pm-
midnight, til-2am Fri-Sun • lesbians/gay
men • dancing/DJ • call for events •
non-smoking bar upstairs • espresso
bar
**The Mint** 1207 19th St. **325-4048** 6pm-
2am • gay-friendly • more gay wknds •
neighborhood bar

**Town Casino Lounge** 1813 'H' St.
(Padre Hotel) **324-2594** 10am-2am •
gay-friendly • live piano Th-Sun

SPIRITUAL GROUPS
**MCC of the Harvest** 2421 Alta Vista Dr.
**327-3724** 7pm Sun

EROTICA
**Deja Vu** 1524 Golden State Hwy. **322-
7300**
**Wildcat Books** 2620 Chester Ave. **324-
4243**

### Benicia (707)

ACCOMMODATIONS
**Captain Walsh House** 235 E. 'L' St. **747-
5653** gay-friendly • gracious gothic
charm • full brkfst • wheelchair access •
$125-150

### Berkeley

*(see East Bay)*

### Big Bear Lake (909)

ACCOMMODATIONS
**Eagles' Nest B&B** 41675 Big Bear Blvd.
**866-6465** gay-friendly • 5 cottages • spa
• 85-170
**Grey Squirrel Resort** 866-4335 gay-
friendly • 18 private cabins • hot tub •
swimming • kids/pets ok • women-
owned/run • $75-300
**Hillcrest Lodge** 40241 Big Bear Blvd.
**866-6040/(800) 843-4449** gay-friendly •
motel • cabins • hot tub • kitchens •
fireplaces • non-smoking rms. avail. •
kids ok • gay-owned/run • $35-169
▲ **Smoke Tree Resort** 40154 Big Bear
Blvd. **866-2415/(800) 352-8581** gay-
friendly • B&B • cabins • near outdoor
recreation • hot tub • fireplaces •
kids/pets ok • gay-owned/operated •
$59-180

RESTAURANTS
**Ché Faccia** 607 Pine Knot Ave. **878-
3222** dinner 7 nights, lunch Fri-Sun only
• Italian • plenty veggie • beer/wine •
$10-15

### Big Sur (408)

ACCOMMODATIONS
**Lucia Lodge** Hwy. 1 **667-2391** gay-
friendly • cabins • kids ok • store •
ocean view • also restaurant •
American/seafood • full bar • $8-24 •
IGLTA

## Bishop (760)

ACCOMMODATIONS
**Starlite Motel** 192 Short St. 873-4912
gay-friendly • swimming • kids ok • 1
rm. avail. for pets • $40+

BOOKSTORES & RETAIL SHOPS
**Spellbinder Books** 124 S. Main 873-
4511 9:30am-5:30pm, clsd Sun •
women's section • wheelchair access

## Buena Park (714)

BARS & NIGHTCLUBS
**Ozz Supper Club** 6231 Manchester
Blvd. 522-1542 6pm-2am, clsd Mon •
popular • lesbians/gay men •
dancing/DJ • live shows • cabaret •
women's country/western dancing Wed •
call for events • also restaurant • some
veggie • $9-25

## Burlingame (650)

TRAVEL AGENTS
**Confident Travel** 1499 Bayshore Hwy.
#126 697-7274 IGLTA

## Cambria (805)

ACCOMMODATIONS
**The J. Patrick House B&B** 2990 Burton
Dr. 927-3812/(800) 341-5258 gay-friendly • authentic log cabin • fireplaces •
smokefree • inquire about kids • $110-
170

## Carmel (408)

*(see also Monterey)*

ACCOMMODATIONS
**Happy Landing Inn** 624-7917 gay-
friendly • Hansel & Gretel 1925 inn • full
brkfst • smokefree • kids 13+ okay •
$90-175

TRAVEL AGENTS
**Carmel Travel** 626-2000 IGLTA
**Four Winds Travel** 3662 The Barnyard
622-0800 IGLTA

## Chico (916)

INFO LINES & SERVICES
**Stonewall Alliance Center** 820 W. 7th
St. 893-3338/893-3336 social 6pm-
10pm Fri • Gay AA 7pm Tue • hotline

# All Season Resort!

- Individual cabins
- Fireplaces
- Kitchens
- Heated pool & spa
- Children's playground
- BBQs & picnic tables
- Volleyball, basketball, horseshoes
- Close to Village – Shops & Restaurants

**800.352.8581**
**909.866.2415**

40210 Big Bear Boulevard, Big Bear, CA

## BOOKSTORES & RETAIL SHOPS
**Travellin' Pages** 1174 East Ave. **342-6931** hours vary • lesbigay section

## TRAVEL AGENTS
**Gheller-vers Travel** 1074 E. Ave. #H **891-1633/(888) 891-1633** IGLTA

## Chula Vista (619)

### EROTICA
▲ **F St. Bookstore** 1141 3rd Ave. **585-3314** 24hrs

## Clearlake (707)

### ACCOMMODATIONS
**Blue Fish Cove Resort** 10573 E. Hwy. 20, Clearlake Oaks **998-1769** gay-friendly • lakeside resort cottages • kitchens • kids ok • pets ok by arr. • boat facilities • $45-95

**Edgewater Resort** 6420 Soda Bay Rd., Kelseyville **279-0208** gay-friendly • cabin • camping • $25-65

**Lake Vacations Reservations** 1855 S. Main St., Lakeport **263-7188** vacation-home rental service

**Sea Breeze Resort** 9595 Harbor Dr., Glenhaven **998-3327** gay-friendly • cottages • swimming • inquire about kids • gay-owned/operated • $55-85

### RESTAURANTS
**The Brentwood** 6271 E. Hwy. 20, Lucerne **274-2301** $7-14

**Kathy's Inn** 14677 Lake Shore Dr. **994-9933** lunch Wed-Fri, open from 4pm wknds, clsd Mon-Tue • full bar • wheelchair access

## Cloverdale (707)

### ACCOMMODATIONS
**Vintage Towers B&B** 302 N. Main St. **894-4535/(888) 886-9377** gay-friendly • Queen Anne mansion • full brkfst • smokefree • kids 10+ ok • $75-135

## Columbia (209)

### ENTERTAINMENT & RECREATION
**Ahwahnee Whitewater Expeditions** **533-1401** women-only, co-ed and charter rafting

## Concord (510)

### EROTICA
**Pleasant Hill Adult Books & Videos** 2294 Monument **676-2962**

## Corte Madera (415)

### ACCOMMODATIONS
**Marin Suites Hotel** 45 Tamal Vista Blvd. **924-3608** gay-friendly • variety of apt-style rooms

## Costa Mesa (714)

### INFO LINES & SERVICES
**Shalom Chavurah** 529-4201

### BARS & NIGHTCLUBS
**Lion's Den** 719 W. 19th St. **645-3830** 8pm-2am • lesbians/gay men • dancing/DJ • women's night Sat

**Metropolis** 4255 Campus Dr., Irvine **725-0300** 7pm-2am, from 8pm Tue, clsd Mon & Wed • gay-friendly • more gay Sun • dancing/DJ • 18+ Fri & Sun • also restaurant • Californian & sushi • strict dress code wknds

**Newport Station** 1945 Placentia **631-0031** 9pm-2am Th-Sat • dancing/DJ • live shows • videos • more women Th • wheelchair access

**Tin Lizzie Saloon** 752 St. Clair **966-2029** 11am-2am • mostly gay men • neighborhood bar • more women Sun • wheelchair access

## Cupertino (408)

### BARS & NIGHTCLUBS
**Silver Fox** 10095 Saich Wy. **255-3673** 2pm-2am • mostly gay men • neighborhood bar • live shows • wheelchair access

## Davis (916)

### INFO LINES & SERVICES
**DavisDykes** 752-2452 (CENTER#) social group • call for events

**LGBT Resource Center** 105 University House, UCDavis **752-2452** info • referrals • mtgs. • call for hours • wheelchair access

### CAFES
**Cafe Roma** 231 'E' St. **756-1615** 6:30am-11pm • coffee & pastries • student hangout

## East Bay (510)

*(includes Berkeley & Oakland)*

### INFO LINES & SERVICES

**La Peña** 3105 Shattuck Ave., Berkeley **849-2568/849-2572** 10am-5pm Mon-Fri • also cafe 6pm-10pm Wed-Sun • multi-cultural center • hosts meetings, dances, events • mostly Latino-American /African-American

**Pacific Center** 2712 Telegraph Ave., Berkeley **548-8283** 10am-10pm, from noon Sat, 6pm-9pm Sun • also 'Lavender Line' (841-6224) also TDD • 4pm-10pm Mon-Fri, 6pm-9pm Sat

**What's Up! Events Hotline for Sistahs** **835-6126** for lesbians of African descent

### ACCOMMODATIONS

**Elmwood House** 2609 College Ave., Berkeley **540-5123/(800) 540-3050** gay-friendly • guesthouse • gay-owned/run • $60-85 (double occupancy)

### BARS & NIGHTCLUBS

**Bench & Bar** 120 11th St., Oakland **444-2266** 3pm-2am • popular • mostly men • dancing/DJ • professional • live shows • Latin nights Fri, Sat & Mon • wheelchair access

**Cabel's Reef** 2272 Telegraph Ave., Oakland **451-3777** noon-2am • lesbians/gay men • women's night Wed • dancing/DJ • multi-racial

**Club Salsa Dance Club** 6401 Stockton, El Cerrito **428-2144** 7:30pm-11pm 2nd Sat • women only • smoke- & alcohol-free • lessons 7:30pm

**Country Nights** 3903 Broadway (Masonic Hall), Oakland **421-2144** 7:30pm-11:30pm Fri • women only • lessons at 7:30pm • smoke-, alcohol- & scent-free

**Town & Country** 2022 Telegraph Ave., Oakland **444-4978** 11am-2am • mostly gay men • neighborhood bar • wheelchair access

---

## East Bay (510)

**Where the Girls Are:** Though there's no lesbian ghetto, you'll find more of us in north Oakland and north Berkeley, Lake Merritt, around Grand Lake & Piedmont, the Solano/Albany area, or at a cafe along 4th St. Berkeley.

**Lesbigay Pride:** June in Berkeley.

**Annual Events:**

June - **Gay Prom** / Project Eden: 247-8200. $15. For ages 16-25, preregistered.

October - **Halloween Spiral Dance**: 893-3097. Annual rite celebrating the crone.

**City Info:** Oakland Visitors Bureau: 839-9000.

**Attractions:** Jack London Square, Oakland. Emeryville Marina Public Market. UC Berkeley. Telegraph Ave., Berkeley. The Claremont Hotel Restaurant, Berkeley. The Paramount Theater, Oakland.

**Best View:** Claremont Hotel, or various locations in Berkeley and Oakland Hills.

**Weather:** While San Francisco is fogged in during the summers, the East Bay remains sunny and warm. Some areas even get hot (90°s-100°s). As for the winter, the temperature drops along with rain (upper 30°s-40°s in the winter). Spring is the time to come – the usually brown hills explode with the colors of green grass and wildflowers.

**Transit:** Yellow Cab (Berkeley): 848-3333.
Yellow Cab (Oakland): 836-1234.

# East Bay:
# Berkeley and Oakland

*S*o what exactly is the East Bay? To most Northern Californians, it's simply the string of cities and counties across the Bay Bridge from San Francisco—with weather that's consistently sunnier and 10-20° warmer than Fog City. For the Damron Women's Traveller, it is the more lesbian-friendly cities of Berkeley and Oakland.

Berkeley—both the campus of the University of California and the city where it's located—was immortalized in the '60s as a hotbed of student/counterculture activism. Today, most of the people taking to the streets, especially Telegraph and College Avenues, are tourists or kids from the suburbs in search of consumer thrills in the form of a good book, exotic cuisine, the perfect cup of java, and anything tie-dyed.

Locals and visitors alike will enjoy people-watching on Telegraph or University Avenues. Or you can just take to the hills—Tilden Park offers incredible views and trails to hike and bike.

As for Oakland, Gertrude Stein once said, "There is no there there." Well, Caesar, a lot has happened since you were in Oakland!

Today Oakland is a city with an incredible diversity of races, cultures, and classes. The birthplace of the Black Panthers, this city has been especially influential in urban African-American music, fashion, and politics. Lately Oakland has also become a vital artists' enclave, as Bay Area artists flee high rent in San Francisco for spacious lofts downtown or in West Oakland.

And where are all the women? Well, many are in couples or covens or both, which can make them hard to find. But if you want to start a couple or a coven of your own, stop by **Mama Bears** or one of the other women's bookstores—they're also great informal resource centers, and often host popular performances and author signings. And speaking of "hot mamas," try the popular weekend brunch at **Mama's Royale.**

For info on groups and events, cruise by the **Pacific Center,** still the Bay Area's only lesbian/gay center, located in Berkeley. The center hosts meetings for lesbian moms & kids, bisexuals, transgendered women, separatists, and more. Those interested in women's spirituality should drop by **Ancient Ways,** the pagan emporium extraordinaire.

If you're the outdoors type, consider an adventure in Northern California with **Mariah Wilderness Expeditions.** Or make a day of it at one of the nearby state parks: Point Reyes is a beautiful destination with a hostel, and Point Isabel is rumored to be a good meeting place for dykes with dogs. We've heard that Sister Boom, a multicultural women's drum corps, practices at Waterfront Park in Jack London Square (left onto 11th St. exit off I-80, then right on Broadway), and the Emeryville Marina Public Market off I-80 is popular with gastronomically inclined lesbians.

If you'd rather exercise indoors, make some moves on the dancefloor of the **White Horse** or at the Masonic Hall in downtown Oakland on **Country Dance Night.** For plays, performances and events, grab a copy of the **Bay Times** and check out the calendar section. Or pick up some entertainment of your own at the East Bay **Good Vibrations** or **Passion Flower**—both are women-friendly, clean sex toy stores.

There are also lots of resources for women of color in the East Bay. Start with **La Peña Cultural Center,** an active center with many events for Latina-Americans and African-Americans. Then there's **What's Up!,** an events hotline for lesbian sistahs of African descent.

**White Horse** 6551 Telegraph Ave., Oakland **652-3820** 1pm-2am, from 3pm Mon-Tue • popular Fri night • lesbians/gay men • dancing/DJ • wheelchair access

### CAFES

**Cafe Sorrento** 2510 Channing, Berkeley **548-8220** 7am-8pm, 9am-4pm Sat, clsd Sun • multi-racial • Italian • vegetarian • $5-10

**Cafe Strada** 2300 College Ave., Berkeley **843-5282** 6:30am-midnight • popular • students • great patio & bianca (white choc.) mochas

**The Edible Complex** 5600 College, Oakland **658-2172** 7am-midnight, til 1am Fri-Sat • popular • mostly students • some sandwiches & soups • cafe • $5-10

**Mimosa Cafe** 462 Santa Clara, Oakland **465-2948** 11am-9pm, til 2pm Sun, clsd Mon • natural & healthy • plenty veggie • beer/wine • $7-12

### RESTAURANTS

**Betty's To Go** 1807 4th St., Berkeley **548-9494** 6:30am-5pm, 8am-4pm Sun • sandwiches • some veggie • $5

**Bison Brewery** 2598 Telegraph, Berkeley **841-7734** 7:30am-1am • live music • sandwiches • some veggie • beer/wine • wheelchair access • $5-10

**Chez Panisse** 1517 Shattuck Ave., Berkeley **548-5525** nouvelle Californian • beer/wine • $38-68

**La Mediterranée** 2936 College Ave., Berkeley **540-7773** 10am-10pm • beer/wine • $12-17

**Mama's Royale** 4012 Broadway, Oakland **547-7600** 7am-3pm, from 8am wknds • popular • come early for excellent weekend brunch • beer/wine • wheelchair access • $5-10

### ENTERTAINMENT & RECREATION

**Dyke TV** Channel 8 7:30pm Wed • 'weekly half-hour TV show produced by lesbians for lesbians'

### BOOKSTORES & RETAIL SHOPS

**Ancient Ways** 4075 Telegraph Ave., Oakland **653-3244** 11am-7pm • extensive occult supplies • classes • readings • woman-owned

# Mama Bears
## WOMEN'S BOOKSTORE-COFFEEBAR

*The full-spectrum women's bookstore
serving the Greater Bay Area
since 1983*

■ **open every day** ■
**including all holidays**

**6536 Telegraph
Oakland, CA 94609**
(between Ashby & Alcatraz)

Phone: (510) 428-9684 • (800) 643-8629
Fax: (510) 654-2774

**Boadecia's Books** 398 Colusa Ave., Kensington **559-9184** 11am-9pm, til 7pm Sun • lesbigay • readings • wheelchair access • lesbian-owned/run

**Cody's** 2454 Telegraph Ave., Berkeley **845-7852** 10am-10pm • general • lesbigay section • frequent readings & lectures • wheelchair access

**Easy Going** 1385 Shattuck, Berkeley **843-3533** 10am-7pm, til 6pm Sat, noon-6pm Sun • travel books & accessories • also 1617 Locust, Walnut Creek 947-6660

**Gaia Bookstore & Catalogue Co.** 1400 Shattuck Ave., Berkeley **548-4172** 10am-7:30pm • feminist • eco-spiritual/goddess

▲**Mama Bears Bookstore** 6536 Telegraph Ave., Oakland **428-9684** 10:30am-8pm • women's books • readings & performances • coffeebar • also 'Mama Bears News & Notes' book review • lesbian-owned/run

**Shambhala Booksellers** 2482 Telegraph Ave., Berkeley **848-8443** 10am-8pm • metaphysical feminist/goddess section • wheelchair access

PUBLICATIONS

**San Francisco Bay Times** (415) 626-8121 popular • a 'must read' for Bay Area resources & personals

TRAVEL AGENTS

**New Venture Travel** 404 22nd St., Oakland **835-3800** women-owned/run • IGLTA

**Northside Travel** 1824 Euclid Ave., Berkeley **843-1000** IGLTA

SPIRITUAL GROUPS

**Albany Unified Methodist Church** 980 Stannage Ave., Albany **526-7346** 10am Sun

**MCC New Life** 1823 9th St., Berkeley **843-9355** 12:30pm Sun • wheelchair access

EROTICA

▲ **Good Vibrations** 2504 San Pablo, Berkeley **841-8987** 11am-7pm • clean, well-lighted sex toy store • also mail order • wheelchair access • see ad in SF section

**Hollywood Adult Books** 5686 Telegraph Ave., Oakland **654-1169**

**L'Amour Shoppe** 1905 San Pablo Ave., Oakland **465-4216**

**Passion Flower** 4 Yosemite Ave., Oakland **601-7750** toys • lingerie • leather

## El Cajon (619)

EROTICA

▲ **F St. Bookstore** 158 E. Main **447-0381** 24hrs • wheelchair access

## Escondido (619)

TRAVEL AGENTS

**Discovery-Costa Travels** 886 Overlook Cir., San Marcos **744-6536** IGLTA

EROTICA

▲ **F St. Bookstore** 237 E. Grand Ave. **480-6031** 24hrs

**Video Specialties** 2322 S. Escondido Blvd. **745-6697**

## Eureka (707)

INFO LINES & SERVICES

**Northcoast Lesbian, Gay, Bisexual & Transgender Alliance** 445-9760/444-1061 hours vary, clsd Mon • various services • wheelchair access

ACCOMMODATIONS

**An Elegant Victorian Mansion** 1406 'C' St. **444-3144** gay-friendly • full brkfst • smokefree • $95-185

**Carter House Victorians** 301 'L' St. **444-8062/(800) 404-1390** gay-friendly • enclave of 4 unique inns • full brkfst • smokefree • kids ok • wheelchair access • $65-350

BARS & NIGHTCLUBS

**Club Triangle (Club West)** 535 5th St. **444-2582** 8pm-2am • gay-friendly • dancing/DJ • alternative • 18+ • gay Sun • also restaurant • wheelchair access

**Lost Coast Brewery Pub** 617 4th St. **445-4480** 11am-1am • gay-friendly • food served • beer/wine • wheelchair access • women-owned/run

RESTAURANTS

**Folie Deuce** 1551 'G' St., Arcata **822-1042** dinner only, clsd Sun-Mon • bistro • $8-20

**Seafood Grotto** 605 Broadway **443-2075** low prices • informal setting • also a fish market

BOOKSTORES & RETAIL SHOPS

**Booklegger** 402 2nd St. **445-1344** 10am-5:30pm, noon-5pm Sun • mostly used • some lesbian titles • women-owned/run • wheelchair access

PUBLICATIONS
**The 'L' Word** lesbian newsletter for Humboldt Co. • available at 'Booklegger'

## Fairfield

*(see Vacaville)*

## Ferndale (707)

ACCOMMODATIONS
**The Gingerbread Mansion Inn** 400 Berding St. **786-4000/(800) 952-4136** popular • gay-friendly • a grand lady w/beautifully restored interior • full brkfst • afternoon tea • near outdoor recreation • smokefree • kids ok • $140-350

## Fort Bragg (707)

ACCOMMODATIONS
**Annie's Jug Handle Beach B&B** 32980 Gibney Ln. **964-1415/(800) 964-9957** gay-friendly • full brkfst • kids ok • $75-159
**Aslan House** 24600 N. Hwy. 1 **964-2788/(800) 400-2189** gay-friendly • cottages • ideal place for romance & privacy on the Mendocino Coast • partial ocean view • hot tub • kids 10+ ok • $135 + $10 extra person (4 max)
**Cleone Lodge Inn** 24600 N. Hwy. 1 **964-2788/(800) 400-2189** gay-friendly • cottages • country garden retreat on 9-1/2 acres • hot tub • $74-130 (2 persons)

RESTAURANTS
**Purple Rose** Mill Creek Dr. **964-6507** dinner only, clsd Mon-Tue • Mexican

BOOKSTORES & RETAIL SHOPS
**Windsong Books & Records** 324 N. Main **964-2050** 10am-5:30pm, til 4pm Sun • mostly used • large selection of women's titles

## Fremont (510)

EROTICA
**Cupid's Corner** 34129 Fremont Blvd. **796-8697** boutique • lingerie • large sizes • videos
**L'Amour Shoppe** 40555 Grimmer Blvd. **659-8161** 24hrs

## Fresno (209)

INFO LINES & SERVICES
**Bulletin Board at Valley Women's Books** popular resource for community info

**Community Link 266-5465** info • lesbi-gay support • also publishes 'Pink Pages'
**GUS (Gay United Service)** 1999 Tuolumne #625 **268-3541** 8am-5pm Mon-Fri • counseling & referrals
**Serenity Fellowship AA** 2812 N. Blackstone **221-6907** various mtg. times • women's mtg. 7pm Mon

BARS & NIGHTCLUBS
**The Express** 708 N. Blackstone **233-1791** hours vary • lesbians/gay men • dancing/DJ • piano bar • cafe • videos • popular patio • wheelchair access
**Palace** 4030 E. Belmont Ave. **264-8283** 3pm-2am • mostly women • neighborhood bar • dancing/DJ • country/western • live shows • wheelchair access
**Red Lantern** 4618 E. Belmont Ave. **251-5898** 2pm-2am • mostly men • neighborhood bar • country/western • wheelchair access

CAFES
**Java Cafe** 805 E. Olive **237-5282** 6:30am-11pm, til midnight Fri-Sat • popular • bohemian • plenty veggie • live shows • wheelchair access • women-owned/run • $8-12

RESTAURANTS
**Cafe Express** 708 N. Blackstone **233-1791** 6pm-9pm, champagne brunch 10am-3pm Sun, clsd Mon • fine dining

BOOKSTORES & RETAIL SHOPS
**Valley Women's Books** 1118 N. Fulton St. **233-3600** 10am-6pm, til 9pm Th-Fri, clsd Mon • women's • lesbigay section • wheelchair access

TRAVEL AGENTS
**A&D Travel Agency** 2547 W. Shaw Ave. #108 **224-1200/(800) 645-1213** IGLTA

SPIRITUAL GROUPS
**Wesley United Methodist Church** 1343 E. Barstow Ave. **224-1947** 8:30am & 11am Sun • reconciling congregation

EROTICA
**Only For You** 1460 N. Van Ness Ave. **498-0284** noon-9pm, til 10pm Th-Sat • lesbigay
**Wildcat Book Store** 1535 Fresno St. **237-4525**

## Garberville (707)

### ACCOMMODATIONS
**Giant Redwoods RV & Camp** 943-3198
gay-friendly • campsites • RV • located
off the Avenue of the Giants on the Eel
River • shared baths • kids/pets ok •
$20-25

## Garden Grove (714)

### INFO LINES & SERVICES
**AA Gay/Lesbian** 9872 Chapman Ave. #15
(Ash Inc.) 534-5820/537-9968 6pm-
10pm, clsd Fri

### BARS & NIGHTCLUBS
**Frat House** 8112 Garden Grove Blvd.
897-3431 9am-2am • popular • les-
bians/gay men • dancing/DJ • multi-racial
• live shows • theme nights • piano bar
• wheelchair access
**Happy Hour** 12081 Garden Grove Blvd.
537-9079 2pm-2am, from noon wknds •
mostly women • dancing/DJ • wheelchair
access • women-owned/run

### TRAVEL AGENTS
**Craig's Travel Service** 12089 Euclid St.
638-7381 IGLTA

### EROTICA
**Hip Pocket** 12686 Garden Grove Blvd.
638-8595

## Glendale (818)

### TRAVEL AGENTS
**Superior Travel Associates** 715 N.
Central #218 549-8755 IGLTA

### SPIRITUAL GROUPS
**MCC Divine Redeemer** 346 Riverdale
Dr. 500-7124 10:45am Sun, 7:30pm Wed

## Grass Valley (916)

### ACCOMMODATIONS
**Murphy's Inn** 318 Neal St. 273-6873 gay-
friendly • full brkfst • smokefree

### RESTAURANTS
**Friar Tucks** 111 N. Pine St., Nevada City
265-9093 dinner from 5pm •
American/fondue • full bar • wheelchair
access • $15-20

### BOOKSTORES & RETAIL SHOPS
**Nevada City Postal Company** 228
Commercial St., Nevada City 265-0576
9am-6pm, til 5pm Sat, clsd Sun • community bulletin board avail.

## Gualala (707)

### ACCOMMODATIONS
**Starboard House Ranch Vacation
Home** 140 Starboard 884-4808 gay-
friendly • vacation house • ocean views •
hot tub • smokefree • kids ok • wheelchair access • women-owned/run • $165

## Half Moon Bay (650)

### ACCOMMODATIONS
**Mill Rose Inn** 615 Mill St. 726-
8750/(800) 900-7673 gay-friendly • classic European elegance by the sea • full
brkfst • hot tub • smokefree • kids 10+
ok • $165-285

### RESTAURANTS
**Moss Beach Distillery** Beach & Ocean
728-5595 lunch & dinner • $9-20
**Pasta Moon** 315 Main St. 726 5125
beer/wine • wheelchair access
**San Benito House** 356 Main St. 726-
3425 Mediterranean • full bar • wheelchair access • $11-17

## Hawthorne (310)

### BARS & NIGHTCLUBS
**El Capitan** 13825 S. Hawthorne Blvd.
675-3436 4pm-2am, from noon Fri-Sun •
lesbians/gay men • neighborhood bar •
beer/wine • more women Tue

## Hayward (510)

### BARS & NIGHTCLUBS
**Driftwood Lounge** 22170 Mission Blvd.
581-2050 2pm-2am, from noon wknds •
mostly women • dancing/DJ • wheelchair
access • women-owned/run
**Rainbow Room** 21859 Mission Blvd.
582-8078 noon-2am • lesbians/gay men
• dancing/DJ • women-owned/run
**Rumors** 22554 Main St. 733-2334 10am-
2am • mostly men • neighborhood bar •
dancing/DJ • wheelchair access
**Turf Club** 22517 Mission Blvd. 881-9877
10am-2am • lesbians/gay men • danc-
ing/DJ • country/western • live shows •
patio bar in summer

### EROTICA
**L'Amour Shoppe** 22553 Main St. 886-
7777

# Healdsburg (707)

## ACCOMMODATIONS

**Camellia Inn** 211 North St. **433-8182/(800) 727-8182** gay-friendly • full brkfst • $75-145

**Madrona Manor 433-4231** gay-friendly • elegant Victorian country inn • full brkfst • swimming • smokefree • some rooms okay for kids • pets ok • wheelchair access

**Twin Towers River Ranch** 615 Bailhache **433-4443** gay-friendly • 1864 Victorian farmhouse located on 5 rolling acres • also vacation house • kids & pets by arr. • B&B:$105 Apt: $450-570/week

## RESTAURANTS

**Chateau Souverain** 400 Souverain Rd., Geyserville **433-8281**

# Hermosa Beach (310)

## EROTICA

**U.S.J. Video & Books** 544 Pacific Coast Hwy. **374-9207**

# Huntington Beach (714)

## TRAVEL AGENTS

**KB Travel & Tours** 8907 Warner Ave. #162 **848-7272** IGLTA

## EROTICA

**Paradise Specialties** 7344 Center **898-0400**

# Idyllwild (909)

## ACCOMMODATIONS

**The Pine Cove Inn** 23481 Hwy. 243 **659-5033** gay-friendly • on 3 wooded acres • full brkfst • fireplaces • kids ok • $70-90

**The Rainbow Inn 659-0111** gay-friendly • full brkfst • shared/private baths • hot tub • kitchen • smokefree • patio • conference rooms avail. • gay-owned/run • $75-105

**Wilkum Inn B&B 659-4087/(800) 659-4086** gay-friendly • 1938 shingle-style inn • shared/private baths • fireplaces • smokefree • kids ok • women-owned/run • wheelchair access • $75-100 (plus tax)

# Inglewood (310)

## BARS & NIGHTCLUBS

**Annex** 835 S. La Brea **671-7323** noon-2am • mostly men • neighborhood bar

**Caper Room** 244 S. Market St. **677-0403** 5:30pm-2am, from 4pm Sun, clsd Mon • mostly gay men • dancing/DJ • mostly African-American

# Lafayette (510)

## RESTAURANTS

**Java Jones** 100 Lafayette Cir. #101 **284-5282** 9am-9pm, til 10pm Th-Sat, clsd Mon • lesbians/gay men • brunch Sun • some veggie • wheelchair access • lesbian-owned/run • $6-13

# Laguna Beach (714)

## INFO LINES & SERVICES

**AA Gay/Lesbian** 31872 Coast Hwy. (South Coast Medical Hospital) **499-7150** 8:30pm Fri

**Laguna Outreach 497-4237** educational/social group for Orange County • call for details

## ACCOMMODATIONS

**Best Western Laguna Brisas Spa Hotel** 1600 S. Coast Hwy. **497-7272/(800) 624-4442** gay-friendly • resort • swimming • kids ok • non-smoking rms avail. • wheelchair access • $99-229

**By The Sea Inn** 475 N. Coast Hwy. **497-6645/(800) 297-0007** gay-friendly • hot tub • swimming • kids ok • wheelchair access

**California Riviera** 800 1400 S. Coast Hwy. #104 **(800) 621-0500** extensive reservation & accommodation services • IGLTA

▲ **Casa Laguna B&B Inn** 2510 S. Coast Hwy. **494-2996/(800) 233-0449** gay-friendly • also cottages • overlooks Pacific • swimming • non-smoking rms avail. • kids/pets ok • $89-249

**The Coast Inn** 1401 S. Coast Hwy. **494-7588/(800) 653-2697** lesbians/gay men • resort • swimming • oceanside location • 2 bars & restaurant • $60-140

**Holiday Inn Laguna Beach** 696 S. Coast Hwy. **494-1001/(800) 228-5691** gay-friendly • swimming • kids ok • food served • wheelchair access

## BARS & NIGHTCLUBS

**Boom Boom Room** 1401 S. Coast Hwy. (at the Coast Inn) **494-7588** 10am-2am • popular • lesbians/gay men • dancing/DJ • live shows • videos • wheelchair access

**Main St.** 1460 S. Coast Hwy. **494-0056**
noon-2am • mostly gay men • piano bar
• women-owned/run

**Newport Station** 1945 Placentia, Costa
Mesa **631-0031** 9pm-2am Th-Sat • more
women Th • dancing/DJ • live shows •
videos • wheelchair access

### CAFES

**Cafe Zinc** 350 Ocean Ave. **494-6302**
7am-5:30pm, til 5pm Sun • vegetarian •
beer/wine • patio • also market • wheelchair access • $5-10

### RESTAURANTS

**Cafe Zoolu** 860 Glenneyre **494-6825**
dinner • Californian • some veggie •
wheelchair access • $10-20

**The Cottage** 308 N. Coast Hwy. **494-
3023** lunch & dinner • homestyle cooking • some veggie • $10-12

**Dizz's As Is** 2794 S. Coast Hwy. **494-
5250** open 5:30pm, seating at 6pm, clsd
Mon • cont'l • full bar • patio • $16-27

**Leap of Faith** 1440 Pacific Coast Hwy.
**494-8595** 11am-11pm, til midnight Fri-
Sat, from 8:30am wknds • lesbians/gay
men • American/gourmet desserts •
plenty veggie • beer/wine • patio • $10-
20

### BOOKSTORES & RETAIL SHOPS

**A Different Drummer** 1294-C S. Coast
Hwy. **497-6699** 11am-8pm • women's •
lesbigay section • wheelchair access •
women-owned/run

**Fahrenheit 451 Booksellers &
Coffeehouse** 540 S. Coast Hwy. Ste. 100
**376-3451** 10am-10pm • readings • patio
• wheelchair access

▲ **Jewelry by Poncé** 1417 S. Coast Hwy.
**494-1399/(800) 969-RING** 11am-7pm
Wed-Sun, by appt. Mon-Tue • lesbigay
commitment rings & other jewelry • see
ad in mail order section

### PUBLICATIONS

**Orange County/ Long Beach Blade**
494-4898

*Casa Laguna* INN

A Romantic - Intimate Setting - Spectacular Ocean Views
Tropical Gardens - Heated Pool - Continental Plus
Breakfast - Afternoon Tea & Wine

20 Lovely Rooms - Suites - Cottages

**From $69 - Ocean Views $89**

2510 S. Pacific Coast Hwy
Laguna Beach
800-233-0449

*Laguna Beach*

*Holly's*

A SPECIAL PLACE
FOR ALL WOMEN
Lake Tahoe California

Cozy Cabins

**Only 2-Blocks From The Lake!**
▼
**Casinos, Fine Dining, Hiking,
Skiing,Bicycling, & Boating!**

**Website: www.hollysplace.com**
e-mail: Hollys@oakweb.com

business calls
916-544-7040

reservations
800-745-7041

## SPIRITUAL GROUPS
**Christ Chapel of Laguna** 286 St. Anne's Dr. **376-2099** 10am Sun

**Congregation Kol Simcha** 499-3500

**Unitarian Universalist Fellowship** 429 Cypress Dr. **497-4568/645-8597** 10:30am Sun

## EROTICA
**Gay Mart** 168 Mountain Rd. **497-9108**

**Video Horizons** 31674 Coast Hwy **499-4519**

# Lake Tahoe                    (530)

*(see also Lake Tahoe, Nevada)*

## ACCOMMODATIONS
**Bavarian House B&B** 544-4411/(800) **431-4411** exclusively gay/lesbian • smokefree • $75-125

▲ **Holly's Place** 544-7040/(800) 745-7041 women only • guesthouse • cabin • kitchens • nudity • smokefree • kids/pets ok • lesbian-owned/run • $85-155

**Inn Essence** 865 Lake Tahoe Blvd., S. Lake Tahoe **577-0339/(800) 578-2463** lesbians/gay men • $79-125

**Ridgewood Inn** 1341 Emerald Bay Rd. **541-8589/(800) 800-4640** gay-friendly • hot tub • pets ok • quiet wooded setting • $40-150

**Secrets Honeymooners' Inn** 924 Park Ave., S. Lake Tahoe **544-6767/(800) 441-6610** gay-friendly • quiet, romantic adult-only inn • spas

**Sierrawood Guest House** 577-6073/700-3802 lesbians/gay men • hot tub • cozy, romantic chalet • gay-owned/run • $110-150

**Silver Shadows Lodge** 1251 Emerald Bay Rd., S. Lake Tahoe **541-3575** gay-friendly • motel • swimming • kids/pets ok • $35 & up

**Tradewinds Motel** 944 Friday, S. Lake Tahoe **544-6459/(800) 628-1829** gay-friendly • swimming • suite w/spas & fireplace avail.

## BARS & NIGHTCLUBS
**Faces** 270 Kingsbury Grade NV **(702) 588-2333** 5pm-4am, from 9pm Mon-Wed • lesbians/gay men • dancing/DJ

## CAFES
**Syd's Bagelry** 550 North Lake Rd., Tahoe City **583-2666** 6:30am-6:30pm daily • bagel sandwiches • plenty veggie

## RESTAURANTS
**Driftwood Cafe** 4119 Laurel Ave. **544-6545** 7:30am-2pm • homecooking • some veggie • $4-8

**Passaretti's** 1181 Emerald Bay Rd. (Hwy.50) **541-3433** 9am-9:30pm • Italian

## BOOKSTORES & RETAIL SHOPS
**The Funkyard** 265-A North Lake Blvd., Tahoe City **581-3483** 11am-7pm • eccentric consignment/thrift store • women-owned/run

# Lakeport                    (707)

## ACCOMMODATIONS
**Lake Vacation Rentals** 1855 S. Main St. **263-7188** gay-friendly • $110-400

# Lakewood                    (310)

## TRAVEL AGENTS
**Action Travel Service** 6416 Del Amo Blvd. **420-3316** IGLTA

# Lancaster                    (805)

## INFO LINES & SERVICES
**Antelope Valley Gay/Lesbian Alliance** 942-2812 call for events

## BARS & NIGHTCLUBS
**Back Door** 1255 W. Ave. 'I' **945-2566** 6pm-2am • lesbians/gay men • dancing/DJ

## SPIRITUAL GROUPS
**Antelope Valley Unitarian Universalist Fellowship** 43843 N. Division St. **272-0530** 11am Sun

**Sunrise MCC of the High Desert** 45303 23rd St. W. **942-7076** 11am Sun

# Lompoc                    (805)

## TRAVEL AGENTS
**Cruise & Travel International** 1313 N. 'H' St. #E **737-9668** IGLTA

## Long Beach (310)

INFO LINES & SERVICES

**AA Gay/Lesbian (Atlantic Alano Club)** 441 E. 1st St. **432-7476** hours vary

**Lesbian/Gay Center & Switchboard** 2017 E. 4th St. **434-4455** 9am-10pm, til 6pm Sat, 3pm-9pm Sun • also newsletter

**South Bay Lesbian/Gay Community Organization 379-2850** support/education for Manhattan, Hermosa & Redondo Beaches, Torrance, Palos Verdes, El Segundo

ACCOMMODATIONS

**Bed & Breakfast California** 3924 E. 14th St. **(800) 383-3513** reservation service

BARS & NIGHTCLUBS

**The Brit** 1744 E. Broadway **432-9742** 10am-2am • mostly gay men • neighborhood bar

**The Broadway** 1100 E. Broadway **432-3646** 10am-2am • mostly gay men • neighborhood bar

**The Bulldogs (The Crest)** 5935 Cherry Ave. **423-6650** 2pm-2am • lesbians/gay men

**Club 5211** 5211 N. Atlantic St. **428-5545** 6am-2am • mostly gay men • neighborhood bar • karaoke Wed • wheelchair access

**Club Broadway** 3348 E. Broadway **438-7700** 11am-2am • mostly women • neighborhood bar • wheelchair access • women-owned/run

**De De's** locations vary **433-1470** mostly women • dancing/DJ • call for events

**Executive Suite** 3428 E. Pacific Coast Hwy. **597-3884** 8pm-2am, clsd Tue • popular • lesbians/gay men • more women wknds • dancing/DJ • wheelchair access

---

## Long Beach

*T*hough it's often overshadowed by its neighbor Los Angeles, Long Beach is a large harbor city with plenty of bars and shopping all its own...and of course, lesbians.

According to local rumor, Long Beach is second only to San Francisco in lesbian/gay population, at approximately 45,000— though many of these gay residents are "married," making Long Beach a bedroom community of professional couples.

The city itself is melded from overlapping suburbs and industrial areas. The cleaner air, mild weather, and reasonable traffic make it an obvious choice for those looking for a livable refuge away from L.A. Of course the nightlife is milder as well, but nobody's complaining about the women's bars—**Club Broadway** for casual hanging out, and **Que Será** for dancing and shows. Though it's a mixed lesbigay club, we hear that the **Executive Suite** is popular with lesbians on weekends. For other events, check with **Pearls Booksellers,** the women's bookstore, or the **Lesbian/Gay Center.**

**Floyd's** 2913 E. Anaheim St. (entrance on Gladys St.) **433-9251** 6pm-2am, from 2pm Sun, clsd Mon • lesbians/gay men • more women Fri • dancing/DJ • country/western • dance lessons Tue-Th • wheelchair access

**Pistons** 2020 E. Artesia **422-1928** 6pm-2am, til 4am Fri-Sat • mostly gay men • leather • patio

**Que Será** 1923 E. 7th St. **599-6170** 3pm-2am, from 2pm wknds • mostly women • dancing/DJ • live shows • wheelchair access • women-owned/run

**Ripples** 5101 E. Ocean **433-0357** noon-2am • popular • mostly gay men • dancing/DJ • piano bar • videos • food served • patio

**Silver Fox** 411 Redondo **439-6343** noon-2am, from 8am Sun • popular happy hour • mostly gay men • karaoke 9pm Wed & Sun • videos

**Sweetwater Saloon** 1201 E. Broadway **432-7044** 6am-2am • mostly gay men • neighborhood bar • popular days

### Restaurants

**Birds of Paradise** 1800 E. Broadway **590-8773** 10am-1am • lesbians/gay men • Sun brunch • cocktails • live piano Wed-Sun • some veggie • wheelchair access • $10

**Cha Cha Cha** 762 8th **436-3900** lunch & dinner • Caribbean • plenty veggie • wheelchair access • $20-30

**Egg Heaven** 4358 E. 4th St. **433-9277** 7am-2pm, til 3pm wknds • some veggie • $4-7

**House of Madame JoJo** 2941 E. Broadway **439-3672** 5pm-10pm • popular • lesbians/gay men • Mediterranean • some veggie • beer/wine • wheelchair access • $12-20

**Original Park Pantry** 2104 E. Broadway **434-0451** lunch & dinner • Mexican/American/Asian • some veggie • $8-12

### Bookstores & Retail Shops

**By the Book** 2501 E. Broadway **930-0088** 10am-8pm, til 6pm Sun • large lesbigay section • wheelchair access

# Long Beach (310)

**Where the Girls Are:** Schmoozing with the boys on Broadway between Atlantic and Cherry Avenues, or elsewhere between Pacific Coast Hwy. and the beach. Or at home snuggling.

**Lesbigay Pride:** May. 987-9191.

**Annual Events:**

April - **AIDSWalk.**

September - **Pride Picnic.**

November - **The Gatsby.** A benefit for the Center at the Sheraton.

**City Info:** 436-3645.

**Attractions:** The Queen Mary. Long Beach Downtown Marketplace, Fri 10am-4pm: 436-4259.

**Best View:** On the deck of the Queen Mary, docked overlooking most of Long Beach. Or Signal Hill, off 405. Take the Cherry exit.

**Weather:** Quite temperate: highs in the mid-80°s July through September, and cooling down at night. In the "winter," January to March, highs are in the upper 60°s, and lows in the upper 40°s.

**Transit:** Long Beach Yellow Cab: 435-6111. Super Shuttle: 213/338-1111 (from LAX). Long Beach Transit & Runabout (free downtown shuttle): 591-2301.

**Dodd's Bookstore** 4818 E. 2nd St. **438-9948** 10am-10pm, noon-6pm Sun • strong lesbigay section • wheelchair access

**Hot Stuff** 2121 E. Broadway **433-0692** 11am-7pm, til 5pm wknds • cards • gifts • toys

**Out & About On Broadway** 1724 E. Broadway **436-9930** 12:30pm-10pm, noon-8pm Sun • clothing • videos • books

**Pearls Booksellers** 224 Redondo Ave. **438-8875** 11am-7pm, noon-5pm wknds • women's • wheelchair access • women-owned/run

### TRAVEL AGENTS

**Blaze Travel** 1349 E. Broadway **628-0555** IGLTA

**Touch of Travel** 3918 Atlantic Ave. **427-2144**/**(800) 833-3387**IGLTA

**Two Brothers Travel** 6280 Bridle Cir. **938-8650** IGLTA

### SPIRITUAL GROUPS

**Christ Chapel** 3935 E. 10th St. **438-5303** 10am & 6pm Sun, 7pm Wed • non-denominational • wheelchair access

**Dignity 984-8400** call for service times & locations

**First United Methodist Church** 507 Pacific Ave. **437-1289** 9am & 11am Sun • wheelchair access

**Lesbian/Gay Chavurah** 3801 E. WIllow St. (Jewish Comm. Ctr.) **426-7601 x31**

**Trinity Lutheran Church** 759 Linden Ave. **437-4002** 10am Sun • wheelchair access

### EROTICA

**The Crypt on Broadway** 1712 E. Broadway **983-6560** leather • toys

**The Rubber Tree** 5018 E. 2nd St. **438-7600**

# damronatlas
## WORLDTRAVEL

• offices nationwide
• great rates on airfare
• gay cruises & tours
• groups & special events welcome
• fully accredited IATA agency

*finally the most popular gay guidebooks and the most popular gay travel agency team up!*

**Call toll-free: (888) 907•9771
or (310) 670•6991**

# LOS ANGELES

*Los Angeles is divided into 7 geographical areas (see map on pages 70-71):*

## L.A.—Overview

## L.A.—West Hollywood

## L.A.—Hollywood

## L.A.—West L.A. & Santa Monica

## L.A.—Silverlake

## L.A.—Midtown

## L.A.—Valley

## L.A.—Overview

### INFO LINES & SERVICES

**Alcoholics Together Center** 1773 Griffith Park Blvd. **(213) 663-8882/(213) 936-4343 (AA#)** call for mtg. times • 12-step groups

**Asian/Pacific Gays & Friends (213) 980-7874** call for events

**Bi-Social (Pansocial) Center & Bi-Line** 7136 Matilija Ave., Van Nuys **(213) 873-3700/(818) 989-3700** 24hr hotline for bi, transgender & gay info/referrals

**Gay/Lesbian Youth Talk Line (213) 993-7475** 7pm-10pm, clsd Sun • referrals & support for those 23 & under • women's night Mon

▲ **Los Angeles Gay/Lesbian Community Center** 1625 N. Shrader **(213) 993-7400** 9am-10pm, til 6pm Sun • wide variety of services

**South Bay Lesbian/Gay Community Organization (310) 379-2850** support/education for Manhattan, Hermosa & Redondo Beaches, Torrance, Palos Verdes, El Segundo

### ACCOMMODATIONS

**Bed & Breakfast California (310) 498-0552/(800) 383-3513** reservation service

### BARS & NIGHTCLUBS

**Meow Mix West 969-4666** mostly women • live shows • call for events

### ENTERTAINMENT & RECREATION

**The Celebration Theatre** 7051-B Santa Monica Blvd. **(213) 957-1884** lesbigay theater • call for more info

**Highways** 1651 18th St., Santa Monica **453-1755** 'full-service performance center'

# WHAT'S WRONG WITH THIS PICTURE?

## . . .NOTHING

# 1 (888) 44 DINAH
## CLUB SKIRTS & GIRL BAR

# Los Angeles

*T*here is no city that better embodies the extremes of American life than Los Angeles. Here fantasy and reality have become inseparable. The mere mention of the 'City of Angels' conjures up images of palm-lined streets, sun-drenched beaches, and wealth beyond imagination, along with smog, over-crowded freeways, searing poverty, and urban violence.

Most travellers come only for the fantasy. They want to star-gaze at Mann's Chinese Theatre in Hollywood, at movie and television studios (Fox, Universal) in Burbank, at famous restaurants (Spago, The City, Chasen's, Citrus, Ivy's, Chaya Brasserie, Morton's, etc.) and, of course, all along Rodeo Drive. (Our favorite star-gazing location is **Canter's Deli** after 2am.)

But if you take a moment to focus your sights past the usual tourist traps, you'll see the unique—and often tense—diversity that L.A. offers as a city on the borders of Latin America, the Pacific Rim, Suburbia USA, and the rest of the world. You'll find museums, centers, and theatres celebrating the cultures of the many peoples who live in this valley. An excellent example is West Hollywood's June Mazer Lesbian Collection. Other cultural epicenters include Olvera Street, Korea Town, China Town and the historically Jewish Fairfax District. Call the L.A. Visitor's Bureau for directions and advice.

L.A.'s art scene rivals New York's, so if you're an art-lover be sure to check out the galleries and museums, as well as the performance art scene (check a recent LA Weekly). Our favorite gallery, reknowned for its trashy kitsch art, is La Luz de Jesus Gallery ( 213/651-4875).

Other kitsch fans should explore cult store **Archaic**

**Idiot/Mondo Video** or the many thrift shops in hip neighborhood Los Feliz (pronounced anglo-style: *Lahss Feel-iss*) or video theater EZTV (on Melrose, 310/657-1532), while trash or kink fans should schedule time at Trashy Lingerie (on LaCienega, 310/652-4543) and the **Pleasure Chest,** or pick up some new body ornaments at the **Gauntlet.**

L.A. is a car-driven city—remember the song, "Nobody Walks in L.A.?" Nobody takes the bus, either, if they can avoid it. So plan on spending a day just driving; don't miss Mulholland Drive at night.

As for lesbian nightlife in L.A., there are several full-time women's bars (some of them in the Valley), and many women's nights. L.A. is where the one-nighter women's dance bar revolution began, so make sure to double-check the papers before you go out.

But the big deal for women in L.A. is the retro-chic supperclub—a perfect combo of the food, schmoozing, and entertainment that define L.A. nightlife. Try the Women's Night at **Atlas** or call to find out about the latest **Klub Banshee** event. For serious girl-watching, cruise by **Michele's XXX All-Female Topless Revue** at **7969** on Tuesdays. For coffee and girls with British accents, stop by **Van Go's Ear** in Venice. And you can always visit that perennially popular night spot, **The Palms.**

Check out Los Feliz, the new neighborhood to cruise between Silverlake and Hollywood. We hear tell that Madonna is making a home there with baby Lourdes.

You'll really find out the buzz at **Sisterhood Bookstore,** another great spot to get caught up or checked out. While you're there pick up a copy of **Female FYI** or the more topical **Lesbian News.**

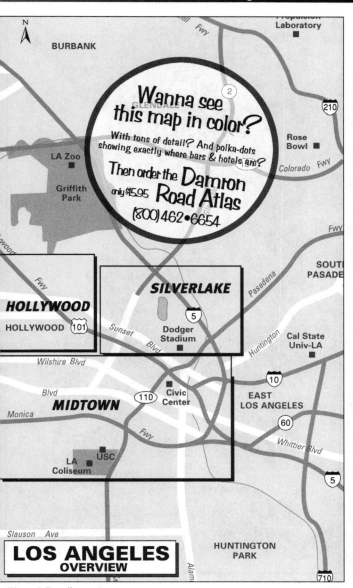

LOS ANGELES OVERVIEW

Wanna see this map in color?
With tons of detail? And polka-dots showing exactly where bars & hotels are?
Then order the Damron Road Atlas
only $15.95
(800) 462•6654

# Gay & Lesbian Center

"The world's largest gay & lesbian organization"

Pride. Purpose. Progress.
25 years strong.

1625 North Schrader Boulevard
Los Angeles, California 90028
(213)993-7400

**Los Angeles**

(213/310/818)

**Where the Girls Are:** Hip dykes hang out in West Hollywood, with the boys along Santa Monica Blvd., or cruising funky Venice Beach and Santa Monica. The S&M ("Stand & Model") glamour-dykes pose in chichi clubs and posh eateries in West L.A. and Beverly Hills. There's a scattered community of women in Silverlake. And more suburban lesbians frequent the women's bars in Studio City and North Hollywood. If you're used to makeup-free lesbians, you may be surprised that coiffed and lipsticked lesbian style is the norm in LA.

**Entertainment:** Celebration Theatre: 213/957-1884. 7051-B Santa Monica Blvd. Highways: 310/453-1755. 1651 18th St., Santa Monica. Theatre Geo: 213/466-1767. 1229 N. Highland Ave. Gay Men's Chorus: 213/650-0756.

**Lesbigay Pride:** June: 213/860-0701 (Christopher St. West).

**Annual Events:**

April - AIDS Dance-a-thon: 213/466-9255.

May - **California AIDS Ride:** 213/874-7474 & 800/474-3395. AIDS benefit bike ride from San Francisco to LA.

July 11-20 - **Outfest:** 213/951-1247. Los Angeles' lesbian & gay film and video festival.

August 23-24 - **Sunset Junction Fair:** 213/661-7771. Carnival, arts & information fair on Sunset Blvd. in Silverlake benefits Sunset Junction Youth Center. **Labor Day L.A.:** 800/522-7329. Weekend-long AIDS fundraising celebration with many events.

September - AIDS Walk LA: 213/466-9255. AIDS benefit. **Gay Night at Knotts Berry Farm:** 805/222-7788.

November - **Gay Night at Disneyland:** 805/222-7788.

**City Info:** 800/228-2452.

**Attractions:** Melrose Ave. in West Hollywood. City Walk in Universal Studios. Venice Beach. Sunset Blvd. in Hollywood. Westwood Village. Chinatown. Theme Parks: Disneyland, Knotts Berry Farm or Magic Mountain.

**Best View:** Drive up Mulholland Drive, in the hills between Hollywood and the Valley, for a panoramic view of the city, and the Hollywood sign.

**Weather:** Summers are hot, dry and smoggy with temperatures in the 80's -90's. L.A.'s weather is at its finest — sunny, blue skies and moderate temperatures (mid 70's) — during the months of March, April and May.

**Transit:** Green & White Taxi: 213/870-4664. United Yellow: 310/855-7070. LA Express: 800/427-7483. Super Shuttle: 310/782-6600. Metro Transit Authority: 213/626-4455.

**IMRU Gay Radio** KPFK LA 90.7 FM **(818) 985-2711** 10pm Sun • also 'This Way Out' 4:30pm Tue

### PUBLICATIONS

**4-Front Magazine** (213) 650-7772
**The Edge** (213) 962-6994
**fab!** (213) 655-5716 free club listings
**Female FYI** (213) 938-5969 monthly • lesbian lifestyle/entertainment magazine
**Genre** (213) 896-9778 slick nat'l magazine
**L.A. Girl Guide** (310) 391-8877
**Leather Journal** (213) 656-5073 lifestyle newsmagazine
▲ **Lesbian News** (310) 787-8658/(800) 458-9888 see ad front color section
**Nightlife** (213) 462-5400 club listings
**SBC Magazine** 1155 4th Ave. (213) 733-5661
**The Women's Yellow Pages** (818) 995-6646

### TRAVEL AGENTS

**By Exposure** (213) 913-1300 IGLTA
**Damron Atlas World Travel** 8923 S. Sepulveda Blvd. (310) 670-6991/(888) 907-9771 IGLTA

### SPIRITUAL GROUPS

**Beth Chayim Chadashim** 6000 W. Pico Blvd. (213) 931-7023 8pm Fri

## L.A.—West Hollywood    (310)

### ACCOMMODATIONS

**The Grove Guesthouse** 1325 N. Orange Grove Ave. (213) 876-7778 lesbians/gay men • 1-bdrm cottage • hot tub • designated smoking areas • kitchens • pets ok by arr. • gay-owned/run • $125-150
**Holloway Motel** 8465 Santa Monica Blvd. (213) 654-2454/(888) 654-6400 lesbians/gay men • kitchens • centrally located • gay-owned/run • IGLTA • $55-85
▲ **Le Montrose Suite Hotel** 900 Hammond St. 855-1115/(800) 776-0666 gay-friendly • hot tub • swimming • kitchens • fireplaces • smokefree • gym • kids/pets ok • also full restaurant • rooftop patio • IGLTA • wheelchair access • $150-475
**Le Parc Hotel de Luxe** 733 N. West Knoll Dr. 855-8888/(800) 578-4837 popular • gay-friendly • swimming • tennis courts • kids/pets ok • also restaurant • IGLTA • wheelchair access • $165-265

**Le Reve** 8822 Cynthia St. 854-1114/(800) 835-7997 gay-friendly • swimming • kids ok • IGLTA • wheelchair access
**Ma Maison Sofitel** 8555 Beverly Blvd. 278-5444/(800) 521-7772 gay-friendly • swimming • food served • wheelchair access • IGLTA
**Ramada West Hollywood** 8585 Santa Monica Blvd. 652-6400/(800) 845-8585 gay-friendly • modern art deco hotel & suites • swimming • kids ok • IGLTA • wheelchair access • $79-250
**San Vincente B&B Resort** 845 San Vincente Blvd. 854-6915 mostly gay men • swimming • hot tub • nudity • $59-129

### BARS & NIGHTCLUBS

**7702 SM Club** 7702 Santa Monica Blvd. (213) 654-3336 24hrs • lesbians/gay men • neighborhood bar • dancing/DJ • wheelchair access
**7969** 7969 Santa Monica Blvd. (213) 654-0280 9pm-2am • gay-friendly • live shows • transgender-friendly • 'Michele's XXX Review' 9pm Tue
**Axis** 652 N. La Peer 659-0471 9pm-2am Tue-Sun • mostly gay men • dancing/DJ • alternative • live shows • videos • 'Girl Bar' Fri (women only)
**Checca Bar & Cafe** 7323 Santa Monica Blvd. (213) 850-7471 11:30am-2am • popular • gay-friendly • dancing/DJ • live shows • theme nights • also restaurant (dinner only) • French/Italian • some veggie • patio
**Comedy Store** 8433 Sunset Blvd. (213) 656-6225 8pm-1am • gay-friendly • stand-up club • lesbigay comedy Sat in 'Belly Room'
**Fuel** 394-6541 women's nightclub Wed & Sun • call for events
▲ **Girl Bar** (213) 460-2531 9pm-2am Fri-Sat • popular • women only • dancing/DJ • call hotline for events & locations
**Improvisation** 8162 Melrose Ave. (213) 651-2583 gay-friendly • stand-up comedy • also restaurant
**Klub Banshee Hotline** 8512 Santa Monica (Benvenuto Cafe) 288-1601 8pm-2am Mon • popular • mostly women • call for events • dance parties in the L.A. area
**Love Lounge** 657 N. Robertson Blvd. 659-0471 9pm-2am, clsd Mon • lesbians/gay men • dancing/DJ • alternative • live shows • theme nights • women only Sat

WEST LA'S FINEST ALL SUITE HOTEL

WEST HOLLYWOOD CALIFORNIA

REVOLVER ▪ MICKY'S ▪ MOTHER LODE ▪ AXIS ▪ ABC ▪ CBS

BEVERLY CENTER ▪ SUNSET STRIP ▪ SPAGO ▪ HOLLYWOOD BOWL

PARAMOUNT STUDIOS ▪ ORSO ▪ CAFFE LUNA

ARENA

RAGE

UNIVERSAL STUDIOS HOLLYWOOD ▪ BILLBOARD LIVE ▪ PARADISE GRILL

JACKSON'S ▪ HOLLYWOOD BOWL

PACIFIC DESIGN CENTER

HOUSE OF BLUES ▪ RODEO DRIVE ▪ SANTA MONICA BLVD.

## WE RUN IN VERY EXCLUSIVE CIRCLES

Le Montrose is nestled on a quiet lane just below the Sunset Strip. A stone's throw from Beverly Hills. Closest hotel to West Hollywood hot spots.

128 charming suites, some with kitchenettes, each featuring color TV's and VCR's, individual air conditioning, multi-line telephones with voice mail, fireplace, private balcony, twice daily maid service.

Delightful private restaurant, rooftop pool & jacuzzi, lighted free tennis court, health club, tennis pro, private trainer on staff, bicycles, jogging, non-smoking, and handicapped rooms, meeting facilities, suite service. Bilingual staff, currency exchange, In-suite movies, fax machines, Nintendo.

## le montrose
SUITE HOTEL DE GRAN LUXE

Internet Address: http://www.travelweb.com
Internet http://www.travel2000.com
310-855-1115
900 Hammond Street, Los Angeles, CA 90069

(800) 776-0666

MEMBER

**IGTA**

INTERNATIONAL · GAY · TRAVEL · ASSOCIATION

# Girl Bar Los Angeles

## 7 Years and Going Strong!

Co-Producers of the Dinah Shore Weekend & the Nation's Largest Dance and Entertainment Club

For Women
located in the heart of West Hollywood, California

## Every Friday Night

West Hollywood's Largest Dance Club
652 N. La Peer Drive

## Every Saturday Night

LOVE LOUNGE

Live Entertainment & DJ Dancing
657 N. RoberTson Blvd.

For more information call our hotline
213 - 460 - 2531

Simply...The Place To Be!

or Visit our website @ www.girlbar.com

**Maverick Productions** (714) 854-4337 special events for women including 'Singlefest' & 'Country Fever'

**Meow Mix West** (213) 969-4666 women's nightclub Wed • call for events

**The Normandie Room** 8737 Santa Monica Blvd. **659-6204** 5pm-2am

▲ **The Palms** 8572 Santa Monica Blvd. **652-6188** noon-2am • popular • mostly women • neighborhood bar • dancing/DJ • wheelchair access

**Rage** 8911 Santa Monica Blvd. **652-7055** noon-2am • popular • mostly gay men • dancing/DJ • live shows • videos • lunch daily • wheelchair access

**Revolver** 8851 Santa Monica Blvd. **659-8851** 4pm-2am, til 4am Fri-Sat, from 2pm Sun • popular • mostly gay men • alternative • videos

**Union** 8210 Sunset Blvd. (213) 654-1001 8pm-2am • gay-friendly

**Viper Room** 8852 Sunset Blvd. **358-1880** 9pm-2am • gay-friendly

**Wildfire Productions** (213) 960-4329 mostly gay men • after hours club • call for events

## CAFES

**Club Cafe** 8560 Santa Monica Blvd. (in Athletic Club) **659-6630** 7am-9pm, til 6pm Sat, til 5pm Sun • salads & sandwiches • $5-10

**The Heights Cafe** 1118 N. Crescent Heights Blvd. (213) 650-9688 7am-11pm, 8pm-midnight Fri-Sat, til 9pm Sun • lesbians/gay men • bistro • plenty veggie • BYOB

**Little Frida's Coffee House** 8730 Santa Monica Blvd. **854-5421** 11am-11pm, til midnight Fri-Sat, clsd Mon • popular

**Mani's Bakery** 519 S. Fairfax Ave. (213) 938-8800 6:30am-midnight, 7:30am-1am wknds • coffee & dessert bar • wheelchair access

**Who's On Third Cafe** 8369 W. 3rd St. (213) 651-2928 8am-6pm, til 3pm Sun • $8-12

## RESTAURANTS

**The Abbey** 692 N. Robertson **289-8410** 7am-3am • lesbians/gay men • patio • wheelchair access

**Alto Palato** 755 N. La Cienega Blvd. **657-9271** 6pm-11pm • bargain pasta & comfortable chairs • full bar • $12-17

THE·PALMS

COCKTAIL LOUNGE

PARKING AVAILABLE — CALL FOR INFO
8572 SANTA MONICA BOULEVARD • (310) 652-6188

**Baja Bud's** 8575 Santa Monica Blvd. **659-1911** 7am-10pm, til 11pm Fri-Sat • healthy Mexican • under $10

**Benvenuto** 8512 Santa Monica Blvd. **659-8635** lunch Mon-Fri, dinner 5:30pm-10:30pm, til 11pm Fri-Sat • Italian • $8-16

**Bossa Nova** 685 N. Robertson Blvd. **657-5070** 11am-11pm • Brazilian • patio • wheelchair access • $7 & up

**Caffe Luna** 7463 Melrose Ave. **(213) 655-9177** 8am-3am, til 4am wknds • popular afterhours • Italian country food • some veggie • wheelchair access • $15-25

**Canter's Deli** 419 N. Fairfax **(213) 651-2030** 24hrs • hip afterhours • Jewish/American • some veggie • wheelchair access

**Crostini** 846 N. La Cienega Blvd. **652-8254** lunch & dinner, clsd Sun • Italian bistro • $7-16

**Eclipse** 8800 Melrose Ave. **724-5959** see and be seen • specialty is oven-baked fish • $17-30

**Figs** 7929 Santa Monica Blvd. **(213) 654-0780** dinner, Sun brunch • Californian • some veggie • full bar • $8-15

**French Quarter Market Place** 7985 Santa Monica Blvd. **(213) 654-0898** 7am-midnight, til 3:30am Fri-Sat • popular • lesbians/gay men • some veggie • $5-12

**The Greenery** 8945 Santa Monica Blvd. **275-9518** 8am-1am, til 3am Fri-Sat • Californian • some veggie • wheelchair access • $7-12

**Hoy's Wok** 8163 Santa Monica Blvd. **(213) 656-9002** noon-11pm, from 4pm Sun • Mandarin • plenty veggie • wheelchair access • $8-12

**Il Pastaio** 400 N. Cannon Dr., Beverly Hills **205-5444** homemade pasta & great colorful risotto • $8-12

**Il Piccolino Trattoria** 350 N. Robertson Blvd. **659-2220** 11am-11pm, clsd Sun, patio

**L'Orangerie** 903 N. La Cienega Blvd. **652-9770** lunch & dinner, clsd Mon • haute French • patio • $28-38

**La Masía** 9077 Santa Monica Blvd. **273-7066** clsd Mon-Tue • Spanish/cont'l • $14-24

**Luna Park** 655 N. Robertson **652-0611** dinner • eclectic European/Mediterranean • some veggie • cabaret • wheelchair access • $10-15

**Marix Tex Mex** 1108 N. Flores **(213) 656-8800** 11am-midnight • lesbians/gay men • TexMex • some veggie • great margaritas • $10-15

**Mark's Restaurant** 861 N. La Cienega Blvd. **652-5252** 6pm-10pm, til 11:30pm Fri-Sat, Sun brunch • plenty veggie • full bar • $7-16

**Melrose Place** 650 N. La Cienega Blvd. **657-2227** 5pm-11pm • cont'l/Californian • some veggie • full bar • wheelchair access • $8-15

**The Shed** 8474 Melrose Ave. **(213) 655-6277** clsd Sun • dinner • cont'l • $12-17

**Skewers** 8939 Santa Monica Blvd. **271-0555** 11am-2am • grill, salads, dips • beer/wine • under $10

**Tango Grill** 8807 Santa Monica Blvd. **659-3663** noon-11pm • lesbians/gay men • some veggie • beer/wine • wheelchair access • $6-12

**Tommy Tang's** 7313 Melrose Ave. **(213) 937-5733** noon-11pm • popular Tue nights w/'Club Glenda' • beer/wine

**Trocadero** 8280 Sunset Blvd. **(213) 656-7161** 6pm-3am, clsd Sun • pastas & salads • full bar • patio • $6-14

**Yukon Mining Co.** 7328 Santa Monica Blvd. **(213) 851-8833** 24hrs • popular • champagne Sat & Sun brunch • beer/wine • $6-11

## BOOKSTORES & RETAIL SHOPS

**A Different Light** 8853 Santa Monica Blvd. **854-6601** 10am-11pm, til midnight Fri-Sat • popular • lesbigay

**Book Soup** 8818 Sunset Blvd. **659-3110**

**Dorothy's Surrender** 7985 Santa Monica Blvd. #111 **(213) 650-4111** 10am-11:30pm • cards • magazines • gifts

## TRAVEL AGENTS

**Azzurro Travel** 7985 Santa Monica Blvd. #109 **(213) 654-3700/(800) 864-6567** IGLTA

**Cassis Travel Services** 9200 W. Sunset Blvd. #320 **246-5400** IGLTA

**Classic Travel PHONE ME** 7985 Santa Monica Blvd. #103 **(213) 650-8444** IGLTA

**Club Travel** 8739 Santa Monica Blvd. **358-2207/(800) 429-8747** IGLTA

**Embassy Travel** 906 N. Harper Ave. #B **(213) 656-0743/(800) 227-6668** IGLTA

**Friends Travel** 322 Huntley Dr. #100 **652-9600/(800) 429-0069**

**Gunderson Travel** 8543 Santa Monica Blvd. #8 **657-3944/(800) 872-8457** IGLTA

**Magnum/Select Travel** 9056 Santa Monica Blvd. #304 **887-0930** IGLTA

**Travel, Etc.** 8764 Holloway Dr. **652-4430** IGLTA

**Traveline** 8721 Santa Monica Blvd. #845 **(213) 654-3000** IGLTA

**West Hollywood Travel** 801 Larrabee St. **289-5900/(800) 893-7846** IGLTA

### SPIRITUAL GROUPS

**Congregation Kol Ami** 7350 Sunset Blvd. **248-6320** 8pm Fri

**MCC LA** 8714 Santa Monica Blvd. **854-9110** 9am, 11am & 6pm Sun

**West Hollywood Presbyterian Church** 7350 Sunset Blvd. **(213) 874-6646** 11am Sun • wheelchair access

### GYMS & HEALTH CLUBS

**Athletic Club** 8560 Santa Monica Blvd. **659-6630**

**Easton's Gym** 8053 Beverly Blvd. **(213) 651-3636** gay-friendly

### EROTICA

**Circus of Books** 8230 Santa Monica Blvd. **(213) 656-6533** videos • erotica • toys

**Drake's** 8932 Santa Monica Blvd. **289-8932** gifts • toys • videos • also at 7566 Melrose Ave. **(213) 651-5600**

**Gauntlet** 8720-1/2 Santa Monica Blvd. **657-6677** body piercings

**Pleasure Chest** 7733 Santa Monica Blvd. **(213) 650-1022**

**Skin Graffiti Tattoo** 8722 Santa Monica Blvd. (upstairs) **358-0349**

## L.A.—Hollywood (213)

### ACCOMMODATIONS

**Hollywood Celebrity Hotel** 1775 Orchid Ave. **850-6464/(800) 222-7017** gay-friendly • 1930s Art Deco hotel • kids/pets ok • non-smoking rms avail. • IGLTA • $55-115

**Hollywood Metropolitan Hotel** 5825 Sunset Blvd. **962-5800/(800) 962-5800** gay-friendly • kids ok • also restaurant • $49-129

### BARS & NIGHTCLUBS

**Blacklite** 1159 N. Western **469-0211** 6am-2am • lesbians/gay men • neighborhood bar

**Faultline** 4216 Melrose **660-0889** 3pm-2am • beer/soda bust 3pm-7pm Sun • popular • mostly gay men • leather • occasional leatherwomen's events • videos • food served • patio • also 'Faultline Store' 660-2952

**Octopussy (213) 390-2663** women's nightclub Sat • call for events

**Temple** (call for location) **243-5221** mostly gay men • dancing/DJ • alternative • underground house Sat • call for events

**Tempo** 5520 Santa Monica Blvd. **466-1094** from 8pm, from 6pm Sun, til 4am wknds • mostly gay men • dancing/DJ • mostly Latino-American • live shows

### RESTAURANTS

**360° Restaurant & Lounge** 6290 Sunset Blvd. **871-2995** lunch & dinner til midnight Th-Sat

**Hollywood Canteen** 1006 Seward St. **465-0961** 11:30am-10pm • popular • classic

**La Poubelle** 5907 Franklin Ave. **465-0807** 6pm-midnight • French/Italian • some veggie • wheelchair access • $20-25

**Prado** 244 N. Larchmont Blvd. **467-3871** lunch & dinner • Caribbean • some veggie • wheelchair access • $20-30

**Quality** 8030 W. 3rd St. **658-5959** 8am-4pm • homestyle brkfst • some veggie • wheelchair accessible • $8-12

### BOOKSTORES & RETAIL SHOPS

**Archaic Idiot/Mondo Video** 1724 N. Vermont **953-8896** noon-10pm • vintage clothes • cult & lesbigay videos

**Videoactive** 2522 Hyperion Ave. **669-8544** 10am-11pm, 10am-midnight Fri-Sat • lesbigay section • adult videos

### PUBLICATIONS

**Community Yellow Pages (213) 469-4454** annual survival guide to lesbigay southern CA

### TRAVEL AGENTS

**Jacqleen's Travel Service** 6222 Fountain Ave. #314 **463-7404** IGLTA

**Travel Lab** 1943 Hillhurst Ave. **660-9811/(800) 747-7026** IGLTA

**Travel Management Group** 832 N. La Brea Ave. **993-0444/(800) 666-6717** IGLTA

### SPIRITUAL GROUPS
**Dignity LA** 126 S. Ave. 64 **344-8064** 5:30pm Sun • Spanish Mass 3rd Sat

### GYMS & HEALTH CLUBS
**Gold's Gym** 1016 N. Cole Ave. **462-7012**

## L.A.—West L.A. &
## Santa Monica                     (310)

### INFO LINES & SERVICES
**Women Motorcyclists of Southern California** (213) 664-3964 monthly Sun brunch • social events open to all interested women

### ACCOMMODATIONS
**The Georgian** 1415 Ocean Ave., Santa Monica **395-9945/(800) 538-8147** gay-friendly • food served • wheelchair access

**Malibu Beach Inn** 22878 Pacific Coast Hwy. **456-5428/(800) 462-6444** gay-friendly • on the ocean • kids ok • wheelchair access

**Rose Avenue Beach House** 55 Rose Ave., Venice **396-2803** gay-friendly • Victorian beach house • 1 blk. from ocean & boardwalk

**Westwood Marquis Hotel & Gardens** 730 Hilgard Ave. **208-8765/(800) 421-2317** IGLTA

### BARS & NIGHTCLUBS
**Babylon** 2105 Artesia Blvd., Redondo Beach **793-9393** 4pm-2am • patio

**Connection** 4363 Sepulveda Blvd., Culver City **391-6817** 2pm-2am, from noon wknds • popular • mostly women • neighborhood bar • dancing/DJ • women-owned/run

**Dolphin** 1995 Artesia Blvd., Redondo Beach **318-3339** 1pm-2am • mostly gay men • neighborhood bar • wheelchair access

**J.J.'s Pub** 2692 S. La Cienega **837-7443** 11am-2am • mostly gay men • neighborhood bar • wheelchair access

**Studio City Bar & Grill** 11002 Ventura Blvd. **763-7912** 6pm-2am • mostly women • dancing/DJ • food served • woman-owned/run

**Trilogy** 2214 Stoner Ave., West Los Angeles **477-2844** from 6pm, clsd Mon-Tue • gay-friendly • transgender-friendly • dinner theater w/drag waitresses/performers

### CAFES
**Van Go's Ear** 796 Main St., Venice **314-0022** 24hrs • $2-9

**Wolfgang Puck Cafe** 1323 Montana Ave., Santa Monica **393-0290** colorful entrees à la Puck (fast food versions) • $10-13

### RESTAURANTS
**12 Washington** 12 Washington Blvd., Venice **822-5566** dinner from 6pm • cont'l • $10-30

**Baja Cantina** 311 Washington Blvd., Venice **821-2252** 11am-2am, from 10am wknds

**Cheesecake Factory** 4142 Via Marina, Venice **306-3344** 11:30am-noon, 10am-10:30pm Sun • full menu • $5-20

**Drago** 2628 Wilshire Blvd., Santa Monica **828-1585** lunch & dinner • Sicilian Italian

**Golden Bull** 170 W. Channel Rd., Santa Monica **230-0402** full bar

**Joe's** 1023 Abbot Kinney Blvd., Venice **399-5811** French/Californian, clsd Mon

**The Local Yolk** 3414 Highlands Ave., Manhattan Beach **546-4407** 6:30am-2:30pm

**Siamese Princess** 8048 W. 3rd St. **(213) 653-2643** 5:30pm-11pm, clsd Mon & Th • lunch wkdays • Thai • beer/wine • $6-10

### BOOKSTORES & RETAIL SHOPS
**Her Body Books** 433 S. Beverly Dr., Beverly Hills **553-5821** 9am-6pm, clsd wknds • women's health books • gifts & supplies • women-owned/run

**NaNa** 1228 3rd St., Santa Monica **394-9690** 11am-9pm, til 11pm Fri-Sat • hip shoes & clothes • also Nana outlet at 8727 W. 3rd St. (213) 653-1252

**Sisterhood Bookstore** 1351 Westwood Blvd., Westwood **477-7300** 10am-8pm • women's • periodicals • music & more • women-owned/run

### ENTERTAINMENT & RECREATION
**Women on a Roll** 578-8888

### TRAVEL AGENTS
**Atlas Travel Service** 8923 S. Sepulveda Blvd. **670-3574/(800) 952-0120 (OUTSIDE L.A.)** IGLTA

**Firstworld Travel Express** 1990 S. Bundy Dr. #175 **820-6868/(800) 366-0815** IGLTA

**The Traveler's Edge** 9363 Wilshire Blvd. #216, Beverly Hills **271-2208/(888) 777-5959** IGLTA

**Wilson's Travel** 9359 Wilshire Blvd., Beverly Hills **275-4131** IGLTA

### SPIRITUAL GROUPS
**St. Andrew's Episcopal Church** 1432 Engracia Ave., Torrance **328-3781** 8am & 10am Sun

### EROTICA
**The Love Boutique** 2924 Wilshire Blvd., Santa Monica **453-3459** toys

## L.A.—Silverlake (213)

### BARS & NIGHTCLUBS
**Drag Strip 66** 2500 Riverside Dr. (Rudolpho's) **969-2596** popular • queer dance club • call for events
**The Garage** 4519 Santa Monica Blvd. **683-3447** gay-friendly • call for events

### RESTAURANTS
**Casita Del Campo** 1920 Hyperion Ave. **662-4255** 11am-10pm • popular • Mexican • patio • also 'Plush Cabaret' Sat • call 969-2596 for details
**Cha Cha Cha** 656 N. Virgil **664-7723** 8am-10pm, til 11pm Fri-Sat • lesbians/gay men • Caribbean • plenty veggie • wheelchair access • $20-30
**The Cobalt Cantina** 4326 Sunset Blvd. **953-9991** 11am-11pm • lesbians/gay men • Cal-Mex • some veggie • full bar • patio • wheelchair access • $10-15
**The Crest Restaurant** 3725 Sunset Blvd. **660-3645** 6am-11pm • diner/Greek • $5-10
**Da Giannino** 2630 Hyperion Ave. **664-7979** lunch (Tue-Fri) & dinner, clsd Mon
**El Conquistador** 3701 Sunset Blvd. **666-5136** 5pm-11pm, from 11am wknds • Mexican • $5-10
**Rudolpho's** 2500 Riverside Dr. **669-1226** 8pm-2am • lesbians/gay men • salsa music & dancing lessons • patio
**Vida** 1930 Hillhurst Ave., Los Feliz **660-4446** hip with Asian accent • $12-17
**Zen Restaurant** 2609 Hyperion Ave. **665-2929/665-2930** 11:30am-2am • Japanese • some veggie • $9-12

### TRAVEL AGENTS
**Burgan Travel** 428 N. Azusa Ave., West Covina **(818) 915-8617**
**Pernell Carson Wagonlit Travel** 2616 Hyperion Ave. **660-2946** IGLTA

### SPIRITUAL GROUPS
**Holy Trinity Community Church** 4209 Santa Monica Blvd. **662-9118** 10am Sun

### GYMS & HEALTH CLUBS
**Body Builders** 2516 Hyperion Ave. **668-0802** gay-friendly

### EROTICA
**Circus of Books** 4001 Santa Monica Blvd. **666-1304** 24hrs Fri-Sat

## L.A.—Midtown (213)

### BARS & NIGHTCLUBS
**Jewel's Catch One Disco** 4067 W. Pico Blvd. **734-8849** noon-2am, til 5am Fri-Sat • upstairs opens 9pm Th-Sun for dancing • popular • lesbians/gay men • multi-racial • wheelchair access • women-owned/run
**The Red Head** 2218 E. 1st St. **263-2995** 2pm-midnight, til 2am wknds • mostly women • neighborhood bar • beer only

### RESTAURANTS
**Atlas** 3760 Wilshire Blvd. **380-8400** lunch & dinner except Sun • global cuisine • some veggie • full bar • $8-19
**Cassell's** 3266 W. 6th St. **480-8668** 10:30am-4pm, clsd Sun • great burgers

## L.A.—Valley (818)

### BARS & NIGHTCLUBS
**Apache Territory** 11608 Ventura Blvd., Studio City **506-0404** 3pm-2am, til 4am Fri-Sat • popular • lesbians/gay men • dancing/DJ • live shows
**Escapades** 10437 Burbank Blvd., N. Hollywood **508-7008** 1pm-2am • popular • lesbians/gay men • neighborhood bar • live shows • wheelchair access
**Gold 9** 13625 Moorpark St., Sherman Oaks **986-0285** 11am-2am, from 7am wknds • mostly gay men • neighborhood bar
**Incognito Valley** 7026 Reseda Blvd., Reseda **996-2976** noon-2am • popular • mostly gay men • dancing/DJ • wheelchair access
**Mag Lounge** 5248 N. Van Nuys Blvd., Van Nuys **981-6693** 11am-2am • popular • mostly gay men • wheelchair access
**Oasis** 11916 Ventura Blvd., Studio City **980-4811** 3pm-2am • lesbians/gay men • piano bar
**Oxwood Inn** 13713 Oxnard, Van Nuys **997-9666** (PAY PHONE) 3pm-2am, from noon Fri & Sun • mostly women • neighborhood bar • one of the oldest bars in the country • women-owned/run

*Sea View Inn*
At The Beach

• Ocean View
Rooms & Suites

• Courtyard & Pool

• 10 Minutes to LAX

• 100 Meters to
the Beach

• Voice Mail

• Cable T.V. & VCRs

3400 Highland Avenue
Manhattan Beach,
California 90266
310-545-1504
FAX: 310-545-4052

**Queen Mary** 12449 Ventura Blvd., Studio City **506-5619** 11am-2am, clsd Mon-Tue • popular • gay-friendly • shows wknds

**Rawhide** 10937 Burbank Blvd., N. Hollywood **760-9798** 7pm-2am, from 2pm Sun, clsd Mon-Wed • popular • mostly gay men • dancing/DJ • country/western

**Rumors** 10622 Magnolia Blvd. **506-9651** 6pm-2am, from 3pm Fri-Sun • mostly women • neighborhood bar • women-owned/run

RESTAURANTS
**Venture Inn** 11938 Ventura Blvd., Studio City **769-5400** lunch & dinner, champagne brunch Sun • popular • lesbians/gay men • full bar • $10-15

TRAVEL AGENTS
**Classic Cruise & Travel** 19626 Ventura Blvd. #216, Tarzana **346-8747** IGLTA

**JP Travel** 11632 Luanda St., Sylmar **834-2125** IGLTA

**Meridian Destinations** 13400 Riverside Dr. #111, Sherman Oaks **986-6868** IGLTA

**Southern Horizons Travel & Tours** 6100 Simpson Ave., N. Hollywood **980-7011/(800) 333-9361** IGLTA

SPIRITUAL GROUPS
**Christ Chapel of the Valley** 5006 Vineland Ave., N. Hollywood **985-8977** 10am Sun, 7:30pm Wed • full gospel fellowship

**MCC in the Valley** 5730 Cahuenga Blvd., N. Hollywood **762-1133** 10am Sun

GYMS & HEALTH CLUBS
**Gold's Gym** 6233 N. Laurel Canyon Blvd., N. Hollywood **506-4600**

EROTICA
**Le Sex Shoppe** 4539 Van Nuys Blvd., Sherman Oaks **501-9609** 24hrs

**Stan's Video** 7505 Foothill Blvd., Tujunga **352-8735**

## Manhattan Beach (310)

*(see also L.A.—West L.A. & Santa Monica)*

ACCOMMODATIONS
▲ **Seaview Inn at the Beach** 3400 Highland Ave. **545-1504** gay-friendly • swimming • non-smoking rms avail. • kids ok • courtyard

TRAVEL AGENTS
**Touches of Travel** 1015 1st St. **937-6724** IGLTA

## Marina del Rey (310)

### ACCOMMODATIONS

**The Mansion Inn** 327 Washington Blvd., Venice **821-2557/(800) 828-0688** gay-friendly • European-style inn • kids ok • wheelchair access • $69-125

## Mendocino (707)

### ACCOMMODATIONS

**Agate Cove Inn** 11201 N. Lansing **937-0551/(800) 527-3111** gay-friendly • full brkfst • fireplaces • smokefree • $99-250

**Bellflower 937-0783** lesbians only • secluded cabin with kitchen • near outdoor recreation • hot tub • fireplaces • smokefree • kids/pets ok • 2-night min. • $65

**Blair House & Cottage** 45118 Little Lake St. **937-1800** gay-friendly

**Glendeven** 8221 N. Hwy. 1, Little River **937-0083** gay-friendly • charming farmhouse on the coast • full brkfst • smokefree • kids ok

**McElroy's Inn** 998 Main St. **937-1734/937-3105** gay-friendly • pleasant rms & suites • located in the village • smokefree • kids ok

**Mendocino Coastal Reservations (800) 262-7801** 9am-6pm • gay-friendly • call for available rentals

**Sallie & Eileen's Place 937-2028** women only • cabins • hot tub • kitchens • fireplaces • kids/pets ok • 2 night min. • A-frame: $65; Cabin: $80; $15 each additional person

**Seagull Inn** 44594 Albion St. **937-5204** gay-friendly • 9 units in the heart of historic Mendocino • smokefree • kids ok • wheelchair access

**Stanford Inn by the Sea** Coast Hwy. 1 & Comptche-Ukiah Rd. **937-5615/(800) 331-8884** gay-friendly • full brkfst • hot tub • swimming • kitchens • fireplaces • smokefree • kids/pets ok • wheelchair access • $175-275

**Wildflower Ridge (510) 735-2079** women only • secluded cabin in Medocino • kids/pets ok ($5/night for dogs) • women-owned/run

### CAFES

**Cafe Beaujolais** 961 Ukiah **937-5614** dinner from 5:45pm • California country food • some veggie • wheelchair access • women-owned/run • $20-30

### BOOKSTORES & RETAIL SHOPS

**Book Loft** 45050 Main **937-0890** 10am-6pm • wheelchair access

## Menlo Park

*(see Palo Alto)*

## Midway City (714)

### BARS & NIGHTCLUBS

**The Huntress** 8122 Belsa Ave. **892-0048** 2pm-2am, from noon wknds • mostly women • dancing/DJ • wheelchair access

## Mission Viejo (714)

### TRAVEL AGENTS

**Sunrise Travel** 23891 Via Fabricante #603 **837-0620**

## Modesto (209)

### INFO LINES & SERVICES

**AA Gay/Lesbian** 1203 Tully Rd. #B **531-2040** 8pm daily, 7pm Sun

### BARS & NIGHTCLUBS

**Brave Bull** 701 S. 9th **529-6712** 7pm-2am, from 4pm Sun • mostly men • leather

**The Mustang Club** 413 N. 7th St. **577-9694** 4pm-2am, from 2pm Fri-Sun • open 30+ years! • lesbians/gay men • dancing/DJ • live shows • women-owned/run

### CAFES

**Espresso Caffe** 3025 Mettenig Ave. **571-3337** 7am-11pm, til midnight Fri-Sat • $4-7

### BOOKSTORES & RETAIL SHOPS

**Bookstore** 1700 McHenry Ave. **521-0535** 8am-9pm, 9am-6pm Sat, til 5pm Sun • readings • also espresso bar • wheelchair access

### TRAVEL AGENTS

**Tempo Travel** 1600 McHenry #A **521-2000** IGLTA

### EROTICA

**Liberty Adult Book Store** 1030 Kansas Ave. **524-7603** 24hrs

## Monterey (408)

### INFO LINES & SERVICES

**AA Gay/Lesbian** 373-3713 (AA#)

## ACCOMMODATIONS

**Gosby House Inn** 643 Lighthouse Ave., Pacific Grove **375-1287** gay-friendly • full brkfst • smokefree • kids ok • wheelchair access • $90-150

**Misty Tiger** 9422 Acorn Circle, Salinas **633-8808** women only • hot tub • video library • smokefree • women-owned/run

**Monterey Fireside Lodge** 1131 10th St. **373-4172/(800) 722-2624** gay-friendly • hot tub • fireplaces • non-smoking rms avail. • kids ok • $79-250

**Sapaque Valley Ranch Inn** 48491 Sapaque Valley Rd., Bradley **(805) 963-2860 (RESERVATIONS ONLY)/(805) 472-2750** gay-friendly • B&B • vacation home rental • near Big Sur & San Simeon • food served • group facilities avail.

## BARS & NIGHTCLUBS

**After Dark** 214 Lighthouse Ave. **373-7828** 8pm-2am • lesbians/gay men • dancing/DJ • videos • patio

**Title IX** 281 Lighthouse Ave., New Monterey **373-4488** 6pm-2am • lesbians/gay men • soon to be renamed

## RESTAURANTS

**The Clock Garden Restaurant** 565 Abrego **375-6100** 11am-midnight • American/cont'l • some veggie • patio • wheelchair access • $10-20

**Fisherman's Grotto** 39 Fisherman's Wharf #1 **375-4604** 11am-9pm • $20-40

**Tarpy's Roadhouse** 2999 Hwy. 68 at Canyon Dr. **647-1444** lunch & dinner

## Moraga (510)

### BOOKSTORES & RETAIL SHOPS

**Lonesome Traveller** 376-8846 traveling book mobile • call for details

## Mountain View (650)

### BARS & NIGHTCLUBS

**Daybreak** 1711 W. El Camino Real **940-9778** 3pm-2am, from 4pm wknds • mostly women • dancing/DJ • karaoke Th & Sun • wheelchair access

## Napa (707)

### ACCOMMODATIONS

**Bed & Breakfast Inns of Napa Valley** **944-4444** reservation service

**The Ink House B&B** 1575 St. Helena Hwy., St. Helena **963-3890** gay-friendly • 1884 Italianate Victorian among the vineyards • full brkfst • smokefree • kids ok • $110-155

### TRAVEL AGENTS

**Destinations** 1734 Jefferson St. #C **256-3078/(800) 509-3322**

## Novato (415)

### TRAVEL AGENTS

**Dimensions in Travel** 2 Commercial Blvd. #101 **883-3245 x202/(800) 828-2962** IGLTA

## Oakland

*(see East Bay)*

## Oceanside (619)

### BARS & NIGHTCLUBS

**Capri Lounge** 207 N. Tremont **722-7284** 10am-2am • mostly gay men • neighborhood bar • wheelchair access

### RESTAURANTS

**Greystokes** 1903 S. Coast Hwy. **757-2955** 9am-2am • lesbians/gay men • live shows • $8-14

## Orange

*(see also Anaheim)*

## Orland (530)

### ACCOMMODATIONS

**Inn at Shallow Creek Farm** 4712 Road DD **865-4093/865-4093** gay-friendly • smokefree • $55-75

## Palm Springs (760)

INFO LINES & SERVICES

**AA Gay/Lesbian** 324-4880 (AA#) call for mtg. schedule

**SCWU Desert Women** 363-7565 social/support group

ACCOMMODATIONS

**The Abbey West** 772 Prescott Cir. **416-2654/(800) 223-4073** mostly gay men • hot tub • swimming • gym • kitchens • private patios • wheelchair access • IGLTA • $135-250

**Aruba Hotel Suites** 671 S. Riverside Dr. **325-8440/(800) 842-7822** lesbians/gay men • apts on 2 levels • hot tub • swimming • kitchens • nudity • IGLTA • $109-169

▲ **Bee Charmer Inn** 1600 E. Palm Canyon Dr. **778-5883** women only • swimming • smokefree • lesbian-owned/run • $77-97

**Casa Rosa** 589 Grenfall Rd. **322-4143/(800) 322-4151** mostly gay men • B&B service in a private resort • full brkfst • hot tub • swimming • mist system • kitchens • nudity • private patios • wheelchair access • $65-120

**Desert Palms Inn** 67-580 E. Palm Canyon Dr., Cathedral City **324-3000/(800) 801-8696** lesbians/gay men • hot tub • swimming • huge courtyard • also restaurant • some veggie • full bar • wheelchair access • IGLTA

**Desert Shadows** 260 Chuckwalla **325-6410/(800) 292-9298** gay-friendly • naturist hotel • hot tub • swimming • nudity • kids ok • also restaurant • $5-20

**El Mirasol Villas** 525 Warm Sands Dr. **327-5913/(800) 327-2985** mostly gay men • hot tub • swimming • kitchens • nudity • food served • IGLTA • gay-owned/run • $95-180

**The Enclave** 641 San Lorenzo Rd. **325-5269/(800) 621-6973** mostly women • hotel • hot tub • swimming • nudity • pets ok • private patios • wheelchair access

**Ingleside Inn** 200 W. Ramon Rd. **325-0046** gay-friendly • hot tub • swimming • also restaurant • French con'tl • $25 • wheelchair access

*The Palm Springs Private Hotel For Women*

**BEE CHARMER INN**

• Pool and Private Courtyard
• Outdoor Misting System
• Refrigerators and Microwaves
• Cable Television
• Air Conditioning
• Continental Breakfast
• Minutes from Clubs, Restaurants, Hiking, Golf, and Tennis

*For Reservations or Brochure Call:* (760) 778-5883

**Le Garbo Inn** 287 W. Racquet Club Rd. **325-6737** mostly women • hot tub • swimming • nudity • lesbian-owned/run • $55-120

**Mira Loma Hotel** 1420 N. Indian Canyon Dr. **320-1178** lesbians/gay men • swimming • smokefree • kids ok

**The Villa Resort** 67-670 Carey Rd., Cathedral City **328-7211/(800) 845-5265** mostly men • individual bungalows • hot tub • swimming • sauna • massage • kitchens • IGLTA • $45-120

## BARS & NIGHTCLUBS

**Backstreet Pub** 72-695 Hwy. 111 #A-7, Palm Desert **341-7966** 2pm-2am • lesbians/gay men • neighborhood bar • wheelchair access • women-owned/run

**Choices** 68-352 Perez Rd., Cathedral City **321-1145/321-6167** 7pm-2am • popular • lesbians/gay men • dancing/DJ • live shows • videos • patio • wheelchair access

**Delilah's** 68-657 E. Palm Canyon Dr., Cathedral City **324-3268** 5pm-2am, clsd Mon-Tue • mostly women • dancing/DJ • live shows • country/western & karaoke Sun

**The Speakeasy** 2400 N. Palm Canyon Dr. **322-3224** 4pm-2am, clsd Mon • mostly gay men • piano bar • also restaurant (lesbians/gay men) • wheelchair access • women-owned/run

**Streetbar** 224 E. Arenas **320-1266** 2pm-2am • popular • lesbians/gay men • neighborhood bar • live shows • wheelchair access

**The Sundance Saloon** 38-737 Cathedral Canyon Dr., Cathedral City **321-0031** 2pm-2am • lesbians/gay men • dancing/DJ • also 'Love Shack' • mostly women • open 5pm Wed-Sun

**Sweetwater Saloon** 2420 N. Palm Canyon **320-8878** 11am-2am • mostly gay men • neighborhood bar

# Palm Springs  (760)

**Where the Girls Are:** Socializing with friends at private parties – you can meet them by getting in touch with a women's social organization like the SCWUDesert Women. Vacationers will be staying on E. Palm Canyon near Sunrise Way. Women do hang out at the boys' bars too. Try the popular disco Choices, the bar at The Desert Palms Inn, or just about anywhere on Perez Rd.

**Lesbigay Pride:** November: 322-8769.

## Annual Events:

March – **Nabisco Dinah Shore Golf Tournament:** 310/281-7358. One of the biggest gatherings of lesbians on the continent. **White Party:** popular circuit party. Mostly gay men.

**City Info:** Palm Springs Visitors Bureau: 778-8418. Desert Gay Tourism Guild: (888) 200-4469.

**Attractions:** Palm Springs Aerial Tramway to the top of Mt. San Jacinto, on Tramway Rd.

**Best View:** Top of Mt. San Jacinto. Driving through the surrounding desert, you can see great views of the mountains. But be careful in the summer. Always carry water in your vehicle, be sure to check all fluids in your car before you leave and frequently during your trip.

**Weather:** Palm Springs is sunny and warm in the winter, in the 70°s. Summers are torrid (100°+).

**Transit:** Airport Taxi: 321-4470. Rainbow Cab: 327-5702. Desert City Shuttle: 329-3334. Sun Line Transit Agency: 343-3451.

## CAFES

**Ivan's Cafe** 2466 N. Palm Canyon Dr. **320-2100** 9am-10pm, from 7am Sun • Bulgarian specialities

## RESTAURANTS

**Bangkok 5** 69-930 Hwy. 111, Rancho Mirage **770-9508** lunch & dinner, seasonal • Thai • $8-15

**Billy Reed's** 1800 N. Palm Canyon Rd. **325-1946** some veggie • full bar • also bakery • $7-13

**Blue Angel** 777 E. Tahquitz Canyon **778-4343**

**El Gallito Mexican Restaurant** 68820 Grove St., Cathedral City **328-7794** Mexican • beer/wine • $3-8

**Elan Brasserie** 415 N. Palm Canyon Dr. **323-5554** lunch & dinner • Provençal/ Mediterranean • full bar • live shows

**Las Casuelas** 368 N. Palm Canyon Dr. **325-3213** 10am-9:30pm • Mexican • some veggie

**Maria's Italian Cuisine** 67-778 Hwy. 111, Cathedral City **328-4378** 5:30pm-9:30pm dinner only, clsd Mon • plenty veggie • beer/wine • $8-15

**Mortimer's** 2095 N. Indian Canyon (at Casablanca) **320-4333** lunch & dinner • California/French • full bar • live shows • $15-30

**Paoli's Pizza & Pasta House** 71-380 Hwy. 111, Cathedral City **324-3737** $8-15

# Palm Springs

*P*alm Springs has a well-deserved reputation as one of the top resort destinations for lesbian and gay travellers. However, it's a man's world—except during **Dinah Shore Weekend** in late March.

The same is true for this desert resort's bumper crop of gay inns and guesthouses. Most are men only, either in practice or policy. However, there are three women's inns: the **Enclave, Le Garbo Inn,** and the **Bee Charmer Inn.** Wherever you're staying, make sure they have a misting machine to take the edge off dry desert summers.

For nightlife, you have **Choices** for dancing with the boys, and **Backstreet Pub** for more casual pursuits. To find out what's on for women, call **SCWU Desert Women.**

For a little danger and an amazing view, catch a ride on the Aerial Tram that goes from the desert floor to the top of Mount San Jacinto. When you come back to earth, it's time to lay back and treat yourself to some sun and outdoor fun.

By far the most popular event for women—a sort of informal Lesbian Festival, attracting thousands of lesbians from all over the western United States—is the Nabisco Dinah Shore Golf Tournament (call 619/324-4546 for details) in late March. The local lesbian and gay paper, the **Bottom Line,** and L.A.'s **Lesbian News,** publish special editions in March just to keep up with all the parties, contests and jubilation. See you there!

**Rainbow Cactus Cafe** 212 S. Indian Canyon **325-3868** 11am-2am • Mexican • full bar

**Red Tomato** 68-784 Grove St., Cathedral City **328-7518** 5pm-10pm • pizza & pasta • beer/wine • plenty veggie • wheelchair access • $10-15

**Robí** 78-085 Avenida La Fonda, La Quinta **564-0544** dinner only, clsd Mon (seasonal April-Oct) • cont'l • some veggie • wheelchair access • $45

**Shame on the Moon** 69-950 Frank Sinatra Dr., Rancho Mirage **324-5515** 5:30pm-10:30pm, clsd Mon (summer only) • cont'l • plenty veggie • full bar • patio • wheelchair access • $10-20

**Silas' on Palm Canyon** 664 N. Palm Canyon Dr. **325-4776** from 6pm, clsd Mon-Tue • intimate dining • cont'l • full bar • patio • $11-19

**Simba's** 190 N. Sunrise **778-7630** lunch & dinner • ribs

**Sorrentino's** 1032 N. Palm Canyon Dr. **325-2944** from 5pm, seafood

**Venezia Ristorante** 70-065 Hwy. 111, Rancho Mirage **328-5650** clsd Mon, seasonal • Italian • some veggie

**The Wilde Goose** 67-938 Hwy. 111, Cathedral City **328-5775** from 5:30pm • cont'l/wild game • plenty veggie • full bar • live shows • $20-40

## BOOKSTORES & RETAIL SHOPS

**Bloomsbury Books** 555 S. Sunrise Wy. **325-3862** 11am-9pm, clsd Sun • lesbigay • gay-owned/run

**Moonlighting** (at Desert Palms Inn) **770-8833** 6pm-2am, til 6am Th-Sun

## PUBLICATIONS

**The Bottom Line 323-0552** lesbigay newsmagazine

**Hijinx 329-2421** free lesbigay guide to Palm Springs & desert resorts

**Lifestyle Magazine 321-2685**

## TRAVEL AGENTS

**Anderson Travel Service** 700 E. Tahquitz Canyon Dr. #A **325-2001**/**(800) 952-5068** IGLTA

**Canyon Travel** 67-555 Hwy. 111 #C-110, Cathedral City **324-3484** IGLTA

**Journey's Travel** 42462 Bob Hope Dr. at Hwy. 111, Rancho Mirage **340-4545**/**(800) 733-3646**

**Las Palmas Travel** 403 N. Palm Canyon Dr. **325-6311**/**(800) 776-6888** IGLTA

**Rancho Mirage Travel** 71-428 E. Palm Canyon Dr., Rancho Mirage **341-7888**/**(800) 369-1073** IGLTA

## SPIRITUAL GROUPS

**Unity Church of Palm Springs** 815 S. Camino Real **325-7377** 11am Sun, 7:30pm Tue • also bookstore & classes

## GYMS & HEALTH CLUBS

**Gold's Gym** 40-70 Airport Center Dr. **322-4653** gay-friendly

**The Guest House** 246 N. Palm Canyon Dr. **320-3366** tropical day spa

**Palm Springs Athletic Club** 543 S. Palm Canyon **323-7722** gay-friendly

## EROTICA

**Black Moon Leather** 68-449 Perez Rd. #7, Cathedral City **770-2925**/**(800) 945-3284** 3pm-midnight, til 2am wknds

**Gay Mart** 305 E. Arenas **320-0606**

## Palo Alto (650)

### INFO LINES & SERVICES

**Palo Alto Lesbian Rap** 4161 Alma (YMCA) **583-1649** 7:30pm Th

**Peninsula Women's Group** (at 'Two Sisters Bookstore'), Menlo Park  7:30pm Wed

### BOOKSTORES & RETAIL SHOPS

**Books Inc.** 157 Stanford Shopping Center **321-0600** 9:30am-9pm, 10am-8pm Sat, til 6pm Sun • general • lesbigay section

**Stacey's Bookstore** 219 University Ave. **326-0681** 9am-9pm, til 10pm Fri-Sat, 11am-6pm Sun • general • lesbigay section

▲ **Two Sisters** 605 Cambridge Ave., Menlo Park **323-4778** 11am-9pm, 10am-5pm Sat, from noon Sun, clsd Mon • women's • wheelchair access • women-owned/run

## Pasadena (818)

### INFO LINES & SERVICES

**Hugo Au Go-Go's Video Lending Library** 1030 S. Arroyo Pkwy. **441-8495** free video lending library for people w/ HIV/AIDS

### BARS & NIGHTCLUBS

**Boulevard** 3199 E. Foothill Blvd. **356-9304** 1pm-2am • mostly gay men • neighborhood bar • piano bar Sun

**Club Three-Seven-Two** 3772 E. Foothill Blvd. **578-9359** 4pm-2am, from noon Fri, clsd Sun-Mon • mostly women • dancing/DJ • live bands Fri-Sat • country/western dance lessons Tue • wheelchair access

**Encounters** 203 N. Sierra Madre Blvd. **792-3735** 2pm-2am • mostly gay men • dancing/DJ

**Nardi's** 665 E. Colorado Blvd. **449-3152** 1pm-2am • mostly gay men • neighborhood bar • wheelchair access

### RESTAURANTS

**Twin Palms** 101 W. Green St. **577-2567** chic decor • reasonable prices • huge menu w/unusual combinations • $7-15

### BOOKSTORES & RETAIL SHOPS

**Page One Books** 1200 E. Walnut **796-8418** 11am-6:30pm, noon-5pm Sun, clsd Mon • women's • wheelchair access • women-owned/run

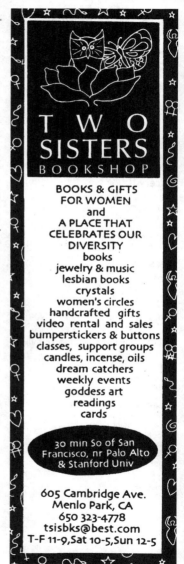

**T W O SISTERS BOOKSHOP**

**BOOKS & GIFTS FOR WOMEN**
and
**A PLACE THAT CELEBRATES OUR DIVERSITY**
books
jewelry & music
lesbian books
crystals
women's circles
handcrafted gifts
video rental and sales
bumperstickers & buttons
classes, support groups
candles, incense, oils
dream catchers
weekly events
goddess art
readings
cards

30 min So of San Francisco, nr Palo Alto & Stanford Univ

605 Cambridge Ave.
Menlo Park, CA
650 323-4778
tsisbks@best.com
T-F 11-9, Sat 10-5, Sun 12-5

SPIRITUAL GROUPS
**First Congregational United Church of Christ** 464 E. Walnut **795-0696** 10am Sun

## Pescadero (650)

ACCOMMODATIONS
**Oceanview Farms** 879-0698/(800) 642-9438 lesbians/gay men • on working horse breeding farm • full brkfst • nudity • smokefree • $75

## Pismo Beach (805)

ACCOMMODATIONS
**The Palomar Inn** 1601 Shell Beach Rd., Shell Beach **773-4204** lesbian/gay men • close to nude beach • gay-owned/run

## Placerville (209)

ACCOMMODATIONS
**Rancho Cicada Retreat** 245-4841 mostly gay men • secluded riverside retreat in the Sierra foothills w/two-person tents & cabin • swimming • nudity • gay-owned/run • $100-200 (lower during wk)

## Pleasant Hill (510)

EROTICA
**Pleasant Hill Books** 2298 Monument Blvd. **676-2962**

## Pomona (909)

INFO LINES & SERVICES
**Gay/Lesbian Community Center Hotline** **882-4488** 6:30pm-10pm

BARS & NIGHTCLUBS
**Alibi East** 225 San Antonio Ave. **623-9422** 10am-2am, til 4am Fri-Sat • mostly gay men • dancing/DJ • live shows Wed
**Mary's** 1047 E. 2nd St. **622-1971** 2pm-2am • lesbians/gay men • dancing/DJ • also restaurant • wheelchair access
**Robbie's** 390 E. 2nd St. (at College Plaza) **620-4371** 6pm-2am, clsd Tue-Wed • lesbians/gay men • ladies night Th • dancing/DJ • live shows • call for events

EROTICA
**Mustang Books** 961 N. Central, Upland **981-0227**

## Redding (916)

BARS & NIGHTCLUBS
**Club 501** 1244 California St. (enter rear) **243-7869** 6pm-2am, from 4pm Sun • lesbians/gay men • dancing/DJ • food served

## Redondo Beach (310)

INFO LINES & SERVICES
**South Bay Lesbian/Gay Community Organization** (310) 379-2850 support/education for Manhattan, Hermosa & Redondo Beaches, Torrance, Palos Verdes, El Segundo

ACCOMMODATIONS
**Palos Verdes Inn** 1700 S. Pacific Coast Hwy. **316-4211** IGLTA

## Redwood City (650)

BARS & NIGHTCLUBS
**Shouts** 2034 Broadway **369-9651** 11am-2am • lesbians/gay men • neighborhood bar • dancing/DJ • wheelchair access

BOOKSTORES & RETAIL SHOPS
**Bean's on Broadway** 2209 Broadway **369-3335** noon-9pm, til 10pm Fri-Sat, clsd Sun-Mon • also cafe

## Riverside (909)

*(see also San Bernardino)*

BARS & NIGHTCLUBS
**Menagerie** 3581 University Ave. **788-8000** 4pm-2am • mostly gay men • dancing/DJ • wheelchair access • women-owned/run
**VIP Club** 3673 Merrill Ave. **784-2370** 4pm-2am, til 3am Fri-Sat • lesbians/gay men • dancing/DJ • food served • wheelchair access

SPIRITUAL GROUPS
**St. Bride's** 3645 Locust St. **369-0992** 11am Sun • Celtic Catholic service

## Russian River (707)

*(includes Cazadero, Forestville, Guerneville & Monte Rio)*

### INFO LINES & SERVICES

**Russian River Tourist Bureau** (800) 253-8800

### ACCOMMODATIONS

**Applewood—An Estate Inn** 13555 Hwy. 116, Guerneville **869-9093/(800) 555-8509** gay-friendly • 21+ • full brkfst • swimming • smokefree • food served • wheelchair access • $125-250

**Avalon** 4th & Mill St., Guerneville **869-9566** gay-friendly • swimming

**The Chalet** 864-4061 rental home on 1/4 acre • sleeps 6 • 4 min. to downtown Guerneville

**Country Inns of the Russian River** (800) **927-4667** info & referrals for 6 inns

**Faerie Ring Campground** 16747 Armstrong Woods Rd., Guerneville **869-2746** gay-friendly • on 14 acres • RV spaces • near outdoor recreation • pets ok • $20-25

## Russian River

*T*he Russian River resort area is hidden away in the redwood forests of Northern California, an hour and a half north of the San Francisco Bay Area. The warm summer days and cool starlit nights have made it a favorite secret getaway for many of San Francisco's lesbians and gays—especially when they can't stand another foggy, cold day in the City.

Life at "the River," as it's fondly called, is laid back. You can take a canoe ride, hike under the redwoods, or just lie back on the river bank and soak up the sun. There's plenty of camping and RV parking, including the **Redwood Grove, The Willows** (camping) and **Fife's Resort** (camping & RV). If you're in the mood for other soothing and sensual delights, you're in luck. The River is in the heart of the famous California Wine Country. Plan a tour to the many wineries, and don't forget to designate a sober driver, so you can taste the world-class wines as you go. Or see some of the world's most beautiful coastline as you cruise the car along the Pacific Coast Highway—only fifteen minutes away!

The River becomes a lesbian garden of earthly delights several times a year. **Women's Weekend** happens in May and late September, with shuttles taking women from resort to resort as they enjoy the many entertainers, dances, and barbecues.

Cabins with fireplaces
Rooms, Camping and
Day use.
Swimming Pool and
Hot Tub.
**Nude Sunbathing**

Located a short walk
from town on 3 acres
of redwood trees and
beautiful gardens..

**Open all year!**

# HIGHLANDS RESORT

P.O. Box 346/14000 Woodland Dr.
Guerneville, CA 95446
http://travel.org/HighlandsResort
**(707) 869-0333  Fax (707) 869-0370**

# HIGHLAND DELL INN
### Bed and Breakfast on the River's Edge

*A warm and sumptous atmosphere, new
friends, hosts who truely care*

## For Reservations or *Free* Brochure Call:

## 800.767.1759

Rich stained glass windows · Heirloom antiques
Uniquely different bedrooms decorated in harmony
with the Inn · Rooms & Suites all with TV· Phone
Suites with VCR and Small Refrig.
Gourmet breakfasts · buffet weekends, individual weekdays
Summer pool · Just 4 miles to Guerneville
Gay owned & operated

▲ **Fern Falls** 632-6108 lesbians/gay men •
main house w/deck overlooking creek •
also cabin • hot tub • waterfall •
smokefree • kids ok by arr. • pets ok •
$85-135

**Fern Grove Inn** 16650 River Rd.,
Guerneville 869-9083/(800) 347-9083
gay-friendly • California craftsman cottages circa 1926 • swimming • kids ok •
$79-199

**Fife's Resort** 16467 River Rd.,
Guerneville 869-0656/(800) 734-3371
lesbians/gay men • cabins • campsites
• also restaurant • some veggie • full
bar • $10-20 • IGLTA • $50-215

**Golden Apple Ranch** 17575 Fitzpatrick
Ln., Occidental 874-3756 gay-friendly

▲ **Highland Dell Inn** 21050 River Blvd.,
Monte Rio 865-1759/(800) 767-1759
gay-friendly • serene retreat on the river
• full brkfst • swimming • smokefree •
wheelchair access • $95-160

▲ **Highlands Resort** 14000 Woodland Dr.,
Guerneville 869-0333 lesbians/gay men
• country retreat on 4 wooded acres •
hot tub • swimming • nudity • pets ok •
$45-105

**House of a Thousand Flowers** 11
Mosswood Cir., Cazadero 632-5571 gay-
friendly • country B&B overlooking the
Russian River • full brkfst • kids ok •
pets ok by arr. • $80-85

**Huckleberry Springs Country Inn** 8105
Old Beedle, Monte Rio 865-2683/(800)
822-2683 gay-friendly • private cottages
• swimming • Japanese spa • massage •
smokefree • dinner served • $25 • IGLTA
• women-owned/run • $145

**Jacques' Cottage at Russian River**
6471 Old Trenton Rd., Forestville 575-
1033 lesbians/gay men • hot tub •
swimming • nudity • pets ok

**Mountain Lodge** 16350 First St.,
Guerneville 869-3722 lesbians/gay men
• condo-style 1-bdrm apts on the river •
hot tub • swimming • kids ok • wheelchair access • $50-125

**Paradise Cove Resort** 14711 Armstrong
Woods Rd., Guerneville 869-2706 les-
bians/gay men • studio units • hot tub
• fireplaces • decks

**Redwood Grove RV Park &
Campground** 16140 Neely Rd.,
Guerneville 869-3670 gay-friendly

**Redwood Properties** 869-7368/(800)
939-7368 rental homes

*Fern Falls*

*Romance & Redwoods*
*A spirtual habitat*
*in a hillside canyon,*

*with natural waterfall,*
*swimming hole,*
*creeks,*
*gardens,*
*gazebo,*
*jacuzzi....*

*private cabins:*
*w/fireplaces*
*elegant furn.*
*kitchens*
*decks*
*pets ok.*

*Close to Guerneville,*
*Coast & Russian River*
*Darrel / Peter PO 228*
*Cazadero Ca. 95421*
*PH: 707/ 632- 6108*
*FAX: 707/ 632- 6216*

*Bruce's* BARBER SHOP

869-4539
OPEN
TUES-SAT

16005 RIVER ROAD
(TWO BLOCKS EAST OF
DOWNTOWN GUERNEVILLE)

**Rio Villa Beach Resort** 20292 Hwy. 116, Monte Rio **865-1143** gay-friendly • on the river • cabins • kids ok • $68-179

**Riverbend Campground & RV Park** 11820 River Rd., Forestville **887-7662** gay-friendly • kids ok • wheelchair access

**Russian River Resort/Triple 'R' Resort** 16390 4th St., Guerneville **869-0691/(800) 417-3767** lesbians/gay men • hot tub • swimming • also restaurant • some veggie • full bar • $5-10 • wheelchair access • $40-90

**Schoolhouse Canyon Park** 12600 River Rd. **869-2311** gay-friendly • campsites • RV • private beach • kids/pets ok

**Tim & Tony's Treehouse** 887-9531/(888) 887-9531 lesbians/gay men • studio cottage • hot tub • sauna • smokefree

**Wildwood Resort Retreat** Old Cazadero Rd., Guerneville **632-5321** gay-friendly • facilities are for groups of 20 or more • swimming • smokefree • kids ok • wheelchair access

**The Willows** 15905 River Rd., Guerneville **869-2824/(800) 953-2828** lesbians/gay men • old-fashioned country lodge & campground • smokefree • $49-119

## BARS & NIGHTCLUBS

**Molly's Country Club** 14120 Old Cazadero Rd., Guerneville **869-0511** 4pm-2am, from noon wknds, til midnight Sun-Th • country/western • food served

**Mr. T's Bullpen** 16246 1st St., Guerneville **869-3377** 10am-2am • lesbians/gay men • neighborhood bar • patio • wheelchair access

**Rainbow Cattle Co.** 16220 River Rd., Guerneville **869-0206** 6am-2am • mostly gay men • neighborhood bar

**River Business** 16225 Main St., Guerneville **869-3400** mostly gay men • neighborhood bar • food served • wheelchair access

## CAFES

**Coffee Bazaar** 14045 Armstrong Woods Rd., Guerneville **869-9706** 7am-8pm • cafe • soups/salads/pastries

**International Cafe** 10940 River Rd., Forestville **887-4644** 6am-8pm, 8am-10pm wknds • cybercafe • wheelchair access

## RESTAURANTS

**Big Bertha's Burgers** 16357 Main St., Guerneville **869-2239** 11am-8pm • beer/wine

## Russian River   (707)

**Where the Girls Are:** Guerneville is a small town, so you won't miss the groups of vacationing women strolling along Main St.

**Annual Events:**

May & Sept-Women's Weekend: 869-9000 ext. 8, ext. 3.

**City Info:** Russian River Visitors Info: 800/253-8800.

**Attractions:** Armstrong Redwood State Park. Bodega Bay. Mudbaths of Calistoga. Wineries of Napa and Sonoma counties.

**Best View:** Anywhere in Armstrong Woods, the Napa Wine Country and on the ride along the coast on Highway 1.

**Weather:** Summer days are sunny and warm (80°s-90°s) but usually begin with a dense fog. Winter days have the same pattern but are a lot cooler and wetter. Winter nights can be very damp and chilly (low 40°s).

**Transit:** Bill's Taxi Service: 869-2177.

**Burdon's** 15405 River Rd., Guerneville **869-2615** call for hours • lesbians/gay men • cont'l/pasta • plenty veggie • wheelchair access • $10-15

**Flavors Unlimited** 16450 Main St. (River Rd.), Guerneville **869-0425** hours vary • custom-blended ice cream • women-owned/run

**Hiding Place** 15025 River Rd., Guerneville **869-2887** 8am-9pm • home-cooking • some veggie • $5-12

**Mill St. Grill** (at Triple 'R' Resort), Guerneville **869-0691** lesbians/gay men • some veggie • full bar • patio • wheelchair access • $10-15

**River Inn Restaurant** 16141 Main St., Guerneville **869-0481** seasonal • local favorite • wheelchair access • $10-15

**Sweet's River Grill** 16251 Main St., Guerneville **869-3383** noon-9pm • popular • beer/wine

### BOOKSTORES & RETAIL SHOPS

**River Reader** 16355 Main St., Guerneville **869-2240** 10am-6pm, extended hours during summer

**Up the River** 16212 Main St., Guerneville **869-3167** cards • gifts • T-shirts

### SPIRITUAL GROUPS

**MCC of the Redwood Empire** 14520 Armstrong Woods Rd. (Guerneville Community Church), Guerneville **869-0552** 6pm Sun

## Sacramento (916)

### INFO LINES & SERVICES

**Lambda Community Center** 919 20th St. **442-0185/442-7960** 10am-7pm • youth groups & more

**Northall Gay AA** 2015 'J' St. #32 **454-1100** 8pm Mon, noon Wed

### ACCOMMODATIONS

**Hartley House B&B Inn** 700 22nd St. **447-7829/(800) 831-5806** gay-friendly • turn-of-the-century mansion • full brkfst • smokefree • older kids ok • conference facilities • $90-155

**Verona Village River Resort** 6985 Garden Hwy., Nicholas **656-1320** lesbians/gay men • RV space • full bar • restaurant • store • marina

## Bars & Nightclubs

**Faces** 2000 'K' St. **448-7798** 4pm-2am, from 2pm wknds • mostly gay men • dancing/DJ • country/western • transgender-friendly • karaoke • live shows • videos • wheelchair access

**Joseph's Town & Country Bar** 3514 Marconi **483-1220** 11am-2am • lesbians/gay men • dancing/DJ • live shows • also restaurant • Italian • some veggie • $7-12

**Mirage** 601 15th St. **444-3238** 5pm-2am • lesbians/gay men • neighborhood bar • wheelchair access • women-owned/run

**The Townhouse** 1517 21st St. **441-5122** 3pm-2am, from 10am wknds • also dinner Fri-Sat, Sun brunch • mostly gay men • neighborhood bar • wheelchair access

## Cafes

**Triangle Cafe** (at the Lambda Center) **442-0185** 7pm-midnight Fri • lesbians/gay men • live shows • drug/alcohol-free

## Restaurants

**Ernesto's** 1901 16th St. **441-5850** 11am-10pm, from 9am wknds • Mexican • full bar

**Hamburger Mary's** 1630 'J' St. **441-4340**

**Rick's Dessert Diner** 2322 'K' St. **444-0969** 10am-11pm Sun-Mon, til midnight Tue-Th, til 1am Fri-Sat • coffee & dessert

## Bookstores & Retail Shops

**Lioness Book Store** 2224 'J' St. **442-4657** 11am-7pm, noon-6pm Sat, til 5pm Sun, clsd Mon • women's • wheelchair access • women-owned/run

**The Open Book** 910 21st St. **498-1004** 9am-midnight • lesbigay bookstore & coffeehouse

## Publications

**MGW (Mom Guess What) 441-6397** women-owned/run

**Outword 329-9280**

**Travel Books Worldwide 452-5200** newsletter reviewing travel books

## Travel Agents

**Patterson Travel** 1107 21st St. **441-1526/(800) 283-2772** IGLTA

**Sports Leisure Travel** 9527-A Folsom Blvd. **361-2051/(800) 951-5556** IGLTA

## Spiritual Groups

**Integrity Northern California** 2620 Capital Ave. **394-1715** 4pm 2nd Sun • lesbigay Episcopalians • group meets at Trinity Cathedral

## Erotica

**Adult Discount Center** 1800 Del Paso Blvd. **920-8659**

**Goldies I** 201 N. 12th St. **447-5860** 24hrs • also 2138 Del Paso Blvd. location 922-0103

**Kiss-N-Tell** 4201 Sunrise Blvd. **966-5477**

**L'Amour Shoppe** 2531 Broadway **736-3467**

# Salinas (408)

## Spiritual Groups

**St. Paul's Episcopal Church** 1071 Pajaro St. **424-7331**

## Erotica

**L'Amour Shoppe** 325 E. Alisal St. **758-9600**

# San Bernardino (909)

*(see also Riverside)*

## Info Lines & Services

**AA Gay/Lesbian 825-4700** numerous mtgs. for Inland Empire • call for times

**Gay/Lesbian Community Center** 1580 N. 'D' St. #7 **892-4488** 6:30pm-10pm • raps • counseling • library

**Project Teen 335-2005** 7:30pm Tue • support group for lesbigay teens

## Restaurants

**Tradewinds Bistro** 155 W. Highland Ave. **883-1100** 5pm-midnight • full bar • wheelchair access

## Travel Agents

**Go Aweigh! Travel** 2584 Carbon Ct. #2, Colton **370-4554** IGLTA

## Spiritual Groups

**St. Aelred's Parish** 161 W. Highland Ave. **883-0900** 11am Sun, 7pm Wed

## Erotica

**Bearfacts Book Store** 1434 E. Baseline **885-9176** 24hrs

## San Diego (619)

### INFO LINES & SERVICES

**AA Gay/Lesbian** 1730 Monroe St. **298-8008** 10:30am-10pm • 'Live & Let Live Alano' • also contact for 'Sober Sisters'

**Gay/Lesbian Info Line** 294-4636 24hrs

**Lesbian/Gay Men's Community Center** 3916 Normal St. **692-4297** 9am-10pm

**Lesbians in North County** 744-0780 Fri night • social group

**SAGE of California** 282-1395 seniors' social group • 1st Wed

### ACCOMMODATIONS

**Balboa Park Inn** 3402 Park Blvd. **298-0823/(800) 938-8181** gay-friendly • charming guest house in the heart of San Diego • wheelchair access • IGLTA • $80-190

**Banker's Hill B&B** 3315 2nd Ave. **260-0673/(800) 338-3748** lesbians/gay men • gay-owned/run • $85-125

**The Beach Place** 2158 Sunset Cliffs Blvd. **225-0746** lesbians/gay men • hot tub • nudity • kids ok • pets by arr. • 4 blks from beach • IGLTA • $50-60 (nightly); $300-350 (weekly)

**The Blom House B&B** 1372 Minden Dr. **467-0890/(800) 797-2566** gay-friendly • charming 1948 cottage style home • magnificent view • smokefree • $55-85

**Carole's B&B Inn** 3227 Grim Ave. **280-5258** gay-friendly • comfy early California bungalow • full brkfst • swimming • smokefree • kids ok • $65-85

**Dmitri's B&B** 931 21st St. **238-5547** lesbians/gay men • swimming • hot tub • smokefree • overlooks downtown • wheelchair access • $60-85

**Elsbree House** 5054 Narragansett Ave. **226-4133** gay-friendly • near beach • smokefree • kids ok

**Friendship Hotel** 3942 8th Ave. **298-9898** gay-friendly • kids/pets ok • $18-27

**Harbor Lights Inn** 1765 Union **234-6787** lesbians/gay men

**Heritage Park B&B** 2470 Heritage Park Row **239-4738/(800) 995-2470** gay-friendly • full brkfst • afternoon tea • smokefree • kids ok • wheelchair access

▲ **Hillcrest Inn Hotel** 3754 5th Ave. **293-7078/(800) 258-2280** lesbians/gay men • int'l hotel in the heart of Hillcrest • wheelchair access • IGLTA • $49-55

**Kasa Korbett** 1526 Van Buren Ave. **291-3962/(800) 757-5272** lesbians/gay men • comfortable craftsman-designed B&B in Hillcrest • wheelchair access • spa • smokefree • kids ok

**Keating House** 2331 2nd Ave. **239-8585/(800) 995-8644** gay-friendly • graceful 150-yr-old Victorian on Bankers Hill • full brkfst • smokefree • kids ok • $60-85

## San Diego (619)

**Where the Girls Are:** Lesbians tend to live near Normal Heights, in the northwest part of the city. But for partying, women go to the bars near I-5, or to Hillcrest to hang out with the boys.

**Entertainment:** Diversionary Theatre: 220-0097. Gay & lesbian theater. Labrys Productions: 297-0220 (M-F, 8am-5pm). Lesbian theater company. Aztec Bowl, 4356 30th St., North Park, 283-3135. Gay Mon night.

**Lesbigay Pride:** July: 297-7683.

**City Info:** San Diego Visitors Bureau: 232-3101.

**Attractions:** Balboa Park. Cabrillo National Monument. La Jolla. Sea World. Torrey Pines State Park.

**Best View:** Cabrillo National Monument on Point Loma or from a harbor cruise.

**Weather:** San Diego is sunny and warm (upper 60°s-70°s) year-round, with higher humidity in the summer.

**Transit:** Yellow Cab: 234-6161. Radio Cab: 232-6566. Silver Cab/Co-op: 280-5555. Cloud Nine Shuttle: 800/974-8885. San Diego Transit System: 233-3004. San Diego Trolley (through downtown or to Tijuana).

# San Diego's
# Hillcrest Inn

## An international hotel in the heart of Hillcrest.

Walk to Bars, Restaurants, Shopping and Balboa Park. Easy drive to Zoo, Sea World, Horton Plaza and Beaches.

Lounge on our new Sun Patio or relax in the Jacuzzi. Our reasonable rates and friendly staff will always make you feel welcome.

3754 Fifth Ave., San Diego, CA
**800-258-2280 • 619-293-7078**

**Park Manor Suites** 525 Spruce St. **291-0099/(800) 874-2649** gay-friendly • 1926 hotel • kids/pets ok • IGLTA • $69-169

**Ramada Inn** 2223 El Cajon Blvd. **296-2101** gay-friendly • swimming • kids ok • also restaurant • wheelchair access

**Villa Serena B&B** 2164 Rosecrans St. **224-1451/(800) 309-2778** gay-friendly • Italian villa in residential neighborhood • full brkfst • swimming • hot tub

**Welcome Inn** 1550 E. Washington St. **298-8251** gay-friendly • kids ok • wheelchair access • $30-50

## BARS & NIGHTCLUBS

**Club Bombay** 3175 India St. (enter from Spruce St.) **296-6789** 4pm-2am, from 2pm wknds • popular • mostly women • dancing/DJ • live shows • Sun BBQ • patio • wheelchair access • women-owned/run

**Club Montage** 2028 Hancock St. **294-9590** 8pm-2am, til 4am Fri-Sat • mostly gay men • dancing/DJ • patio • wheelchair access

**Eagle** 3040 North Park Wy. **295-8072** 4pm-2am • mostly gay men • leather • wheelchair access

**The Flame** 3780 Park Blvd. **295-4163** 5pm-2am, from 4pm Fri • popular • mostly women • dancing/DJ • theme nights • women-owned/run

**Kickers** 308 University Ave. **491-0400** 7pm-2am • mostly gay men • dancing/DJ • country/western • lessons at 7pm • wheelchair access

**The No. 1 Fifth Ave. (no sign)** 3845 5th Ave. **299-1911** noon-2am • mostly gay men • professional • videos • patio

**Redwing Bar & Grill** 4012 30th St. **281-8700** 10am-2am • mostly gay men • neighborhood bar • food served • $5-10

**Tidbits** 3838 5th Ave. **543-0300** 6pm-2am • gay-friendly • lives shows • also restaurant

## CAFES

**Cafe Roma** UCSD Price Center #76, La Jolla **450-2141** 7am-midnight

**Claire de Lune** 2906 University Ave. **291-7070** 6am-10pm, til midnight Fri-Sat, 7am-9pm Sun • lesbians/gay men • live shows • call for events

**David's Place** 3766 5th Ave. **294-8908** 7am-midnight, til 3am wknds • lesbians/gay men • non-profit coffeehouse for positive people & their friends • live shows • wheelchair access

**Pannikin** 523 University Ave. **295-1600** 6am-11pm, til midnight wknds • cafe

## RESTAURANTS

**Bayou Bar & Grill** 329 Market St. **696-8747** lunch & dinner, Sun champagne brunch • Creole/Cajun • full bar • $12-16

**Beaux Cantina** 2770 5th Ave. **294-7002** lunch, dinner & Sun Brunch • Mexican • video cantina • gay-owned/run • wheelchair access • $11

**Big Kitchen** 3003 Grape St. **234-5789** 7:30am-2pm, 8am-3pm wknds • some veggie • wheelchair access • women-owned/run • $5-10

**Cafe Eleven** 1440 University Ave. **260-8023** dinner, clsd Mon • country French • some veggie • wheelchair access • $15-20

**California Cuisine** 1027 University Ave. **543-0790** 11am-10pm, from 5pm wknds, clsd Mon • French/Italian • some veggie • wheelchair access • women-owned/run • $15-20

**City Deli** 535 University Ave. **295-2747** 7am-midnight, til 2am Fri-Sat • NY deli • plenty veggie • beer/wine • $5-10

**The Cottage** 7702 Fay, La Jolla **454-8409** brkfst & lunch only • fresh-baked items

**Crest Cafe** 425 Robinson **295-2510** 7am-midnight • some veggie • wheelchair access • $5-10

**Grill 2201 & Desserts** 2201 Adams Ave. **298-8440** dinner & wknd brunch • bistro • plenty veggie • beer/wine • gay-owned/run

**Hamburger Mary's** 308 University Ave. **491-0400** 11am-10pm, from 9am wknds • some veggie • full bar • wheelchair access • $5-10

**Liaison** 2202 4th Ave. **234-5540** dinner & Sun brunch, clsd Mon • French country • wheelchair access • $18-24 (prix fixe)

**Picciurro's Ristorante** 1288 University Ave. **293-0299** Italian • gay-owned/run

## BOOKSTORES & RETAIL SHOPS

**Auntie Helen's** 4028 30th St. **584-8438** 10am-5pm, clsd Sun-Mon • thrift shop benefits PWAs

**Blue Door Bookstore** 3823 5th Ave. **298-8610** 9am-9:30pm, 10am-9pm Sun • large lesbigay section

**Groundworks Books** UCSD Student Center 0323, La Jolla **452-9625** 9am-7pm, 10am-6pm Fri-Sat, clsd Sun • alternative • lesbigay section • wheelchair access

# San Diego

**S**an Diego is a west coast paradise. This city sprawls from the bays and beaches of the Pacific to the foothills of the desert mountains. The days are always warm, and the nights can be refreshingly cool.

Stay at one of the city's quaint lesbian-friendly inns. During the days, follow the tourist circuit which includes the world-famous San Diego Zoo and Sea World. Call the Visitor's Center for a brochure on all the sites.

Once the sun sets, you're ready to tour the lesbian circuit. Where to begin? Check out **Club Bombay** and **The Flame,** San Diego's two lesbian dance bars. If you're a country/western gal, **Kickers** is a popular place to two-step. In the mood for theater? Look up Labris Productions (297-0220), the city's own lesbian theater group, or check out Diversionary Theatre (574-1060) for gay & lesbian performances.

If you'll be in town in early December, don't miss the annual Lesbian Community Cultural Arts festival (phone 281-0406 or 464-3831 for details), with multicultural performances, workshops, and more. In mid-August, there's the Hillcrest Street Fair, popular with the many lesbian and gay residents of the happening Hillcrest district. (Be warned though. Because of its location between super-freeways and construction, rush-hour traffic has been known to crawl through Hillcrest.) If you're staying in North County, contact the **Lesbians in North County** for casual fun.

If you're feeling adventurous, cruise by the **Crypt** for some sex toys or a piercing, and pick up your safer sex supplies at **Condoms Plus.** If you just want to network, stop in at the **Community Center** or pick up one of the lesbigay papers for all the latest information about San Diego's lesbian community.

**WHERE'S THE LOVE?**
**WHERE'S THE**
**ROMANCE?**

# F Street

VISA

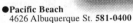
MasterCard

- ●**Pacific Beach**
  4626 Albuquerque St. **581-0400**
- ●**San Ysidro**
  4650 Border Village Dr. **690-2070**
- ●**Sports Arena**
  3112 Midway Dr. **221-0075**
- ●**Gaslamp**
  4th & F. **236-0841**
- ●**Kearny Mesa**
  7865 Balboa **292-8083**
- ● **Chula Vista**
  3rd Ave. **585-3314**
- ● **Mira Mesa**
  7998 Miramar Rd. **549-8014**
- ● **North Park**
  2002 University Ave. **298-2644**
- ● **Escondido**
  237 E. Grand **480-6031**†
- ● **El Cajon**
  158 E. Main **447-0381**

**Our Selection says it all!**
**OPEN 24 HOURS**

**Moose Leather** 2923 Upas St. **297-6935** noon-9pm, clsd Sun-Mon

**Obelisk the Bookstore** 1029 University Ave. **297-4171** 11am-10pm, noon-9pm Sun • lesbigay • wheelchair access

## PUBLICATIONS

**Gay/Lesbian Times** 3636 5th Ave. #101 **299-6397**

**Update** 2801 4th Ave. **299-4104**

## TRAVEL AGENTS

**The Art Of Travel** 294-3598/(888) 294-3598 IGLTA

**Firstworld Travel of Mission Gorge** 7443 Mission Gorge Rd. **265-1916** contact Dennis • IGLTA

**Hillcrest Travel** 431 Robinson Ave. **291-0758**/(800) 748-5502 IGLTA

**Jerry & David's Travel** 1025 W. Laurel St. **233-5199**/(800) 748-6968 IGLTA

**Midas Travel** 525 University Ave. **298-1160** IGLTA

**Mission Center Travel** 3108-A 5th Ave. **299-2720** IGLTA

**Sports Travel International Ltd.** 4869 Santa Monica Ave. **225-9555**/(800) 466-6004 IGLTA

**Sun Travel** 3545 Midway Dr. **222-2786** IGLTA

**Travel 800** 3530 Camino del Rio N. #300 **624-2000**/(800) FLY-GAYS IGLTA

## SPIRITUAL GROUPS

**Anchor Ministries** 3441 University Ave. **284-8654** 10am Sun • non-denominational

**Dignity** 4190 Front St. (First Unitarian Universalist Church), Hillcrest **645-8240** 6pm Sun

**First Unitarian Universalist Church** 4190 Front St. **298-9978** 10am (July-Aug); 9am & 11am (Sept-June)

**MCC** 4333 30th St. **280-4333** 6:30pm Sat, 9am & 11am Sun, 5pm Sun bilingual

**Yachad** 492-8616 Jewish lesbian/gay/bisexual social group

## GYMS & HEALTH CLUBS

**Frog's Athletic Club** 901 Hotel Circle South, Mission Valley **291-3500**

**Hillcrest Gym** 142 University Ave. **299-7867** lesbians/gay men

## EROTICA

▲ **Condoms Plus** 1220 University Ave. **291-7400** safer sex gifts for women & men

**The Crypt** 1515 Washington **692-9499** also 30th St. location 284-4724

▲ **F St. Bookstore** 2004 University Ave. **298-2644** 24hrs

▲ **F St. Bookstore** 3112 Midway Dr. **221-0075** 24hrs

▲ **F St. Bookstore** 4626 Albuquerque **581-0400** 24hrs

▲ **F St. Bookstore** 751 4th Ave. **236-0841** 24hrs

▲ **F St. Bookstore** 7865 Balboa Ave., Kearney Mesa **292-8083** 24hrs

▲ **F St. Bookstore** 7998 Miramar Rd. **549-8014** 24hrs

**Flesh Skin Grafix** 1228 Palm Ave., Imperial Beach **424-8983** tattoos • piercing

**Gay Mart** 550 University Ave. **543-1221**

**Mastodon** 4638 Mission Bvld., Pacific Beach **272-1188**/(800) 743-8743 body piercing

**Trademark** 3701-A 6th Ave. **296-1700** 2pm-10pm, til 11pm Fri-Sat, clsd Mon • videos • fetish clothing • toys

# No Centerfolds.
# No Fashion Spreads.
# No Astrology or Gossip.

## Icon
### The Thinking Lesbian's Newsmagazine

## A monthly publication that's more about Lesbian *Lives* than Lesbian *Lifestyle*.

*Icon is a nonprofit sponsored project of the SF Women's Center/The Women's Building. Become a member for $25 and get 12 issues of Icon mailed discretely to your home.*

❑ *Yes! I am a Thinking Lesbian! Sign me up!*

❑ Here's my check/money order for $25 ($US45 intl)

❑ Please charge my ❑MasterCard ❑Visa

Acct #_____ Exp. _____

_____
name

_____
mailing address

_____
city/state/zip

_____
phone                          signature

**Icon Newsmagazine: 3543 18th St. #2, SF/CA 94110
415.863.9536 Fax: 415.863.0245 iconlesmag@aol.com**

## SAN FRANCISCO

*San Francisco is divided into 7 geographical areas (see map on pages 106-107):*

**S.F.–Overview**

**S.F.–Castro & Noe Valley**

**S.F.–South of Market**

**S.F.–Polk Street Area**

**S.F.–Downtown & North Beach**

**S.F.–Mission District**

**S.F.–Haight, Fillmore & West**

**S.F.—Overview**

**INFO LINES & SERVICES**

**AA Gay/Lesbian** (415) 621-1326

**APSLBN (Asian Pacific Sisters Lesbian/Bisexual Network)** (510) 814-2422 social/support group for lesbian/bi women of Asian/Pacific Islander descent • special events • newsletter

**The Bay Area Bisexual Resource Line** (415) 703-7977

**Brothers Network** 973 Market St. #650 (415) 356-8140 1:30pm-3:30pm Tue • transgender support group

**FTM International** (415) 553-5987 2pm-5pm 2nd Sun • info & support for female-to-male transgendered people • newsletter • resource guide

**Gay/Lesbian Sierrans** (415) 281-5666 outdoor group

**Lavender Line** (510) 841-6224 10am-10pm Mon-Fri • info • referrals • rap line

**LGBA (Lesbian/Gay/Bisexual Alliance)** (415) 338-1952 student group

**LINKS** (415) 703-7159 S/M play parties & calendar • transgender-friendly

**LYRIC (Lavender Youth Recreation/Information Cntr)** 127 Collingwood (415) 703-6150/(800) 246-7743 (**OUTSIDE BAY AREA**) support & social groups • also crisis counseling for lesbigay & transgendered youth under 24 at 863-3636 (hotline #)

# DINAH SHORE
## PALM SPRINGS WEEKEND
### MARCH 26-29, 1998

The Ultimate Hotel & Entertainment Package at the All Inclusive

**DOUBLE TREE RESORT**

Book today to ensure availability. For hotel and party ticket Info Call

**310.281.7358**

Advocate · SKYY VODKA · Lesbian Dining Club · W WOMEN'S TRAVELLER · CURVE magazine · AA AmericanAirlines

For Airline reservations call 1•800•433•1790

Produced by JOANI WEIR PRODUCTIONS • POM POM PRODUCTIONS • KLUB BANSHEE

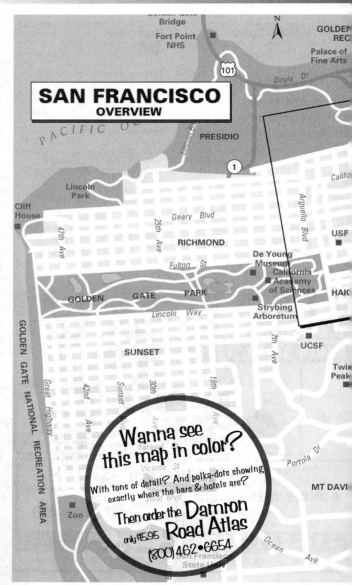

Wanna see this map in color?

With tons of detail? And polka-dots showing exactly where the bars & hotels are?

Then order the Damron Road Atlas

only $15.95

(800) 462•6654

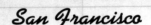

# San Francisco

**S**an Francisco may be a top tourist destination because of its cable cars, beatniks, quaint beauty, and the Haight-Ashbury district, but we know what really makes it shine: its legendary lesbian and gay community. So unless kitsch is your thing, skip Fisherman's Wharf and the cable cars, and head for the Mission, the Castro, Noe Valley, or South of Market (SoMa).

Any lesbian walking along Valencia between Market Street and 24th Street can't miss all the hot women of all sizes and colors that live in this neighborhood. Valencia Street borders the upscale, predominantly gay Castro area, and the Mission, San Francisco's largest Latino neighborhood. This intersection of cultures results in a truly San Franciscan mix of punk dykes, dykes of color, lesbian-feminists, working class straights, and funky artists.

Your first stop in the Mission should be either punk dyke hangout **Red Dora's Bearded Lady Café & Gallery** (be sure to check out the dyke-run **Black & Blue Tattoo** next door) or the more traditional resource center, the **Women's Building,** on 16th Street. (You can't miss their stunning murals.) After that, rush to **Good Vibrations** women's sex toy store before they close at 7pm. Pick up a famous "San Francisco Mission-Style Burrito" (as they're advertised in New York these days) at one of the many cheap and delicious taquerias.

You might have heard the legends about the Mission's one-time women's bar, Amelia's. Sadly, it's long gone. Instead, head for the **Lexington Club,** a popular dyke hangout. Another must for lesbians along Valencia Street is **Osento,** the women's bathhouse. Just off Valencia on 16th is The Roxie (957-1212), a dyke-friendly repertory cinema.

For nightlife, you'll have to head to SoMa for dancing, but the Mission has lots of fun queer performance at places like **Build** and **Brava!** and **Luna Sea**—check the bi-weekly **Bay Times** calendar. If you're into artsy or radical video, get a calendar from Artists' Television Access (824-3890).

You'll also find lots of lesbians in nearby Noe Valley, though this area tends to be a couples heaven for professional women and lesbian moms. If that's your dream, call **Bay Area Career Women**

(495-5393) about their upcoming social events, or drop in on their TGIF social, downtown. You'll also enjoy an afternoon in one or all of the many quirky shops and cafes along 24th Street.

If you cruise the Castro, you'll be surprised how many sisters—ranging from executives to queer chicks—you'll see walking the streets of what was the "Boys' Town" of the 1970s. Drop in at **A Different Light,** the lesbigay bookstore, or **The Cafe** for a game of pool or girl-watching from the balcony. The Castro also hosts three great 24-hour diners—**Bagdad Cafe, Sparky's,** and **Orphan Andy's**—as well as **Josie's Cabaret & Juice Joint,** great for vegetarian brunch, comedy and performance. For lesbian/gay-themed films, don't miss an evening at The Castro Theater (621-6120).

SoMa (South of Market) also contains lots of art, poetry, and kink for the daring. And plenty of schmoozing for women of color and friends at the **CoCo Club** (8th & Minna), a small but lively women's cabaret & speakeasy, with events seven nights a week (Tuesday is Xena night)!

You might also want to check out the women's S/M scene in this kinky city: **Stormy Leather** is a women-owned fetish store. And if you're inspired to get that piercing you've been thinking about, visit one of the queer-friendly piercing parlors in town—we like **Body Manipulations,** right between the Mission and the Castro on 16th Street at Guerrero.

You still have energy? Wanna dance? Then boogie on down to the ever-popular **G-Spot** (Girl-Spot) on Saturday nights. If you're in town on the first Friday of the month, don't miss **Club Q** – a huge dance club crowded with hundreds of women of all colors and styles. For a truly hot dance party, call the **ABLUNT** hotline to find out when their latest dance for Asian, Black and Latina women (and their friends) will be. Also check the calendar of **ICON,** the city's lesbian newspaper, or the extensive listings in **Oblivion** and the "Jet Girl" section of **Odyssey.**

Finally, if you're a fan of Diane Di Prima, Anne Waldman, the late Allen Ginsberg, or other beatniks, **City Lights Bookstore** in North Beach is a required pilgrimage. Afterward, have a drink or an espresso at beatnik hangout Café Vesuvius, just across Jack Kerouac Alley from City Lights.

Sound like a lot? They don't call it Mecca for nothing.

**San Francisco**

**(415)**

**Where the Girls Are:** Younger, radical dykes call the Mission or the lower Haight home, while upwardly-mobile couples stake out Bernal Heights and Noe Valley. Hip, moneyed dykes live in the Castro. The East Bay is home to lots of lesbian feminists, older lesbians and lesbian moms (see East Bay listing).

**Entertainment:** Theatre Rhinoceros: 861-5079, 2926 16th St.

**Lesbigay Pride:** June. 864-3733.

**Annual Events:**

March - **AIDS Dance-a-thon:** 392-9255. AIDS benefit dance at the Moscone Center.

April - **Readers/Writers Conference:** 431-0891. 4th annual weekend of workshops at Women's Building.

May - **California AIDS Ride:** 800/474-3395. AIDS benefit bike ride from San Francisco to L.A.

June - **San Francisco Int'l Lesbian/Gay Film Festival:** 703-8650. Get your tickets early for a slew of films about us. Physique'98: 978-9495, national gay/lesbian body building championships.

July - **Up Your Alley Fair:** 861-3247. Local SM/leather street fair held in Dore Alley, South-of-Market. Mostly gay men.

September - **Folsom St. Fair:** 861-3247. Huge SM/leather street fair, topping a week of kinky events. **Mr. Drummer Contest:** 252-1195. International leather title contest & vendors. **Festival of Babes:** 510/428-1489. Annual women's soccer tournament.

October - **Castro St. Fair:** 467-3354. Arts and community groups street fair.

**City Info:** San Francisco Convention & Visitors Bureau: 391-2000.

**Attractions:** Alcatraz. Chinatown. Coit Tower. Fisherman's Wharf. Exploratorium. Golden Gate Park. Haight & Ashbury Sts. North Beach. Mission San Francisco de Assisi. Twin Peaks.

**Best View:** After a great Italian meal in North Beach, go to the top floor of the North Beach parking garage on Vallejo near Stockton, next to a police station. If you're in the Castro or the Mission, head for Dolores Park, at Dolores & 20th St. Other good views: Golden Gate Bridge, Kirby Cove (a park area to the left just past Golden Gate Bridge in Marin), Coit Tower, Twin Peaks, the beach at sunset.

**Weather:** A beautiful summer comes at the end of August and lasts through October. Much of the city is cold and fogged-in June through August, though the Castro and Mission are usually sunny. The winter is cold & damp, so bring lots of layers.

**Transit:** Yellow Cab: 626-2345. Luxor Cab: 282-4141. Quake City Shuttle: 255-4899. Muni: 673-6864. Bay Area Rapid Transit (BART): 673-6864, subway.

**New Leaf (415) 626-7000** 9am-7pm Mon-Fri • lesbigay AA mtgs. at 15th & Market • offices at 217 Church St.

**TARC Transgender Support Group** 187 Golden Gate Ave. **(415) 431-7476** 3pm Tue, 1pm-3pm Wed & Fri

**Transgender Support Groups** 50 Lech Walesa (Tom Waddell Clinic) **(415) 554-2940** 6pm-7:30 pm Tue • support groups & counseling for MTF & FTM transsexuals • low-cost TG health clinic

## ACCOMMODATIONS

**American Property Exchange** 2800 Van Ness Ave. **(415) 863-8484/(800) 747-7784** daily, weekly & monthly furnished rentals • women-owned/run

**Bed & Breakfast California (415) 696-1690** reservation service • IGLTA

**Dockside Boat & Bed (510) 444-5858/(800) 436-2574** gay-friendly • private houseboats • kitchen • smokefree • kids ok • $95-275

**Mi Casa Su Casa (510) 268-8534/(800) 215-2272** lesbians/gay men • int'l home exchange network

**One In Ten Guesthouse (415) 664-0748** women only • smokefree • kids ok • kitchen use • right on the beach in the Sunset district • near Golden Gate Park • $35-60

## BARS & NIGHTCLUBS

**Club Q** 177 Townsend **(415) 647-8258** 1st Fri • women only • popular • dance party DJ'd by 'mixtress' Page Hodel

**Fence Sitter's Lounge (415) 703-7977** bisexual dance club, call for info

**Just-Us** 139 8th St (CoCo Club) **(415) 703-0862** 1st & 3rd Wed • popular • multi-racial • roving dance parties • call to verify location

▲ **MT Productions (415) 337-4962** mostly women • dance parties including 'Girl Spot' & 'Club Skirts' and weekend events (see ad in front color section)

## ENTERTAINMENT & RECREATION

**Beach Blanket Babylon** 678 Green St. (Club Fugazi) **(415) 421-4222** the USA's longest running musical revue & wigs that must be seen to be believed

**Brava!** 2180 Bryant St. #208 **(415) 641-7657** culturally diverse performances by women • theater at 2789 24th St. (formerly 'York Theater') • wheelchair access

**Castro Theatre** 429 Castro **(415) 621-6120** art house cinema • many lesbigay & cult classics • live organ evenings

**Cruisin' the Castro (415) 550-8110** guided walking tour of the Castro • IGLTA

**Dyke TV** Channel 53 0 6pm Sun • 'weekly half hour TV show produced by lesbians for lesbians'

**Frameline** 346 9th St. **(415) 703-8650/(800) 869-1996 (OUTSIDE CA)** lesbigay media arts foundation • sponsors annual SF Int'l Lesbian/Gay Film Festival in June (see ad in front color section)

**Josie's Cabaret & Juice Joint** 3583 16th St. **(415) 861-7933** from 9am • lesbians/gay men • cabaret • live comedy • call for events • food served • healthy American • plenty veggie • $8-12

**Luna Sea** 2940 16th St. Rm. 216-C **(415) 863-2989** lesbian performance space

**The Marsh** 1062 Valencia **(415) 641-0235** queer-positive theater

**Theatre Rhinoceros** 2926 16th St. **(415) 861-5079** lesbigay theater

**Victorian Home Walks (415) 252-9485** custom-tailored walking tours w/San Francisco resident • IGLTA

## PUBLICATIONS

**Anything That Moves (415) 626-5069** bisexual magazine • published by Bay Area Bisexual Network (BABN)

**BAR (Bay Area Reporter) (415) 861-5019**

**Cuir Underground (415) 487-7622** local pansexual S/M magazine • e-mail: cuirpaper@aol.com

▲ **Curve (415) 863-6538** popular • lesbian magazine (see ad front color section)

**Fat Girl (415) 522-8733** fat dyke 'zine

**FBN (Feminist Bookstore News) (415) 642-9993** nat'l journal about feminist bookstores & publications

▲ **Girlfriends (415) 648-9464/(800) 475-3763** lesbian lifestyle magazine (see front color section) • also 'On Our Backs'

**GirlJock (415) 282-6833** pan-athletic magazine for lesbians

**Hype (415) 202-0898/(888) 497-3634** club listings & dirt-dishing columns

▲ **ICON: The Thinking Lesbian's Newspaper (415) 282-0942**

**Maiden Voyages (800) 528-8425** nat'l magazine on women's travel w/tour calendar

**Oblivion Magazine (415) 554-0565** extensive listings for clubs, arts & entertainment

**Odyssey Magazine (415) 621-6514/(888) 945-8777** all the dish on SF's club scene

**Q San Francisco (800) 999-9718 (SUB-SCRIPTIONS)** newsmagazine w/extensive arts & entertainment listings for the City

**San Francisco Bay Times (415) 227-0800** popular • a 'must read' for Bay Area resources

**San Francisco Frontiers (415) 487-6000** newsmagazine

**Women's Sports Connection (415) 241-8879** general women's quaterly newsletter • provides game schedules & ticket info

TRAVEL AGENTS

**Damron Atlas World (888) 907-9771** IGLTA

SPIRITUAL GROUPS

**Bay Area Pagan Assemblies (408) 559-4242**

**Dharma Sisters (415) 285-8850** events & weekly meditations for lesbian/bi women interested in practicing Buddhism

**Dignity San Francisco** 1329 7th Ave. **(415) 681-2491** 5:30pm Sun • lesbigay Roman Catholic services

**Hartford Street Zen Center** 57 Hartford St. **(415) 863-2507**

**Oasis/California** 110 Julian Ave. **(415) 522-0222/(800) 419-0222** lesbian/gay ministry of the Episcopal Diocese of California

**Q-Spirit (415) 281-9377** queer spirituality

**Reclaiming (415) 929-9249** pagan info-line & network • classes • newsletter

## S.F.—Castro & Noe Valley(415)

INFO LINES & SERVICES

**Gay/Lesbian Outreach to Elders** 1853 Market St. **626-7000**

**Harvey Milk Public Library** 3555 16th St. **554-9445** call for hours

ACCOMMODATIONS

**24 Henry** 24 Henry St. **864-5686/(800) 900-5686** mostly gay men • smokefree • one-bdrm apt also available 1 blk from guesthouse • IGLTA • $55-120

▲ **Albion House Inn** 135 Gough St. **621-0896/(800) 625-2466** gay-friendly • smokefree • kids ok • also restaurant • $85-195

**Beck's Motor Lodge** 2222 Market St. **621-8212** gay-friendly

"For a romantic getaway at a fabulous deal!"

# The Albion House Inn

- An antique furnished room
- Welcome glass of brandy or wine
- Full American Breakfast

CASTRO LOCATION/NEXT TO PUBLIC TRANS.
2 blks from symphony and opera

135 Gough Street
San Francisco, CA 94102
(415) 621-0896
(800) 6ALBION

## SAN FRANCISCO VIEWS

### The Villa

SHORT TERM RENTALS
GUEST HOUSE

Fabulous Executive Suites & Rooms
Pool • Decks • Views
Nightly, Weekly & Monthly Rates
*(Hotel Alternative)*

BEST CASTRO LOCATIONS

379 Collingwood Street    San Francisco, CA 94114
415/282-1367 • Fax: 415/821-3995

## 1-800-358-0123

# PENSION
## SAN FRANCISCO

☆ Centrally Located ☆ On San Francisco's main corridor of public transportation
☆ Hotel recently renovated ☆ Charming rooms ☆ City Tours available
☆ Also tours to Muir Woods, the Wine Country, and Monterey/Carmel
with hotel pickup ☆ Visa, Mastercard, American Express welcome

*Pension San Francisco, a hotel with a distinctly European flavor, is
pleased to offer accommodations featuring rooms at very low rates.*

**1668 MARKET STREET • SAN FRANCISCO, CA 94102
TEL (415) 864-1271 • 1-800-886-1271 • FAX (415) 861-8116**

ALWAYS A CROWD.

NEVER A COVER.

The Café

The Bay Area's HOTTEST dance bar for women. (...and a few good men)

• BALCONY OVERLOOKING THE CASTRO
• PRIVATE SUNDECK
• CITY'S TOP DJS SPIN THE HITS
• 2 FULL BARS
• BEER ON TAP
• PINBALL & POOL TABLES

MONDAYS: Domestic bottled beer only $1.25

OPEN 7 DAYS • NOON-2AM
2367 MARKET STREET @ CASTRO • INFO: 415.861.3846

**The Cumberland** 255-3086/(800) 605-1357 gay-friendly • guesthouse above the Castro • full brkfst • $100-175

**Dolores Park Inn** 3641 17th St. 621-0482 gay-friendly • historic two-story Italianate Victorian mansion • hot tub • private/shared baths • kitchens • fireplaces • smokefree • kids ok • $60-200

**Ethel's Garden in the Castro** 864-6171 women only • hot tub • near everything • $40-75

**House O' Chicks Guesthouse** 861-9849 women only • $50-100

**Inn on Castro** 321 Castro St. 861-0321 lesbians/gay men • B&B known for its hospitality & friendly atmosphere • full brkfst • smokefree • $80-150

**Le Grenier** 347 Noe St. 864-4748 lesbians/gay men • suite • kitchen • $60-90

**Nancy's Bed** 239-5692 women only • private home • kitchen • smokefree • kids ok

**Noe's Nest B&B** 3973 23rd St. 821-0751 gay-friendly • kitchens • fireplace • smokefree • kids ok • dogs ok (no cats) • IGLTA • $75-125

**The Parker House** 520 Church St. 621-3222 mostly gay men • IGLTA

▲**Pension San Francisco** 1668 Market St. 864-1271 gay-friendly • shared/private baths • kids ok • $42-55

**Ruth's House** 641-8898 women only • shared bath • smokefree • small kids ok • lesbian owned/run • $35-45

**San Francisco Cottage** 224 Douglass St. 861-3220 lesbians/gay men • self-catering cottage & studio apt • smokefree • IGLTA • $105

**Terrace Place** 241-0425 lesbians/gay men • guest suite • $75-175

**Travelodge Central** 1707 Market St. 621-6775/(800) 578-7878 gay-friendly • non-smoking rms. avail. • $59-159

▲ **The Villa/San Francisco Views** 379 Collingwood St. 282-1367/(800) 358-0123 lesbians/gay men • swimming • kids ok • wheelchair access • IGLTA • $90-150

**The Willows B&B Inn** 710 14th St. 431-4770 mostly gay men • B&B in the true European country tradition • non-smoking rms avail. • IGLTA • $70-125

## BARS & NIGHTCLUBS

▲ **The Cafe** 2367 Market St. 861-3846 noon-2am • lesbians/gay men • dancing/DJ • deck overlooking Castro & Market Sts. • more women Fri night

**Cafe du Nord** 2170 Market St. 861-5016 4pm-2am • gay-friendly • supper club • some veggie • theme nights • live jazz • $5-10

**Castro Country Club** 4058 18th St. 552-6102 11am-midnight, til 11am Fri-Sat, from 10am Sun • mostly gay men • alcohol & drug-free club

**Daddy's** 440 Castro St. 621-8732 9am-2am, from 6am wknds • popular • mostly gay men • neighborhood bar • leather • women genuinely welcome

**Harvey's** 500 Castro St. 431-4278 lesbians/gay men • neighborhood bar • live shows • also restaurant • wheelchair access • under $10

**Martuni's** 4 Valencia St. 241-0205 mostly gay men • neighborhood bar • professional • piano bar

**The Metro** 3600 16th St. 703-9750 2:30pm-2am • mostly gay men • karaoke Tue • also restaurant • Chinese

**The Mint** 1942 Market St. 626-4726 11am-2am • lesbians/gay men • karaoke • videos • also restaurant

**Moby Dick's** 4049 18th St. mostly gay men • neighborhood bar • videos • cool dykes often at pool table

**Pilsner Inn** 225 Church St. 621-7058 gay men/lesbians • 6am-2am • patio

**Uncle Bert's Place** 4086 18th St. 431-8616 6am-2am • mostly gay men • neighborhood bar • patio

## CAFES

**Cafe Flore** 2298 Market St. 621-8579 7:30am-11:30pm, til midnight Fri-Sat • popular • lesbians/gay men • some veggie • great patio • $5-8

**Castro Country Club** 4058 18th St. 552-6102 11am-midnight, til 11am Fri-Sat, from 10am Sun • alcohol & drug-free club

**Jumpin' Java** 139 Noe St. 431-5282 7am-10pm

**Just Desserts** 248 Church St. 626-5774 7am-11pm • lesbians/gay men • cafe • great patio

**Orbit Room Cafe** 1900 Market St. 252-9525 7am-midnight, til 2am Fri-Sat • full bar • great view of Market St. & street cars

## RESTAURANTS

**2223 Market** 2223 Market St. 431-0692 popular • contemporary American • full bar • wheelchair access • $13-16

**Alfred Schilling** 1695 Market St. **431-8447** lunch & dinner • gourmet fare • also cafe & chocolatier

**Amazing Grace** 216 Church St. **626-6411** 11am-10pm • cafeteria-style vegetarian • wheelchair access • $5-10

**Anchor Oyster Bar** 579 Castro St. **431-3990** lesbians/gay men • seafood • some veggie • beer/wine • women-owned/run • $10-20

**Bad Man Jose's** 4077 18th St. **861-1706** 11am-11pm • healthy Mexican • some veggie • $5-7

**Bagdad Cafe** 2295 Market St. **621-4434** 24hrs • lesbians/gay men • diner • some veggie • $5-10

▲ **Cafe Cuvee** 2073 Market St. **621-7488** brkfst & lunch, call for dinner hours, clsd wknds • lesbian owned/run

**Caffe Luna Piena** 558 Castro St. **621-2566** lunch & dinner • lesbians/gay men • Californian • patio

**Carta** 1772 Market St. **863-3516** lunch & dinner, Sun brunch, clsd Mon • changing theme menus • gay-owned/run

**China Court** 599 Castro **626-5358** 5pm-11pm • Chinese • some veggie • beer/wine • $5-10

**Chloe's Cafe** 1399 Church St., Noe Valley **648-4116** 8am-3:30pm, til 4pm wknds • popular • come early for the excellent weekend brunch

**Cove Cafe** 434 Castro St. **626-0462** 7am-10pm • lesbians/gay men • some veggie • wheelchair access • $8-12

**Dame** 1815 Market St. **255-8818** lunch & dinner, Sun brunch

**Eric's Chinese Restaurant** 1500 Church St., Noe Valley **282-0919** 11am-9pm • popular • some veggie • $5-10

**Hot 'N Hunky** 4039 18th St. **621-6365** 11am-midnight • lesbians/gay men • hamburgers • some veggie • $5-10

**It's Tops** 1801 Market St. **431-6395** 7am-3pm, 8pm-3am • diner • $5-7

**Little Italy** 4109 24th St. **821-1515** dinner only • plenty veggie • beer/wine • $15-20

**M&L Market (May's)** 691 14th St. **431-7044** great huge sandwiches • some veggie

# CAFE CUVEE
## 2073 MARKET @ CHURCH
## SAN FRANCISCO, CA

### 415. 621.7488

A SEASONAL

INNOVATIVE

CASUAL RESTAURANT

LIGHT BREAKFAST AND LUNCH MONDAY THROUGH FRIDAY
PLEASE CALL FOR DINNER HOURS

ANNE O'DRISCOLL, CHEF/PROPRIETOR

**Ma Tante Sumi** 4243 18th St. **552-6663**
5:30pm-10pm • cont'l cuisine w/Japanese accent

**Mecca** 2029 Market St. **621-7000** dinner from 6pm • popular • Mediterranean • full bar • $13-19 • wheelchair access

**Orphan Andy's** 3991 17th St. **864-9795** 24hrs • diner • gay-owned/run

**Pasta Pomodoro** 2304 Market St. open til midnight • Italian • $5-10

**Patio Cafe** 531 Castro St. **621-4640** lesbians/gay men • enclosed patio dining • Californian • $10-20

**Pozole** 2337 Market St. **626-2666** healthy Mexican specialties • some veggie • beer/wine • $5-10

**The Sausage Factory** 517 Castro St. **626-1250** noon-1am • lesbians/gay men • pizza & pasta • some veggie • beer/wine • $8-15

**Sparky's** 242 Church St. **626-8666** 24hrs • diner • some veggie • popular late night • $8-12

▲ **Valentine's Cafe** 1793 Church St., Noe Valley **285-2257** clsd Mon, call for hours • lunch, dinner, wknd brunch • plenty veggie

**Welcome Home** 464 Castro St. **626-3600** 8am-11pm • popular • lesbians/gay men • homestyle • some veggie • beer/wine • JJ's favorite • $7-12

**Without Reservations** 460 Castro St. **861-9510** 8am-midnight • lesbians/gay men • diner • some veggie • wheelchair access • $7-12

**Zuni Cafe** 1658 Market St. **552-2522** clsd Mon • popular • upscale cont'l/Mediterranean • full bar • $30-40

## BOOKSTORES & RETAIL SHOPS

**A Different Light** 489 Castro St. **431-0891** 10am-11pm, til midnight Fri-Sat • lesbigay • bookstore & queer info clearinghouse • readings

**Aardvark Books** 227 Church St. **552-6733** 10:30am-10:30pm, 9:30am-9pm Sun • mostly used • good lesbigay section • say hello to Ace, the bookstore cat par excellence

# Valentine's
C A F E

GOURMET INTERNATIONAL VEGETERIAN CUISINE

# FABULOUS DINNER
# AND
# WEEKEND BRUNCH!

1793 Church St. @ 30th, SF
415.285.2257
Off the "J" Church & 24 Divisadero Lines

**Books Etc.** 538 Castro St. **621-8631**
11am-10pm, til midnight Fri-Sat • mostly
used

**Botanica** 1478 Church St., Noe Valley
**285-0612** 11am-7pm • Afro-Caribbean
religious articles

**Does Your Father Know?** 548 Castro St.
**241-9865** lesbigay gifts & videos

**Does Your Mother Know?** 4079 18th St.
**864-3160** 10am-11pm • cards • T-shirts

**Don't Panic** 541 Castro St. **553-8989**
10am-9pm • T-shirts • gifts

**Headlines** 557 Castro St. **626-8061**
10am-9pm • clothes • cards • novelties

**Headlines for Women** 549 Castro St.
**252-1280** 10am-9pm • clothing • jewelry

**Image Leather** 2199 Market St. **621-
7551** 9am-10pm, 11am-9pm Sun • custom leather clothing • accessories • toys

**Just for Fun** 3982 24th St., Noe Valley
**285-4068** 9am-9pm, til 7pm Sun • gift
shop

**Leather Zone** 2352 Market St. **255-8585**
11am-7pm • new & used fetishwear

**Rolo** 2351 Market St. **431-4545** designer
labels • also 450 Castro location 626-
7171

**Under One Roof** 2362 Market St. **252-
9430** 11am-7pm • 100% of sales are
donated for AIDS relief

TRAVEL AGENTS

**Acento Travel** 864-1630

**Bottom Line Travel** 1236 Castro St. **826-
8600**/(800) 456-9833 IGLTA

**Doin' It Right Tours & Travel** 621-
3576/(800) 936-3646 Gay Travel Club
meets 1st Wed • IGLTA • women-
owned/run

**Now, Voyager** 4406 18th St. **626-
1169**/(800) 255-6951 IGLTA

**Outbound Travel** 143 Collingwood St.
**626-0649** IGLTA

**Passport To Leisure** 2265 Market St.
**621-8300**/(800) 322-1204 (OUTSIDE CA)
IGLTA

**Scandia Travel** 76 Gough St. **552-
5300**/(800) 536-4359

**Travel Trends** 431 Castro St. **558-6922**
IGLTA

**Winship Travel** 2321 Market St. **863-
2555**/(800) 545-2557 ask for Susan •
IGLTA

SPIRITUAL GROUPS

**Congregation Sha'ar Zahav** 220
Danvers St. **861-6932** 8:15pm Fri • les-
bian/gay synagogue

**MCC of San Francisco** 150 Eureka St.
**863-4434** 9am, 11am & 7pm Sun, 7pm
Wed

**Most Holy Redeemer Church** 100
Diamond St. **863-6259** 7:30am & 10am
Sun, 5pm Sat (vigil mass) • mostly
gay/lesbian Roman Catholic parish

GYMS & HEALTH CLUBS

**Market Street Gym** 2301 Market St.
**626-4488** lesbians/gay men • day passes
avail.

**Women's Training Center** 2164 Market
St. **864-6835** women only • day passes
avail.

EROTICA

**The Gauntlet** 2377 Market St. **431-3133**
noon-7pm • piercing parlor • jewelry

**Jaguar** 4057 18th St. **863-4777**

**Le Salon** 4126 18th St. **552-4213**

**The MMO (Mercury Mail Order)** 4084
18th St. **621-1188** leather • toys

**Rob Gallery** 1925 Market St. **252-1198**
11am-7pm • leather • latex • artwork

## S.F.—South of Market (415)

ACCOMMODATIONS

**Ramada Market St.** 1231 Market St.
**626-8000**/(800) 227-4747 gay-friendly •
wheelchair access • IGLTA

**Victorian Hotel** 54 4th St. **986-
4400**/(800) 227-3804 gay-friendly • 1913
landmark hotel • private/shared baths •
also restaurant • SF cuisine • full bar •
$49-89

BARS & NIGHTCLUBS

**The Box** 715 Harrison St. **647-8258**
9pm-2:30am Th only • popular • les-
bians/gay men • dancing/DJ • multi-
racial

**C.W. Saloon** 917 Folsom St. **974-1585**
10am-2am • gay-friendly • neighborhood
bar

**Club Asia** 174 King St. (King St. Garage)
**285-2742** 10pm-? 2nd & 4th Fri • popular • mostly gay men • dancing/DJ •
mostly Asian-American • live shows

**Club Universe** 177 Townsend **985-5241**
9:30pm-7am Sat • popular • lesbians/gay
men • dancing/DJ • alternative

**The CoCo Club** 139 8th St. (enter on
Minna) **626-2337** mostly women • multi-
racial • live shows • call for events

**Endup** 401 6th St. **495-9550** mostly gay
men • dancing/DJ • multi-racial • many
different theme nights • esp. popular
Sun mornings

# The hottest Women's dance club on the planet!

Every Saturday Night at the **ENDup**
**401 6th Street at Harrison**

Call our event line for info on The Girl Spot events
at our Club Skirts circuit party events (415) 337-4962

An MT Production

Producer of The Club Skirts Labor Day in Monterey Women's Weekend
and co-producer of The Club Skirts & Girl Bar Dinah Shore Weekend

**Futura** 174 King St. (King St. Garage) **665-6715** 10pm-3am 2nd & 4th Sat • popular • mostly gay men • dancing/DJ • mostly Latino-American • live shows

▲ **Girl Spot (G-Spot)** 401 6th St. (at the 'Endup') **337-4962** 9pm Sat only • popular • mostly women • dancing/DJ • go-go dancers

**Jaded** 314 11th St. (at Transmission) **697-0375x3** monthly • lesbians/gay men • dancing/DJ • multi-racial • transgender-friendly

**Litter Box** 683 Clementina Alley at 8th & Folsom (Cat's Alley Club) **431-3332** 9pm-2am Fri • lesbians/gay men • dancing/DJ • alternative

**Pleasuredome** 177 Townsend **985-5256** Sun night dance club • mostly gay men • dancing/DJ • call hotline for details

**Rawhide II** 280 7th St. **621-1197** noon-2am • mostly gay men • dancing/DJ • country/western

**San Francisco Eagle** 398 12th St. **626-0880** 4pm-2am, from 2pm Sat, from noon Sun • mostly gay men • leather • occasional women's leather events • patio

**Sound Factory** 525 Harrison St. **979-8686** 9:30pm-6am Fri-Sat only • mostly gay men • dancing/DJ

**The Stud** 399 9th St. **863-6623** 5pm-2am • lesbians/gay men • dancing/DJ • theme nights • outrageous 'Trannyshack' Tue • mostly men Wed

**Twenty Tank Brewery** 316 11th St. **255-9455** gay-friendly • microbrewery • food served • some veggie

### CAFES

**Brain Wash** 1122 Folsom St. **431-9274** 7:30am-midnight, til 1am Fri-Sat • popular • gay-friendly • live shows • beer/wine • laundromat & cafe • brkfst & lunch menu

**Chat House** 139 8th St. **255-8783** brkfst & lunch menu • cute staff • 'Xena Night' 8pm Tue • women-owned

**Cyberworld Cafe** 528 Folsom St. **278-9669** 6am-midnight, til 2am Fri-Sat, from 8am Sat, 9am-6pm Sun • internet cafe • Californian cuisine • live shows • classes • theme parties • patio • pets ok

### RESTAURANTS

**42 Degrees** 235 16th St. (3rd St.) **777-5558**

# STORMYLEATHER

*San Francisco's Premier Fetish Boutique Retailing One Of The World's Largest Collections Of Leather, Latex and PVC.*

1158 Howard St SF CA 94103 415.626.1672
Store Hours: Mon thru Sat 12-7 Sun 2-6
Website: www.stormyleather.com

**Bistro Roti** 155 Steuart **495-6500** lunch & dinner • country French • full bar • $15-20

**Boulevard** 1 Mission St. **543-6084**

**Caribbean Zone** 55 Natoma St. **541-9465** lunch & dinner • some veggie • cocktails • festive decor • $7-15

**Fringale** 570 4th St. **543-0573** lunch & dinner • Mediterranean • wheelchair access • $11-16

**Hamburger Mary's** 1582 Folsom St. **626-5767/626-1985** 10am-2am, clsd Mon • some veggie • wheelchair access • $7-15

**Hawthorne Lane** 22 Hawthorne St. **777-9779**

**Le Charm** 315 5th St. **546-6128**

**Line Up** 398 7th St. **861-2887** 11am-10pm • lesbians/gay men • Mexican • some veggie • $8-15

**Lulu** 816 Folsom St. **495-5775** lunch & dinner • upscale Mediterrranean • some veggie • full bar • $12-20

**Manora's Thai Cuisine** 1600 Folsom **861-6224** 11:30am-2pm & 5:30pm-10:30pm, some veggie

**Slow Club** 2501 Mariposa **241-9390** 7am-2am, clsd Sun • full bar • wheelchair access

**Wa-Ha-Ka!** 1489 Folsom **861-1410** Mexican • plenty veggie • $5-10

**Woodward's Garden** 1700 Mission St. **621-7122**

### BOOKSTORES & RETAIL SHOPS

**Leather Etc.** 1201 Folsom St. **864-7558** 10:30am-7pm, from 11am Sat

**Stompers** 323 10th St. **255-6422** noon-8pm, clsd Mon • boots • cigars • gloves

### TRAVEL AGENTS

**Above & Beyond Travel** 330 Townsend #107 **284-1666/(800) 397-2681** IGLTA

**Castro Travel Company** 435 Brannan #214 **357-0957/(800) 861-0957** IGLTA

**China Basin Travel Center** 185 Berry St. **777-4747**

**Gregory Howell & Assoc.** 118 King St. #530 **541-5388** IGLTA

### EROTICA

**A Taste of Leather** 317-A 10th St. **252-9166/(800) 367-0786** noon-8pm

**City Entertainment** 960 Folsom St. **543-2124** 24hrs wknds

**Mr. S Leather** 310 7th St. **863-7764** 11am-7pm, noon-6pm Sun • erotic goods • leather • latex

▲ **Stormy Leather** 1158 Howard St. **626-1672** noon-7pm • leather • latex • toys • magazines • women-owned/run

## S.F.—Polk Street Area    (415)

### ACCOMMODATIONS

**Atherton Hotel** 685 Ellis St. **474-5720/(800) 474-5720** gay-friendly • non-smoking rms. avail. • also restaurant • full bar • IGLTA • $59-119

▲ **Essex Hotel** 684 Ellis St. **474-4664/(800) 443-7739** gay-friendly • boutique hotel w/European-style hospitality • wheelchair access • IGLTA • $59-89

**Hotel Richelieu** 1050 Van Ness Ave. **673-4711/(800) 227-3608** lesbians/gay men • gym • full bar • wheelchair access • $99-169

**Pensione International Hotel** 875 Post St. **775-3344/(800) 358-8123** gay-friendly • Victorian-styled hotel built in early 1900s • shared/private baths • $30-65

▲ **The Phoenix Hotel** 601 Eddy St. **776-1380/(800) 248-9466** gay-friendly • 1950s-style motor lodge • popular • swimming • kids ok • fabulous 'Back Flip' bar • IGLTA • $89-150

**The Super 8 Lombard Hotel** 1015 Geary St. **673-5232/(800) 777-3210** gay-friendly • kids ok • non-smoking rms. avail. • up to $100

### BARS & NIGHTCLUBS

**Mother Lode** 1002 Post St. **928-6006** 6am-2am • mostly gay men • neighborhood bar • dancing/DJ • multi-racial • transsexuals, transvestites & their admirers • live shows

### CAFES

**Quetzal** 1234 Polk St. **673-4181** 6am-11pm • food served • live entertainment • internet connections • beer/wine

**Rendezvous Cafe** 1760 Polk St. **292-4033** 7am-10pm • some veggie • $6-10

### RESTAURANTS

**Caffe Monda** 2032 Polk St. **923-9984** 6pm-10pm, 5:30pm-11pm Fri-Sat • southern Italian • beer/wine • gay-owned/operated

**Grubstake II** 1525 Pine St. **673-8268** 5pm-4am, 10am-4am wknds • lesbians/gay men • beer/wine

**Spuntino** 524 Van Ness Ave. **861-7772** 7am-8pm, from 10am wknds • Italian • also cafe & desserts • beer/wine • $8-12

# San Francisco's small hotels,

## UNION SQUARE . . . . . . . . . . . .

### THE ANDREWS HOTEL
**from $92** *"One of SF's Top Ten for value."* —NY Times •Down comforters & floral decor •FREE gourmet breakfast •Italian restaurant •Walk to Cable Cars & Chinatown
624 POST  1-800-926-3739

### THE NOB HILL LAMBOURNE
**from $165** *"A holistic approach to hospitality."* —USA Today  •SF's ultra-pampering spa hotel •In-room business center & kitchenettes •FREE gourmet breakfast & wine hour •Massage & Aromatherapy  725 PINE  1-800-274-8466

### THE COMMODORE
**from $79** *This is..."where to stay in San Francisco!"* —NY Times •Stylish & contemporary •Unusually spacious & comfortable rooms •Sophisticated cocktail lounge: The Red Room •Charming diner-style cafe: Titanic •Walk to Cable Cars & Chinatown
825 SUTTER  1-800-338-6848

### HOTEL REX
**from $125** *"New SF hotel goes big on the ambiance."* —SF Chronicle •1920's club-like atmosphere inspired by SF arts & literary spirit •Antiquarian bookstore •Restaurant & stylish lounge •Walk to Cable Cars & Chinatown
562 SUTTER  1-800-433-4434

. . . . . . . . . . . . . . . **PACIFIC HEIGHTS**

### THE HOLIDAY LODGE
**from $99** *"A refreshing oasis edged by palm trees."* —NY Times •Secluded atmosphere •Heated pool & lush gardens •Free parking •AAA approved •Near Fisherman's Wharf & Marina
1901 VAN NESS  1-800-367-8504

# most unique inns and B&Bs.

### CIVIC CENTER
. . . . . . . . . . . . & HISTORIC DISTRICT

**THE ABIGAIL**
**from $79** *"Absolutely perfect for travelers who like charm, great food and international company." —Frommer's Guide* •Antiques & down comforters •FREE continental breakfast •Vegetarian restaurant •Steps from Symphony Hall & new Main Library •Near Castro, SOMA and The Mission   246 McALLISTER  1-800-243-6510

**THE PHOENIX**
**from $99**  *"Ambiance is pure Fantasy Island" —People Magazine*
•Tropical, fun, hip & artistic •Pool
•New Blackflip Restaurant
•Bungalow-style rooms •FREE
breakfast & parking •Near Castro,
SOMA and Mission
562 SUTTER  1-800-433-4434

**THE ARCHBISHOP'S MANSION**
**from $149**  *"Most elegant small hotel on the West Coast."*
*—USA Today* •Historic chateau
•15 romantic rooms •Jacuzzi tubs & fireplaces •FREE breakfast-in-bed & parking •Walk to Castro
1000 FULTON  1-800-543-5820

Visit all these hotels on the Internet:
www.sftrips.com   Or call JOIE DE VIVRE:
# 1-800-SF-TRIPS for centralized
info & reservations at all these fine hotels.

*the* **Essex**
**HOTEL**

**W**ith a European charm and tradition, the Essex is only one block from Polk Street. Close to shopping, bars, restaurants, theatres, and the City's gay life!

**415-474-4664**
***Rooms from $69***

- Toll free for reservation -
1-800-453-7739 USA • 1-800-443-7739 CA
684 Ellis Street · S.F., CA · 94109

**Stars Cafe** 500 Van Ness Ave. **861-4344** lunch & dinner • full bar • $15-25

## BOOKSTORES & RETAIL SHOPS

**A Clean Well Lighted Place For Books** 601 Van Ness Ave. **441-6670** 10am-11pm, til midnight Fri-Sat • general • lesbigay section • call for events

**Hog On Ice** 1630 Polk St. **771-7909** 10am-10pm, til 6pm Sat • novelties • books • CDs

**My Boyfriend's Closet** 1390 Larkin St. **563-5999** opens 11am, clsd Mon • women's clothing • jewelry • art

## TRAVEL AGENTS

**Jackson Travel** 1829 Polk St. **928-2500** IGLTA

**Left Coast Travel** 1655 Polk St. #1 **771-5353/(800) 823-5338** IGLTA

# S.F.—Downtown & North Beach (415)

## ACCOMMODATIONS

▲ **The Abigail Hotel** 246 McAllister St. **861-9728/(800) 243-6510** gay-friendly • also 'Millennium' restaurant • gourmet vegetarian • IGLTA • $84-139

**Allison Hotel** 417 Stockton St. **986-8737/(800) 628-6456** gay-friendly • $69-109

**Amsterdam Hotel** 749 Taylor St., Nob Hill **673-3277/(800) 637-3444** gay-friendly • charming European-style hotel • shared/private baths • $69-89

**The Andrews** 563-6877/(800) 926-3739 gay-friendly • also restaurant • Italian • $10-15

**Canterbury Hotel** 750 Sutter St. **474-6464/(800) 528-1234** gay-friendly

**Cartwright Hotel** 524 Sutter St. **983-6243/(800) 227-3844** gay-friendly • free gym passes • afternoon tea • wine hour • IGLTA • $99-149

▲ **The Commodore International Hotel** 825 Sutter St. **923-6800/(800) 338-6848** gay-friendly • $69-109

**Dakota Hotel** 931-7475 gay-friendly • near Union Square • $65-105

**Glenwood Hotel at Union Square** 717 Sutter St. **673-0700/(888) 442-2020** gay-friendly

**Grand Hyatt San Francisco** 345 Stockton St. **398-1234** gay-friendly • IGLTA

**Hotel Diva** 440 Geary **202-8700/(800) 553-1900** gay-friendly • IGLTA • $135-155

**Hotel Griffon** 155 Steuart St. **495-2100/(800) 321-2201** gay-friendly • fitness center • non-smoking rms. avail. • kids ok • also restaurant • bistro/cont'l • wheelchair access • $155-250

**Hotel Monaco** 501 Geary St. **292-8132/(800) 214-4220** gay-friendly • full bar • IGLTA • $195-375

▲ **The Hotel Rex** 562 Sutter St. **433-4434/(800) 433-4434** gay-friendly • full bar • non-smoking rms. avail. • wheelchair access

**Hotel Triton** 342 Grant Ave. **394-0500/(800) 433-6611** gay-friendly • wheelchair access • IGLTA • $135-185

**Hotel Vintage Court** 650 Bush St. **392-4666/(800) 654-1100** gay-friendly • fireplaces • also world-famous 5-star 'Masa's' restaurant • French • $75 prix fixe • wheelchair access • IGLTA • $129-169

**Hyde Park Suites** 771-0200/(800) 227-3608 gay-friendly • Mediterranean-inspired 1- & 2-bdrm suites • gym • sundeck • kitchens • IGLTA • $165-220

**King George Hotel** 334 Mason St. **781-5050/(800) 288-6005** gay-friendly • European-style boutique hotel • non-smoking rms. avail. • kids ok • also 'The Bread & Honey Tearoom' w/morning & afternoon teas • $115-125

**Maxwell Hotel** 386 Geary **986-2000/(888) 734-6299** gay-friendly • wheelchair access • $99-145

▲ **Nob Hill Lambourne** 725 Pine St., Nob Hill **433-2287/(800) 274-8466** gay-friendly • luxurious 'business accommodation' • kitchens • kids ok • $155-275

**Nob Hill Pensione** 835 Hyde St. **885-2987** gay-friendly • European-style hotel • shared/private baths • smokefree • kids ok • also restaurant • $30-60

**The Pacific Bay Inn** 520 Jones St. **673-0234** gay-friendly • also 'Dottie's True Blue Cafe' • $225-300 (weekly)

**Pensione International Hotel** 775-3344/(800) 358-8123 gay-friendly • Victorian-styled hotel built in early 1900s • shared/private baths • $30-65

**Ramada Union Square** 345 Taylor St. **673-2332/(800) 228-2828** gay-friendly • also restaurant & full bar • wheelchair access

**Savoy Hotel** 580 Geary St. **441-2700/(800) 227-4223** gay-friendly • non-smoking rms. avail. • IGLTA • $105-195

**The York Hotel** 940 Sutter St. **885-6800/(800) 808-9675** gay-friendly • boutique hotel • $99-210

MensWear
Tailored for
Women

54 Geary
at Grant
Union Square

ANGELA KWAN CHRISTENSEN
*Recreational Therapist*

# BILLYBLUE
## SAN FRANCISCO

## BARS & NIGHTCLUBS

**Moze** 1093 Pine St. **885-2852** 4pm-2am, 11am-2am wknds, Sun brunch • mostly gay men • neighborhood bar

## CAFES

**Cafe Claude** 7 Claude **392-3505** 10am-9pm, clsd Sun • live jazz • as close to Paris as you can get in SF • beer/wine

**Dottie's True Blue Cafe** 522 Jones St. **885-2767** 7:30am-2pm, clsd Tue • plenty veggie • great brkfst • gay-owned/run

## RESTAURANTS

**Akimbo** 116 Maiden Ln. **433-2288** lunch & dinner, clsd Sun • lesbians/gay men • beer/wine • gay-owned/run

**Bistro Roti** 155 Steuart St. (Hotel Griffon) **495-6500** lunch & dinner • country French • full bar • $15-20

**Campo Santo** 240 Columbus Ave., North Beach **433-9623** lunch & dinner, clsd Mon night • Mexican • some veggie • beer/wine • hip decor • $8-15

**Gracie's** 398 Geary St. **646-8600**

**Mario's Bohemian Cigar Store Cafe** 566 Columbus Ave. **362-0536** great foccacia sandwiches • some veggie

**Millennium** 246 McAllister St. (at Abigail Hotel) **487-9800** 11:30am-2:30pm Tue-Fri, 5pm-9:30pm Tue-Sun, clsd Mon • Euro-Mediterranean • upscale vegetarian

**Moose's** 1652 Stockton **989-7800** upscale bistro menu

**New Moon Cafe** 639 Post St. **775-4789** lunch & dinner • California nouvelle w/Chinese accent • some veggie • $15-25

**US Restaurant** 431 Columbus Ave., North Beach **362-6251** 7am-9pm, clsd Sun-Mon • Italian food just like home • beer/wine

## BOOKSTORES & RETAIL SHOPS

▲ **Billy Blue** 54 Geary (at Grant) **781-2111/(800) 772-BLUE** 10am-6pm, clsd Sun • men's clothing

**City Lights Bookstore** 261 Columbus Ave., North Beach **362-8193** 10am-midnight • historic beatnik bookstore • many progressive titles

## TRAVEL AGENTS

**Beyond the Bay** 520 Davis St. **421-7721/(800) 542-1991** women-owned/run • IGLTA

**De Rose Travel Group** 1177 California St. #B **865-0100**

**European Travel** 442 Post St. #301 **981-5518/(800) 635-6463** IGLTA

**Franciscan Travel** 323 Geary St. #701 **391-6592** IGLTA

**SF Travelers** 870 Market St. #578 **433-9621** IGLTA

**Travel Time** One Hallidie Plaza #406 **677-0799** IGLTA

damron online
www.damron.com
damronco@aol.com

## S.F.—Mission District (415)

### INFO LINES & SERVICES

**Women's Building** 3543 18th St. **431-1180** hours vary • space for many women's organizations • social/support groups • housing & job listings • beautiful murals

### ACCOMMODATIONS

▲ **Andora Inn** 2434 Mission **282-0337/(800) 967-9219** lesbians/gay men • guesthouse • near Castro & public transportation • smokefree • also restaurant • full bar • IGLTA • $79-185

▲ **The Inn San Francisco** 943 S. Van Ness Ave. **641-0188/(800) 359-0913** gay-friendly • Victorian mansion • full brkfst • hot tub • shared/private baths • kitchens • fireplaces • patio • IGLTA • $75-195

### BARS & NIGHTCLUBS

**El Rio** 3158-A Mission St. **282-3325** 3pm-2am, til midnight Mon • gay-friendly • neighborhood bar • mostly Latino-American • live bands • patio • popular Sun afternoons • 'Red' on Sat (women's night)

**Esta Noche** 3079 16th St. **861-5757** 1pm-2am • mostly men • dancing/DJ • mostly Latino-American • live shows • salsa & disco

**Lexington Club** 3464 19th St. **863-2052** 2pm-2am • mostly women • neighborhood bar • lesbian-owned/run

**Phone Booth** 1398 S. Van Ness Ave. **648-4683** 10am-2am • lesbians/gay men • neighborhood bar • piano bar wknds

**Red** 540 Valencia (at 'Blondies') **864-2419** 2pm-2am Sun • women only • dancing/DJ • also Sat at 'El Rio'

**Wild Side West** 424 Cortland **647-3099** 1pm-2am • gay-friendly • neighborhood bar • patio • magic garden

### CAFES

**Cafe Commons** 3161 Mission St. **282-2928** 7am-7pm, from, from 8am wknds • sandwiches • plenty veggie • patio • wheelchair access • women-owned/run • $4-7

**Farleys** 1315 18th St., Potrero Hill **648-1545** 7am-10pm, from 8am wknds • coffeehouse

# Andora Inn . . . The Jewel of the Mission ꙮ in The Heart of San Francisco ꙮ

Historic Andora Inn, a beautifully restored 1875 Italianate Victorian is conveniently located in the historic Mission district offering unique shops, restaurants, coffee houses, nightspots, and within easy walking distance to The Castro! Adjacent to a Bay Area Rapid Transit Station, the Andora Inn is just minutes from Union Square with its cable cars, museums, shopping, theaters and access to the Wharf, Northbeach, Chinatown and Folsom Street (SOMA).

★★★★

• 14 Elegant Rooms & Suites
• Some City views, private baths, fireplace
• Complimentary Breakfast
• Telephones
• Color remote TV and VCR
• Garage Parking Available
• Library with Fireplace
• Patio
• Conference Room featuring:
THE COLA CABANA
Contemporary Cuisine
Restaurant & Bar

2434 Mission Street, San Francisco, CA 94110 • Ph: 415-282-0337 800-967-9219
Website: www.gayglobal.com/sf/andora • Email: AndoraSF@aol.com

**Radio Valencia** 1199 Valencia St. **826-1199** 5pm-midnight Mon-Tue, noon-midnight Wed-Sun • sandwiches & dessert • artsy cafe

**Red Dora's Bearded Lady Dyke Cafe & Gallery** 485 14th St. **626-2805** 7am-7pm, from 9am wknds • mostly women • funky brunch & sandwiches • plenty veggie • performances Fri-Sat nights (call for events) • patio • women-owned/run • $4-7

### RESTAURANTS

**The Barking Basset Cafe** 803 Cortland Ave. **648-2146** 8am-9pm, til 3pm Sun-Mon, clsd Tue

**Cafe Istanbul** 525 Valencia St. **863-8854** noon-11pm, Fri-Sat til midnight • Mediterranean • some veggie • authentic Turkish coffee • bellydancers Sat • wheelchair access

**Firecracker** 1007 1/2 Valencia St. **642-3470** Chinese

**Just For You** 1453 18th St., Potrero Hill **647-3033** hours vary • popular • lesbians/gay men • Southern breakfast • some veggie • women-owned/run • $4-7

**Klein's Delicatessen** 501 Connecticut St., Potrero Hill **821-9149** 7am-7pm, 8am-5:30pm Sun • patio • sandwiches & salads • some veggie • beer/wine • women-owned/run • $4-10

**Pancho Villa** 3071 16th St. **864-8840** 10am-midnight • best 'Mission-style' burritos in city • some veggie • $4-8 • wheelchair access • also 'El Toro' at 18th & Valencia

**Pauline's Pizza Pie** 260 Valencia St. **552-2050** 5pm-10pm Tue-Sun, clsd Mon • popular • lesbians/gay men • beer/wine

**Picaro** 3120 16th St. **431-4089** 11am-2pm, 5pm-10pm, til 11pm Fri-Sun • Spanish tapas bar

**The Slanted Door** 584 Valencia St. **861-8032** popular • Vietnamese

**Ti-Couz** 3108 16th St. **252-7373** 11am-11pm, 10am-11pm Sat, 10am-10pm Sun • Breton dinner & dessert crepes • plenty veggie • beer/wine • wheelchair access • $5-10

**Val 21** 995 Valencia St. **821-6622** dinner, wknd brunch • eclectic Californian • some veggie • $7-15

*Bed AND Breakfast*

Distinct San Franciscan hospitality.
Gracious 1872 Victorian Mansion.
Historic residential neighborhood.
Antiques, fresh flowers, beverages.
Spa tubs, hot tubs, fireplaces.
Sundeck, lovely English Garden.
Full Buffet Breakfast.

# The Inn San Francisco

943 SOUTH VAN NESS AVENUE
SAN FRANCISCO, CA 94110
FACSIMILE (415) 641-1701

*For Reservations*
**(415) 641-0188    (800) 359-0913**

"First
Good Vibrations
Then the
Golden Gate
Bridge..."

No visit to San Francisco
is complete without a stop
at The City's legendary
feminist vibrator store and
museum. We carry the
highest quality vibrators,
books and toys, the wildest
selection of silicone dildos,
and individually reviewed
videos. Or send $4 for our
two catalogs
(applied to first order).

GOOD VIBRATIONS

11am-7pm, daily
1210 Valencia #WT
San Francisco, CA 94110
(415) 974-8980

Also in Berkeley:
2504 San Pablo Avenue
(510) 841-8987

### BOOKSTORES & RETAIL SHOPS

**381** 381 Guerrero St. **621-3830** noon-6pm, 11am-7pm Fri-Sat • great kitsch & candles

**Bernal Books** 401 Cortland Ave., Bernal Hts. **550-0293** 10am-7pm, til 4pm Sun, clsd Mon • lesbigay section

**Dog Eared Books** 900 Valencia St. **282-1901** 10am-9pm, new & used • good lesbigay section

**Leather Tongue Video** 714 Valencia St. **552-2900** noon-11pm, til midnight Fri-Sat • great collection of camp, cult & obscure video

**Modern Times Bookstore** 888 Valencia St. **282-9246** 11am-9pm, til 6pm Sun • alternative • lesbigay section • readings • wheelchair access

### SPIRITUAL GROUPS

**The Episcopal Church of St. John the Evangelist** 1661 15th St. (enter on Julian Ave.) **861-1436** 11am Sun • Oasis congregation • wheelchair access

### GYMS & HEALTH CLUBS

**Osento** 955 Valencia St. **282-6333** 1pm-midnight • women only • baths • hot tub • massage

### EROTICA

**Body Manipulations** 3234 16th St. **621-0408** noon-7pm, clsd Wed • piercing (walk-in basis)

▲ **Good Vibrations** 1210 Valencia St. **550-7399** 11am-7pm • mostly women • clean, well-lighted sex toy store • also mail order • women-owned/run

## S.F.—Haight, Fillmore & West (415)

### ACCOMMODATIONS

**Alamo Square Inn** 719 Scott St. **922-2055/(800) 345-9888** gay-friendly • 1895 Queen Anne & 1896 Tudor Revival Victorian mansions • full brkfst • smoke-free • kids ok • $85-275

▲ **The Archbishops Mansion** 1000 Fulton St. **563-7872/(800) 543-5820** gay-friendly • one of SF's grandest homes • $129-385

**Auberge des Artistes** 829 Fillmore **776-2530** gay-friendly • full brkfst • hot tub • shared/private baths • kids ok • computer access • $55-100

**Bella Vista Inn** 114 Divisadero St. **255-3167/(800) 428-8559** gay-friendly • rental apt. B&B • IGLTA • $225-295

**Bock's B&B** 1448 Willard St. **664-6842** gay-friendly • restored 1906 Edwardian residence • shared/private baths • smokefree • lesbian-owned/run • $40-75

**Carl Street Unicorn House** 156 Carl St. **753-5194** gay-friendly • 1895 Victorian house • shared baths • smokefree • kids 6+yrs ok • women-owned/run • $40-55

**Casa Loma Hotel** 610 Fillmore St. **552-7100** gay-friendly • shared bath • kids ok • $28-45

**The Chateau Tivoli** 1057 Steiner St. **776-5462/(800) 228-1647** gay-friendly • historic San Francisco B&B • $80-200

**Gough Hayes Hotel** 417 Gough St. **431-9131** lesbians/gay men • $55

▲ **Holiday Lodge** 1901 Van Ness Ave., Pacific Heights **776-4469/(800) 367-8504** gay-friendly • motel • tropical resort & pool oasis in the heart of San Francisco • kitchens • IGLTA • $59-109

**Hotel Majestic** 1500 Sutter St., Pacific Heights **441-1100/869-8966** gay-friendly • one of SF's earliest grand hotels • also restaurant • Mediterranean • full bar • wheelchair access • $135-260

**Inn 1890** 1890 Page St. **386-0486/(888) INN-1890** lesbians/gay men • kitchens • fireplaces • apt. avail. • $69-79

**Inn at the Opera** 333 Fulton St. **863-8400/(800) 325-2708** gay-friendly • also restaurant • Mediterranean • $165-275

**Jackson Court** 2198 Jackson St. **929-7670** gay-friendly • $139-195

**Lombard Plaza Motel** 2026 Lombard St. **921-2444** gay-friendly • $49-79

**The Mansions** 2220 Sacramento St., Pacific Heights **929-9444/(800) 826-9398** gay-friendly • full brkfst • IGLTA • $129-350

**Metro Hotel** 319 Divisadero St. **861-5364** gay-friendly • food served • $50-94

**The Queen Anne Hotel** 1590 Sutter St., Pacific Heights **441-2828/(800) 227-3970** gay-friendly • beautifully restored 1890 landmark • popular • fireplaces • non-smoking rms. avail. • kids ok • IGLTA • $110-170

**Radisson Miyako Hotel** 1625 Post St. **922-3200/(800) 533-4567** gay-friendly • located in the heart of Japantown • non-smoking rms. avail. • wheelchair access • IGLTA • $149-169

**Stanyan Park Hotel** 750 Stanyan St. **751-1000** gay-friendly • fireplaces • kids ok • $85-185

## BARS & NIGHTCLUBS

**Alta Plaza** 2301 Fillmore **922-1444** 4pm-2am • mostly gay men • professional • also restaurant • cont'l • some veggie • gay-owned/run • wheelchair access • $10-15

**Hayes & Vine** 377 Hayes St. **626-5301** 5pm-midnight, til 1am Fri-Sat • lesbians/gay men • wine bar

**The Lion Pub** 2062 Divisadero St. **567-6565** 3pm-2am • mostly gay men • professional • theme nights

**Marlena's** 488 Hayes St. **864-6672** 10am-2am • lesbians/gay men • neighborhood bar • drag shows Fri-Sat nights • wheelchair access

**Noc Noc** 557 Haight St. **861-5811** 5pm-2am • gay-friendly • beer/wine

**The Top** 424 Haight St. **864-7386** gay-friendly • dancing/DJ • alternative • theme nights • call for events

**Traxx** 1437 Haight St. **864-4213** noon-2am • mostly gay men • neighborhood bar • wheelchair access

## CAFES

**Mad Magda's Russian Tearoom & Cafe** 579 Hayes St. **864-7654** popular • lesbians/gay men • eclectic crowd • magic garden • tarot & palm readers daily

## RESTAURANTS

**Alta Plaza** 2301 Fillmore St. **922-1444** 5:30pm-10pm, Fri-Sat til 11pm, Sun brunch • some veggie • $10-15

**Blue Muse** 409 Gough St. **626-7505** 8am-10pm, wknd brunch • some veggie • $10-15

**Cafe Delle Stelle** 395 Hayes **252-1110** popular • Italian • beer/wine

**Cha Cha Cha's** 1801 Haight St. **386-7670** til 11pm • Cuban/Cajun • excellent sangria • worth the long wait!

**Charpe's Grill** 131 Gough St. **621-6766** dinner nightly • some veggie • full bar • wheelchair access • $10-15

**Garibaldi's** 347 Presidio **563-8841** lunch & dinner • Italian • full bar • wheelchair access • gay-owned/run

**Greens** Fort Mason **771-6222** dinners, Sun brunch, clsd Mon • gourmet prix fixe vegetarian • $20-40

**Kan Zaman** 1793 Haight **751-9656** noon-midnight, til 2am Fri-Sat • Mediterranean • some veggie • beer/wine • hookahs & tobacco avail.

**Ya Halla** 494 Haight St. **522-1509** lunch & dinner • Middle Eastern • plenty veggie • $4-9

### BOOKSTORES & RETAIL SHOPS
**La Riga** 1391 Haight St. **552-1525** 11am-7pm • leather

**Mainline Gifts** 1928 Fillmore St. **563-4438** hours vary

**Nomad** 1881 Hayes St. **563-7771** noon-6pm, clsd Wed • piercing (walk-in) • jewelry

### TRAVEL AGENTS
**Deeds & Daily World Travel** 311 9th Ave. **221-6760** IGLTA • contact Don Wilson

### EROTICA
**Romantasy** 199 Moulton St. **673-3137** books • videos • toys • clothing • women-owned/run

## San Jose (408)

### INFO LINES & SERVICES
**AA Gay/Lesbian 374-8511** call for mtg. schedule

**Billy DeFrank Lesbian/Gay Community Center** 175 Stockton Ave. **293-2429** 3pm-9pm, from noon Sat, 9am-6pm Sun

**Rainbow Gender Association 984-4044** transgender group • recorded info

### ACCOMMODATIONS
**Hensley House B&B** 456 N. 3rd St. **298-3537/(800) 498-3537** lesbians/gay men • located in a historic landmark • gay-owned/operated

### BARS & NIGHTCLUBS
**641 Club** 641 Stockton **998-1144** 2pm-2am, from 11am wknds • lesbians/gay men • dancing/DJ • multi-racial

**Buck's** 301 W. Stockton Ave. **286-1176** noon-2am, 24hrs wknds • lesbians/gay men • neighborhood bar • dancing/DJ

**Greg's Ballroom** 551 W. Julian **286-4388** noon-2am • lesbians/gay men • dancing/DJ • live shows • leather night Th

### CAFES
**Cafe Leviticus** 1445 The Alameda **279-8877** 7am-midnight • lesbians/gay men

### RESTAURANTS
**El Faro** 610 Coleman Ave. **294-1846** lunch & dinner, Sun champagne brunch 10am-3pm • Mexican • some veggie • $10-20

**Hamburger Mary's** 170 W. St. John St. **947-1667** 11:30am-2am, from 9am wknds • lesbians/gay men • some veggie • full bar • live shows

### BOOKSTORES & RETAIL SHOPS
**Sisterspirit** 175 Stockton Ave. **293-9372** 6:30pm-9pm, from 4pm Wed, noon-6pm Sat, 1pm-4pm Sun • women's • periodic coffeehouse

### PUBLICATIONS
**Entre Nous 378-7787** lesbian news-magazine & calendar for South Bay

**Out Now! 991-1873**

**Trikone 270-8776** magazine for lesbigay South Asians

### TRAVEL AGENTS
**Damron Atlas World Travel 776-1660/(888) 907-9771**

**Out & About Travel** 864 Apricot Ave. #D, Campbell **369-1739** IGLTA

**Yankee Clipper Travel** 260 Saratoga Ave., Los Gatos **354-6400/(800) 624-2664** contact Jim • IGLTA

### SPIRITUAL GROUPS
**MCC of San Jose** 65 S. 7th St. **279-2711** 10:30am Sun

### EROTICA
**Leather Masters** 969 Park Ave. **293-7660** leather & fetish • clothes • toys • publications

## San Lorenzo (510)

### SPIRITUAL GROUPS
**MCC of Greater Hayward** 100 Hacienda (Christ Lutheran Church) **481-9720** 12:30pm Sun

## San Luis Obispo (805)

### INFO LINES & SERVICES
**Central Coast Community Center** 1306-B Higuera St. **541-4252** call for hrs, clsd Sun

**Lesbian Rap Groups** in Santa Maria **928-8630 (EVES)** social/support groups • lesbians of color meet 3rd Sat

**Women's Resource Center** 1009 Morro St. #201 **544-9313** counseling • support • referrals

### ACCOMMODATIONS
**Adobe Inn** 1473 Monterey St. **549-0321** gay-friendly • cozy, comfortable & congenial inn • full brkfst • kitchens • smoke-free • kids ok • $55-95

**Amber Hills B&B** 239-2073 gay-friendly
• rural setting • kids/pets ok ($5 extra
per) • women-owned/run • $65 ($5 /extra
person)

**Casa De Amigas B&B** 1202 8th St., Los
Osos **528-3701** lesbians/gay men • suite
• smokefree • women-owned/run * $65
(2-night min.)

**The Madonna Inn** 1000 Madonna Rd.
**543-3000/(800) 543-9666** gay-friendly •
theme rooms

**Palomar Inn** 1601 Shell Beach Rd., Shell
Beach **773-4204** lesbians/gay men •
close to nude beach • gay-owned/run

## BARS & NIGHTCLUBS

**Breezes Pub & Grill** 11560 Los Osos
Valley Rd., Laguna Village #160 **544-8010**
8pm-midnight, 6pm-2am Fri-Sat, clsd
Sun-Tue • lesbians/gay men • dancing/DJ
• patio • wheelchair access

## CAFES

**Linnea's Cafe** 1110 Garden **541-5888**
7am-midnight, til 2am wknds • plenty
veggie • $5

## BOOKSTORES & RETAIL SHOPS

**Coalesce Bookstore & Garden
Wedding Chapel** 845 Main St., Morro
Bay **772-2880** 10am-5:30pm, 11am-4pm
Sun • lesbigay section • women-
owned/run

**Twisted Orbits** 778 Marsh St. **782-0278**
11am-7pm, noon-5pm Sun, clsd Mon •
cards • lesbigay gifts

**Volumes of Pleasure** 1016 Los Osos
Valley Rd., Los Osos **528-5565** 10am-
6pm, clsd Sun • general • lesbigay section • wheelchair access • lesbian-
owned/run

## SPIRITUAL GROUPS

**Integrity** 467-3042/534-0332 5:30pm 3rd
Sun

**MCC of the Central Coast** 2333 Meadow
Ln. **481-9376** 10:30am Sun

## San Rafael                    (415)

### BARS & NIGHTCLUBS

**Aunt Ruby's** 815 W. Francisco Blvd. **459-
6079** 4pm-11pm, 2pm-2am Fri-Sat, from
noon Sun • lesbians/gay men • danc-
ing/DJ • wheelchair access

## San Ysidro                    (619)

### EROTICA

**F St. Bookstore** 4650 Border Village
497-6042

## Santa Ana                    (714)

### SPIRITUAL GROUPS

**Christ Chapel MCC** 720 N. Spurgeon
**835-0722** 10am Sun

## Santa Barbara                    (805)

### INFO LINES & SERVICES

**Gay/Lesbian Resource Center** 126 E.
Haley St. #A-17 **963-3636/965-2925 (CRI-
SIS HOTLINE ONLY)** 10am-5pm Mon-Fri •
social/educational & support services •
youth groups • newsletter

### ACCOMMODATIONS

**Glenborough Inn** 1327 Bath St. **966-
0589/(800) 962-0589** lesbians/gay men •
3 different homes w/3 different personali-
ties • full brkfst • private/shared baths •
fireplaces • smokefree • kids ok • $100-
250

**Ivanhoe Inn** 1406 Castillo St. **963-
8832/(800) 428-1787** gay-friendly • lovely old Victorian house • private/shared
baths • kitchens • smokefree • kids/pets
ok • $95-195

### BARS & NIGHTCLUBS

**Chameleon Restaurant & Bar** 421 E.
Cota **965-9536** 5pm-2am • lesbians/gay
men • Californian • plenty veggie • patio
• wheelchair access

**Fathom** 423 State St. **730-0022** les-
bians/gay men • call infoline for events
882-2082

**Gold Coast** 30 W. Cota **965-6701** 4pm-
2am • mostly gay men • dancing/DJ •
wheelchair access

### CAFES

**Hot Spot Espresso Bar & Reservation
Service** 564-1637 24hrs

### RESTAURANTS

**Mousse Odile** 18 E. Cota St. **962-5393**
brkfst, lunch & dinner • French • patio

**Sojourner Cafe** 134 E. Canon Perdido
**965-7922** 11am-11pm • veggie •
beer/wine • wheelchair access

**Zelo's** 630 State **966-5792** 10am-2am •
popular • dancing/DJ • full bar

### BOOKSTORES & RETAIL SHOPS
**Chaucer's Books** 3321 State St. **682-6787** 9am-9pm, til 10pm Fri-Sat, 10am-5pm Sun • general • lesbigay section

**Earthling Books & Cafe** 1137 State St. **965-0926** 9am-11pm, til midnight Fri-Sat • lesbigay

### PUBLICATIONS
**We Are Visible** PO Box 91304, 93190-1304

## Santa Clara (408)

### BARS & NIGHTCLUBS
**New Savoy** 3546 Flora Vista **247-7109** 3pm-2am • popular • mostly women • dancing/DJ • live shows • wheelchair access • women-owned/run

**Tynker's Damn** 46 N. Saratoga **243-4595** 3pm-2am, 1pm-2am wknds • mostly gay men • dancing/DJ

### TRAVEL AGENTS
**Rainbow Travel** 1055 Monroe St. **246-1414** IGLTA

### EROTICA
**Borderline** 36 N. Saratoga Ave. **241-2177** toys • videos

## Santa Cruz (408)

### INFO LINES & SERVICES
**AA Gay/Lesbian** 475-5782 call for mtgs.
**Lesbian/Gay/Bisexual/Transgender Community Center** 1328 Commerce Ln. 425-5422 noon-8pm • call for events

### ACCOMMODATIONS
**Chateau Victorian B&B Inn** 118 1st St. **458-9458** lesbians/gay men • 1885 Victorian inn w/warm friendly atmosphere • fireplaces • smokefree • women-owned/run • $110-140

### BARS & NIGHTCLUBS
**Blue Lagoon** 923 Pacific Ave. **423-7117** 4pm-2am • lesbians/gay men • dancing/DJ • alternative • transgender-friendly • live shows • videos • wheelchair access

### CAFES
**Herland Book Cafe** 902 Center St. **429-6641(CAFE)/429-6636 (BOOKSTORE)** 10am-6pm, bookstore from noon wknds • vegetarian & vegan • wheelchair access • $3-6

**Saturn Cafe** 1230 Mission **429-8505** noon-midnight • light fare • plenty veggie • $4-7

### RESTAURANTS
**Costa Brava Taco Stand** 505 Seabright **423-8190** 11am-11:30pm • Mexican • some veggie • $4-8

**Crêpe Place** 1134 Soquel Ave. **429-6994** 11am-midnight, 10am-1am wknds • plenty veggie • beer/wine • garden patio • wheelchair access • $5-11

### BOOKSTORES & RETAIL SHOPS
**Book Loft** 1207 Soquel Ave. **429-1812** 10am-10pm, noon-6pm Sun, 10am-6pm Mon • mostly used books

**Bookshop Santa Cruz** 1520 Pacific Garden Mall **423-0900** 9am-11pm • general • lesbigay section • cafe • wheelchair access

**Chimney Sweep Books** 419 Cedar St. **458-1044** hours vary • lesbigay section • mostly used books

### PUBLICATIONS
**Manifesto** 425-5422

### TRAVEL AGENTS
**Pacific Harbor Travel** 519 Seabright Ave. **427-5000/(800) 435-9463** women-owned/run • IGLTA

**Waldorf Travel** 20920 E. Cliff Dr. **475-6149** IGLTA

### GYMS & HEALTH CLUBS
**Heartwood Spa Hot Tub & Sauna Garden** 3150-A Mission Dr. **462-2192** noon-11pm • women only 6:30pm-11pm Sun

**Kiva Retreat House Spa** 702 Water St. **429-1142** noon-11pm, til midnight Fri-Sat • women-only 9am-noon Sun

## Santa Maria (805)

### INFO LINES & SERVICES
**Gay/Lesbian Resource Center** 2255 S. Broadway #4 349-9947

### CAFES
**Cafe Monet** 1555 S. Broadway **928-1912** 7am-7pm, til 10pm Wed & Fri, 9am-5pm Sun • wheelchair access

### EROTICA
**Book Adventure** 306 S. Blosser Blvd. **928-7094**

## Santa Rosa (707)

### BARS & NIGHTCLUBS
**Club Heaven** 120 5th St. (Railroad Sq.) **544-6653** 9pm-4am Sun only • lesbians/gay men • dancing/DJ

**Girl's Night Out** 1801 Cleveland **(510) 428-2144** 4pm-7pm 1st Sun • women only • smoke- & alcohol-free • dance lessons 4pm

**Santa Rosa Inn** 4302 Santa Rosa Ave. **584-0345** noon-2am • lesbians/gay men • dancing/DJ

### CAFES
**Aroma Roasters** 95 5th St. (Railroad Sq.) **576-7765** 7am-midnight, til 11pm wknds • lesbians/gay men • wheelchair access • lesbian-owned/run

### BOOKSTORES & RETAIL SHOPS
**North Light Books** 95 5th St. (Railroad Sq.) **579-9000** 9am-9pm, til 11pm Fri-Sat, 10am-8pm Sun • anti-establishment • strong lesbigay emphasis • also coffeehouse • lesbian-owned/run

**Sawyer's News** 733 4th St. **542-1311** 7am-9pm, til 10pm Fri-Sat • general news & bookstand

### PUBLICATIONS
**We the People** 573-8896

### TRAVEL AGENTS
**Just Corporate, A Travel Company** 510 5th St. **525-5105** IGLTA

**Santa Rosa Travel** 542 Farmers Ln. **542-0943/(800) 227-1445**

### SPIRITUAL GROUPS
**1st Congregational United Church of Christ** 2000 Humboldt St. **546-0998** 10:30am Sun

**New Hope MCC** 200 5th St. **526-4673** 11:30am & 6pm Sun

### EROTICA
**Santa Rosa Adult Books** 3301 Santa Rosa Ave. **542-8248**

## Sausalito (415)

### ACCOMMODATIONS
**Design Hotels** 323 Pine St. #B **332-4885/(800) 337-4685** reservation service • IGLTA

## Sebastopol (707)

### BOOKSTORES & RETAIL SHOPS
**Milk & Honey** 137 N. Main St. **824-1155** 10am-6pm, til 5pm Sun • goddess- & woman-oriented crafts

## St. Helena (707)

### ACCOMMODATIONS
**The Ink House B&B** 1575 St. Helena Hwy., St. Helena **963-3890** gay-friendly • 1884 Italianate Victorian among the vineyards • full brkfst • smokefree • kids ok • $110-155

### RESTAURANTS
**Mustard's Grill** 7399 Hwy. 29 **944-2424** lunch & dinner

**Travigne** 1050 Charter Oak Ave. **963-4444** 11:30am-10pm • Northern Italian • $15

## Stockton (209)

### BARS & NIGHTCLUBS
**Paradise** 10100 N. Lower Sacramento Rd. **477-4724** 6pm-2am, from 4pm wknds • lesbians/gay men • dancing/DJ • live shows • live bands

## Tiburon (415)

### ACCOMMODATIONS
**Tiburon Lodge** 1651 Tiburon Blvd. **435-3133** gay-friendly • hotel • $104-289

## Ukiah (707)

### BARS & NIGHTCLUBS
**Perkins St. Grill** 228 E. Perkins St. **463-0740** lunch & dinner, clsd Mon • gay-friendly • dancing/DJ • also restaurant • Californian • $10-15

## Vacaville (707)

### INFO LINES & SERVICES
**Solano County Gay/Lesbian Infoline** 448-1010

### SPIRITUAL GROUPS
**St. Paul's United Methodist Church** 101 West St. **448-5154** 10:30am Sun

## Vallejo (707)

### BARS & NIGHTCLUBS
**Nobody's Place** 437 Virginia St. **645-7298** 10am-2am • mostly gay men • dancing/DJ • live shows • patio • wheelchair access

# RECIPE FOR THE PERFECT GETAWAY

*START* with two people who want to be alone.

*BLEND* with a cozy four cottage getaway on 160 wooded acres at the gateway to YOSEMITE National Park.

*SIMMER* a few days or a week for romance, relaxation, and pampering.

**THE HOMESTEAD** is a great place to do nothing, or take advantage of the nearby sight-seeing, golf, horseback riding, hiking, antique shops & restaurants. **Call** proprietors Cindy & Larry for planning that well-deserved getaway! **(209) 683-0495**

**41110 Road 600   Ahwahnee, CA   93601** or www.sierranet.net/~homestead

**The Q** 412 Georgia St. **644-4584** noon-2am, from 4pm Mon-Wed • mostly gay men • dancing/DJ • wheelchair access

## Ventura (805)

### INFO LINES & SERVICES
**AA Gay/Lesbian** 739 E. Main **389-1444** women's mtg. 6:30pm Wed at G/L Comm. Ctr.

**Gay/Lesbian Community Center** 1995 E. Main **653-1979** 10am-4pm & 6:30pm-9pm Mon-Th, clsd wknds

### BARS & NIGHTCLUBS
**Club Alternatives** 1644 E. Thompson Blvd. **653-6511** 2pm-2am • lesbians/gay men • dancing/DJ • live shows • patio

**Paddy McDermott's** 577 E. Main St. **652-1071** 2pm-2am • lesbians/gay men • dancing/DJ • live shows • karaoke

### SPIRITUAL GROUPS
**MCC Ventura** 1848 Pacific (Church of Latter Day Saints) **643-0502** 6:30pm Sun

### EROTICA
**Three Star Books** 359 E. Main St. **653-9068** 24hrs

## Victorville (619)

### BARS & NIGHTCLUBS
**West Side 15** 16868 Stoddard Wells Rd. **243-9600** 2pm-2am • lesbians/gay men • beer/wine

## Walnut Creek (510)

### INFO LINES & SERVICES
**AA Gay/Lesbian** 1924 Trinity Ave. (St. Paul's Episc. Church) **939-4155** 8:30pm Fri • 5:30pm Sat at 193 Mayhew Wy.

### BARS & NIGHTCLUBS
**D.J.'s** 1535 Olympic Blvd. **930-0300** 4pm-2am • lesbians/gay men • piano bar • also restaurant • some veggie • wheelchair access • $8-12

**J.R.'s** 2520 Camino Diablo **256-1200** 5pm-2am, til 4am Fri-Sat • lesbians/gay men • more women Sat • dancing/DJ • country/western • wheelchair access

**Twelve Twenty** 1220 Pine St. **938-4550** 4pm-2am, from 3pm wknds • mostly gay men • dancing/DJ • wheelchair access

### TRAVEL AGENTS
**Special Service Travel** 747 Wimbledon Rd. **939-4300** IGLTA

**Travex** 1875 Olympic Blvd. #100 **932-5276** IGLTA

### SPIRITUAL GROUPS
**MCC of the New Vision** 1543 Sunnyvale (United Methodist Church) **283-2238** 1pm Sun

## Whittier (310)

### INFO LINES & SERVICES
**Together in Pride AA** 11931 Washington Blvd. (church) **696-6213** (CHURCH #) 7:30pm Th

### ACCOMMODATIONS
**Whittier House** 12133 S. Colima Blvd. **(310) 941-7222** mostly women • full brkfst • hot tub • smokefree • kids/pets ok • IGLTA

### SPIRITUAL GROUPS
**Good Samaritan MCC** 11931 Washington Blvd. **696-6213** 10am Sun, 7:30pm Wed Bible study

## Willits (707)

### RESTAURANTS
**Tsunami** 50 S. Main St. **459-4750** 9:30am-8pm • Japanese/int'l • $8-13

### ENTERTAINMENT & RECREATION
**Skunk Train California Western** 299 E. Commercial St., **459-5248** scenic train trips

### BOOKSTORES & RETAIL SHOPS
**Leaves of Grass** 630 S. Main St. **459-3744** 10am-5:30pm, noon-5pm Sun • alternative

## Yosemite Nat'l Park (209)

### ACCOMMODATIONS
**The Ahwahnee Hotel** Yosemite Valley Floor **252-4848** gay-friendly • incredibly dramatic & expensive grand fortress • swimming • also restaurant

▲ **The Homestead** 41110 Rd. 600, Ahwahnee **683-0495** gay-friendly • cottages • full brkfst • kitchens • fireplaces • smokefree • $125-175

## COLORADO

### Alamosa (719)

#### ACCOMMODATIONS
**Cottonwood Inn** 123 San Juan Ave. 589-3882/(800) 955-2623 gay-friendly • smokefree • $64-85

### Aspen (970)

#### INFO LINES & SERVICES
**Aspen Gay/Lesbian Community** 925-9249 8pm-midnight (live) • recorded local info & events

#### ACCOMMODATIONS
**Aspen B&B Lodge** 311 W. Main 925-7650/(800) 362-7736 gay-friendly • hot tub • swimming
**Hotel Aspen** 110 W. Main St. 925-3441/(800) 527-7369 gay-friendly • mountain brkfst • hot tub • swimming • wheelchair access
**Hotel Lenado** 200 S. Aspen St. 925-6246/(800) 321-3457 gay-friendly • full brkfst • hot tub • full bar
**Rising Star Guest Ranch** (888) 429-7624 lesbians/gay men • call for location • swimming • IGLTA
**Rising Star Ranch** (281) 820-0880/(888) 429-7624 lesbians/gay men • may be opening in '98 • IGLTA
**Sardy House** 128 E. Main St. 920-2525/(800) 321-3457 gay-friendly • hot tub • swimming • also restaurant

#### BARS & NIGHTCLUBS
**Club Soda** Hyman Ave. Mall 925-8154 10pm-2am • gay-friendly • dancing/DJ • live shows • wheelchair access
**Double Diamond** 450 S. Galena 920-6905 seasonal • gay-friendly • live shows
**Freedom** 426 E. Hyman Ave. 925-6523 from 9pm • gay-friendly
**Howling Wolf** 316 E. Hopkins Ave. 920-7771 gay-friendly • live shows • also restaurant
**The Tippler** 535 E. Dean 925-4977 11:30am-2am (seasonal) • gay-friendly • dancing/DJ • live entertainment • also restaurant • Italian • wheelchair access

#### RESTAURANTS
**Syzygy** 520 E. Hyman 925-3700 seasonal • 5pm-10pm, bar til 2am • live shows • some veggie • wheelchair access

#### BOOKSTORES & RETAIL SHOPS
**Explore Booksellers & Bistro** 221 E. Main 925-5336 10am-10pm • vegetarian menu • wheelchair access

### Boulder (303)

#### INFO LINES & SERVICES
**LBGT (Lesbian/Bisexual/Gay/Trans-gendered) Alliance** 492-8567 student group • events schedule & resource info
**TLC (The Lesbian Connection)** 2525 Arapahoe Ave. 443-1105 social/network-ing group • newsletter • info & referrals

#### ACCOMMODATIONS
**Boulder Guesthouse** 938-8908 women only • private home • hot tub • kitchen privileges • smokefree • kids/pets ok • $63-69
**Boulder Victorian Historic B&B** 1305 Pine St. 938-1300 gay-friendly • patio
**The Briar Rose B&B** 2151 Arapahoe Ave. 442-3007 gay-friendly

#### BARS & NIGHTCLUBS
**The Foundry** 1109 Walnut 447-1803 7pm-2am • gay-friendly • dancing/DJ • live shows • wheelchair access
**The Yard** 2690 28th St. #C 443-1987 4pm-2am, from 2pm wknds • lesbians/gay men • dancing/DJ • wheelchair access • women-owned/run

#### CAFES
**Walnut Cafe** 3073 Walnut 447-2315 7am-11pm, til 3pm Sun-Mon • popular • plenty veggie • patio • wheelchair access • women-owned/run • $5-9

#### BOOKSTORES & RETAIL SHOPS
**Aria** 2043 Broadway 442-5694 10am-6pm, noon-5pm Sun • cards • T-shirts • gifts • wheelchair access
**Left Hand Books** 1825 Pearl St., 2nd flr. 443-8252 noon-9pm, 1pm-4pm Sun
**Word Is Out** 1731 15th St. 449-1415 10am-6pm, noon-5pm Sun, clsd Mon • women's • lesbigay section • wheelchair access

#### PUBLICATIONS
**Rainbow List** 443-7768 extensive statewide resources

#### EROTICA
**The News Stand** 1720 15th St. 442-9515

## Breckenridge (970)

### ACCOMMODATIONS

**Allaire Timbers Inn** 9511 Hwy. 9, S. Main St. 453-7530/(800) 624-4904 gay-friendly • full brkfst • hot tub • wheelchair access

**Mountain Lodge** 453-6475 rental home • sleeps 8 • sauna

## Colorado Springs (719)

### INFO LINES & SERVICES

**Pikes Peak Gay/Lesbian Community Center Helpline** 471-4429 6pm-9pm Mon-Fri • call for events

### ACCOMMODATIONS

**Amara's Guesthouse** 9425 Mohawk Tr., Chipita Park 684-9169 gay-friendly • full brkfst • private entrance • smokefree • $73

**Authentic Inns of the Pikes Peak Region** (888) 892-2237

**Pikes Peak Paradise** Woodland Park (800) 354-0989 gay-friendly • mansion w/view of Pikes Peak • full brkfst • hot tub • fireplaces • smokefree • kids 12+ ok • $95-195

**Quality Inn—Garden of the Gods** 555 W. Garden of the Gods 593-9119 IGLTA

### BARS & NIGHTCLUBS

**Hide & Seek Complex** 512 W. Colorado 634-9303 10:30am-2am, til 4am Fri-Sat • popular • lesbians/gay men • dancing/DJ • country/western • live shows • also restaurant • some veggie • wheelchair access • $5-12

**Hour Glass Lounge** 2748 Airport Rd. 471-2104 10am-2am • gay-friendly • neighborhood bar

**True Colors** 1865 N. Academy Blvd. 637-0773 3pm-2am, clsd Sun-Tue • mostly women • dancing/DJ • multi-racial • wheelchair access • women-owned/run

### RESTAURANTS

**Dale Street Cafe** 115 E. Dale 578-9898 11am-9pm, clsd Sun • vegetarian • full bar • $6-11

### PUBLICATIONS

**New Phazes** 634-0236 women's newspaper

### SPIRITUAL GROUPS

**Pikes Peak MCC** 730 N. Tejon (Unitarian Church) 634-3771 5pm Sun

### EROTICA

**First Amendment Adult Bookstore** 220 E. Fillmore 630-7676

## Denver (303)

### INFO LINES & SERVICES

**AA Gay/Lesbian** 322-4440 many mtgs.

**Colorado Tourism Board** (800) 265-6723

**Gay/Lesbian/Bisexual Community Center** 1245 E. Colfax Ave. #125 831-6268/837-1598 10am-6pm Mon-Fri • extensive resources & support groups • wheelchair access

**Gender Identity Center of Colorado (GIC)** 202-6466 transgender resources & support

### ACCOMMODATIONS

**Elyria's Western Guest House** 1655 E. 47th Ave. 291-0915 lesbians/gay men • Western ambiance in historic Denver neighborhood • hot tub • shared baths • smokefree • $30-40

**Lumber Baron Inn** 2555 W. 37th Ave. 477-8205/(800) 697-6552 gay-friendly • furnished w/antiques • full brkfst • hot tub • $125-185

**The Queen Anne Inn** 2147 Tremont Pl. 296-6666/(800) 432-4667 gay-friendly • full brkfst

**Stapleton Plaza Hotel** 3333 Quebec St. 321-3500/(800) 950-6070 gay-friendly • swimming • also restaurant • wheelchair access

**Twin Maples** 1401 Madison St. 393-1832/(888) 835-5738 patio • gay-owned/run

**Victoria Oaks Inn** 1575 Race St. 355-1818/(800) 662-6257 gay-friendly • fireplaces • gay-owned/run • $50-85

### BARS & NIGHTCLUBS

**B.J.'s Carousel** 1380 S. Broadway 777-9880 noon-2am, from 10am wknds • popular • mostly men • neighborhood bar • live shows • volleyball court • patio • also restaurant • wheelchair access

**Brick's** 1600 E. 17th Ave. 377-5400 11am-2am • lunch daily, dinner Mon-Fri • mostly men • neighborhood bar • wheelchair access

**C's** 7900 E. Colfax Ave. 322-4436 5pm-midnight, til 2am Fri-Sat, from 2pm Sun • lesbians/gay men • dancing/DJ • multi-racial • wheelchair access

**Club Proteus** 1669 Clarkson **869-4637** 9pm-2am, from 5pm Fri & Sun • lesbians/gay men • dancing/DJ • videos • patio • wheelchair access

**Club Synergy** 3240 Larimer **575-5680** 9pm-5am Th-Sun • popular • mostly women • dancing/DJ • alternative

**Colfax Mining Co.** 3014 E. Colfax Ave. **321-6627** 10am-2am • lesbians/gay men • neighborhood bar • dancing/DJ • wheelchair access

**The Compound** 145 Broadway **722-7977** 7am-2am, from 8am Sun • mostly gay men • neighborhood bar

**Den** 5110 W. Colfax Ave. **534-9526** 10am-2am • lesbians/gay men • neighborhood bar • food served • wheelchair access

**Denver Detour** 551 E. Colfax Ave. (back entrance) **861-1497** 11am-2am • popular • lesbians/gay men • live shows • lunch & dinner daily • some veggie • $5-9 • wheelchair access

**The Elle** 716 W. Colfax **572-1710** 8pm-2am, 2pm-midnight Sun, clsd Mon-Tue • mostly women • dancing/DJ • alternative • live shows • patio • wheelchair access

**The Grand** 538 E. 17th Ave. **839-5390** 3pm-2am • lesbians/gay men • upscale piano bar • patio • wheelchair access

**Highland Bar** 2532 15th St. **455-9978** 2pm-2am • mostly women • neighborhood bar • wheelchair access

**Maximilian's** 2151 Lawrence St. **297-0015** 9pm-2am Fri-Sat • gay-friendly • dancing/DJ • multi-racial

**Mike's** 60 S. Broadway **777-0193** noon-2am • lesbians/gay men • dancing/DJ • wheelchair access • women-owned/run

**R&R Denver** 4958 E. Colfax Ave. **320-9337** mostly gay men • 9am-2am

**Rock Island** 1614 15th St. **572-7625** gay-friendly • dancing/DJ • alternative • call for events • wheelchair access

**Snake Pit** 608 E. 13th Ave. **831-1234** 5pm-2am • popular • mostly gay men • dancing/DJ • alternative • wheelchair access

**Tequila Rosa's** 314 E. 13th Ave. **839-5426** 8pm-2am

**Tracks 2000** 2975 Fox St. **292-6600** 9pm-2am, from 8pm Sun, clsd Mon-Tue & Th • 18+ Wed & Fri

**Ye O' Matchmaker Pub** 1480 Humboldt **839-9388** 10am-2am • lesbians/gay men • dancing/DJ • multi-racial • live shows • also restaurant • Mexican/American

## CAFES

**9th Avenue West** 99 W. 9th Ave. **572-8006** 6pm-1am, from 4pm Fri • swing dance club/lessons • live shows • food served

**Basil's Cafe** 30 S. Broadway **698-1413** lunch & dinner, clsd Sun • beer/wine • nouvelle Italian • plenty veggie • wheelchair access • women-owned/run • $6-16

**Dads** 282 S. Pennsylvania St. **744-1258** 5pm-midnight, from 1pm Sun • coffeehouse • buffet Sat

**Euphemia's Place** 70 S. Broadway **744-6774** 7am-9pm, til midnight Fri-Sat, 9am-9pm Sun, clsd Mon, coffee & more

**Java Creek** 287 Columbine St. **377-8902** 7am-7pm, til 8pm Sun • coffeehouse • live shows • sandwiches & desserts • wheelchair access • lesbian-owned

## RESTAURANTS

**Cindy Lynn Cafe** 1650 E. 47th Ave. **295-9004** 5:30am-2pm • American/Mexican

**City Spirit** 1434 Blake St. **575-0022** 11am-11pm • live shows • full bar • wheelchair access

**Daily Planet Cafe** 1560 Broadway **894-8308** 11:30am-2:30pm, clsd wknds • full bar • wheelchair access

**Denver Sandwich Co.** 1217 E. 9th Ave. **861-9762** 10:30am-5pm (later summers) • some veggie • wheelchair access

**Diced Onions** 609 Corona St. **831-8352** 7am-3pm, clsd Mon • diner/deli • under $10

**Hugh's New American Bistro** 1469 S. Pearl **744-1940** 11am-10pm, from 5pm wknds • some veggie • full bar • $7-18

**Judy, Judy, Judy** 104 S. Broadway **722-3430** lunch & dinner daily, brkfst wknds • lesbians/gay men • some veggie • full bar • wheelchair access • $8-12

**Las Margaritas** 1066 Old S. Gaylord St. **777-0194** from 11am, bar til 2am • Mexican • some veggie • wheelchair access • $6-14

**Lincoln Diner** 100 E. 9th **894-0600** 8am-2pm • some veggie • full bar • great patio

**Michael's Supper Club & Lounge** 1509 Marion **863-8433** 5pm-10pm, clsd Sun, lounge til 2am Fri-Sat • piano bar • patio • $10

**Racine's** 850 Bannock St. **595-0418** brkfst, lunch, dinner & Sun brunch • plenty veggie • full bar

# Denver

**D**enver is a big city with a friendly small town feel. To get the most out of your stay, start with a visit to the women's **Book Garden**, and pick up at copy of **Lesbians in Colorado** (LIC) or **Colorado Woman News**. Next, drop by the **Gay/Lesbian/ Bisexual Center** for the inside scoop on where to go and what to do in Denver. For night-time fun, taste the local cuisine at **Basil's Cafe**, have a cocktail at **The Elle** women's bar, check out the shows at the **Denver Detour**, or get down at **C's** dance club.

Outside the Mile-High City, be sure to take advantage of the Rocky Mountain snows with a ski trip to one of the many nearby resorts: Aspen, Telluride or Rocky Mountain National Park.

## Denver (303)

**Where the Girls Are:** Many lesbians reside in the Capitol Hill area, near the gay and mixed bars, but hang out in cafes and women's bars scattered around the city.

**Entertainment:** Denver Women's Chorus: 274-4177.

**Lesbigay Pride:** 831-6268 ext. 18.

**City Info:** 892-1112.

**Attractions:** Black American West Museum. Denver Art Museum. Larimer Square. Mile High Flea Market. Lower Downtown (LoDo). Coors Field.

**Best View:** Lookout Mountain (at night especially) or the top of the Capitol rotunda.

**Weather:** Summer temperatures average in the 90's and winter ones in the 40's. The sun shines an average of 300 days a year with humidity in the single digits.

**Transit:** Yellow Cab: 777-7777. Metro Taxi: 333-3333. Super Shuttle: 342-5450. RTD: 628-9000 / 299-6000 (infoline).

**Sfuzzi** 3000 E. 1st Ave. (Cherry Creek Mall) **321-4700** 11am-10pm • Italian • some veggie • full bar

**Wazee Supper Club** 1600 15th St. **623-9518** 11am-2am • beer/wine

ENTERTAINMENT & RECREATION

**Dyke TV** Channel 12 call (212) 343-9335 for more information

**Q TV** 595-5776 lesbigay cable TV program • call for times

BOOKSTORES & RETAIL SHOPS

**Book Garden** 2625 E. 12th Ave. **399-2004/(800) 279-2426** 10am-6pm, til 8pm Th • women's bookstore • also jewelry • posters • spiritual items • wheelchair access • women-owned/run

**Isis Bookstore** 5701 E. Colfax Ave. **321-0867** 10am-7pm, til 6pm Fri-Sat, noon-5pm Sun • new age • metaphysical • wheelchair access

**Magazine City** 200 E. 13th Ave. **861-8249** 10am-6pm, 11am-5pm wknds

**Newsstand Cafe** 630 E. 6th Ave. **777-6060** 7am-10pm, til 4pm Sun • popular • wheelchair access • women-owned/run

**Tattered Cover Book Store** 2955 E. 1st Ave. **322-7727/(800) 833-9327** 9:30am-11pm, 10am-6pm Sun also 1536 Wynkoop St. • 4 flrs.

**Thomas Floral & Adult Gifts** 1 Broadway #108 **744-6400** 8:30am-6pm, 9am-5pm Sat, clsd Sun • wheelchair access

**Unique of Denver** 2626 E. 12th Ave. **355-0689** 10am-6pm, til 7pm in summer • lesbigay gift shop

PUBLICATIONS

**Colorado Woman News** 355-9229 professional/feminist newspaper

**Lesbians in Colorado** (970) 482-4393 statewide • calendar w/political, social & arts coverage

**Out Front** 778-7900 statewide lesbigay newspaper

**Quest/H. Magazine** 722-5965 news & bar guide

TRAVEL AGENTS

**B.T.C. World Travel** 2120 S. Holly #100 **691-9200** women-owned/run

**Business & Leisure Travel** 1775 Sherman St. **830-8928** IGLTA

**Compass Travel** 1001 16th St. #A-150 **534-1292/(800) 747-1292** women-owned/run • IGLTA

**Metro Travel** 90 Madison #101 **333-6777** IGLTA

**Travel 16th St.** 535 16th St. #250 **595-0007/(800) 222-9229** IGLTA

**Travel Junction** 5455 W. 38th Ave. #C **420-4646/(800) 444-8980** women-owned/run

**Travel Square One** 608 Garrison St. #G, Lakewood **233-8457** IGLTA

SPIRITUAL GROUPS

**Congregation Tikvat Shalom** 331-2706 lesbigay Jewish fellowship

**Dignity Denver** 1100 Fillmore (Capitol Hts. Presb. Church) **322-8485** 5pm Sun

**MCC of the Rockies** 980 Church St. **860-1819** 9am & 11am Sun • wheelchair access

**St. Paul's United Methodist Church** 1615 Ogden **832-4929** 10:30am Sun • reconciling congregation • also Buddhist-Christian contemplative prayer • 5pm Sun

GYMS & HEALTH CLUBS

**Broadway Bodyworks** 160 S. Broadway **722-4342** gay-friendly • wheelchair access

EROTICA

**The Crypt** 131 Broadway **733-3112** leather & more

## Durango (970)

ACCOMMODATIONS

**The Guest House** 477 E. 4th Ave. **382-8161** women only • historic Victorian • smokefree • women-owned/run

**Leland House** 721 2nd Ave. **385-1920/(800) 664-1920** popular • gay-friendly • full brkfst

## Estes Park (970)

ACCOMMODATIONS

**Sundance Cottages** 586-3922 gay-friendly • women-owned/run • wheelchair access

## Florissant (719)

ENTERTAINMENT & RECREATION

**McNamara Ranch** 4620 County Rd. 100, Floreissant **748-3466** horseback tours for 2-3

## Fort Collins (970)

### ACCOMMODATIONS

**Never Summer Nordic** 482-9411 lesbians/gay men • camping in yurts (portable Mongolian round houses) in Colorado Rockies • sleep 8-12 • mountain-biking & skiing

### BARS & NIGHTCLUBS

**Nightingales** 1437 E. Mulberry St. **493-0251** 4pm-2am, clsd Mon • lesbians/gay men • dancing/DJ • country/western Th • 18+ Fri • call for events • patio • wheelchair access

### TRAVEL AGENTS

**Fort Collins Travel** 333 W. Mountain Ave. **482-5555/(800) 288-7402**

## Grand Lake (970)

### ACCOMMODATIONS

**Grandview Lodge** 12429 Hwy. 34 **627-3914** popular • gay-friendly • hot tub • sundeck • women-owned/run

## Greeley (970)

### INFO LINES & SERVICES

**Greeley Gay/Lesbian/Bisexual Alliance** U. of Northern Colorado **351-1484** hours vary • call for events • leave message for referrals

### BARS & NIGHTCLUBS

**C Double R Bar** 1822 9th St. Plaza **353-0900** 4pm-2am, from 2pm Sun • lesbians/gay men • dancing/DJ • alternative • country/western • wheelchair access

### BOOKSTORES & RETAIL SHOPS

**Wild Woman** 915 13th St. **356-7705**

## Pueblo (719)

### INFO LINES & SERVICES

**Pueblo After 2** 564-4004 social/educational network • monthly mtgs. • newsletter

### BARS & NIGHTCLUBS

**Aqua Splash** 806 S. Santa Fe Dr. **543-3913** 4pm-2am, from noon (summers), clsd Mon • lesbians/gay men • dancing/DJ • food served • live shows • wheelchair access

**Pirate's Cove** 409 N. Union **542-9624** 2pm-2am, from 4pm Sun, clsd Mon • lesbians/gay men • neighborhood bar • wheelchair access

# DINAH SHORE WEEKEND
## MARCH 26-29, 1998
## PALM SPRINGS

The Ultimate Hotel & Entertainment Package at the All Inclusive

**DOUBLE TREE RESORT**

Book today to ensure availability. For hotel and party ticket Info Call

# 310.281.7358

For Airline reservations call
**1•800•433•1790**

Produced by JOANI WEIR PRODUCTIONS
POM POM PRODUCTIONS • KLUB BANSHEE

## SPIRITUAL GROUPS
**MCC Pueblo** Bonforte & Liberty (United Church of Christ), Belmont **543-6460** 5pm Sun

## Steamboat Springs (970)

### ACCOMMODATIONS
**Elk River Estates** 879-7556 gay-friendly • suburban townhouse B&B near hiking, skiing & natural hot springs • full brkfst • $35-40

## Vail (970)

### ACCOMMODATIONS
**Antlers at Vail** 680 W. Lionshead Pl. 476-2471/(800) 843-8245 gay-friendly • apts • hot tub • swimming • fireplace • balcony • kids ok • $205-755

### RESTAURANTS
**Sweet Basil** 193 E. Gore Creek Dr. 476-0125 lunch & dinner • some veggie • full bar • wheelchair access

## Winter Park (970)

### ACCOMMODATIONS
**Beau West B&B** 148 Fir Dr. 726-5145/(800) 473-5145 gay-friendly • full brkfst
**Silverado II** 490 Kings Crossing Rd. 726-5753 gay-friendly • condo ski resort

### RESTAURANTS
**Silver Zephyr** (at Silverado II) 726-8732 5pm-10pm • full bar • wheelchair access

# CONNECTICUT

## Bethel (203)

### RESTAURANTS
**Bethel Pizza House** 206 Greenwood Ave. 748-1427
**Emerald City Cafe** 269 Greenwood Ave. 778-4100 dinner & Sun brunch, clsd Mon • cont'l

## Bridgeport (203)

### RESTAURANTS
**Bloodroot Restaurant** 85 Ferris St. 576-9168 clsd Mon • women's night Wed • vegetarian • call for events • patio • wheelchair access • women-owned/run • $8-12

### BOOKSTORES & RETAIL SHOPS
**Bloodroot** 85 Ferris St 576-9168 clsd Mon • wheelchair access

## Collinsville (860)

### BOOKSTORES & RETAIL SHOPS
**Gertrude & Alice's** 2 Front St. 693-3816 10am-9pm, til 11pm wknds • live shows • cafe • patio • wheelchair access

## Danbury (203)

### INFO LINES & SERVICES
**Women's Center of Danbury** 256 Main St. 731-5200 9am-5pm, clsd wknds • extensive info & referrals • support groups

### BARS & NIGHTCLUBS
**Triangles Cafe** 66 Sugar Hollow Rd. Rte. 7 798-6996 5pm-2am • popular • lesbians/gay men • dancing/DJ • live shows • patio

### RESTAURANTS
**Goulash Place** 42 Highland Ave. 744-1971 lunch & dinner • Hungarian • beer/wine

### TRAVEL AGENTS
**Aldis The Travel Planner** 46 Mill Plain Rd. 778-9399/(800) 442-9386 IGLTA

## East Windsor (860)

### RESTAURANTS
**The Eatery** 297 S. Main St. 627-7094 lunch Mon-Fri, dinner nightly • full bar • wheelchair access • $6-12

## Enfield (860)

### EROTICA

**Bookends** 44 Enfield St. (Rte. 5) **745-3988**

## Hartford (203)

### INFO LINES & SERVICES

**Gay/Lesbian Guide Line (203) 366-3734** 7pm-10pm Tue-Th • statewide info

**Info Line for Southeastern Connecticut** Rocky Hill **886-0516/(800) 203-1234 (IN CT)** 8am-8pm Mon-Fri • info & referrals • crisis counseling

**Lesbian Rap Group** 135 Broad St. (YWCA) **525-1163** 7:30pm Tue

**Project 100/ The Community Center** 1841 Broad St. **724-5542** 10am-10pm, wknd hours vary • wheelchair access

### ACCOMMODATIONS

**The 1895 House B&B** 97 Girard Ave. **232-0014** gay-friendly • Victorian home designed by woman architect, Genevra Whittemore Buckland • $60-75

### BARS & NIGHTCLUBS

**A Bar With No Name** 115 Asylum St. **522-4646** 4pm-2am, 7pm-1am wknds, clsd Mon-Wed • gay-friendly • dancing/DJ • Sun gay night • wheelchair access

**Chez Est** 458 Wethersfield Ave. **525-3243** 3pm-1am, from noon Sun, Sun brunch • popular • mostly gay men • dancing/DJ • patio

**Metro Club & Cafe** 22 Union Pl. **549-2083** 4pm-1am, til 2am Fri-Sat, from 3pm Sun • lesbians/gay men • women's night Sun • dancing/DJ • live shows • food served • patio

**Nick's Cafe** 1943 Broad St. **956-1573** 4pm-1am, til 2am Fri-Sat • lesbians/gay men • quiet front cafe • disco in back • dancing/DJ • Latin night Sat

**The Polo Club** 678 Maple Ave. **278-3333** 3pm-1am, til 2am wknds • lesbians/gay men • live shows

**The Sanctuary** 2880 Main St. **724-1277** 8pm-2am, from 6pm Sun, clsd Mon-Tue • mostly gay men • dancing/DJ • videos • wheelchair access

**Starlight Playhouse & Cabaret** 1022 Main St., E. Hartford **289-0789** 4:30pm-1am Th (club), Fri-Sat (shows) • lesbians/gay men • call for events • food served • deli menu • wheelchair access • gay-owned/run

**Til Dawn** 495 Farmington Ave., 2nd flr. **305-9695** midnight-dawn Fri-Sat only

### BOOKSTORES & RETAIL SHOPS

**MetroStore** 493 Farmington Ave. **231-8845** 8am-8pm, til 5:30pm Tue, Wed, Sat, clsd Sun • magazines • travel guides • leather • more

**Reader's Feast Bookstore Cafe** 529 Farmington Ave. **232-3710** 10am-9pm, til 10pm Fri-Sat, til 2:30pm Sun • feminist progressive bookstore & cafe • some veggie • live shows

### PUBLICATIONS

**Metroline 570-0823** regional newspaper & entertainment guide

### TRAVEL AGENTS

**Damron Atlas World Travel 653-2492/(888) 907-9777**

### SPIRITUAL GROUPS

**Congregation Am Segulah 674-5095/(800) 734-8524 (IN CT ONLY)** call for service times & location

**Dignity Hartford** 144 S. Quaker Ln. (Quaker Mtg. House) **522-7334** 6pm Sun

**MCC 724-4605** call for info

### EROTICA

**Water Hole Custom Leather** 982 Main St., E. Hartford **528-6195**

## Manchester (860)

### INFO LINES & SERVICES

**Women's Center at Manchester Community College** 60 Bidwell **647-6056** hours vary

## Middletown (860)

### INFO LINES & SERVICES

**Wesleyan Women's Resource Center** 287 High St. **347-9411** library

## Milford (203)

### TRAVEL AGENTS

**Cruisetime** 35 Point Beach Dr. **877-6967/(800) 427-9402** IGLTA

## New Britain (860)

### TRAVEL AGENTS

**Weber's Travel Services** 24 Cedar St. **229-4846**

## New Haven (203)

INFO LINES & SERVICES
**New Haven Gay/Lesbian Community Center** 1 Long Wharf Dr., E. Haven **777-7780** 6pm-7:45pm Mon, Wed & Th • also mtgs.

**Yale Women's Services** 198 Elm St. **432-0388** 10am-10pm, til 5pm Fri, noon-5pm Sat, clsd Sun • resources • support groups • library • wheelchair access

BARS & NIGHTCLUBS
**168 York St. Cafe** 168 York St. **789-1915** 3pm-1am • lesbians/gay men • also restaurant • some veggie • patio • $6-14

**The Bar** 254 Crown St. **495-8924** 4pm-1am • gay-friendly • more gay Tue • dancing/DJ • wheelchair access

**Bash** 239 Crown St. **562-1957** from 8pm Tue only • mostly gay men • dancing/DJ

**Gotham Citi Cafe** 130 Crown St. **498-2484** Happy Hour Mon-Fri • dance club from 10pm Tue & Th, Fri-Sun

RESTAURANTS
**Claire's Corner** 1000 Chapel St. **562-3888** 8am-10pm • vegetarian Mexican cafe • great soup • wheelchair access

TRAVEL AGENTS
**Adler Travel** 2323 Whitney Ave., Hamden **288-8100/(800) 598-2648** IGLTA

**Hamden Travel** 2911 Dixwell Ave. #208, Hamden **288-7718** IGLTA

**Plaza Travel Center** 208 College St. **777-7334/(800) 887-7334** IGLTA

SPIRITUAL GROUPS
**MCC** 34 Harrison St. (United Church) **389-6750** 9:30am & 4pm Sun

## New London (860)

INFO LINES & SERVICES
**New London People's Forum Affirming Lesbian/Gay Identity** 76 Federal (St. James Church) **443-8855** 7:30pm Wed • educational/support group

BARS & NIGHTCLUBS
**Frank's Place** 9 Tilley St. **443-8883** 4pm-1am, til 2am Fri-Sat • lesbians/gay men • dancing/DJ • live shows • patio • wheelchair access

**Heroes** 33 Golden St. **442-4376** 4pm-1am • lesbians/gay men • more women Th • neighborhood bar • dancing/DJ

BOOKSTORES & RETAIL SHOPS
**Greene's Books & Beans** 140 Bank St. **443-3312** 7am-5:30pm, til 9pm Fri, 8am-5pm Sat, clsd Sun • wheelchair access

## Norfolk (860)

ACCOMMODATIONS
**Manor House B&B** 69 Maple Ave. **542-5690** gay-friendly • elegant & romantic 1898 Victorian Tudor estate • full brkfst • fireplaces • hot tubs • smokefree • kids 12+ ok • $95-190

## Norwalk (203)

INFO LINES & SERVICES
**Triangle Community Center** 25 Van Zant St. #7-C, E. Norwalk **853-0600** 7:30pm-9:30pm Mon-Fri • activities • newsletter

ACCOMMODATIONS
**Silk Orchid** 847-2561 women only • 1 suite • full brkfst • swimming • $95 • unconfirmed

## Old Saybrook (860)

RESTAURANTS
**Kountry Kitchen** Rte. 154 & Mill Rock Rd. **388-4784** unique seafood dishes • also gift shop

TRAVEL AGENTS
**Klingerman Travel** 900 Boston Post Rd. **388-1423** IGLTA

## Portland (860)

TRAVEL AGENTS
**Brownstone Travel Agency** 278 Main St. **342-3450** IGLTA

## Southbury (203)

TRAVEL AGENTS
**Rainbow Destinations** 791-1535/(800) 387-2462 IGLTA

## Southington (860)

TRAVEL AGENTS
**Copper Coyote Cruises & Travel** 104 Waterbury Rd. **620-0776** IGLTA

## Stamford (203)

INFO LINES & SERVICES
**Gay/Lesbian Guide Line** 366-3734 7pm-10pm Tue-Th • statewide

BARS & NIGHTCLUBS
**Art Bar** 84 W. Park Pl. **973-0300** 9pm-1am • gay-friendly • gay night Sun from 8pm • dancing/DJ • alternative

## Stratford (203)

BARS & NIGHTCLUBS
**Stephanie's Living Room 377-2119** popular • mostly women • 'quality social events for women' • dances • multi-racial • wheelchair access • discounts for physically challenged

## Wallingford (203)

BARS & NIGHTCLUBS
**Choices** 8 North Turnpike Rd. **949-9380** 8pm-1am Th-Sat • mostly gay men • 'Girl Twirl' Fri (women only) • dancing/DJ • live shows

TRAVEL AGENTS
**Tower Travel** 600 N. Colony Rd. **284-8747** IGLTA

## Waterbury (203)

BARS & NIGHTCLUBS
**The Brownstone** 29 Leavenworth St. **597-1838** 5pm-1am, til 2am Fri-Sat, clsd Mon • lesbians/gay men • women's night Th • live shows • also restaurant • wheelchair access
**Maxie's Cafe** 2627 Waterbury Rd. **574-1629** from 11am, from 7pm Sat, from 6pm Sun • lesbians/gay men • dancing/DJ • live shows • women-owned/run

TRAVEL AGENTS
**Paradise Travel** 34 Waterbury Rd., Prospect **758-6132** IGLTA

SPIRITUAL GROUPS
**Integrity/Waterbury Area** 16 Church St. (St. John's) **754-3116** call for mtg. times

## Westport (203)

BARS & NIGHTCLUBS
**The Brook Cafe** 919 Post Rd. E. **222-2233** 5pm-1am, til 2am Fri-Sat, 4pm-11pm Sun • popular • mostly gay men • dancing/DJ • patio • wheelchair access downstairs

ENTERTAINMENT & RECREATION
**Sherwood Island State Park Beach** left to gay area

TRAVEL AGENTS
**Travelstar** 15 Apple Tree Trl. **227-7233**/**(800) 338-1414** IGLTA

## Willimantic (860)

BARS & NIGHTCLUBS
**Purple Monkey** 103 Union St. **456-8311** from 8pm Wed-Fri • mostly gay men • more women on karaoke night

## DELAWARE

### Bethany Beach (302)

BARS & NIGHTCLUBS

**Nomad Village** Rte. 1 (3 mi. N. in Tower Shores) 539-7581 10am-1am (seasonal) • lesbians/gay men • neighborhood bar • also 'Oasis' • dancing/DJ

### Claymont (302)

RESTAURANTS

**Queen Bean Cafe** 8 Commonwealth Ave. 792-5995 lunch & dinner • hours vary

### Dover (800)

INFO LINES & SERVICES

**Delaware Tourism Office** (800) 441-8846 (OUTSIDE DE)/(800) 282-8667 (IN-STATE ONLY) info

BARS & NIGHTCLUBS

**Rumors** 2206 N. DuPont Hwy. 678-8805 11am-2am, from 7pm Sun, clsd Mon • popular • lesbians/gay men • ladies night Wed • dancing/DJ • live shows • also restaurant • wheelchair access • $10-15

TRAVEL AGENTS

**Gulliver's Travel** 171 N. Dupont Hwy. 678-3747 IGLTA

### Milton (302)

ACCOMMODATIONS

▲ **Honeysuckle** 330 Union St. 684-3284 women only • full brkfst • swimming • nudity • women-owned/run • $85-105 • rental houses $135-175

### Rehoboth Beach (302)

INFO LINES & SERVICES

**Camp Rehoboth** 39-B Baltimore Ave. 227-5620 10am-5pm, clsd wknds • info service for lesbigay businesses • newsletter w/extensive listings

ACCOMMODATIONS

**At Melissa's B&B** 36 Delaware Ave. 227-7504/(800) 396-8090 gay-friendly • women-owned/run

▲ **Beach House B&B** 15 Hickman St. 227-7074/(800) 283-4667 gay-friendly • swimming

**Cabana Gardens B&B** 20 Lake Ave. 227-5429 lesbians/gay men • lake & ocean views • deck • smokefree

**Chesapeake Landing B&B** 101 Chesapeake St. 227-2973 gay-friendly • full brkfst • swimming • smokefree • lakefront • near Poodle Beach • $95-175

**The Lighthouse Inn** 20 Delaware Ave. 226-0407/600-9092 lesbians/gay men • B&B • also apt w/full kitchen & private deck (weekly rental)

**Rehoboth Guest House** 40 Maryland Ave. 227-4117 lesbians/gay men • Victorian beach house • near boardwalk & beach

**Renegade Restaurant & Lounge/Motel** 4274 Hwy. 1 227-4713 lesbians/gay men • 10-acre resort • swimming • full bar • dancing/DJ • also restaurant (dinner only) • some veggie • wheelchair access • $7-14

**Sand in My Shoes** Canal & 6th St. 226-2006/(800) 231-5856 lesbians/gay men • full brkfst • hot tub • sundeck • kitchens • pets ok

---

### Rehoboth Beach (302)

**City Info:** Rehoboth Beach-Dewey Beach Chamber of Commerce: 227-2233 & 800/441-1329.

**Attractions:** Anna Hazard Museum. Cape Henlopen State Park. Poodle Beach. Zwaanendael Museum.

**Transit:** Seaport Taxi: 645-8100.

*Now in Our 10th Year!*

**Honeysuckle**

*A Women's Victorian Inn & Adjoining Houses near the Delaware beaches*

### By Day:

- Inn guests will enjoy a great breakfast
- Go to the women's beach
- Swim nude in our pool
- Schedule a massage
- Use our hot tubs & sauna
- Enjoy our women-only space
- Go out to a marvelous restaurant

### By Night:
Well, use your imagination!

*Reservations Required • Mary Ann & Julie • 302-684-3284 • www.honeysuckleinn.com*

**THE BEACH HOUSE**

*A Bed & Breakfast*

15 Hickman Street
Rehoboth Beach, DE 19971
302-227-7074
800-283-1NNS

OCEAN BLOCK, CONTINENTAL BREAKFAST, PRIVATE BATHS, INDIVIDUAL AIR/HEAT, BBQ GRILL AND PATIO, HEATED SWIMMING POOL, OFF STREET PARKING, CONFERENCE ROOM, STEPS AWAY FROM BEACH, BOARDWALK, DINING, SHOPPING, AND ENTERTAINMENT. Great for R&R, business conferences, and retreats.

*"A House for All Seasons and All Reasons"*

**Shore Inn at Rehoboth** 703 Rehoboth Ave. **227-8487/(800) 597-8899** mostly gay men • hot tub • swimming

▲ **Silverlake** 133 Silver Lake Dr. **226-2115/(800) 842-2115** lesbians/gay men • near Poodle Beach • IGLTA

**Summer Place Hotel** 30 Olive Ave. **226-0766/(800) 815-3925** gay-friendly • also apts.

### BARS & NIGHTCLUBS

**The Blue Moon** 35 Baltimore Ave. **227-6515** 4pm-2am, clsd Jan • gay-friendly • popular happy hour • T-dance • also restaurant • Sun brunch • plenty veggie • $12-26

### CAFES

**Java Beach** 59 Baltimore Ave. **227-8418** 7am-6pm • cafe • patio

**Lori's** 39 Baltimore Ave. **226-3066** 8am-10pm, til midnight Fri-Sat

**The West Side Cafe** 137 Rehoboth Ave. **226-0888** 6pm-1am, bar opens 5pm • lesbians/gay men • dancing/DJ • 18+ • wheelchair access • $7-11

### RESTAURANTS

**Back Porch Cafe** 59 Rehoboth Ave. **227-3674** lunch & dinner • Sun brunch • seasonal • some veggie • full bar • wheelchair access • $9-20

**Celsius** 50-C Wilmington Ave. **227-5767** 5:30pm-11pm • Italian/French • some veggie • wheelchair access • $15-20

**Cloud Nine** 234 Rehoboth Ave. **226-1999** bistro menu • full bar

**Dos Locos** 42 1/2 Baltimore Ave. **227-5626** 5pm-11pm • Mexican • some veggie • full bar • patio

**Dream Cafe** 26 Baltimore Ave. **226-2233** espresso bar & gourmet deli • full brkfst menu

**Iguana Grill** 52 Baltimore Ave. **227-0948** 11am-1am • Southwestern • full bar • patio • $7-12

**La La Land** 22 Wilmington Ave. **227-3887** 6pm-1am (seasonal) • full bar • patio • $18-24

**Mano's Restaurant & Bar** 10 Wilmington Ave. **227-6707** 5pm-10pm • $9-14

## SILVER LAKE
The guest house on the lake ... by Poodle Beach

*"The best of the bunch."* <u>Fodor's Gay Guide</u>
*"The best option."* <u>Out & About</u>
133 Silver Lake Drive • Rehoboth Beach, DE 19971
302/226-2115 • 800/842-2115

Plumb Loco 10 N. 1st St. **227-6870** popular • mostly women • 3pm-1am • American/Southwestern • full bar

**Savannah's** 37 Wilmington Ave. **227-1994** 5pm-1am (seasonal) • lesbians/gay men • full bar • $14-22

**Sydney's Side Street Restaurant & Blues Place** 25 Christian St. **227-1339** 5pm-1am, from 11am Sun, clsd Mon-Tue • healthy entrees • full bar • live shows • patio • $12-20

**Tijuana Taxi** 207 Rehoboth Ave. **227-1986** 5pm-10pm, from noon wknds • full bar • wheelchair access • $5-11

## BOOKSTORES & RETAIL SHOPS

**Lambda Rising** 39 Baltimore Ave. **227-6969** 10am-midnight (seasonal) • lesbi-gay • wheelchair access

## SPIRITUAL GROUPS

**MCC of Rehoboth Beach** Rte. 271 (Glade Rd.) **226-0816** 10am Sun

## GYMS & HEALTH CLUBS

**Body Shop** 401 N. Boardwalk **226-0920** lesbians/gay men

## Wilmington (302)

### BARS & NIGHTCLUBS

**814 Club** 814 Shipley St. **657-5730** 5pm-1am • lesbians/gay men • dancing/DJ • also restaurant • $8-15

**Porky's** 1206 N. Union St. **429-6645** gay night Wed • 9pm-1:30am • dancing/DJ

**Roam** 913 Shipley St. (upstairs) **658-7626** 5pm-1am • popular • lesbians/gay men • dancing/DJ • multi-racial

### RESTAURANTS

**Mrs. Robino's** 520 N. Union **652-9223** family-style Italian

**The Shipley Grill** 913 Shipley St. **652-7797** lunch & dinner • fine dining • full bar • live shows • $13-22

### TRAVEL AGENTS

**All Around Travel** 911 Orange St. **657-2104** IGLTA

### SPIRITUAL GROUPS

**More Light** Hanouver Presb. Church (18th & Baynard) **764-1594** 1st & 3rd Sun • dinner 5:30pm & worship 6:45pm

## Finally

# Damron does Europe!

- no ads – so we can be as opinionated as you are!
- absolutely everything the gay tourist needs
- sleek, practical design
- handy indexes
- color maps
- Gay Games section
- only $9.95!

available now! call **(800) 462-6654** to order
or turn to the **Damron Mail Order** form on page 12

## DISTRICT OF COLUMBIA

### Washington (202)

INFO LINES & SERVICES

**Asians & Friends 387-2742** Tue happy hour 5:30pm-7:30pm at 'Trumpets' • call for more info

**BiCentrist Alliance 828-3065** national bisexual organization with mtgs. & newsletter • taped info

**Black Lesbian Support Group** 1736 14th St. NW **797-3593** 3pm 2nd & 4th Sat

**Bon Vivant (301) 907-7920** social club for lesbian professionals • dance parties 1st Sat • call for details

**Coalition of Gay Sisters (301) 868-8225** social group for DC area • unconfirmed

**Gay/Lesbian Hotline** (Whitman-Walker Clinic) **833-3234** 7pm-11pm • resources • crisis counseling

**HIV+ Coffeehouse** 2111 Florida Ave. NW (Friends Meeting House, enter on Decatur Pl.) **483-3310** 7:30pm-10pm Sat • HIV+ & friends

**Hola Gay 332-2192** 7pm-11pm Th • hotline en español

**Kasper's Livery Service** 201 'I' St. #512 **554-2471/(800) 455-2471** limousine service serving DC, MD & VA • gay-owned/run

**Lesbian/Gay Youth Helpline** (at Sexual Minority Youth Assistance League) **546-5911** 7pm-10pm Mon-Fri, drop-in 6pm-8pm Fri • for youth under 21

**LLEGO (Latino/a Lesbian/Gay Organization)** 1612 'K' St. NW #500 **466-8240** 9am-6pm Mon-Fri • also produces newsletter 'Noticias de LLEGO'

**Nubian Womyn** Box 65274, 20035-5274 group for Black lesbians over 35

**OWLS (Older, Wiser Lesbians) (301) 588-7247/(202) 363-9647** for women '39 & better'

## Washington (202)

**Where the Girls Are:** Strolling around DuPont Circle or cruising a bar in the lesbigay bar ghetto southeast of The Mall.

**Entertainment:** Gay Men's Chorus: 338-7464.

**Lesbigay Pride:** June: 986-1119.

**Annual Events:**

May - Black Lesbian/Gay Pride Weekend: 843-6786.

October - Reel Affirmations Film Festival: 986-1119.

**City Info:** D.C. Visitors Assoc.: 789-7000.

**Attractions:** Ford's Theatre. Jefferson Memorial. JFK Center for the Performing Arts. National Museum of Women in the Arts.

Smithsonian. Vietnam Veterans Memorial.

**Best View:** From the top of the Washington Monument.

**Weather:** Summers are hot (90°s) and MUGGY. (Someone had the brilliant idea to build the city on marshes.) In the winter, temperatures drop to the 30°s and 40°s with rain. Spring is the time of cherry blossoms.

**Transit:** Yellow Cab: 544-1212. Washington Flier: 703/685-1400 (from Dulles or National). Metro Transit Authority: 637-7000.

# Washington D.C.

Even though Washington D.C. is known worldwide as a showcase of American culture and a command center of global politics, many people overlook this international "hot spot" when travelling in the United States. But D.C. is not all boring museums and stuffy bureaucrats.

For instance, begin your stay in D.C. at one of the gay-friendly hotels or guesthouses in and around the city. **Creekside B&B** in Maryland has a strong lesbian following.

Of course, you could tour the usual sites—starting with the heart of D.C., the "Mall", a two-mile-long grass strip bordered by many museums and monuments: the Smithsonian, the National Air and Space Museum, the National Gallery of Art, the Museum of Natural History, the Museum of American History, the Washington Monument, the Lincoln Memorial and the Vietnam Veterans Memorial.

But for real fun and infotainment, check out these less touristy attractions: the outstanding National Museum of Women in the Arts, the hip shops and exotic eateries along Massachusetts Ave., and of course, DuPont Circle, the pulsing heart of lesbigay D.C. The Circle is also home to the oldest modern art museum in the country, the Phillips Collection, as well as the popular women's bookstore **Lammas**, the lesbigay bookstore **Lambda Rising** and the kinky **Pleasure Place.**

For nightlife, don't miss the **Hung Jury,** D.C.'s hippest dyke dancespot. **Phase One** is a more casual bar for lesbians, and there are several women's nights at the mixed bars.

Still can't find your crowd? Try **Hola Gay,** the lesbian/gay hotline in Spanish and English, call the **Black Lesbian Support Group** or drop by the **Asians & Friends** happy hour at **Trumpet's.**

**Transgender Education Association** (301) 949-3822 social/support group for crossdressers & transsexuals

**Triangle Club** 2030 'P' St. NW 659-8641 site for various 12-step groups • see listings in 'The Washington Blade'

## ACCOMMODATIONS

**1836 California** 1836 California St. NW 462-6502 gay-friendly • 1900s house w/period furnishings & sundeck • $60-115

**The Brenton B&B** 1708 16th St. NW 332-5550/(800) 673-9042 mostly gay men • IGLTA • $69-79

**Capitol Hill Guest House** 101 5th St. NE 547-1050 gay-friendly • Victorian rowhouse in historic Capitol Hill district • gay-owned/run • $50-120

**The Carlyle Suites** 1731 New Hampshire Ave. NW 234-3200/(800) 964-5377 gay-friendly • art deco hotel • 'Randolph's Grill' on premises • wheelchair access

**Creekside B&B** (301) 261-9438 mostly women • private home south of Annapolis, MD • 45 min. from DC • swimming

**The Embassy Inn** 1627 16th St. NW 234-7800/(800) 423-9111 gay-friendly • small hotel w/B&B atmosphere • $69-125

**Embassy Suites—Chevy Chase Pavilion** 4300 Military Rd. NW 362-9300 IGLTA

▲ **Kalorama Guest House at Kalorama Park** 1854 Mintwood Pl. NW 667-6369 gay-friendly • IGLTA • $50-95

▲ **Kalorama Guest House at Woodley Park** 2700 Cathedral Ave. NW 328-0860 gay-friendly • IGLTA • $45-95

**Maison Orleans** 414 5th St. SE 544-3694 gay-friendly • smokefree • shared/private baths • $65-85

**Radisson Barcelo Hotel** 2121 'P' St. NW 956-6612 IGLTA

**The River Inn** 924 25th St. NW 337-7600/(800) 424-2741 gay-friendly • also 'Foggy Bottom Cafe' • wheelchair access

**Savoy Suites Hotel** 2505 Wisconsin Ave. NW, Georgetown 337-9700/(800) 944-5377 gay-friendly • also restaurant • Italian • wheelchair access

**The William Lewis House B&B** 1309 'R' St. NW 462-7574 turn-of-the-century building near Logan & Dupont Circles • $65-75

*Fashionable Inns In Fashionable Neighborhoods*

o *Walk to Dupont Circle, fashionable clubs and restuarants, and the subway (Metro)*
o *Enjoy breakfast and evening aperitif*

*THE KALORAMA GUEST HOUSES*
*Kalorama Park (202) 667-6369*
*Woodley Park (202) 328-0860*

**The Windsor Inn** 1842 16th St. NW 667-0300/(800) 423-9111 gay-friendly • small hotel w/B&B atmosphere • $69-150

## BARS & NIGHTCLUBS

**Bachelors Mill** (downstairs at 'Back Door Pub') 544-1931 8pm-2am, til 5am Fri-Sat, clsd Mon • lesbians/gay men • more women Wed • dancing/DJ • multiracial • live shows • wheelchair access

**Chief Ike's Mambo Room** 1725 Columbia Rd. NW 332-2211 4pm-2am • gay-friendly • dancing/DJ

**The Circle** 1629 Connecticut Ave. NW 462-5575 11am-2am • popular • mostly gay men • women's night Wed • dancing/DJ • live shows

**Cobalt** 17th & 'R' Sts. NW 232-6969 4pm-2am, til 3am Fri-Sat • lesbians/gay men • dancing/DJ • videos • also 'La Fonda' restaurant

**D.C. Eagle** 639 New York Ave. NW 347-6025 6pm-2am, from noon Fri-Sun, til 3am Fri-Sat • popular • mostly gay men • leather • wheelchair access

**Diversité** 1526 14th St. NW 234-5740 Fri & Sun only • gay-friendly • dancing/DJ

**El Faro** 2411 18th St. NW 387-6554 noon-2am • lesbians/gay men • mostly Latino-American • live shows • also restaurant • Mexican/El Salvadorean • some veggie • $9-14

**Escandalo** 2122 'P' St. NW 822-8909 4pm-2am, til 5am Fri-Sat • lesbians/gay men • women's night Th • dancing/DJ • mostly Latino-American • also 'Breadbasket Cafe' • tapas • some veggie • patio • $5-13

**The Fireplace** 2161 'P' St. NW 293-1293 1pm-2am • mostly gay men • neighborhood bar • videos

**Full House** 811 Virginia Ave. SE 544-9800 4pm-11pm, noon-2am Sat • mostly gay men • neighborhood bar • mostly African-American • karaoke Mon • special events • also dinner Mon-Fri • down-home cooking

**Hung Jury** 1819 'H' St. NW 785-8181 open Fri-Sat only • mostly women • dancing/DJ • call for events • wheelchair access

**J.R.'s Bar & Grill** 1519 17th St. NW 328-0090 11am-2am, til 3am Fri-Sat • popular • mostly gay men • videos

**Larry's Lounge** 1836 18th St. NW 483-1483 5pm-midnight, til 2am Fri-Sat • lesbians/gay men • neighborhood bar • food served • Malaysian • wheelchair access

**Mr. Henry's Capitol Hill** 601 Pennsylvania Ave. SE 546-8412 11am-1am • popular • gay-friendly • live jazz • also restaurant • lunch & dinner • wheelchair access

**Nob Hill** 1101 Kenyon NW 797-1101 5pm-2am, from 6pm wknds • mostly gay men • dancing/DJ • mostly African-American • live shows • food served

**Ozone** 1214 18th St. NW 293-0303 10pm-4am, 4pm-9pm Sun, clsd Mon-Wed • mostly gay men • Sun women's night • dancing/DJ • live shows • videos

**Phase One** 525 8th St. SE 544-6831 7pm-2am, til 3am Fri-Sat • mostly women • dancing/DJ • neighborhood bar • wheelchair access

**Remington's** 639 Pennsylvania Ave. SE 543-3113 4pm-2am • popular • mostly gay men • dancing/DJ • country/western • videos • wheelchair access

**Tavern Terrace** 1629 Connecticut Ave. NW (at 'The Circle' bar) 462-5575 2pm-2am, til 3am Fri-Sat • popular Happy Hour • lesbians/gay men • karaoke • videos

**Tracks** 1111 First St. SE 488-3320 9pm-4am • popular • lesbians/gay men • women's T-dance last Tue • dancing/DJ • live shows • food served • call for events • wheelchair access

**Trumpets** 1603 17th St. NW 232-4141 4pm-2am, from 11am Sun (brunch) • popular • lesbians/gay men • ladies night Wed • also restaurant • some veggie • wheelchair access • $10-18

**The Underground** 1629 Connecticut Ave. NW (at 'The Circle' bar) 462-5575 9pm-2am • popular • lesbians/gay men • women's night Wed • dancing/DJ • live shows

**The Wave** 1731 New Hampshire (at 'Carlyle Suites') 518-5011 mostly gay men • dancing/DJ • also restaurant • wheelchair access

**Ziegfield's** 1345 Half St. SE 554-5141 8pm-3am Th-Sun • lesbians/gay men • dancing/DJ • alternative • live shows • wheelchair access

### CAFES

**Cafe Luna** 1633 'P' St. NW **387-4005** 11am-11pm • popular • lesbians/gay men • multi-racial • healthy • plenty veggie

**Cusano's Meet Market** 1613 17th St. NW **319-8757** 8am-11pm, til midnight wknds • lesbians/gay men • newspapers & magazines • wheelchair access

**Hannibal's** Connecticut Ave. at 'Q' St. NW **232-5100** 7am-10pm, til 11pm Fri-Sat • coffee/desserts • wheelchair access

**Pop Stop** 1513 17th St. NW **328-0880** 7:30am-2am, til 3am wknds

### RESTAURANTS

**Annie's Paramount Steak House** 1609 17th St. NW **232-0395** opens 11am, 24hrs Fri-Sat • popular • full bar

**Arizona** 1211 Connecticut Ave. NW **785-1211** 11:30am-9:30pm, clsd Sun • Southwestern • plenty veggie • dance club til 2am Th-Sat • $6-11

**Armand's Chicago Pizza** 4231 Wisconsin Ave. NW **686-9450** 10am-11pm, til 1am Fri-Sat • full bar • also Capitol Hill location: 226 Massachusetts Ave. NE 547-6600

**Banana Cafe** 500 8th St. SE **543-5906** lunch & dinner, Sun brunch w/Mariachi trio • Puerto Rican/Cuban • some veggie • also piano bar til 1am Tue-Sat

**The Belmont Kitchen** 2400 18th St. NW **667-1200** clsd Tue • popular brunch • plenty veggie • full bar • patio • wheelchair access • women-owned/run • $12-18

**Cafe Berlin** 322 Massachusetts Ave. NE **543-7656** lunch & dinner, dinner only Sun • German • some veggie • $7-20

**Cafe Japoné** 2032 'P' St. NW **223-1573** 5:30pm-2am • mostly Asian-American • Japanese food • full bar • live shows • karaoke • $10-15

**Cafe Parma** 1724 Connecticut Ave NW **462-8771** lunch & dinner • full bar

**Dupont Italian Kitchen** 1635 17th St. NW **328-3222/328-0100** some veggie • full bar upstairs • 4pm-2am

Jason Harvey

*Look, darling, our beloved Lammas has moved to 17th Street!*

**Books, CDs, gifts, video rentals & more for women and men of quality.**

Women's Books & More

**1607 17th St, NW (at Q)**
**202-775-8218**
**Mail order: 1-800-955-2662**

**Fio's** 3636 16th St. NW (at the 'Woodner') **667-3040** dinner • Italian

**Gabriel** 2121 'P' St. NW **956-6690** 10:30am-midnight • Southwestern • some veggie • full bar • live shows • wheelchair access • $13-18

**Greenwood** 1990 'K' St. NW **833-6572** lunch & dinner, clsd Sun • vegetarian/seafood • full bar • wheelchair access

**Guapo's** 4515 Wisconsin Ave. NW **686-3588** lunch & dinner • Mexican • some veggie • full bar • wheelchair access • $5-11

**The Islander** 1201 'U' St. **234-4955** noon-midnight, til 2am Fri-Sat, clsd Mon • Caribbean • some veggie • full bar

**Jaleo** 480 7th St. NW **628-7949** til 10pm • tapas

**Jenkins Hill Bar & Grill** 319 Pennsylvania Ave. SE **543-2850** 11am-2am • lesbians/gay men • some veggie • full bar • wheelchair access

**La Frontera Cantina** 1633 17th St. NW **232-0437** 11:30am-11pm, til 1:30am Fri-Sat, clsd Sun • Tex-Mex

**Las Cruces** 1524 'U' St. NW **328-3153** clsd Mon

**Lauriol Plaza** 1801 18th St. NW **387-0035** noon-midnight • Latin American

**Mediterranean Blue** 1910 18th St. NW **483-2583** dinner

**Mr. Henry's** 601 Pennsylvania Ave. SE **546-8412** til 1am

**Occidental Grill** 1475 Pennsylvania Ave. NE **783-1475** political player hangout

**Pepper's** 1527 17th St. NW **328-8193** int'l • full bar • wheelchair access • $7-14

**Perry's** 1811 Columbia Rd. NW **234-6218** 5:30pm-11:30pm

**Randy's Cafe** 1517 17th St. NW **387-5399** noon-11:30pm, til 2am wknds • lesbians/gay men • Italian/American • inexpensive

**Rocklands** 2418 Wisconsin Ave. NW **333-2558** barbecue & take-out

**Roxanne** 2319 18th St. NW **462-8330** 5pm-11pm, bar til 2am wknds • also 'Peyote Cafe' • Tex/Mex • some veggie • $8-18

**Sala Thai** 2016 'P' St. NW **872-1144** lunch & dinner • some veggie

**Skewers** 1633 'P' St. NW **387-7400** noon-11pm • Middle-Eastern • full bar • $7-13

**Stage Door** 1433 'P' St. NW **234-4050** open 5pm for cocktails, 6pm for dinner • full bar • transgender-friendly

**Straits of Malaya** 1836 18th St. NW **483-1483** lunch & dinner • Singaporean/Malaysian • full bar • rooftop patio • gay-owned/run

**Trio** 1537 17th St. NW **232-6305** 7:30am-midnight • some veggie • full bar • wheelchair access • $6-10

**Trocadero Cafe** 1914 Connecticut Ave. (Hotel Sofitel) **797-2000** French • intimate setting • wheelchair access • $25-35

**Trumpets** 1603 17th St. NW **232-4141** mostly gay men • videos

**Two Quail** 320 Massachusetts Ave. NE **543-8030** lunch Mon-Fri & dinner nightly • popular • New American • some veggie • full bar • $10-18

## ENTERTAINMENT & RECREATION

**Anecdotal History Tours** (301) 294-9514 variety of guided tours

**Dyke TV** Channel 25 9pm Wed • weekly half-hour TV show produced by lesbians for lesbians

**Gross National Product** (310) 587-4291/(800) 758-7687 comedy troupe w/"Scandal Tour' of DC • 1pm Sat (April-Labor Day) • also topical show 7:30pm Sat at 'Bayou Club'

**Phillips Collection** 1612 21st St. NW **387-0961** clsd Mon • America's oldest museum of modern art • near Dupont Circle

## BOOKSTORES & RETAIL SHOPS

**Kramer Books & Afterwords** 1517 Connecticut Ave. NW **387-1400** opens 7:30am, 24hrs wknds • general • cafe • wheelchair access

**Lambda Rising** 1625 Connecticut Ave. **462-6969** 10am-midnight • lesbigay • wheelchair access

▲ **Lammas Women's Books & More** 1607 17th St. NW **775-8218** 10am-10pm, 11am-8pm Sun • lesbian/feminist • readings • gifts • music • wheelchair access • women-owned/run

**The Map Store** 1636 'I' St. NW **628-2608**/(800) 544-2659 many maps & travel guides

# off our backs
## 27 years of the finest feminist journalism

News        **International**
Health         Conferences
*Lesbian issues*      **Interviews**
*Sexuality*      *Radical*

## Subscribe Today!
ONE YEAR FOR JUST $25

Name _____

Address _____

City, State, Zip _____

*Or write for a **free** 2-issue
trial subscription*

**off our backs**
2337B 18th St. NW
Washington, DC 20009

ex

**Outlook** 1706 Connecticut Ave. NW **745-1469** 10am-10pm, til midnight Fri-Sat • cards • gifts • wheelchair access

**The Pride Emporium** 2147 'P' St. NW (above 'Mr. P's' bar) variety of pride gifts

**Vertigo Books** 1337 Connecticut Ave. NW **429-9272** 10am-7pm, noon-5pm Sun • global politics • literature • African-American emphasis • wheelchair access

## PUBLICATIONS

**MW (Metro Arts & Entertainment)** **588-5220** extensive club listings

▲ **Off Our Backs** **234-8072** international feminist newspaper

**Washington Blade** **797-7000** extensive resource listings

**Women's Monthly** (703) **527-4881** covers DC & VA community events

## TRAVEL AGENTS

**Act Travel** 1629 'K' St. NW #401 **463-6380/(800) 433-3577** IGLTA

**Executive Travel Associates** 1101 17th St. NW #412 **828-3501** IGLTA

**Freedom Travel** 1750 'K' St. NW #510 **496-1810** IGLTA

**Passport Executive Travel** 1025 Thomas Jefferson St. NW **337-7718/(800) 222-9800** IGLTA

**Personalized Travel** 1325 'G' St. NW #915 **508-8656** IGLTA

**Travel Escape** 1725 'K' St. NW **223-9354/(800) 223-4163** IGLTA

## SPIRITUAL GROUPS

**Bet Mishpachah** 5 Thomas Cir. NW **833-1638** 8:30pm Fri • lesbigay synagogue

**Dignity Washington** 1820 Connecticut Ave. NW (St. Margaret's Church) **387-4516** 4:30pm & 7:30pm Sun

**Faith Temple (Evangelical)** 1313 New York Ave. NW **232-4911** 1pm Sun

**Friends (Quaker)** 2111 Florida Ave. NW (enter on Decatur) **483-3310** 9am, 10am, 11am Sun, 7pm Wed

# WHAT'S THE BUZZ ABOUT?
## ...IT'S TIME YOU FOUND OUT

**1 (888) 44 DINAH**
CLUB SKIRTS & GIRL BAR

**MCC Washington** 474 Ridge St. NW **638-7373** 9am, 11am & 7pm Sun, 6:30pm Wed

**More Light Presbyterians** 400 'I' St. SW (Westminister Church) **484-7700** 11am & 7pm Sun

### GYMS & HEALTH CLUBS

**Results—The Gym** 1612 'U' St. NW **518-0001** aerobics, spinning, tanning, massage • women-only fitness area • also 'Aurora Basics Health Cafe' • 234-6822

**Washington Sports Club** 1835 Connecticut Ave. NW **332-0100** gay-friendly

### EROTICA

**Leather Rack** 1723 Connecticut Ave. NW **797-7401**

**Perforations** 900 'M' St. NW **289-8863** 1pm-8pm Mon-Th, til 9pm Sat, til 6pm Sun • piercing • tattooing

▲ **Pleasure Place** 1710 Connecticut Ave. NW **483-3297** leather • body jewelry • wheelchair access

▲ **Pleasure Place** 1063 Wisconsin Ave. NW Georgetown **333-8570** leather • body jewelry • wheelchair access

# The Pleasure Place

### WASHINGTON'S PREMIER EROTIC BOUTIQUE

*"Everything for the Sophisticated Adult"*

*Lingerie • Stockings • Patent Thigh-High Boots & 6" Heels Adult Novelties Lotions & Potions Leather Clothes & Toys Adult Videos, CD-Roms & More ...*

Open 7 days
Mon. & Tues. 10am-10pm
Wed.-Sat. 10am-Midnight
Sunday 12-7pm

*1063 Wisc. Avenue, NW*
*202-333-8570*
*1710 Conn. Avenue, NW*
*202-483-3297*

FOR CATALOG ($3) & MAIL ORDER CALL
*1-800-386-2386*
*Email: pleasure@pleasureplace.com*
*Web Site: http://pleasureplace.com*

Photo by Martin Schulman

## FLORIDA

### Amelia Island (904)

ACCOMMODATIONS
**The Amelia Island Williams House** 103 S. 9th St. **277-2328/(800) 414-9257** gay-friendly • magnificent 1856 antebellum mansion • hot tub • fireplace • $135-175

RESTAURANTS
**Beech Street Grill** 810 Beech St., Fernandina Beach **277-3662** dinner only
**Bretts** 1 Front St. **261-2660**
**Southern Tip** 4802 First Coast Hwy. **261-6184** lunch & dinner • cont'l • full bar

### Boca Raton (561)

INFO LINES & SERVICES
**Boca Lesbian Rap Group** 2601 St. Andrews Blvd., Deerfield Beach **368-6051** 7:30pm Tue

ACCOMMODATIONS
**Floresta Historic B&B** 755 Alamanda St. **391-1451** lesbians/gay men • swimming

BARS & NIGHTCLUBS
**Choices** 21073 Powerline Rd. 2nd flr. **482-2195** 3pm-2am, til 3am Fri-Sat • mostly gay men • dancing/DJ • videos • wheelchair access

TRAVEL AGENTS
**Preferred Travel & Tours** 9144 Glades Rd. **852-4400/(800) 764-3522** IGLTA

SPIRITUAL GROUPS
**Church of Our Savior MCC** 4770 NW 2nd Ave. #C **998-0454** 10:30am Sun

### Bonita Springs (941)

TRAVEL AGENTS
**Bonita Beach Travel** 4365 Bonita Beach Rd. #124 **498-0877/(800) 856-4575** IGLTA

### Boynton Beach (561)

SPIRITUAL GROUPS
**Church of Our Savior MCC** 2011 S. Federal Hwy. **773-4000** 10:30am Sun • wheelchair access

### Bradenton Beach (941)

ACCOMMODATIONS
**Bungalow Beach Resort** 2000 Gulf Dr. N. **778-3600/(800) 779-3601** gay-friendly • hot tub • kitchens • grills avail. • non-smoking rms. avail. • private beach on Gulf of Mexico • wheelchair access • $75-175

### Clearwater (813)

*(see also St. Petersburg)*

BARS & NIGHTCLUBS
**Lost & Found** 5858 Roosevelt Blvd. (State Rd. 686) **539-8903** 4pm-2am • mostly gay men • live shows • karaoke • patio • wheelchair access
**Pro Shop Pub** 840 Cleveland **447-4259** 11:30am-2am, from 1pm Sun • mostly gay men • neighborhood bar
**Turtle Club** 15481 49th St. N. **524-8777** gay-friendly • dancing/DJ • gay night Sun only • wheelchair access

### Cocoa Beach (407)

BARS & NIGHTCLUBS
**Blondies** 5450 N. Atlantic Ave. **783-5339** 2pm-2am • lesbians/gay men • dancing/DJ • live shows • wheelchair access
**Club Chances Cocoa** 610 Forrest Ave., Cocoa **639-0103** 4pm-2am • mostly gay men • dancing/DJ • patio • wheelchair access

RESTAURANTS
**Flaminias** 3210 S. Atlantic Ave. **783-9908** Italian • beer/wine
**Lobster Shanty** 2200 S. Orlando Ave. **783-1350** lunch & dinner • full bar • wheelchair access
**Mango Tree** 118 N. Atlantic Ave. **799-0513** opens 6pm, clsd Mon • fine dining • full bar • wheelchair access • $12-17

TRAVEL AGENTS
**Aerospace Travel** 205 Parnell St., Merritt Island **453-1702** IGLTA

SPIRITUAL GROUPS
**Breaking the Silence MCC** 1261 Range Rd., Cocoa **631-4524** 7pm Sun

## Crescent City (904)

### ACCOMMODATIONS
**Crescent City Campground** 698-2020/(800) 634-3968 gay-friendly • tenting sites • RV hookups • swimming • laundry • showers • $15 day, $90 week, $230 month

## Daytona Beach (904)

### INFO LINES & SERVICES
**Lambda Center** 320 Harvey Ave. 255-0280 support groups • youth services

### ACCOMMODATIONS
**Best Western Mayan Inn Beachfront** 103 S. Ocean Ave. (904) 252-2378/(800) 237-8238 gay-friendly

**Buccaneer Motel** 2301 N. Atlantic Ave. 253-9678/(800) 972-6056 gay-friendly • swimming • $30-90

**Coquina Inn** 544 S. Palmetto Ave. 254-4969/(800) 805-7533 gay-friendly • fireplaces • hot tub • smokefree • IGLTA

**The Villa B&B** 801 N. Peninsula Dr. 248-2020 gay-friendly • historic Spanish mansion • swimming • nudity • IGLTA • $65-250

### BARS & NIGHTCLUBS
**7-69 Restaurant & Lounge** 769 Alabama Ave. 253-4361 5pm-2am • lesbians/gay men • neighborhood bar • food served • wheelchair access • $3-4

**Barndoor** 615 Main St. 252-3776 11am-3am • lesbians/gay men • neighborhood bar • also restaurant • $3-7 • also 'Hollywood Complex' • mostly gay men • dancing/DJ

**The Barracks & Officers Club** 952 Orange Ave. 254-3464 3pm-3am, from noon wknds • popular • mostly gay men • dancing/DJ • live shows • theme nights • wheelchair access

**Hot Nights** 542-U Seabreeze Blvd. 257-4020 lesbians/gay men • Fri women's night

**Mike & Hank's** 415 Main St. noon-3am • popular • mostly gay men • dancing/DJ • live shows

### CAFES
**Euro Cafe** 113 Flagler Ave., New Smyrna Beach 428-8784 8am-10pm, til 5pm Mon • sandwiches • salads

### RESTAURANTS
**Anna's** 304 Seabreeze 239-9624 dinner only, clsd Sun • Italian • beer/wine

**Cafe Frappes** 174 Beach St. 254-7999 lunch & dinner, clsd Sun • some veggie • patio

**Sapporo** 501 Seebreeze Ave. 257-4477 lunch Mon-Fri only, dinner 7 days • Japanese • full bar

**Sweetwater's** 3633 Halifax Dr., Port Orange 761-6724 seafood & steaks • wheelchair access

### PUBLICATIONS
**Our World** 441-5367 glossy magazine focusing on lesbigay travel

### TRAVEL AGENTS
**Monahan Travel Services** 485 S. Nova Rd., Daytona 677-4495/(800) 476-5876

### SPIRITUAL GROUPS
**Hope MCC** 56 N. Halifax (Unitarian Church) 254-0993 7pm Sun • also 320 Harvey St. 10am Sun

## De Land (904)

### ENTERTAINMENT & RECREATION
**'Alley-Gator' Houseboat** 2161 Saragossa Ave. 775-7423 houseboat tour on St. Johns River

## Delray Beach (561)

### BARS & NIGHTCLUBS
**Lulu's Place** 640 E. Atlantic Ave. Bay 6 278-4004 4pm-2am, from noon Sun • lesbians/gay men • piano bar • also restaurant

### RESTAURANTS
**Masquerade Cafe** 640 E. Atlantic Ave. 279-0229 lunch & dinner • wheelchair access

## Deltona (407)

### TRAVEL AGENTS
**Triangles Unltd. Travel** 1332 Hartley Ave. 574-3481 IGLTA

## Dunedin (813)

*(see also St. Petersburg)*

### BARS & NIGHTCLUBS
**1470 West** 325 Main St. 736-5483 4pm-2am, clsd Mon • lesbians/gay men • dancing/DJ • live shows • patio • wheelchair access

## Fort Lauderdale

*F*ort Lauderdale, one of Florida's most popular cities and resort areas, has everything that makes the whole state a natural paradise—sunny skies, balmy nights, hot sands and a clear blue sea. Honeycombed by the Intercoastal Waterway of rivers, bays, canals and inlets, Fort Lauderdale is known as the American Venice. If you like to keep your feet on solid ground, you can tour the Seminole Indian Reservation, shop at Sawgrass Mills outlet mega-mall, or take in a jai alai game.

For more breathtaking attractions, however, check out Fort Lauderdale's growing lesbian community. First, you'll find a number of lesbian-friendly accommodations, including **Rainbow Ventures— The Inn**; ask about their chartered cruises, too. Then replenish your erotica collection from the supply of fetish and sex toys at **Fallen Angel**.

Next pay a visit to Fort Lauderdale's women's bar, **Otherside**. Of course, there are several lesbian-friendly bars like **The Copa**, a complete bar complex, where women can mix it up with the gay boys, or women's night at **Club Electra** on Saturday. Or check out Gay Skate Night on Tuesdays at **Gold Coast Roller Rink**.

## Fort Lauderdale (954)

### INFO LINES & SERVICES

**The Eden Society** 316-8470 transgender social/support group • excellent newsletter

**Gay/Lesbian Community Center** 1164 E. Oakland Park Blvd. **563-9500** 10am-10pm • wheelchair access

**Lambda South** 1231 E. Las Olas Blvd. **761-9072** 12-step clubhouse • wheelchair access

### ACCOMMODATIONS

**215 Guesthouse** 215 SW 7th Ave. **527-4900** gay-friendly • $85-125

**Admiral's Court** 21 Hendricks Isle **462-5072/(800) 248-6669** lesbians/gay men • motel • swimming • IGLTA

**Bahama Hotel** 401 N. Atlantic Blvd. **467-7315/(800) 622-9995** full gym • also 'The Deck' restaurant & bar • IGLTA

**Flamingo Resort** 2727 Terramar St. **561-4658/(800) 283-4786** effeciencies • intimate Art Deco setting

**Hunter Cove** 1752 NE 12th St. **523-7208/(888) 434-2929** gay-friendly • vacation rental near beach • fireplace • sleeps 4-6 • IGLTA • $130-160

# JP's Beach Villas

### F o r t   L a u d e r d a l e

## An all Suites Hotel featuring Luxurious 1 and 2 Bedroom Apartments only a 1/2 Block from the Beach

Lush Tropical Landscaping ■ Heated Pool

Tennis ■ Near Shopping, Clubs, and Restaurants

Outdoor Barbeque ■ Fully Equipped Kitchens

Cable TV and Telephone ■ Daily Maid Service

| DAILY RATES | 12/15 - 4/15 | 4/16 - 12/14 |
|---|---|---|
| 1 Bedroom | $150 | $100 |
| 2 Bedrooms | $200 | $135 |
| Efficiency | $100 | $70 |

Weekly rates available

### For more information call
### 954/772-3672 ■ Fax 954/776-0889

▲ **JP's Beach Villas** 772-3672 all-suite hotel • 1- & 2-bdrm apts • full kitchens • swimming • 1/2 blk to ocean

**King Henry Arms Motel** 543 Breakers Ave. **561-0039/(800) 205-5464** lesbians/gay men • small & friendly motel just steps from the ocean • swimming • IGLTA

**La Casa del Mar** 3003 Granada St. **467-2037/(800) 739-0009** full brkfst • swimming • IGLTA • $90-140

**Midnight Sea** 3005 Alhambra St. **463-4827** mostly gay men • guesthouse on beach • hot tub • nudity • IGLTA

**Orton Terrace** 606 Orton Ave. **566-5068/(800) 323-1142** gay-friendly • apts & motel units • swimming • IGLTA • gay-owned/run

**Rainbow Ventures—The Inn** 1520 NE 26th Ave. **568-5770/(800) 881-4814** women only • also sailing charters • commitment ceremonies • IGLTA

## BARS & NIGHTCLUBS

**Adventures** 303 SW 6th St., Pompano Beach **782-9577** 2pm-2am • lesbians/gay men • neighborhood bar • food served • wheelchair access

**The Bushes** 3038 N. Federal Hwy. **561-1724** 9am-2am, til 3am Sat • mostly men • neighborhood bar • piano bar • wheelchair access

**Club Electra** 1600 SE 15th Ave. **764-8447** 9pm-3am • lesbians/gay men • women's night Sat • dancing/DJ

**Copa** 2800 S. Federal Hwy. **463-1507** 9pm-4am • popular • lesbians/gay men • dancing/DJ • live shows • videos • 2 patio bars

**Eagle** 1951 Powerline Rd. (NW 9th Ave.) **462-7224** 2pm-2am • mostly gay men • leather • wheelchair access

**End Up** 3521 W. Broward Blvd. **584-9301** 11pm-4am • mostly gay men • dancing/DJ • T-dance Sun

**Everglades Bar** 1931 S. Federal Hwy. **462-9165** 9am-2am, from noon Sun • mostly gay men • neighborhood bar • wheelchair access

**Jungle** 545 S. Federal Hwy. **832-9550** 9am-2am, from noon Sun • mostly gay men • videos • patio

**O'Reilly's Cybercafe** 1608 E. Commercial Blvd. **771-0001** 4pm-4am, from 2pm Sun • lesbians/gay men • internet cafe

## Fort Lauderdale (954)

**Where the Girls Are:** On the beach near the lesbigay accommodations, just south of Birch State Recreation Area. Or at one of the cafes or bars in Wilton Manors or Oakland Park.

**Lesbigay Pride:** June: 771-1653.

**Annual Events:**

February - **Winter Gayla**. 525-4567. Circuit Party.

**City Info:** 765-4466.

**Attractions:** Butterfly World. Broward Center for the Performing Arts. Everglades. Flamingo Gardens. Museum of Art. Museum of Discovery & Science. Sawgrass Mills (world's largest outlet mall). Six Flags

Atlantis:The Water Kingdom.

**Weather:** The average year-round temperature in this sub-tropical climate is 75-90°.

**Transit:** Yellow Cab: 565-5400. Super Shuttle: 764-1700. Broward County Transit: 357-8400.

**Otherside of Fort Lauderdale** 2283 Wilton Dr. (NE 4th Ave.) **565-5538** 6pm-2am, til 3am Sat • popular • mostly women • dancing/DJ • wheelchair access

**Tropics Cabaret & Restaurant** 2004 Wilton Dr. **537-6000** 4pm-2am • mostly gay men • neighborhood bar • dancing/DJ • live shows • also restaurant • wheelchair access • $4-12

**The Whale and Porpoise** 2750 E. Oakland Park Blvd. **565-2750** 4pm-2am Mon-Fri, til 3am Sat • lesbians/gay men • dancing/DJ • karaoke • food served

## CAFES

**Courtyard Cafe** 2211 Wilton Dr. **564-9365** 7am-4pm, til 2pm wknds

## RESTAURANTS

**Chardee's** 2209 Wilton Dr. **563-1800** 5pm-2am • lesbians/gay men • some veggie • full bar • live shows • wheelchair access • $12-30

**The Deck** 401 N. Atlantic (Bahama Hotel) **467-7315** some veggie • also oceanfront cafe • $8-12

**Hi-Life Cafe** 3000 N. Federal Hwy. **563-1395** dinner Tue-Sun • bistro • some veggie

**Legends Cafe** 1560 NE 4th Ave. (Wilton Manors Dr.) **467-2233** 6pm-10pm, clsd Mon • lesbians/gay men • multi-ethnic homecooking • some veggie • BYOB • wheelchair access • $8-14

**Lester's Diner** 250 State Rd. 84 **525-5641** 24hrs • popular • more gay late nights • $5-10

**Sukothai** 1930 E. Sunrise Blvd. **764-0148** popular • Thai • some veggie

**Victor Victoria's** 2345 Wilton Dr. **563-6296** 6pm-2am • Italian • some veggie • full bar • wheelchair access • $10-26

**Victoria Park** 900 NE 20th Ave. **764-6868** dinner only • popular • beer/wine • some veggie • call for reservations

## ENTERTAINMENT & RECREATION

**Gold Coast Roller Rink** 2604 S. Federal Hwy. **523-6783** 8pm-midnight Tue • gay skate

## BOOKSTORES & RETAIL SHOPS

**Fallen Angel** 3045 N. Federal Hwy. **563-5230** opens 11am • leather • cards • toys

**Pride Factory** 400 N. Federal Hwy. **463-6600** call for hours • pride gifts • also coffee house

**Rainbow Wear Clothing** 2215 Wilton Dr. **563-4545** 10am-5pm Sun-Mon, til 8pm Tue-Sat • pride gifts

## PUBLICATIONS

**Fountain** 565-7479 statewide lesbian magazine

**Hot Spots** 928-1862/(800) 522-8775 weekly bar guide

**Scoop Magazine** 561-9707

**Unique** 463-8640 lesbigay magazine

## TRAVEL AGENTS

**Beach Travel Service** 3280 NE 32nd St. **564-2323** IGLTA

**Certified Vacations** 110 E. Broward Blvd. **522-1440** IGLTA

**Cliff Petit Travel Service** 1975 E. Sunrise Blvd. #714 **463-4630** IGLTA

**Four Seasons Travel** 3528 N. Federal Hwy. **566-1900** IGLTA

**Olwell Travel Service** 100 NE 3rd Ave. #110 **764-8510** IGLTA

**Southport Travel** 14256 SE 17th St. **761-1500** IGLTA

**Tom Rosenblatt Travel** 927-8697/(800) 877-8389 IGLTA

**Up, Up & Away** 701 E. Broward Blvd. **523-4944**/(800) 234-0841 IGLTA

**Worldwide Vacations** 1400 E. Oakland Park Blvd. #216 **630-0242**/(800) 841-8222 IGLTA

## SPIRITUAL GROUPS

**Congregation Etz Chaim** 3970 NW 21st Ave. **714-9232** 8:30pm Fri • lesbigay synagogue

**Dignity Fort Lauderdale** 330 SW 27th St. (Sunshine Cathedral MCC) **463-4528** 7pm Sun • Roman Catholic liturgy

**Sunshine Cathedral MCC** 330 SW 27th St. **462-2004** 8:30am, 10am, 11:30am, 7pm Sun • wheelchair access

## EROTICA

**Fetish Factory** 821 N. Federal Hwy. **462-0032**

## Fort Myers                    (941)

## INFO LINES & SERVICES

**Gay Switchboard** 332-2272 24hrs • also publishes 'Support-line' newsletter

## ACCOMMODATIONS

▲ **Carefree Resort** 3000 Carefree Blvd. **(800) 326-0364** women's community development on 50 acres • homes to buy or rent • recreation • nature trails

*Wish you were here!*

With people like you, who dream of a comfortable, fun community. One that's perfect for an active retirement or for relaxing vacations.

At The Resort on Carefree Boulevard, you'll find affordable luxury:
- 10,000 sq. ft. clubhouse complex
- three-acre nature preserve and trails
- tennis court and putting green
- lakes for boating and fishing

and much more— all within 25 miles of Sanibel and Captiva Islands. Home and RV sites from $26,500. For sales and rental information, call 1-800-326-0364.

## THE RESORT
*on Carefree Boulevard*

3000 Carefree Blvd., Ft. Myers, FL 33917
1-800-326-0364   http://www.resortoncb.com

OBTAIN THE FEDERAL PROPERTY REPORT REQUIRED BY FEDERAL LAW AND READ IT BEFORE SIGNING ANYTHING. NO FEDERAL AGENCY HAS JUDGED THE MERITS OR VALUE, IF ANY, OF THIS PROPERTY. AD#9723471

**Golf View Motel** 3523 Cleveland Ave. **936-1858** gay-friendly • swimming • wheelchair access • $28+

## BARS & NIGHTCLUBS

**The Bottom Line (TBL)** 3090 Evans Ave. **337-7292** 3pm-2am • lesbians/gay men • dancing/DJ • live shows • wheelchair access

**Office Pub** 3704 Grove **936-3212** noon-2am • mostly men • neighborhood bar • beer/wine

## CAFES

**Black Coffee Cafe** 2236 First St. **332-3779** 10am-6pm, til 1am Fri, 4pm-midnight Sat, clsd Sun-Mon • coffeehouse • deli • wheelchair access

## RESTAURANTS

**Oasis** 2222 McGregor Blvd. **334-1566** brkfst & lunch only • beer/wine • wheelchair access • women-owned/run • $4-6

**Palate Pleasers** 3512 Del Prado S., Cape Coral **945-6333** clsd Sun • some veggie • beer/wine • wheelchair access

## SPIRITUAL GROUPS

**St. John the Apostle MCC** 2209 Unity St. **278-5181** 10am Sun & 7pm Wed • wheelchair access

## Fort Walton Beach          (904)

## BARS & NIGHTCLUBS

**Frankly Scarlett** 223 Hwy. 98 E. **664-2966** 8pm-2am, til 4am wknds • lesbians/gay men • dancing/DJ • live shows • patio • wheelchair access

## Gainesville          (352)

## INFO LINES & SERVICES

**Gay Switchboard** 332-0700 live 6pm-11pm, 24hr touchtone service • extensive info on Gainesville area • AA info

## BARS & NIGHTCLUBS

**Ambush Room** 4130 NW 6th St. **376-3772** 4pm-2am • popular • lesbians/gay men • country/western

**Club Diversity** 22822 N. Hwy. 441, Micanopy **591-2525** lesbians/gay men • dancing/DJ • live shows • 18+ • multi-bar complex • full restaurant • wheelchair access

**The University Club** 18 E. University Ave. (enter rear) **378-6814** 5pm-2am, til 4am Fri-Sat, til 11pm Sun • lesbians/gay men • more women Fri • dancing/DJ • live shows • patio • wheelchair access

## BOOKSTORES & RETAIL SHOPS

**Wild Iris Books** 802 W. University Ave. **375-7477** 10am-6pm, til 7pm Sat, 11am-5pm Sun • feminist bookstore • lesbigay • wheelchair access

## SPIRITUAL GROUPS

**Trinity MCC** 11604 SW Archer Rd. **495-3378** 10:15am Sun • wheelchair access

## Hallandale          (305)

## ACCOMMODATIONS

**Club Atlantic Resort** 2080 S. Ocean Dr. **458-6666/(800) 645-8666** gay-friendly • rooms & suites on the beach • swimming • also restaurant • wheelchair access

## Holiday          (813)

## BARS & NIGHTCLUBS

**Lovey's Pub** 338 US 19 **849-2960** 10am-2am, from 1pm Sun • lesbians/gay men • neighborhood bar • wheelchair access

## Hollywood          (954)

## BARS & NIGHTCLUBS

**Partners** 625 Dania Beach Blvd., Dania **921-9893** noon-3am • gay-friendly • neighborhood bar • dancing/DJ • live shows

**Zachary's** 2217 N. Federal Hwy. **920-5479** 4pm-2am, from 11am wknds • mostly women • neighborhood bar • beer/wine • wheelchair access • women-owned/run

## TRAVEL AGENTS

**Carrie-Me-Away Travel** 5650 Sterling Rd. **987-9770** IGLTA

## EROTICA

**Hollywood Book & Video** 1235 S. State Rd. 7 **981-2164** 24hrs

## Jacksonville          (904)

## BARS & NIGHTCLUBS

**616** 616 Park St. **358-6969** 2pm-2am, from 5pm wknds • mostly gay men • neighborhood bar • beer/wine • patio

**Boot Rack Saloon** 4751 Lenox Ave. **384-7090** 4pm-2am • mostly gay men • country/western • patio

**Eagle** 1402-6 San Marco Blvd. **396-8551** 9am-2am • mostly gay men • leather • food served • patio • wheelchair access

**Edgewater Junction** 1261 King St. 388-3434 2pm-2am • lesbians/gay men • neighborhood bar • live shows • beer/wine • food served

**HMS** 1702 E. 8th St. 353-9200 2pm-2am • mostly gay men • neighborhood bar • beer/wine • patio

**In Touch Tavern** 10957 Atlantic Blvd. 642-7506 noon-2am, from 3pm Sun • lesbians/gay men • neighborhood bar • beer/wine • wheelchair access

**The Metro** 2929 Plum St. 388-8719 4pm-2am • lesbians/gay men • dancing/DJ • patio

**My Little Dude/Jo's Place** 2952 Roosevelt Blvd. 388-9503 4pm-2am • mostly women • dancing/DJ • live shows • wheelchair access

**Park Place Lounge** 931 King St. 389-6616 noon-2am • mostly gay men • neighborhood bar • wheelchair access

**Third Dimension** 711 Edison Ave. 353-6316 3pm-2am, from 6pm Sat, from 5pm Sun • mostly gay men • dancing/DJ • alternative • live shows • wheelchair access

## PUBLICATIONS

**The Last Word (TLW)** 384-6514/(800) 677-0772

## TRAVEL AGENTS

**A Beeline Travel Center** 6937 St. Augustine Rd. 739-3349/(800) 528-6560 IGLTA

**A World Of Travel** 3947 Boulevard Center Dr. #101 398-6638/(800) 253-9846 IGLTA

**Cruise Market/US Travel** 1300 Riverplace Blvd. #400 858-0123 IGLTA

## SPIRITUAL GROUPS

**St. Luke's MCC** 1140 S. McDuff Ave. 389-7726 10am & 6pm Sun

## Jacksonville Beach (904)

### BARS & NIGHTCLUBS

**Bo's Coral Reef** 201 5th Ave. N. 246-9874 2pm-2am • lesbians/gay men • dancing/DJ • live shows

## Jasper (904)

### ACCOMMODATIONS

**The J&J Farms B&B** 792-2771 lesbians/gay men • full brkfst • hot tub • swimming • nudity

**DINAH SHORE WEEKEND**

**MARCH 26-29, 1998**

**PALM SPRINGS**

The Ultimate Hotel & Entertainment Package at the All Inclusive

**DOUBLE TREE RESORT**

Book today to ensure availability. For hotel and party ticket Info Call

**310.281.7358**

For Airline reservations call
**1•800•433•1790**

Produced by JOANI WEIR PRODUCTIONS
POM POM PRODUCTIONS • KLUB BANSHEE

*Tasteful gay & lesbian accommodations*

## ALEXANDER'S
G U E S T H O U S E

### 1-800-654-9919

Fax 1-305-295-0357

1118 Fleming, Key West, FL 33040

Visit us online:

E-mail: alexghouse@aol.com
Website: www.http://home.aol.com/alexghouse

## Key West (305)

### INFO LINES & SERVICES

**Commitment Ceremonies by Capt. Linda Schuh** 294-4213 on the sea or shore • certificate

**Helpline** 296-8654 24hrs • info • support

### ACCOMMODATIONS

**Alexander Palms Court** 715 South St. 296-6413/(800) 858-1943 gay-friendly • swimming • $85-395

▲ **Alexander's Guest House** 1118 Fleming St. 294-9919/(800) 654-9919 lesbians/gay men • swimming • nudity • IGLTA • $130-275

**Ambrosia House Tropical Lodging** 615 Fleming St. 296-9838/(800) 535-9838 gay-friendly • swimming • turn-of-the-century sea captain's house

**Andrew's Inn** Zero Whalton Ln. 294-7730/(888) 263-7393 popular • lesbians/gay men • elegantly restored rooms & garden cottages • swimming • wheelchair access • $148-378

**The Artist House** 534 Eaton St. 296-3977/(800) 593-7898 gay-friendly • Victorian guesthouse • hot tub • patio

**Atlantic Shores Resort** 510 South St. 296-2491/(800) 526-3559 gay-friendly • swimming • also restaurant • 2 bars • IGLTA • $75-135

**Author's of Key West** 725 White St. 294-7381/(800) 898-6909 gay-friendly • swimming

**Banana's Foster Bed** 537 Caroline St. 294-9061/(800) 653-4888 gay-friendly • historic conch house B&B • swimming • wheelchair access • $170-190

**Big Ruby's Guesthouse** 409 Appelrouth Ln. 296-2323/(800) 477-7829 mostly gay men • full brkfst • swimming • nudity • evening wine service • wheelchair access • IGLTA

**Blue Parrot Inn** 916 Elizabeth St. 296-0033/(800) 231-2473 gay-friendly • swimming • nudity • IGLTA • $70-180

**The Brass Key Guesthouse** 412 Frances St. 296-4719/(800) 932-9119 popular • mostly gay men • luxury guesthouse • full brkfst • swimming • spa • IGLTA • wheelchair access • $130-215

▲ **Chelsea House** 707 Truman Ave. 296-2211/(800) 845-8859 gay-friendly • swimming • nudity • wheelchair access • IGLTA • $79-305

# RED ROOSTER INN

**A LOT FOR A LITTLE**

**709 Truman Avenue • Key West, FL 33040**
**Reservations 1-800-845-0825 • 305 296-6558**
**Fax 305 296-4822 • chelseahse@aol.com**

# Chelsea House

*Two blocks from Duval, this meticulously restored 19th century mansion has beautifully appointed rooms, most with private balconies. Enjoy the clothing optional sun deck and lush tropical gardens in the finest Key West tradition.*

707 Truman Avenue
Key West, FL 33040
305 296-2211 • Fax 305 296-4822
Reservations 1-800-845-8859
chelseahse@aol.com

**Colours—The Guest Mansion** 410 Fleming St. **294-6977/(800) 459-6212** popular • lesbians/gay men • swimming • complimentary sunset cocktails • IGLTA

**Cuban Club Suites** 1102-A Duval St. **296-0465/(800) 432-4849** gay-friendly • award-winning historic hotel overlooking Duval St. • IGLTA • $200-300

**Cypress House** 601 Caroline **294-6969/(800) 525-2488** popular • gay-friendly • guesthouse • $100-180

**Deja Vu Resort** 611 Truman Ave. **292-1424/(800) 724-5351** gay-friendly • hot tub • swimming • $59-165

**Duval House** 815 Duval St. **292-9491/(800) 223-8825** popular • gay-friendly • swimming • IGLTA • $75-250

**Duval Suites** 724 Duval St. (upstairs) **293-6600/(800) 648-3780** lesbians/gay men • nudity • non-smoking rms avail. • $80-275

**Eaton Lodge** 511 Eaton St. **292-2170/(800) 294-2170** gay-friendly • 1886 mansion & conch house adjacent to Duval St. • hot tub • swimming • $139-219

**Garden House** 329 Elizabeth St. **296-5368/(800) 695-6453** gay-friendly • swimming • hot tub • $75-125

**Heron House** 512 Simonton St. **294-9227/(800) 294-1644** gay-friendly • swimming • hot tub • wheelchair access • $99-249

**Incentra Carriage House Inn** 729 Whitehead St. **296-5565** gay-friendly • 3 houses surrounding lush garden • swimming • $90-275

▲ **The Island Key Courts** 910 Simonton St. **296-1148/(800) 296-1148** gay-friendly • inquire about packages for women

**Key Lodge Motel** 1004 Duval St. **296-9915/(800) 458-1296** popular • gay-friendly • swimming • $75-165

**Knowles House** 1004 Eaton St. **296-8132/(800) 352-4414** lesbians/gay men • restored 1880s conch house • swimming • nudity • $99-149

**La Casa de Luces** 422 Amelia St. **296-3993/(800) 432-4849** gay-friendly • early 1900s conch house • wheelchair access • IGLTA • $70-175

BEST VALUES! BEST RATES!

# The Island Key Courts of Key West

❦❦❦❦❦❦❦

SPECIAL WELCOME PACKAGE FOR WOMEN, with free gifts & a unique Key West For Women Insider's Guide, plus friendly concierges!

Guestrooms & Apartment Suites (studios, 1&2 bedrooms, sleeping 1-9), with kitchens, gardens, AC, TV, in Old Town. Very Private! Very Key West!

FREE membership to nearby private beach club, with pool, gym, spa, 2 restaurants, 3 bars. Minutes to Atlantic beaches & Duval Street bars!

**(305) 296-1148; (800) 296-1148; Fax: (305) 292-7924**
Email: rayebv@aol.com  910 Simonton St., Key West, FL 33040

# Key West

*T*his tiny Caribbean island at the very tip of Florida, closer to Cuba than to Miami, is a lesbian and gay tropical paradise. Key West is a way of life, not just an exotic resort. Locals have perfected a laissez-faire attitude and visitors quickly fall into the relaxed rhythm.

The famous Old Town area is dotted with Victorian homes and mansions. Many of them are now fully renovated as accommodations, such as the women-only **Rainbow House.**

Perhaps because Key West life is so laid back, there's only one women's bar, **Club International,** and a few boys' bars. But you'll be thoroughly entertained spending your days lounging poolside with warm tropical breezes in your hair and a cool drink in your hand.

Or get out of that lounge chair and sail the emerald waters around Key West on the **Mangrove Mistress.** The ocean is home to the hemisphere's largest living coral reef, accessible by snorkeling and scuba vessels. For an inexpensive and fun way to get around, rent a moped from one of the many bike rental shops to cruise the island.

Don't miss **Womenfest** in September, the annual women's week in Key West—the ideal time and place to experience women entertainers, sailing, boating, snorkeling, a street fair, dances, and more. **Fantasy Fest** in October is seven days of Halloween in a tropical heaven: costumes, contests, parades, and parties galore. For information on other fun events, pick up a **Southern Exposure** paper.

## Key West (305)

**Where the Girls Are:** You can't miss 'em during Women In Paradise in September, but other times they're just off Duval St. somewhere between Eaton and South Streets. Or on the beach. Or in the water.

**Annual Events:**

December - Int'l Gay Arts Fest: 800/535-7797. Cultural festival of film, theatre, art, concerts, seminars, parties and a parade.

September - **Women Fest:** 296-4238 & 800/535-7797.

October - **Fantasy Fest:** 800/535-7797. Week-long Halloween celebration with masquerade balls & parades.

**City Info:** Key West Chamber of Commerce: 294-2587.

**Attractions:** Audubon House and Gardens. Dolphin Research Center. Glass-bottom boats. Mallory Market. Red Barn Theatre. Southernmost Point U.S.A. Hemingway House.

**Best View:** Old Town Trolley Tour (1/2 hour).

**Weather:** The average temperature year-round is 78°, and the sun shines nearly everyday. Any time is the right time for a visit.

**Transit:** Yellow Cab: 294-2227. 5 Sixes: 296-6666.

**La Te Da** 1125 Duval St. **296-6706/(800) 528-3320** popular • lesbians/gay men • tropical setting • swimming • gourmet restaurant • 2 bars • Sun T-dance • IGLTA

**Lightbourne Inn** 907 Truman Ave. **296-5152/(800) 352-6011** gay-friendly

**Marquesa Hotel** 600 Fleming St. **292-1919/(800) 869-4631** gay-friendly • swimming • also restaurant • some veggie • full bar • $17-26 • wheelchair access

**Merlinn Guesthouse** 811 Simonton St. **296-3336/(800) 642-4753** gay-friendly • full brkfst • swimming • wheelchair access • $70-160

**The Mermaid and the Alligator** 729 Truman Ave. **294-1894/(800) 773-1894** gay-friendly • full brkfst • swimming • smokefree • gay-owned/operated • $65-155

**Pegasus International** 501 Southard **294-9323/(800) 397-8148** gay-friendly • swimming • also restaurant

**Pier House Resort & Caribbean Spa** 1 Duval St. **296-4600/(800) 327-8340** gay-friendly • private beach • swimming • restaurants • bars • spa • fitness center • IGLTA • $195 and up

**Pilot House Guest House** 414 Simonton St. **294-8719/(800) 648-3780** lesbians/gay men • 19th century Victorian in Old Town • hot tub • swimming • nudity • non-smoking rms avail. • $80-300

▲ **The Rainbow House** 525 United St. **292-1450/(800) 749-6696** women only • hot tub • swimming • nudity • smokefree • wheelchair access • IGLTA • lesbian-owned/run • $99-169 • (see inside back cover)

**Red Rooster Inn** 709 Truman Ave. **296-6558/(800) 845-0825** gay-friendly • 19th century wooden 3-story inn • swimming • smokefree • $59-150

**Sea Isle Resort** 915 Windsor Ln. **294-5188/(800) 995-4786** mostly gay men • hot tub • swimming • nudity • large private courtyard • gym • sundeck • IGLTA • $75-250

**Seascape Guest House** 420 Olivia **296-7776/(800) 765-6438** gay-friendly • recently restored inn circa 1889 located in the heart of Old Town • swimming • $69-129

**Discover A True Women's Paradise**

# The Rainbow House®

*Key West's Only Exclusively Women's Guest House*

## has <u>Expanded</u>!

*2 Swimming Pools!*
*2 Hot Tubs!*
*38 Rooms*
*& Suites!*

**Our Lovely Accommodations Include:**
- *Bedroom with Queen or King Bed*
- *Private Bath* • *Color TV*
- *Air Conditioning & Bahama Fan*
- *Deluxe Continental Breakfast in our Air Conditioned Pavilion*

**Other Amenities for your Vacationing Pleasure Include:** *2 Swimming Pools • 2 Hot Tubs*
• *Massage Available • Extensive Decks for Sunbathing • Shaded Tropical Pavilion for Lazy Day Lounging • Restaurants & Nightlife within walking distance • 1/2 block to shopping district*
• *1 block to Atlantic Ocean & Southernmost Point in Continental United States*

*Call for a free color brochure.*

**1-800-74-WOMYN • 1-800-749-6696
(305) 292-1450
525 United Street, Key West, FL 33040 USA**

**Sheraton Suites—Key West** 2001 S. Roosevelt Blvd. **292-9800/(800) 452-3224** gay-friendly • non-smoking rms avail. • IGLTA

▲ **Simonton Court Historic Inn & Cottages** 320 Simonton St. **294-6386/(800) 944-2687** popular • gay-friendly • 23-unit compound built in 1880s • hot tub • 4 pools • IGLTA • $110-350

**White Street Inn** 905-907 White St. **295-9599/(800) 207-9767** gay-friendly • swimming • IGLTA • $85-220

**William Anthony House** 613 Caroline St. **294-2887/(800) 613-2276** gay-friendly • award-winning historic inn • swimming • social hour • wheelchair access

**The William House** 1317 Duval St. **294-8233/(800) 848-1317** gay-friendly • turn-of-the-century guesthouse • spa • $125-180

### BARS & NIGHTCLUBS

**801 Bar** 801 Duval St. **294-4737** 11am-4am • mostly gay men • neighborhood bar • live shows • also 'Dan's Bar' from 9pm • mostly gay men • leather

**Bourbon Street Pub** 730 Duval St. **296-1992** noon-4am • lesbians/gay men • live shows • videos • wheelchair access

**Club International** 900 Simonton St. **296-9230** 1pm-4am • mostly women • neighborhood bar • videos

**Donnie's** 618 Duval St. (enter rear) **294-5620** 24hrs • gay-friendly • neighborhood bar • also restaurant • wheelchair access

**Epoch** 623 Duval St. **296-8522** 10pm-4am, clsd Mon • mostly gay men • dancing/DJ • live shows • patio • also 'Terrace Bar' 2pm-4am

**One Saloon** 524 Duval St. (enter on Appelrouth Ln.) **296-8118** 9pm-4am • mostly gay men • 3 bars • dancing/DJ • patio • wheelchair access

### CAFES

**Croissants de France** 816 Duval St. **294-2624** 7:30am-9pm • lesbians/gay men • French pastries/crepes/gallettes • some veggie • beer/wine • patio • $5-7

### RESTAURANTS

**Al Fresco's** 416 Appelrouth Ln. **296-6670** lunch & dinner • Italian • $7-15

# SIMONTON COURT
## The Island Resort
### Historic Inn & Cottages

*Secluded Rendezvous*

Quiet. Romantic. A block from Duval Street in Key West.

*For more information call:*
**1-800-944-2687**

**Antonia's** 615 Duval St. **294-6565** 6pm-11pm • popular • Northern Italian • beer/wine • some veggie • $16-22

**B.O.'s Fish Wagon** corner of Duval & Fleming Sts. **294-9272** popular • lunch • 'seafood & eat it' • $3-8

**Cafe des Artistes** 1007 Simonton St. **294-7100** 6pm-11pm • tropical French • full bar • $22-30

**Cafe Europa** 1075 Duval St. C-13 **294-3443** brkfst, lunch & dinner • bistro • beer/wine • German & Island cuisine • also cafe & bakery

**Camille's** 703 Duval St. **296-4811** 8am-3pm, 6pm-10pm, no dinner Sun-Mon • bistro • hearty brkfst

**Dim Sum** 613-1/2 Duval St. **294-6230** 6pm-11pm • Pan-Asian • plenty veggie • beer/wine • sake cocktails • $13-17

**Duffy's Steak & Lobster House** 1007 Simonton **296-4900** 11am-11pm • full bar • $15-30

**Dynasty** 918 Duval St. **294-2943** lunch & dinner • Chinese • beer/wine • $7-16

**Kelly's Caribbean Bar Grill & Brewery** 301 Whitehead St. **293-8484** owned by actress Kelly McGillis

**La Trattoria Venezia** 524 Duval St. **296-1075** 6pm-11pm • lesbians/gay men • Italian • full bar • $12-22

**Lobos** 611 1/2 Duval St. **296-5303** 11am-6pm, clsd Mon • plenty veggie • $4-7

**Louie's Backyard** 700 Waddell Ave. **294-1061** lunch & dinner, bar 11:30am-2am • popular • fine cont'l dining • $22-30

**Mangia Mangia** 900 Southard St. **294-2469** fresh pasta • beer/wine • patio

**Mango's** 700 Duval St. **292-4606** 11am-2am • int'l • plenty veggie • full bar • wheelchair access • $10-22

**Palm Grill** 1029 Southard St. **296-1744** 6pm-10pm • some veggie • $16-20

**The Quay** 12 Duval St. **294-4446** gourmet • some veggie • $13-18

**Rooftop Cafe** 310 Front St. **294-2042** American/Caribbean • some veggie • $10-22

**South Beach Seafood & Raw Bar** 1405 Duval St. **294-2727** 7am-10pm • full bar • around $15 for dinner

**Square One** 1075 Duval St. **296-4300** 6:30pm-10:30pm • full bar • wheelchair access • $14-22

# WOMEN ONLY TRIPS

## SNORKEL & EXPLORE
## ABOARD THE 30' CRUISER
## MANGROVE MISTRESS

### CEREMONIES OUR SPECIALTY

### NO SEASICKNESS

### PRIVATE SUNSET
### CHARTERS AVAILABLE

## OWNED & OPERATED BY CAPT. LYNDA SCHUH
## 305-294-4213

**Yo Sake** 722 Duval St. **294-2288** 6pm-11pm • Japanese/sushi bar • beer/wine • $10-18

## ENTERTAINMENT & RECREATION

▲ **Mangrove Mistress (formerly Women on the Water)** 294-4213 sailing charters • no seasickness • lesbian-owned/run

**Water Sport People** 511 Greene St. **296-4546** scuba-diving instruction and group charters

## BOOKSTORES & RETAIL SHOPS

**Blue Heron Books** 1014 Truman Ave. **296-3508** 9am-9pm, 1pm-5pm Sun • general • lesbian's section

**Fast Buck Freddie's** 500 Duval St. **294-2007** 10am-6pm, 10am-10pm Sat • clothing • gifts

**Flaming Maggie's** 830 Fleming St. **294-3931** lesbigay bookstore

**In Touch** 715 Duval St. **292-7293** 10am-11pm • gay gifts

**Key West Aloe** 524 Front St. **(800) 445-2563** mail order avail.

**Key West Island Books** 513 Fleming St. **294-2904** 10am-6pm • new & used rare books • lesbigay section

**Lido** 532 Duval St. **294-5300** clothing • gifts • gay-owned/run

## PUBLICATIONS

**Key West Pride Connections** 292-5972
**Southern Exposure** 294-6303

## TRAVEL AGENTS

**Colours Destinations Int'l (800) ARRIVAL** hotel reservation service • IGLTA • gay-owned/run

**IGLTA (International Gay/Lesbian Travel Association)** 296-6673/**(800) 448-8550** active organization for worldwide lesbian/gay travel industry

**Regency Travel** 1075 Duval St. #19 **294-0175**/**(800) 374-2784** IGLTA

## SPIRITUAL GROUPS

**MCC Key West** 1215 Petronia St. **294-8912** 9:30am & 11am Sun • wheelchair access

**St. Paul's Episcopal Church** 401 Duval **296-5142** 7:30am, 9am & 11am Sun

## GYMS & HEALTH CLUBS

**Club Body Tech** 1075 Duval St. **292-9683** lesbians/gay men • full gym • sauna • massage therapy avail.

**Pro Fitness** 1111 12th St. **294-1865**

## EROTICA

**Leather Masters** 418-A Appelrouth Ln. **292-5051** custom leather

# Lake Worth                    (561)

## BARS & NIGHTCLUBS

**Club 502 & The Birdcage Cabaret** 502 Lucerne Ave. **540-8881/540-4663** 4pm-2am, 11am-midnight Sun, clsd Mon • lesbians/gay men • dancing/DJ • T-dance Sun • also restaurant • some veggie • wheelchair access

**Inn Exile** 6 S. 'J' St. **582-4144** 3pm-2am, til midnight Sun • mostly gay men • live shows • videos

**K & E's** 29 S. Dixie Hwy. **533-6020** 4pm-2am, from 2pm wknds • lesbians/gay men • food served

## SPIRITUAL GROUPS

**Yeladim Shel Yisrael** 4938 S. Davis Rd. 967-4267

# Lakeland                    (941)

## INFO LINES & SERVICES

**PGLA (Polk Gay/Lesbian Alliance)** 299-8126

## ACCOMMODATIONS

**Sunset Motel & RV Resort** 2301 New Tampa Hwy. **683-6464** gay-friendly • motels, apts & private home on 3 acres • swimming • wheelchair access

## BARS & NIGHTCLUBS

**Dockside** 3770 Hwy. 92 E. **665-2590** 4pm-2am • lesbians/gay men • dancing/DJ • live shows • gay-owned/run

**Roy's Green Parrot** 1030 E. Main St. **683-6021** 4pm-2am, til midnight Sun • popular • mostly gay men • dancing/DJ • live shows • beer/wine

# Largo                    (813)

## BARS & NIGHTCLUBS

**Sports Page Pub** 13344 66th St. N. **538-2430** noon-2am, from 1pm Sun • lesbians/gay men • sports bar • food served • wheelchair access

# Madeira Beach                    (813)

## BARS & NIGHTCLUBS

**Surf & Sand Lounge/Back Room Bar** 14601 Gulf Blvd. **391-2680** 1pm-2am • mostly gay men • neighborhood bar • beach access • wheelchair access

# Melbourne (407)

## BARS & NIGHTCLUBS

**Cold Keg** 4060 W. New Haven Ave. **724-1510** 2pm-2am • popular • lesbians/gay men • dancing/DJ • live shows • wheelchair access

**Loading Zone** 4910 Stack Blvd. **727-3383** 8pm-2am, clsd Mon • popular • lesbians/gay men • dancing/DJ • videos • wheelchair access

## TRAVEL AGENTS

**Beyond & Back** 401 Ocean Ave. #101, Melbourne Beach **725-9720** IGLTA

# Miami (305)

*(see also Miami Beach/South Beach)*

## INFO LINES & SERVICES

**Gay/Lesbian/Bisexual Hotline of Greater Miami** 759-3661

**Lambda Dade AA** 410 NE 22nd St. **573-9608** 8:30pm daily • call for other mtg. times • wheelchair access

**Lesbian/Gay/Bisexual Community Center** 6445 NE 7th Ave. **759-5210** 10am-4pm

**PALS-Lesbian Social** 759-6423 2nd Fri • call for location

**Switchboard of Miami** 358-4357 24hrs • gay-friendly info & referrals for Dade County

## BARS & NIGHTCLUBS

**Splash** 5922 S. Dixie Hwy. **662-8779** 4pm-2am • mostly gay men • dancing/DJ • live shows • 'Bliss' Fri only • mostly women

**Sugar's** 17060 W. Dixie **940-9887** 3pm-6am • mostly gay men • more women Fri • neighborhood bar • dancing/DJ • videos • wheelchair access

## BOOKSTORES & RETAIL SHOPS

**Lambda Passages Bookstore** 7545 Biscayne Blvd. **754-6900** 11am-9pm, noon-6pm Sun • lesbigay/ feminist bookstore

# Miami/South Beach (305)

**Where the Girls Are:** In Miami proper, Coral Gables and the University district, as well as Biscayne Blvd. along the coast, are the lesbian hangouts of choice. You'll see women everywhere in South Beach, but especially along Ocean Dr., Washington, Collins and Lincoln Roads.

**Entertainment:** Bridge Theater Play Readings at the Community Center, Wednesdays.

**Lesbigay Pride:** June: 771-1653.

**Annual Events:**

March - **Winter Party**: 460-3115. AIDS benefit dance on the beach

November - **White Party Vizcaya**: 757-4444. AIDS benefit circuit party.

**City Info:** Greater Miami Visitors Bureau 701 Brickell Ave. 539-3000.

**Attractions:** Bass Museum of Art (673-7533). Bayside Market Place (577-3344). Art Deco Welcome Center (672-2014). Miami Museum of Science & Space Transit Planetarium (854-4247). Miami Seaquarium (361-5705). Parrot Jungle and Gardens (666-7834). Vizcaya Estate & Gardens (250-9133).

**Best View:** If you've got money to burn, a helicopter flight over Miami Beach is a great way to see the city. Otherwise, hit the beach.

**Weather:** Warm all year. Temperatures stay in the 90°s during the summer and drop into the mid-60°s in the winter. Be prepared for sunshine!

**Transit:** Yellow Cab: 444-4444. Metro Taxi: 888-8888.

## Miami/South Beach

*A*s a key center of business and politics in the Americas, Miami has an incredibly multicultural look and feel. You'll discover a diversity of people, from a growing population of transplanted seniors to large communities of Cubans, Latin-Americans, and Americans of African descent.

Miami is also a tourist's winter wonderland of sun, sand and sea. Make the most of it with trips to Seaquarium, Key Biscayne or the nearby Everglades. For a relaxing evening with the girls, try the **PALS Lesbian Social** or the Women's Film Series on the 4th Friday at the New Alliance Theater (600 Lincoln Rd. #219 at Penn Ave.).

Or make reservations to dine at **Something Special,** a women-only restaurant in a private home. Get the latest on local nightlife from **Lips,** South Florida's contemporary woman's newspaper or **Fountain** women's magazine, both available at **Lambda Passages,** the lesbigay bookstore.

But if you're really hungry for loads of lesbigay culture, head directly for South Beach. This section of Miami Beach has been given an incredible makeover by gays and lesbians, and is fast becoming the hot spot on the East Coast—even Madonna and (TAFKA) Prince have staked out the area! If you're dazzled by South Beach's historic Art Deco architecture, take the walking tour that leaves from the Miami Welcome Center at 1224 Ocean Dr. (672-2014) for under $10.

Much of the SoBe scene is gay boys and drag queens, but svelte, hot-blooded women are in abundance too. During the day, 12th St.reet gay beach is the place to be seen. Try the **Palace Grill** for a queer mid-afternoon munch and great people-watching. **821** attracts professional women on their women's nights hosted by Mary D, while Ladies' Happy Hour at **The Penguin Hotel** is the place for lesbian lounge lizards. For a see-and-be-seen dining experience, head to **Wolfie's** or the **News Cafe** for a late-night meal.

TRAVEL AGENTS

**Jacquin Travel** 10530 NW 26th St. #F-105 **592-5882/(800) 367-3249** IGLTA

**Leutner Travel Service** 1322 NE 105th St. #10, Miami Shores **895-1229** IGLTA

**Professional Travel Management** 195 SW 15th Rd. #403 **858-5522/(800) 568-4064** IGLTA

**The Travel House** 3801 N. Miami Ave. **576-5550/(888) 878-5473** IGLTA

**Vision Travel: Carlson Travel Network** **444-8484/(800) 654-4544** IGLTA

SPIRITUAL GROUPS

**Christ MCC** 7701 SW 76th Ave. **284-1040** 9:30am & 7pm Sun • wheelchair access

**Grace MCC** 10390 NE 2nd Ave., Miami Shores **758-6822** 11:30am Sun

EROTICA

**Le Jeune Road Books** 928 SW 42nd Ave. **443-1913** 24hrs

## Miami Beach/South Beach (305)

INFO LINES & SERVICES

**South Beach Business Guild** 234-7224 maps & info

ACCOMMODATIONS

**Abbey Hotel** 300 21st St. **531-0031/(888) 612-2239** gay-friendly • studios • kitchens

**The Astor** 956 Washington Ave. **531-8081/(800) 270-4981** popular • gay-friendly • food served • swimming • wheelchair access

**Bohemia Gardens** 825 Michigan Ave. **758-3902/(800) 472-4102** gay-friendly • hot tub • $75-150

**Collins Plaza** 318 20th St. **532-0849** gay-friendly • hotel

**The Colony Hotel** 736 Ocean Dr. **673-0088/(800) 226-5669** gay-friendly • food served • wheelchair access

**The Colours—The Mantell Guest Inn** 255 W. 24th St. **538-1821/(800) 277-4825** lesbians/gay men • several art deco hotels & apts avail. • swimming • IGLTA • $79-159

**The Delano Hotel** 1685 Collins Ave. **534-6300/(800) 555-5001** gay-friendly • food served • swimming

**Fairfax Hotel** 1776 Collins Ave. **538-3837** IGLTA

**Florida Sunbreak** 532-1516/(800) 786-2732 reservation service • IGLTA

IT ONLY HAPPENS ONCE A YEAR

...CURIOUS

1 (888) 44 DINAH
GIRL BAR & CLUB SKIRTS

**Fountainbleu Hilton Resort & Spa** 4441 Collins Ave. **538-2000/(800) 445-8667** gay-friendly • swimming • wheelchair access

**The Governor Hotel** 435 21st St. **532-2100/(800) 542-0444** gay-friendly • swimming

**Hotel Impala** 1228 Collins Ave. **673-2021/(800) 646-7252** gay-friendly • luxury hotel near beach • wheelchair access • IGLTA

**The Indian Creek Hotel** 2727 Indian Creek Dr. **531-2727/(800) 491-2772** gay-friendly • food served • swimming • IGLTA

**Jefferson House B&B** 1018 Jefferson **534-5247** lesbians/gay men • tropical garden • IGLTA • $80-130

**Kenmore Hotel** 1050 Washington Ave. **674-1930** gay-friendly • swimming • IGLTA • $69-89

**The Kent** 1131 Collins Ave. **531-6771/(800) 688-7678** gay-friendly • wheelchair access

**Lily Guesthouse** 835 Collins Ave. **535-9900** gay-friendly • studios • suites • sundeck • IGLTA

**Lord Balfour** 350 Ocean Dr. **673-0401/(800) 501-0401** gay-friendly

**Marlin Hotel** 1200 Collins Ave. **673-8770/(800) 688-7678** gay-friendly • upscale • wheelchair access

**Meridian Villas** 1545 Meridian Ave. **531-4989** IGLTA

**Ocean Front Hotel** 1230 Ocean Dr. **672-2579/(800) 783-1725** great location

**The Park Central & Imperial Hotel** 640 Ocean Dr. **538-1611** IGLTA

**Park Washington** 1020 Washington Ave. **532-1930** gay-friendly • hotel • swimming

**The Pelican** 826 Ocean Dr. **673-3373/(800) 773-5422** designer theme rms

**Penguin Hotel & Bar** 1418 Ocean Dr. **534-9334/(800) 235-3296** lesbians/gay men • also restaurant • plenty veggie

**The Raleigh Hotel** 1775 Collins Ave. **534-6300/(800) 848-1775** IGLTA

**Richmond Hotel** 1757 Collins Ave. **538-2331/(800) 327-3163** IGLTA

**The Shelborne Beach Resort** 1801 Collins Ave. **531-1271/(800) 327-8757** gay-friendly • poolside bar • terrace cafe • IGLTA

**South Florida Hotel Network** 538-3616/(800) 538-3616 gay-friendly • hotel reservations • vacation rentals • IGLTA • gay-owned/run

**Villa Paradiso Guesthouse** 1415 Collins Ave. **532-0616** gay-friendly • studios • $75-115

**The Winterhaven** 1400 Ocean Dr. **531-5571/(800) 395-2322** gay-friendly • classic Deco architecture • also restaurant • full bar • cafe • IGLTA • $45-125

## Bars & Nightclubs

**821** 821 Lincoln Rd. **531-1188** 3pm-4am • gay-friendly • popular women's night Th from 6pm • neighborhood bar • dancing/DJ • live shows

**Amnesia** 136 Collins Ave. **531-5535** 6pm-3am Sun • mostly gay men • dancing/DJ

**Bash** 655 Washington Ave. **538-2274** 10pm-5am, clsd Mon • gay-friendly • dancing/DJ • patio

**Comedy Zone** 1121 Washington Ave. **672-4788** clsd Mon-Wed • gay-friendly • call for events

**Groove Jet** 323 23rd St. **532-2002** gay-friendly • dancing/DJ • live shows • call for events

**Liquid** 1439 Washington Ave. **532-9154** 11pm-5am, clsd Tue • lounge (decorated by Madonna's brother) open from 9pm nightly • more gay Sun

**Salvation** 1771 West Ave. **673-6508** Sat only • lesbians/gay men • dancing/DJ • alternative

**Swirl** 1049 Washington Ave. **534-2060** clsd Mon • lesbians/gay men • dancing/DJ • call for events

**Twist** 1057 Washington Ave. **538-9478** 1pm-5am • popular • mostly gay men • neighborhood bar • dancing/DJ • wheelchair access

**The Warsaw** 1450 Collins Ave. **531-4555** 9:30pm-5am, clsd Mon-Tue & Th • popular • mostly gay men • dancing/DJ • live shows • alternative

## Cafes

**Hollywood Juice Bar** 704 Lincoln Rd. **538-8988**

**News Cafe** 800 Ocean Dr. **538-6397** 24hrs • popular • healthy sandwiches • some veggie • $4-6

## Restaurants

**11th Street Diner** 11th & Washington **534-6373** til midnight, 24hrs on wknds • some veggie • full bar • $6-14

**A Fish Called Avalon** 700 Ocean Dr. **532-1727** 6pm-11pm • popular • some veggie • full bar • patio • wheelchair access • $12-22

**Bang** 1516 Washington **531-2361** popular • int'l • full bar • $17-28

**Beehive** 630 Lincoln Rd. **538-7484** noon-midnight • pizza/pasta • patio

**El Rancho Grande** 1626 Pennsylvania Ave. **673-0480** Mexican

**The Front Porch** 1420 Ocean Dr. **531-8300** 8am-midnight • healthy homecooking • some veggie • full bar • $6-10

**Jams Tavern & Grill** 1331 Washington **532-6700** 11am-5am • full bar

**Jeffrey's** 1629 Michigan Ave. **673-0690** 6pm-11pm, from 5pm Sun, clsd Mon • bistro

**Joe's Stone Crab** 227 Biscayne St. **673-0365**

**Larios on the Beach** 820 Ocean Dr. **532-9577** 11am-midnight, til 2am Fri-Sat • Cuban • $5-12

**The Living Room** 671 Washington Ave. **532-2340** 8:30pm-2am • some veggie • full bar • wheelchair access • $7-12

**Lucky Cheng's** 600 Lincoln Rd. **672-1505** 6pm-midnight • popular • live shows • full bar • 'fabulous Latasian cuisine'

**Lulu's** 1053 Washington **532-6147** 11am-2am • popular • Southern homecooking • full bar • wheelchair access • $5-11

**Norma's on the Beach** 646 Lincoln Ave. **532-2809** opens 4pm, clsd Mon • popular • Caribbean • full bar • $11-19

**Oak Feed** 2911 Grand Ave. **446-9036** 11am-10pm • health food store

**Pacific Time** 915 Lincoln Rd. **534-5979** lunch & dinner weekdays • Pan-Pacific • some veggie • beer/wine • $10-30

**Palace Bar & Grill** 1200 Ocean Dr. **531-9077** 8am-2am • full bar • $10-15

**Something Special** 7762 NW 14th Ct. (private home) **696-8826** noon-9pm, 2pm-7pm Sun • women only • vegetarian • plenty veggie • also tent space

**Sushi Rock Cafe** 1351 Collins Ave. **532-2133** full bar

**Wolfie's Jewish Deli** 2038 Collins Ave. (at 21st) **538-6626** 24hrs • $6-8

## BOOKSTORES & RETAIL SHOPS

**The 9th Chakra** 817 Lincoln Rd. **538-0671** clsd Mon • metaphysical books • supplies • gifts

**GW's** 720 Lincoln Rd. Mall **534-4763** 11am-10pm, til midnight Fri-Sat • lesbigay emporium • wheelchair access

**The Seeker of The Light** 536 Lincoln Rd. **531-1455** 11am-8pm, til midnight Fri-Sat, from noon Sun • metaphysical bookstore • lesbigay section • supplies • readings

**Whittal & Schön** 1319 Washington **538-2606** 11am-9pm, til midnight Fri-Sat • funky clothes

**WOW Boutique** 3415 Main Hwy. **443-9993** noon-8pm • club clothes

## PUBLICATIONS

**The Fountain (954) 565-7479** statewide lesbian magazine

**Lips 534-4830** 'Florida's newspaper for the contemporary woman'

**Wire 538-3111** guide to South Beach

## TRAVEL AGENTS

**Colours Destinations** 255 W. 24th St. **532-9341/(800) 277-4825** IGLTA • gay-owned/run

**Distinctive Travel Company** 18327 NE 19th Ave. **931-4443/(800) 216-6170** IGLTA

**Florida Best Travel Services** 1905 Collins Ave. **673-0909** IGLTA

**Z-Max Travel** 420 Lincoln Rd. #239 **532-0111/(800) 864-6429** hotel reservations, tours & events • call for special bar admissions • IGLTA

## GYMS & HEALTH CLUBS

**Body Tech** 1253 Washington Ave. **674-8222** popular • gay-friendly

**David Barton Gym** 1685 Collins Ave. **674-5757**

## EROTICA

**Pleasure Emporium** 1019 5th St. **673-3311** large section for women only

# Naples                                    (941)

## INFO LINES & SERVICES

**Lesbian/Gay AA 262-6535** several mtgs.

## ACCOMMODATIONS

**Festive Flamingo B&B 455-8833** lesbians/gay men • swimming

## BARS & NIGHTCLUBS

**The Galley** 509 3rd St. S. **262-2808** 11am-2am, from 1pm Sun • lesbians/gay men • more women Fri • neighborhood bar • food served

## CAFES

**Cafe Flamingo** 536 9th St. N. **262-8181**
7:30am-2:30pm • some veggie • women-
owned/run • $3-7

## BOOKSTORES & RETAIL SHOPS

**Book Nook** 824 5th Ave. S. **262-4740**
8am-7pm • general • wheelchair access
**Lavender's** 5600 Trail Blvd. #4 **594-9499**
noon-5pm, til 4pm Sat, clsd Sun-Mon •
lesbigay bookstore & pride shop

## Ocala                              (352)

### BARS & NIGHTCLUBS

**Connection** 3331 S. Pine Ave. (US 441)
**620-2511** 2pm-2am • lesbians/gay men •
neighborhood bar • wheelchair access

### BOOKSTORES & RETAIL SHOPS

**Barnes & Noble** 3500 SW College Rd.
**854-3999** lesbigay section

### EROTICA

**Secrets of Ocala** 815 N. Magnolia Ave.
**622-3858**

## Orlando                          (407)

### INFO LINES & SERVICES

**Gay/Lesbian Community Center** 714 E.
Colonial Ave. **425-4527** 11am-9pm, noon-
5pm Sat, clsd Sun • also lesbigay library
**Gay/Lesbian Community Services of
Central Florida** 843-4297 24hr touchtone helpline • extensive referrals
**LCN (Loving Committed Network)** 332-
2311 lesbian community social/support
group • monthly events • 'LCN Express'
newsletter

### ACCOMMODATIONS

**The Garden Cottage B&B** 1309 E.
Washington Ave. **894-5395** popular • les-
bians/gay men • quaint & romantic
1920s private cottage in gay downtown
area • women-owned/run • $70-95
**Leora's B&B** 649-0009 women only •
$45-75
**Parliament House Motor Inn** 410 N.
Orange Blossom Trail **425-7571** popular
• mostly gay men • swimming • live
shows • food served • full bar from 8pm
• $44
**Rick's B&B** 396-7751 lesbians/gay men
• full brkfst • swimming • patio

**Things Worth Remembering B&B** 7338
Cabor Ct. **291-2127/(800) 484-3585
x6908** gay-friendly • collection of memo
rabilia from TV, movies, Broadway •
kitchen use • smokefree • $65-70
**The Veranda B&B** 115 N. Summerlin
Ave. **849-0321/(800) 420-6822** gay-
friendly • located in downtown Orlando
• hot tub • wheelchair access • $99-189

### BARS & NIGHTCLUBS

**The Cactus Club** 1300 N. Mills Ave. **894-
3041** 3pm-2am • mostly gay men • professional • patio
**Cairo** 22 S. Magnolia **422-3595** gay-
friendly • clsd Sun-Tue • dancing/DJ •
more gay Th • rooftop patio
**The Club** 578 N. Orange Ave. **426-0005**
popular • lesbians/gay men • dancing/DJ
• 18+ • live shows • videos • call for
events
**Copa** 5454 International Dr. **351-4866**
4pm-2am • gay-friendly • more gay Sun-
Wed • appetizers • wheelchair access
**Copper Rocket** 106 Lake Ave., Maitland
**645-0069** 11:30am-2am, from 4pm wknds
• gay-friendly • also restaurant • micro
brews • wheelchair access
**Faces** 4910 Edgewater Dr. **291-7571**
4pm-2am • popular • mostly women •
dancing/DJ • live shows • wheelchair
access
**Full Moon Saloon** 500 N. Orange
Blossom Tr. **648-8725** noon-2am • mostly gay men • leather • country/western •
patio
**The Galleria** 3400 S. Orange Blossom Tr.
**423-7590** noon-2am • lesbians/gay men
• dancing • live shows
**Hank's** 5026 Edgewater Dr. **291-2399**
noon-2am • mostly gay men • neighborhood bar • patio • wheelchair access
**Mannequins** Pleasure Island at Disney
World popular on Th (Employee Night)
• otherwise very straight • dancing/DJ
**Metopolis** 8562 Palm Bay (shopping center) **239-4919** gay-friendly • more gay
Wed
**Phoenix** 7124 Aloma Ave., Winter Park
**678-9220** 4pm-2am, clsd Mon-Wed •
gay-friendly • more gay Sat • Goth bands
other nights • call for events
**Sadie's Tavern** 415 S. Orlando Ave.,
Winter Park **628-4562** 4pm-2am, til midnight Sun • mostly women • neighborhood bar • patio • wheelchair access

# Orlando

or most vacationers, Orlando means one thing: Disney World. Disney has been in the news of late as a supporter of gay civil rights. If you're a fan of the Mouse, show your appreciation during the first weekend of June at Disney's (unofficial) Gay Days. "Family" traditionally wear red T-shirts, while protesters wear white. Queer Christians go for red-and-white stripes!

But save some time for the enormous Epcot Center and MGM Studios, too. You'll need at least three days to traverse the 27,000 acres of this entertainment mecca. And if you still crave infotainment, visit Universal Studios, Wet 'n' Wild, Sea World, the Tupperware Museum (yes, Tupperware), Busch Gardens, or Cypress Gardens, a natural wonderland of lagoons, moss-draped trees and exotic plants from around the world. Call the **GLCS** to find out when the next Gay Day in the Busch (Gardens, that is) will be. If you like fairs, be sure to stop by the Central Florida Fair in February for Gay/Lesbian day at the fair.

**Faces** is the neighborhood dyke bar, while **Southern Nights** and **The Club** (aka Firestone) are the places to dance. For education, stop by the local lesbigay store, **Out & About Books,** or the **Gay/Lesbian Community Center,** and pick up a copy of the **Watermark** or **The Triangle.**

And for fun, watch a lesbian/gay-themed movie at The Club on Monday nights. The lesbian social group **LCN** sponsors plenty of other events, including picnics at Wekiva Falls in the spring and around Halloween, and a dance in mid-January.

**Southern Nights** 375 S. Bumby Ave. **898-0424** 4pm-2am • lesbians/gay men • more women Sat • dancing/DJ • live shows • wheelchair access

**Stable** 410 N. Orange Blossom Tr. (at 'Parliament House') **425-7571** 8pm-2am • mostly gay men • country/western

**Union** 337 N. Shine Ave. **894-5778** 11am-11pm • lesbians/gay men • neighborhood bar • food served

**Will's Pub** 1820-50 N. Mills Ave. **898-5070** 4pm-2am • gay-friendly • many lesbians • neighborhood bar • food served • beer/wine • wheelchair access • also 'Loch Haven Motor Inn' • 896-3611

CAFES

**White Wolf Cafe & Antique Shop** 1829 N. Orange Ave. **895-5590** 10am-midnight, clsd Sun • salads/sandwiches • plenty veggie • beer/wine • live shows • wheelchair access • $5-12

## RESTAURANTS

**Cafe Citron** 1869 W. SR 434 (Longwood Village Shoppes), Longwood **831-2504** lunch & dinner, clsd Sun • Happy Hour 5pm-7pm

**Dug Out Diner** (at 'Parliament House') **425-7571x711** 24hrs • lesbians/gay men

**Hemingway's at the Hyatt** 1 Grand Cypress Blvd., Lake Buena Vista **239-1234** cont'l • $20-25

**Le Cordon Bleu** 537 W. Fairbanks Ave., Winter Park **647-7575** French • $20-25

**Le Provence** 50 E. Pine St. **843-1320** lunch & dinner, clsd Sun • French bistro • full bar • live jazz

**Taqueria Queztzalcoatl** 350 W. Fairbanks Ave., Winter Park **629-4123** 11am-11pm, from noon Sun • Mexican • some veggie • beer/wine

**Thorton Park Cafe** 900 E. Washington **425-0033** 11am-10pm • seafood/Italian • some veggie • beer/wine • patio • wheelchair access • $9-17

## ENTERTAINMENT & RECREATION

**Family Values** WPRK 91.5 FM 7pm Wed • lesbigay radio from Rollins College

**Universal Studios Florida** 1000 Universal Studios Pl. **363-8000/(800) 232-7827**

## BOOKSTORES & RETAIL SHOPS

**Out & About Books** 930 N. Mills Ave. **896-0204** 10am-8pm, noon-6pm Sun • lesbigay

**Rainbow City** 934 N. Mills Ave. **898-6096** lesbigay giftshop

## PUBLICATIONS

**The Triangle** 849-0099

**Watermark** 481-2243

**Women's Network Yellow Pages** 896-4444

## TRAVEL AGENTS

**Odyssey** 334 E. Michigan St. **841-8686/(800) 327-4441** IGLTA

**Priority Travel Services** 291 E. Altamonte Dr. #1, Altamonte Springs **830-7198/(800) 899-3506** IGLTA

**Tuscawilla Travel** 1020 Spring Villas Pt., Winter Springs **699-4700/(800) 872-8566** IGLTA

**Universal Travel Services** 5728 Major Blvd. #611 **345-0368** IGLTA

## SPIRITUAL GROUPS

**Integrity/Central Florida** 332-2743 4th Sun • call for time & location

**Joy MCC** 2351 S. Ferncreek Ave **894-1081** 9:15am & 11am, 7:15pm Sun • wheelchair access

## EROTICA

**Absolute Leather** 942 N. Mills Ave. **896-8808/(800) 447-4820** wheelchair access

**Fairvilla Video** 1740 N. Orange Blossom Tr. **425-5352**

**The Leather Closet** 498 N. Orange Blossom Tr. **649-2011** noon-2am • wheelchair access

# Orlando (407)

**Where the Girls Are:** Women who live here hang out at Will's Pub. Tourists are—where else?—at the tourist attractions, including the Mannequins bar in Disney World.

**Entertainment:** Orlando Gay Chorus: 645-5866.

**Lesbigay Pride:** June.

**Annual Events:**

June (1st Sat) - **Gay Day at Disney World:** 857-5444.

**City Info:** 363-5871.

**Attractions:** Walt Disney World (824-4321). Universal Studios. Wet & Wild Waterpark. Sea World.

**Weather:** Mild winters, hot summers.

**Transit:** Yellow Cab: 699-9999. Gray Line: 422-0744. Lynx: 841-8240.

## Palm Beach (561)

### ACCOMMODATIONS

**Heart of Palm Beach** 160 Royal Palm Wy. **655-5600** gay-friendly • charming, friendly European-style hotel • swimming • kids ok • also restaurant • full bar • $69-199

### RESTAURANTS

**Ta-Boo** 221 Worth Ave. **835-3500** 11:30am-10:30pm • French/Italian • live shows • wheelchair access • $12-25

### TRAVEL AGENTS

**Royal Palm Travel** 223 Sunset Ave. **659-6080** IGLTA

## Palm Beach Gardens (561)

### TRAVEL AGENTS

**Vagabond Travels** 601 Northlake Blvd. **848-0648/(800) 226-3830** IGLTA

## Panama City (904)

### BARS & NIGHTCLUBS

**Fiesta Room** 110 Harrison Ave. **784-9285** 8pm-3am • popular • lesbians/gay men • dancing/DJ • live shows • wheelchair access

**La Royale Lounge & Liquor Store** 100 Harrison **784-9311** 3pm-3am • lesbians/gay men • neighborhood bar • courtyard • wheelchair access

## Pembroke Pines (954)

### RESTAURANTS

**Blue Goose Cafe** 1491 N. Palm Ave. **436-8677** from 5:30pm, clsd Mon • game • some veggie • beer/wine • wheelchair access • $7-15

## Pensacola (904)

### INFO LINES & SERVICES

**AA Gay/Lesbian** 415 N. Alcaniz (MCC location) **433-8528** 7:30pm Mon & Fri

### ACCOMMODATIONS

**Noble Manor B&B** 110 W. Strong St. **434-9544** gay-friendly • hot tub

### BARS & NIGHTCLUBS

**Club Heat** 406 E. Wright St. **438-1112** 9pm-3am, clsd Mon-Tue • mostly gay men • dancing/DJ • wheelchair access

**Numbers Pub** 200 S. Alcaniz **438-9004** 4pm-3am • mostly men • dancing/DJ

**The Office** 406 E. Wright St. **433-7278** 11am-3am • mostly women • neighborhood bar

**Red Carpet** 937 Warrington Rd. **453-9918** 3pm-3am • mostly women • dancing/DJ • live shows • patio • wheelchair access

**Red Garter** 1 W. Main St. **433-9292** 8pm-3am • lesbians/gay men • dancing/DJ • live shows • wheelchair access

**The Riviera** 120 E. Main St. **432-1234** noon-3am • lesbians/gay men • more women Wed • live shows • patio • wheelchair access

**Round-up** 706 E. Gregory **433-8482** 2pm-3am • popular • mostly gay men • videos • patio • wheelchair access

**Seville Park Lounge** 312 E. Government St. **434-3506** 2pm-3am • lesbians/gay men • dancing/DJ • live shows • wheelchair access

### CAFES

**The Secret Cafe** 23 S. Palafox Pl. **444-9020** call for hours • coffeehouse & gallery • women-owned/run

### BOOKSTORES & RETAIL SHOPS

**Pensacola Pride** 9 E. Gregory **435-7272** 11am-7pm • lesbigay

**Silver Chord Bookstore** 10901 Lillian Hwy. **453-6652** 10am-6pm, clsd Mon • metaphysical • lesbigay section • wheelchair access

### SPIRITUAL GROUPS

**Holy Cross MCC** 415 N. Alcaniz **433-8528** 11am Sun & 7pm Wed

## Port Richey (813)

### BARS & NIGHTCLUBS

**BT's** 7737 Grand Blvd. **841-7900** 6pm-2am • lesbians/gay men • dancing/DJ • live shows • wheelchair access

### SPIRITUAL GROUPS

**Spirit of Life MCC** 4133 Thys Rd., New Port Richey **849-6962** 10am Sun & 7:30pm Wed • wheelchair access

## Port St. Lucie (561)

### BARS & NIGHTCLUBS

**Bourbon St. Cabaret & Cafe** 2727 SE Morningside Blvd. **335-8608** 11:30am-2am, from 1pm Sun • popular • lesbians/gay men • more women Tue • live shows • food served • steak & seafood • some veggie • wheelchair access • $6-14

## Sarasota (941)

### INFO LINES & SERVICES
**ALSO** 252-2576 **(PAGER)** gay, lesbian & bisexual youth • confidential weekly mtgs.

**Friends Group (Gay AA)** 2080 Ringling Blvd. #302 **951-6810** 8pm Mon, Wed & Fri

**Gay Info Line** 923-4636

### ACCOMMODATIONS
**The Cypress** 621 Gulfstream Ave. S. **955-4683** gay-friendly • B&B inn on historic grounds overlooking Sarasota Bay • full gourmet brkfst

**Normandy Inn** 400 N. Tamiami Tr. **366-8979/(800) 282-8050** gay-friendly

**Siesta Holiday House** 1011-1015 Crescent St., Siesta Key **488-6809/(800) 720-6885** gay-friendly • smokefree • gay-owned

### BARS & NIGHTCLUBS
**Bumpers (Club X)** 1927 Ringling Blvd. **951-0335** 9pm-2:30am • gay-friendly • more gay Th & Sun • dancing/DJ • live shows

**Christopher Street** 6543 Gateway Ave. (behind Gulf Gate Mall) **927-8766** 4pm-2am, from 6pm wknds • mostly gay men • dancing/DJ • live shows

**Club Chada** 2941 N. Tamiani **355-7210** 3pm-2am • mostly women • neighborhood bar • live shows

**HG Rooster's** 1256 Old Stickney Pt. Rd. **346-3000** 3pm-2am • mostly gay men • neighborhood bar • live shows

**Ricky J's** 1330 Martin Luther King Jr. Wy. **953-5945** 3pm-2am • popular • mostly gay men • dancing/DJ • live shows • patio • wheelchair access

### ENTERTAINMENT & RECREATION
**Sarasota Bay Watcher** 377-0799 fishing from the shore • everything provided • woman-owned/run

### BOOKSTORES & RETAIL SHOPS
**Charlie's** 1341 Main St. **953-4688** 9am-10pm, til 5pm Sun • books • magazines • cards

### PUBLICATIONS
**Rainbow Pages Magazine** 488-4496

### TRAVEL AGENTS
**A+ Travel of Sarasota** 230 N. Lime Ave. **951-6866/(800) 275-8779** IGLTA

**Forest Lakes Travel** 3618 Webber St. #101 **923-6474/(800) 922-4818** IGLTA

**Horizon Travel** 1516 Main St. **362-0166/(800) 719-7892** IGLTA

### SPIRITUAL GROUPS
**Church of the Trinity MCC** 7225 N. Lockwood Ridge Rd. **355-0847** 10am Sun • wheelchair access

**Suncoast Cathedral MCC** 3276 Venice Ave. **484-7068** 11am Sun • women's 45+ group last Sat of month

## Satellite Beach (407)

### EROTICA
**Space Age Books & Temptations** 63 Ocean Blvd. **773-7660**

## Sebastian (561)

### ACCOMMODATIONS
**The Pink Lady Inn** 1309 Louisiana Ave. **589-1345** mostly women • swimming • kitchens • women-owned/run

## South Beach
*(see Miami Beach/South Beach)*

## St. Augustine (904)

### ACCOMMODATIONS
**Pagoda** 2854 Coastal Hwy. **824-2970** women only • guesthouse • near beach • swimming • kitchen privileges • wheelchair access • women-owned/run • $20-35

## St. Cloud (407)

### TRAVEL AGENTS
**Get Outta Town! Travel** 2532 Longpine Ln. **957-8870/(800) 849-6545** IGLTA

## St. Petersburg (813)
*(see also Tampa)*

### INFO LINES & SERVICES
**Gay Information Line (The Line)** 586-4297 volunteers 7pm-11pm • touchtone 24hrs

**WEB (Women's Energy Bank)** 823-5353 many services & activities for lesbians

### ACCOMMODATIONS
**The Barge House** 360-0729 women only • cabana & cottages • 1/2 blk to beach • hot tub • women-owned/run • $74-85

**Bay Gables B&B and Garden** 136 4th Ave. NE **822-8855/(800) 822-8803** gay-friendly • smokefree • kids ok

**Boca Ciega** 3526 Boca Ciega Dr. N. **381-2755** women only • swimming • lesbian-owned/run • $40-50

**Feathers B&B** 2107 Burlington Ave. N. **321-1766** women only • full brkfst

**Frog Pond Guesthouse** 145 29th Ave. N. **823-7407** gay-friendly • smokefree • $65

**Pass-A-Grille Beach Motel** 709 Gulfway Blvd., St. Petersburg Beach **367-4726** gay-friendly • swimming

**Sea Oats & Dunes** 12620 Gulf Blvd., Treasure Island **367-7568** gay-friendly • motel & apts on the Gulf of Mexico • $295-595/week

### BARS & NIGHTCLUBS

**D.T.'s** 2612 Central Ave. **327-8204** 2pm-2am • mostly gay men • neighborhood bar • wheelchair access

**The Hideaway** 8302 4th St. N. **570-9025** 2pm-2am • mostly womens • neighborhood bar • live shows • wheelchair access

**The New Connection** 3100 3rd Ave. N. **321-2112** 1pm-2am • lesbians/gay men • 3 bars • neighborhood bar • dancing/DJ

**Sharp A's** 4918 22nd Ave. S., Gulfport **327-4897** 4pm-2am • popular • lesbians/gay men • dancing/DJ • wheelchair access

**VIP Lounge & Mexican Food Grill** 10625 Gulf Blvd. **360-5062** 10am-2am • gay-friendly • wheelchair access

### CAFES

**Beaux Arts** 2635 Central Ave. **328-0702** noon-5pm • historic gallery w/coffeehouse • sponsors events

### RESTAURANTS

**Magnolia R&B Cafe** 5853 Haines Rd. N. **527-1611** 4pm-9pm, til 10pm Fri-Sat, clsd Sun • live shows • beer/wine • wheelchair access • women-owned • $8-14

### BOOKSTORES & RETAIL SHOPS

**Affinity Books** 2435 9th St. N. **823-3662/(800) 355-3662** 10am-6pm, til 8pm Wed-Fri, til 5pm Sat, noon-5pm Sun • lesbigay • wheelchair access

**Brigit Books** 3434 4th St. N. **522-5775** 10am-8pm, til 6pm Fri-Sat, 1pm-5pm Sun • women's/feminist

**P.S.** 111 2nd Ave. NE **823-2937** 10am-6pm • cards • gifts

### PUBLICATIONS

**Womyn's Words** 823-5353

### TRAVEL AGENTS

**Travel Beyond** 2525 Pasadena Ave. #N **367-3737/(800) 237-4070** IGLTA

### SPIRITUAL GROUPS

**King of Peace MCC** 3150 5th Ave. N. **323-5857** 10am • wheelchair access

### EROTICA

**Triskel Leather Customs** 5924 4th St. N. 6-A **528-8992** call first • toys • novelties • body jewelry

## Tallahassee                    (850)

### INFO LINES & SERVICES

**Florida Division of Tourism** 487-1462

### BARS & NIGHTCLUBS

**Brothers Bar** 926 W. Tharpe St. **386-2399** 4pm-2am • lesbians/gay men • dancing/DJ • 18+ • live shows • videos • wheelchair access

**Club Park Ave.** 115 E. Park Ave. **599-9143** 10pm-2am • popular • gay-friendly • more gay wknds • mostly African-American Sun • dancing/DJ • live shows

### RESTAURANTS

**The Village Inn** 2690 N. Monroe St. **385-2903** dinner • 24hrs wknds • popular

### BOOKSTORES & RETAIL SHOPS

**Rubyfruit Books** 739 N. Monroe St. **222-2627** 10:30am-6:30pm, til 8pm Th, clsd Sun • alternative bookstore • gay titles • coffeehouse • wheelchair access

## Tampa                    (813)

*(see also St. Petersburg)*

### INFO LINES & SERVICES

**Gay Information Line (The Line)** 586-4297 volunteers 7pm-11pm • touchtone service 24hrs

**Gay/Lesbian Community Center of Tampa** 273-8919 soon to open • call for location

**University of South Florida Gay/Lesbian/Bisexual Coalition** CTR 2466, 4202 E. Fowler Ave. **974-4297**

**Women's Center** 677-8136 women's helpline

## ACCOMMODATIONS

**Gram's Place B&B & Artist Retreat**
3109 N. Ola Ave. **221-0596** lesbians/gay men • nudity • hot tub • BYOB • $45-100

**Ruskin House B&B** 120 Dickman Dr. SW, Ruskin **645-3842** gay-friendly • 1910 multi-story home • 30 min. S. of Tampa & 30 min. N. of Sarasota • full brkfst • $45-65

## BARS & NIGHTCLUBS

**2606** 2606 N. Armenia Ave. **875-6993** 3pm-3am • popular • mostly gay men • also leather shop from 9pm • wheelchair access

**Cherokee Club** 1320 E. 9th Ave., 2nd flr., Ybor City **247-9966** 9pm-3am Fri-Sat only • mostly women • dancing/DJ • live shows • call for events

**City Side** 3810 Neptune St. **254-6466** noon-3am • mostly gay men • neighborhood bar • professional • patio

**The Factory at the Garage** 802 E.Whiting **221-2582** gay Fri only • mostly gay men • dancing/DJ

**Flavour** Palm Ave. & 15th, Ybor City **242-8007** lesbians/gay men • dancing/DJ

**Impulse Channelside Village** 302 S. Nebraska Ave. **223-2780** 3pm-3am • T-dance Sun • mostly gay men • dancing/DJ • videos • patio • wheelchair access

**Jungle** 3703 Henderson Blvd. **877-3290** 1pm-3am • mostly gay men • neighborhood bar • gourmet buffet Fri & Sun • patio

**Metropolis** 3447 W. Kennedy Blvd. **871-2410** noon-3am, 1pm-3am Sun • mostly gay men • neighborhood bar • live shows Fri • wheelchair access

**Northside Lounge** 9002 N. Florida Ave. **931-3396** noon-3am • mostly gay men • neighborhood bar

**Pleasuredome** 1430 E. 7th Ave. **247-2711** 9pm-3am, clsd Sun-Mon & Wed • gay-friendly • dancing/DJ • wheelchair access

**Rascal's** 105 W. Martin Luther King Blvd. **237-8883** 4pm-3am, from noon Sun • lesbians/gay men • also restaurant • cont'l/American • some veggie • $4-13

**Sahara's** 4643 W. Kennedy Blvd. **282-0183** noon-3am • mostly women • neighborhood bar

**Solar** 911 Franklin St. **226-9227** 10am-3am • lesbian/gay men • live shows • patio • wheelchair access

## CAFES

**Sacred Grounds** 11118 30th St. N. **631-0035** 5:30pm-1am Mon-Th, til 2am wknds, 6:30pm-midnight Sun • lesbians/gay men • women-owned/run

## RESTAURANTS

**Boca** 20th & 7th Ave., Ybor City **241-2622** lunch & dinner • 4-course Sun brunch • 2 full bars

**Ho Ho Chinese** 720 S. Howard **254-9557** 11:30am-10pm • full bar • wheelchair access • gay-owned

**La Tereseta** 3248 W. Tampa **879-4909** Cuban/Spanish • full bar

**Taqueria Queztzalcoatl** 402 S. Howard Ave. **259-9982** 11am-11pm, from noon Sun • Mexican • some veggie • beer/wine

## ENTERTAINMENT & RECREATION

**The Women's Show** WMNF (88.5 FM) **238-8001** 10am-noon Sat

## BOOKSTORES & RETAIL SHOPS

**Tomes & Treasures** 408 S. Howard Ave. **251-9368** 11am-8pm, 1pm-6pm Sun • lesbigay

## PUBLICATIONS

**Encounter** 877-7913
**Gazette** 689-7566
**Stonewall** 832-2878

## TRAVEL AGENTS

**Deluxe Travel Professionals Int'l** 13186 N. Dale Mabry Hwy. **784-1831/(888) 375-9622** IGLTA

**First Travel** 337 S. Plant Ave. **254-2007/(800) 327-3367** IGLTA

**Millennium Travel** 761 S. Pinellas Ave., Tarpon Springs **944-2000/(800) 585-9757** IGLTA

**Passport Travel Management Group** 1503 W. Busch Blvd. #A **931-3166** IGLTA

**Tampa Bay Travel Corp.** 4830 W. Kennedy #148 **286-4202/(800) 298-3740** IGLTA

**Travel Agents International** 4559 Gunn Hwy. **968-3600** IGLTA

**Travel Services Unlimited** 726 S. Dale Mabry **877-4040/(800) 874-4711** IGLTA

## SPIRITUAL GROUPS

**Dignity** 3010 Perry Ave. **238-2868** 7pm Sun

**MCC** 408 Cayuga St. **239-1951** 10:30am Sun

### GYMS & HEALTH CLUBS
**Metro Flex Fitness** 2511 Swann Ave. 876-3539

## Venice (941)

### RESTAURANTS
**Maggie May's** 1550 US 41 Bypass South **497-1077** 8am-3pm, til 2pm wknds • home cooking • some veggie • beer/wine • women-owned/run • wheelchair access

## Vero Beach (561)

### TRAVEL AGENTS
**Radcliff Travel & Tours** 13090 North A1A **388-9035/(800) 398-7522** IGLTA

## West Palm Beach (561)

### INFO LINES & SERVICES
**Compass Community Center** 1700 N. Dixie Hwy. **833-3638** 10am-10pm • wheelchair access

**The Whimsey 686-1354** resources & archives • political clearinghouse • also camping/RV space & apt • wheelchair access

### ACCOMMODATIONS
**Hibiscus House B&B** 501 30th St. **863-5633/(800) 203-4927** lesbians/gay men • full brkfst • swimming • smokefree • IGLTA • $75-160

**Tropical Gardens B&B** 419 32nd St. Old Northwood **848-4064/(800) 736-4064** mostly gay men • swimming • $65-125

### BARS & NIGHTCLUBS
**5101 Bar** 5101 S. Dixie Hwy. **585-2379** 7am-3am, til 4am Fri-Sat, from noon Sun • mostly gay men • neighborhood bar

**B.G.'s Bar** 5700 S. Dixie Hwy. **533-3800** 7am-3am, from noon Sun • mostly gay men • neighborhood bar • live shows • karaoke • wheelchair access

**Enigma** 109 N. Olive Ave. **832-5040** 9pm-3am, clsd Mon-Wed • lesbians/gay men • dancing/DJ • alternative

**H.G. Rooster's** 823 Belvedere Rd. **832-9119** 3pm-3am, til 4am Fri-Sat • popular • mostly gay men • neighborhood bar • wheelchair access

**Heartbreaker** 2677 Forrest Hill Blvd. **966-1590** 10pm-5am Wed-Sun • popular • lesbians/gay men • more women Fri • 'Chatters Lounge' from 5pm daily • dancing/DJ • live shows • karaoke • videos

**Kozlow's** 6205 Georgia Ave. **533-5355** noon-2am • popular • mostly gay men • neighborhood bar • country/western • private club • patio • wheelchair access

**Leather & Spurs WPB** 5004 S. Dixie Hwy. **547-1020** 7pm-3am, til 4am wknds • mostly gay men • leather • food served • beer only

**Respectable Street Cafe** 518 Clematis St. **832-9999** 9pm-2am, clsd Sun-Tue • live shows • ladies night Wed

### RESTAURANTS
**Antonio's South** 3001 S. Congress Ave., Palm Springs **965-0707** dinner only, clsd Sun • popular • southern Italian • beer/wine • $9-18

**Down Dixie Grill** 3815 S. Dixie Hwy. **832-4959** lunch Mon-Fri & dinner nightly

**Rhythm Does Ranch** 3800 S. Dixie Hwy. **833-3406** 7am-10pm, clsd Sun • some veggie • beer/wine • $12-19

### BOOKSTORES & RETAIL SHOPS
**Changing Times Bookstore** 911 Village Blvd. #806 **640-0496** 10am-7pm, noon-5pm Sun • spiritual • lesbigay section • community bulletin board • wheelchair access

**Eurotique** 3109 45th St. #300 **684-2302** 11am-7pm Mon-Fri, noon-6pm Sat • leather • books • videos

### PUBLICATIONS
**Community Voice** 471-1528

### SPIRITUAL GROUPS
**MCC** 3500 W. 45th St. #2-A **687-3943** 11am Sun

**DON'T WAIT ANOTHER YEAR!**
YOU AIN'T GETTING ANY YOUNGER, HONEY!

1 (888) 44 DINAH
CLUB SKIRTS & GIRL BAR

## GEORGIA

### Athens (706)

#### INFO LINES & SERVICES
**Lesbian Support Group** 546-4611 unconfirmed

**LGBSU (Lesbian/Gay/Bisexual Student Union)** Tate Center Rm. 137 549-9368 7pm Mon

#### BARS & NIGHTCLUBS
**Boneshakers** 433 E. Hancock Ave. 543-1555 9pm-2am, 9:30pm-3am Fri, til 4am Sat, clsd Sun • lesbians/gay men • dancing/DJ • 18+ • wheelchair access

**Forty Watt Club** 285 W. Washington St. 549-7871 gay-friendly • alternative • theme nights • wheelchair access

**Georgia Bar** 159 W. Clayton 546-9884 4pm-2am, clsd Sun • gay-friendly • more gay wknights • neighborhood bar • wheelchair access

**The Globe** 199 N. Lumpkin 353-4721 4pm-2am, clsd Sun • gay-friendly • 30 single-malt scotches

#### CAFES
**Espresso Royale Cafe** 297 E. Broad St. 613-7449 7am-midnight, from 8am wknds • best coffee in Athens • gallery • wheelchair access

#### RESTAURANTS
**The Bluebird** 493 E. Clayton 549-3663 8am-3pm, dinner Fri-Sat only • popular Sun brunch • plenty veggie • $5-10

**The Grit** 199 Prince Ave. 543-6592 11am-10pm • ethnic vegetarian • great wknd brunch • wheelchair access • $5-10

#### BOOKSTORES & RETAIL SHOPS
**Barnett's Newsstand** 147 College Ave. 353-0530 8am-10pm

### Atlanta (404)

#### INFO LINES & SERVICES
**Atlanta Gay/Lesbian Center** 71 12th St. NE 876-5372 1pm-5pm Mon-Fri • social services center • clinic

**Galano Club** 585 Dutch Valley Rd. 881-9188 lesbigay club for recovery • mtgs.

**Gay Helpline** 892-0661 24hrs • live 6pm-11pm • info & counseling

**WINK (Women in Kahoots)** (770) 438-1421 lesbian social group • monthly parties • newsletter • unconfirmed

# Atlanta

*I*f you watched the 1996 Olympic Games, you saw how proud the residents of Atlanta are of their city. Today's Southerners have worked hard to move beyond stereotypes of the Old South. Of course, Atlanta's large population of lesbians and gay men is an integral part of that work.

But the South's checkered past is a powerful agent for future understanding. Atlanta houses the must-see Martin Luther King Jr. Center and the Carter Presidential Center—tributes to icons of peace and positive change—as well as the nationally known Black Arts Festival (730-7315).

Lesbian culture in Atlanta is spread out (a car is a must) between **Charis** women's bookstore in L'il Five Points (cruise their readings), the **Atlanta Gay/Lesbian Center** in posh Midtown, and in between, along Piedmont and Cheshire Bridge roads. Midway between the gay Ansley Square area (Piedmont at Monroe) and downtown, stop by **Outwrite**, Atlanta's lesbian/gay bookstore. Pick up a copy of **Southern Voice** to scope out the political scene or Etc. to dish the bar scene. For more shopping, **Brushstrokes** is Atlanta's lesbigay goodies store.

Unless you're a serious mall-crawler, skip the overly commercial (but much hyped) Underground Atlanta, and head for Lenox Mall instead, where you'll see more stylish queers. And, just a couple miles south on Highland, you'll run smack into funky shopping, dining, and live music in the punk capital of Atlanta: L'il Five Points (not to be confused with 'Five Points' downtown).

If you're looking for women's accommodations, try the lesbian-owned **Bonaventure**. Or head an hour north to lush, wooded Dahlonega to one of the women's guesthouses.

If you're a fan of R.E.M., head northeast on Hwys. 306 or 78 about an hour-and-a-half to the university town of Athens, Georgia. Avoid visiting on weekends during footbal season, though, since traffic is hellish. Pick up a Flagpole magazine to find out what's going on, and stop by **Boneshakers**, Athens' lesbian/gay dancebar.

### ACCOMMODATIONS

**The Bonaventure** 650 Bonaventure Ave. **817-7024** gay-friendly • restored Victorian • French spoken • $100-150 • gay-owned/run

**Cottage Grove B&B** 1055 Delaware Ave. SE **622-9821** gay-friendly

**Hello B&B 892-8111** mostly gay men • private home

**Lismore House** 855 Penn Ave. **817-9640** gay-friendly

**Magnolia Station B&B** 1020 Edgewood Ave. NE **522-3923** mostly gay men • swimming • smokefree • $50-80

▲ **Midtown Manor** 811 Piedmont Ave. NE **872-5846/(800) 724-4381** gay-friendly • charming Victorian guesthouse • $65+

**Our Place 297-9825** fully furnished vacation home in N. Georgia Mtns. • lesbian-owned/run

**Quality Inn—Midtown** 870 Peachtree St. **875-5511/(800) 228-5151** gay-friendly

**Sheraton Colony Square Hotel** 188 14th St. **892-6000/(800) 325-3535** gay-friendly • gym • food served • full bar

### BARS & NIGHTCLUBS

**Armory** 836 Juniper St. NE **881-9280** 4pm-4am • popular • mostly gay men • dancing/DJ • videos • 3 bars

**Backstreet** 845 Peachtree St. NE **873-1986** 24hrs • popular • mostly gay men • dancing/DJ • live shows • videos • 3 flrs.

**Burkhart's Pub** 1492-F Piedmont Rd. (Ansley Sq. Shopping Center) **872-4403** 4pm-4am, from 2pm wknds • lesbians/gay men • neighborhood bar • wheelchair access

**The Chamber** 2115 Faulkner Rd. **248-1612** 10pm-3am, clsd Sun-Wed • gay-friendly • dancing/DJ • live shows • fetish crowd

**Circles** 710 Peachtree St. **815-6687** mostly women • mostly African-American

**E.S.S.O.** 489 Courtland St. **872-3776** 10pm-3am, clsd Sun-Wed • gay-friendly • dancing/DJ • rooftop deck • wheelchair access

# MIDTOWN MANOR

### ATLANTA'S FINEST ONCE LIVED HERE... NOW THEY DO AGAIN...HERE'S WHY:

- Authentic Victorian manor
- Private Phones & Color TV
- Close to public transportation
- Centrally located
- Off-street parking
- Laundry facilities

LOCATED IN THE HEART OF ATLANTA'S GAY DISTRICT

(800) 724-4381        (404) 872-5846
811 Piedmont Avenue N.E.    •    Atlanta, GA 30308

**Atlanta**

(404/770)

**Where the Girls Are:** Many lesbians live in DeKalb county, in the northeast part of the city Decatur. For fun, women head for Midtown or Buckhead if they're professionals, Virginia-Highlands if they're funky or 30ish, and Little Five Points if they're young and wild.

**Entertainment:** Atlanta Feminist Women's Chorus: 770/438-5823. Lefont Screening Room: 231-1924, gay film.

**Lesbigay Pride:** June.

**Annual Events:**

April- **Lesbian/Gay Arts Fest:** 874-8710. Gallery, performances. **Gay/Lesbian Film Festival:** 733-6112.

May- **Wigswood:** 874-6782. Annual festival of peace, love and wigs & street party Act Up fundraiser. Wig watchers welcome. May 22-25 - **Armory Sports Classic:** 874-2710. Softball & many other sports competitions.

August - **Hotlanta:** 874-3976. A weekend of river rafting, pageants & parties for boys. Aug 11-16 - **Gay World Series.**

December - **Women's Christmas Ball**/Good Friends for Good Causes: 770/938-1194.

**City Info:** 521-6600.

**Attractions:** Martin Luther King Memorial Center. Atlanta Botanical Gardens. Piedmont Park. CNN Center. Coca-Cola Museum. Underground Atlanta.

**Best View:** 70th floor of the Peachtree Plaza, in the Sun Dial restaurant. Also from the top of Stone Mountain.

**Weather:** Summers are warm and humid (upper 80°s to low 90°s) with occasional thunderstorms. Winters are icy with occasional snows. Temperatures can drop into the low 30°s. Spring and fall are temperate—spring brings blossoming dogwoods and magnolias, while fall festoons the trees with Northeast Georgia's awesome fall foliage.

**Transit:** 521-0200. Atlanta Airport Shuttle: 524-3400. Marta: 848-4711.

**Guys & Dolls** 2788 E. Ponce de Leon Ave., Decatur **377-2956** 11:30am-4am, from 7pm Sat, from 6pm Sun • gay-friendly • more gay Tue & Sun • live shows • stripper bar • food served • wheelchair access

**Hoedowns** 931 Monroe Dr. **876-0001** 3pm-3am • popular • mostly gay men • dancing/DJ • country/western • live shows • wheelchair access

**Kaya** 1068 Peachtree St. NE **874-4460** 6pm-midnight, til 4am Fri • lesbians/gay men • dancing/DJ • mostly African-American • also restaurant • some veggie • live shows • patio • $6-12

**Le Buzz** 585 Franklin Rd. (Longhorn Plaza), Marietta **(770) 424-1337** 6pm-2am, from noon during summer • mostly gay men • neighborhood bar

**Loretta's** 708 Spring St. NW **874-8125** 6pm-4am • gay-friendly • neighborhood bar • dancing/DJ • mostly African-American • live shows • wheelchair access

**Model T** 699 Ponce de Leon **872-2209** 9am-4am • lesbians/gay men • neighborhood bar • live shows • wheelchair access

**Moreland Tavern** 1196 Moreland Ave. SE **622-4650** 11am-4am • lesbians/gay men • neighborhood bar • food served • patio • wheelchair access

**My Sister's Room** 931 Monroe Dr. (upstairs in the back) **875-6699** 5pm-2am • mostly women • food served • some veggie

**Opus I** 1086 Alco St. NE **634-6478** 9pm-4am • mostly gay men • neighborhood bar • wheelchair access

▲ **The Otherside of Atlanta** 1924 Piedmont Rd. **875-5238** 6pm-4am • popular • lesbians/gay men • dancing/DJ • country/western • live shows • food served • videos • patio • women-owned/run

**Revolution—Midtown** 1492-B Piedmont Ave. (Ansley Sq. Shopping Cntr.) **874-8455** 4pm-2am, call for summer hours • mostly women • dancing/DJ • live shows • deck • wheelchair access

**Scandals** 1510-G Piedmont Rd. NE (Ansley Sq. Shopping Ctr.) **875-5957** 11:30am-4am • popular • mostly gay men • neighborhood bar • wheelchair access

**Sol** 917 Peachtree St. **815-8070** gay-friendly • dancing/DJ • live shows • call for events

**The Tower 2** 735 Ralph McGill Blvd. NE **523-1535** 5pm-4am, from 2pm Sun • mostly women • neighborhood bar • wheelchair access

## CAFES

**Cafe Diem** 640 N. Highland Ave. **607-7008** salad & sandwich menu • coffee til midnight

**Caribou Coffee** 1551 Piedmont Ave. **733-5539** til midnight wknds

**Intermezzo** 1845 Peachtree Rd. NE **355-0411** 8am-2am, 9am-3am Fri-Sat • classy • plenty veggie • full bar • $7-10

## RESTAURANTS

**The Big Red Tomato Bistro** 980 Piedmont Rd. **870-9881** lunch, dinner & Sun brunch • Italian • full bar • patio • $8-18

**Bridgetown Grill** 689 Peachtree (across from Fox Theater) **873-5361** noon-11pm • popular • funky Caribbean • some veggie • $5-10 • also Li'l 5 Points location 653-0110

**Camille's** 1186 N. Highland **872-7203** dinner only • beer/wine • Italian • wheelchair access

**Chow** 1026-1/2 N. Highland Ave. **872-0869** lunch & dinner • popular Sun brunch • some veggie • $8-15

**Cowtippers** 1600 Piedmont Ave. NE **874-3469** 11:30am-11pm • transgender-friendly • wheelchair access

**Dunk N' Dine (aka Drunk N' Dyke)** 2276 Cheshire Bridge Rd. **636-0197** 24hrs • popular • lesbians/gay men • downscale diner • some veggie • $4-10

**Edelweiss** 6075 Roswell Rd., Sandy Springs **303-8700** German • full bar

**Einstein's** 1077 Juniper **876-7925** noon-1am • some veggie • full bar • $8-12

**The Flying Biscuit Cafe** 1655 McLendon Ave. **687-8888** 8:30am-10pm, clsd Mon • healthy brkfst all day • plenty veggie • beer/wine • wheelchair access • lesbian-owned/run • $6-12

**Majestic Diner** 1031 Ponce de Leon (near N. Highland) **875-0276** 24hrs • popular diner right from the '50s • cantankerous waitresses included (at your own risk) • some veggie • $3-8

**Murphy's** 997 Virginia Ave. **872-0904** 7am-10pm, til midnight Fri-Sat • popular • cont'l • plenty veggie • great brunch • wheelchair access • $5-15

**Pleasant Peasant** 555 Peachtree St. **874-3223** lunch & dinner • full bar

Live Female Impersonation

12 Big Screen TVs

Billiard areas

Starlit Weatherized Patio

9200 Sq Ft
High Energy Dance

Martini Room

Live DJs and VJs

OTHERSIDE

Live Bands

Valet Parking

THE OTHERSIDE
CONTINUOUS ENTERTAINMENT COMPLEX
1924 PIEDMONT RD NE ATLANTA  404. 875. 5238

**R. Thomas** 1812 Peachtree Rd. NE 872-2942 24hrs • popular • beer/wine • healthy Californian/juice bar • plenty veggie • $5-10

**Swan Coach House** 3130 Slaton Dr., Buckhead **261-0636** lunch & dinner

**Veni Vidi Vici** 41 14th St. **875-8424** lunch & dinner • upscale Italian • some veggie • $14-25

### ENTERTAINMENT & RECREATION

**Alternative Talk** WRFG 89.7 FM 523-8989 6pm 2nd & 4th Fri • radio program for Atlanta's African-American lesbigay community

**Dyke TV** Channel 12 'weekly, half hour TV show produced by lesbians for lesbians' • call (212) 343-9335 for more info

**Funny That Way Theatre Company** 893-3344 lesbigay theater company • fall & spring musicals • call for schedule

**Gay Graffiti** WRFG 89.7 FM **523-8989** 7pm Th • lesbigay radio program

**Little 5 Points, Moreland & Euclid Ave.** S. of Ponce de Leon Ave. hip & funky area w/too many restaurants & shops to list

### BOOKSTORES & RETAIL SHOPS

**Bill Hallman's** 792 N. Highland Ave. 876-6055 noon-8pm, til 10pm Wed-Sat, til 6pm Sun • hip designer fashions

**The Boy Next Door** 1447 Piedmont Ave. NE 873-2664 11am-7pm • clothing

▲ **Brushstrokes** 1510-J Piedmont Ave. NE 876-6567 10am-10pm, noon-9pm Sun • lesbigay variety store

**Charis Books & More** 1189 Euclid St. 524-0304 10:30am-6:30pm, til 8pm Wed, til 9pm Fri-Sat, noon-6pm Sun • lesbigay/feminist • wheelchair access

**Condomart** 632 N. Highland Ave. NE 875-5665 11am-11pm, noon-7pm Sun • wheelchair access

**The Junkman's Daughter** 464 Moreland Ave. 577-3188 11am-7pm • hip stuff

**Metropolitan Deluxe** 1034 N. Highland 892-9337 11am-10pm, til 7pm Sun • flowers • chocolates • artful gifts • wheelchair access

▲ **Outwrite Books** 991 Piedmont Ave. NE 607-0082 8am-11pm, til midnight Fri-Sat • lesbigay • cafe • wheelchair access

# YOUR VISITORS CENTER IN ATLANTA

## OUTWRITE BOOKSTORE & COFFEEHOUSE

- ■ BOOKS
- ■ MAGAZINES
- ■ CARDS
- ■ MUSIC
- ■ VIDEOS
- ■ GIFTS
- ■ SANDWICHES
- ■ DESSERTS
- ■ JUICE
- ■ COFFEE

ATLANTA'S GAY & LESBIAN

**OUTWRITE** BOOKSTORE & COFFEEHOUSE

RIGHT ON PIEDMONT PARK!

**PIEDMONT AVENUE AT TENTH STREET MIDTOWN/ ATLANTA (404) 607-0082**

*The South's Source for Information on Our Lives*

**W**hile traveling
we can help you
find these
*among your
souvenirs:*

▼ Cards
▼ Jewelry
▼ T-Shirts
▼ Books
▼ Flags
▼ Stickers
▼ Wind Socks
▼ Videos
▼ Towels

*Brushstrokes* ©

SENSORY ⚡ OVERLOAD™

*STOP BY AND COLLECT
SOME MEMORIES*

ANSLEY SQUARE • 404 876 6567

ACCEPTING DISCOVER • AMEX • VISA • MASTERCARD • DEBIT CARDS

Sun-Thurs 10-10 • Fri-Sat 10-11

**Oxford Books** 2345 Peachtree **364-2700** 9am-midnight, til 2am Fri-Sat • many lesbigay books & magazines • also at 360 Pharr Rd. 262-3333 • 'Cup & Chaucer' cafe at both locations

### PUBLICATIONS

**Atlanta Community Yellow Pages** (602) 277-0105/(800) 849-0406

**ETC Magazine 888-0063** bar & restaurant guide for Southeast

**The News 876-5372**

**Southern Voice 876-1819** newspaper w/extensive resource listings

**Venus Magazine 755-8711** for lesbians & gays of color

**Women's Yellow Pages of Greater Atlanta 255-4144**

### TRAVEL AGENTS

**All Points Travel** 1544 Piedmont Ave. #107 **873-3631**/(800) 246-1756 IGLTA

**Conventional Travel** 1658 Lavista Rd. NE **315-0107**/(800) 747-7107 IGLTA

**Cumberland Travel Services** 2675 Cumberland Pkwy. #260 **(770) 438-2555** IGLTA

**Esquire Travel Service** 5446 Peachtree Industrial Blvd. #240 **457-6696**/(800) **786-6402** IGLTA

**Grand Destination Management** 2255 Cumberland Pkwy. #200 **(770) 333-9396**/(800) 472-6593 IGLTA

**IMTC** 3025 Maple Dr. #5 **240-0949**/(800) **790-4682** IGLTA

**Midtown Travel Consultants** 1830 Piedmont Rd. #F **872-8308**/(800) 548-**8904** IGLTA

**Out & About Travel Advisors** 587 Virginia Ave. Ste. 3-A **892-8998**/(800) **914-8232** IGLTA

**Real Travel** NE Plaza #1030, 3375 Buford Hwy. **636-8500**/(800) 551-4202 IGLTA

**Travel Affair** 1069 Juniper St. **892-9400**/(800) 332-3417 IGLTA

**Trips Unlimited** 1004 Virginia Ave. NE **872-8747**/(800) 275-8747 IGLTA

### SPIRITUAL GROUPS

**All Saints MCC** 957 N. Highland Ave. **524-9090** 11am Sun

**Christ Covenant MCC** 109 Hibernia Ave., Decatur **373-2933** 9am & 11am Sun

**Congregation Bet Haverim** 701 W. Howard Ave., Decatur **(770) 642-3467** 8pm Fri • lesbigay synagogue

**First MCC of Atlanta** 1379 Tullie Rd. NE **325-4143** 9am,11am & 7:30pm Sun, 7:30pm Wed • wheelchair access

**Integrity Atlanta** 2089 Ponce de Leon (church) **(770) 642-3183** 7:30pm 2nd & 4th Fri • lesbigay Episcopalians

**Redefined Faith Worship Center** 743 Virginia Ave. **872-2133** 2:30pm Sun • 'a place of worship in the African-American (Black Church) tradition where all are welcome'

### GYMS & HEALTH CLUBS

**Boot Camp** 1544 Piedmont Ave. #105 **876-8686** gay-friendly • full gym

**The Fitness Factory** 500 Amsterdam **815-7900** popular • gay-friendly • full gym

**Mid-City Fitness Center** 2201 Faulkner Rd. **321-6507** lesbians/gay men

### EROTICA

**9 1/2 Weeks** 505 Peachtree St. **888-0878** call for other locations

**Piercing Experience** 1654 McLendon Ave. NE **378-9100** noon-9pm

**The Poster Hut** 2175 Cheshire Bridge Rd. **633-7491** clothing • toys

**Starship** 2275 Cheshire Bridge Rd. **320-9101** leather • novelties • 5 locations in Atlanta

## Augusta (706)

### BARS & NIGHTCLUBS

**Walton Way Station** 1632 Walton Wy. **733-2603** 9pm-3am, clsd Sun • lesbians/gay men • dancing/DJ • live shows

### SPIRITUAL GROUPS

**MCC** 924 Green St. **722-6454** 7pm Sun

## Carrollton (770)

### BOOKSTORES & RETAIL SHOPS

**Blue Moon Gifts** 113 Newnan St. **836-0014** 10:30am-6:30pm, til 7pm Fri-Sat, clsd Sun

## Columbus (706)

### BARS & NIGHTCLUBS

**PTL Club** 1207 1st Ave. **322-8997** 8pm-3am, clsd Mon • lesbians/gay men • dancing/DJ • multi-racial • transgender-friendly • live shows

### TRAVEL AGENTS

**Century Travel Service** 5256 Armour Rd Ste.A **322-6385**/(800) 828-0487 IGLTA

## Dahlonega (706)

### ACCOMMODATIONS
**Above the Clouds** 864-5211 women only • mountainside B&B • full brkfst • 1 ste. w/hot tub • 1 bdrm w/private bath • wheelchair access • lesbian-owned/run
**Swiftwaters** (706) 864-3229 seasonal • women only • on scenic river • full brkfst • hot tub • smokefree • deck • women-owned/run • $69-95 (B&B)/ $40-50 (cabins)/ $10 (camping)
**Triangle Pointe** (706) 867-6029 lesbians/gay men • full brkfst • hot tub • $69

### RESTAURANTS
**Renee's Cafe** 135 N. Chestatee 864-6829 clsd Sun-Mon • gourmet wine bar
**Smith House** 202 S. Chestatee St. 864-3566 clsd Mon • family-style Southern

## Dalton (706)

### RESTAURANTS
**Applebee's** 1322 W. Walnut Ave. 278-5776 full bar
**Dalton Depot** 110 Depot St. 226-3160 clsd Sun

## Lawrenceville (770)

### ENTERTAINMENT & RECREATION
**Pathways 'The Walking Folk'** 867 John Court 339-3640/707-9255 walking tours of the Southeast

## Macon (912)

### BARS & NIGHTCLUBS
**Cherry St. Pub** 425 Cherry St. 755-1400 7:30pm-2am, clsd Sun-Mon • lesbians/gay men • live shows
**Topaz** 695 Riverside Dr. 750-7669 5pm-2am, clsd Sun • lesbians/gay men • dancing/DJ • live shows • wheelchair access

## Mountain City (706)

### ACCOMMODATIONS
**The York House** York House Rd. 746-2068 gay-friendly • 1896 historic country inn • $59-139

## Norcross (770)

### TRAVEL AGENTS
**American Express Travel** 400 Pinnacle Wy. #460 246-3500 IGLTA

## Savannah (912)

### INFO LINES & SERVICES
**First City Network** 335 Tatnall St. 236-2489 complete info & events line • social group

### ACCOMMODATIONS
**912 Barnard Victorian B&B** 912 Barnard 234-9121 lesbians/gay men • shared baths • fireplaces • smokefree • balcony • $79
**Park Avenue Manor** 107-109 W. Park Ave. 233-0352 lesbians/gay men • 1897 Victorian B&B • full brkfst • $69-110

### BARS & NIGHTCLUBS
**Club One** 1 Jefferson St. 232-0200 5pm-3am • lesbians/gay men • dancing/DJ • food served • live shows Wed, Fri-Sun
**Faces II** 17 Lincoln St. 233-3520 noon-3am • mostly gay men • neighborhood bar • also restaurant • patio • $8-10
**Felicia's** 416 W. Liberty St. 238-4788 5pm-3am, from 12:30pm wknds • lunch served • mostly gay men • dancing/DJ • live shows

## Valdosta (912)

### BARS & NIGHTCLUBS
**Club Paradise** 2100 W. Hill Ave. (exit 4 I-95) 242-9609 8pm-2am, clsd Sun-Mon • lesbians/gay men • dancing/DJ • live shows • patio • wheelchair access

### SPIRITUAL GROUPS
**Family of God MCC** 1442 Double Churches Rd. (Unitarian Church) 321-9202 6:30pm Sun

## HAWAII

*(Please note that cities are grouped by islands)*

## HAWAII (BIG ISLAND)

### Captain Cook (808)

ACCOMMODATIONS

**Hale Aloha Guest Ranch** 84-4780 Mamalahoa Hwy. **328-8955/(800) 897-3188** lesbians/gay men • full brkfst • hot tub • nudity • smokefree • $65-120

**Kealakekua Bay B&B** 328-8150/(800) 328-8150 gay-friendly • hot tub • smokefree

**Merryman's B&B** 323-2276 gay-friendly • full brkfst • hot tub • smokefree

**Rainbow Plantation** 323-2393 gay-friendly • on coffee & macadamia plantation • smokefree

▲**RBR Farms** 328-9212/(800) 328-9212 popular • lesbians/gay men • swimming • nudity • on working macadamia nut & coffee plantation • IGLTA • $60-150

**Samurai House** 328-9210 popular • gay-friendly • traditional house brought from Japan • hot tub • wheelchair access

### Hilo (808)

INFO LINES & SERVICES

**Gay & Lesbian AA** 219 Ululani St. (Religious Science Bookstore) **935-9851** 8pm Fri

ACCOMMODATIONS

**The Butterfly Inn** 966-7936/(800) 546-2442 women only • tropical brkfst • hot tub • kitchens • smokefree • women-owned/run • $55-65

**Oceanfront B&B** 1923 Kalanianaole St. **934-9004** 2 units • ocean views

**Rainbow Dreams Cottage** 13-6412 Kalapana Beach Rd. **936-9883** gay-friendly • oceanfront cottage • smokefree

Plantation-style home on a gated tropical estate

Expansive covered decks, ceilings fans & jacuzzi

Interior atrium with lava rock falls & koi pond

Only 5 miles to the beach and all activities

Large bungalow & kitchen

# HALE KIPA 'O PELE

*A distinctive Bed & Breakfast on the Big Island*

PO Box 5252 Kailua-Kona, Hawaii 96745

## 1-800-LAVAGLO

## Honokaa (808)

### ACCOMMODATIONS

**Paauhau Plantation Inn** 775-7222/(800) 789-7614 gay-friendly • B&B w/cottages built on ocean point

## Kailua-Kona (808)

### INFO LINES & SERVICES

**Kona Lesbian Support Group** 322-2306 ask for Denise • Kona location

### ACCOMMODATIONS

**Dolores B&B** 77-6704 Kilohana **329-8778** gay-friendly • ocean views • full gourmet brkfst

▲**Hale Kipa 'O Pele** 329-8676/(800) 528-2456 lesbians/gay men • plantation-style B&B • hot tub • IGLTA • $65-135

▲**Royal Kona Resort** 75-5852 Alii Dr. **329-3111/(800) 222-5642** gay-friendly • set atop dramatic lava outcroppings overlooking Kailua Bay • swimming • private beach • $99-250 • see ad in front color section

**Tropical Tune-ups** (800) 587-0405 women only • small group retreats for women • B&B avail. on off-weeks • full brkfst • jacuzzi • sweat lodge • kids ok • lesbian-owned/run • $350-1495/week

### BARS & NIGHTCLUBS

**Mask Bar & Grill** 75-5660 Kopiko St. **329-8558** 6pm-2am • popular • lesbians/gay men • neighborhood bar • dancing/DJ • live shows • karaoke • only lesbian/gay bar on the island

### TRAVEL AGENTS

**Eco-Adventures** 75-5626 Kuakini Hwy. #1 **329-7116/(800) 949-3483** IGLTA

## Kamuela (808)

### ACCOMMODATIONS

**Ho'onanea** 882-1177 women only • hot tub • near beaches & outdoor recreation • women-owned/run

**RBR FARMS**

**Bed and Breakfast**
on the Big Island of Hawaii

For More Information and Reservations
Call: **1-800-328-9212**
Or
**1-808-328-9212**
Or Write: P.O. Box 930, Captain Cook, Hawaii 96704

This secret little hideaway
will offer you a quiet and
memorable look back to
mother nature.
You truly have reached...

## The
# RAINBOW'S INN
### B&B Hideaway

Located on
the Big Island of Hawaii.

Private and comfortable
king size bedroom,
living/dining room,
full kitchen and
full private bath.

A stone's throw away from
the ocean, you can stroll
along the lava cliff coast
line or explore the thick,
luscious jungle or just lay
in the double hammock
and watch the ocean,
clouds and world go by.

PO Box 983
Pahoa, HI 96778
Phone/fax: 808-965-9011
Email: RainbwAdv@aol.com

Also featuring:

## Rainbow
## Adventures

•Excursions
•Rental equipment
•Classes

## Kohala Coast (808)

### ACCOMMODATIONS
**Ka Hale Na Pua** 329-2960/(800) 595-3458 gay-friendly • swimming • massage therapist avail.

## Na'alehu (808)

### ACCOMMODATIONS
**Earthsong** 929-8043 women only • retreat center w/cottages on 3 acres • Hawaiian massage • Goddess temple • substance-free • lesbian-owned/run

## Pahala (808)

### ACCOMMODATIONS
**Wood Valley B&B Inn** 928-8212 mostly women • plantation home B&B • tent sites • full veggie brkfst • sauna • smokefree • nudity • women-owned/run • $35-55

## Pahoa (808)

### ACCOMMODATIONS
**Huliaule'a B&B** 965-9175 lesbians/gay men • smokefree • gay-owned/run • $45-80

**Kalani Oceanside Eco-Resort** 965-7828/(800) 800-6886 gay-friendly • coastal retreat • conference center & campground w/in Hawaii's largest conservation area • full brkfst • swimming • food served • IGLTA

**Pamalu** 965-0830 gay-friendly • country retreat on 5 secluded acres • swimming • near hiking • snorkeling • warm ponds

▲**Rainbow's Inn** 965-9011 gay-friendly • B&B hideaway by the sea • $60-80 • (see sweepstakes in front)

**The Volcano Ranch Inn & Hostel** 13-3775 Kalapana Hwy. **965-8800** gay-friendly

### CAFES
**Mady's Cafe Makana** 152923 Gov't Main Rd. **965-0608** 8am-3pm, clsd Sat • vegetarian cafe & gift shop

### ENTERTAINMENT & RECREATION
**Rainbow Adventures** 965-9011 hiking, bicycling, scuba & more

### PUBLICATIONS
**Outspoken** 936-7073/934-7178 seasonal newsletter

## Volcano Village (808)

### ACCOMMODATIONS

**Chalet Kilauea/The Inn at Volcano** 967-7786/(800) 937-7786 gay-friendly • full brkfst • hot tub • smokefree

**Hale Ohia Cottages (808)** 967-7986/(800) 455-3803 gay-friendly • wheelchair access • IGLTA • $75-95

**The Lodge at Volcano** 967-7244 gay-friendly • hot tub • smokefree• private trail • lanai

**Volcano B&B** 967-7779/(800) 736-7140 gay-friendly • smokefree

# KAUAI

## Anahola (808)

### ACCOMMODATIONS

**Mahina Kai B&B** 4933 Aliomanu Rd. #699 822-9451/(800) 337-1134 popular • lesbians/gay men • country villa rental overlooking Anahola Bay • swimming • hot tub • smokefree • $95-175

## Hanalei (808)

### BARS & NIGHTCLUBS

**Tahiti Nui** Kuhio Hwy. 826-6277 gay-friendly • 8am-2am • more gay Fri-Sat • luau Fri • country/western Mon • live bands wknds • food served • wheelchair access • $12-18

## Kalaheo (808)

### INFO LINES & SERVICES

**Black Bamboo Reservation Service** 332-9607/(800) 527-7789 free reservation service

## Kapaa (808)

### ACCOMMODATIONS

**Aloha Kauai B&B** 156 Lihau St. 822-6966/(800) 262-4652 lesbians/gay men • full brkfst • swimming • smokefree • wheelchair access • $60-95

**Hale Kahawai** 185 Kahawai Pl., Wailua 822-1031 lesbians/gay men • hot tub • smokefree • mountain views • $60-90

**Kauai Coconut Beach Resort** 822-3455/(800) 222-5642 gay-friendly • newly redecorated oceanfront resort • swimming • tennis • nightly torchlighting ceremony & luau • $150-500 • see ad in front color section

**Kauai Waterfall B&B** 5783 Haaheo St. 823-9533/(800) 996-9533 gay-friendly • swimming • hot tub • overlooking Wailua River State Park Waterfall

**Mahina's** 4433 Panihi Rd. 823-9364 women-only beach house • hostel-style accommodations • $20-40/night

**Royal Drive Cottages** 147 Royal Dr., Wailua 822-2321 gay-friendly • private garden cottages w/kitchenettes • smokefree • $50-90

### BARS & NIGHTCLUBS

**Sideout** 4-1330 Kuhio Hwy. 822-0082 noon-1:30am • popular • gay-friendly • live bands Tue, Th & wknds • wheelchair access

### RESTAURANTS

**Bull Shed** 796 Kuhio Hwy. 822-3791 5:30pm-10pm

**Me Ma's Thai** 4361 Kuhio Hwy. (shopping Center) 823-0899 lunch Mon-Fri, dinner nightly

**Pacific Cafe** 4831 Kuhio Hwy. #200 822-0013

## Kilauea (808)

### ACCOMMODATIONS

**Kai Mana** 828-1280/(800) 837-1782 gay-friendly • Shakti Gawain's paradise home set on a cliff surrounded by ocean & mountains • cottages • kitchens • smokefree • $75-150

**Kalihiwai Jungle Home** 828-1626 gay-friendly • clifftop hideaway overlooking jungle & waterfalls • near beaches • nudity • smokefree • $100-135

▲**Pali Kai** 828-6691/(888) 828-6691 popular • lesbians/gay men • hilltop B&B w/ocean view • cottages • hot tub • women-owned/run

### CAFES

**Mango Mamas Fruitstand Cafe** Kuhio Hwy. & Hookui Rd. 828-1020 fruit smoothies & more • lesbian-owned

## Lihue (808)

### INFO LINES & SERVICES

**AA Alternative Lifestyles** 4364 Hardy St. (St. Michael's Episcopal Church) 821-1911 7:30pm Sun

## Puunene (808)

### RESTAURANTS

**Roy's Bar & Grill** 2360 Kiahuna Plantation Dr. 742-5000 5:30pm-9:30pm

## MAUI

### Haiku (808)

ACCOMMODATIONS

**Golden Bamboo Ranch** 422 Kaupakalua Rd. **572-7824/(800) 344-1238** gay-friendly • 7-acre estate • panoramic ocean views • cottages • IGLTA • $69-90

**Halfway to Hana House** 572-1176 gay-friendly • private studio w/ocean view • smokefree

**Kailua Maui Gardens** 572-9726/(800) 258-8588 gay-friendly • also suites • hot tub • swimming • nudity • wheelchair access • IGLTA • $70-200

### Hana (808)

ACCOMMODATIONS

**Hana Alii Holidays** Hana 248-7742/(800) 548-0478 accommodations reservations service

**Hana Plantation Houses** 923-0772/(800) 228-4262 popular • mostly gay men • tropical cottages & houses in exotic gardens • swimming • IGLTA • $60-200

**Napualani O'Hana** 248-8935 gay-friendly • 2 full units • ocean & mtn. views • non-smoking rms avail. • lanai • wheelchair access

### Huelo (808)

ACCOMMODATIONS

**Waipi'o Bay Lookout** 572-4530 gay-friendly • seasonal • $100-115

### Kahului (808)

INFO LINES & SERVICES

**AA Gay & Lesbian** 101 W. Kam Ave. (Kahului Union Church) **874-3589** 8pm Wed

PUBLICATIONS

**Out In Maui** 244-4566

## PALI KAI

*Bed and breakfast hide-away on Kauai's spectacular North Shore*

**P.O. Box 450, Kilauea, HI 96754 • 888 828 6691**

MAUI • HAWAII

# ANDREA & JANET HAVE GOT YOU COVERED ON MAUI

## Andrea & Janet's Maui Condos
## Andi's Bed & Breakfast

Savor a postcard-perfect Maui sunset from our 1 & 2 bedroom spacious ocean/beach front suites. Pool, jacuzzi, tennis, golf, snorkeling, and TONS of amenities. Meticulously owned and maintained by lesbian owners who can give you the *best* that Maui has to offer.

Call Andi on Maui for reservations:

**1-800-289-1522**  Fax: 808-879-6430 •

or preview from our web site: http://www.maui.net/~andrea

## Express your love, show your pride—on Maui, the most beautiful place in the world.

Andrea and Janet started it all—the first in the world to offer lesbian weddings. Call us to find out why we are the leader in lesbian ceremonies. Enjoy the experience you've been waiting for all your life—on Maui, the most beautiful place on earth. Call us on Maui toll free:

**1-800-659-1866** or preview our

web site: http://www.hawaiigaywed.com

*"You're there, I'm here. Allow me to help you with your best vacation ever."*
—Andrea Thomas

Royal Hawaiian Weddings

MEMBERS IGLTA

## Kihei (808)

INFO LINES & SERVICES
**AA Gay & Lesbian** Kapalama Park
Gazebo **874-3589** 9am Sun

ACCOMMODATIONS
▲ **Andrea & Janet's Maui Vacation
Rentals 875-1558/(800) 289-1522**
women only • 1- & 2-bdrm
oceanfront/beachfront condos • swimming • near outdoor recreation • IGLTA
• lesbian-owned/run
▲**Anfora's Dreams (213) 737-0731/(800)
788-5046** gay-friendly • rental condo
near ocean • hot tub • swimming • $60-
135
▲**Hale Makaleka 879-2971** women only •
full brkfst • smokefree • women-
owned/run • $60
**Jack & Tom's Maui Condos 874-1048**
gay-friendly • fully equipped condos &
apts • non-smoking rms avail.
**Ko'a Kai Rentals 879-6058/(800) 399-
6058 x33** gay-friendly • inexpensive
rentals • swimming • $38 day/ $225
weekly

**Koa Lagoon** 800 S. Kihei Rd. **879-
3002/(800) 367-8030** gay-friendly •
oceanfront suites • 5 night min. • swimming • wheelchair access
**Triple Lei B&B 874-8645/(800) 871-
8645** mostly gay men • full brkfst • hot
tub • swimming • nudity • near nude
beach

CAFES
**Stella Blues** 1215 Kihei Rd. **874-3779**
deli

## Kula (808)

ACCOMMODATIONS
**Camp Kula - Maui B&B 876-0000** popular • lesbians/gay men • on the slopes of
Mt. Haleakala • HIV+ welcome • wheelchair access • $35-78

## Lahaina (800)

INFO LINES & SERVICES
▲ **Maui Dreamtime Weddings (800) 779-
1320** traditional & non-traditional commitment ceremonies in secluded Maui
locations

# Affordable Maui Condo's
## (800) 788-5046
## (213) 737-0731
### The Best Deal On Maui!
**Deluxe - Completely Furnished Units
From singles to Large Homes With
Your Total Comfort In Mind!
Pool - Jacuzzi - Beach Access
Starting From $65.00/Day**
# Anfora's Dreams Maui
## Post Office Box 74030
## Los Angeles, Ca. 90004

# Hale Makaleka
## Women's B & B

**Hale Makaleka is a Bed & Breakfast for
Women Travelers located on the sunny side of Maui.**

Resort activities, dining experiences and yellow sand beaches are
all within four miles of your comfortable, spacious room. Or, you
can escape it all and come "home" to restful seclusion. Private
garden entrance and bath offer the opportunity for serene solitude.
"Natural" sunbathing is also available if you wish.

We can exchange information with you on activities in
the Women's Community during your tropical breakfast,
which is served on our upstairs view deck.

Accommodations for two are $60 per night,
with a three-day minimum stay.

**Hale Makaleka, Kihei, Maui
(808) 879-2971**

*Maui Dreamtime Weddings*

Actual photo of couple we married.

## You can get married!
## We're doing it now on Maui!

Moderate to deluxe wedding packages. Your dreams can come
ture at Maui Dreamtime Weddings. Call toll free for more info.

### 1-800-779-1320

See us on the internet at http://randm.com/mmw.html

**Royal Hawaiian Weddings** 875-0625/(800) 659-1866 specializes in scenic gay weddings • IGLTA • women-owned/run

### ACCOMMODATIONS

▲ **Kahana Beach Condominium Hotel** 4221 Lower Honoapiilani Rd. 669-8611/(800) 222-5642 gay-friendly • oceanfront studios & 1-bdrm suites • kitchenettes • private lanai • $120-225 • see ad in front color section

▲ **The Royal Lahaina Resort** 2780 Kekaa Dr. 661-3611/(800) 222-5642 gay-friendly • full service resort on 27 tropical acres of Ka'anapali • world-class tennis courts & golf courses • swimming • wheelchair access • $215-1,500 • see ad in front color section

### ENTERTAINMENT & RECREATION

**Maui Surfing School** 875-0625/(800) 851-0543 lessons for beginners, cowards & non-swimmers • 'surf-aris' for advanced • women-owned/run

### TRAVEL AGENTS

**Gay Hawaiian Excursions** 667-7466/(800) 311-4460 extensive activities, tours & travel arrangements

### EROTICA

▲ **Skin Deep Tattoo** 626 Front St. 661-8531 traditional, custom, fine line & Hawaiian tattoos

## Makawao (808)

### INFO LINES & SERVICES

**Personal Maui** 572-1589 guide & driver for tours of the hidden Maui

### ACCOMMODATIONS

**Maui Network** 572-9555/(800) 367-5221 condo reservation service

### RESTAURANTS

**Casanova's** 1188 Makawao Ave. 572-0220 lunch & dinner • Italian • full bar til 2am

## Paia (808)

### INFO LINES & SERVICES

**Women's Event Hotline** 573-3077 covers entire island

### ACCOMMODATIONS

**Huelo Point Flower Farm** 572-1850 gay-friendly • vacation rental • oceanfront estate & organic farm • swimming • kids 10+ ok • $110-300 + 10.17% state tax

Skin Deep TATTOO Hawaii ®

626 FRONT STREET
LAHAINA TOWN
MAUI
661-8531

PUBLICATIONS

**Island Lesbian Connection** 575-2681 newsletter • covers all islands • unconfirmed

## Pukalani (808)

ACCOMMODATIONS

**Heavenly Gate B&B** 276 Hiwalani Loop 572-0321 cottage • smokefree • $100

## Wailea (800)

ACCOMMODATIONS

**Coconuts** Wailea (800) 289-1522 lesbians/gay men • swimming • hot tub • kitchens • wheelchair access

## Wailuku (808)

BARS & NIGHTCLUBS

**Hamburger Mary's** 2010 Main St. 244-7776 10am-2am • popular • lesbians/gay men • dancing/DJ • videos • food served til 10pm • plenty veggie • $7-15

TRAVEL AGENTS

**Remote Possibilities** 875-7438 IGLTA

# MOLOKAI

## Kaunakakai (808)

ACCOMMODATIONS

**Kainehe Retreat Home** 558-8207 gay-friendly • kitchen • smokefree • kids ok • beachfront • lesbian-owned/run

**Molokai Beachfront Escapes** 248-7868/(800) 228-4262 gay-friendly • beachfront units on the exotic island of Molokai • IGLTA • $89-109

# OAHU

## Honolulu (808)

INFO LINES & SERVICES

**Always Yours by The Wedding Connection** Honolulu 537-9427/(800) 388-6933 lesbigay commitment ceremonies

**Gay/Lesbian AA** 277 Ohua (Waikiki Health Ctr.) 946-1438 8pm daily

**Gay/Lesbian Community Center** 1566 Wilder Ave. (YWCA) 951-7000 9am-5pm, clsd wknds

**Hawaii Transgendered Outreach** 923-4270 social mtgs. bi-weekly Fri

**Hawaii Visitors Bureau** 2270 Kalakaua Ave. #801 923-1811

**Island Pride Taxi & Tour** 3151 Monsarrat Ave. #402 732-6518 IGLTA

**Leis of Hawaii** (888) 534-7644 personalized Hawaiian greeting service complete w/ fresh flower leis

ACCOMMODATIONS

**Aston Waikiki Terrace Hotel** 2045 Kalakaua Ave. 955-6000/(800) 922-7866 gay-friendly • IGLTA

**Bed & Breakfast Honolulu (Statewide)** 3242 Kaohinani Dr. 595-7533/(800) 288-4666 clientele & ownership vary (most gay-friendly) • represents 350 locations on all islands • $40-175

**Bed & Breakfast in Manoa Valley** 2651 Terrace Dr. 988-6333 gay-friendly • spectacular views • women-owned/run

**Breakers Hotel** 250 Beach Walk 923-3181/(800) 426-0494 gay-friendly • swimming • full bar & grill • great burgers

**The Coconut Plaza Hotel** 450 Lewers St. 923-8828/(800) 882-9696 gay-friendly • swimming • near beach • wheelchair access • $87-150

**Hawaiian Waikiki Beach Hotel** 2570 Kalakaua Ave. 922-2511/(800) 877-7666 gay-friendly • IGLTA

**Hotel Honolulu** 376 Kaiolu St. 926-2766/(800) 426-2766 popular • mostly gay men • IGLTA • $79-115

**Outrigger Hotels & Resorts** 921-6820/(800) 688-7444 gay-friendly • IGLTA

**Pleasant Holiday Isle Hotel** 270 Lewers St. 923-0777/(800) 222-5642 gay-friendly • swimming • private lanai • 1 blk from Waikiki beach • also full restaurant & lounge • see ad in front color section

**Waikiki Parkside Hotel** 1850 Ala Moana Blvd. 955-1567/(800) 237-9666 gay-friendly • IGLTA

**Waikiki Vacation Condos** 1580 Makaloa St. #770 946-9371/(800) 543-5663 furnished 1- & 2-bdrm units • smokefree • also reservation service • $75-175

BARS & NIGHTCLUBS

**Angles** 2256 Kuhio Ave., 2nd flr. 926-9766/923-1130 (INFOLINE) 10am-2am • lesbians/gay men • neighborhood bar • dancing/DJ

**Club Michaelangelo** 444 Hobron Ln. #P-8 951-0008 4pm-2am • lesbians/gay men • dancing/DJ • karaoke

## Honolulu

*T*he city of Honolulu suffers from a bad case of mistaken identity. The highrise tourist hotels of Waikiki, six miles away, overshadow the downtown area of Honolulu, the center of the state government and teems with a vibrant culture all its own. Chinatown, a designated National Historic Landmark, offers a living history of Asian immigration to Hawaii, with street vendors, grocers, herbalists, acupuncture clinics. Authentic Chinese, Vietnamese and Filipino restaurants cram the area north of downtown, off of North King Street.

On the other side of downtown, on South King St., sits 'Iolani Palace, the heart and soul of modern Hawaiian history. The graceful structure served as a prison for Queen Lili'uokalani, Hawaii's last reigning monarch, when she was placed under house arrest by armed US forces intent on her signing over the nation's sovereignty. Don't miss the Hawaii Maritime Center next door for a glance back at the history of the islands and the often injurious effects Western culture has had on this most isolated of island chains. If you're staying in Waikiki, you can catch a trolley downtown from any of the main streets, saving yourself a mountain of parking headaches.

Waikiki sits on the Southwest corner of Oahu and offers a mind-boggling number of hotels, restaurants and shops that are just waiting to consume your tourist dollars. Campy though it is, enjoy the postcard pleasure of a mai tai on the patio of the magnificently restored Sheraton Moana Surfrider while the sun sets over the Pacific. Old Waikiki, situated along Kuhio Avenue, is where you'll find a small collection of men's bars, a couple of shops, one restaurant, **Hamburger Mary's**, and a hotel, Hotel Honolulu, that cater to the gay and lesbian community. **Hula's**, a neighborhood bar with a homey feel, is the most welcoming of the bunch. Down the street you can dance the night away at **Fusion**. **Island Lifestyle**, the lesbigay monthly, runs a complete calendar, and offers a better bet for locating events of interest to local lesbians.

*– By reader Deirdre S. Green. Updated by Damron editors.*

**Dis 'N Dat Lounge** 1315 Kalakaua Ave. **946-0000** lesbians/gay men • 4pm-2am • karaoke • live bands

**Fusion Waikiki** 2260 Kuhio Ave., 3rd flr. **924-2422** 10pm-4am, from 8pm wknds • popular • mostly gay men • dancing/DJ • transgender-friendly • live shows

**Hula's Bar & Lei Stand** 2103 Kuhio Ave. **923-0669** 10am-2am • popular • lesbians/gay men • dancing/DJ • live shows • videos • patio

**Metropolis** 611 Cooke St. **593-2717** 8pm-2am, clsd Mon-Th • mostly women • dancing/DJ

**Trixx** 2109 Kuhio Ave. **923-0669** 5pm-2am, from 3pm Sun (barbecue) • lesbians/gay men • dancing/DJ • also 'Treats' deli & the 'Fruit Bar' from 10am • wheelchair access

**Windows** 444 Hobron Ln., Waikiki **946-4442** 11am-2am • lesbians/gay men • more women Wed • lunch & Sun brunch • live shows • wheelchair access

## CAFES

**Java Java Cafe** 760 Kapahulu Ave. **732-2670** 8am-midnight • psychic readings Tue • shows Fri

**Mocha Java Cafe** 1200 Ala Moana Blvd. (Ward Center) **591-9023** 8am-9pm, til 4pm Sun • plenty veggie

## RESTAURANTS

**Banana's** 2139 Kuhio Ave. #125, Waikiki **922-6262** 5pm-2am, clsd Mon • lesbians/gay men • Thai • full bar • wheelchair access

**Cafe Sistina** 1314 S. King St. **596-0061** lunch Mon-Fri, dinner nightly • northern Italian • some veggie • full bar • wheelchair access • $9-16

**Caffe Aczione** 1684 Kalakaua Ave. **941-9552** 9am-midnight, til 2am Fri-Sat, til 10pm Sun • Italian • some veggie • BYOB

**The Jungle** 311 Lewers St. **922-7808** pasta plus • some veggie • full bar • dancing/DJ • live shows • wheelchair access

---

# Honolulu (808)

**Where the Girls Are:** Where else? On the beach. Or cruising Kuhio Ave.

**Lesbigay Pride:** June: 951-7000.

**Annual Events:**

April - Merrie Monarch Festival.

May 25-June 2: Golden Week. Celebration of Japanese culture.

September - Aloha Week.

**City Info:** 923-1811.

**Attractions:** Bishop Museum. Foster Botanical Gardens. Hanauma Bay. Honolulu Academy of Arts. Polynesian Cultural Center (800/367-7060). Sea Life Park (800/767-8046). Waimea Falls Park.

**Best View:** Helicopter tour.

**Weather:** Usually paradise perfect, but humid. It rarely gets hotter than the upper 80°s.

**Transit:** Charley's: 955-2211. Island Pride Taxi: 732-6518.

**Kahala Moon Cafe** 4614 Kilauea **732-7777** lunch & dinner, clsd Mon • Pacific Rim cuisine

**Keo's Thai** 1200 Ala Moana Blvd. **533-0533** dinner • popular

**Pacific Cafe** 1200 Ala Moana Blvd. **593-0035** dinner nightly • lunch weekdays • Pacific Rim & classical Mediterranean cuisine • wheelchair accessible

**Pieces of Eight** 250 Lewers St., Waikiki **923-6646** 5pm-11pm • steak & seafood • full bar • wheelchair access • $8-15

**Singha Thai** 1910 Ala Moana **941-2898** 11am-11pm • live shows

## BOOKSTORES & RETAIL SHOPS

**Daäk's Body Splash** 343-3333

**Eighty Percent Straight** 2139 Kuhio Ave., 2nd flr., Waikiki **923-9996** 10am-midnight • lesbigay clothing • books • cards

## PUBLICATIONS

**Island Lifestyle Magazine** 737-6400 inquire about resource/travel guide • women-owned/run

## TRAVEL AGENTS

**Bird of Paradise Travel** 735-9103 IGLTA

**Pacific Ocean Holidays** 923-2400/(800) **735-6600** IGLTA • also publishes semi-annual 'Pocket Guide to Hawaii'

**Travel Travel** 320 Ward Ave. #204 **596-0336** IGLTA

## SPIRITUAL GROUPS

**Dignity Honolulu** 539 Kapahulu Ave. (St. Mark's Church) **536-5536** 7:30pm Sun

**Ke Annenue O Ke Aloha MCC** 1212 University Ave. (Church of the Crossroads) **942-1027** 7pm Sun

**Unitarian Universalists for Lesbian/Gay Concerns (Interweave)** 2500 Pali Hwy. **595-4047** 10:15am Sun • wheelchair access

**Unity Church of Hawaii** 3608 Diamond Head Cir. **735-4436** 7:30am, 9am & 11am Sun • wheelchair access

## EROTICA

**Diamond Head Video** 870 Kapahulu Ave. **735-6066** also 25 Kaneohe Bay Dr., Kailau 254-6066

# Windward Coast      (808)

## ACCOMMODATIONS

**Ali'i Bluffs Windward B&B** 46-251 Ikiiki St. **235-1124/(800) 235-1151** gay-friendly

## Boise (208)

### INFO LINES & SERVICES
**AA Gay/Lesbian** 23rd & Woodlawn (First Cong. Church) **344-6611** 8pm Sun & Tue
**Boise Bisexual Network** (at Community Ctr.) **331-1101** (BI-LINE) 8pm Sun
**Boise Bloomers 388-3864** social group for the gender gifted & friends
**Community Center** 919-A N. 27th St. **939-1629/336-3870** live 7pm-10pm • 24hr touchtone info line
**Women's Night 336-8471** 7pm 2nd Tue at 'Dreamwalker Cafe'

### BARS & NIGHTCLUBS
**8th Street Balcony Pub** 150 N. 8th St. **336-1313** 2pm-2am • gay-friendly • gay-owned/run
**Emerald City Club** 415 S. 9th **342-5446** 10am-2:30am • lesbians/gay men • dancing/DJ • live shows • women-owned/run
**Papa's Club 96** 1108 Front St. **333-0074** 4pm-2am, from 2pm wknds • mostly gay men • neighborhood bar • patio
**Partners** 2210 Main St. **331-3551** 2pm-2am • lesbians/gay men • dancing/DJ • live shows • wheelchair access

### CAFES
**Dreamwalker** 1015 W. Main St. **343-4196** 7am-12:30am, til 2:30am Fri, 3pm-5am Sat, 3pm-12:30am Sun • pastries • beer/wine • women's night 7pm 2nd Tue • live shows • dance parties Sat • wheelchair access • women-owned/run
**Flying M** 500 W. Idaho **345-4320** espresso & coffeehouse (soy milk) • food served • some veggie & vegan
**Jumpin' Juice & Java** 6748 Glenwood Ave. (Plantation Shopping Ctr.), Garden City **853-6264** 6am-8pm, til midnight Fri-Sat, 8am-6pm Sun

### ENTERTAINMENT & RECREATION
**Flicks & Rick's Cafe American** 646 Fulton St. **342-4288** 4:30pm-10pm, from noon wknds • 4 movie theaters • multi-racial • live shows • beer/wine • patio
**Triangle Connection 939-1627** 24hr activities hotline

### BOOKSTORES & RETAIL SHOPS
**Blue Unicorn** 107 N. 9th St. **345-9390** 10am-9pm, til 6pm Sat, 11am-5pm Sun • self-help • women's • lesbigay section • wheelchair access

**The Edge** 1101 W. Idaho St. **344-5383** gifts, cards, some lesbigay magazines • also coffee & pastries
**Retrospect** 113 N. 11th St. **336-5034** 11am-6pm, til 9pm Fri, noon-5pm Sun • sassy stuff • pride gifts

### PUBLICATIONS
**Diversity 323-0805** monthly

### SPIRITUAL GROUPS
**MCC** 408 N. Garden St. **342-6764** 5:45pm Sun

## Coeur D'Alene (208)
*(see also Spokane, Washington)*

### ACCOMMODATIONS
**The Clark House on Hayden Lake** 4550 S. Hayden Lake Rd., Hayden Lake **772-3470/(800) 765-4593** popular • gay-friendly • mansion on a wooded 12-acre estate • full brkfst • also fine dining • $125-200

### BARS & NIGHTCLUBS
**Mik-N-Mac's** 406 N. 4th **667-4858** noon-2am, til midnight Sun • lesbians/gay men • neighborhood bar • DJ or live shows Fri-Sat

## Lava Hot Springs (208)

### ACCOMMODATIONS
**Lava Hot Springs Inn 776-5830** gay-friendly • full brkfst • hot tub • mineral pool • wheelchair access • $59-145

### BOOKSTORES & RETAIL SHOPS
**Aura Soma Lava** 97 N. Portneuf River Rd. **776-5800/(800) 757-1233** seasonal • 10am-6pm • metaphysical & lesbigay books

## Moscow (208)

### INFO LINES & SERVICES
**Inland Northwest 882-8034** 1st Mon
**University of Idaho Gay/Lesbian/Bisexual Group 885-2691**
**Women's Center (Univ. of Idaho)** corner of Idaho & Line Sts. **885-6616** library & resources • support • limited outreach • call first

### BOOKSTORES & RETAIL SHOPS
**Bookpeople** 512 S. Main **882-7957** 9am-8pm • general

## Pocatello (208)

### BARS & NIGHTCLUBS
**Charleys** 331 E. Center **232-9606** 2pm-2am, clsd Sun-Mon • lesbians/gay men • dancing/DJ • live shows • wheelchair access

**Continental Bistro** 140 S. Main St. **233-4433** 11am-1am, clsd Sun • gay-friendly • also restaurant • northern Italian • plenty veggie • patio • $7-20

### CAFES
**Main St. Coffee & News** 234 N. Main **234-9834** 7am-6pm, 10am-4pm Sun

### EROTICA
**The Silver Fox** 143 S. 2nd St. **234-2477**

## Stanley (208 )

### ACCOMMODATIONS
**Las Tejanas B&B** Hwy. 75, Lower Stanley **376-6077/774-3301** May-Sept • gay-friendly • full brkfst • natural hot tub • btwn. 2 wilderness areas in the Sawtooth Mtns. • near outdoor recreation

## ILLINOIS

## Alton (618)

### ACCOMMODATIONS
**MotherSource Travels** 187 W. 19th St. **462-4051/(314) 569-5795** B&B network • St. Louis & Alton locations

### BARS & NIGHTCLUBS
**Mabel's Budget Beauty Shop & Chainsaw Repair** 602 Belle **465-8687** 4pm-1:30am, from 2pm wknds • mostly gay men • dancing/DJ • live shows • wheelchair access

## Arlington Heights (847)

*(see also Chicago)*

### BOOKSTORES & RETAIL SHOPS
**Prairie Moon** 8 N. Dunton Ave. **342-9608** 11am-6pm, til 8pm Th, clsd Mon • feminist • special events • wheelchair access • women-owned/run

## Aurora (630)

*(see also Chicago)*

### EROTICA
**Denmark Book Store** 1300 US Hwy. 30 **898-9838** 24hrs

## Bloomington (309)

### BARS & NIGHTCLUBS
**Bistro** 316 N. Main St. **829-2278** 4pm-1am, from 8pm Sat, from 6pm Sun • lesbians/gay men • dancing/DJ • wheelchair access

### BOOKSTORES & RETAIL SHOPS
**Once Upon a Time (O.U.T.)** 311 N. Main **828-3998** 1pm-8pm,10am-6pm Sat, noon-5pm Sun, clsd Mon • lesbigay

### EROTICA
**Risques** 1506 N. Main **827-9279** 24hrs

## Blue Island (708)

### BARS & NIGHTCLUBS
**Clubhouse Players** 13126 S. Western **389-6688** 8pm-2am, til 3am Fri-Sat • lesbians/gay men • dancing/DJ • transgender-friendly • live shows • wheelchair access

## Calumet City (708)

*(see also Chicago & Hammond, IN)*

### BARS & NIGHTCLUBS

**Are You Crazy** 48 154th Pl. **862-4605**
7pm-2am • mostly gay men

**Intrigue** 582 State Line Rd. **868-5240**
6pm-2am, 7pm-3am Sat, 2pm-2am Sun •
mostly women • dancing/DJ • women-
owned/run

**Mr. B's** 606 State Line Rd. **862-1221**
2pm-2am, til 3am Wed & Fri-Sat • popular • mostly gay men • dancing/DJ

**Patch** 201 155th St. **891-9854** 4pm-2am,
from noon Th, from 6pm Sun, clsd Mon •
mostly women • neighborhood bar •
women-owned/run

**Pour House** 103 155th Pl. **891-3980**
9:30pm-2am, clsd Mon-Tue, til 3am Wed
& Fri-Sat • mostly gay men • dancing/DJ

## Carbondale (618)

### INFO LINES & SERVICES

**AA Lesbian/Gay 549-4633**

**Gay/Lesbian/Bisexuals & Friends**
(Southern Illinois University) **453-5151**

**Women's Services 453-3655** 8am-
4:30pm

### BARS & NIGHTCLUBS

**Club Traz** 213 E. Main St. **549-4270**
8pm-2am, clsd Mon • lesbians/gay men
• dancing/DJ • alternative • wheelchair
access

## Champaign/Urbana (217)

### INFO LINES & SERVICES

**Outpost Community Center** 123 W.
Church St., Champaign **239-4688** 6pm-
9pm, noon-5pm Sat, clsd Sun • site for
lesbigaytrans events & groups • events
for teens every Sat

**People for Lesbian/Gay/Bisexual
Concerns of Illinois** (at University of
Illinois) **333-1187** 5:30pm Tue • student
group

### BARS & NIGHTCLUBS

**Chester Street** 63 Chester St. **356-5607**
5pm-1am • lesbians/gay men • danc-
ing/DJ • 'Trash Disco' Wed • wheelchair
access

### BOOKSTORES & RETAIL SHOPS

**Horizon Book Store** 603 S. Wright St.
**356-9113** 10am-6pm, clsd Sun

**Jane Addams Book Shop** 208 N. Neil
**356-2555** 10am-5pm, til 8pm Fri, noon-
5pm Sun • lesbigay & women's sections

## CHICAGO

*Chicago is divided into 5 geographical areas:*

### Chicago—Overview

### Chicago—North Side

### Chicago—New Town

### Chicago—Near North

### Chicago—South Side

### Chicago—Overview

### INFO LINES & SERVICES

**AA Gay/Lesbian-Newtown Al-Anon Club**
909 W. Belmont St. 2nd flr. **(773) 529-
0321** 3pm-11pm, from 11am Fri, from
8am wknds • wheelchair access

**Chicago 35** (at 'Ann Sather's' restaurant)
**(773) 271-5909** 3:30pm-6pm 3rd Sun •
group for women over 35

**The Chicago Area Gay/Lesbian
Chamber of Commerce (888) 452-4262**
call for maps, member lists & more

**Chicago Black Lesbians/Gays (312)
409-4917 (HOTLINE#)** citywide group for
lesbigaytrans activism & visibility • 24hr
touchtone events line

**Chicagoland Bisexual Network (312)
458-0983** variety of political, social &
support resources

**Gerber/Hart Library & Archives** 3352 N.
Paulina St. **(773) 883-3003** 6pm-9pm
Wed-Th, noon-4pm wknds • lesbigay
resource center

**Horizons Community Services** 961 W.
Montana **(773) 472-6469** 9am-10pm
Mon-Th, til 5pm Fri

**Illinois Tourist Information Center** 310
S. Michigan #108 **(800) 822-0292**

**Lesbian/Gay Helpline (773) 929-4357**
6pm-10pm

**SANGAT (Gay/Lesbian South Asians)
(773) 506-8810**

### ENTERTAINMENT & RECREATION

**Bailiwick Arts Center** 1229 W. Belmont
**(773) 883-1090** Bailiwick Repertory presents many lesbigay-themed productions
w/popular Pride Series

**Leather Archives & Museum** 5007 N.
Clark St. **(773) 275-1570** 4pm-midnight
Sat or by appt.

# Chicago

Not just another big Midwestern city, Chicago is home to strong communities of political radicals, African-Americans, artists and performers, and of course, lesbians and gays.

If you remember the Chicago 7, you might want to stop by the Heartland Cafe (465-8005) in Rogers Park for a drink, some food, or a T-shirt from their radical variety store. Or check in with **Horizons Community Services** to find out about local lesbigay political and social groups.

The African-American communities in Chicago are large and influential, making up about 40% of Chicago's population. In fact, Chicago was settled by an African-French man, whose name graces the Du Sable Museum of African-American History (947-0600). The South Side is the cultural center for Chicagoans of African descent and houses the South Side Community Art Center (373-1026) and the Olivet Baptist Church (842-1081), a station on the Underground Railroad and site of Mahalia Jackson's 1928 debut. We've heard the home cooking at Army & Lou's Restaurant (483-3100) will make you stand up and holler.

Many of Chicago's other immigrant neighborhoods also house the museums, centers and restaurants the city is famous for—call the Chicago Office of Tourism for details. However, if you love Indian food, don't miss the many delicious and cheap Indian buffets on Devon, just west of Sheridan.

What else is there to do? For starters, take a cruise on Lake Michigan. You have your choice of wine-tasting cruises, narrated history cruises, brunch, dinner or cocktail cruises. On land, you'll find superb shopping, real Chicago-style deep dish pizza, a great arts and theater scene. Don't miss the thriving blues and jazz clubs, like the Green Mill (878-5552), known for originating "poetry slams," and for its house big band.

And you'll never have a dull moment in Chicago's women's scene. For a good book or a good time, seek out **People Like Us,** the city's lesbigay bookstore, or **Women & Children First** bookstore. Pick up a copy of **Outlines** or **Nightlines** for the dish on what's hot. And while you're in New Town, cruise by **Girlbar.** On the Northside, treat yourself to the art at **Womanwild** women's gallery, grab a cup of java at the truly **Mountain Moving Coffeehouse** on Saturday.

## BOOKSTORES & RETAIL SHOPS

**Barbara's Bookstore** 1350 N. Wells St. **(312) 642-5044** 9am-10pm, 10am-9pm Sun • women's/lesbigay • other locations: 700 E. Grand Ave. 222-0897 • Oak Park (708) 848-9140

## PUBLICATIONS

**The Alternative Phone Book (773) 472-6319** directory of local businesses
**Gab (773) 248-4542**
**Gay Chicago (773) 327-7271** weekly • extensive resource listings
▲**Outlines/Nightlines (773) 871-7610** monthly
**Windy City Times (312) 397-0020**

## TRAVEL AGENTS

**All-Ways Travel** 111 N. Canal **(312) 255-9297/(800) 536-3876** IGLTA
**The Concierge Exclusif (312) 849-3604** personalized assistance for visitors

## SPIRITUAL GROUPS

**Congregation Or Chadash** 656 W. Barry (2nd Unitarian Church) **(773) 248-9456** 8pm Fri • Shabbat services & monthly activities
**Dignity Chicago** 3344 N. Broadway **(773) 296-0780** mass & social hour 7pm Sun
**Integrity/Chicago (773) 348-6362** 7:30pm 1st & 3rd Fri • call for location
**MCC Good Shepherd** 615 W. Wellington Ave. **(773) 262-0099** 7pm Sun
**Presbyterians for Lesbian/Gay Concerns** 600 W. Fullerton Pkwy. (Lincoln Park Preb.) **(312) 784-2635** 10am Sun • 'More Light' congregation

## Chicago—North Side     (773)

### ACCOMMODATIONS
**A Sister's Place** Andersonville **275-1319** women only • guestrooms in artist's flat • women-owned/run • $25-45

### BARS & NIGHTCLUBS
**Augenblick** 3907 N. Damen **929-0994** 7pm-3am • lesbians/gay men • live shows • patio

---

## Chicago     (312/773)

**Where the Girls Are:** In the Belmont area—on Halsted or Clark streets—with the boys, or hanging out elsewhere in New Town. Upwardly-mobile lesbians live in Lincoln Park or Wrigleyville, while their working-class sisters live in Andersonville (way north).

**Lesbigay Pride:** June: 773/348-8243.

**Annual Events:**

February- Hearts Party: 773/404-3784.

May - International Mr. Leather: 800/545-6753. Weekend of events and contest on Sunday.

June- Lambda Literary Awards: 202/462-7924. The 'Lammies' are the Oscars of lesbigay writing & publishing. Chicago Blues Festival: 744-3315.

November - Chicago Gay/Lesbian Film Festival: 773/384-5533.

**City Info:** Chicago Office of Tourism: 744-2400/ 800/487-2446.

**Attractions:** 900 North Michigan Shops. Historic Water Tower. Leather Archives and Museum (773/275-1570). Museum of Science and Industry. Sears Tower Skydeck Observatory. Second City and the Improv Comedy Clubs. The Art Institute of Chicago.

**Best View:** Skydeck of the 110-story Sears Tower.

**Weather:** "The Windy City" earned its name. Winter temperatures have been known to be as low as -46°. Summers are humid, normally in the 80's.

**Transit:** Yellow & Checker Cabs: 829-4222. Chicago Airport Shuttle Service: 773/247-7678. Chicago Transit Authority: 836-7000.

**Big Chicks** 5024 N. Sheridan 728-5511 3pm-2am, from 1pm wknds • lesbians/gay men • neighborhood bar • wheelchair access

**Boom Boom Room at Red Dog** 1958 W. North Ave. 278-1009 9pm-4am Mon • gay-friendly • dancing/DJ

**Chicago Eagle** 5015 N. Clark St. 728-0050 8pm-4am • lesbians/gay men • women's night Th • leather • wheelchair access

**Clark's on Clark** 5001 N. Clark St. 728-2373 4pm-4am • popular • mostly gay men • neighborhood bar

**Different Strokes** 4923 N. Clark St. 989-1958 noon-2am, til 3am Sat • mostly gay men • neighborhood bar

**Estelle's** 2013 W. North Ave. 486-8760 gay-friendly

**Friends Pub** 3432 W. Irving Park Rd. 539-5229 noon-2am • lesbians/gay men • dancing/DJ • wheelchair access

**Lost & Found** 3058 W. Irving Park Rd. 463-9617 7pm-2am, from 4pm wknds, clsd Mon • mostly women • neighborhood bar

**Madrigal's** 5316 N. Clark St. 334-3033 2pm-2am • lesbians/gay men • live shows

**Paris Dance** 1122 W. Montrose 769-0602 5pm-2am • mostly women • dancing/DJ • also cafe • clsd Mon-Tue • wheelchair access

**Rainbow Room** 4539 N. Lincoln 271-4378 6pm-2am, from 4pm Sat, from noon Sun • mostly women • dancing/DJ

**Scot's** 1829 W. Montrose 528-3253 3pm-2am, from 11am wknds • lesbians/gay men • neighborhood bar

**Touché** 6412 N. Clark St. 465-7400 5pm-4am, from 3pm wknds • mostly gay men • leather

CAFES

**I.Net@Cafe** 5243 N. Clark St., 2nd flr. 784-4075 11am-midnight, til 1am Sat, til 11pm Sun • espresso & deli • internet • gay-owned

**Mountain Moving Coffeehouse** 1545 W. Morse 477-8362 Sat only • women & girls only • non-alcoholic beverages • live shows • collectively run

**Lambda Publications**
*since 1987*

1115 West Belmont, Suite 2-D, Chicago, IL 60657-3312

(773) 871-7610
FAX (773) 871-7609

e-mail:
outlines@suba.com

*send $5 for sample of all products*

**World Wide Web Page**
http://www.suba.com/~outlines/
*All our products are now ONLINE!*

**OUTLINES**
The Monthly Voice of the Gay & Lesbian Community

**NIGHTLINES** *Weekly*

**OUT! Resource Guide**
a twice-yearly resource guide

**CLOUT! Business Report**
a quarterly glossy magazine

**BLACKlines**
for Black lesbians, gays, bi/trans

**En La Vida**
for Latino/a lesbigays/trans

## Restaurants

**Fireside** 5739 N. Ravenswood **878-5942** 11am-4am • plenty veggie • full bar • patio • wheelchair access • $6-15

**Julie Mai's** 5025 N. Clark **784-6000** 3pm-10pm • French/Vietnamese • full bar

**Lolita's Cafe** 4400 N. Clark **561-3356** noon-11pm, til 2am Fri & 3am Sat • lesbians/gay men • multi-racial (Latino/a) • transgender-friendly • authentic Mexican food • full bar • also club from 11pm Fri-Sat • dancing/DJ • live shows

**Tendino's** 5335 N. Sheridan **275-8100** 11am-11pm • pizzeria • full bar • wheelchair access

**Tomboy** 5402 N. Clark **907-0636** 5pm-10pm, clsd Mon • popular • BYOB • lesbian-owned • wheelchair access

## Bookstores & Retail Shops

**KOPI: A Traveler's Cafe** 5317 N. Clark St. **989-5674** 8am-11pm • live shows • also boutique & gallery

**WomanWild/Treasures by Women** 5237 N. Clark St. **878-0300** 11am-7pm, til 6pm wknds • art & gift gallery • commitment rings & gift registry • wheelchair access • lesbian-owned/run

**Women & Children First** 5233 N. Clark St. **769-9299** 11am-7pm, til 9pm Wed-Fri, til 6pm Sun • women's bookstore • also videos & music • wheelchair access • women-owned/run

## Travel Agents

**Ivory Isle Travel** 1 N. Franklin #350 **726-8998** IGLTA

**Yellow Brick Road, The Travel Agency** 1500 W. Balmoral Ave. **561-1800/(800) 642-2488** IGLTA

## Chicago—New Town (773)

## Accommodations

**City Suites Hotel** 933 W. Belmont **404-3400/(800) 248-9108** gay-friendly • accommodations w/touch of European style • IGLTA • $79-89

**Park Brompton Inn** 528 W. Brompton Pl. **404-3499/(800) 727-5108** gay-friendly • romantic 19th century atmosphere • $75-89

**Surf Hotel** 555 W. Surf St. **528-8400/(800) 787-3108** gay-friendly • 1920s hotel in Lincoln Park

**Villa Toscana Guesthouse** 3447 N. Halsted St. **404-2643/(800) 684-5755** lesbians/gay men • full brkfst

## Bars & Nightclubs

**Annex 3** 3160 N. Clark St. **327-5969** noon-2am, til 3am Sat • lesbians/gay men • videos • sports bar • wheelchair access

**Beat Kitchen** 2100 W. Belmont **281-4444** noon-2am • gay-friendly • live shows • also grill • some veggie • wheelchair access

**Berlin** 954 W. Belmont **348-4975** opening time varies, closes 4am • popular • lesbians/gay men • women's night w/dancers 1st & 3rd Wed • dancing/DJ • live shows • videos • wheelchair access

**Blues** 2519 N. Halsted **528-1012** classic Chicago blues spot

**Buddies** 3301 N. Clark St. **477-4066** 7am-2am, from 9am Sun • lesbians/gay men • some veggie • $8-12

**Cell Block** 3702 N. Halsted **665-8064** 6pm-2am, 2pm-3am Sat, til 2am Sun • also 'Holding Cell' from 10pm Th-Sat w/strict uniform code, from 6pm Sun w/ no dress code • also 'Leather Cell' store

**Circuit** 3641 N. Halsted St. **325-2233** 7pm-2am, from 1pm wknds • gay-friendly • dancing/DJ • live shows • karaoke

**The Closet** 3325 N. Broadway St. **477-8533** 2pm-4am, from noon wknds • popular • lesbians/gay men • videos

**Cocktail** 3359 Halsted St. **477-1420** 4pm-2am, from 2pm wknds • lesbians/gay men • wheelchair access

**Dandy's Piano Bar** 3729 N. Halsted St. **525-1200** noon-2am • lesbians/gay men • neighborhood bar • piano bar • wheelchair access

**Fusion** 3631 N. Halsted **975-6622** 10pm-4am Fri, til 5am Sat • lesbians/gay men • monthly women's parties • dancing/DJ • alternative • live shows • videos • wheelchair access

**Gentry** 3320 N. Halsted **348-1053** 4pm-2am • lesbians/gay men • live shows

**Girlbar** 2625 N. Halsted **871-4210** 6pm-2am, from 3pm Fri & Sun • mostly women • 'Boybar' Wed • dancing/DJ • patio

**Roscoe's** 3354-3356 N. Halsted St. **281-3355** 2pm-2am, noon-3am Sat • popular • lesbians/gay men • neighborhood bar • dancing/DJ • videos • food served • patio

**Smart Bar/Metro** 3730 N. Clark St. **549-4140** 9:30pm-4am • gay-friendly • dancing/DJ • live shows

**Spin** 3200 N. Halsted **327-7711** 4pm-2am • mostly gay men • 2nd & 4th Tue women's night • dancing/DJ • videos

## CAFES

**Mike's Broadway Cafe** 3805 N. Broadway **404-2205** 7am-10pm, 24hrs Fri-Sat • lesbians/gay men • some veggie • wheelchair access • $5-10

## RESTAURANTS

**Angelina Ristorante** 3561 Broadway **935-5933** 5:30pm-11pm, Sun brunch • Italian • $10-20

**Ann Sather's** 929 W. Belmont Ave. **348-2378** 7am-10pm, til midnight Fri-Sat • popular • some veggie • $5-10

**Bossa Nova** 1960 N. Clybourn Ave. **248-4800** dinner Tue-Sat • tapas

**Buddies Restaurant & Bar** 3301 N. Clark St. **477-4066** 7am-2am, from 9am Sun • lesbians/gay men • some veggie • $8-12

**Cornelia's** 750 Cornelia Ave. **248-8333** dinner, clsd Mon • some veggie • full bar • wheelchair access • $10-20

**The Pepper Lounge** 3441 N. Sheffield **665-7377** 6pm-2am, clsd Mon • lesbians/gay men • supper club • gourmet Italian • plenty veggie • full bar • $12-20

**The Raw Bar & Grill** 3720 N. Clark St. **348-7291** 5pm-2am • seafood • $8-12

## BOOKSTORES & RETAIL SHOPS

**People Like Us** 1115 W. Belmont **248-6363** 10am-9pm • Chicago's only exclusively lesbigay bookstore

**Unabridged Books** 3251 N. Broadway St. **883-9119** 10am-10pm, til 8pm wknds

**We're Everywhere** 3434 N. Halsted St. **404-0590/(800) 772-6411** noon-9pm, 11am-8pm wknds • also mail order catalog

## TRAVEL AGENTS

**Action Travel** 2256 W. Roscoe **929-4600/(800) 397-2749** IGLTA

**All Points Travel Services** 3405 N. Broadway **525-4700/(800) 774-3329** IGLTA

**American Express Travel Lincoln Park** 2338 N. Clark St. **477-4000/(800) 477-3661** IGLTA

**Time Travelers** 822 W. Roscoe **248-8173** IGLTA

## GYMS & HEALTH CLUBS

**Chicago Sweat Shop** 3215 N. Broadway **871-2789** gay-friendly

IT'S **YOUR** WEEKEND

...TAKE ADVANTAGE OF IT

**1 (888) 44 DINAH**
CLUB SKIRTS & GIRL BAR

## EROTICA
**Male Hide Leathers** 2816 N. Lincoln Ave. **929-0069**

**The Pleasure Chest** 3143 N. Broadway **525-7152**

# Chicago—Near North    (312)

## ACCOMMODATIONS
**Best Western Inn of Chicago** 162 E. Ohio St. **787-3100**/**(800) 557-2378** gay-friendly • food service • wheelchair access • IGLTA

**Gold Coast Guesthouse** 113 W. Elm St. **337-0361** gay-friendly • women-owned/run • $105-150

**Hotel Lincoln (Days Inn)** 1816 N. Clark St. **664-3040**/**(800) 329-7466** gay-friendly

**Hyatt Regency Chicago** 151 E. Wacker Dr. **565-1234**/**(800) 233-1234** gay-friendly

**Old Town B&B 440-9268** lesbians/gay men • patio • $75

## BARS & NIGHTCLUBS
**Artful Dodger** 1734 W. Wabansia **(773) 227-6859** 5pm-2am, from 8pm Sat • gay-friendly • dancing/DJ

**Baton Show Lounge** 436 N. Clark St. **644-5269** 8pm-4am Wed-Sun • lesbians/gay men • live shows • wheelchair access

**Club B.A.D. (House of Blues)** 329 N. Dearborn St. **(888) 777-8886** mostly gay men • dancing/DJ

**The Crowbar** 1543 N. Kingsbury **243-4800** 10pm-4am, clsd Mon-Tue • popular • gay-friendly • more gay Sun • dancing/DJ

**Elixir** 325 N. Jefferson St. **258-0523** 10pm-4am Th-Sat • gay-friendly • hip fashion crowd

**The Generator** 306 N. Halsted **243-8889** 9pm-4am, clsd Mon-Tue • lesbians/gay men • dancing/DJ • alternative • mostly African-American • wheelchair access

**Gentry** 440 N. State **664-1033** 1pm-2am • popular • mostly gay men • live shows • videos

**Second City** 1616 N. Wells St. **337-3992** legendary comedy club • call for reservations

**Vinyl** 1615 N. Clybourn **587-8469** opens 5:30pm daily, Sun brunch 10am-3pm

## CAFES
**Urbis Orbis Coffeehouse** 1934 W. North Ave. **(773) 252-4446** 9am-midnight • lesbigay periodicals

## RESTAURANTS
**The Berghoff** 17 West Adams St. **427-3170** 11am-9pm, til 10pm Sat, clsd Sun great mashed potatoes

**Blue Mesa** 1729 N. Halsted St. **944-5990** lunch & dinner • Southwestern • full bar

**Fireplace Inn** 1448 N. Wells St. **664-5264** 4:30pm-midnight, from 11am wknds (summer) • lesbians/gay men • BBQ/American • full bar • $10-20

**Iggy's** 700 N. Milwaukee, River North **829-4449** dinner nightly, til 4am Th-Sat • Italian • some veggie • full bar • $8-12

**Kiki's Bistro** 900 N. Franklin St. **335-5454** French • full bar

**Manny's** 1141 S. Jefferson St. **939-2855** 5am-4pm, clsd Sun • killer corned beef

**The Mashed Potato Club** 316 W. Erie St., downtown **255-8579** 11am-10:30pm, til 1:30am Fri-Sat • homecooking • plenty veggie • patio • wheelchair access

**Shaw's Crab House** 21 E. Hubbard **527-2722** lunch & dinner • full bar

## TRAVEL AGENTS
**Business Travel Advisors** 875 N. Michigan Ave. #1355 **266-8700** IGLTA

**C.R.C. Travel** 2121 N. Clybourn **(773) 525-3800**/**(800) 874-7701** IGLTA

**Envoy Travel** 740 N. Rush St. **787-2400**/**(800) 443-6869** IGLTA

**Hemingway Travel** 1640 N. Wells, 2nd flr. **440-9870** IGLTA

**River North Travel** 432 N. Clark St. **527-2269** IGLTA

**Travel With Us, Ltd.** 919 N. Michigan Ave. #3102 **944-2244**/**(800) 775-0919** IGLTA

## GYMS & HEALTH CLUBS
**Thousand Waves** 1212 W. Belmont Ave. **(773) 549-0700** women only • martial arts & self-defense for women & children • health spa • women-owned/run

# Chicago—South Side    (773)

## BARS & NIGHTCLUBS
**Escapades** 6301 S. Harlem **229-0886** 10pm-4am, til 5am Sat • mostly gay men • videos

**Inn Exile** 5758 W. 65th St. **582-3510** 6pm-2am, from noon Sun • mostly gay men • dancing/DJ • wheelchair access

**Jeffery Pub/Disco** 7041 S. Jeffery **363-8555** 11am-4am • mostly gay men • dancing/DJ • multi-racial • wheelchair access

### BOOKSTORES & RETAIL SHOPS
**57th St. Books** 1301 E. 57th St., Hyde Park **684-1300** lesbigay section • readings

### SPIRITUAL GROUPS
**Resurrection MCC** 5757 S. University, Hyde Park **288-1535** 10:30am Sun

## Decatur (217)

### BARS & NIGHTCLUBS
**The Flashback Lounge** 2239 E. Wood St. **422-3530** 11am-2am, from 4pm Sun • gay-friendly • neighborhood bar

### TRAVEL AGENTS
**Village Travel** 3008 N. Water **875-5640**/(800) 373-8747 IGLTA

## Deerfield (847)

### TRAVEL AGENTS
**Ridgebrook Travel** 104 Wilmot Rd. #100 **(847) 374-0077**/(800) 962-0560 IGLTA

## Elgin (847)
*(see also Chicago)*

### INFO LINES & SERVICES
**Fox Valley Gay Association** 392-6882 7pm-10pm Mon-Fri

## Elk Grove Village (847)
*(see also Chicago)*

### BARS & NIGHTCLUBS
**Hunters** 1932 E. Higgins **439-8840** 4pm-4am • popular • mostly gay men • dancing/DJ • videos

## Evanston (847)

### INFO LINES & SERVICES
**Kinheart Women's Center** 2214 Ridge Ave. **604-0913** lesbian-only programs 8pm 2nd, 3rd & 4th Fri

## Evansville (812)

### TRAVEL AGENTS
**Evansville Travel** 970 S. Hebron Ave. **471-4000** IGLTA

## Forest Park (708)
*(see also Chicago)*

### BARS & NIGHTCLUBS
**Nut Bush** 7201 Franklin **366-5117** 3pm-2am, til 3am Fri-Sat • mostly gay men • dancing/DJ • videos

## Frankfort (815)

### TRAVEL AGENTS
**Triangle Travel & Cruise** 464-6460 IGLTA

## Franklin Park (847)

### BARS & NIGHTCLUBS
**Temptations** 10235 W. Grand Ave. **455-0008** 4pm-4am, from 6pm Fri-Sun • popular • mostly women • dancing/DJ • transgender-friendly • live entertainment • wheelchair access

## Galesburg (309)

### ACCOMMODATIONS
**The Fahnestock House** 591 N. Prairie St. **344-0270** gay-friendly • full brkfst • Queen Anne Victorian • gay-owned

## Granite City (618)
*(see also St. Louis, MO)*

### BARS & NIGHTCLUBS
**Club Zips** 3145 W. Chain of Rocks Rd. **797-0700** 7pm-2am, til 3am Sat, 5pm-midnight Sun, clsd Mon-Tue • popular • lesbians/gay men • live entertainment • videos • outdoor complex

## Hinsdale (630)

### SPIRITUAL GROUPS
**MCC Holy Covenant** 17 W. Maple (Unitarian Church) **325-8488** 6pm Sun • wheelchair access

## Joliet (815)

### BARS & NIGHTCLUBS
**Maneuvers** 118 E. Jefferson **727-7069** 8pm-2am, til 3am Fri-Sat • lesbians/gay men • dancing/DJ • patio

## Lake County (847)

### BARS & NIGHTCLUBS
**Emerald City** 26029 W. Rte. 173, Antioch **838-1888** 7pm-2am, til 3am Fri-Sat • lesbians/gay men • dancing/DJ • wheelchair access

## Lansing (708)
*(see also Chicago & Hammond, IN)*

### RESTAURANTS
**Outriggers** 2352 172nd St. **418-0202** 11am-11pm • popular • seafood • some veggie • full bar • live shows • wheelchair access • $11-18

## Lincolnwood (847)

### TRAVEL AGENTS
**Bonanza Travel** 3952 W. Touhy **674-3770** IGLTA

**Edward's Travel Advisors** 7301 N. Lincoln Ave. #215 **677-4420/(800) 541-5158** IGLTA

## Naperville (630)

### TRAVEL AGENTS
**Classic Travel** 1271 E. Ogden Ave. #123 **963-3030/(800) 932-5789** IGLTA

## Oak Park (708)

*(see also Chicago)*

### BOOKSTORES & RETAIL SHOPS
**The Left Bank Bookstall** 104 S. Oak Park Ave. **383-4700** 10am-8pm, til 9pm Fri-Sat, noon-5pm Sun

**The Pride Agenda** 1109 Westgate **524-8429** 11am-7pm, til 8pm Th-Fri, 11am-5pm wknds • lesbigay • wheelchair access

### TRAVEL AGENTS
**Gone With The Wind Travel** 212 S. Marion #5 **383-6960/(888) 429-8785** IGLTA

### SPIRITUAL GROUPS
**MCC of the Incarnation** 460 Lake **383-3033** 11am Sun • wheelchair access

## Peoria (309)

### BARS & NIGHTCLUBS
**D.J.'s Timeout** 703 SW Adams **674-5902** 1pm-1am • lesbians/gay men • dancing/DJ • wheelchair access

**Quench Room** 631 W. Main **676-1079** 5pm-1am, from 1pm wknds • lesbians/gay men • neighborhood bar • wheelchair access

**Red Fox Den** 800 N. Knoxville Ave. **674-8013** 9pm-4am • lesbians/gay men • dancing/DJ • food served • live shows

### PUBLICATIONS
**The Alternative Times** 688-1930

## Quincy (217)

### INFO LINES & SERVICES
**AA Gay/Lesbian** 124-1/2 N. 5th (MCC) **224-2800** 7pm Th

### BARS & NIGHTCLUBS
**Irene's Cabaret** 124 N. 5th St. **222-6292** 9pm-2:30am, from 7pm Fri-Sat, clsd Mon • lesbians/gay men • dancing/DJ • live shows • wheelchair access

### SPIRITUAL GROUPS
**MCC** 124-1/2 N. 5th **224-2800** 6pm Sun

## Rock Island (309)

*(see also Davenport, IA)*

### BARS & NIGHTCLUBS
**Augie's** 313 20th St. **788-7389** 6am-3am, from 10am Sun • mostly women • neighborhood bar

**J.R.'s** 325 20th St. **786-9411** 3pm-3am, from noon Sun • lesbians/gay men • dancing/DJ • live shows • wheelchair access

### BOOKSTORES & RETAIL SHOPS
**All Kinds of People** 1806 2nd Ave. **788-2567** 10am-11pm • alternative • food served • wheelchair access

## Rockford (815)

### BARS & NIGHTCLUBS
**Office** 513 E. State St. **965-0344** 5pm-2am, noon-midnight Sun • popular • lesbians/gay men • dancing/DJ • videos • beer only

**Oh Zone** 1014 Charles St. **964-9663** 5pm-2am, 11am-midnight Sun • lesbians/gay men • dancing/DJ • wheelchair access

### CAFES
**Cafe Esperanto** 107 N. Main **968-0123** 3pm-1am, noon-2am Sat, 7pm-midnight Sun • full bar • also gallery

### RESTAURANTS
**Lucernes** 845 N. Church St. **968-2665** 5pm-11pm, clsd Mon • fondue • full bar • wheelchair access

**Maria's** 828 Cunningham **968-6781** 5pm-9pm, clsd Sun-Mon • Italian • full bar • Denise's favorite • $6-12

## South Holland (708)

### TRAVEL AGENTS
**South Holland Travel & Cruise** 550 E. 162nd St., C-East **333-0360** IGLTA

## Springfield (217)

### BARS & NIGHTCLUBS

**New Dimensions** 3036 Peoria Rd. **753-9268** 9pm-3am, clsd Mon • mostly gay men • dancing/DJ • beer only

**Smokey's Den** 411 E. Washington **522-0301** 6pm-1am, til 3am Fri-Sat • lesbians/gay men • dancing/DJ • wheelchair access

**The Station House** 306 E. Washington **525-0438** 7am-1am, from noon Sun • gay-friendly • neighborhood bar • wheelchair access

### BOOKSTORES & RETAIL SHOPS

**Sundance** 1428 E. Sangamon Ave. **788-5243** 11am-7pm, 10am-6pm Sat, clsd Sun-Mon • New Age books & gifts • lesbigay titles

### PUBLICATIONS

▲ **Prairie Flame** PO Box 2483, 62705-2483 **753-2887** covers central IL

### TRAVEL AGENTS

**World Travel Associates** 2816 Plaza Dr. (at the Gables) **793-9006/(800) 298-9200**

### SPIRITUAL GROUPS

**Faith Eternal MCC** 304 W. Allen **525-9597** 10am & 6pm Sun

## Waukegan

*(see Chicago)*

## Wood River

*(see Alton)*

# Prairie Flame

**Where Lesbian & Gay Readers in Central Illinois get the news**

**Free Directory of Local GLBT Friendly Businesses
Free Event Listings - Free Personals
Reasonable Subscription & Advertising Rates**

phone-FAX 217/753-2887
e-mail pflame@eosinc.com
write P. O. Box 2483, Springfield, IL 62705-2483
To place personal ads
phone 1-800-536-6896 Ext 186C

# INDIANA

## Bloomington (812)

### INFO LINES & SERVICES
**Indiana University Gay/Lesbian/Bisexual Student Services** 705 E. 7th St. **855-4252** hours vary • recorded info 24hrs • 855-5688

**Indiana Youth Group (800) 347-8336 (IN-STATE)** 7pm-midnight Th-Fri • lesbigay youth hotline

**Office for Women's Affairs** Memorial Hall East #123 **855-3849** 8am-noon & 1pm-5pm, clsd wknds • support/discussion groups • call for info

### ACCOMMODATIONS
**Enchanted Otter 323-9800** women only • lake retreat for all seasons • full brkfst • hot tub • kitchen • smokefree • women-owned/run • $60-85

**Holiday Inn Bloomington** 1710 Kinser Pike **334-3252/(800) 465-4329** gay-friendly

### BARS & NIGHTCLUBS
**Bullwinkle's** 201 S. College St. **334-3232** 7pm-3am, clsd Sun • lesbians/gay men • more women Th • dancing/DJ • live shows

**The Other Bar** 414 S. Walnut **332-0033** 4pm-3am, clsd Sun • lesbians/gay men • neighborhood bar • patio • wheelchair access

### RESTAURANTS
**Village Deli** 409 E. Kirkwood **336-2303** 8am-7pm, 7am-4pm wknds • some veggie

### BOOKSTORES & RETAIL SHOPS
**Athena Gallery** 108 E. Kirkwood Ave. **339-0734** 11am-6pm, til 8pm Fri-Sat, til 4pm Sun • wheelchair access

### SPIRITUAL GROUPS
**Integrity Bloomington** 400 E. Kirkwood Ave. (Trinity Episcopal Church) **336-4466** 7:30pm 2nd Wed • wheelchair access

## Elkhart (219)

*(see also South Bend)*

### INFO LINES & SERVICES
**Switchboard Concern 293-8671 (CRISIS ONLY)** 24hrs

### SPIRITUAL GROUPS
**Unitarian Universalist Fellowship** 1732 Garden **264-6525** 10:30am Sun • wheelchair access

## Evansville (812)

### INFO LINES & SERVICES
**Tri-State Alliance 474-4853** info • monthly social group • newsletter

### BARS & NIGHTCLUBS
**Someplace Else** 930 Main St. **424-3202** 4pm-3am, clsd Sun • lesbians/gay men • dancing/DJ • also 'Down Under' pride gift shop

**Uptown Bar** 201 W. Illinois St. **423-4861** 1pm-1am, til 3am Fri-Sat, clsd Sun • lesbians/gay men • dancing/DJ • videos • pizza served • patio • wheelchair access

### BOOKSTORES & RETAIL SHOPS
**A.A. Michael Books** 1541 S. Green River Rd. **479-8979** 10am-6pm, til 8pm Fri, 10am-5pm Sat, noon-5pm Sun • spiritual • wheelchair access

## Fort Wayne (219)

### INFO LINES & SERVICES
**Gay/Lesbian AA** (at Up the Stairs Community Center) **744-1199** 7:30pm Tue & Sat, 4:30pm Sun

**Up the Stairs Community Center** 3426 Broadway **744-1199** helpline 7pm-10pm, til midnight Fri-Sat, 6:30pm-9pm Sun • drop-in 8pm-midnight Fri • space for various groups

### BARS & NIGHTCLUBS
**After Dark** 231 Pearl St. **424-6130** 6pm-3am, clsd Sun • lesbians/gay men • dancing/DJ • live shows • wheelchair access

**Downtown On The Landing** 110 W. Columbia St. **420-1615** 7pm-3am, clsd Sun-Tue • lesbians/gay men • dancing/DJ

**Riff Raff's** 2809 W. Main St. **436-4166** 6pm-3am, 4pm-midnight Sun • mostly gay men • neighborhood bar • food served • wheelchair access

**Up the Street** 2322 S. Calhoun **456-7166** 5pm-3:30am, clsd Sun • lesbians/gay men • dancing • live shows • food served • wheelchair access

### SPIRITUAL GROUPS
**Open Door Chapel** (at Up the Stairs Community Center) **744-1199** 7pm Sun

## Hammond (219)

RESTAURANTS

**Phil Smidt & Son** 1205 N. Calumet Ave. **659-0025** lunch & dinner • seafood • full bar

## Indianapolis (317)

INFO LINES & SERVICES

**AA Gay/Lesbian** 632-7864

**Fellowship Indianapolis** 328-8061 social & support groups for lesbians/gay men

**Gay/Lesbian Hotline** 630-4297 7pm-11pm • resources • crisis counseling

ACCOMMODATIONS

**The Nuthatch B&B** 7161 Edgewater Pl. **257-2660** gay-friendly • full brkfst • smokefree

BARS & NIGHTCLUBS

**501 Tavern** 501 N. College Ave. **632-2100** 5:30pm-3am, clsd Sun • popular • mostly gay men • country/western Tue • dancing/DJ Fri-Sat • also leather shop

**Betty Boop's Lounge** 637 Massachusetts Ave. **637-2310** 10am-midnight, til 3am wknds, clsd Sun • gay-friendly • neighborhood bar • food served

**Brothers Bar & Grill** 822 N. Illinois St. **636-1020** 11am-midnight, 4pm-1am wknds • lesbians/gay men • live shows • also restaurant • some veggie • wheelchair access • $7-14

**Club Cabaret** 151 E. 14th St. **767-1707** 9pm-3am Wed, Fri & Sat only • lesbians/gay men • dancing/DJ • patio • call for events • wheelchair access

**Illusions** 1446 E. Washington **266-0535** 7am-3am • lesbians/gay men • dancing/DJ • live shows

**The Metro** 707 Massachusetts **639-6022** 4pm-3am, noon-12:30am Sun • lesbians/gay men • dancing/DJ • also restaurant • some veggie • patio • wheelchair access • $5-11

**The Ten** 1218 N. Pennsylvania St. (enter rear) **638-5802** 6pm-3am, clsd Sun • popular • mostly women • dancing/DJ • country/western Mon • live shows • wheelchair access

**Tomorrow's** 2301 N. Meridian **925-1710** 5pm-3am, til 12:30am Sun • lesbians/gay men • more women Tue & Th • dancing/DJ • live shows • also restaurant • Chinese/American • wheelchair access • $7-10

## Indianapolis (317)

**Where the Girls Are:** Spread throughout the city.

**Entertainment:** Women's Chorus: 931-9464. Men's Chorus at the Crossroads Performing Arts: 931-9464.

**Lesbigay Pride:** June: 634-9212, Justice Inc.

**Annual Events:**

Memorial Day Weekend: **Indy 500** auto race.

June - **National Women's Music Festival** (in Bloomington, IN): 927-9355.

**City Info:** Indianapolis Visitor's Bureau: 639-4282.

**Attractions:** Art Museum. Zoo. Speedway 500.

**Weather:** The spring weather is moderate (50°s-60°s) with occasional storms. The summers are typically midwestern: hot (mid-90°s) and humid. The autumns are mild and colorful in southeastern Indiana. As for winter, it's the wind chill that'll get to you.

**Transit:** Yellow Cab: 487-7777. Metro Transit: 635-3344.

**The Varsity** 1517 N. Pennsylvania St. **635-9998** 10am-3am, noon-midnight Sun • mostly gay men • neighborhood bar • food served • $4-10

**The Vogue** 6259 N. College Ave. **259-7029** 9pm-1am • gay-friendly • more gay Sun • dancing/DJ • alternative • live shows

CAFES

**The MT Cup** 314 Massachusetts Ave. **639-1099** 7am-11pm, til midnight Fri-Sat, 8am-6pm Sun • espresso & coffee bar • deli menu

RESTAURANTS

**Aesop's Tables 631-0055** 11am-9pm, til 10pm Fri-Sat • authentic Mediterranean • some veggie • beer/wine • wheelchair access • $9-12

BOOKSTORES & RETAIL SHOPS

**Borders** 5612 Castleton Corner Ln. **849-8660** 9am-10pm, 11am-6pm Sun • general

**Indy News** 121 S. Pennsylvania **632-7680** 6am-7pm, til 6pm wknds

**Just Cards** 145 E. Ohio St. **638-1170** 9am-5:30pm, clsd Sun • wheelchair access

**Southside News** 8063 Madison Ave. **887-1020** 6am-8pm, til 6pm Sun

PUBLICATIONS

**The Indiana Word 725-8840** lesbigay newspaper

**Outlines 923-8550** lesbigay news-magazine w/extensive resources

TRAVEL AGENTS

**Ross & Babcock Travel** 832 Broad Ripple Ave. **259-4194/(800) 229-4194** IGLTA

**UniWorld Travel** 1010 E. 86th St. #24E **573-4919/(800) 573-4919**

SPIRITUAL GROUPS

**Jesus MCC** 3620 N. Franklin Rd. (church) **894-5110** 6pm Sun • wheelchair access

# Indianapolis

*I*ndianapolis, the capital of the Hoosier state, may look like your typical midwestern industrial city, but you'll find a few surprises under the surface.

You probably won't find lesbians dancing in the streets (unless it's Pride Day), but they're there. Check out some of the fun boutiques and restaurants in the Broad Ripple district. Later fuel up on caffeine at **The MT Cup** and dance with the girls at **The Ten**.

If you're into women's music, plan to be in Indiana during the first weekend in June for the **National Women's Music Festival** in Bloomington. You can stay at the **Enchanted Otter**, a lakeside women's retreat and visit the **Athena Gallery** while you're in town.

If fast cars are more your style, be sure to be in Indianapolis for the Indy 500 on Memorial Day weekend.

## Lafayette (765)

BARS & NIGHTCLUBS
**The Sportsman** 644 Main St. 742-6321
9am-3am, from 5pm Sat, clsd Sun • lesbians/gay men • neighborhood bar • dancing/DJ

EROTICA
**The Fantasy** 119 N. River Rd., W. Lafayette 743-5042
**Fantasy East** 2311 Concord Rd. 474-2417 books & videos

## Lake Station (219)

BARS & NIGHTCLUBS
**Axcis Nightclub** 2415 Rush St. 962-1017
7pm-3am, clsd Sun • lesbians/gay men • dancing/DJ • live shows • ladies night Tue • wheelchair access

## Merrillville

*(see Gary & Hammond)*

## Michigan City (219)

BARS & NIGHTCLUBS
**Total Eclipse** 4960 W. US 20 874-1100
7pm-2am, from 5pm Fri, 7pm-midnight Sun • lesbians/gay men • dancing/DJ • transgender-friendly • food served • live shows Th • fish-fry Fri • wheelchair access

## Mishawaka

*(see South Bend)*

## Monroe City (812)

TRAVEL AGENTS
**The Travel Club** 743-2919 int'l members-only non-profit travel club

## Muncie (765)

BARS & NIGHTCLUBS
**Carriage House** 1100 Kilgore 282-7411
gay-friendly • neighborhood bar • also restaurant • steak/seafood • wheelchair access • gay-owned/run • $9-14
**Mark III Tap Room** 107 E. Main St. 282-8273 11am-3am, clsd Sun • lesbians/gay men • dancing/DJ

## Richmond (765)

INFO LINES & SERVICES
**Earlham Lesbian/Bisexual/Gay Peoples Union** Box E-565 Earlham College, 47373

BARS & NIGHTCLUBS
**Coachman** 911 E. Main St. 966-2835
6pm-3am, clsd Sun • lesbians/gay men • more women Sat • dancing/DJ • alternative • wheelchair access • unconfirmed

## South Bend (219)

INFO LINES & SERVICES
**Community Resource Center Helpline** 232-2522 9am-5pm Mon-Fri • limited gay/lesbian info • also 24hr crisis hotline

ACCOMMODATIONS
**Kamm's Island Inn** 700 Lincoln Wy. W., Mishawaka 256-1501/(800) 955-5266 gay-friendly • wheelchair access • $44-71

BARS & NIGHTCLUBS
**Sea Horse II Cabaret** 1902 Western Ave. 237-9139 8pm-3am, clsd Sun • lesbians/gay men • dancing/DJ • live shows • wheelchair access
**Starz Bar & Restaurant** 1505 S. Kendall St. 288-7827 9pm-3am, clsd Sun • mostly gay men • dancing/DJ • live shows • wheelchair access • unconfirmed
**Truman's** The 100 Center, Mishawaka 259-2282 8pm-3am, clsd Mon-Tue • popular • lesbians/gay men • dancing/DJ

## Terre Haute (812)

BARS & NIGHTCLUBS
**R-Place** 684 Lafayette Ave. 232-9119
8pm-3am, clsd Sun-Mon • lesbians/gay men • dancing/DJ • alternative

## Whiting (219)

RESTAURANTS
**Vogel's** 1250 Indianapolis Blvd. 659-1250
from 11am, clsd Mon

# Iowa

## Ames (515)

### INFO LINES & SERVICES
**Gay/Lesbian Alliance** 294-2104 11am-5pm • LGBT Student Services 294-1020

**Help Central** 232-0000 8:30am-4:30pm • community info service • some lesbigay referrals

**Margaret Sloss Women's Center** Sloss House (ISU) 294-4154 8am-5pm, clsd wknds • call for programs

### RESTAURANTS
**Lucallen's** 400 Main St. 232-8484 11am-11pm • Italian • some veggie • full bar • $6-12

**Pizza Kitchen** 120 Hayward 292-1710 11am-10pm • beer/wine

## Burlington (319)

### ACCOMMODATIONS
**Arrowhead Motel** 2520 Mt. Pleasant St. 752-6353/(800) 341-8000 gay-friendly • suites avail. • kitchenettes

### BARS & NIGHTCLUBS
**Steve's Place** 852 Washington 752-9109 9am-2am • gay-friendly • neighborhood bar • wheelchair access

## Cedar Falls (319)

*(see also Waterloo)*

### BOOKSTORES & RETAIL SHOPS
**Gateways** 109 E. 2nd St. 277-3973 10:30am-5:30pm Mon, Tue & Fri , til 7pm Wed-Th, 9:30am-4pm Sat • gay section

## Cedar Rapids (319)

### INFO LINES & SERVICES
**Gay/Lesbian Resource Center** 366-2055 live 6pm-9pm Mon, 24hr info

### BARS & NIGHTCLUBS
**Rockafellas** 119-1/2 3rd Ave. SE 399-1623 4:30pm-2am, from 5pm wknds • lesbians/gay men • dancing/DJ

### SPIRITUAL GROUPS
**Faith United Methodist Church** 1000 30th St. NE 363-8454/895-6678 10:30am Sun

## Council Bluffs (712)

*(see also Omaha, NE)*

## Davenport (319)

*(see also Rock Island, IL)*

### BARS & NIGHTCLUBS
**Club Marquette** 3923 Marquette St. 386-0700 11am-2am • mostly gay men • dancing/DJ • food served • live shows • patio • wheelchair access

### SPIRITUAL GROUPS
**MCC Quad Cities** 3025 N. Harrison 324-8281 11am Sun & 7pm Wed

## Des Moines (515)

### INFO LINES & SERVICES
**GLRC (Gay/Lesbian Resource Center)** 414 E. 5th St. 281-0634 (24HR INFO) live 7pm-9pm Mon-Sat • youth groups • many other mtgs.

**Iowa Division of Tourism** (800) 345-4692

**Out-Reach** 830-1777 social/support group

**Young Women's Resource Center** 1909 Ingersoll Ave 244-4901 8:30am-5pm, clsd wknds

### ACCOMMODATIONS
**Kingman House** 2920 Kingman Blvd. 279-7312 lesbians/gay men • turn-of-the-century B&B • full brkfst • wheelchair access • $40

**Racoon River Resort** 2920 Kingman Blvd. 279-7312 lesbians/gay men • on the river • available for large groups • full brkfst • hot tub • nudity • food served • wheelchair access

### BARS & NIGHTCLUBS
**Blazing Saddles** 416 E. 5th St. 246-1299 2pm-2am, from noon wknds • popular • mostly gay men • leather • wheelchair access

**Faces** 416 E. Walnut 280-5463 noon-2am

**Garden** 112 SE 4th St. 243-3965 8pm-2am, from 7pm Mon-Wed • popular • lesbians/gay men • dancing/DJ • live shows • patio

## CAFES

**Chat Noir Cafe** 644 18th St. **244-1353** 10am-11pm, til midnight Fri-Sat, clsd Sun-Mon • some veggie • beer/wine • wheelchair access • $6-12

**Java Joe's** 214 4th St. **288-5282** 8am-11pm, til 1am Fri-Sat, 9am-11pm Sun • live shows

## BOOKSTORES & RETAIL SHOPS

**Borders** 4100 University, West Des Moines **223-1620** 9am-9pm, 11am-6pm Sun • wheelchair access

## PUBLICATIONS

**Outword** 281-0634

## SPIRITUAL GROUPS

**Church of the Holy Spirit MCC** 1548 8th St. (Trinity United Methodist) **284-7940** 6pm Sun

## EROTICA

**Axiom** 412-1/2 E. 5th St. **246-0414** piercings

**Gallery Book Store** 1114 Walnut St. **244-2916** 24hrs

## Fort Dodge                    (515)

### EROTICA

**Mini Cinema** 15 N. 5th St. **955-9756**

## Grinnell                    (515)

### INFO LINES & SERVICES

**Stonewall Resource Center Grinnell College** 269-3327 4pm-11pm, til 6pm Fri, 1pm-4pm Sat • also quarterly newsletter

## Iowa City                    (319)

### INFO LINES & SERVICES

**AA Gay/Lesbian** 338-9111 (AA#)

**Gay/Lesbian/Bisexual People's Union** 335-3251 also publishes 'Gay Hawkeye' newsletter

**Women's Resource/Action Center** 130 N. Madison **335-1486** 10am-5pm • community center & lesbian support group • wheelchair access

### BARS & NIGHTCLUBS

**6:20 Club** 620 S. Madison St. **354-2494** from 9pm Sat only • popular • lesbians/gay men • dancing/DJ • wheelchair access

## BOOKSTORES & RETAIL SHOPS

**Alternatives** 323 E. Market St. **337-4124** 10am-6pm, noon-4pm Sun • pride gifts • wheelchair access

**Moon Mystique** 114-1/2 E. College St. (Hall Mall) **338-5752** 10am-9pm, noon-6pm Sun • esoterica • magazines • piercing • gifts

**Prairie Lights Bookstore** 15 S. Dubuque St. **337-2681** 9am-10pm, til 6pm wknds • wheelchair access

## Newton                    (515)

### ACCOMMODATIONS

**La Corsette Maison Inn** 629 1st Ave. E. **792-6833** gay-friendly • 3-course brkfst • antique jacuzzi • 4-star restaurant • $70-170

## Sioux City                    (712)

### BARS & NIGHTCLUBS

**3 Cheers** 414 20th St. **255-8005** Wed-Sat • lesbians/gay men • neighborhood bar • dancing/DJ • live shows • wheelchair access

**Kings & Queens** 417 Nebraska St. **252-4167** 7pm-2am • lesbians/gay men • dancing/DJ • unconfirmed

## Waterloo                    (319)

### INFO LINES & SERVICES

**Access** 232-6805 weekly info & support

**Lesbian/Bisexual Support Group** 233-7519 7pm 1st Fri • call evenings

### BARS & NIGHTCLUBS

**The Bar** 903 Sycamore **232-0543** 7pm-2am • lesbians/gay men • dancing/DJ • live shows • wheelchair access

### RESTAURANTS

**Joe's Country Grill** 4117 University, Cedar Falls **277-8785** 11am-10pm, 24hrs wknds

### PUBLICATIONS

**Access Line** 232-6805

# KANSAS

## Abilene (913)

### BOOKSTORES & RETAIL SHOPS
**Triangle Artworks** 1605 W. 3rd St. 263-7849 gallery & gifts • ask about gay discount

## Kansas City

*(see also Kansas City, Missouri)*

## Lawrence (913)

### INFO LINES & SERVICES
**Decca Center AA Support & Counseling** 841-4138 call for lesbigay mtg. info
**KU Queers & Allies** 864-3091 student group

### BARS & NIGHTCLUBS
**3-GALS Coffeehouse** 842-2147 women only • 2nd Sat • call for location & events • wheelchair access
**Jazzhaus** 926-1/2 Massachusetts 749-3320 4pm-2am • gay-friendly • live shows
**Teller's Restaurant & Bar** 746 Massachusetts Ave. 843-4111 11am-2am • gay-friendly • more gay Tue • live shows • also restaurant • southern Italian/pizza • some veggie • $9-15

## Lenoxa (913)

### TRAVEL AGENTS
**Travel Quest** 599-3700 IGLTA

## Matfield Green (316)

### ACCOMMODATIONS
**Prairie Women Adventures** 753-3465 women only • working cattle ranch • full brkfst & dinner avail. • women-owned/run

## Topeka (913)

### INFO LINES & SERVICES
**AA Gay/Lesbian** 2425 SE Indiana St. (MCC) 271-6183 call for info
**Gay Rap Telephone** 233-6558 24hr recorded info • live 8pm-midnight Wed-Sun
**Kansas Travel & Tourism Department** (800) 252-6727

**LIFT (Lesbians in Fellowship Together)** (at 'MCC Topeka') 232-6196 6pm 3rd Th • call for details

### BARS & NIGHTCLUBS
**Classics** 110 SW 8th 233-5153 4pm-2am, from noon Sun • lesbians/gay men • dancing/DJ • live shows
**The Mark** 601 SE 8th St. 233-2447 til 2am

### BOOKSTORES & RETAIL SHOPS
**Town Crier Books** 1301 SW Gage Blvd. #120 272-5060 9am-9pm, noon-6pm Sun

### SPIRITUAL GROUPS
**MCC Topeka** 2425 SE Indiana Ave. 232-6196 10am & 6pm Sun

## Wichita (316)

### INFO LINES & SERVICES
**Land of Oz Info Line** 269-0913 touch-tone info
**Support Group** 687-3524 mtgs. 1st Tue • call for location
**Transitions** 687-3524 Sat mtgs. for lesbigay youth 18-24 • also 'Project Acceptance' Tue • for ages 14-18

### BARS & NIGHTCLUBS
**America's Pub** 900 E. 1st St. 267-1782 8pm-2am • gay Mon night only
**Casablanca Club** 4916 E. Lincoln 686-6092 11am-2am • gay-friendly • karaoke • food served • gay-owned/run
**Dreamers** 3210 E. Osie 682-4461 4pm-2am, from 3pm wknds, clsd Mon • lesbians/gay men • neighborhood bar • karaoke
**Dreamers II** 2835 S. George Washington Blvd. 682-4490 4pm-2am, from 3pm wknds, clsd Mon • mostly women • dancing/DJ • women-owned/run
**The Fantasy Complex** 3201 S. Hillside 682-5494 8pm-2am Wed-Sun • lesbians/gay men • dancing/DJ • live shows • swimming • also 'South Forty' • from 4pm • country/western • patio • wheelchair access
**Kirby's Beer Store** 3227 E. 17th 685-7013 2pm-2am • lesbians/gay men • live bands • food served
**Metro** Central & Waco 262-8130 5pm-2am Wed-Sun, clsd Mon-Tue • mostly gay men • dancing/DJ • live shows • also restaurant • kitchen open til 10pm • women's night Th

# The Liberty Press

**The Official Lesbian and Gay News magazine of Kansas**

# "One of the most refreshing lesbigay magazines in the country."

**-Girlfriends Magazine**

## Serving Queer Kansans Since 1994

**See Us For:**
- News
- Entertainment
- Personals
- Comics
- Around Kansas
  (A Comprehensive, Up-to-date Resource Directory)

## Call For Your FREE Sample Issue!

P.O. Box 16315 • Wichita, KS 67216-0315
voice/fax (316) 262-8289 e-mail LibrtyPrs@aol.com
**In Lawrence:**
P.O. Box 82 • Lawrence, KS 66044
(785) 841-2771 e-mail abfab@falcon.cc.ukans.edu
**On The Web:** http://eagle.cc.ukans.edu/~deer/libprs.htm

**R&R Brass Rail** 2828 E. 31st St. S. **685-9890** noon-2am • lesbians/gay men • dancing/DJ • country/western • live shows • food served • wheelchair access

**Side Street Saloon** 1106 S. Pattie **267-0324** 2pm-2am • lesbians/gay men • neighborhood bar

**Silky's Restaurant & Bar** 126 N. Mosley **267-1309** 11am-9pm, til 2am Th-Sat, til 6pm Sun • food til 10pm • dancing/DJ Sat • karaoke Th

**The T-Room** 1507 E. Pawnee **262-9327** 3pm-2am, from noon wknds • lesbians/gay men • leather

### RESTAURANTS

**Bohemian Bean Company** 511 E. Douglas **263-2882** open til 2am, til 3am Th-Sat • live shows

**Dakotas** 229 E. William **267-4407** lunch Mon-Fri & dinner Tue-Sat, clsd Sun • steak & seafood • some veggie

**The Lassen** 155 N. Market St. **263-2777** lunch & dinner, clsd Sun • some veggie • full bar • $9-12

**Moe's Sub Shop** 2815 S. Hydraulic **524-5511**

**Old Mill Tasty Shop** 604 E. Douglas **264-6500** 11am-3pm, 8am-5pm Sat, clsd Sun • old-fashioned soda fountain • lunch menu • some veggie

**Riverside Perk** 1142 Bidding at 11th St. **264-6464** 7am-10pm, til midnight Fri-Sat, 10am-10pm Sun

**The Upper Crust** 7038 E. Lincoln **683-8088** lunch only, clsd wknds • homestyle • some veggie • $4-7

### BOOKSTORES & RETAIL SHOPS

**Mother's** 3100 E. 31st St. S. **686-8116** noon-10pm, til 2:30am Fri-Sat • lesbigay gifts

**Puttin' on the Glitz** 3343 E. 47th St. S. **524-6455** 1pm-8pm, clsd Sun • custom-made lingerie • transgender-friendly

**Triangle Community Outlet** 1607 S. Broadway **267-1965** noon-5pm Wed-Fri, noon-6pm Sat, clsd Sun-Tue • lesbigay gifts • magazines • videos

### PUBLICATIONS

▲ **The Liberty Press** 262-8289 statewide lesbigay newspaper

**Triangle** 943-9902/(888) 843-7273

### TRAVEL AGENTS

**Major Travel** 6611 E. Central **682-5151/(800) 489-7151**

**Nova Travel** 1117 S. Rock Rd. #4 **683-4200/(800) 995-6682**

**Triangle Travel** 889 N. Maize Rd. Ste. 101 **722-7202/945-0676**

### SPIRITUAL GROUPS

**College Hill United Methodist Church** 2930 E. 1st St. **683-4643** 8:30am & 11am Sun • also lesbigay group • 3rd Th

**First Metropolitan Community Church** 156 S. Kansas Ave. **267-1852** 10:30am & 6:30pm Sun

**First Unitarian Universalist Church** 1501 Fairmount **684-3481** 11am Sun

**Wichita Praise & Worship Center** 1607 S. Broadway **267-6270** 11am Sun

### EROTICA

**Holier Than Thou Body Piercing** 3700 E. Douglas #55 (Clifton Shopping Square) **652-7267**

# KENTUCKY

## Covington (606)

*(see also Cincinnati, Ohio)*

### BARS & NIGHTCLUBS
**Rosie's Tavern** 643 Bakewell St. 291-9707 3pm-1am, from1pm wknds • gay-friendly • gay-owned/run

## Harrodsburg (606)

### ACCOMMODATIONS
**Baxter House B&B** 1677 Lexington Rd. 734-5700 gay-friendly • kids/pets ok • 30 min. from Lexington

## Lexington (606)

### INFO LINES & SERVICES
**Gay/Lesbian AA** 224-4067/276-2917 (AA#) 8pm Wed, 7:30pm Fri & 7pm Sun
**Lexington Pride Center** 387 Waller Ave.

### BARS & NIGHTCLUBS
**The Bar Complex** 224 E. Main St. 255-1551 4pm-1am, til 3:30am Fri-Sat, clsd Sun • popular • lesbians/gay men • dancing/DJ • live shows • wheelchair access

**Club 141** 141 W. Vine St. 233-4262 8:30pm-1am, til 3am Sat, clsd Sun-Mon • lesbians/gay men • dancing/DJ • live shows • wheelchair access

**The Watering Hole** 147 N. Limestone St. 223-0495 7pm-1am, clsd Sun • lesbians/gay men • neighborhood bar

### RESTAURANTS
**Alfalfa** 557 S. Limestone 253-0014 11am-9pm, til 5pm Mon, 10am-2pm Sun • live folk music Fri-Sat • healthy multi-ethnic • plenty veggie • $6-12

### BOOKSTORES & RETAIL SHOPS
**Joseph-Beth** 3199 Nicholasville Rd. 271-5330 9am-10pm, til 11pm Fri-Sat, 11am-8pm Sun

### PUBLICATIONS
**GLSO (Gay/Lesbian) News** calendar

### TRAVEL AGENTS
**Pegasus Travel** 245 Lexington Ave. 253-1644 IGLTA • women-owned/run

### SPIRITUAL GROUPS
**Lexington MCC** 134 Church St. 271-1407 11:30am Sun • wheelchair access

**Pagan Forum** 268-1640 call for info on 10+ area pagan groups

## Louisville (502)

### INFO LINES & SERVICES
**AA Gay/Lesbian** 454-7613 call for mtg. schedule
**Gay/Lesbian/Bisexual Hotline** 897-2475/454-7613 6pm-10pm
**Louisville Gender Society** 222-3182 transgender group • contact Michelle
**Louisville Youth Group** 894-9787 bi-weekly mtgs. • call for location
**The Williams-Nichols Institute** 636-0935 6pm-9pm • lesbigay archives • library • referrals

### ACCOMMODATIONS
**Beharrell House** 343 Beharrell Ave., New Albany IN (812) 944-0289/(800) 728-3262 lesbians/gay men • Queen Anne B&B • 4 miles to Louisville • gay-owned/operated

### BARS & NIGHTCLUBS
**Connection Complex** 120 S. Floyd St. 585-5752 8pm-4am, clsd Mon • popular • lesbians/gay men • dancing/DJ • live shows • also restaurant • from 6pm Wed-Sun • some veggie • $5-15

**Magnolia's** 1398 S. 2nd St. 637-9052 noon-4am • gay-friendly • neighborhood bar

**Murphy's Place** 306 E. Main St. 587-8717 11am-4am • mostly gay men • neighborhood

**Sparks** 104 W. Main St. 587-8566 10pm-4am • lesbians/gay men • dancing/DJ • alternative • live shows • wheelchair access

**Town Cafe** 414 W. Oak St. 637-7730 mostly gay men • neighborhood bar • live shows • karaoke

**Tryangles** 209 S. Preston St. 583-6395 4pm-4am, from 1pm Sun • mostly gay men • dancing/DJ

**Tynkers Too/The Rage** 319 Market 561-0752 2pm-4am, from 5pm wknds • lesbians/gay men • women-owned/run

**The Upstairs** 306 E. Main St. (at 'Murphy's Place') 587-1432 9pm-4am, clsd Mon • lesbians/gay men • dancing/DJ

### BOOKSTORES & RETAIL SHOPS
**Carmichael's** 1295 Bardstown Rd. 456-6950 8am-10pm, 10am-6pm Sun • lesbigay section • women-owned/run

# *Louisville*

*B*eautiful Louisville sits on the banks of the Ohio River and is home to the world famous Kentucky Derby. This spectacular race occurs during the first week of May at Churchill Downs.

Louisville is also home to many whiskey distilleries. If neither watching horses run in circles, nor swilling home-grown booze excites you, check out the **Louisville Slugger Museum** (588-7228). Whatever you do, you're certain to enjoy this city's slower pace of life and Southern charm— Louisville is, after all, known as the 'Northern border for Southern hospitality.'

Before you leave, sample the whiskey and the hospitality at several of the city's lesbian and gay bars. And only a few hours to the east, make sure to rest a spell in the beautiful bluegrass country of Lexington, Kentucky.

## Louisville (502)

**Where the Girls Are:** On Main or Market Streets near 1st, and generally in the north-central part of town, just west of I-65.

**Entertainment:** Bowling League: 456-5780, Monday nights. Community Chorus: 327-4099. The Vogue: 893-3646.

**Lesbigay Pride:** June.

**Annual Events:**

May - **Kentucky Derby.**

October - **Halloween Cruise** on the Ohio River.

**City Info:** Louisville Tourist Commission: 800/626-5646.

**Attractions:** Kentucky Derby. The Waterfront. Belle Of Louisville. Churchill Downs. Farmington. Hadley Pottery. Locust Grove. St. James Court. West Main Street Historic District.

**Best View:** The Spire Restaurant and Cocktail Lounge on the 19th floor of the Hyatt Regency Louisville.

**Weather:** Mild winters and long, hot summers!

**Transit:** Yellow Taxi: 636-5511.

**Hawley Cooke Books** 3024 Bardstown Rd. **456-6660** 9am-9pm, 10am-6pm Sun • also 27 Shelbyville Rd. Plaza 893-0133

**MT Closets** 310 E. Main St. **587-1060**/**(800) 606-4524** hours vary • call first • gay gifts • unique clothing

## PUBLICATIONS

**The Furies** 899-3551 lesbian publication

**The Kentucky Word (317) 725-8840**

**The Letter** 772-7570 statewide lesbigay newspaper

**Rainbow Pages** 899-3551 lesbigay resource guide

## TRAVEL AGENTS

**Blue Planet Travel** 833 W. Main St. #102-B **584-1799**/**(800) 960-2001** IGLTA

## SPIRITUAL GROUPS

**B'nai Shalom** 896-0475 lesbigay Jewish group

**Central Presbyterian Church** 587-6935 11am Sun • 'More Light' congregation

**Dignity** 1864 Frankfurt Ave. (Third Lutheran) **(888) 625-0005** 7pm 2nd & 4th Sun

**MCC Louisville** 4222 Bank St. **775-6636** 11am Sun • wheelchair access

## Paducah                              (502)

## BARS & NIGHTCLUBS

**Bar One** 417 Broadway **443-7277** lesbians/gay men • dancing/DJ • live shows

## SPIRITUAL GROUPS

**MCC of Paducah** 2201 Broadway (Ritz Hotel, 6th flr.) **441-2330** 11am Sun • wheelchair access

## Somerset                            (606)

## INFO LINES & SERVICES

**Lesbigay Info** 678-5814 call Linda for info

# LOUISIANA

## Alexandria                          (318)

## BARS & NIGHTCLUBS

**Unique Bar** 3117 Masonic Dr. 448-0555 7pm-2am, clsd Sun-Mon • popular • mostly gay men • dancing/DJ • unconfirmed

## TRAVEL AGENTS

**Over the Rainbeaux Travel** 1706 Pierce Rd. 442-0540

## Baton Rouge                        (504)

## INFO LINES & SERVICES

**AA Gay/Lesbian** 924-0030 7pm Mon, 8pm Th, 9pm Sat

## BARS & NIGHTCLUBS

**Baton Rouge Time Zone** 668 Main St. 344-9714 6pm-2am Mon-Sat • lesbians/gay men

**The Blue Parrot** 450 Oklahoma St. 267-4211 2pm-2am • mostly gay men

**George's Place** 860 St. Louis 387-9798 3pm-2am, clsd Sun • popular • mostly gay men • neighborhood bar • wheelchair access

**Hideaway** 7367 Exchange Pl. 923-3632 8pm-2am, clsd Sun-Tue • mostly women • neighborhood bar • dancing/DJ • wheelchair access • women-owned/run

**Mirror Lounge** 111 3rd St. 387-9797 3pm-2am, from 6pm Sat, clsd Sun • lesbians/gay men • dancing/DJ • live shows • wheelchair access • unconfirmed

**Traditions** 2183 Highland Rd. 344-9291 9pm-2am, clsd Sun-Tue • lesbians/gay men • dancing/DJ • alternative • 18+ • wheelchair access • unconfirmed

## RESTAURANTS

**Chalet Brant** 7655 Old Hammond Hwy. 927-6040 5:30pm-9pm, lunch Th & Fri only • cont'l • $15-50

**Drusilla Seafood** 3482 Drusilla Lane 923-0896 dinner til 10pm • $8-15

**Ralph & Kacoo's** 6110 Bluebonnet 766-2113 dinner til 10pm • Cajun • $8-20

## BOOKSTORES & RETAIL SHOPS

**Hibiscus Bookstore** 635 Main St. 387-4264 11am-6pm • lesbigay

## PUBLICATIONS

**Voices Magazine** 665-7815 off-beat articles on everything • original artwork & writings

## TRAVEL AGENTS

**Out & About Travel** 11528 Old Hammond Hwy. #610 **272-7448** IGLTA

**Trips Unlimited** 10249 Cashel Ave. **927-7191/(800) 256-9661** gay-owned/run

## SPIRITUAL GROUPS

**Church of Mercavah** 665-7815 5pm Sun • interfaith • call for locations

**Joie de Vivre MCC** 333 E. Chimes St. **383-0450** 11am Sun

## Bossier City (318)

### INFO LINES & SERVICES

**Homosexual Info Center** 115 Monroe St. **742-4709** 9am-5pm

## Gretna (504)

### BARS & NIGHTCLUBS

**Cheers** 1711 Hancock **367-0149** 10am-3am • gay-friendly • neighborhood bar

## Hammond (504)

### BARS & NIGHTCLUBS

**Chances** 42357 Veterans **542-9350** 9pm-2am Fri-Sat • lesbians/gay men • dancing/DJ • wheelchair access

## Houma (504)

### BARS & NIGHTCLUBS

**Kixx** 112 N. Hollywood **876-9587** 6pm-2am, clsd Sun-Mon • lesbians/gay men • dancing/DJ • live shows • wheelchair access

## Lafayette (318)

### INFO LINES & SERVICES

**AA Gay/Lesbian** 234-7814 call for mtg. schedule

### BARS & NIGHTCLUBS

**Images** 524 W. Jefferson **233-0070** 9pm-2am, clsd Mon-Tue • lesbians/gay men • dancing/DJ • food served • live shows • wheelchair access

## Lake Charles (318)

### BARS & NIGHTCLUBS

**Crystal's** 112 W. Broad St. **433-5457** 9pm-2am, clsd Sun-Tue • lesbians/gay men • dancing/DJ • country/western • live shows • food served • wheelchair access

## New Orleans (504)

### INFO LINES & SERVICES

**AA Lambda Center** 2106 Decatur **947-0548** daily mtgs.

**Lesbian/Gay Community Center** 816 N. Rampart **522-1103** hours vary • call first • wheelchair access

**Louisiana Office of Tourism** (800) 334-8626

### ACCOMMODATIONS

**A Private Garden** 1718 Philip St. **523-1776** lesbians/gay men • B&B-private home • hot tub • 2 private apts • enclosed garden • $50-75 (special holiday rates)

**Alternative Accommodations/French Quarter Accommodation Service** 828 Royal St. #233 **552-2910/(800) 209-9408**

**Andrew Jackson Hotel** 919 Royal St. **561-5881/(800) 654-0224** gay-friendly • historic inn

**The B&W Courtyards B&B** 2425 Chartres St. **949-5313/(800) 585-5731** gay-friendly • jacuzzi • gay-owned/run

**Big D's B&B** 704 Franklin Ave. **945-8049** lesbians/gay men • women-owned/run

**The Big Easy Guest House** 2633 Dauphine St. **943-3717** gay-friendly • 8 blks from French Quarter

**Big Easy/Gulf Coast Reservations** 433-2563/(800) 368-4876

**The Biscuit Palace** 730 Dumaine **525-9949** gay-friendly • B&B & apts • in the French Quarter

**Bon Maison Guest House** 835 Bourbon St. **561-8498** popular • gay-friendly • 3 studio apts • 2 suites • $65-115

**Bourbon Orleans Hotel** Bourbon & Orleans **523-2222/(800) 521-5338** popular • gay-friendly • IGLTA

**Bourgoyne Guest House** 839 Bourbon St. **524-3621** popular • lesbians/gay men • 1830s Creole mansion • courtyard • $60-150

**Bywater B&B** 1026 Clouet St. **944-8438** gay-friendly • kitchen • fireplace • smokefree • kids/pets ok • women-owned/run • $60/shared bath • $75/private bath

**Casa de Marigny Creole Guest Cottages** 818 Frenchmen St. **948-3875** lesbians/gay men • swimming

**Chateau Negara Guest House** 1923 Esplanade Ave. **947-1343** gay-friendly • IGLTA

# The Greenhouse

## A New Orleans Tropical Guest House

# 800-966-1303

## 1212 Magazine Street
## New Orleans

# FRENCH QUARTER ACCOMMODATIONS

# French Quarter Reservation Service

*N'awlins Oldest & Largest Gay Reservation Service*
*NEVER A FEE*

## 1-800-523-9091
### 504-523-1246 • FAX 504-527-6327

### e-mail • fqrsinc@linknet.net
### www.neworleans-gay.com

IGLTA

## New Orleans

*I*f you haven't been to New Orleans for Mardi Gras, you've missed the party of the year. But there's still time to plan next year's visit to the French Quarter's blowout of a block party—complete with its elaborate balls, parades and dancing in the streets. It all starts the day before Ash Wednesday (usually in February).

Of course, there's more to New Orleans than Mardi Gras, especially if you like life hot, humid and spiced with steamy jazz and hot pepper. Park your bags in one of the dozen lesbian/gay inns in the area. Then venture into the French Quarter, where you'll find the infamous Bourbon Street with people strolling—or occasionally staggering—from jazz club to jazz club, bar to bar, restaurants to shops, twenty-four hours a day. Kitsch-lovers won't want to miss Pat O'Brien's, home of the Hurricane and the #1 bar in the country for alcohol volume sold—even if you don't drink, a campy photo in front of the fountain is a must. Jazz lovers, make a pilgrimmage to Preservation Hall.

If you love to shop, check out the French Market, the Jackson Brewery and Riverwalk. Antique hunting is best on Rue Royal or Decatur Street. And you can't leave New Orleans without a trip through the Garden District to see the incredible antebellum and revival homes—a trip best made on the St. Charles Trolley.

Gourmands must try real Cajun & Creole food in its natural environment—though if you're vegetarian, the **Old Dog New Trick Cafe** is your best bet. For melt-in-your-mouth, hot, sugar-powdered beignets, run, don't walk to Café du Monde (525-4544).

For the morbidly inclined among us, you're bound to see shadows of vampires and other creatures of the night in this town of mysticism and the occult. With residents like Anne Rice, Poppy Z. Brite, and (the late) Marie LaVeau stirring up the spirits, perhaps a protective amulet from Marie LaVeau's House of Voodoo (581-3751; 739 Bourbon St.) would be a good idea. For a peek at traditional voodoo— the Afro-Caribbean religion, not the B-movie shlock—take the swamp tour that ends at a cottage in the bayou, with gumbo dinner and a performance by the Mask Dance Voodoo Theater (522-2904) for $75. Or sate that urge for blood with a body piercing at **Rings of Desire** or some fresh fetish wear from **Second Skin Leather.**

So, pick a realm of the senses and go wild. You'll be happy to know that the women-loving-women of New Orleans know how to do wild very well. Try **Charlene's** for drinks and tall tales, or get crazy with the boys (try **Rubyfruit Jungle**) in the French Quarter—this Gay Central in New Orleans is also party central for everyone. And during Southern Decadence, the gay Mardi Gras on Labor Day weekend, the quarter becomes a little queerer.

To find out the current women's nights at the guys' bars, stop by the lesbigay **Faubourg Marigny Bookstore** and pick up an **Impact** or **Ambush** newspaper. Or drop by the **Lesbian/Gay Community Center** on North Rampart.

## New Orleans (504)

**Where the Girls Are:** Wandering the Quarter, or in the small artsy area known as mid-city, north of the Quarter up Esplanade St.

**Lesbigay Pride:** June.

**Annual Events:**

February - **Mardi Gras**: 566-5011. North America's rowdiest block party.

April - **Gulf Coast Womyn's Festival** at Camp SisterSpirit (in Ovett, MS): 601/344-1411.

September - **Southern Decadence**: 529-2860. Gay mini-Mardi Gras.

**City Info:** 566-5011.

**Attractions:** Bourbon St. in the French Quarter. Cafe du Monde for beignets. Pat O'Brien's for a hurricane. Preservation Hall. Moon Walk. Top of the Market.

**Best View:** Top of the Mart Lounge (522-9795) on the 33rd floor of the World Trade Center of New Orleans.

**Weather:** Summer temperatures hover in the 90's with subtropical humidity. Winters can be rainy and chilly. The average temperature in February (Mardi Gras month) is 58° while the average precipitation is 5.23".

**Transit:** United Cab: 522-9771. Airport Shuttle: 522-3500. Regional Transit Authority: 242-2600.

**The Chimes B&B** Constantinople at Coliseum **488-4640/(800) 729-4640** gay-friendly • 5 guest suites & rms in an 1876 home • smokefree • kids/pets ok • $51-161

**Dauzat House** 337 Burgundy St. **524-2075** gay-friendly

**Deja Vu Guest House** 1835 N. Rampart St. **945-5912/(800) 238-1577** mostly gay men • individual Creole cottages

**Doubletree Hotel** 300 Canal St. **581-1300** gay-friendly • IGLTA

**Faubourg Guest House** 1703 2nd St. **895-2004** mostly gay men • 1860s Greek Revival • pets ok • gay-owned/run • $40-125

**Fourteen Twelve Thalia—A B&B** 1412 Thalia **522-0453** gay-friendly • 1-bdrm apt in the Lower Garden District • patio • $75-150

**French Quarter B&B** 1132 Ursulines **525-3390** lesbians/gay men • apt • full brkfst • swimming • $65-125

▲ **French Quarter Reservation Service** **523-1246/(800) 523-9091**

**The Frenchmen Hotel** 417 Frenchmen St. **948-2166/(800) 831-1781** popular • lesbians/gay men • 1860s Creole townhouses • spa • swimming • wheelchair access

▲ **The Greenhouse** 1212 Magazine St. **561-8400/(800) 966-1303** lesbians/gay men • swimming • hot tub • non-smoking rms avail. • $65-125

**Hotel de la Monnaie** 405 Esplanade Ave. **947-0009** gay-friendly • wheelchair accesss • IGLTA • $140-190

**Ingram House** 1012 Elysian Fields Ave. **949-3110** gay-friendly

▲ **Inn The Quarter (888) 523-5235** gay-friendly • townhouse • private courtyard

**La Dauphine, Residence des Artistes** 2316 Dauphine St. **948-2217** mostly gay men • smokefree • free airport pickup (call for details) • IGLTA • $55-100

**La Residence** 1300 Marais St. **522-4828/(800) 826-9718 x11** lesbians/gay men • 1- & 2-bdrm apts • kitchens

**Lafitte Guest House** 1003 Bourbon St. **581-2678/(800) 331-7971** popular • gay-friendly • elegant French manor house • smokefree • full bar • gay-owned/run • $85-165

# INN THE QUARTER

Rooftop View Balcony • Townhouse • Courtyard Apartment

## Call Toll Free **888-523-5235**

**G**o for a splash in our refreshing heated pool. Enjoy beautiful cottages and rooms with color cable TV, phone, private baths, gym and continental breakfast. Great romantic getaway.

## MACARTY PARK
### GUEST HOUSE

3820 Burgundy Street • New Orleans, LA 70117
(504) 943-4994 • (800) 521-2790
faxmehard@aol.com • www.macartypark.com

**Lamothe House Hotel** 621 Esplanade Ave. **947-1161/(800) 367-5858** gay-friendly • fine hotel

**Lions Inn** 2517 Chartres St. **945-2339** mostly gay men • handsome 1850s home • swimming • smokefree • patio • $65-125 (higher special events)

▲ **Macarty Park Guesthouse** 3820 Burgundy St. **943-4994/(800) 521-2790** lesbians/gay men • swimming • rooms & cottages • 5 min. from the French Quarter • IGLTA

**Maison Burgundy** 1860 Burgundy St. **948-2355/(800) 863-8813** gay-friendly • swimming • hot tub

**Maison Dauphine** 2460 Dauphine St. **943-0861** mostly gay men • near French Quarter • gay-owned/run

**Marigny Guest House** 621 Esplanade **944-9700/(800) 367-5858** gay-friendly • quaint Creole cottage

**Mazant St. Guest House** 906 Mazant **944-2662** gay-friendly • $21-48 (higher Mardi Gras & other events)

**The McKendrick-Breaux House** 1474 Magazine St. **586-1700** gay-friendly

**Mentone B&B** 1437 Pauger St. **943-3019** gay-friendly • suite in a Victorian home in the Faubourg Marigny district • smokefree • $100-150

**New Orleans Guest House** 1118 Ursulines St. **566-1177/(800) 562-1177** gay-friendly • Creole cottage dated back to 1848 • courtyard • $79-99

**Parkview Marigny B&B** 726 Frenchmen St. **945-7875/(800) 749-4640** lesbians/gay men • apt • IGLTA • $82-150

**Pauger Guest Suites** 1750 N. Rampart St. **944-2601/(800) 484-8334x9834** mostly gay men • near French Quarter • gay-owned/run

**Radisson Hotel New Orleans** 1500 Canal St. **522-4500** gay-friendly • IGLTA

**Rainbow House** 2311-15 N. Rampart St. **943-5805** lesbians/gay men • walking distance to French Quarter • also apts

**Rathbone Inn** 1227 Esplanade Ave. **947-2100/(800) 947-2101** 1850s Greek Revival mansion • 2 blks from the French Quarter • IGLTA • $95-145

**Renaissance Realty** (800) 238-1577 fully equipped rental properties

# Rue Royal Inn

*An 1830's Creole Townhouse in the Heart of the French Quarter Accommodations range from economical courtyard units to large balcony suites with jacuzzi bath...complete with refrigerators and wet bars.*

*1006 Rue Royal New Orleans, LA 70116 (504) 524-3900 • (800) 776-3901 FAX (504) 558-0566 credit cards accepted*

**Rober House Condos** 822 Ursulines Ave. **529-4663** gay-friendly • apt • swimming • non-smoking rm avail. • courtyard • IGLTA • gay-owned/run • $110-150

**The Robert Gordy House** 2630 Bell St. **486-9424/(800) 889-7359** gay-friendly

**Royal Barracks Guest House** 717 Barracks St. **529-7269** lesbians/gay men • hot tub • private patios

**Royal St. Courtyard** 2446 Royal St. **943-6818/(888) 846-4004** lesbians/gay men • historic 1884 guesthouse • full kitchens • hot tub

▲ **Rue Royal Inn** 1006 Royal St. **524-3900/(800) 776-3901** gay-friendly • historic 1830s Creole townhouse in the heart of the French Quarter • IGLTA • $75-145

**St. Charles Guest House** 1748 Prytania St. **523-6556** gay-friendly • pensione-style guest house • swimming • patio • $30-85 (higher special events)

**St. Peter Guest House** 1005 St. Peter St. **524-9232/(800) 535-7815** gay-friendly • historic location • authentically appointed

**Sun Oak Museum & Guesthouse** 2020 Burgundy St. **945-0322** lesbians/gay men • Greek Revival Creole cottage circa 1836 • gardens • $75-125

**Ursuline Guest House** 708 Ursulines St. **525-8509/(800) 654-2351** popular • mostly gay men • hot tub • evening socials w/wine

**Vieux Carre Rentals** 841 Bourbon St. **525-3983** gay-friendly • 1- & 2-bdrm apts

## BARS & NIGHTCLUBS

**Angel Club** 2441 Bayou Rd. **940-0666** lesbians/gay men • dancing/DJ • gothic/industrial

**Angles** 2301 N. Causeway, Metairie **834-7979** 4pm-4am • lesbians/gay men • neighborhood bar • dancing/DJ • wheelchair access

**Big Daddy's** 2513 Royal **948-6288** 24hrs • lesbians/gay men • neighborhood bar • wheelchair access

**Buffa's** 1001 Esplanade Ave. **945-9373** 11am-3am • gay-friendly • neighborhood bar • food served

**Cafe Lafitte in Exile/The Corral** 901 Bourbon St. **522-8397** 24hrs • popular • mostly gay men • videos

**PLANS FOR MARCH?**
**IT'S TIME YOU MADE THEM**

**1 (888) 44 DINAH**
**CLUB SKIRTS & GIRL BAR**

**Charlene's** 940 Elysian Fields Ave. **945-9328** 5pm-close, from 2pm Fri-Sun, clsd Mon • mostly women • neighborhood bar • dancing/DJ • live shows • B&B avail.

**Copper Top** 706 Franklin Ave. **948-2300** 24hrs • lesbians/gay men • neighborhood bar • dancing/DJ • Cajun & country/western • wheelchair access

**Country Club** 634 Louisa St. **945-0742** 10am-11pm • lesbians/gay men • neighborhood bar • live shows • swimming

**The Double Play** 439 Dauphine **523-4517** 24hrs • mostly gay men • neighborhood bar

**Footloose** 700 N. Rampart **524-7654** 24hrs • lesbians/gay men • dancing/DJ • transgender-friendly • shows on wknds

**The Four Seasons** 3229 N. Causeway, Metairie **832-0659** 3pm-4am • lesbians/gay men • neighborhood bar • dancing/DJ

**The Friendly Bar** 2801 Chartres St. **943-8929** 11am-3am • lesbians/gay men • neighborhood bar • wheelchair access • women-owned/run

**Good Friends Bar** 740 Dauphine **566-7191** 24hrs • popular • gay-friendly • professional • good cocktails • wheelchair access • also 'Queens Head Pub' 6pm-3am Wed-Sun • mostly gay men • neighborhood bar

**Metro** 2004 A.P. Tureaud **943-7788** lesbians/gay men • dancing/DJ • live shows • mostly African-American

**The Mint** 504 Esplanade **525-2000** noon-3am • popular • lesbians/gay men • professional • live shows • wheelchair access

**Oz** 800 Bourbon St. **593-9491** 24hrs • lesbians/gay men • dancing/DJ • wheelchair access

**Rawhide** 2010 740 Burgundy **525-8106** 24hrs • popular • mostly gay men • neighborhood bar • leather/ fetish • alternative

**Rubyfruit Jungle** 640 Frenchmen **947-4000** 4pm-close, from 1pm wknds • popular • lesbians/gay men • dancing/DJ • alternative • live shows • wheelchair access

# Out of Focus

## art & photography

### 1119-A Saint Mary Street
### New Orleans LA 70130
### 504.586.1888
Between Camp St. & Magazine St.

candles, jewelry & other cool stuff
no longer having clear image
out of the way, off the beaten path,
out of this world, off center, out of focus

**Xis** 1302 Allo St., Marrero **340-0049** 5pm-close • lesbians/gay men • neighborhood bar • dancing/DJ • wheelchair access

## CAFES

**St. Ann's Cafe & Deli** 800 Dauphine **529-4421** 24hrs • popular • American • some veggie • wheelchair access • $5-10

## RESTAURANTS

**Cafe Sbisa** 1011 Decatur **522-5565** dinner & Sun brunch • French Creole • patio

**Casamento's** 4330 Magazine **895-9761** 5:30pm-9pm • best oyster loaf in city

**Clover Grill** 900 Bourbon St. **523-0904** 24hrs • popular • diner fare • $5-10

**Commander's Palace** 1427 Washington Ave. **899-8221** lunch & dinner • Creole • $30-50

**Feelings Cafe** 2600 Chartres St. **945-2222** dinner nightly, Fri lunch, Sun brunch • Creole • piano bar wknds • $10-20

**Fiorella's Cafe** 45 French Market Pl. **528-9566** dinner & Sun brunch • homecooking

**Gram's Cafe Creole** 533 Toulouse **524-1479** 11:30am-close • wheelchair access

**Jack Sprat** 3240 S. Carrollton **486-2200** 11am-10pm, noon-5pm Sun • healthy vegetarian • $6-12

**La Peniche** 1940 Dauphine St. **943-1460** 24hrs • diner • some veggie • $5-10

**Lucky Cheng's** 720 St. Louis **529-2045** lunch & dinner

**Mama Rosa** 616 N. Rampart **523-5546** 11am-10pm, clsd Mon • Italian • $5-10

**Mona Lisa** 1212 Royal St. **522-6746** 11am-11pm • Italian • some veggie • $8-15

**Nola** 534 St. Louis St. **522-6652** lunch & dinner • Creole

**Old Dog New Trick Cafe** 307 Exchange Alley **522-4569** 11am-9pm • vegetarian • wheelchair access • $5-10

**Olivier's** 911 Decatur **525-7734** 10am-10pm • Creole • wheelchair access • $10-15

**Petunia's** 817 St. Louis **522-6440** 8am-midnight • popular • Cajun/Creole • $10-20

**PJ's** 634 Frenchmen St. **949-2292** 7am-11pm, til midnight Fri-Sat, from 8am wknds • popular • wheelchair access

**Pontchartrain Cafe** 2031 St. Charles Ave. **524-0581** 5:30pm-9pm • $8-15

**Poppy's Grill** 717 St. Peter **524-3287** 24hrs • diner • wheelchair access

**Praline Connection** 542 Frenchmen St. **943-3934** til 10pm • soul food • $9-16

**Quarter Scene** 900 Dumaine St. **522-6533** 24hrs, clsd Tue • homecooking • some veggie • $8-15

**Sammy's Seafood** 627 Bourbon St. **525-8442** 11am-midnight • Creole/Cajun • $9-28

**Sebastian's** 538 St. Philip St. **524-2041** 5:30pm-10pm • Creole plus

**Vera Cruz** 1141 Decatur St. **561-8081** noon-11pm, clsd Mon-Tue • Mexican • wheelchair access • $8-20

**Whole Foods Market** 3135 Esplanade Ave. **943-1626** 9am-9pm • healthy deli • plenty veggie • $5-10

## ENTERTAINMENT & RECREATION

**Gay Heritage Tour** 907 Bourbon St. (at 'Alternatives' bookstore) **945-6789** call for details

## BOOKSTORES & RETAIL SHOPS

**Alternatives** 907 Bourbon St. **524-5222** 11am-9pm, til 11pm Fri-Sat • lesbigay

**Bookstar** 414 N. Peters **523-6411** 10am-midnight, til 8pm Sun • wheelchair access

**Faubourg Marigny Bookstore** 600 Frenchmen St. **943-9875** 10am-8pm, til 6pm wknds • lesbigay • wheelchair access

**Gay Mart** 808 Rampart St. **523-6005** noon-7pm • gifts • T-shirts

▲ **Out of Focus** 1119-A St. Mary **586-1888** 11am-5pm Wed-Sat • art gallery

**Postmark New Orleans** 631 Toulouse St. **529-2052/(800) 285-4247**

**Sidney's News Stand** 917 Decatur St. **524-6872** 8am-9pm • general magazine store w/lesbigay titles

**Something Different** 5300 Tchoupitoulas **891-9056**

## PUBLICATIONS

**Ambush** 522-8049

**Exit** 482-1743

**Impact** 944-6722

**The Pink Pages** 947-3969

## TRAVEL AGENTS

**Alternative Tours & Travel** 3003 Chartres **949-5815/(800) 576-0238** IGLTA

**Avalon Travel Advisors** 1206 Magazine 561-8400/(800) 966-1303 IGLTA

**Community Travel** 612 N. Rampart 552-2913/(800) 811-5028 IGLTA

**Destination Management PHONE ME** 610 S. Peters St. #200 592-0500 IGLTA

**Uptown Travel & Tours** 4001 Toulouse St. #101 488-9993/(800) 566-9312 IGLTA

### SPIRITUAL GROUPS

**Jewish Gay/Lesbian Alliance** 1228 Bourbon St. #D 525-8286

**Vieux Carre MCC** 1128 St. Roch 945-5390 11am & 4:15pm Sun, 6pm Wed

### EROTICA

**Gargoyle's** 1205 Decatur St. 529-4387 11am-7pm, til 10pm Fri-Sat • leather/fetish store

**Panda Bear** 415 Bourbon St. 529-3593 leather • toys

**Paradise** 41 W. 24th St., Kenner 461-0000

**Rings of Desire** 1128 Decatur St., 2nd flr. 524-6147 piercing studio

**Second Skin Leather** 521 St. Philip St. 561-8167 also 'Above & Below' piercing studio upstairs

## Shreveport                    (318)

### BARS & NIGHTCLUBS

**Central Station** 1025 Marshall 222-2216 4pm-6am • popular • lesbians/gay men • dancing/DJ • country/western • transgender-friendly • wheelchair access

**Korner Lounge** 800 Lousiana 222-9796 5pm-2am, clsd Sun • mostly gay men • neighborhood bar • unconfirmed

### EROTICA

**Fun Shop** 1601 Marshall 226-1308

## Slidell                       (504)

### BARS & NIGHTCLUBS

**Billy's** 2600 Hwy. 190 W. 847-1921 5pm-2am • mostly gay men • neighborhood bar

**Pier 11** 4809 Pontchartrain Dr. 645-0603 lesbians/gay men • food served

# MAINE

## Augusta                       (207)

### ACCOMMODATIONS

**Maple Hill Farm B&B Inn** 622-2708 gay-friendly • 1890s Victorian farmhouse on 62 acres • full brkfst

### BARS & NIGHTCLUBS

**P.J.'s** 80 Water St. 623-4041 7pm-1am Tue-Sat • popular • lesbians/gay men • dancing/DJ

## Bangor                        (207)

### BARS & NIGHTCLUBS

**The Bar** 123 Franklin St. 941-8966 6pm-1am, 7pm-midnight Sun & Wed • lesbians/gay men • dancing/DJ • chem/alcohol-free Mon

## Bar Harbor                    (207)

### ACCOMMODATIONS

**Devilstone** 288-2933 IGLTA

**Manor House Inn** 106 West St. 288-3759 open May-Nov • gay-friendly • full brkfst

## Bath                          (207)

### ACCOMMODATIONS

**The Galen C. Moses House** 1009 Washington St. 442-8771 gay-friendly • 1874 Victorian • full brkfst • gay-owned/run

## Bethel                        (207)

### ACCOMMODATIONS

**Speckled Mountain Ranch** 836-2908 gay-friendly • on a horse farm • full brkfst • lesbian-owned • $55-65

## Brunswick                     (207)

### INFO LINES & SERVICES

**Bowdin College BGLAD** 725-3620 9pm Wed • call for location

### ACCOMMODATIONS

**The Vicarage by the Sea B&B** 833-5480 gay-friendly • full brkfst • wheelchair access • women-owned/run • $55-80

### BOOKSTORES & RETAIL SHOPS

**Gulf of Maine Books** 134 Maine St. 729-5083 9:30am-5pm, clsd Sun • alternative

## Camden (207)

ACCOMMODATIONS

**The Old Massachusetts Homestead Campground** 789-5135/(800) 213-8142 open May-Nov • gay-friendly • cabins • tentsites • RV hookups • swimming

## Caribou (207)

INFO LINES & SERVICES

**Gay/Lesbian Phoneline** 398 S. Main St. 498-2088/(800) 468-2088 (ME ONLY) social & networking group for northern ME & NW New Brunswick, Canada

## Corea (207)

RESTAURANTS

**Fisherman's Inn** 963-5585

## Corea Harbor (207)

ACCOMMODATIONS

**The Black Duck Inn on Corea Harbor** 963-2689 gay-friendly • full brkfst • $65-135

## Dexter (207)

ACCOMMODATIONS

**Brewster Inn** 37 Zions Hill 924-3130 gay-friendly • historic mansion

## Ellsworth (207)

RESTAURANTS

**Le Domaine Restaurant & Inn** 422-3395 dinner only, clsd Tue

## Freeport (207)

ACCOMMODATIONS

**The Bagley House** 1290 Royalsborough Rd., Durham 865-6566/(800) 765-1772 gay-friendly • lesbian-run • $65-120
**Country at Heart B&B** 37 Bow St. 865-0512 gay-friendly • full brkfst • located in Maine's outlet shopping mecca

RESTAURANTS

**Harraseeket Lunch & Lobster Co.** 865-3535

## Kennebunk (207)

ACCOMMODATIONS

**Arundel Meadows Inn** 1024 Portland Rd., Arundel 985-3770 gay-friendly • full brkfst • $85-125

## Kennebunkport (207)

ACCOMMODATIONS

**The Colony Hotel** Ocean Ave. & Kings Hwy. 967-3331/(800) 552-2363 gay-friendly •1914 grand oceanfront property
**White Barn Inn** 37 Beach St. 967-2321 gay-friendly • dinner served

RESTAURANTS

**Bartley's Dockside** by the bridge 967-5050 seasonal • 11am-10pm • seafood • some veggie • full bar • wheelchair access

## Kittery Point (207)

RESTAURANTS

**Chauncey Creek Lobster Pier** Chauncey Creek 439-1030 seasonal • 11am-8pm • BYOB

## Lewiston (207)

INFO LINES & SERVICES

**Bates Gay/Lesbian/Straight Alliance** Hirasawa Lounge, Chase Hall, Bates College 786-6255 8:30pm Sun

BARS & NIGHTCLUBS

**The Sportsman's Club** 2 Bates St. 784-2251 8pm-1am • popular • lesbians/gay men • dancing/DJ

EROTICA

**Paris Book Store** 297 Lisbon St. 783-6677

## Lincolnville Beach (207)

ACCOMMODATIONS

**Sign of the Owl B&B** 243 Atlantic Hwy., Northport 338-4669 lesbians/gay men • full brkfst • $35-65

RESTAURANTS

**Chez Michael** Rte. 1 789-5600 dinner & Sun brunch, clsd Mon • full bar
**Lobster Pound** Rte. 1 789-5550 11:30am-8pm • full bar

## Lovell (207)

ACCOMMODATIONS

**The Stone Wall B&B** 925-1080/(800) 413-1080 lesbians/gay men • full brkfst • IGLTA • $85-135

## Milbridge (860)

ACCOMMODATIONS

**Bay View Cottage** 289-8026 mostly gay men • 1 hour from Bangor

TRAVEL AGENTS
**Alpine Travel Services** (800) 564-3395

## Mt. Desert Island (207)

ACCOMMODATIONS
**Duck Cove Retreat** W. Tremont 244-9079/(617) 864-2372 women only • swimming • seasonal • wheelchair access • $10-15
**Mountain View** Southwest Harbor 885-5026 seasonal • weekly home rental • no pets

## Naples (207)

ACCOMMODATIONS
▲ **Lambs Mill Inn** 693-6253 mostly women • full brkfst • hot tub • swimming • IGLTA • women-owned/run • $75-105

RESTAURANTS
**Sydney's** Rte. 302 693-3333 4pm-9pm, til 10pm Fri-Sat

## Ogunquit (207)

ACCOMMODATIONS
**Admiral's Inn** 70 S. Main St. 646-7093 lesbians/gay men • swimming
**The Clipper Ship B&B** 646-9735 gay-friendly
**The Gazebo B&B** 646-3733 gay-friendly • 165-yr-old Greek Revival farmhouse • full brkfst • swimming • $95-105
▲ **The Heritage of Ogunquit** 14 Marginal Ave. 646-7787 mostly women • lesbian-owned/run • $70-80
**The Inn at Tall Chimney** 94 Main St. 646-8974 open April-Nov • lesbians/gay men
**The Inn at Two Village Square** 135 Main St. 646-5779 seasonal • mostly gay men • oceanside Victorian • $50-120
**Leisure Inn** 6 School St. 646-2737 seasonal • lesbians/gay men • B&B & apts • $60-95

Ewe Hike • Ewe Bike • Ewe Ski • Ewe zzzzz

Small country inn nestled in the heart of Maine's western lakes and mountains
• Hot Tub
• Full Country Breakfast
• Private Baths

**Lamb's Mill Inn**

Box 676, Lamb's Mill Rd.
Naples, Me. 04055
207-693-6253

Innkeepers
Laurie Tinkham • Sandy Long
Reservations suggested

▲ **Moon Over Maine** Berwick Rd. 646-6666/(800) 851-6837 gay-friendly

**Ogunquit Beach Inn** 8 School St. 646-1112/(888) 976-2463 lesbians/gay men • cottage suites • $65-125

**The Ogunquit House** 7 Kings Hwy. 646-2967 popular • lesbians/gay men • Victorian B&B w/beautiful gardens • $59-130

**Old Village Inn** 30 Main St. 646-7088 gay-friendly • dinner served

**Rockmere Lodge B&B** 40 Stearns Rd. 646-2985 gay-friendly

**The Seasons Hotel** 646-6041/(800) 639-8508 seasonal • gay-friendly

**Shore House** 7 Shore Rd. 646-0627 gay-friendly

**Yellow Monkey Guest Houses/Hotel** 168 Main St. 646-9056 seasonal • lesbians/gay men

## BARS & NIGHTCLUBS

**The Club** 13 Main St. 646-6655 9pm-1am, from 4pm Sun, clsd Wed (seasonal) • popular • mostly gay men • dancing/DJ • food served

**Front Porch Cafe** Ogunquit Sq. 646-3976 4pm-1am (seasonal) • gay-friendly • full menu • $6-16

**Maxwell's Pub** 27 Main St. 646-2345 noon-1am (seasonal) • gay-friendly food served • patio

## CAFES

**Cafe Amoré** 37 Shore Rd. 646-6661 from 7:30am daily • wheelchair access

## RESTAURANTS

**Arrows** Berrick Rd. (1.8 mi. W. of Center) 361-1100 6pm-9pm, clsd Mon (seasonal) • popular • cont'l • some veggie • $20-27

**The Cape Neddick Inn** 1233 Rte. 1 363-2899 5:30pm-9pm • also a brewery

**Clay Hill Farm** Agamenticus Rd. (2 miles W. of Rte. 1) 646-2272 some veggie • also piano bar • $13-24

**Grey Gull Inn** 321 Webhannet Dr., Wells 646-7501 dinner • New England fine dining • $13-22

**Johnathan's** Bourne Ln. 646-4777 5pm-9pm • veggie/seafood • full bar • wheelchair access • $13-25

**The Moonsnail Grill & Tavern** 188 Main St. 646-2259 brkfst & dinner

**Poor Richard's Tavern** Perkins Cove at Shore Rd. & Pine Hill 646-4722 5:30pm-9:30pm • New England fare • some veggie • full bar • $10-18

# THE HERITAGE OF OGUNQUIT

*"Beautiful Place by the Sea"*

*5 min walk to Beach*
*NON-SMOKING*
*private or shared baths*
*lesbian owned*
*hot tub & deck*

## P.O. BOX 1295 OGUNQUIT, ME 03907

## (207)646-7787
www.one-on-onepc.com/ heritage

email:heritageo @cybertours.com

## Old Orchard Beach (207)

ACCOMMODATIONS
**Sea View Motel** 65 W. Grand Ave. **934-4180** gay-friendly

## Orono (207)

INFO LINES & SERVICES
**Wilde-Stein Club** Sutton Lounge, Memorial Union, Univ. of Maine **581-1731** Sept-May only • 6pm Th

ACCOMMODATIONS
**Maine Wilderness Lake Island 990-5839** lesbians/gay men • rental cabins in the forest

## Pembroke (207)

ACCOMMODATIONS
**Yellow Birch Farm 726-5807** mostly women • B&B on working farm • daily & weekly rates • also cottage • lesbian-owned/run • $45 night/$250 wk

## Portland (207)

INFO LINES & SERVICES
**Bob's Livery & Tour** 25 Alton St. **773-5135** transportation to Portland, Ogunquit, Boston, Logan Airport, and other New England areas
**Gays in Sobriety** 32 Thomas St. (Williston W. Church) **774-4060** 6:30pm Sun & 8pm Th
**Maine Publicity Bureau** (800) 533-9595 ME vacation info
**Out Among Friends** 87 Spring St. (YWCA, downstairs club room) **879-1037** 7pm-8:30pm 1st & 3rd Th • lesbian social/discussion group
**Outright** 1 Pleasant St. (4th Fl.) **828-6560**/(888) 567-7600 6pm Tue & 7:30pm Fri • youth organization
**Queer Alliance** 874-6596
**W.O.W. (Wild Outdoor Women)** 787-2379 monthly mtg. • recreational group

ACCOMMODATIONS
**Andrews Lodging B&B** 417 Auburn St. **797-9157** gay-friendly • full brkfst • kitchens • pets ok • patio

Center of Town
All Private Baths
Cable TV
Air Conditioning
Free Soft Drinks
Continental Breakfast
Outdoor Hot Tub
and Old-Fashioned
Hospitality!

**Moon Over Maine**
Bed & Breakfast ★ Ogunquit, ME
(800) 851-6837  (207) 646-MOON

**The Danforth** 163 Danforth St. **879-8755** gay-friendly • 1823 mansion • conference/reception facilities • woman-owned

▲ **The Inn at St. John** 939 Congress St. **773-6481/(800) 636-9127** gay-friendly • unique historic inn • $30-90

**The Inn By The Sea** 40 Bowery Beach Rd., Cape Elizabeth **799-3134** gay-friendly • condo-style suites w/ocean views • woman-owned

**The Pomegranate Inn** 49 Neal St. **772-1066/(800) 356-0408** gay-friendly • upscale B&B

**West End Inn** 146 Pine St. **772-1377** gay-friendly • 1870 townhouse

## BARS & NIGHTCLUBS

**The Blackstones** 6 Pine St. **775-2885** 4pm-1am • mostly gay men • neighborhood bar

**Cosmo's Bar & Video Lounge** 117 Spring St. **874-2041** mostly gay men • neighborhood bar

**Raoul's Roadside Attraction** 865 Forest Ave. **773-6886** 4pm-1am, from noon wknds • gay-friendly • live shows • also restaurant • Mexican/American • $5-7

**Sisters** 45 Danforth St. **774-1505** 5pm-1am, clsd Mon-Tue • mostly women • live shows • food served

**Underground** 3 Spring St. **773-3315** 4pm-1am • popular • lesbians/gay men • dancing/DJ • live shows

**Zootz** 31 Forest Ave. **773-8187** 9pm-1am • gay-friendly • dancing/DJ • alternative music • live shows

## RESTAURANTS

**Cafe Always** 47 Middle St. **774-9399** dinner Wed-Sat, Sun brunch • some veggie • full bar • $10-20

**Katahdin** 106 Spring St. **774-1740** 5pm-10pm, clsd Sun-Mon • full bar

**Street & Co.** 33 Wharf St. **775-0887** 5:30pm-9:30pm, til 10pm Fri-Sat • seafood • $12-18 • Nancy's favorite

**Tabitha Jean's Restaurant** 94 Free St. **780-8966** lunch & dinner • some veggie • woman-owned

**Walter's Cafe** 15 Exchange St. **871-9258** 11am-9pm, from 5pm Sun • some veggie • $10-14

# Quiet Gentility with European Charm
### ...in the heart of Portland

# INN AT ST. JOHN

- *Free Airport Pick-up*
- *Convenient Intown Location*
- *Minutes to Historic Old Port and Arts District*
- *Extended Stays Available*

- *Continental Breakfast*
- *Free Local Calls*
- *Free Bicycle Storage*
- *An Easy Walk to Everything that Portland Has to Offer*

## 800-636-9127 • 207-773-6481
939 Congress Street • Portland, Maine 04102

# *C*ommunity *P*ride *R*eporter

*Proudly serving the Lesbian, Gay,*
*Bisexual, Transgender Community*

Community Pride Reporter serves as a source of local, state, national and international news, information, idea and opinions by and for the lesbian, gay, bisexual and transgendered Community.

Subscription rates are $25.00 per year. If you would like a subscription, please fill out the information below and mail it to: Community Pride Reporter; 175 Lancaster Street Suite 214 B; Portland, ME 04072.

Name: _____

Address: _____

_____

Phone: _____

Please make checks payable to : Community Pride Reporter. We acknowledge the varying degrees to which members of our community are out and respect their choice, CPR is mailed in a plain envelope, the return address reads "CPR 175 Lancaster St. Suite 214 B  Portland ME 04101" If printing a return address is ever a problem, please let us know.

**Westside** 58 Pine St. 773-8223 lunch & dinner, clsd Mon • Maine game & seafood • some veggie • wheelchair access • $14-20

**Woodford's Cafe** 129 Spring St. 772-1374 11am-10pm, til midnight Fri-Sat, clsd Mon • full bar • wheelchair access • $5-9

### ENTERTAINMENT & RECREATION

**Bob's Airport Livery** 25 Alton St. 773-5135 shuttle and tour service for Portland and also covers Ogunquit

### BOOKSTORES & RETAIL SHOPS

**Communiques** 3 Moulton St. 773-5181 10am-7pm, til 9pm summers • cards • gifts • clothing

**Condom Sense** 424 Fore St. 871-0356 hours vary

**Drop Me A Line** 611 Congress St. 773-5547 10am-6pm, til 7pm Th-Fri, noon-5pm Sun

### PUBLICATIONS

▲**Community Pride Reporter** 282-4311 extensive resource listings for ME & NH

### TRAVEL AGENTS

**Adventure Travel** 2 Elsie Wy., Scarborough 885-5060 IGLTA

### SPIRITUAL GROUPS

**Am Chofshi** 833-6004 lesbigay Jews

**Circle of Hope MCC** 156 High St. 773-0119 4pm Sat

**Congregaton Bet Ha'am** 81 Westbrook St., S. Portland 879-0028 7:30pm Fri • gay-friendly synagogue

**Dignity Maine** 143 State St. (St. Luke's Cathedral, side chapel ) 646-2820 6pm 3rd Sun

**Feminist Spiritual Community** 797-9217 7pm Mon • call for info

### EROTICA

**Video Expo** 666 Congress St. 774-1377

## Rockland (207)

### ACCOMMODATIONS

**The Old Granite Inn** 546 Main St. 594-9036/(800) 386-9036 gay-friendly • wheelchair access

## Rockport (207)

### ACCOMMODATIONS

**White Cedar Accommodations** 378 Commercial St. 236-9069 lesbians/gay men • weekly apt. rental • seasonal • lesbian-owned

## Saco Bay (207)

### ACCOMMODATIONS

**Sea Forest Women's Retreat** 282-1352 women only • full brkfst • lesbian-owned/run • $50

## Sebago Lake (207)

### ACCOMMODATIONS

**Maine-ly For You** 583-6980 gay-friendly • cottages • campsites

## Stonington (207)

### ACCOMMODATIONS

**Sea Gnomes Home** 367-5076 clsd Oct-May • women only • lesbian-owned/run • $40

### RESTAURANTS

**Fisherman's Friend** School St. 367-2442 11am-8pm

## Tennants Harbor (207)

### ACCOMMODATIONS

**Eastwind Inn** 372-6366 gay-friendly • full brkfst • also restaurant • old fashioned New England fare • $14-18

## Waterville (207)

### INFO LINES & SERVICES

**Colby College Bi/Lesbian/Gay Community** Bridge Room 872-4149 7:30pm Mon

### EROTICA

**Priscilla's Book Store** 18 Water St. 873-2774 clsd Sun

## Windham (207)

### RESTAURANTS

**The Olde House** Rte. 85 off 302, Raymond 655-7841 clsd Mon-Tue • cont'l

## York Harbor (207)

### ACCOMMODATIONS

**Canterbury House** 432 York St. 363-3505 gay-friendly • spacious Victorian home • $69-120

### RESTAURANTS

**York Harbor Inn** Rte. 1A 363-5119 lunch Mon-Fri, dinner nightly

## MARYLAND

### Annapolis                                    (410)

#### INFO LINES & SERVICES
**AA Gay/Lesbian** 199 Duke of Gloucester St. (St. Anne's Parish) **255-9721** 8pm Tue

#### ACCOMMODATIONS
**Bed & Breakfast of Maryland** 269-6232/(800) 736-4667 gay-friendly • accommodations service

**William Page Inn** 8 Martin St. **626-1506**/(800) 364-4160 gay-friendly • elegantly renovated 1908 home • full brkfst • smokefree • older kids ok • gay-owned/run

#### CAFES
**Grattis Cafe** 47 State Cir. **267-0902** 9am-8pm, from 11am Sat, clsd Sun

#### EROTICA
**20/20 Books** 2020 West St. **266-0514**

### Baltimore                                    (410)

#### INFO LINES & SERVICES
**AA Gay/Lesbian** (at 'G/L Community Center') **433-4843** 7:30pm Fri & 6:30pm Sat

**FIST (Females Investigating Sexual Terrain)** 675-0856 leather-S/M group

**Gay/Lesbian Community Center** 241 W. Chase St. **837-5445** 10am-4pm, clsd wknds • inquire about 'Womanspace'

**Gay/Lesbian Switchboard** 837-8888/837-8529 (TDD) live 7pm-10pm

**Maryland Office of Tourism** (800) 543-1036

**PACT (People of all Colors Together)** 323-4720

**Transgender Support Group** (at 'G/L Community Center') **837-5445** 8pm 2nd Tue • also 'Tran-Quility' group • 8pm 4th Sat

#### ACCOMMODATIONS
**Abacrombie Badger B&B** 58 W. Biddle St. **244-7227** gay-friendly • smokefree • also restaurant

**Biltmore Suites** 205 W. Madison St. **728-6550**/(800) 868-5064 gay-friendly

**Chez Claire B&B** 17 W. Chase St. **685-4666** gay-friendly • 4-story townhouse in historic area

**Clarion Hotel** 612 Cathedral St. **727-7101**/(800) 292-5500 gay-friendly • jacuzzis

**Mr. Mole B&B** 1601 Bolton St. **728-1179** popular • gay-friendly • splendid suites on historic Bolton Hill • gay-owned/run • $97-155

#### BARS & NIGHTCLUBS
**The Allegro** 1101 Cathedral St. **837-3906** 6pm-2am, from 4pm Sun • mostly gay men • women's night Th • dancing/DJ

**Atlantis** 615 Fallsway **727-9099** 5pm-2am, from 4pm Sun, clsd Mon • mostly gay men • dancing/DJ • live shows

**Baltimore Eagle** 2022 N. Charles St. (enter on 21st) **823-2453** 6pm-2am • popular • mostly gay men • leather • wheelchair access

**Central Station** 1001 N. Charles St. **752-7133** 11:30am-2am • popular • lesbians/gay men • neighborhood bar • videos • also restaurant • some veggie • $7-15

**Club 1772** 1722 N. Charles St. **727-7431** 1:30am-5am Th-Sun • mostly gay men • dancing/DJ • BYOB

**Club Bunns** 608 W. Lexington St. **234-2866** 5pm-2am • lesbians/gay men • women's night Tue • dancing/DJ • mostly African-American

**Club Mardi Gras** 228 Park Ave. **625-9818** 10am-2am • mostly gay men • neighborhood bar • wheelchair access

**Club Midnite** 2549 N. Howard St. **243-3535** 5pm-midnight Sun • gay-friendly • T-dance

**Coconuts Cafe** 311 W. Madison **383-6064** 11am-2am, from 4pm wknds, clsd Mon • call for summer hours • mostly women • dancing/DJ • food served • light fare • wheelchair access • $5-7

**The Drinkery** 203 W. Read St. **669-9820** 11am-2am • lesbians/gay men • neighborhood bar

**The Gallery Bar & Studio Restaurant** 1735 Maryland Ave. **539-6965** 1pm-2am • lesbians/gay men • dinner nightly • $10-12

**Hepburn's** 504 S. Haven St. **276-9310** 7pm-2am, from 4pm wknds, clsd Mon-Tue • mostly women • dancing/DJ

**Hippo** 1 W. Eager St. **547-0069** 3pm-2am • popular • lesbians/gay men • more women Fri & at Sun T-dance • dancing/DJ • transgender-friendly • karaoke • videos • wheelchair access

**Orpheus** 1001 E. Pratt St. **276-5599** gay-friendly • dancing/DJ • 18+ • call for events

**Port in a Storm** 4330 E. Lombard St. **732-5608** 10am-2am • mostly women • neighborhood bar • dancing/DJ • wheelchair access • women-owned/run

**Randy's Sportsman's Bar** 412 Park Ave. **727-8935** 6am-2am • mostly gay men • neighborhood bar • mostly African-American

**Stagecoach** 1003 N. Charles St. **547-0107** 4pm-2am • lesbians/gay men • dancing/DJ • country/western • piano bar • free dance lessons • also restaurant • Tex/Mex • some veggie • rooftop cafe • $5-18

**Unicorn** 2218 Boston St. **342-8344** 4pm-2am, from 2pm wknds • popular • mostly gay men • neighborhood bar • live shows

## CAFES

**Donna's Coffee Bar** 2 W. Madison **385-0180** beer/wine

**Louie's the Bookstore Cafe** 518 N. Charles **962-1224** live shows • plenty veggie • full bar • wheelchair access • $4-12

## RESTAURANTS

**Cafe Hon** 1009 W. 36th St. **243-1230** 8am-10pm, clsd Sun • some veggie • $6-11

**City Diner** 911 Charles St. **547-2489** 24hrs • full bar

**Gampy's** 904 N. Charles St. **837-9797** 5pm-1am, til 2am Wed-Th, til 3am Fri-Sat • plenty veggie

**Guiseppe's** 3215 N. Charles **467-1177** pizza & pasta • full bar

**Gypsy Cafe** 1103 Hollins St. **625-9310** 11am-1am, til 3pm Sun

**Joy America** 800 Key Hwy., Inner Harbor **244-6500** 11am-10pm, clsd Mon

**Loco Hombre** 413 W. Cold Spring Ln. **889-2233** til 10pm • Mexican

**Mencken's Cultured Pearl Cafe** 1114 Hollins St. **837-1947** Mexican • full bar • wheelchair access • $6-12

**Metropol Cafe & Art Gallery** 1713 N. Charles St. **385-3018** 6pm-11pm, 10am-6pm Sun, clsd Mon

**The Millrace** 5201 Franklintown Rd. **448-3663** 11am-midnight, til 2am Th-Sat • seafood • $5-20

**Mount Vernon Stable & Saloon** 909 N. Charles St. **685-7427** lunch & dinner • some veggie • bar 11:30am-2am • $8-12

## Baltimore (410)

**Where the Girls Are:** The women's bars are in southeast Baltimore, near the intersection of Haven and Lombard. Of course, the boy's playground, downtown around Chase St. and Park Ave., is also a popular hangout.

**Lesbigay Pride:** June: 837-5445.

**City Info:** Baltimore Tourism Office: 659-7300.

**Attractions:** Baltimore Art Museum. Harbor Place. National Aquarium.

**Best View:** Top of the World Trade Center at the Inner Harbor.

**Weather:** Unpredictable rains and heavy winds. In summer, the weather can be hot (90°s) and sticky.

**Transit:** Yellow Cab: 685-1212.

**Rooftop Grill** 120 E. Lombard St. (at 'The Brookshire Hotel') **547-8986** 5pm-10pm, til 11pm Fri-Sat • popular • upscale cont'l • some veggie • rooftop dining • $19-25

**Spike & Charlie's Restaurant & Wine Bar** 1225 Cathedral St. **752-8144** lunch, dinner & Sun brunch, clsd Mon • live shows

BOOKSTORES & RETAIL SHOPS

**Adrian's Book Cafe** 714 S. Broadway, Fells Point **732-1048** 8am-8pm, til 11pm Fri-Sat, from 11am wknds • new & used • some gay titles

**Lambda Rising** 241 W. Chase St. **234-0069** 10am-10pm • lesbigay • wheelchair access

PUBLICATIONS

**The Baltimore Alternative** 235-3401

**The Baltimore Gay Paper** 837-7748

**Gay Community Yellow Pages— Baltimore** 547-0380

TRAVEL AGENTS

**Falls Road Travel** 3649 Falls Rd. **467-2600** IGLTA

**Inner Harbor Travel** 916 Eastern Ave. **837-2909** IGLTA

**Mt. Royal Travel** 1303 N. Charles St. **685-6633/(800) 767-6925** IGLTA

**Safe Harbors Travel** 25 South St. **547-6565/(800) 344-5656**

**Travel By Design** 7516 Belair Rd. **668-9414** IGLTA

SPIRITUAL GROUPS

**Beit Tikvah** 5802 Roland Ave. **560-2062** 7:30pm Fri & 10am Sat • welcoming Jewish congregation

**Dignity Baltimore** 740 N. Calvert St. (St. Ignatius) **325-1519** 7:30pm 1st Sat

**Grace & St. Peter's Episcopal Church** 707 Park Ave. **539-1395** 7:45am & 10am Sun, 6pm daily

**MCC** 3401 Old York Rd. **889-6363** 10am & 4pm Sun

**St. Mark's Lutheran Church** 1900 St. Paul St. **752-5804** 11am Sun & 6:30pm Th

EROTICA

**Leather Underground** 136 W. Read St. **528-0991**

## Beltsville (301)

TRAVEL AGENTS

**Your Travel Agent in Beltsville** 10440 Baltimore Blvd. **937-0966/(800) 872-8537** IGLTA

## Catonsville (410)

TOUR OPERATORS

**Galaxsea Cruises & Vacations** 6400 Baltimore Nat'l Pike #270B **747-5204** IGLTA

## Columbia (410)

TRAVEL AGENTS

**American Express Travel-Related Services** 8857 Youngsea Pl. **715-6826** IGLTA

## Cumberland (301)

ACCOMMODATIONS

**Red Lamp Post B&B** 849 Braddock Rd. **777-3262** lesbians/gay men • full brkfst • dinner avail. • hot tub • smokefree • $55-65

RESTAURANTS

**Acropolis** 25 E. Main St., Frostburg **689-8277** 4pm-10pm

**Au Petite Paris** 86 E. Main St. **689-8946** 6pm-9:30pm, clsd Sun-Mon • French • $12-20

## Frederick (301)

CAFES

**The Frederick Coffee Co. & Cafe** 100 East St. **698-0039** 8am-7pm, til 9pm Fri-Sat, 9am-6pm Sun • women-owned/run

## Gaithersburg (301)

TRAVEL AGENTS

**Monarch Travel Center** 9047 Gaither Rd. **258-0989/(800) 800-4669** IGLTA • gay-owned/run

## Hagerstown (301)

BARS & NIGHTCLUBS

**Headquarters** 41 N. Potomac **797-1553** 5pm-2am, til midnight Sun • lesbians/gay men • dancing/DJ • food served • live shows

## Largo (301)

TRAVEL AGENTS
**Shipmate Cruise & Travel** 1300
Mercantile Ln. #158 **925-7041** IGLTA

## Oxon Hill (301)

TRAVEL AGENTS
**Travel Desk** 6178 Oxon Hill Rd. #103
**567-9550** IGLTA

## Parkton (410)

ACCOMMODATIONS
**Hidden Valley Farm B&B** 1419 Mt.
Carmel Rd. **329-8084** lesbians/gay men •
hot tub • 30 min. N. of Baltimore

## Pasadena (410)

TRAVEL AGENTS
**Show-Me Travel** 245 10th St. **360-6501**
IGLTA

## Rockville (301)

SPIRITUAL GROUPS
**Open Door MCC** 15817 Barnesville Rd.
**601-9112** 9am & 10:30am Sun

## Silver Spring (301)

INFO LINES & SERVICES
**GLASS (Gay/Lesbian Assoc. of Silver
Spring)** 588-7330 x3

TRAVEL AGENTS
**Central Travel of Silver Spring** 8609
2nd Ave. **589-9440**
**Travel Central** 8209 Fenton St. **587-
4000/(800) 783-4000**

## Smith Island (203)

ACCOMMODATIONS
**Smith Island Get-A-Way (203) 579-9400**
gay-friendly • apt • secluded community
accessible only by boat • $150 wknd/
$350 wk

## MASSACHUSETTS

## Acton (978)

RESTAURANTS
**Acton Jazz Cafe** 452 Great Rd. (Rte. 2A)
**263-6161** from 5pm, clsd Mon • live
shows • womens' performances Sun •
full bar

## Amherst (413)

INFO LINES & SERVICES
**Everywomen's Center** Wilder Hall,
UMass **545-0883** call for office hours

ACCOMMODATIONS
**Ivy House B&B** 1 Sunset Ct. **549-7554**
gay-friendly • restored Colonial Cape •
$50-80

ENTERTAINMENT & RECREATION
**Women's Media Project** WMUA (91.1
FM) **545-2876** radio shows • 'Women's
Affairs' 5:30-6:30 Fri • 'Oblivion Express'
6am-9am Wed

BOOKSTORES & RETAIL SHOPS
**Food For Thought** 106 N. Pleasant St.
**253-5432** 10am-6pm, til 8pm Wed-Fri,
noon-5pm Sun • progressive bookstore •
wheelchair access • collectively run

PUBLICATIONS
**Valley Women's Voice** UMass **545-2436**

TRAVEL AGENTS
**Adventura Travel** 233 N. Pleasant St.
**549-1256**

SPIRITUAL GROUPS
**Integrity/Western MA** 14 Boltwood Ave.
(chapel) **532-5060** 7pm last Sun

## Athol (978)

TRAVEL AGENTS
**Athol Travel Agency** 352 Main St. **249-
3543** IGLTA

## Barre (978)

ACCOMMODATIONS
**Jenkins House Inn & Restaurant 355-
6444/(800) 378-7373** gay-friendly •
wrap-around porch • English garden

RESTAURANTS
**Barre Mill** 90 Main St. **355-2987** Italian
• $9-12
**Colonel Isaac** 11 Exchange St. **355-4629**
$12-18

## Boston (617)

### INFO LINES & SERVICES

**BAGLY (Boston Alliance of Gay/Lesbian Youth) (800) 422-2459/(800) 399-7337** extensive services for lesbigay youth 22 & under • women's mtg. 6:45pm Wed

**Bisexual Resource Center** 29 Stanhope St., 3rd flr. **424-9595** also Women's Bi-Network

**Cambridge Women's Center** 46 Pleasant St., Cambridge **354-8807**

**Daughters of Bilitis** 1151 Massachusetts Ave. (Harvard Sq.), Cambridge **661-3633** women's social & support networks • call for schedule

**Entre Nous 282-0522** men's & women's leather group • annual Provincetown wknd in Oct.

**Gay/Lesbian Helpline 267-9001** 4:30pm-10pm, from 6pm wknds

**International Foundation for Gender Education 894-8340/899-2212** transgender info & support

**Lesbian Al-Anon** (at the Women's Center) **354-8807** 6:30pm Wed

**Massachusetts Office of Travel & Tourism** 100 Cambridge St., 13th flr. **(800) 447-6277**

**Tiffany Club of New England 891-9325** transgender hotline Tue night

### ACCOMMODATIONS

**463 Beacon St. Guest House** 463 Beacon St. **536-1302** gay-friendly • IGLTA

**Amsterdammertje 471-8454** lesbians/gay men • Euro-American B&B • full brkfst

**Carolyn's B&B** 102 Holworthy St., Cambridge **864-7042** full brkfst • near Harvard Square

▲ **Chandler Inn** 26 Chandler St. **482-3450/(800) 842-3450** gay-friendly • centrally located • IGLTA

**Citywide Reservation Service** 25 Huntington Ave. #500 **267-7424/(800) 468-3593** covers most of New England

**Clarendon Square B&B** 81 Warren Ave. **536-2229** lesbians/gay men • restored Victorian townhouse • fireplaces • $90-160

**Iris B&B 329-3514** women only • private home • shared baths • $60

# BOSTON

On the edge of historic Back Bay and the wonderfully eclectic South End, Boston's most exciting small hotel offers visitors a myriad of fringe benefits.

## $79 $89
### ONE PERSON TWO PEOPLE

Complimentary continental breakfast served daily in Fritz, one of Boston's most frequented gay bars.

## 1-800-842-3450

# CHANDLER INN
HOTEL

FAX: (617) 542-3428

Website: www.chandlerinn-fritz.com

**26 Chandler St., Boston MA 02116 • (617) 482-3450**

# Boston

*H*ome to 65 colleges and universities, Boston has been an intellectual center for the continent for two centuries. Since that famed tea party, it's also been home to some of New England's most rebellious radicals. The result is a city whose character is both traditional and free-thinking, high-brow and free-wheeling*, stuffy and energetic.

Not only is this city complex, it's cluttered...with plenty of historic and mind-sparking sites to visit. Check out the high/low culture in Harvard Square and the shopping along Newbury Street in the Back Bay, as well as the touristy vendors in Faneuil Hall. Don't miss the North End's fabulous Italian food.

Boston's women's community is, not surprisingly, strong and politically diverse. To find out what the latest hotspots are, pick up a copy of **Bay Windows** or **IN Newsweekly** at the well-stocked women's bookstore, **New Words Books.** While you're there, check out the many national lesbian magazines published in Boston, from feminist newsjournal **Sojourner** to **Bad Attitude,** an erotic 'zine for S/M dykes.

Tired of reading? Cruise by the **Hideaway** on Thursday or Sunday for a game of pool. If you like to dance the night away, try **Diva** on Saturday nights, or **Ryles** all weekend.

* About driving in Boston: its drivers are notoriously the most freeform in the country. The streets of Boston can be confusing—often streets of the same name intersect, and six-way intersections are the rule.

## Boston (617)

**Where the Girls Are:** Sipping coffee and reading somewhere in Cambridge or Harvard Square, strolling the oh-so-gay South End near Columbus & Mass. Avenues, or hanging out in the Fenway or Jamaica Plain.

**Entertainment:** Gay Men's Chorus: 424-8900. Triangle Theatre Co.: 867-9909. United Fruit Company & The Theatre Offensive: 547-7728.

**Lesbigay Pride:** June. 1-976-PRIDE, $1.50 per call.

**Annual Events:**

February - **Outwrite:** 426-4469. Annual national lesbian/gay writers & publishers conference at the Boston Park Plaza Hotel.

**City Info:** Boston Visitor's Bureau: (800) 374-7400 (touchtone).

**Attractions:** Back Bay. Beacon Hill. Black Heritage Trail. Boston Common. Faneuil Hall. Freedom Trail. Harvard University. Museum of Afro-American Artists. Old North Church. Thoreau Lyceum.

**Weather:** Extreme—from freezing winters to boiling summers with a brief-but-beautiful spring and fall.

**Transit:** Boston Cab: 536-5010.

# FEEL RIGHT AT HOME IN BOSTON

Two Townhouses In The Heart of Boston / Telephones / Color TV's / Central Air / Outdoor Decks / Private and Shared Baths Continental Breakfast and Evening Snacks / Walk To Historic Sights, Nightlife, Resturants And Shopping / Reasonable Rates ($65 - 104 Per Night) / MC, V & Amex

## OASIS GUEST HOUSE

22 Edgerly Road, Boston, MA 02115
617-267-2262 / Fax: 617-267-1920
www.oasisgh.com
email: oasisgh @ tiac . net

O·A·S·I·S GUEST HOUSE B·O·S·T·O·N

▲ **Oasis Guest House** 22 Edgerly Rd. **267-2262** mostly gay men • Back Bay location • IGLTA • $55-87

**Royal Sonesta Hotel** 5 Cambridge Pkwy., Cambridge **576-5972** gay-friendly • IGLTA

**Taylor House B&B** 50 Burroughs St. **983-9334/(888) 228-2956** gay-friendly • smokefree • $70-150

**Thoreau's Walden B&B** 2 Concord Rd., Lincoln **259-1899** gay-friendly • near historic Walden Pond • full brkfst • $75

**Victorian B&B** 536-3285 women only • full brkfst • smokefree $50-85 (1-4 guests)

## BARS & NIGHTCLUBS

**The Arena** 835 Beacon St. **424-8350** noon-2am • lesbians/gay men • neighborhood bar • dancing/DJ • food served • wheelchair access

**The Avalon** 15 Lansdowne St. **262-2424** 9pm-2am Sun only • popular • mostly gay men • dancing/DJ

**The Bar** 99 St. Botolph St. **266-3030** 5pm-1am, from noon Sun • lesbians/gay men • neighborhood bar • food served

**Buzz** 67 Stuart St. **267-8969** 10pm Sat only • popular • lesbians/gay men • dancing/DJ

**Chaps** 27 Huntington Ave. **266-7778** noon-2am • popular • mostly gay men • more women Wed • Latin night Wed • dancing/DJ • videos • wheelchair acces

**Club Cafe** 209 Columbus **536-0966** 2pm-2am, from 11:30am Sun • popular • lesbians/gay men • more women Wed • 3 bars • live shows • videos • also restaurant • some veggie • wheelchair access • $10-20

**Diva** 184 High St. (International Restaurant) **542-4747** 7pm-2am Sat only • mostly women • dancing/DJ

**Excalibur** Rte. 1 South, Peabody **(508) 535-3545** 8pm-2am, clsd Sun-Wed • lesbians/gay men • dancing/DJ • wheelchair access

**Heaven** 7 Lansdowne St. **421-9595** 10pm-2am Wed • lesbians/gay men • dancing/DJ

**Hexx** 100 Warrenton St. **348-0594** open Tue & Fri-Sat • gay-friendly • Goth/Industrial • call for events

**Joy Boy** 533 Washington St. **338-6999** 10pm Fri only • mostly gay men • dancing/DJ • alternative

**Luxor** 69 Church **423-6969** 4pm-1am • mostly gay men • videos • also 'Mario's' restaurant • Italian • $9-13

**Man-Ray** 21 Brookline St., Cambridge **864-0400** 9pm-1am, clsd Mon-Tue • gay-friendly • gay night Th • more women Sun • dancing/DJ • alternative

**Paragon** 965 Massachusetts Ave. **427-7807** 9pm-2am • mostly gay men • dancing/DJ

**The Spat** 1270 Boylston St. **424-7747** 9pm-2am, clsd Sun • popular • lesbians/gay men • dancing/DJ • videos • roof deck

**Upstairs at Ryles** 212 Hampshire St. **876-9330** Fri-Sun only • mostly women • dancing/DJ

**Upstairs at the Hideaway** 20 Concord Ln., Cambridge **661-8828** Th & Sun only • mostly women • free pool bar for women

**Venus** 101 Warrenton St. **542-4077** 10pm-2am Fri only • mostly women • dancing/DJ

## RESTAURANTS

**Art Zone/Blue Cafe** 150 Kneeland St. **695-0087** 11am-4pm, til 4am Th, 24hrs Fri-Sat • lesbians/gay men • Southern BBQ • plenty veggie • full bar • $7-15

**Biba** 272 Boylston St. **426-7878** lunch & dinner • upscale dining • $30-45

**The Blue Wave** 142 Berkeley St. **424-6711/424-6664** noon-11pm, til 5pm Sun • lesbians/gay men • plenty veggie • $7-10

**Brandy Pete's** 267 Franklin St. **439-4165** lunch & dinner

**Casa Romero** 30 Gloucester St. **536-4341** 5pm-10pm, til 11pm wknds • Mexican • $10-20

**Cedars** 253 Shawmut Ave. **338-7528** 5pm-11pm, clsd Sun • Lebanese

**Icarus** 3 Appleton St. **426-1790** dinner & Sun brunch • New American • $30-40

**Rabia's** 73 Salem St. **227-6637** lunch & dinner • fine Italian • some veggie • wheelchair access • $10-25

**Regalia Restaurant & Wine Bar** 480 Columbus Ave. **236-5252** dinner nightly, Sun brunch • inventive American & tapas • some veggie • $10-20

**Ristorante Lucia** 415 Hanover St. **367-2353** great North End pasta • some veggie • $8-15

**Santarpio's** 113 Chelsea **567-9871** pizza

## Entertainment & Recreation

**Dyke TV** Cambridge Channel 66, Cambridge 9pm Th • 'weekly half-hour TV show produced by lesbians, for lesbians'

## Bookstores & Retail Shops

**Designs for Living** 52 Queensberry St. 536-6150 7am-6pm • also cafe

**Glad Day Books** 673 Boylston St. 267-3010 9:30am-10pm, til 11pm Fri-Sat, noon-9pm Sun • lesbigay

**New Words Bookstore** 186 Hampshire St., Cambridge 876-5310 10am-8pm, til 6pm wknds, from noon Sun • women's

**Synchronicity Transgender Bookstore** 123 Moody St., Waltham 899-2212 over 100 TG titles

**Trident Booksellers & Cafe** 338 Newbury St. 267-8688 9am-midnight • beer/wine • wheelchair access

**Unicorn Books** 1210 Massachusetts Ave., Arlington 646-3680 10am-9pm, til 5pm wknds • spiritual • women-owned/run

**Waterstone's Booksellers** 26 Exeter 859-7300 9am-11pm • huge general bookstore • wheelchair access

**We Think The World of You** 540 Tremont St. 423-1965 open daily • popular • lesbigay

**Wordsworth** 30 Brattle St., Cambridge 354-5201 9am-11pm, 10am-10pm Sun • general • lesbigay titles

## Publications

**Bad Attitude** PO Box 390110, Cambridge, 02139 magazine of lesbian erotica • women-owned/run

**Bay Windows** 266-6670

**Gay Community News** 262-6969 nat'l lesbigay quarterly

**In Newsweekly** 426-8246/(800) 426-8246 statewide newspaper

**Let's Go** Harvard Student Agencies, Cambridge, 02138 travel info for lesbigay youth

**Sojourner—The Women's Forum** 524-0415

## Travel Agents

**5 Star Travel** 164 Newbury St. 536-1999/(800) 359-1999 IGLTA

**American Express Travel** PHONE ME 12 Melrose St. #4 423-2178 IGLTA

**Blue Hill Travel** 35 Sea St., N. Weymouth 337-3774 IGLTA

**Flight Time International** PHONE ME 651 Washington St. 277-0277 IGLTA

**Friends in Travel** 5230 Washington St., W. Roxbury 327-8600/(800) 597-8267 IGLTA

**Gibb Travel** 673 Boylston St. 353-0595/(800) 541-9949 IGLTA

**Homebase Abroad, Ltd.** 29 Mary's Ln., Scituate 545-5112 IGLTA

**Just Right Reservations** 18 Piedmont St., 2nd flr. 423-3550 covers Boston, NYC & Provincetown

**Omega International Travel** 99 Summer St. 737-8511/(800) 727-0599 IGLTA

**Steven Travels** 14 Dartmouth St., Malden 321-6100/(800) 500-6921 IGLTA

**Travel Management** 160 Commonwealth Ave. 424-1908/(800) 532-0055

## Spiritual Groups

**Am Tikva** 50 Sewall Ave., Brockton 926-2536 lesbigay Jewish services

**Dignity** 35 Bowdin St. 421-1915 5:30pm Sun

**MCC** 131 Cambridge St. (Old West Church) 973-0404 6pm Sun

**R.I. & S.E. Mass. Gay Jewish Group** (508) 992-7927

## Gyms & Health Clubs

**Metropolitan Health Club** 209 Columbus 536-3006 gay-friendly

**Mike's Gym** 560 Harrison Ave. 338-6210 popular • gay-owned/run

## Erotica

**Eros Boutique** 581-A Tremont St., 2nd flr. 425-0345 fetishwear • toys

**Grand Opening** 318 Harvard St., 2nd flr. (Arcade Bldg.), Brookline 731-2626 women's sex toy store

**Marquis de Sade** 73 Berkeley St. 426-2120

**Video Expo** 465 Moody St., Waltham 894-5063

## Charlemont (413)

## Accommodations

**The Inn at Charlemont** Rte. 2, Mohawk Trail 339-5796 gay-friendly • also restaurant • some veggie • full bar • women-owned/run • $10-20

## Chelsea (617)

BARS & NIGHTCLUBS
**Club 9-11** 9-11 Williams St. **884-9533**
5pm-1am • lesbians/gay men • dancing/DJ • live shows • wheelchair access

## Chicopee (413)

BARS & NIGHTCLUBS
**Our Hide-away** 16 Bolduc Ln. **534-6426**
6pm-2am, clsd Mon • mostly women • neighborhood bar • dancing/DJ • outdoor volleyball • women-owned/run • wheelchair access

## Gloucester (978)

BOOKSTORES & RETAIL SHOPS
**The Bookstore** 61 Main St. **281-1548**
9am-6pm

## Great Barrington (413)

ACCOMMODATIONS
**Windflower Inn** 684 S. Egremont Rd.
**528-2720** gay-friendly

## Greenfield (413)

ACCOMMODATIONS
**Brandt House** 29 Highland Ave. **774-3329**/(800) 235-3329 gay-friendly • full brkfst • $85-160

BOOKSTORES & RETAIL SHOPS
**World Eye Bookshop** 60 Federal St. **772-2186** open 9am, from noon Sun • general • community bulletin board • women-owned/run

## Harwich (508)

ACCOMMODATIONS
**Blue Heron B&B** 464 Pleasant Lake Ave.
**430-0219** mostly women • swimming • $50-75

## Haverhill (978)

BARS & NIGHTCLUBS
**Friend's Landing** 85 Water St. **374-9400**
4pm-1am, from noon wknds (summer) • mostly gay men • dancing/DJ • karaoke • wheelchair access

BOOKSTORES & RETAIL SHOPS
**Radzukina's** 714 N. Broadway **521-1333**
call for hours • books • jewelry • music • women-owned/run

## Hyannis (508)

INFO LINES & SERVICES
**Gay/Lesbian AA** Cape Cod Hosp. on Bayview St. **775-7060** 5pm Sun

ACCOMMODATIONS
**Gull Cottage** 10 Old Church St., Yarmouth Port **362-8747** lesbians/gay men • near beach • wheelchair access • $50

BARS & NIGHTCLUBS
**Duval Street Station** 477 Yarmouth Rd.
**775-9835** 6pm-1am • popular • lesbians/gay men • Cape Cod's largest gay complex • dancing/DJ • live shows • food served

## Lenox (413)

ACCOMMODATIONS
**Summer Hill Farm** 950 East St. **442-2057** gay-friendly • colonial guesthouse & cottage • full brkfst • wheelchair access
**Walker House** 64 Walker St. **637-1271**/(800) 235-3098 gay-friendly • wheelchair access • $70-90

RESTAURANTS
**Cafe Lucia** 80 Church St. **637-2640** dinner only, clsd Sun-Mon • $13-22
**Church Street Cafe** 65 Church St. **637-2745** some veggie • $13-22
**Gateways** 51 Walker St. **637-2532** plenty veggie • wheelchair access • $13-30

## Lowell (978)

INFO LINES & SERVICES
**Shared Times** 441-9081 newsletter & dances

## Lynn (781)

BARS & NIGHTCLUBS
**Fran's Place** 776 Washington **598-5618**
1pm-2am • lesbians/gay men • neighborhood bar • dancing/DJ • wheelchair access
**Joseph's** 191 Oxford St. **599-9483** 5pm-2am • lesbians/gay men • dancing/DJ • videos • wheelchair access

## Manchester (603)

INFO LINES & SERVICES
**LINC (Lesbians Inviting New Connections)** 668-9245 network for women in rural areas in southern New England

## Marblehead (617)

INFO LINES & SERVICES
**North Shore Gay/Lesbian Alliance** 745-3848 event line

TRAVEL AGENTS
**Around the World Travel** Townhouse Square 631-8620/(800) 733-4337

## Martha's Vineyard (508)

INFO LINES & SERVICES
**Martha's Vineyard Steamship Authority** 540-2022 call for info & schedule of ferries from Boston

ACCOMMODATIONS
**Captain Dexter House of Edgartown** 627-7289 gay-friendly • country inn circa 1840 • $110-180

**Captain Dexter House of Vineyard Haven** 693-6564 gay-friendly • 1840s sea captain's home • $100-165

▲ **Martha's Place Inn** 693-0253 lesbians/gay men • harbor views • fireplaces • wheelchair access • $175-275

**Webb's Camping Area** 693-0233 open May-Sept • gay-friendly • women-owned/run

CAFES
**Black Dog Bakery** 157 State Rd., Vineyard Haven **693-8190**

**Wintertide Coffee House** 5 Corners, Vineyard Haven **693-8830** also live jazz

RESTAURANTS
**The Black Dog Tavern** Beach St. Extension 693-6962 popular • wheelchair access • $13-25

**Le Grenier** 96 Main St. **693-4906** French • $13-25

**Louis' Cafe** State Rd., Vineyard Haven 693-3255

**O'Brian's** 137 Upper Main 627-5850 $12-25

**"A Distinctly Different Bed & Breakfast"**

Martha's is a stately Greek Revival, overlooking Vineyard Haven Harbor, two blocks from the ferry and beach—an ideal island location!

*Come experience the Vineyard and do something new!*

114 Main Street • P.O. Box 1182
Vineyard Haven, MA 02568

**(508) 693-0253**

*The island's Only Gay-owned and operated B & B*

## BOOKSTORES & RETAIL SHOPS
**Bunch of Grapes** 44 Main St., Vineyard Haven **693-2291** general • some lesbian/gay titles & magazines

## Methuen (978)

### BARS & NIGHTCLUBS
**Sammy's** 280 Merrimack St. **685-9911** 8pm-2am Fri, til 1am Sat only • gay-friendly • dancing/DJ

## Nantucket (508)

### ACCOMMODATIONS
**The Chestnut House** 3 Chestnut St. **229-9521** gay-friendly • full brkfst • $75-245
**House of Orange** 25 Orange St. **228-9287** seasonal • old captain's home

## New Bedford (508)

### BARS & NIGHTCLUBS
**Le Place** 20 Kenyon St. **992-8156** 2pm-2am, from noon wknds • popular • lesbians/gay men • dancing/DJ • women-owned/run

**Puzzles** 428 N. Front St. **991-2306** 4pm-2am • lesbians/gay men • dancing/DJ • live shows • wheelchair access

## Newbury (508)

### ACCOMMODATIONS
**46 High Road B&B** 46 High Rd. **462-4664** gay-friendly • full brkfst

## Newton

### ENTERTAINMENT & RECREATION
**Dyke TV** Channel 13 10pm Tue • 'weekly half-hour TV show produced by lesbians, for lesbians'

## Northampton (413)

### INFO LINES & SERVICES
**Community Pride Line** 585-0683 recorded info
**East Coast FTM Group** 584-7616 support group for FTM transgendered people & their partners only
**Lesbian/Gay Business Guild** 585-8839 call for brochure
**New Alexandria Lesbian Library** 584-7616 archives • library • call for appt.
**Shelix** 584-7616 New England S/M support group for lesbian/bi & transgendered women

### ACCOMMODATIONS
**Clark Tavern Inn B&B** 98 Bay Rd., Hadley **586-1900** gay-friendly • full brkfst • $95-135

### Northampton (413)

**Where the Girls Are:** Just off Main St., browsing in the small shops, strolling down an avenue, or sipping a beverage at one of the cafes.

**Annual Events:**

July - **Northampton Lesbian Festival:** 586-8251. 2nd-largest women's music festival.

June - **Golden Threads:** PO Box 60475, Northampton, MA 01060-0475. Gathering for lesbians over 50 & their admirers, at the Provincetown Inn. Fat Women's Gathering: 212/721-8259.

**Best View:** At the top of Skinner Mountain, up Rte. 47 by bus, car or bike.

**Weather:** Late summer/early fall is the best season, with warm, sunny days. Mid-summer gets to the low 90°s, while winter brings snow from November to March, with temperatures in the 20°s and 30°s.

**Transit:** Mystery Taxi: 584-0055. Peter Pan Shuttle: 586-1030. Pioneer Valley Transit Authority (PVTA): 586-5806.

# Northampton

*W*ith all the hype a while back about Northampton being the lesbian capital of the world, visitors are often surprised by the low-key atmosphere of this quaint and quiet New England town. It's the sort of place where the people are nice, the streets are safe, and most groups come in multiples of two.

Sure, you'll be free to smooch with your honey just about everywhere, but don't expect to see the throngs of sapphic sisters you've heard about in the *National Enquirer* or on *20/20* milling around the streets. They're there all right, but they're probably home with the kids, cuddling with their other half, or studying for that big exam at one of the five colleges in the area.

Still, there's plenty for a visiting lesbian to enjoy in Northampton. There are several lesbian-friendly inns close by: **Little River Farm** in Worthington, **Innamorata** in Goshen, and **Tin Roof** in Hadley. The **Green Street Cafe** is popular with local girls. In this college town, many women indulge in literary pleasures at the **New Alexandria Lesbian Library.** Join them here or take the tour of Emily Dickinson's House in nearby Amherst.

With two women's colleges, Smith and Mount Holyoke, progressive Hampshire College, Amherst College and the University of Massachusetts all in the area, there's something fun to do every night of the week, from readings to performance art. Pick up a copy of Off Campus, an entertainment guide for all five colleges. Also check out the **Lesbian Calendar,** a comprehensive monthly listing of events. It's available at **Pride & Joy** lesbian/gay bookstore, the informal community center. While you're there, pick up a copy of the Lesbian/Gay Business Guild's listing of "family" businesses in the area. Or call the **Community Pride Line**.

If you're in town around late July, look for the Northampton Lesbian Festival, which usually happens in Washington, Mass., in the Berkshires—for lack of enough public space in the town of Northampton!

**Corner Porches** 82 Baptist Corner Rd., Ashfield **628-4592** gay-friendly • full brk-fst

**The Inn at Northampton** 1 Atwood Dr. **586-1211/(800) 582-2929** gay-friendly • swimming • restaurant & bar • wheelchair access

**Innamorata B&B** 268-0300 mostly women • full brkfst • women-owned/run • $70-99

**Little River Farm B&B** 967 Huntington Rd., Worthington **238-4261** seasonal • women only • full brkfst • women-owned/run • $75

**Old Red Schoolhouse** 67 Park St. **584-1228** apts • studios • also 'Lesbian Towers' in East Hampton • gay-owned/run • $40-200

▲ **Tin Roof B&B** 586-8665 mostly women • 1909 farmhouse w/spectacular view of the Berkshires • women-owned/run • $60

## BARS & NIGHTCLUBS

**Club Metro** 492 Pleasant St. **582-9898** clsd Mon • gay-friendly • gay night Wed • dancing/DJ • live shows

**The Grotto** 25 West St. **586-6900** 5pm-1am • lesbians/gay men • dancing/DJ • live shows • food served

**The Iron Horse** 20 Center St. **584-0610** 8:30pm-close • gay-friendly • live shows • food served • some veggie • $5-15

**Pearl Street Cafe** 10 Pearl St. **584-7810** 9pm-1am Wed & Sat • lesbians/gay men • dancing/DJ • women-owned/run

## CAFES

**Haymarket Cafe** 15 Amber Ln. **586-9969** 9am-midnight • fresh pastries

## RESTAURANTS

**Bela** 68 Masonic St. **586-8011** noon-8pm, til 10pm Th-Sat, clsd Sun-Mon • vegetarian • women-owned/run • $5-10

**Green Street Cafe** 64 Green St. **586-5650** lunch & dinner • plenty veggie • beer/wine • $11-17

**Paul & Elizabeth's** 150 Main St. **584-4832** seafood • plenty veggie • beer/wine • wheelchair access • $7-12

---

# Tin Roof Bed & Breakfast

*For Women & Their Friends*

PO Box 296 • Hadley, MA 01035 • 413-586-8665

---

Our 1909 farmhouse has a front porch with swing, comfortable dining and living room area (with TV/VCR) for our guests. The three guestrooms have double beds and share a bath and a half. Breakfast is homemade (extended continental). Laundry facilities are available. We have resident cats and request smoking outside only.

The owners, both long time residents of the valley, have lots of local information to acclimate you to the area.

Located on New England's longest common, this rural setting is close to Northampton and Amherst.

*Reservations required*
*Two night minimum on weekends and holidays*
*Your hostesses are Diane Smith & Jane Nevin*

**Squire's Smoke & Game Club** Rte. 9, Williamsburg **268-7222** from 5pm, clsd Mon-Tue • popular • some veggie • full bar • live shows • Ali & Bear's favorite • $12-17

ENTERTAINMENT & RECREATION
**Dyke TV** Channel 2 10:30pm Mon • 'weekly half-hour TV show produced by lesbians, for lesbians'
**Out & About** Cable TV Channel 2 9pm Mon

BOOKSTORES & RETAIL SHOPS
**Pride & Joy** 20 Crafts Ave. **585-0683** 11am-6pm, til 8pm Th, from noon-6pm Sun • lesbigay books & gifts • wheelchair access
**Third Wave Feminist Booksellers** 90 King St. **586-7851** 10am-6pm, til 8pm Th, noon-5pm Sun-Mon • wheelchair access • lesbian-owned/run

PUBLICATIONS
**Lesbian Calendar** 586-5514
**Metroline** (860) 570-0823 regional newspaper & entertainment guide

TRAVEL AGENTS
**Adventura Travel** 122 Main St. **584-9441**
**Cornerstone Associates** 268-7363/(800) 798-6877 IGLTA

## Orleans (508)

PUBLICATIONS
**Woman of Power** 240-7877 unconfirmed

## Pittsfield (413)

TRAVEL AGENTS
**Troy's Travel Agency** 301 Dalton Ave. **499-1346/(800) 852-3750** IGLTA

## Plymouth (508)

TRAVEL AGENTS
**On Line Travel** 2277 State Rd. **888-2424/(800) 763-3855** IGLTA

## Provincetown (508)

INFO LINES & SERVICES
**Provincetown Business Guild** 487-2313/(800) 637-8696 IGLTA

ACCOMMODATIONS
**155 Bradford St. Guesthouse** 155 Bradford St. **(617) 524-4914** gay-friendly • studios • wheelchair access • IGLTA
▲ **Admiral's Landing Guest House** 158 Bradford St. **487-9665/(800) 934-0925** lesbians/gay men • 1840s Greek Revival home & studio efficiencies

## Provincetown (508)

**Where the Girls Are:** In this small resort town, you can't miss 'em!

**Lesbigay Pride:** June.

**Annual Events:**

August- **Provincetown Carnival:** 800/637-8696.

October - **Women's Week:** 800/933-1963. It's very popular, so make your reservations early!

**City Info:** Chamber of Commerce: 487-3424.

**Attractions:** The beach. Commercial St. Herring Cove Beach. Whale watching.

**Best View:** People-watching from an outdoor cafe or from the beach.

**Weather:** New England weather is unpredictable. Be prepared for rain, snow or extreme heat! Otherwise, the weather during the season consists of warm days and cooler nights.

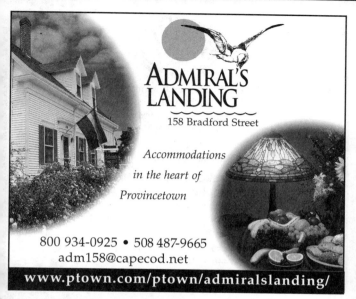

## ADMIRAL'S LANDING

158 Bradford Street

*Accommodations*

*in the heart of*

*Provincetown*

800 934-0925 • 508 487-9665
adm158@capecod.net

www.ptown.com/ptown/admiralslanding/

# Anchor Inn
"Provincetown's Finest Inn on the Beach"

PRIVATE BEACH, COLOR TV, MAJOR CREDIT CARDS HONORED
BROCHURE & RATES ON REQUEST, FREE PARKING

175 Commercial Street, Provincetown, MA
(508) 487-0432

## 800-858-ANKR

**BENCHMARK INN** Top-notch comfort and style. Fireplaces, whirlpool baths, wet bars, private balconied entrances, and stunning harborviews. "Outstanding" 5 Palm Award, Out & About 1997

**Benchmark Inn**
**The Best Is For You.**

**BENCHMARK ANNEX** is a cozy, quiet gem. Beautiful flowering gardens, dip pool, large sundeck, parking and moderate tariffs makes it an attractive choice for your Provincetown getaway.

6 & 8 DYER STREET • PROVINCETOWN • MA 02657
508-487-7440 • TOLL FREE 1-888-487-7440
www.CapeCodAccess.com/benchmark/

**Ampersand Guesthouse** 6 Cottage St. 487-0959/(800) 574-9645 lesbians/gay men

▲ **Anchor Inn Guest House** 175 Commercial St. 487-0432/(800) 858-2657 popular • lesbians/gay men • central location • private beach • harbor view

**Angel's Landing** 353-355 Commercial St. 487-1600 seasonal • lesbians/gay men • efficiency units on waterfront

**Asheton House** 3 Cook St. 487-9966 gay-friendly • restored 1840s captain's house • $80-105

**Beachfront Realty** 145 Commercial St. 487-1397 vacation rentals & housing/condo sales

**Beaconlite Inn** 12 Winthrop St. 487-9603/(800) 696-9603 popular • lesbians/gay men • IGLTA

▲ **Benchmark Inn & Annex** 6-8 Dyer St. 487-7440/(888) 487-7440 lesbians/gay men • fireplace • harbor views • in heart of Provincetown • swimming • IGLTA

**Boatslip Beach Club** 161 Commercial St. 487-1669/(800) 451-7547 seasonal • popular • lesbians/gay men • resort • swimming • also restaurant • cont'l/seafood • some veggie • several bars • popular T-dance • IGLTA • $110-150

**The Bradford Carver House** 70 Bradford St. 487-4966/(800) 826-9083 lesbians/gay men • $80-110

▲ **Bradford Gardens Inn** 178 Bradford St. 487-1616/(800) 432-2334 lesbians/gay men • 1820s colonial • full brkfst • gardens • $65-225

**Bradford House & Motel** 41 Bradford St. 487-0173 gay-friendly • $65-140

**The Brass Key Guesthouse** 12 Carver St. 487-9005/(800) 842-9858 popular • mostly gay men • heated spa • swimming • wheelchair access • IGLTA • $75-265

**The Buoy** 97 Bradford St. 487-3082 lesbians/gay men • $30-115

**Burch House** 116 Bradford St. 487-9170 seasonal • mostly gay men • studios

# Bradford Gardens Inn

Bradford Gardens Inn, woman-owned and featured in most national and international B & B guides, offers you charming, spacious rooms with fireplaces, private baths, cable TV and ceiling fans.

Included are full gourmet breakfasts, such as shirred eggs with tarragon mornay sauce, Portuguese flippers, homemade cinnamon-walnut pancakes with blueberry maple syrup...You can also choose fireplaced cottages situated in our beautiful gardens surrounding the inn.

Just park your car in our lot, and you are 5 minutes from the center of town for fine dining, nightclubs, whalewatching, beaches, galleries and shopping.

Built in 1820, this historic inn offers you New England charm combined with a natural informality. Rates: $69-$145. One block from the beach.

Bradford Gardens Inn
178 Bradford St.
Provincetown, MA 02657
(508) 487-1616

# (800) 432-2334

# Provincetown

**W**ho would have thought that a little New England whaling village at the very tip of Cape Cod would be the country's largest gay and lesbian resort? But Provincetown is just that.

The season in Provincetown (never call it P-Town, it rankles the natives) runs according to a time-honored schedule of who does what when where. According to one regular, the typical lesbian itinerary goes as follows:

Arrival: Rent a bike and explore the town's lesbigay shops and bookstores. (Nobody drives in Provincetown. ) Pick up lunch at a deli on the way to Herring Cove. At the beach, head left to find the women.

At the Beach: Take off your top, if you like. Just keep an eye out for the cops, who'll give you a ticket if they catch you bare-breasted. And a word to the wise: if you're heading toward the sand dunes for a tryst, don't forget your socks. The hot, white sand can burn your feet (Youch!).

3pm: Bike back to your room for a shower, then head to the afternoon T-dance at **Boatslip Beach Club** on Commercial Street. Drink and dance til dinnertime, then take a relaxing few hours for your meal.

After Dinner: Check out the bars; the **Pied Piper** is the pick for women. If you're not into the bar scene or all the sun and surf has tired you out, you can always go shopping. Most stores stay open til 11pm during the summer. When the bars close, grab a slice of pizza and an espresso milkshake at **Spiritus**, and cruise the streets until they're empty—sometimes not til 4 or 5 a.m.

Before you leave, treat yourself to the excitement of a whale-watching cruise. There are several cruise lines, and **Portuguese Princess Whale Watch** is women-owned.

But if you really want a whale of a good time, pencil in **Provincetown's Women's Week**, the third weekend in October. **The Women's Innkeepers of Provincetown** will be sponsoring an opening party, a community dinner, a golf tournament, and fun run, a prom, lots of entertainment...and more. Don't forget to call your favorite guesthouse early to make your reservations!

# DEXTER'S INN

## A Traditional Cape Cod Guest House

Private Baths - Sundeck - Parking - TVs - Fridges
Central Location - Airport Pickup - Brochure
**OPEN YEAR ROUND**
6 Conwell Street, Provincetown, MA 02657
508-487-1911 Toll-free 888-521-1999

---

*The*
# Captain's House

## in Provincetown
350a Commercial St. MA 02657
1-508-487-9353

---

• Immaculate Rooms • Center of Town
• Cable Color TV • Private Patio
• Private and Shared Baths

# 1-800-457-8885

*Carole Whitman*
INNKEEPER

The Dusty Miller Inn

*open year round*

82 Bradford Street
Provincetown, MA 02657

*Telephone*
(508) 487-2213

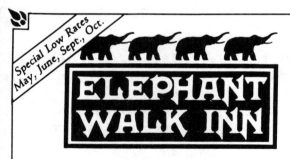

Special Low Rates
May, June, Sept., Oct.

# ELEPHANT WALK INN

## 800-889-WALK

Distinctive, Affordable Accommodations
Private Baths •TVs • Fridges • Parking
Sundeck • Breakfast • Optional A/C
Brochure

156 Bradford St. • Provincetown, MA 02657
(508) 487-2543          (800) 889-9255
Email: elephant@capecod.net

# GABRIEL'S

*Come close to heaven*

## APARTMENTS & GUEST ROOMS

## SIRENS WORKSHOP CENTER

*Conference Center & Holistic Workshops*
*Sauna & Hot Tubs & Steam Room*
*Massage & Exercise Room & Bicycles*
*Gardens & Sundecks & Barbeque*
*Fireplaces & Breakfast*
*Air Conditioning & Cable TV & Phones*
*Internet Access & Computer Facilities*
*Always Open & In the Heart of Town*

*Find us on the World Wide Web:*
***www.provincetown.com/gabriels***

## (800) 9MY-ANGEL

104 Bradford Street
Provincetown, MA
02657-1440

(508) 487•3232
FAX (508) 487•1605
gabriels@provincetown.com

**The Captain & His Ship** 164 Commercial St. **487-1850/(800) 400-2278** seasonal • mostly gay men • 19th century sea captain's home • $75-150

**Captain Lysander's Inn** 96 Commercial St. **487-2253** gay-friendly

▲ **Captain's House B&B** 350-A Commercial St. **487-9353/(800) 457-8885** lesbians/gay men • $40-90

**Chancellor Inn** 17 Center St. **487-9423** mostly gay men

**Check'er Inn** 25 Winthrop St. **487-9029/(800) 894-9029** women only • hot tub • IGLTA • inn: $85-125/apts: $775-1200 wk

**The Clarendon House** 118 Bradford St. **487-1645** gay-friendly

**Commons Guesthouse & Bistro** 386 Commercial St. **487-7800/(800) 487-0784** gay-friendly • $60-140

**Crown & Anchor** 247 Commercial St. **487-1430** mostly gay men • swimming • also restaurant • full bar • $10-20

▲ **Dexter's Inn** 6 Conwell St. **487-1911/(888) 521-1999** lesbians/gay men • smokefree • $50-95

**The Dunes Motel & Apartments** 487-1956 seasonal • lesbians/gay men • $65-145

▲ **Dusty Miller Inn** 82 Bradford St. **487-2213** mostly women • women-owned/run • $45-115

▲ **Elephant Walk Inn** 156 Bradford St. **487-2543/(800) 889-9255** popular • lesbians/gay men • in the heart of Provincetown • $46-95

**Elliot House** 6 Gosnold St. **487-4029** lesbians/gay men • full brkfst • central location • private gardens

▲ **Fairbanks Inn** 90 Bradford St. **487-0386/(800) 324-7265** popular • lesbians/gay men • IGLTA • $49-175

▲ **Gabriel's Guestrooms & Apartments** 104 Bradford St. **487-3232/(800) 969-2643** popular • mostly women • hot tub • gym • workshop center • IGLTA • women-owned/run • $50-175

**Garden at 6 Atwood** 6 Atwood St. **487-2113/(800) 277-5451** mostly gay men • shared baths

## ✿ THE ✿
# FAIRBANKS INN
### Historic Accommodations

1770's Sea Captain's House • Antique Filled Rooms
Wood Burning Fireplaces • Centrally Located

"Exceptional, Exquisite,…Unbeatable Charm and Warmth."
*Five Palms & Editors Choice Award —Out & About*

90 Bradford Street, Provincetown
1-800-FAIRBNK   508-487-0386
E-mail: fairbank@capecod.net

**Visit us on the web: www.capecod.net/fairbank**

*Having a wonderful time... Wish you were here!*

HERITAGE HOUSE

★ Centrally located in the heart of Provincetown
★ Expanded continental breakfast
★ Parking and airport pickup available
★ Open year round

7 Center Street, Provincetown, MA 02657
**(508) 487-3692**

EsCAPE TO

*Halle's*

14 West Vine Street
Provincetown, MA
508-487-6310

Cottages
& Apartments
in the Quiet
West End

# Provincetown
### Invites You To
# Women's Week

Now in its 15th year!
### 3rd Week of October
and

# HollyFolly

The Lesbian & Gay
Holiday Festival
1st Weekend of December

*"Your Room Is Ready"*

The Women Innkeepers
## 1-800-933-1963

Visit us on the web:
### www.provincetown.com/wip

**Grand View Inn** 4 Conant St. **487-9193/(888) 268-9169** lesbians/gay men • $30-100

**The Gull Walk Inn** 300-A Commercial St. **487-9027/(800) 309-4725** women only • sundeck • central location • women-owned/run • $29-72

▲ **Halle's** 14 W. Vine St. **487-6310** mostly women • apt • women-owned/run • $65-95

**Harbor Lights** 163 Bradford St. **487-8246** lesbians/gay men • studio & 1-brm apt • $150-180

**Hargood House at Bayshore** 493 Commercial St. **487-9133** gay-friendly • apts • private beach • women-owned/run • $72-142

▲ **Heritage House** 7 Center St. **487-3692** popular • lesbians/gay men • lesbian-owned/run • $49-85

**Holiday Inn of Provincetown** **487-1711/(800) 422-4224** gay-friendly • swimming • also restaurant • full bar • wheelchair access

**The Inn at Cook Street** 7 Cook St. **487-3894/(888) 266-5655** gay-friendly • intimate & quiet • smokefree

**The Inn at the Egg** 896-3123/(800) 259-8235 gay-friendly • 40 min. from Provincetown • women-owned/run • $65-140

**Ireland House** 18 Pearl St. **487-7132** lesbians/gay men • $62-70

**John Randall House** 140 Bradford St. **487-3533/(800) 573-6700** lesbians/gay men • $40-120

▲ **Lady Jane's Inn** 7 Central St. **487-3387/(800) 523-9526** mostly women • women-owned/run • $60-90

**Lamplighter Inn** 26 Bradford St. **487-2529/(800) 263-6574** lesbians/gay men • wonderful views • $39-185

**Land's End Inn** 22 Commercial St. **487-0706/(800) 276-7088** gay-friendly

**The Lavender Rose Guest House** 186 Commercial St. **487-6648** seasonal • lesbians/gay men • patio • women-owned/run

**Lotus Guest House** 296 Commercial St. **487-4644** seasonal • lesbians/gay men • decks • gardens

**Marigolds B&B 487-9160** seasonal • women only • smokefree • women-owned/run • $40-85

**Mayflower Apartments** 6 Bangs St. **487-1916** gay-friendly • kitchens

# Lady Jane's Inn

- Color remote televisions
- Continental Breakfast
- Hospitality Room
- Full private baths
- On site parking
- Individually heated & Air conditioned
- Open all year

*Lady Jane's Inn is a woman owned and operated guest house in the heart of Provincetown, on a quiet side street, just steps away from shops restaurants and beaches. The Inn has been carefully and tastefully designed to meet the vacationers' need for comfort and privacy.*

*Each spacious room is scrupulously clean and beautifully appointed with turn-of-century furnishings and ceiling fans. Whatever the season, guests will delight in a lovingly prepared continental breakfast served in the cozy common room or in the sunny, flower-filled patio. Provincetown, and Lady Jane's Inn, have much to offer the vacationer.*

Your Innkeepers,
*Jane Antolini & Sharlene Marchette*

7 Central Street, Provincetown, MA 02657
**(508) 487-3387**
ladyjanes@wn.net
www.ladyjanesinn.com

# PILGRIM HOUSE INN

## 336 COMMERCIAL STREET
## PROVINCETOWN, MA 02657

**A Unique Twenty Room Guest House**
In-Room Phones
Color TV
Continental Breakfast
Conference Rooms
Complete Shopping Complex on Premises
Special Off Season and Group Rates
(Ask us!)
Located in the Center of Town

## The Pilgrim House Presents:

# "VIXEN"

**Women's Night Club**
**Dance Bar**
**Lounge Bar**
**Entertainment**

## PILGRIM HOUSE
## RESERVATION SYSTEM
FOR TICKETS TO LIVE SHOWS, CONCERTS,
SPECIAL ENGAGEMENTS AND
ALL YOUR ENTERTAINMENT NEEDS
### TEL. (508) 487-6424
### FAX (508) 487-6296

## Plums
### Bed & Breakfast Inn

Drive past the tumble of Cape Cod houses to Plums Bed & Breakfast, an 1860s Dutch Gambrel. Inside the white picket fence, a garden of lilies, irises and dahlias beckon you across the wisteria-draped porch. Your key unlocks the quiet elegance of the Victorian whaling captain's house.

Inside, wide pine floors shine beneath Eastlake and Renaissance Revival antiques that grace Plums' large rooms. Fresh flowers add to the romance! And white lace curtains adorn windows that reach to high ceilings. Sit at a table of women for breakfast amid sterling silver, brass and period curios. Under a crystal chandelier, enjoy conversation, fresh fruit, baked goods and gourmet entrees like cheese souffle or French toast stuffed with cream cheese and strawberries. Innkeepers to pamper you, parking and private baths for your comfort.

*Come, experience the magic of Plums!*

160 Bradford Street • Provincetown, MA 02657
(508) 487-2283 • Brochure available

# HAVE IT ALL!
# 1 800 648-0364

With over 10 years of experience, we represent the largest selection of accommodations in Provincetown. We can also make all your travel arrangements to anywhere in the world with our on-site ticketing service. Entertainment and Restaurants— one call and we'll take care of your tickets or reservations. It's so easy, when you want the best, call PRS.

**TRAVEL**

**ACCOMMODATIONS**

**ENTERTAINMENT**

PROVINCETOWN RESERVATIONS SYSTEM®

Visit our web site: www.ptownres.com

## Ravenwood

GUESTROOMS & APARTMENTS

Waterviews & Private Sundecks
Parking & Special Amenities
Open Year round

462 Commercial Street
Provincetown, MA 02657

(508) 487. 3203
Diane Corbo, Innkeeper

# Rose Acre

Accommodations for women in a 1840 Cape House.
Apartments, cottage and guest rooms.
Private baths, parking, decks and yard.
Open year-round.

**(508) 487-2347**
**5 Center St.**
**Provincetown, MA 02657**

# WINDAMAR HOUSE

## Guests

This stately, historic home is located in the quiet, residential East End of town directly across from picturesque Cape Cod Bay. We offer guest rooms and apartments distinctively decorated with antiques and original artwork. The front rooms have water views while rooms on the side and back of the house offer views of English flower gardens and manicured lawns. The common room, a central mingling space, is equipped with sink, refrigerator and cable TV with VCR. Homebaked continental breakfast is provided complimentary every morning for our guest rooms. Guests are encouraged to barbeque, picnic or sunbathe on our beautiful, spacious grounds. Ample on-site parking is provided for all our accommodations.

568 Commercial Street
Provincetown, Massachusetts 02657

**508-487-0599**

**Bette Adams • Fax: 508 487-7505**
**E-MAIL: Windamar@tiac.net**

# TUCK HER IN AT
## *The Tucker Inn*
### *A Romantic Country Inn By The Sea*

*circa 1870*

QUIET CENTRAL LOCATION ✹ ANTIQUE-FILLED GUEST ROOMS ✹ QUEEN-SIZE BEDS ✹ PRIVATE BATHS ✹ COLOR CABLE T.V. ✹ CONTINENTAL BREAKFAST WITH HOMEMADE SPECIALTIES ✹ ON-SITE PARKING ✹ PRIVATE PATIO AND GARDEN ✹ APARTMENT AND COTTAGE AVAILABLE ✹

## (508) 487-0381   (800) 477-1867
http:\\www.provincetown\tucker
12 Center Street ✹ Provincetown, MA 02657

# SOME GIRLS JUST WANNA HAVE FUN
## ...OTHERS <u>HAVE</u> FUN

## 1 (888) 44 DINAH
### GIRL BAR & CLUB SKIRTS

# Six Webster Place

**a 1750's Bed & Breakfast**

*It's a dog's life at Six Webster*

**FIREPLACES
JACUZZI
DELICIOUS BREAKFAST
OPEN YEAR ROUND
OFF- SEASON RATES
PRIVATE BATHS
CABLE TV • PARKING
LUXURY APARTMENTS**

*Six Webster Place
Provincetown, MA 02657*

**508-487-2266
1-800-6 WEBSTER**

**Monument House** 129 Bradford St. 487-9664/(888) 487-9664 lesbians/gay men • 1840s banker's home • very central • deck • IGLTA • $60-95

**Normandy House** 184 Bradford St. 487-1197/(800) 487-1197 lesbians/gay men • intimate guest house on the tip of Cape Cod • hot tub • $55-145

**Piaf** 3 Prince St. 487-7458/(800) 340-7423 gay-friendly

▲ **Pilgrim House** 336 Commercial St. 487-6424 mostly women • also restaurant • full bar

▲ **Plums B&B** 160 Bradford St. 487-2283 clsd Jan • women only • full brkfst • also condos & apts • $82-105

**Prince Albert** 166 Commercial St. 487-0859/(800) 992-0859 lesbians/gay men • Victorian • near Cape Cod Bay • $75-150

**Provincetown Inn** 1 Commercial St. 487-9500 gay-friendly • swimming • harbor view restaurant • wheelchair access

▲ **Provincetown Reservations System** 293 Commercial St. #5 487-2400/(800) 648-0364 IGLTA

▲ **Ravenwood Guest House** 462 Commercial St. 487-3203 mostly women • 1830 Greek Revival • also apts & cottage • $75-145

**Red Inn** 15 Commercial St. 487-0050 lesbians/gay men • elegant waterfront lodging & dining

**Renaissance Apartments** 48 Commercial St. 487-4600 seasonal • lesbians/gay men • decks

**Revere Guesthouse** 14 Court St. 487-2292 lesbians/gay men • restored 1820s captain's home • IGLTA

**Roomers** 8 Carver St. 487-3532 seasonal • mostly gay men

▲ **Rose Acre** 5 Center St. 487-2347 women only • shuttle to beach avail. • $65-145

**Rose & Crown Guest House** 158 Commercial St. 487-3332 lesbians/gay men • Victorian antiques

**Sandbars** 570 Shore Rd. 487-1290 seasonal • lesbians/gay men • oceanfront rooms • kitchens • private beach • women-owned/run • $65-115

**Sandpiper Beach House** 165 Commerical St. 487-1928/(800) 354-8628 popular • lesbians/gay men • Victorian • IGLTA • $80-145

**Shamrock Motel, Cottages & Apartments** 49 Bradford St. 487-1133 gay-friendly • swimming • IGLTA

**Six Webster Place** 6 Webster Pl. 487-2266/(800) 693-2783 popular • lesbians/gay men • 1750s B&B & apts • IGLTA • $65-195

**Somerset House** 378 Commercial St. 487-0383/(800) 575-1850 popular • gay-friendly • $60-135

**South Hollow Vineyards** 487-6200 gay-friendly • women-owned/run

**Sunset Inn** 142 Bradford St. 487-9810/(800) 965-1801 seasonal • lesbians/gay men

**Swanberry Inn** 8 Johnson St. 487-4242/(800) 847-7926 lesbians/gay men • $49-110

**Three Peaks** 210 Bradford St. 487-1717/(800) 286-1715 lesbians/gay men • 1870s Victorian • $55-115

**Tradewinds Inn** 12 Johnson St. 487-0138/(800) 487-0132 lesbians/gay men • also condo

**Tucker Inn** 12 Center St. 487-0381/(800) 477-1867 seasonal • gay-friendly • $70-125

**Victoria House** 5 Standish St. 487-4455 lesbians/gay men

**Watermark Inn Guest House** 603 Commercial St. 487-2506 gay-friendly • kitchens • beachside

**Watership Inn** 7 Winthrop 487-0094/(800) 330-9413 popular • lesbians/gay men • $35-175

**Westwinds** 28 Commercial St. 487-1841 seasonal • lesbians/gay men • apts & cottages • swimming

▲ **White Wind Inn** 174 Commercial St. 487-1526 lesbians/gay men • 1800s Victorian • women-owned/run • $105-180

▲ **Windamar House** 568 Commercial St. 487-0599 mostly women • 1840s sea captain's home • $60-125

**Windsor Court** 15 Cottage St. 487-2620 lesbians/gay men • hot tub • swimming • kitchens

## BARS & NIGHTCLUBS

**Back Room** (at 'Crown & Anchor' accommodations) 487-1430 10:30pm-1am (seasonal) • popular • lesbians/gay men • check locally for women's night • dancing/DJ

# White WindInn

Open all year, this sparkling guest house is a favorite in spring and fall when rates are lower! Enjoy a room with fireplace, television in rooms, morning coffee plus harbor view, beach, free parking. More in our brochure!

**174 Commercial Street / Provincetown MA 02657**
**Phone 487-1526**

**The Boatslip Beach Club** (at 'Boatslip' accommodations) **487-1669** seasonal • popular • lesbians/gay men • resort • T-dance every day during season • swimming • also restaurant • cont'l/seafood • some veggie • $10-25

**Governor Bradford** 312 Commercial St. **487-9618** 11am-1am • gay-friendly • food served • check schedule for 'Space Pussy' performance times

**The Iguana Grill** 135 Bradford St. **487-8800** 9am-1am, restaurant from 5pm • mostly gay men • live shows • also restaurant • Mexican • some veggie

**Pied Piper** 193-A Commercial St. **487-1527** noon-1am • popular • mostly women • dancing/DJ • women-owned/run

**Rooster Bar** (at 'Crown & Anchor' accommodations) **487-1430** 6pm-1am • lesbians/gay men • more women off-season • neighborhood bar • videos • food served

**Town House** 291 Commercial St. **487-0292** noon-1am • popular • lesbians/gay men • live shows • food served

▲ **Vixen** 336 Commercial St. **487-6424** 11am-1am • mostly women • dancing/DJ • live shows

### CAFES

**Cafe Express** 214 Commercial St. **487-3382** 9am-2am • lesbians/gay men • vegetarian • wheelchair access • $5-10

**Post Office Cafe Cabaret** 303 Commercial St. (upstairs) **487-3892** 8am-midnight (brkfst til 3pm) • lesbians/gay men • live shows • some veggie • $8-15

### RESTAURANTS

**Cactus Garden** 186 Commercial St. **487-6661** clsd Tue-Wed • Southwestern • plenty veggie • live shows • women-owned/run

**Club Euro** 258 Commercial St. **487-2505** lunch & dinner • some veggie • live shows • wheelchair access • $11-20

**Dodie's Diner** 401-1/2 Commercial St. **487-3868** 8am-10pm • some veggie • women-owned/run • $5-10

**Front Street Restaurant** 230 Commercial St. **487-9715** 6pm-10:30pm, bar til 1am (April-Oct) • lesbians/gay men • full bar • $15-25

14K GOLD AND STERLING SILVER JEWELRY

# Womencrafts

**Jewelry, Bookstore and Gift Gallery**

MUSIC • BOOKS • T-SHIRTS • BABY CLOTHES • CARDS

POTTERY • GLASSWARE • SWEATSHIRTS • SOCKS

...where there's 22 years of Lesbian Pride behind everything we sell...
**376 Commercial Street
Provincetown, MA 02657
508-487-2501**
WE DO MAIL ORDERS AND LAY-AWAYS

# ACCOMMODATIONS

In **Provincetown**, we represent hundreds of inns, b&bs, motels, condos, houses, and cottages. Our experienced, courteous reservationists will help select and confirm just the right place for you. Never a fee for travel and reservation services.

# TRAVEL

With the clout of over 400 Travel Network agencies, our volume buying power guarantees the lowest available airfares, discounted hotels, car rentals, and last minute travel specials.

# REAL ESTATE

We offer the largest selection of vacation rentals...all sizes, types, areas, and price ranges. No wonder we're Provincetown's vacation rental specialists. Our complete real estate services also include the purchase and sale of residential and commercial properties.

# IN TOWN RESERVATIONS
# TRAVEL & REAL ESTATE

# 1-800 67P-TOWN

4 Standish Street, Provincetown, MA 02657
▼ Open Year Round ▼
Fax 508.487.6140 • Local 508.487.1883
E-mail: INTOWNRES@AOL.COM
http://www.travnet.com/provincetown

**Gallerani's** 133 Commercial St. **487-4433** 8am-2pm, 6am-10:30pm Th-Mon • popular • lesbians/gay men • some veggie • beer/wine • $20-30

**Grand Central** 5 Masonic St. **487-7599** seasonal • dinner • full bar • $15-20

**Landmark Inn Restaurant** 404 Commercial St. **487-9319** dinner nightly 5:30pm-10pm (April-Oct) • lesbians/gay men • New England fare • $15-25

**Lobster Pot** 321 Commercial St. **487-0842** noon-10pm • seafood • some veggie • wheelchair access • $15-20

**Martin House 487-1327** $11-19

**The Mews** 429 Commercial St. **487-1500** seasonal • lunch & dinner • popular • cont'l/cafe • some veggie • wheelchair access • $15-30

**Napi's** 7 Freeman St. **487-1145** int'l/seafood • plenty veggie • wheelchair access • $15-25

**Pucci's Harborside** 539 Commercial St. **487-1964** seasonal • popular • some veggie • full bar • wheelchair access • $10-20

**Sal's Place** 99 Commercial St. **487-1279** popular • publisher's choice: cheese & butter pasta

**Sebastian's Long & Narrow** 177 Commercial St. **487-3286** 11am-10pm • wheelchair access • $10-15

**Spiritus** 190 Commercial St. **487-2808** 11am-2am • popular • great espresso shakes & late-night hang out

## Entertainment & Recreation

**Dyke TV** Channel 8 11pm Fri • 'weekly half-hour TV show produced by lesbians, for lesbians'

## Bookstores & Retail Shops

**Don't Panic** 192 Commercial St. **487-1280** lesbigay gifts • T-shirts

**Far Side of the Wind** 389 Commercial St. **487-3963** seasonal • 11am-11pm • New Age books & gifts • Native American artifacts • wheelchair access

**Now, Voyager** 357 Commercial St. **487-0848** 11am-11pm, til 5pm (off-season) • lesbigay bookstore

**Pride's** 182 Commercial St. **487-1127** 10am-11pm (in-season) • lesbigay gifts • T-shirts • books

**Provincetown Bookshop** 246 Commercial St. **487-0964** 10am-11pm, til 5pm (off-season)

**Recovering Hearts** 2-4 Standish St. **487-4875** 10am-11pm (in-season) • recovery • lesbigay & New Age books • wheelchair access

▲ **Womencrafts** 376 Commercial St. **487-2501** seasonal • 10am-11pm

## Publications

**In Newsweekly (617) 426-8246/(800) 426-8246**

**Provincetown Banner 487-7400**

**Provincetown Magazine 487-1000** weekly

## Travel Agents

**All Provincetown** 309 Commercial St. **487-9000/(800) 786-9699** rental hotline

**Cape Air** Barnstable Municipal Airport **771-6944/(800) 352-0714** IGLTA

▲ **In Town Reservations, Travel & Real Estate** 4 Standish St. **487-1883/(800) 67P-TOWN**

**Portuguese Princess Whale Watch** Shank Painter Rd., McMillan Wharf **487-2651** day & evening cruises • women's event cruises • wheelchair access • women-owned/run

**RSVP—Town Reservations 487-1883/(800) 677-8696** IGLTA

## Spiritual Groups

**Dignity** 1 Commercial St. (Provincetown Inn) **487-9500** 10:30am Sun (May-Oct)

## Gyms & Health Clubs

**Mussel Beach** 35 Bradford St. **487-0001** 6am-9pm • lesbians/gay men

**Provincetown Gym** 170 Commercial St. **487-2776** lesbians/gay men

## Erotica

**Wild Hearts** 244 Commercial St. **487-8933** noon-5pm, til 11pm wknds (in-season) • toys for women

# Randolph (781)

## Bars & Nightclubs

**Randolph Country Club** 44 Mazeo Dr. (Rte. 139) **961-2414** 2pm-2am, (10am summer) • popular • lesbians/gay men • dancing/DJ • live shows • volleyball court • swimming • wheelchair access

# Springfield (413)

## Info Lines & Services

**Gay/Lesbian Info Service 731-5403**

## BARS & NIGHTCLUBS

**David's** 397 Dwight St. **734-0566** 6pm-2am, clsd Sun & Tue-Wed • lesbians/gay men • dancing/DJ • wheelchair access

**Friends/Cellblock** 23 Hampden St. **781-5878** 11am-2am • lesbians/gay men • dancing/DJ • videos • wheelchair access

**Pub/Quarry** 382 Dwight **734-8123** 11am-2am, dinner Fri-Sun • mostly gay men • neighborhood bar • dancing/DJ • live shows • wheelchair access

## TRAVEL AGENTS

**A&D Travel** 30 Main St., W. Springfield **737-5706** IGLTA

## EROTICA

**Video Expo** 486 Bridge St. **747-9812**

## Sturbridge (508)

### RESTAURANTS

**The Casual Cafe** 538 Main St. **347-2281** 5pm-9pm, clsd Sun-Mon • Italian/Japanese • plenty veggie • BYOB • wheelchair access • lesbian-owned/run • $7-14

## Ware (413)

### ACCOMMODATIONS

**The Wildwood Inn** 121 Church St. **967-7798**/**(800) 860-8098** gay-friendly • full brkfst • wheelchair access • $50-80

## Wellfleet (508)

### BOOKSTORES & RETAIL SHOPS

**Skin Deep** 25 Bank Street Sq. **349-1300** body care products

### TRAVEL AGENTS

**Outer Cape Travel Agency** 30 Briar Ln. **349-3794** IGLTA

## Williamstown (413)

### ACCOMMODATIONS

**River Bend Farm B&B** 643 Simonds Rd. **458-3121** seasonal • gay-friendly

## Woods Hole (508)

### ACCOMMODATIONS

**The Marlborough B&B Inn** 320 Woods Hole Rd. **548-6218** gay-friendly • full brkfst • $65-125

## Worcester (508)

### INFO LINES & SERVICES

**AA Gay/Lesbian** 1 Freeland St. **752-9000** 7pm Sat

**Floating Dance Floor** **791-1327** produces women's dances • call for info

**Gay/Lesbian Youth Group** **755-0005** 24hrs

**WOBBLES (West of Boston Lesbians)** **478-0242** 3rd Sun • social group • covers eastern MA

### ACCOMMODATIONS

**Winterwood** 19 N. Main St., Petersham **724-8885** gay-friendly • Greek Revival mansion • fireplaces • $60-80

### BARS & NIGHTCLUBS

**A-MEN** 21-23 Foster St. **754-7742** 9pm-2am, clsd Mon-Tue • mostly gay men • dancing/DJ • alternative

**Club 241** 241 Southbridge **755-9311** 6pm-2am, from 2pm wknds, clsd Mon-Th • popular • lesbians/gay men • dancing/DJ • live shows • rooftop deck • wheelchair access

**MB Lounge** 40 Grafton St. **799-4521** 3pm-2am • mostly gay men • leather • wheelchair access

### ENTERTAINMENT & RECREATION

**Face the Music** WCUW (91.3 FM) **753-2284 (REQUEST LINE)** 8pm Th • women's radio show

### SPIRITUAL GROUPS

**Morning Star MCC** 231 Main St. **892-4320** 10am Sun • wheelchair access

### GYMS & HEALTH CLUBS

**Midtown Athletic Club** 22 Front St., 2nd flr. **798-9703** 8am-8pm • gay-friendly

## MICHIGAN

### Ann Arbor (313)

INFO LINES & SERVICES
**Lesbian/Gay AA** 482-5700 (AA#)
**The Office of Lesbian/Gay/Bisexual/Transgender Affairs** 3116 Michigan Union, 530 S. State St. **763-4186** 8am-5pm

BARS & NIGHTCLUBS
**The Ark** 637-1/2 S. Main St. **761-1451** gay-friendly • concert house • women's music shows
**\'aut\ Bar** 315 Braun Ct. **994-3677** 4pm-2am, from 10am Sun (brunch) • lesbians/gay men • food served • American/Mexican • some veggie • patio • wheelchair access • $5-8
**Blind Pig** 208 S. 1st St. **996-8555** 3pm-2am • gay-friendly • neighborhood bar • live bands • wheelchair access
**Club Fabulous** 763-4186 lesbians/gay men • monthly chem-free dances during school
**Flame Bar** 112 W. Liberty 662-9680 7:30pm-2am • popular • mostly gay men • neighborhood bar
**The Nectarine** 516 E. Liberty 994-5835 9pm-2am Tue & Fri only • lesbians/gay men • dancing/DJ • videos

RESTAURANTS
**Dominick's** 812 Monroe St. **662-5414** 10am-10pm Mon-Sat • Italian • full bar • wheelchair access
**The Earle** 121 W. Washington 994-0211 6pm-10pm, til midnight Fri-Sat, clsd Sun (summer) • cont'l • some veggie • beer/wine • wheelchair access • $15-25
**Sweet Lorraines** 303 Detroit St. **665-0700** 11am-10pm, til midnight Fri-Sat • plenty veggie • full bar • patio • wheelchair access • $10-15

BOOKSTORES & RETAIL SHOPS
**Borders Book Shop** 612 E. Liberty 668-7652 9am-9pm, 11am-6pm Sun
**Common Language** 215 S. 4th Ave. 663-0036 open daily • lesbigay • wheelchair access
**Crazy Wisdom Books** 206 N. 4th Ave. 665-2757 10am-7pm Mon-Tue & Sat, til 8pm Wed-Fri, noon-7pm Sun • holistic & metaphysical
**Webster's** 2607 Plymouth Rd. **662-6150** 8am-11pm • lesbigay section

PUBLICATIONS
**Out Post** 332-0066 bi-weekly • newspaper for metro Detroit

TRAVEL AGENTS
**Horizons Travel** 873 W. Eisenhower Pkwy. 663-3434/(800) 878-7477 IGLTA

SPIRITUAL GROUPS
**Beit Chayim** 913-2130 3rd Fri • Shabbat potluck & activities • call for time & location

### Atwood (616)

ACCOMMODATIONS
**Stelle Wunderschönes** 12410 Entrim Dr. 599-2847 lesbians/gay men • red cedar log home • full brkfst • $80

### Battle Creek (616)

BARS & NIGHTCLUBS
**Partners** 910 North Ave. 964-7276 6pm-2am • lesbians/gay men • more women Fri • dancing/DJ • wheelchair access

### Belleville (313)

BARS & NIGHTCLUBS
**Granny's Place** 9800 Haggerty Rd. 699-8862 4pm-2am, from 11am Fri • lesbians/gay men • food served • wheelchair access

### Big Bay (906)

ACCOMMODATIONS
**Big Bay Depot** 345-9350 equipped kitchens • pets ok • $60

### Canton (313)

TRAVEL AGENTS
**Royal Apple Travel** 46000 Geddes Rd. #28 495-1301 IGLTA

### Detroit (313)

INFO LINES & SERVICES
**Affirmations Lesbian/Gay Community Center** 195 W. 9-Mile Rd. #106, Ferndale (248) 398-7105 10am-10pm, noon-5pm Sat, noon-9pm Sun
**Lesbian/Gay Switchboard** (810) 398-4297 4:30pm-11pm, clsd Sat

BARS & NIGHTCLUBS
**Alvins** 5657 Cass St.

**Backstreet** 15606 Joy Rd. **272-8959** 9pm-2am Wed & Sat • popular • mostly gay men • dancing/DJ • wheelchair access

**The Body Shop** 22061 Woodward Ave., Ferndale **(248) 398-1940** 4pm-2am, from 5pm Sat, from 2pm Sun • lesbians/gay men • dancing/DJ • food served • wheelchair access • $5-10

**Club Gold Coast** 2971 E. 7-Mile Rd. **366-6135** noon-2am • popular • mostly gay men • dancing/DJ • live shows • wheelchair access

**Club Ultimate** 22509 Ecorse Rd., Taylor **295-0955** from 8pm Wed & Sun, from 10pm Fri • lesbians/gay men • dancing/DJ • 18+

**The Edge** 12322 Conant **891-3343** 4pm-2am, from 2pm wknds • mostly gay men • dancing/DJ • live shows • patio

**Gigi's** 16920 W. Warren (enter rear) **584-6525** noon-2am, from 2pm wknds • mostly gay men • dancing/DJ • transgender-friendly • live shows • karaoke

**Off Broadway East** 12215 Harper St. **521-0920** 9pm-2am • mostly gay men • more women Sat • dancing/DJ

**Pronto** 608 S. Washington, Royal Oak **(248) 544-7900** 11am-midnight, til 2am Fri-Sat, from 9am wknds • gay-friendly • video bar • food served

**The Rainbow Room** 6640 E. 8-Mile Rd. **891-1020** 7pm-2am, from 2pm Sun • lesbians/gay men • dancing/DJ • live shows

**Silent Legacy** 1641 Middlebelt Rd., Inkster **729-8980** 8pm-2am, clsd Mon • lesbians/gay men • dancing/DJ • live shows

**Stingers Lounge** 19404 Sherwood **892-1765** 6pm-5am, from 8pm wknds • lesbians/gay men • neighborhood bar • grill menu

**Sugarbakers** 3800 E. 8-Mile Rd. **892-5203** 6pm-2am • mostly women • sports bar & grill

# Detroit   (313/810/248)

**Where the Girls Are:** At the bars on 8-Mile Road between I-75 and Van Dyke Ave., with the boys in Highland Park or Dearborn, or shopping in Royal Oak.

**Lesbigay Pride:** May: 810/825-6651.

**Annual Events:** August - Michigan Womyn's Music Festival: 616/757-4766. One of the biggest annual gatherings of lesbians in the continent, in Walhalla.

**City Info:** 313/259-2680.

**Attractions:** Belle Isle Park. Detroit Institute of Arts. Greektown. Montreux Detroit Jazz Festival. Motown Museum. Museum of African-American History. Renaissance Center.

**Best View:** From the top of the 73-story Westin Hotel at the Renaissance Center.

**Weather:** Be prepared for hot, humid summers and cold, dry winters.

**Transit:** Checker Cab: 313/963-7000. Shuttle: 313/283-4800. DOT (bus service): 313/933-1300. Detroit People Mover: 313/962-RAIL

**Zippers** 6221 E. Davison **892-8120**
opens 9pm, from 8pm Sun • popular •
lesbians/gay men • dancing/DJ • mostly
African-American • live shows • wheelchair access

## CAFES

**Lavender Moon Cafe** 205 W. 9-Mile Rd.,
Ferndale **(248) 398-6666** til midnight, til
2am Fri-Sat, from noon Sun • live shows
• wheelchair access • queer-owned/run

## RESTAURANTS

**Como's** 22812 Woodward, Ferndale **(248)
548-5005** 11am-2am, til 3:30am Fri-Sat,
from 2pm wknds • Italian • some veggie
• full bar • wheelchair access • $5-15

**Golden Star** 22828 Woodward Ave.,
Ferndale **(248)** 545-0994 open til midnight, til 10pm Mon • Chinese
**La Dolce Vita** 17546 Woodward Ave.
**865-0331** 4pm-2am, 11am-midnight Sun,
clsd Mon-Tue • lesbians/gay men •
Italian • plenty veggie • full bar • patio •
wheelchair access • $7-16
**Rhinoceros** 265 Riopelle **259-2208**
11:30am-2am • jazz club • $15-25
**Sweet Lorraines** 29101 Greenfield Rd.,
Southfield **(248) 559-5985** 11am-10pm,
til midnight Fri-Sat • plenty veggie • full
bar • wheelchair access • $10-15
**Vivio's** 2460 Market St. **393-1711** 8am-
9pm, clsd Sun • Italian • full bar • $6-11

# *Detroit*

**K**nown for its cars and stars, "Motown" is the home of General
Motors and living legends like Aretha Franklin, Diana Ross & the
Supremes, the Temptations, Stevie Wonder, Anita Baker, and Madonna.

Detroit is also rich in African-American culture. Be sure to check
out the Museum of African-American History, multicultural gallery
Your Heritage House, the Motown Museum...and the lesbian/gay bar
**Zippers.** And just under the river—via the Detroit/Windsor Tunnel—is
the North American Black Historical Museum in Windsor, Canada.

You might want to start your stay with a visit to the
**Affirmations Lesbian/Gay Community Center** or **A Woman's
Prerogative,** the women's bookstore, then check out **Sugarbakers,** a
women's sports bar.

Downtown, discover the impressive Renaissance Center. This
office and retail complex that dominates the city skyline houses
shopping, restaurants, a 73-story hotel, even an indoor lake! Before
moving on to explore the districts of Greektown, Bricktown, or
Rivertown, take a spin around the Civic Center district on the Detroit
People Mover, an elevated transit system that carries travellers in
automated, weatherproof cars.

## BOOKSTORES & RETAIL SHOPS

**A Woman's Prerogative Bookstore** 175 W. 9-Mile Rd., Ferndale **(248) 545-5703** noon-7pm, til 9pm Th, til 5pm Sun, clsd Mon • feminist • wheelchair access

**Chosen Books** 120 W. 4th St., Royal Oak **(248) 543-5758** noon-10pm • lesbigay bookstore • wheelchair access

**The Dressing Room** 42371 Garfield Rd., Clinton Township **(810) 286-0412** noon-9pm, 10am-5pm Sat, clsd Sun • cross-dressing boutique • larger sizes

**Giggles** 309 S. Main St., Royal Oak 414-6850

## PUBLICATIONS

**Between the Lines** **(810) 615-7003** covers southeastern MI

**Cruise Magazine** **(248) 545-9040** entertainment listings

**Metra** **(248) 543-3500** covers IN, IL, MI, OH, PA, WI & Ontario, Canada

**Out Post** 332-0066 bi-weekly • newspaper for metro Detroit

## TRAVEL AGENTS

**Pride Travel Service** 23315 Woodward Ave., Ferndale **(248) 584-4004/(800) 414-7743** IGLTA

**Royal International Travel Services** 31455 Southfield Rd., Birmingham **644-1600/(800) 521-1600** IGLTA

## SPIRITUAL GROUPS

**Dignity Detroit** 6th & Porter St. (Most Holy Trinity) **961-4818** 6pm Sun

**Divine Peace MCC** 23839 John R, Hazel Park **(248) 544-8335** 10am Sun

**MCC of Detroit** Pinecrest & Dreyton (Christ Church), Ferndale **(248) 399-7741** 10am & 7pm Sun

## EROTICA

**Noir Leather** 415 S. Main, Royal Oak **(248) 541-3979** toys • fetishwear

## Escanaba                                    (906)

## BARS & NIGHTCLUBS

**Club Xpress** 904 Ludington St. **789-0140** 8pm-2am, from 6pm Fri-Sat, clsd Sun-Tue • lesbians/gay men • dancing/DJ • wheelchair access

## Flint                                          (810)

## BARS & NIGHTCLUBS

**Club MI** 2402 N. Franklin St. **234-9481** 1pm-2am • popular • lesbians/gay men • neighborhood bar • multi-racial • 18+

**Club Triangle** 2101 S. Dort **767-7552** 7pm-2am • lesbians/gay men • dancing/DJ • 18+

**State Bar** 2510 S. Dort Hwy. **767-7050** 4pm-2am, from 1pm wknds • popular • lesbians/gay men • dancing/DJ • karaoke • wheelchair access

## SPIRITUAL GROUPS

**Redeemer MCC of Flint** 1665 N. Chevrolet Ave. **238-6700** 11am Sun • wheelchair access

## Glen Arbor                                (616)

## ACCOMMODATIONS

**Duneswood Retreat** (at Sleeping Bear Dunes Nat'l Lakeshore) **334-3346** women only • also 'Marge & Joanne's B&B' • $45-85

## Grand Rapids                            (616)

## INFO LINES & SERVICES

**Lesbian/Gay Network** 909 Cherry SE **458-3511** 6pm-10pm, clsd wknds • AA meetings • lounge • library

## BARS & NIGHTCLUBS

**The Apartment** 33 Sheldon **451-0815** 11am-2am, from 1pm Sun • mostly gay men • neighborhood bar • sandwiches served • wheelchair access

**The Cell** 76 S. Division St. **454-4499** 7am-2am, from noon wknds • mostly gay men • dancing/DJ • leather • wheelchair access

**The City Limits** 67 S. Division Ave. **454-8003** 11am-2:30am • popular • lesbians/gay men • dancing/DJ • live shows • videos • wheelchair access

**Diversions** 10 Fountain St. NW **451-3800** 11am-2am, from 8pm wknds • lesbians/gay men • dancing/DJ • live shows • food served • plenty veggie • wheelchair access • $5-10

## RESTAURANTS

**Cherie Inn** 969 Cherry St. **458-0588** 8am-3pm, clsd Mon • some veggie • wheelchair access • $4-6

## BOOKSTORES & RETAIL SHOPS

**Earth & Sky** 6 Jefferson SE **458-3520** 11am-7pm, clsd Sun • feminist • wheelchair access

**Sons & Daughters** 962 Cherry SE **459-8877** noon-midnight, from 10am wknds • lesbigay bookstore • coffeehouse

TRAVEL AGENTS
**Vacation Depot** 907 Cherry SE **454-4339/(888) 872-6292** ask for Karen

SPIRITUAL GROUPS
**Dignity** 1100 Lake Dr. **454-9779** 7:30pm Wed

**Reconciliation MCC** 300 Graceland NE **364-7633** 10am Sun

## Honor (616)

ACCOMMODATIONS
**Labrys Wilderness Resort** 415 Scenic Hwy. **882-5994** women only • $40-65

## Kalamazoo (616)

INFO LINES & SERVICES
**AA Gay/Lesbian** 247 W. Level St. **343-2711** 8pm Tue

**Kalamazoo Lesbian/Gay Resource Line** **345-7878** 7pm-10pm

**Lavender Morning** **388-5656** sponsors women's dances • newsletter

**Office of Lesbian/Gay/Bisexual Issues** **387-2123** 2pm Sun (Kiva Room)

**Women's Resource Center** **387-2995** call for info

BARS & NIGHTCLUBS
**Brother's Bar** 209 Stockbridge **345-1960** 6:30pm-2:30am • lesbians/gay men • more women Sat • dancing/DJ • live shows • karaoke • private club • patio • wheelchair access

**Zoo** 906 Portage St. **342-8888** 2pm-2am • mostly gay men • dancing/DJ • 18+ Sun-Th

BOOKSTORES & RETAIL SHOPS
**Pandora's Books for Open Minds** 226 W. Lovell St. **388-5656** 11am-7pm, til 6pm Fri-Sat, clsd Sun-Mon • feminist/lesbigay

SPIRITUAL GROUPS
**Phoenix Community Church** 394 S. Drake (Sky Ridge Church) **381-3222** 6pm Sun • wheelchair access

EROTICA
**Triangle World** 551 Portage St. **373-4005** noon-10pm, clsd Mon • lesbigay books • leather • gifts • wheelchair access

# It's like having
# a thousand
# brochures
### in one book!

# Damron
# Accommodations
features literally hundreds of **color photographs** – and detailed listings – for gay-friendly B&Bs, hotels, inns & accommodations worldwide! 500 pages – only **$18.95**

To order by credit card, call Damron Mail Order ask for a free catalog
## 800•462•6654 (US)
## 415•255•0404

# Lansing (517)

## INFO LINES & SERVICES
**AA Gay/Lesbian** E. Lansing **321-8781** call for mtg. schedule
**Gender Flex 321-3740** support for female-to-male TS/TG people
**Lansing Lesbian/Gay Hotline 332-3200** 7pm-10pm, 2pm-5pm Sun, clsd Sat

## BARS & NIGHTCLUBS
**Club 505** 505 E. Shiawassee **374-6312** 6pm-2am, clsd Mon • mostly women • neighborhood bar • dancing/DJ
**Esquire** 1250 Turner **487-5338** noon-2am • lesbians/gay men • neighborhood bar • karaoke • wheelchair access
**Paradise** 224 S. Washington Square **484-2399** 9pm-2am • popular • mostly gay men • dancing/DJ • live shows

## ENTERTAINMENT & RECREATION
**Our Living Room Concert Series** 303 S. Holmes **487-6495** 7:30pm 1st Sat • women's music for women only & boys up to 6 yrs. • unconfirmed

## BOOKSTORES & RETAIL SHOPS
**Community News Center** 418 Frandor Shopping Center **351-7562** 9am-9pm, til 7pm Sun • wheelchair access
**Real World Emporium** 1214-16 Turner St. **485-2665** noon-8pm, clsd Mon • lesbigay books • cafe • wheelchair access

## PUBLICATIONS
**Lesbian Connection 371-5257** nationwide grassroots forum for all lesbians

## TRAVEL AGENTS
**Anderson International Travel** 2740 E. Lansing Dr., E. Lansing **337-1300/(800) 723-1233** IGLTA

## SPIRITUAL GROUPS
**Dignity** 327 M.A.C. (St. John's Parish), E. Lansing **351-7341** 8pm Tue

# Marquette (906)

## BOOKSTORES & RETAIL SHOPS
**Sweet Violets** 413 N. 3rd St. **228-3307** 10am-6pm, clsd Sun • feminist bookstore

# Midland (517)

## ACCOMMODATIONS
**Jay's B&B** 4429 Bay City Rd. **496-2498** gay-friendly • deck • $50

## TRAVEL AGENTS
**Travel Together 835-3452/(800) 433-5442**

# Mount Clemens (810)

## BARS & NIGHTCLUBS
**Mirage** 27 N. Walnut **954-1919** 4pm-2am • lesbians/gay men • dancing/DJ • live shows

# New Buffalo (847)

## ACCOMMODATIONS
**A Woman's Place** 17 W. Mechanic St. **(847) 446-7638** women only • rental home • also retreat w/workshops & seminars • house parties • swimming • food served

# Ortonville (248)

## TRAVEL AGENTS
**Your Guy For Travel** 85 Groveland Rd. **627-4393** IGLTA

# Owendale (517)

## ACCOMMODATIONS
**Windover Resort** 3596 Blakely Rd. **375-2586** women only • campsites • swimming • $20/yr membership fee • $13-18 camping fee

# Pontiac (248)

## BARS & NIGHTCLUBS
**Club Flamingo** 352 Oakland Ave. **253-0430** 4pm-2am, from 2pm Sat • lesbians/gay men • dancing/DJ • live shows • wheelchair access

# Port Huron (810)

## BARS & NIGHTCLUBS
**Seekers** 3301 24th St. **985-9349** 7pm-2am, from 4pm Fri-Sun • lesbians/gay men • dancing/DJ

# Saginaw (517)

## BARS & NIGHTCLUBS
**Bambi's** 1742 E. Genessee **752-9179** 7pm-2am • lesbians/gay men • dancing/DJ • live shows
**Heidelberg** 411 S. Franklin **771-9508** 5pm-2am, from 2pm wknds • mostly older gay men • neighborhood bar • wheelchair access

*Saugatuck on the River...*

# DEERPATH LODGE

*...an enchanting retreat*

Bring your bicycle,
fishing gear and Best Pal.

Watch the waterbird rituals from
our private 2000 feet of river frontage.

Bask under sun or stars in a hot tub
overlooking the river.

Saugatuck, the infamous art colony,
is a mecca of innovative shops
and restaurants.

The marina, Lake Michigan beaches,
and all the delights of Saugatuck
are just minutes by car,
longer by boat.

We offer great views, spacious
guestrooms with private baths;
one kitchenette.

The Kalamazoo and 45 wooded acres
seclude us from public access.

*Guest Rooms for Women*

**For Reservations and Information:**
P.O. Box 849 Saugatuck, Michigan 49453
**TOLL FREE 888-DEER-PATH**

## Saugatuck (616)

ACCOMMODATIONS

**Camp It** 543-4335 seasonal • lesbians/gay men • campsites • RV hookups

▲ **Deerpath Lodge** (888) DEER-PATH women only • on 45 secluded acres • $90-95

**Douglas Dunes Resort** 857-1401 mostly gay men • swimming • food served • women's wknds: 1st week in April & Oct • $42-125

**Drift-Woods** 2731 Lakeshore Dr., Fennville **857-2586** mostly women • retreat w/cottages • swimming • kitchens • women-owned/run • $65-200

**Grandma's House B&B** 2135 Blue Star Hwy. **543-4706** lesbians/gay men • Victorian country estate • full brkfst • hot tub • $70-80

**Hillby Thatch Cottages** 71st St., Glenn (847) 864-3553 gay-friendly • cottages • kitchens • fireplaces • women-owned/run

**Kirby House** 857-2904 gay-friendly • Queen Anne Victorian • full brkfst • swimming • $75-115

▲ **The Lighthouse Motel** 857-2271 gay-friendly • swimming • wheelchair access • $50-150

**Moore's Creek Inn** 820 Holland St. **857-2411**/(800) 838-5864 gay-friendly • old-fashioned farmhouse • full brkfst • $65-95

**The New Richmond Guest House** 3037 57th St., New Richmond **561-2591** lesbians/gay men • full brkfst

**The Newnham SunCatcher Inn** 131 Griffith **857-4249** gay-friendly • full brkfst • hot tub • swimming • women-owned/run • $75-120

BARS & NIGHTCLUBS

**Douglas Disco** (at 'Douglas Dunes' resort) **857-1401** mostly gay men • dancing/DJ • live shows

CAFES

**Uncommon Grounds** 123 Hoffman **857-3333** coffee & juice bar

RESTAURANTS

**Cafe Sir Douglas** (at 'Douglas Dunes' resort) **857-1401** 5pm-10pm, til 11pm Fri-Sat, clsd Tue-Wed • cont'l • some veggie • $10-20

# LIGHTHOUSE

# MOTEL

130th at Blue Star
Douglas, MI 49406
• (616) 857-2271 •

**Located in the heart of a gay friendly area.**

**Private and secluded with miles of sandy beaches.**

- Guest rooms, suites, apartments & European style rooms

- Weekend & vacation packages available at reduced rates

- Includes continental breakfast & late check out, upon request

- Overlooks large beautiful pool adjacent to golf course

- Restaurants and shopping nearby

**Come visit Saugatuck**

**Loaf & Mug** 236 Culver St. **857-2974** 8am-3pm, til 8pm Fri-Sat • some veggie • beer/wine • $5-10

**Pumpernickel's** 202 Butler St. **857-1196** seasonal • 8am-4pm • sandwiches & fresh breads • some veggie • $5-10

**Restaurant Toulouse** 248 Culver St. **857-1561** country French • some veggie • full bar • wheelchair access • $10-20

### BOOKSTORES & RETAIL SHOPS

**Hoopdee Scootee** 133 Mason **857-4141** seasonal • 10am-9pm, til 6pm Sun, til 5pm winter • clothing • gifts

## Sault Ste. Marie (906)

### BOOKSTORES & RETAIL SHOPS

**Open Mind Books** 223 Ashmun St. **635-9008** 10am-5pm (9am-7:30pm summer), clsd Sun • progressive

## St. Clair (810)

### ACCOMMODATIONS

**William Hopkins Manor** 613 N. Riverside Ave. **329-0188** gay-friendly • full brkfst • $75-95

## Taylor (313)

### TRAVEL AGENTS

**Wright Way Travel** 24642 Robin **946-9330** IGLTA

## Traverse City (616)

### INFO LINES & SERVICES

**Friends North** 946-1804 networking & social group • newsletter

### ACCOMMODATIONS

**Neahtawanta Inn** 1308 Neahtawanta Rd. **223-7315** gay-friendly • swimming • sauna • wheelchair access • $65-130

### BARS & NIGHTCLUBS

**Side Traxx Nite Club** 520 Franklin **935-1666** 6pm-2am, from 2pm wknds • lesbians/gay men • dancing/DJ • live shows • wheelchair access

### CAFES

**Ray's Coffee House** 129 E. Front St. **929-1006** 7am-7pm, til 10pm Th-Sat (late hours in summer only) • wheelchair access

### BOOKSTORES & RETAIL SHOPS

**The Bookie Joint** 120 S. Union St. **946-8862** 10am-6pm, 1pm-4pm Sun • pride gifts • used books

## Union Pier (616)

### ACCOMMODATIONS

**Warren Woods Inn** 15506 Lakeshore Rd. **469-5880/(800) 358-4754** gay-friendly • full brkfst • jacuzzis • fireplaces • kids ok • $95-160

## Ypsilanti (313)

### SPIRITUAL GROUPS

**Tree of Life MCC** 218 N. Adams St. (1st Congregational Church) **485-3922** 6pm Sun & Wed

### EROTICA

**The Magazine Rack** 515 West Cross **482-6944**

## THE NAMES PROJECT CHAPTERS (U.S.)

**California**

| | |
|---|---|
| Bay Area | (415) 863-1966 |
| Inland Empire | (909) 784-2437 |
| Kern County | (805) 396-8322 |
| Long Beach | (562) 491-9912 |
| Los Angeles | (213) 653-6263 |
| Orange County | (714) 490-3880 |
| Sacramento | (916) 484-5646 |
| San Diego | (619) 492-8452 |
| Ventura County | (805) 650-7382 |

**Connecticut**

| | |
|---|---|
| Central Connecticut | (860) 369-9670 |

**District of Columbia**

| | |
|---|---|
| National Capital Area | (202) 296-2637 |

**Delaware**

| | |
|---|---|
| Delaware | (302) 737-7067 |

**Florida**

| | |
|---|---|
| Central Florida | (407) 589-5076 |

**Georgia**

| | |
|---|---|
| Atlanta | (404) 315-0004 |

**Hawaii**

| | |
|---|---|
| Honolulu | (808) 734-0583 |

**Iowa**

| | |
|---|---|
| Cedar Valley | (319) 266-7903 |

**Illinois**

| | |
|---|---|
| Chicago | (773) 907-9700 |

**Indiana**

| | |
|---|---|
| Indianap· lis | (317) 920-1200 |

**Louisiana**

| | |
|---|---|
| Louisiana Capital Area | (504) 753-0864 |

**Massachusetts**

| | |
|---|---|
| Boston | (617) 262-6263 |
| Southeastern Massachusetts | (508) 992-9273 |

**Maine**

| | |
|---|---|
| Maine | (207) 774-2198 |

**Michigan**

| | |
|---|---|
| Detroit | (313) 541-3160 |
| Thumb Area | (810) 982-6361 |

**Minnesota**

| | |
|---|---|
| Twin Cities | (612) 373-2468 |

**Missouri**

| | |
|---|---|
| Metro St. Louis | (314) 995-4638 |

**New Jersey**

| | |
|---|---|
| Central New Jersey | (908) 249-3933 |

**New Mexico**

| | |
|---|---|
| New Mexico | (505) 466-2637 |

**New York**

| | |
|---|---|
| Buffalo | (716) 838-4860 |
| Long Island | (516) 477-2447 |
| New York City | (212) 226-2292 |
| Syracuse | (315) 498-4940 |

**Ohio**

| | |
|---|---|
| Columbus | (614) 885-3170 |

**Oklahoma**

| | |
|---|---|
| Tulsa Area | (918) 748-3111 |

**Oregon**

| | |
|---|---|
| Portland | (503) 650-7032 |

**Pennsylvania**

| | |
|---|---|
| Philadelphia | (215) 735-6263 |
| Pittsburgh | (412) 343-9846 |
| Susquehanna Valley | (717) 234-0629 |

**Rhode Island**

| | |
|---|---|
| Rhode Island | (401) 434-4880 |

**Texas**

| | |
|---|---|
| Dallas | (214) 520-7397 |
| Fort Worth/Tarrant County | (817) 336-2637 |
| Houston | (713) 526-2637 |

**Utah**

| | |
|---|---|
| Salt Lake City | (801) 487-2323 |

**Virginia**

| | |
|---|---|
| Central Virginia | (804) 346-8047 |

**Washington**

| | |
|---|---|
| Seattle | (206) 285-2880 |

**West Virginia**

| | |
|---|---|
| Upper Ohio Valley | (304) 242-9443 |

THE NAMES PROJECT
FOUNDATION
1987-1997

AIDS
Memorial
Quilt

## MINNESOTA

### Duluth (218)

INFO LINES & SERVICES
**Aurora: A Northern Lesbian Center** 32 E. 1st St. #104 **722-4903** discussion groups & socials

ACCOMMODATIONS
**Rainbow Island** 473-7889 women only • camping • cabin • also workshops
**Stanford Inn B&B** 1415 E. Superior St. **724-3044** gay-friendly • full brkfst • $55-95

BOOKSTORES & RETAIL SHOPS
**At Sara's Table** 728 E. Superior St. **723-8569** 8am-6pm • also cafe • wheelchair access • women-owned/run

### Ely (218)

ACCOMMODATIONS
**Log Cabin Hideaways** 1321 N. Hwy. 21 **365-6045** remote wilderness cabins • smokefree

### Hastings (612)

ACCOMMODATIONS
**Thorwood & Rosewood Inns** 315 Pine St. **437-3297/(888) 846-7966** gay-friendly • circa 1880 mansion • full brkfst

### Hill City (218)

ACCOMMODATIONS
**Northwoods Retreat** 5749 Mt. Ash Dr. **697-8119/(800) 767-3020** lesbians/gay men • 2 cabins w/700 ft. of lakeshore • all meals included • veggie cuisine • wheelchair access

### Hinckley (612)

ACCOMMODATIONS
**Dakota Lodge B&B** 384-6052 gay-friendly • full brkfst • hot tub • wheelchair access • $58-135

### Kenyon (507)

ACCOMMODATIONS
**Dancing Winds Farm** 6863 Country 12 Blvd. **789-6606** lesbians/gay men • B&B on working dairy farm • tentsites • full brkfst • work exchange avail. • women-owned/run

### Mankato (507)

INFO LINES & SERVICES
**Mankato State U. Lesbigay Center** 389-5131

CAFES
**The Coffee Hag** 329 N. Riverfront **387-5533** 9am-11pm, 11am-6pm Sun, clsd Mon • veggie menu • live shows • wheelchair access • women-owned/run • $3-7

### Minneapolis/St. Paul (612)

INFO LINES & SERVICES
**Chrysalis Women's Center** 2650 Nicollett Ave., St. Paul **871-0118** 8:30am-8pm, til 5pm Fri, clsd wknds • many groups
**District 202** 1601 Nicollett Ave., St. Paul **871-5559** 3pm-11pm, til 1am Fri, noon-1am Sat, til 4pm Sun, clsd Tue • resource center for lesbigay youth
**Gay/Lesbian Community Action Council** 310 E. 38th St., Minneapolis **822-0127/(800) 800-0350** 9am-5pm Mon-Fri
**Gay/Lesbian Helpline 822-8661/(800) 800-0907 (IN-STATE)** 2pm-10pm, from 4pm Sat, clsd Sun & holidays • covers IA, MN, NE, ND, SD, WI
**GLEAM (Gay/Lesbian Elders Active in MN)** 1505 Park Ave., Minneapolis **721-8913** 1pm 2nd Sun
**Quatrefoil Library** 1619 Dayton Ave., St. Paul **641-0969** 7pm-9pm, noon-4pm Sat, 1pm-5pm Sun • lesbigay library & resource center
**U of MN Gay/Lesbian/Bi/Transsexual Groups** 230 Coffman Memorial Library, Minneapolis **626-2344** 4:30pm Wed

ACCOMMODATIONS
**Country GuestHouse** 1673 38th St., Somerset WI **(715) 247-3520** lesbians/gay men • rental home on 20 wooded acres in St. Croix River Valley • women-owned • $75
**Eagle Cove B&B** W 4387 120th Ave., Maiden Rock WI **(715) 448-4302/(800) 467-0279** gay-friendly • hot tub • wheelchair access • $50-100
**Garden Gate B&B** 925 Goodrich Ave., St. Paul **227-8430/(800) 967-2703** gay-friendly • massage avail.

# Minneapolis/St. Paul

*I*f you're searching for a liberal oasis in the heartland of America, if you love Siberian winters and if you crave a diverse, intensely political lesbian community, you'll fit right into the Twin Cities of Minneapolis and St. Paul.

Located on the banks of the Mississippi River, these cities share the Minnesota Twins, 936 lakes & 513 parks, and a history of Native American and Northern European settlements. If you want more than glimpses into the various cultures of Minnesota, visit the Minneapolis American Indian Center or the American Swedish Institute.

Of course, you'll probably have more fun checking out the lesbian cultural scene. The place to go to find out about the latest poetry reading, play, or concert is **Amazon Bookstore** in Minneapolis. To find social groups for women of color, call the **Gay/Lesbian Community Action Council.**

Or stop by **Minnesota Women's Press** bookstore & library in St. Paul. Then go cafe-hopping in Minneapolis at the women-owned **Cafe Wyrd** or **Ruby's Cafe.** For a night on the town, you won't find any women's bars, but **Club Metro** is popular on weekends.

Whatever you do, don't stay indoors the whole time. In the summer, boating, fishing, sunbathing, water-skiing, walking, jogging, and bicycling are all popular. With winter, you can enjoy snowmobiling, ice hockey, cross-country skiing or snuggling by a fire. For women's outdoor adventures, try **Women in the Wilderness** in St. Paul or **Woodswomen** in Minneapolis.

**Hotel Amsterdam** 828 Hennepin Ave., Minneapolis **288-0459**/**(800) 649-9500** lesbians/gay men • European-style lodging • $28-49

**Nan's B&B** 2304 Freemont Ave. S., Minneapolis **377-5118** gay-friendly • 1895 Victorian family home • shared bath • $40-50

**Regal Minneapolis Hotel** 1313 Nicollet Mall, Minneapolis **332-6000**/**(800) 222-8888** gay-friendly • food served • swimming • wheelchair access • IGLTA

### BARS & NIGHTCLUBS

**19 Bar** 19 W. 15th St., Minneapolis **871-5553** 3pm-1am, from 1pm wknds • mostly gay men • neighborhood bar • beer/wine • wheelchair access

**Brass Rail** 422 Hennepin Ave., Minneapolis **333-3016** noon-1am • popular • mostly gay men • live shows • karaoke • videos • wheelchair access

**Bryant Lake Bowl** 1810 W. Lake St., Minneapolis **825-3737** 8am-2am • gay-friendly • also theater • restaurant • bowling alley • wheelchair access

**Checkers** 1066 E. 7th St., St. Paul **776-7915** 6pm-1am • mostly gay men • dancing/DJ • live shows • wheelchair access

**Club Metro** 733 Pierce Butler Rte., St. Paul **489-0002** 3pm-1am • popular • lesbians/gay men • dancing/DJ • transgender-friendly • live shows • food served • $5-15 • women-owned/run

**Gay 90s** 408 Hennepin Ave., Minneapolis **333-7755** 8am-1am (dinner nightly 5pm-9pm) • mostly gay men • 7 bar complex • dancing/DJ • live shows • also erotica store • wheelchair access

**Ground Zero/The Front** 15 NE 4th St., Minneapolis **378-5115** 9pm-1am, clsd Sun-Tue, 'The Front' from 7pm, clsd Sun-Mon, • gay-friendly • dancing/DJ • more gay Th w/ 'Bondage-A-Go-Go'

**Innuendo** 510 N. Robert St., St. Paul **224-8996** 4pm-1am, clsd Sun • lesbians/gay men • neighborhood bar • wheelchair access

**Over the Rainbow** 249 W. 7th St., St. Paul **228-7180** 3pm-1am, from noon wknds • lesbians/gay men • dancing/DJ • live shows • karaoke

**Rumours** 490 N. Robert St., St. Paul **224-0703** 4pm-1am, from noon wknds • lesbians/gay men • dancing/DJ • also restaurant • live shows • wheelchair access

## Minneapolis/ (612) St. Paul

**Lesbigay Pride:** July: 362-3680.

**City Info:** 800/445-7412. St. Paul Visitors' Bureau: 297-6985.

**Attractions:** Minneapolis Institute of Arts. Minneapolis Sculpture Garden & Walker Art Center. Minnesota Zoo. St. Anthony Main Historic Waterfront Shopping & Entertainment Center. Mall of America in nearby Bloomington.

**Best View:** Observation deck of the 32nd story of the Foshay Tower (closed in winter).

**Weather:** Winters are harsh. If driving, carry extra blankets and supplies. The average temperature is 19°, and it can easily drop well below 0°, and then there's the wind chill! Summer temperatures are usually in the upper-80°s to mid-90°s, and then there's the humidity!

**Transit:** Town Taxi (Minn): 331-8294. Yellow Cab (St. Paul): 222-4433. Airport Express: 827-7777. MTC: 349-7000.

**The Saloon** 830 Hennepin Ave., Minneapolis **332-0835** 9am-1am, til 3am Fri-Sun • mostly gay men • dancing/DJ • grill menu • $3-6 • wheelchair access • gay-owned/run

**Ten Percent at Tropix** 400 3rd Ave. N., Minneapolis **333-1006** 8pm-midnight Th only • lesbians/gay men

**The Times Bar & Cafe** 1036 Nicollet Ave., Minneapolis **333-2762** 11am-1am • lesbians/gay men • live shows • 'comfort food' • some veggie • $5-19 • wheelchair access

**Town House** 1415 University Ave., St. Paul **646-7087** 2pm-1am, from noon wknds • popular • lesbians/gay men • dancing/DJ • country/western • Mon karaoke

## CAFES

**Cafe Wyrd** 1600 W. Lake St., Minneapolis **827-5710** 7am-1am • lesbians/gay men • plenty veggie • women-owned/run • $3-6

**Cafe Zev** 1362 La Salle Ave., Minneapolis **874-8477** 7am-1am • live shows

**Cahoots** 1562 Selby Ave., St. Paul **644-6778** coffee bar

**Ruby's Cafe** 1614 Harmon Pl., Minneapolis **338-2089** 7am-2pm, from 8am Sun • popular • lesbians/gay men • outdoor seating • women-owned/run • $5

**The Urban Bean** 3255 Bryant Ave. S., Minneapolis **824-6611** also 2717 Hennepin Ave. S. location

## RESTAURANTS

**Al's Breakfast** 413 14th Ave. SE, Minneapolis **331-9991** great hash

**Anodyne at 43rd** 4301 Nicollet Ave., Minneapolis **824-4300** open daily • live shows • wheelchair access

**D'Amico Cucina** 100 N. 6th St., Minneapolis **338-2401**

**Goodfellows** 800 Nicollet Mall, Minneapolis **332-4800**

**La Covina** 1570 Selby Ave., St. Paul **645-5288** Mexican • wheelchair access • $6-10

**Loretta's** 2615 Park Ave. (entrance on 26th St.), Minneapolis **871-1660** 11am-2pm, clsd Sat • homecooking

**Murray's** 26 S. 6th St., Minneapolis **339-0909** meat & potatoes

**Rudolph's Bar-B-Que** 1933 Lyndale, Minneapolis **871-8969** 11am-midnight • wheelchair access

**Sri Lanka Curry House** 2821 Hennepin Ave., Minneapolis **871-2400** Hot!

**To Chau** 823 University Ave., St.Paul **291-2661** Vietnamese

**W.A. Frost & Co.** 374 Selby Ave., St. Paul **224-5715** 11am-11pm • patio • wheelchair access • $11-22

## ENTERTAINMENT & RECREATION

**32nd St. Beach** east side of Lake Calhoun, Minneapolis gay beach

**Dyke TV** Channel 33, Minneapolis 10:30pm Mon • 'weekly half hour TV show produced by lesbians, for lesbians'

**Fresh Fruit** KFAI 90.3 FM, Minneapolis **341-0980** 9pm-midnight Sun, gay radio program

**Twin Lake Beach** in Wirth Park, Minneapolis hard to find, inquire locally • nudity permitted

## BOOKSTORES & RETAIL SHOPS

**A Brother's Touch** 2327 Hennepin Ave., Minneapolis **377-6279** 11am-9pm, til 5pm wknds, til 7pm Mon-Tue • lesbigay bookstore • wheelchair access

**Amazon Bookstore** 1612 Harmon Pl., Minneapolis **338-6560** 10am-9pm, til 10pm Th, 9am-10pm Sat, til 5pm Sun • women's • wheelchair access

**Borders Bookshop** 3001 Hennepin S. (Calhoun Sq.), Minneapolis **825-0336** 10am-10pm, til 11pm Fri-Sat, 11am-6pm Sun

**G.A.L.E.** (inside 'Club Metro'), St. Paul **880-3560** pride accessories • gay-owned/run

**Magus Books** 1316 SE 4th St., Minneapolis **379-7669** noon-8pm, til 5pm wknds • alternative spirituality books • also mail order

**The Rainbow Road** 109 W. Grant, Minneapolis **872-8448** 10am-10pm • lesbigay retail & video • wheelchair access

## PUBLICATIONS

**Focus Point** 288-9008

**Lavender Magazine** 871-2237

**Maize** lesbian country magazine

**Minnesota Women's Press** 771 Raymond Ave., St. Paul **646-3968** newspaper • also bookshop & library • 9am-6pm, til 3pm Sat, clsd Sun

**Woodswomen News** 25 W. Diamond Lake Dr., Minneapolis **822-3809**

### TRAVEL AGENTS

**All Airlines Travel** 111 E. Kellogg Blvd. #225, St. Paul **222-2210/(800) 832-0304** IGLTA

**American Express Travel** 200 S. 6th St., Minneapolis **343-5500** IGLTA

**Hot Spots Travel** 2150 James Ave., St. Paul **699-0403** IGLTA

**New Departures** 625 2nd Ave. S. #408, Minneapolis **305-0025** IGLTA

**Partners In Travel, Ltd.** 825 Nicollet Mall, Minneapolis **338-0004/(800) 333-3177** IGLTA

**Travel About** 400 S. Cedar Lake Rd., Minneapolis **377-8955** IGLTA

**The Travel Company** 2800 University Ave. SE, Minneapolis **379-9000/(800) 328-9131** IGLTA

**Travel Quest International** 2610 Garfield Ave. S. #102, Minneapolis **377-7700** IGLTA

### SPIRITUAL GROUPS

**Dignity Twin Cities** Prospect Park Unitarian Methodist (Malcolm & Orwin), Minneapolis **827-3103** 7:30pm 2nd & 4th Fri

**Lutherans Concerned** 100 N. Oxford, Minneapolis **866-8941** 7:30pm 3rd Fri • wheelchair access

**MCC All God's Children** 3100 Park Ave., Minneapolis **824-2673** 10am & 7pm Sun, 7pm Wed • wheelchair access

**Shir Tikvah** 5000 Girard Ave., Minneapolis **822-1440** 10am 1st Sat, then 8pm every Fri • lesbigay Jewish congregation • wheelchair access

### GYMS & HEALTH CLUBS

**Body Quest** 245 N. Aldrich Ave. N., Minneapolis **377-7222** lesbians/gay men

### EROTICA

**Back in Black Leather, Inc.** 733 Pierce Butler Route (at 'Club Metro'), St. Paul **870-2968** 7pm-close Th-Sat, 1:30pm-6pm Sun

**Broadway Bookstore** 901 Hennepin Ave., Minneapolis **338-7303** 24hrs

**Sexworld** 241 2nd Ave. N., Minneapolis **672-0556** 24hrs

## Rochester (507)

### INFO LINES & SERVICES

**Gay/Lesbian Community Service** 281-3265 5pm-7pm Mon & Wed

## Rushford (507)

### ACCOMMODATIONS

**Windswept Inn** 2070 N. Mill St. 864-2545 gay-friendly

## Two Harbors (218)

### ACCOMMODATIONS

**Star Harbor Resort** 1098 Hwy. 61 E. **834-3796** gay-friendly • log cabins on the N. shore of Lake Superior • wheelchair ramps avail.

## Wolverton (218)

### RESTAURANTS

**District 31 Victoria's** 101 First St. **995-2000** 5:30pm-9:30pm, clsd Sun • cont'l • beer/wine • reservations required • $15-25

# MISSISSIPPI

## Biloxi (601)

### ACCOMMODATIONS

**Lofty Oaks Inn** 17288 Hwy. 67 **392-6722/(800) 280-4361** full brkfst • hot tub • swimming • kids/pets ok by arr. • woman-owned/run • $95-125

### BARS & NIGHTCLUBS

**Joey's** 1708 Beach Blvd. (Hwy. 90) **435-5639** from 8pm, from 6pm Sun, clsd Mon • lesbians/gay men • dancing/DJ • live shows

### EROTICA

**Satellite News** 1632 Pass Rd. **432-8229** clsd Sun

## Columbus (601)

### BARS & NIGHTCLUBS

**Columbus Connection** 851 Island Rd. **329-3926** 6pm-1am Th-Sun • lesbians/gay men • dancing/DJ • mostly African-American • live shows • beer/wine

## Florence (601)

### INFO LINES & SERVICES

**Aurora Transgender Group** 346-4379/845-1328 transgendered support in central MS

## Hattiesburg (601)

### BARS & NIGHTCLUBS
**The Courtyard** 107 E. Front St. **545-2714** hours vary • lesbians/gay men • dancing/DJ • food served • live shows

## Holly Springs (601)

### ACCOMMODATIONS
**Somerset Cottage** 135 Gholson Ave. **252-4513** gay-friendly • smokefree • hot tub • $65

## Jackson (601)

### INFO LINES & SERVICES
**Gay/Lesbian Community Info Line 346-4379/435-2398** voicemail for many organizations • monthly publication
**Lambda AA** 4872 N. State St. (Unitarian Church) **346-4379** 6:30pm Mon & Wed, 8pm Sat
**MGLTF (MS Gay/Lesbian Task Force)** **346-4379** also contact for AIDS project & MS monthly publications

### BARS & NIGHTCLUBS
**Club City Lights** 200 N. Mill St. **353-0059** 10pm-close Wed, Fri-Sun • lesbians/gay men • dancing/DJ • mostly African-American • live shows • beer/wine • BYOB
**Jack's Construction Site (JC's)** 425 N. Mart Plaza **362-3108** 5pm-close, from 2pm Sun • mostly gay men • more women Wed & Fri • neighborhood bar •. beer/wine • BYOB
**Polly-Esther's** 3911 Northview Dr. **366-3247** from 8pm Wed-Sun • mostly gay men • dancing/DJ
**The Village** 206 W. Capitol St. **948-3366** clsd Mon-Tue • lesbians/gay men • ladies night Wed • dancing/DJ • live shows

### PUBLICATIONS
**Mississippi Voice** 346-4378

### SPIRITUAL GROUPS
**Affirmation** 346-4379 United Methodist gays & lesbians
**Integrity Mississippi** 346-4379 lesbigay Episcopalians
**MCC of the Rainbow** 5565 Robinson Rd. #L **372-7979/373-8610 x45** 11:30am Sun

**Safe Harbor Family Church** 2147 Henry Hill Dr. #203 **346-4379** 6pm Sun & 7pm Wed • non-denominational • social events • support groups

### EROTICA
**Terry Road Books** 1449 Terry Rd. **353-9156** 24hrs

## Meridian (601)

### BARS & NIGHTCLUBS
**Crossroads** 655-8415 6pm-1am Fri, til 6am Sat • lesbians/gay men • dancing/DJ • live shows • call for directions • cabins avail. • wheelchair access
**Olie Mae's** at Crossroads, Enterprise **655-8415** 6pm-1am • gay-friendly • wheelchair access

## Ovett (601)

### ACCOMMODATIONS
**Camp Sister Spirit** 344-2005 mostly women • 120 acres of camping & RV sites • cabins • $10-20

## Pascagoula (601)

### TRAVEL AGENTS
**Alternative Tours & Travel** 5918 Meadow Dr., Moss Point **475-9697** IGLTA

## MISSOURI

### Branson (417)

#### ACCOMMODATIONS
**Pine Wood B&B** 779-5514 gay-friendly • full brkfst • hot tub • $65-75

### Cape Girardeau (573)

#### BARS & NIGHTCLUBS
**Independence Place** 5 S. Henderson St. **334-2939** 8:30pm-1:30am, from 7pm Fri-Sat, clsd Sun • lesbians/gay men • dancing/DJ • transgender-friendly • live shows Sat

### Columbia (573)

#### INFO LINES & SERVICES
**Gay/Lesbian Helpline** 449-4477
**Triangle Coalition** 882-4427 meets 7pm Th • also GLBGSA (Gay/Lesbian/Bisexual Graduate Student Association)
**Women's Center** 229 Brady Commons UMC 882-6621

#### BARS & NIGHTCLUBS
**Contacts** 514 E. Broadway 443-0281 8pm-1:30am, clsd Sun • lesbians/gay men • neighborhood bar • dancing/DJ • live shows
**Styx** 3111 Old 63 S. **499-1828** 3pm-1:30am, clsd Sun • lesbians/gay men • dancing/DJ • country/western Tue • patio

#### CAFES
**Ernie's Cafe** 1005 E. Walnut **874-7804** 6:30am-6pm, til 8pm Fri-Sat • brkfst anytime • some veggie

#### SPIRITUAL GROUPS
**Christ the King Agape Church** 515 Hickman Ave. **443-5316** 10:45am Sun & 6:30pm Wed
**United Covenant Church** 449-7194 10am Sun • non-denominational • wheelchair access

#### EROTICA
**Eclectics** 1122-A Wilkes Blvd. **443-0873**

### Imperial (314)

#### TRAVEL AGENTS
**Imperial Travel Experts** 1558 Miller Rd. 464-7077 IGLTA

### Jefferson City (573)

#### ACCOMMODATIONS
**Jefferson Victorian B&B** 801 W. High St. **635-7196** gay-friendly • full brkfst • kids ok • $65-125

### Joplin (417)

#### BARS & NIGHTCLUBS
**Partners** 720 Main St. **781-6453** 3pm-1:30am, clsd Sun • lesbians/gay men • neighborhood bar • dancing/DJ • country/western

### Kansas City (816)

#### INFO LINES & SERVICES
**Gay Chamber of Commerce (UGRC)** 4212 S. Hocker, Bldg. 8 #215, Independence 350-3889/(800) 497-4823
**Gay/Lesbian Phone Tree** 931-4470
**Live & Let Live AA** 4243 Walnut St. 531-9668 many mtgs.

#### ACCOMMODATIONS
**B&B in KC** 9215 Slater, Overland Park KS **(913) 648-5457** women only • full brkfst • smokefree
**Doanleigh Wallagh Inn** 217 E. 37th St. 753-2667 gay-friendly • full brkfst • smokefree • reservations required • lesbian-owned/run
**Inn The Park** 3610 Gillham Rd. **931-0797/(800) 708-6748** gay-friendly • full brkfst • swimming • smokefree

#### BARS & NIGHTCLUBS
**The Cabaret** 5024 Main St. **753-6504** 6pm-3am, from 3pm Sun, clsd Mon • popular • mostly gay men • dancing/DJ • food served • wheelchair access
**Dixie Belle Complexx** 1922 Main St. **471-2424** 11am-3am • popular • mostly gay men • leather • live shows • also leather shop • wheelchair access
**The Edge** 323 W. 8th (in the 'Lucas Place Bldg.') 221-8900 popular • lesbians/gay men • dancing/DJ • alternative • live shows • wheelchair access
**The Fox** 7520 Shawnee Mission Pkwy., Overland Park KS **(913) 384-0369** noon-2am, from 6pm Sat, clsd Sun • gay-friendly • neighborhood bar • more gay evenings
**Jamie's** 528 Walnut 471-2080 10am-2am • mostly women • neighborhood bar • dancing/DJ • country/western • grill menu • wheelchair access

**Mari's Saloon & Grill** 1809 Grand Blvd. **283-0511** 5pm-10pm, from 11am Sun • lesbians/gay men • dancing/DJ • videos • food served • $5-12 • wheelchair access

**Missie B's** 805 W. 39th St. **561-0625** 11am-3am • mostly gay men • neighborhood bar • live shows

**The Other Side** 3611 Broadway **931-0501** 3:30pm-1:30am, clsd Sun • mostly gay men • neighborhood bar • videos

**Sidekicks** 3707 Main St. **931-1430** 2pm-3am, clsd Sun • mostly gay men • dancing/DJ • country/western • wheelchair access

**Soakie's** 1308 Main St. **221-6060** 9am-1:30am, til 3am Fri-Sat, from 11am Sun • mostly gay men • dancing/DJ • mostly African-American • food served

**Ted's Bar & Grill** 529 Walnut **472-0569** 7am-1:30am, 11am-midnight Sun • gay-friendly • neighborhood bar • country/western • lunch served daily

**Tootsie's** 1818 Main **471-7704** 11:30am-1am • popular • mostly women • dancing/DJ • grill menu • some veggie • $3-6

**View on the Hill** 204 Orchard KS **(913) 371-9370** 4pm-2am, from noon wknds • mostly gay men • neighborhood bar

## Cafes

**The Coffeehouse** 1719 W. 39th St. **756-1997** 7am-midnight, from 8am wknds • also 318 E. 51st St. 756-3121 • plenty veggie

## Restaurants

**Classic Cup Cafe** 301 W. 47th St. **753-1840** 7am-midnight, til 1am Fri-Sat • cont'l • some veggie • full bar • wheelchair access • $9-17

**The Corner Restaurant** 4059 Broadway **931-6630** 7am-9pm, til 2am wknds • some veggie • beer/wine • wheelchair access • $5-7

**Metropolis** 303 Westport Rd. **753-1550** lunch & dinner, clsd Sun • popular • lesbians/gay men • wheelchair access • $9-17

**Otto's Malt Shop** 3903 Wyoming **756-1010** 11am-midnight, 24hrs wknds • burgers & malts

**Sharp's 63rd St. Grill** 128 W. 63rd St. **333-4355** 7am-10pm, til 11pm Fri-Sat, from 8am Sat, from 9am Sun • wheelchair access • women-owned/run

**Strouds** 1014 E. 85th St. **333-2132** dinner • fried chicken

## Entertainment & Recreation

**Unicorn Theatre** 3820 Main **531-3033** contemporary American theater

## Bookstores & Retail Shops

**Larry's Gifts & Cards** 205 Westport Rd. **753-4757** 10am-7pm, til 5pm Sun • lesbigay books

## Publications

**The Alternative** 471-2595

**Current News** 561-2679

**News Telegraph** 561-6266/(800) 303-5468

## Spiritual Groups

**MCC of Johnson County** 87th & Lamar (Overland Park Comm. Ctr.), Shawnee KS **(913) 236-4313** 10:30am Sun & 7:30pm Wed

**Spirit of Hope MCC** 3801 Wyandotte **931-0750** 10:15am Sun & 7:15pm Wed

## Erotica

**Erotic City** 8401 E. Truman Rd. **252-3370** 24hrs • boutique • books • lounge

**Extremus** 4037 Broadway **756-1142** body piercing

**Hollywood at Home** 9063 Metcalf, Overland Park KS **(913) 649-9666**

# Noel                                              (417)

## Accommodations

**Sycamore Landing** 475-6460 open May-Sept • campsites • canoe rental

# Springfield                                     (417)

## Info Lines & Services

**AA Gay/Lesbian** SMS University at Ecumenical Ctr. (National off Cherry) **862-9264** 6pm Sat

## Bars & Nightclubs

**The Gallery** 424 N. Boonville **865-1266** 1pm-1:30am, clsd Sun • lesbians/gay men

**Martha's Vineyard** 219 W. Olive St. **864-4572** 4pm-1:30am, from 11am Sat, clsd Sun • lesbians/gay men • neighborhood bar • dancing/DJ • 18+

## Bookstores & Retail Shops

**Renaissance Books & Gifts** 1337 E. Montclair **883-5161** 10am-7pm, noon-5pm Sun • women's/alternative

## Erotica

**Bolivar Road News** 4030 N. Bolivar Rd. 833-3354

## St. Joseph (816)

### BARS & NIGHTCLUBS

**Club 705** 705 Esmond St. **364-9748**
5pm-1:30am, clsd Sun • lesbians/gay
men • neighborhood bar • dancing/DJ •
wheelchair access

## St. Louis (314)

### INFO LINES & SERVICES

**The Center** 2256 S. Grand Ave. **771-7995**
lesbigay/transgender community center

**Gay/Lesbian Hotline** 367-0084 6pm-
10pm

**PACT (People of All Colors Together)**
The Center **995-4683/997-9897** mtgs.
2nd Wed

**Steps Alano Club** 1935-A Park Ave. **436-
1858** call for mtg. schedule

### ACCOMMODATIONS

**A St. Louis Guesthouse** 1032-38 Allen
Ave. **773-1016** lesbians/gay men • located in historic Soulard district

**Brewers House B&B** 1829 Lami St. **771-
1542** lesbians/gay men • 1860s vintage
house

**Lafayette House B&B** 2156 Lafayette
Ave. **772-4429/(800) 641-8965** gay-
friendly • full brkfst • hot tub • kids/pets
ok • women-owned/run

**MotherSource Travels** 187 W. 19th St.,
Alton IL **569-5795/(618) 462-4051**
women only • reservation service

**Napoleon's Retreat B&B** 1815 Lafayette
Ave. **772-6979** lesbians/gay men •
restored 1880s townhouse

### BARS & NIGHTCLUBS

**Alton Metro** 602 Belle St., Alton IL **(618)
465-8687** 4pm-1:30am, from 2pm wknds
• mostly gay men • dancing/DJ • live
shows • wheelchair access

**Atlantis** 4901 Washington Ave. **367-4496**
8pm-1:30am Wed-Sat • popular • gay-
friendly • ladies' night Wed • dancing/DJ
• alternative

**Attitudes** 4100 Manchester **534-3858**
6pm-3am, clsd Sun-Mon • popular •
mostly women • dancing/DJ

**Char-Pei Lounge** 400 Mascoutah Ave.,
Belleville IL **(618) 236-0810** 6pm-2am •
lesbians/gay men • dancing/DJ • unconfirmed

**Clementine's** 2001 Menard **664-7869**
10am-1:30am, from 11am wknds, til midnight Sun • popular • mostly gay men •
leather • also restaurant • dinners &
wknd brunch • wheelchair access • $4-10

## St. Louis (314)

**Where the Girls Are:** Spread out
across the city, yet somewhat concentrated in the Central West End
near Forest Park. Younger, funkier
crowds hang out in the Delmar
Loop, west of the city limits, packed
with ethnic restaurants.

**Lesbigay Pride:** October: 772-8888.

**City Info:** 421-1023.

**Attractions:** Forest Park. Gateway
Arch. Laclede's Landing. Scott Joplin
House. Six Flags Over Mid-America.
St. Louis Cathedral.

**Best View:** Where else? Top of the
Gateway Arch in the Observation
Room.

**Weather:** 100% midwestern. Cold
winters—little snow and the temperatures can drop below 0°. Hot,
muggy summers raise temperatures
back up into the 100°s. Spring and
fall bring out the best in Mother
Nature.

**Transit:** County Cab: 991-5300.
Airport Express: 429-4950. The Bi-
State Bus System: 231-2345.

# St. Louis

**M**ost visitors come to St. Louis see the famous Gateway Arch, the tallest monument in the US at 630ft, designed by renowned architect Eero Saarinen.

After you've ridden the elevators in the Arch and seen the view, come down to earth and take a trip to historic Soulard, the "French Quarter of St. Louis." Established in 1779 by Madame and Monsieur Soulard as an open air market, it's now the place for great food and jazz. And the Market still attracts crowds—lesbigay and straight—on the weekends.

Laclede's Landing is also a popular attraction. While you're down by the Gateway Arch, treat yourself to riverfront dining aboard any of the several riverboat restaurants on the Mississippi. For accommodations, try **MotherSource Travels,** a women's B&B reservations service in nearby Alton, Illinois. Dining and shopping is most fun in the Central West End on Euclid Street between Delmar and Forest Park Blvds. or in the University City Loop area near Washington University.

Women-who-love-their-women-well-read rejoice! St. Louis has two bookstores of note: lesbigay **Our World Too** and **Left Bank Books,** an independent literary haven featuring extensive lesbian and gay sections. And check out the two women's bars: **Attitudes** is a loud-and-rowdy dance bar, and **Ernie's Class Act** is a mellower neighborhood place, perfect for drinks and conversation.

**Club Zips** 3145 W. Chain of Rocks Rd., Granite City IL **(618) 797-0700** 7pm-2am, til 3am Sat, 5pm-midnight Sun, clsd Mon-Tue • popular • lesbians/gay men • outdoor complex • live shows • videos

**The Complex/Angles** 3511 Chouteau **772-2645** 11am-3am, from 3pm Mon • popular • mostly gay men • multiple bars • patio • food served • $3-15 • wheelchair access

**Drake Bar** 3502 Papin St. **865-1400** 5pm-1:30am, clsd Sun • lesbians/gay men • live shows • wheelchair access

**Ernie's Class Act Restaurant & Lounge** 3756 S. Broadway **664-6221** 3pm-1:30am, from 11am Fri-Sat, clsd Sun • mostly women • dancing/DJ • transgender-friendly • food served • $5-7

**Faces Complex** 130 4th St., E. St. Louis IL **(618) 271-7410** 3pm-6am • mostly gay men • dancing/DJ • leather • live shows • 3 levels

**The Green Room** 1312 Washington Ave. **421-4221** til 3am, clsd Sun • gay-friendly • dancing/DJ • also 'Black List Lounge'

**Loading Zone** 16 S. Euclid **361-4119** 2pm-1:30am, clsd Sun • popular • lesbians/gay men • videos • wheelchair access

**Magnolia's** 5 S. Vandeventer **652-6500** 6pm-3am, dinner nightly • popular • mostly gay men • multi-racial • live shows • wheelchair access

**Tangerine** 1405 Washington Ave. **621-7335** 11am-1am, clsd Sun • gay-friendly • lounge • dancing/DJ • 18+ Tue • ladies' night Wed • food served

### CAFES

**Einstein Bagels** 2 N. Euclid Ave. **367-7999** 6am-8pm, 7am-5pm wknds

**Moka Be's** S. Grand & Arsenal **865-2009**

### RESTAURANTS

**Busch's Grove** 9160 Clayton Rd. **993-0011** lunch & dinner, clsd Sun-Mon

**Cafe Balaban** 405 N. Euclid Ave. **361-8085** popular • fine dining • some veggie • wonderful Sun brunch • full bar • wheelchair access • $10-16

**Dressel's** 419 N. Euclid **361-1060** great Welsh pub food • full bar

**Duff's** 392 N. Euclid Ave. **361-0522** clsd Mon • fine dining • some veggie • full bar • wheelchair access • $12-16

**Majestic Bar & Restaurant** 4900 Laclede **361-2011** 6am-1:30am • diner fare • $4-7

**On Broadway Bistro** 5300 N. Broadway **421-0087** 11am-3am • full bar • wheelchair access • $4-12

**Redel's** 310 De Baliviere **367-7005** hours vary • popular • some veggie • full bar • wheelchair access • $4-16

**Sunshine Inn** 8-1/2 S. Euclid Ave. **367-1413** 11:30am-9pm, from 10:30am Sun, clsd Mon • vegetarian • $5-8

**Ted Drewes Frozen Custard** 4224 S. Grand Blvd. **352-7376** seasonal • a St. Louis landmark

**Tony's** 410 Market St. **231-7007** Italian fine dining • reservations recommended

**Zinnia** 7491 Big Bend Blvd. **962-0572** lunch & dinner • bistro

### ENTERTAINMENT & RECREATION

**Wired Women Productions** 352-9473 concerts & events

### BOOKSTORES & RETAIL SHOPS

**Boxers** 310 N. Euclid Ave. **454-0209** 11am-6pm, 1pm-5pm Sun • boy underwear

**Daily Planet News** 243 N. Euclid Ave. **367-1333** 7am-8:30pm

**Friends & Luvers** 3550 Gravois **771-9405** 10am-10pm, noon-7pm Sun • novelties • videos • dating service

**Heffalump's** 387 N. Euclid Ave. **361-0544** 11am-8pm, til 10pm Fri-Sat, noon-5pm Sun • gifts

**Left Bank Books** 399 N. Euclid Ave. **367-6731** 10am-10pm, 11am-5pm Sun • strong lesbigay section

**Our World Too** 11 S. Vandeventer **533-5322** 10am-9:30pm, noon-8pm Sun • lesbigay

**Pages, Video & More** 10 N. Euclid Ave. **361-3420** 9am-8pm, til 5pm Sun

### PUBLICATIONS

**The News-Telegraph** 664-6411/(800) 301-5468

**SLAM!** 771-7739/752-3190 lesbigay newsmagazine

**Women's Yellow Pages of Greater St. Louis** 725-1452

### TRAVEL AGENTS

**Action Travel** 13035 Olive Blvd. #218 576-9736 IGLTA

**Dynamic Travel** 7750 Clayton Rd. #105 781-8400/(800) 237-4083 IGLTA

**First Discount Travel** 1749 Clarkson Rd., Chesterfield **532-8888** IGLTA

**Lafayette Square Travel Co.** 1801 Lafayette Ave. **776-8747** IGLTA

**Park Avenue Travel Services** 2347 Park Ave. #C **771-8031** IGLTA

**Patrik Travel** 22 N. Euclid Ave. # 101 **367-1468/(800) 678-8747** IGLTA

## SPIRITUAL GROUPS

**Agape Church** 2109 S. Spring St. **664-3588** 2pm Sun

**Dignity St. Louis** 6400 Minnesota Ave. **997-9897 x63** 7:30pm Sun

**MCC Living Faith** 6501 Wydown, Clayton **926-6387** 5pm Sun

**MCC of Greater St. Louis** 5000 Washington Pl. **361-3221** 9:30am & 11am Sun

**St. Louis Gay & Lesbian Chavurah** 77 Maryland Plaza (Central Reform Cong.) **361-3919**

**Trinity Episcopal Church** 600 N. Euclid Ave. **361-4655** 8am & 10:30am Sun

## EROTICA

**Cheap Trx** 3211 S. Grand **664-4011** body piercing

# MONTANA

## Billings (406)

### INFO LINES & SERVICES

**AA Gay/Lesbian** (at MCC location) **245-7066** 8pm Sat

### BARS & NIGHTCLUBS

**Monte Carlo** 2824 1st Ave. **259-3393** 10am-2am • gay-friendly • neighborhood bar

### RESTAURANTS

**Stella's Kitchen & Bakery** 110 N. 29th St. **248-3060** 6am-4pm, bakery til 6pm, clsd Sun • some veggie

### BOOKSTORES & RETAIL SHOPS

**Barjon's** 2718 3rd Ave. N. **252-4398** 9:30am-5:30pm, clsd Sun • spiritual • women-owned/run

### SPIRITUAL GROUPS

**Spirit of the Valley MCC** 645 Howard St. **245-7066** 11am Sun • moving at press time • call for new location

### EROTICA

**The Adult Shop** 2019 Minnesota Ave. **245-4293**

**Big Sky Books** 1203 1st Ave. N. **259-0051**

## Boulder (406)

### ACCOMMODATIONS

**Boulder Hot Springs Hotel & Retreat** **225-4339** gay-friendly • spiritual/recovery retreat • camping avail. • swimming • spas • food served • smokefree • call for info

## Bozeman (406)

### INFO LINES & SERVICES

**Lambda Alliance of Gay Men/Lesbians/Bisexuals** **994-4551** 3:30pm Sun • call for location

**Women's Center** Hamilton Hall, MSU **994-3836** some lesbian referrals

### ACCOMMODATIONS

**Gallatin Gateway Inn** 76405 Gallatin Rd., Gallatin Gateway **763-4672/(800) 676-3522** gay-friendly • dinner nightly • hot tub • swimming • non-smoking rms. avail. • wheelchair access • $60-135

# The River Inn

Bed & Breakfast,
Cowgirl Cabin
Sheepherder's Wagon

Secluded 100 year old
farmhouse on the banks of
the Yellowtone River

Spectacular River and
Mountain View

We guide hike, bike,
& canoe trips.

*Women Owned & Operated*

*4950 Highway 89 South*
**Livingston, Montana 59047**
www.wtp.net/go/riverinn
riverinn@alpinet.net

## (406) 222-2429

CAFES
**The Leaf & Bean** 35 W. Main **587-1580**
6:30am-10pm, til 11pm Fri-Sat • desserts
• live shows • wheelchair access •
women-owned/run

RESTAURANTS
**Spanish Peaks Brewery** 120 N. 19th St.
**585-2296** 11:30am-10:30pm, noon-10pm
Sun • Italian • some veggie • $8-15

## Butte (406)

ACCOMMODATIONS
**Skookum** 3541 Harrison Ave. **494-5353**
lesbians/gay men • kitchens • full bar &
restaurant • $32-37

BARS & NIGHTCLUBS
**Snookum's at the Skookum** 3541
Harrison Ave. **494-5353** noon-2am • les-
bians/gay men • also restaurant

RESTAURANTS
**Matt's Place** 2339 Placer **782-8049**
11:30am-7pm, clsd Sun-Mon • classic
soda fountain diner
**Pekin Noodle Parlor** 117 S. Main, 2nd
flr. **782-2217** 5pm-9pm, clsd Tue •
Chinese • some veggie • $3-7
**Pork Chop John's** 8 W. Mercury **782-0812**
10:30am-7:45pm, clsd Sun • $3-5
**Uptown Cafe** 47 E. Broadway **723-4735**
lunch & dinner • bistro • full bar • $15-
20

## Corwin Springs (406)

RESTAURANTS
**The Ranch Kitchen** Hwy. 89 **848-7891**
clsd Tue • lunch & dinner • some veggie
• $3-15

## Great Falls (406)

RESTAURANTS
**Black Diamond Bar & Supper Club** 64
Castner, Belt **277-4118** 5pm-10pm, clsd
Mon • steaks & seafood • 20 mi. from
Great Falls

SPIRITUAL GROUPS
**MCC Shepherd of the Plains** 1501 &
1505 17th Ave. SW **771-1070/771-1173**
11am Sun, 7pm Wed

EROTICA
**After Dark** 209 4th St. S. **771-7266**

# Helena (406)

INFO LINES & SERVICES
**PRIDE** 442-9322/(800) 610-9322 (IN MT)
info & newsletter

TRAVEL AGENTS
**Travel Montana** Dept. of Commerce
(800) 541-1447

# Livingston (406)

ACCOMMODATIONS
▲ **The River Inn** 4950 Hwy. 89 S. **222-2429**
gay-friendly • full brkfst • kitchen use •
horse-boarding avail.

# Missoula (406)

INFO LINES & SERVICES
**AA Gay/Lesbian** KC Hall 312 E. Pine
**523-7799** 9:30pm Wed
**Lambda Alliance (U of MT)** 243-5922
10am-4pm Mon-Fri
**Women's Resource Center (U of MT)**
University Ctr. #210, Campus Dr. **243-4153** 10am-3pm, clsd wknds

ACCOMMODATIONS
**Foxglove Cottage B&B** 2331 Gilbert Ave.
**543-2927** gay-friendly • swimming • gay-owned/run

BARS & NIGHTCLUBS
**Amvets Club** 225 Ryman **543-9174** noon-2am, more gay after 8pm • gay-friendly •
dancing/DJ

RESTAURANTS
**Black Dog Cafe** 138 W. Broadway **542-1138** lunch & dinner, dinner only Sat,
clsd Sun • vegetarian • wheelchair
access
**Heidelhaus/Red Baron Casino** 2620
Brooks **543-3200** 6am-11pm, til midnight
wknds, casino 24hrs • full bar • wheelchair access

ENTERTAINMENT & RECREATION
**Pangaea Expeditions** 721-7719 river
rafting in Montana • call for complete
calendar

BOOKSTORES & RETAIL SHOPS
**Freddy's Feed & Read** 1221 Helen Ave.
**549-2127** 7:30am-8pm, 9am-7pm Sat,
10am-5pm Sun • alternative books • deli
**Second Thought** 529 S. Higgins **549-2790** 6:30am-10pm • bookstore • cafe &
bakery • wheelchair access

**University Center Bookstore** Campus
Drive (U of MT) **243-4921** 8am-6pm, from
10am Sat, clsd Sun • gender studies section

EROTICA
**Fantasy for Adults Only** 210 E. Main St.
**543-7760** also 2611 Brooks Ave. 543-7510

# Ovando (406)

ACCOMMODATIONS
**Lake Upsata Guest Ranch** 793-5890
seasonal • gay-friendly • cabins • hot
tub • wildlife programs & outings • outdoor recreation • meals provided • $195

# Ronan (406)

ACCOMMODATIONS
**North Crow Vacation Ranch** 2360 North
Crow Rd. **676-5169** seasonal •
lesbians/gay men • cabin • tipis • camping • 80 mi. S. of Glacier Park • hot tub •
nudity • $10-20

# Three Forks (406)

ACCOMMODATIONS
**Sacajawea Inn** 5 N. Main St. **285-6515/(800) 821-7326** gay-friendly • food
served • wheelchair access • $69-99

## NEBRASKA

### Grand Island (308)

INFO LINES & SERVICES
**Helpline** 384-7474 24hrs • some gay referrals • crisis calls

ACCOMMODATIONS
**Midtown Holiday Inn** 2503 S. Locust 384-1330 gay-friendly • non-smoking rms. avail. • kids/pets ok • hot tub • also 'Images Pink Cadillac Lounge' • wheelchair access
**Relax Inn** 507 W. 2nd St. 384-1000 gay-friendly • non-smoking rms. avail. • wheelchair access

BARS & NIGHTCLUBS
**Desert Rose Saloon** 3235 S. Locust 381-8919 6pm-2am • gay-friendly • wheelchair access

RESTAURANTS
**Tommy's** 1325 S. Locust 381-0440 24hrs

GYMS & HEALTH CLUBS
**Health Plex Fitness Center** 2909 W. Hwy. 30 384-1110 gay-friendly

EROTICA
**Exclusively Yours Shop** 216 N. Locust 381-6984 adult toys • lingerie
**Sweet Dreams Shop** 217 W. 3rd St. 381-6349 10am-6pm, til 5pm Sat, clsd Sun • lingerie • adult toys

### Hastings (402)

INFO LINES & SERVICES
**GLB (Gay/Lesbian/Bisexual Alliance)** Health Center, Hastings College 461-7372

### Lincoln (402)

INFO LINES & SERVICES
**AA Gay/Lesbian** 28th & 'S' (at 'The Meeting Place') 438-5214 7:30pm Mon
**Crisis Center** 476-2110/475-7273 (24HRS)
**Nebraska Travel & Tourism** (800) 228-4307
**Women's Resource Center** Nebraska Union Rm. 340, UNL 472-2597 lesbian support services • wheelchair access
**Youth Talkline** 473-7932 7pm-midnight Fri-Sat • lesbigay info & referrals for ages 23 & under

BARS & NIGHTCLUBS
**Panic** 200 S. 18th St. 435-8764 4pm-1am, from 1pm wknds • lesbians/gay men • dancing/DJ • live shows • videos • wheelchair access
**The Q** 226 S. 9th 475-2269 8pm-1am, clsd Mon • lesbians/gay men • dancing/DJ • 18+ Tue • alternative Wed

ENTERTAINMENT & RECREATION
**Wimmin's Radio Show** KZUM (89.3 FM) 474-5086 12:30pm-3pm Sun • also 'TGI-Femme' 10am-noon Fri

BOOKSTORES & RETAIL SHOPS
**Avant Card** 1323 'O' St. 476-1918 hours vary

TRAVEL AGENTS
**Good Life Tour & Travel** 8200 Fletcher Ave. 467-3900/(800) 233-0404 IGTA
**MIC/Lincoln Travel** 233 N. 48th #F 466-1520

### Omaha (402)

INFO LINES & SERVICES
**AA Gay/Lesbian** 345-9916 call for mtg. schedule
**HGRA (Heartland Gay Rodeo Association)** 344-3103 contact David
**OPC (Omaha Players Club)** 451-7987 S/M education & play group • pansexual mtgs. • 2nd Sat 2pm
**Rainbow Outreach & Resource Center** 1719 Leavenworth St. 341-0330 6pm-9pm Mon-Fri, also noon-6pm Tue & Th, noon-6pm Sat • 24hr info
**River City Gender Alliance** 398-1255 7pm 1st Sat (at 'Hawthorne Suites') • for CD, TS & inquiring • all orientations • newsletter
**WomenSpace** annual women's music festival • newsletter • unconfirmed

BARS & NIGHTCLUBS
**The Chesterfield** 1901 Leavenworth St. 345-6889 2pm-1am • lesbians/gay men • dancing/DJ • live shows • food served • gay-owned/run • wheelchair access
**Club 15** 1421 Farnam 341-5705 10am-1am, from noon Sun • lesbians/gay men • dancing/DJ • live shows • wheelchair access • also cafe
**Club James Dean** 1507 Farnam 341-2500 3:30pm-1am • mostly women • dancing/DJ • karaoke

**D.C.'s Saloon** 610 S. 14th St. **344-3103**
3pm-1am, from 2pm wknds • mostly gay men • neighborhood bar • country/western • leather • live shows • wheelchair access

**Diamond Bar** 712 S. 16th St. **342-9595**
9am-1am, from noon Sun • mostly gay men • neighborhood bar • wheelchair access

**Gilligan's Bar** 1823 Leavenworth St. **449-9147** 2pm-1am, til 4am Fri-Sat • lesbians/gay men • neighborhood bar • karaoke • also restaurant • burgers

**The Max** 1417 Jackson **346-4110** 4pm-1am • popular • mostly gay men • 5 bars • dancing/DJ • live shows • videos • wheelchair access

### CAFES
**Neon Goose Cafe/Bar** 1012 S. 10th **341-2063** lunch & dinner, clsd Mon • some veggie • wheelchair access • $7-14 • unconfirmed

### RESTAURANTS
**French Cafe** 1013 Howard St. **341-3547** lunch & dinner, Sun brunch • full bar • $11-22

### BOOKSTORES & RETAIL SHOPS
**New Realities** 1026 Howard St. **342-1863** 11am-10pm, til 6pm Sun • progressive • wheelchair access

### PUBLICATIONS
**New Voice** 556-9907

### SPIRITUAL GROUPS
**MCC of Omaha** 819 S. 22nd St. **345-2563** 9am & 10:30am Sun • also support groups

**Mishpachat Chaverim** 959 S. 51st St. (Emintove) **551-0510**

### EROTICA
**Custom Leather Works** 3026 20th St. **344-7638** noon-8pm, til 10pm Sat, til 6pm Sun

**Nuclear Ink** 1116 Jackson St. (at 'Atomic') **348-1997** from 2pm, clsd Mon • tattoos

**Villain's** 3629 'Q' St. **731-0202** tattooing • piercing • leather

## Scotts Bluff                    (308)

### INFO LINES & SERVICES
**Panhandle Gay/Lesbian Support Service** 635-8488 social/support

## NEVADA

## Carson City

### INFO LINES & SERVICES
**NV AIDS Hotline** 505 E. King St. #304 **(800) 842-2437** 8am-10pm • community info & resources • Spanish spoken

## Lake Tahoe                    (702)

*(see also Lake Tahoe, CA)*

### ACCOMMODATIONS
**BeachSide Inn & Suites** 930 Park Ave., S. Lake Tahoe CA **(916) 544-2400/(800) 884-4920** gay-friendly • walk to casinos & private beach access • outdoor spa & sauna • $35-100

**Haus Bavaria** 831-6122/(800) 731-6222 gay-friendly • mountain views • full brkfst • $125-155

**Lakeside B&B** 831-8281 mostly gay men • full brkfst • near great skiing • hot tub • sauna • smokefree • kids/pets ok

### BARS & NIGHTCLUBS
**Faces** 270 Kingsbury Grade, Stateline **588-2333** from 9pm Mon-Wed, from 5pm Th-Sun • lesbians/gay men • dancing/DJ

## Las Vegas                    (702)

### INFO LINES & SERVICES
**Alcoholics Together** 2630 State St. **737-0035** 12:15pm & 8pm, 9pm Tue, noon wknds • lesbigay club for 12-step recovery programs

**Gay/Lesbian Community Ctr.** 912 E. Sahara Ln. **733-9800** 10am-8pm, til 5pm wknds

**Gender Concepts** 1121 Almond Tree Ln. (at Comm. Counseling Ctr.) **639-9458** 7pm 1st & 3rd Mon • support group

### ACCOMMODATIONS
**Center Strip Inn** 3688 Las Vegas Blvd. S. **739-6066/(800) 777-7737** on the Strip

**Las Vegas Private B&B** 384-1129 mostly gay men • swimming • hot tub • sauna • nudity • smokefree • pets ok

**Oasis Guest House** 662 Rolling Green Dr. **369-1396** lesbians/gay men • swimming

### BARS & NIGHTCLUBS
**Angles** 4633 Paradise Rd. **791-0100** 24hrs • mostly gay men • neighborhood bar • videos • wheelchair access

**Angles Annex** 4633 Paradise Rd. (enter rear) **791-1947** from 6pm Th-Sat • popular • mostly women • dancing/DJ

**Backdoor** 1415 E. Charleston **385-2018** 24hrs • mostly gay men • neighborhood bar • dancing/DJ • wheelchair access

**Backstreet** 5012 S. Arville St. **876-1844** lesbians/gay men • dancing/DJ • country/western • wheelchair access

**Badlands Saloon** 953 E. Sahara #22-B **792-9262** 24hrs • mostly gay men • dancing/DJ • country/western • wheelchair access

**Buffalo** 4640 Paradise Rd. **733-8355** 24hrs • popular • mostly gay men • leather • videos • wheelchair access

**Choices** 1729 E. Charleston **382-4791** 24hrs • mostly gay men • neighborhood bar • live shows • wheelchair access

**Gipsy** 4605 Paradise Rd. **731-1919/796-8793** from 10pm • popular • mostly gay men • dancing/DJ • call for women's nights

**Goodtimes** 1775 E. Tropicana (at 'Liberace Plaza') **736-9494** 24hrs • mostly gay men • more women Mon • neighborhood bar • dancing/DJ • piano bar

**Inferno** 3340 S. Highland Ave. **734-7336** 24hrs • mostly gay men • dancing/DJ • live shows • videos

**The Las Vegas Eagle** 3430 E. Tropicana **458-8662** 24hrs • mostly gay men • leather • DJ Wed & Fri

**Tropical Island** 3430 E. Tropicana **456-5525** 6pm-2am, 4pm-midnight Sun, clsd Wed-Sat • mostly women • neighborhood bar

## CAFES

**Cyber City Cafe** Flamingo & Maryland **732-2001** 24hrs • Internet cafe • beer/wine

**Mariposa Cafe** 4643 S. Paradise Rd. **650-9009** 24hrs

## RESTAURANTS

**Coyote Cafe** (at 'MGM Grand') **891-7349** 8:30am-11pm • the original Santa Fe chef • $8-13

**Garlic Cafe** 3650 S. Decatur Blvd. **221-0266** dinner, lunch Mon-Fri • int'l • full bar • $8 & up

**Rocky's of New York** 6370 Windy St. **896-1993** 5pm-midnight, clsd Sun • lesbians/gay men • live shows • some veggie • wheelchair access • $9-15

## ENTERTAINMENT & RECREATION

**Crystal Palace Skate Center** 4680 Boulder Hwy. **458-7107** 8:30pm-11:30pm 3rd Mon • gay/lesbian skate

**Lesbigay Cafe** KLAV AM1230 **391-7960** 8pm-10m Mon • radio show

## BOOKSTORES & RETAIL SHOPS

**Borders** 2323 S. Decatur **258-0999** 9am-11pm, 9am-9pm Sun • lesbigay section • cafe • call for gay events • wheelchair access

## Las Vegas                    (702)

**Lesbigay Pride:** June: 225-3389.

**City Info:** Chamber of Commerce: 457-4664. Convention & Visitors Authority: 892-0711.

**Attractions:** Downtown Las Vegas (Glitter Gulch). Guinness World Records Museum. Imperial Palace Auto Collection. Liberace Museum. University of Nevada–Las Vegas Museum of Natural History.

**Transit:** Western Cab: 382-7100. Yellow Cab: 873-2000. Various resorts have their own shuttle service. CAT (Citizens Area Transit): 228-7433.

**Cat O'Nine Tails Boutique** 1717 S. Decatur Blvd. (at 'Fantastic Indoor Swap Meet') 258-9754 10am-6pm Fri-Sun • contemporary evening wear • transgender-friendly

**Get Booked** 4640 Paradise #15 737-7780 10am-midnight, til 2am Fri-Sat • lesbigay/feminist • videos

**Lock, Stock & Leather** 4640 Paradise Rd. #10 796-9801 3pm-10pm, noon-2am Fri-Sat, from 4pm Sun • bearwear & leather

PUBLICATIONS

**Las Vegas Bugle** 369-6260
**Night Beat** 734-7223
**Q-Tribe** 871-6981 monthly newspaper
**Women's Yellow Pages of Southern Nevada** 362-6507

TRAVEL AGENTS

**Cruise One** 5030 Paradise Dr. #B-101 256-8082/(800) 200-3012 IGLTA
**Good Times Travel** 624 N. Rainbow 878-8900/(800) 638-1066
**Players Express Vacations** 2980 W. Meade Ave. #A (800) 667-5607

SPIRITUAL GROUPS

**Christ Church Episcopal** 2000 Maryland Pkwy. 735-7655 8am, 10:30am & 6pm Sun • 10am & 6pm Wed
**Dignity Las Vegas** 1420 E. Harmon Ave. 593-5395 5:30pm Sat
**MCC of Las Vegas** 3616 Lake Mead Blvd. 369-4380 1pm Sun
**Valley Outreach Synagogue** 2 S. Pecos 436-4900 8pm 1st Fri

EROTICA

**Price Video** 4640 Paradise Rd. #11 734-1342
**Pure Pleasure Book & Video** 3177 S. Highland 369-8044 24hrs
**Rancho Adult Entertainment Center** 4820 N. Rancho #D 645-6104 24hrs
**Tattoos R Us** 320 E. Charleston #E 387-6969 piercing & tattoo studio
**Video West** 5785 W. Tropicana 248-7055 gay-owned/run

**Laughlin**

(see Bullhead City, AZ)

## Reno (702)

INFO LINES & SERVICES

**Cornerstones Gay/Lesbian AA** 2850-J Wrondel Way 673-9633 noon daily, 6pm Tue & Fri, 8pm Fri & Sat

BARS & NIGHTCLUBS

**1099 Club** 1099 S. Virginia 329-1099 24hrs wknds • popular • lesbians/gay men • neighborhood bar • live shows • wheelchair access
**Bad Dolly's** 535 E. 4th 348-1983 3pm-3am, 24hrs Fri-Sun • popular • mostly women • dancing/DJ • live shows • wheelchair access
**Five Star Saloon** 132 West St. 329-2878 24hrs • mostly gay men • dancing/DJ • wheelchair access
**The Quest** 210 Commercial Row 333-2808 noon-5am, 24hrs Fri-Sat • mostly gay men • dancing/DJ • live shows
**Shouts** 145 Hillcrest St. 829-7667 10am-2am • gay-friendly • neighborhood bar • wheelchair access
**Visions** 340 Kietzke Ln. 786-5455 noon-4am, 24hrs Fri-Sun • popular • mostly gay men • dancing/DJ • theme nights • also 'Glitter Palace' gift shop wknds

BOOKSTORES & RETAIL SHOPS

**Grapevine Books** 1450 S. Wells Ave. 786-4869 10am-6pm, til 8pm Fri-Sat, til 4pm Sun • lesbigay/feminist • wheelchair access

PUBLICATIONS

**Reno Informer** 747-8833
**Sierra Voice** fax for info: 322-6513

TRAVEL AGENTS

**Deluxe Travel/American Express** 102 California Ave. 686-7000 IGLTA

SPIRITUAL GROUPS

**MCC of the Sierras** 3405 Gulling Wy. (at 'Temple Sinai') 829-8602 5pm Sun

EROTICA

**The Chocolate Walrus** 2490 Wrondell 825-2267 10:30am-6:30pm Fri, til 5pm Sat, clsd Sun • videos • novelties
**Fantasy Faire** 1298 S. Virginia 323-6969 leather • fetishwear
**Suzie's** 195 Kietzke Ln. 786-8557 24hrs

## NEW HAMPSHIRE

### Ashland (603)

ACCOMMODATIONS
▲ **Country Options** 27-29 N. Main St. **968-7958** gay-friendly • full brkfst • smokefree

### Bethlehem (603)

ACCOMMODATIONS
▲ **Highlands Inn 869-3978** a lesbian paradise • women only • hot tub • swimming • 15 miles of walking & ski trails • wheelchair access • IGLTA • $55-110 (20% off for 7 nights—except holidays)

### Bridgewater (603)

ACCOMMODATIONS
**The Inn on Newfound Lake** 1030 Mayhew Trpk. Rte. 3-A **744-9111/(800) 745-7990** gay-friendly • swimming • also restaurant • 5pm-9pm • full bar • $65-185

### Centre Harbor (603)

ACCOMMODATIONS
**Red Hill Inn 279-7001/(800) 573-3445** gay-friendly • overlooking Squam Lake & White Mtns. • also restaurant • wheelchair access • IGLTA

### Chocorua (603)

ACCOMMODATIONS
**Mount Chocorua View House** Rte. 16 **323-8350** gay-friendly • smokefree • kids ok • 10 mi. S. of N. Conway

### Concord (603)

INFO LINES & SERVICES
**Gay Info Line 224-1686** 6pm-8pm, clsd Tue & wknds • active social & support groups • also 'Citizens Alliance for Gay/Lesbian Rights'
**Travel & Tourism Office 271-2666/(800) 386-4664**

PUBLICATIONS
**WomenWise 225-2739** published by NH Federation of Feminist Health Centers • also many support groups

# COUNTRY OPTIONS

**A SMALL BED & BREAKFAST CONVENIENTLY LOCATED IN CENTRAL NEW HAMPSHIRE'S LAKES REGION AT THE FOOTHILLS OF THE WHITE MOUNTAINS**

*Four light airy rooms, comfortably furnished with antiques. Share two Baths. Full Country breakfast included. Reasonable Rates year round. No smoking.*
*INNKEEPERS:*
*Sandra Ray*
*& Nancy Puglisi*

27-29 N. MAIN ST., ASHLAND, NEW HAMPSHIRE 03217 • (603) 968-7958

# The Highlands Inn

## A LESBIAN PARADISE

*Secluded, romantic mountain hideaway on 100 scenic acres, centrally located between Boston, Montreal & the Maine coast. Close to Provincetown.*

*Experience the warm hospitality of a New England country inn YOUR way... a lesbian paradise!*

## THE HIGHLANDS INN
PO BOX 118WT
VALLEY VIEW LANE
BETHLEHEM, NEW HAMPSHIRE 03574
603 • 869 • 3978
*See Our Listing Under New Hampshire*

EDITOR'S CHOICE AWARD 1995 OUT & ABOUT

## SPIRITUAL GROUPS
**Spirit of the Mountain** 177 N. Main (1st Cong. Church) 225-5491 5pm 2nd & 4th Sun

# Dover (603)

## INFO LINES & SERVICES
**Gay/Lesbian/Bisexual/Transgender Helpline** 141 Central St. (Quaker Mtg. House) 743-4292 7pm Sun, support group

## ACCOMMODATIONS
**Payne's Hill B&B** 141 Henry Law Ave. 742-4139 mostly women • smokefree • $49-69

## CAFES
**Cafe on the Corner** 478 Central Ave. 742-0414 8am-10pm • wheelchair access • lesbian-owned/run

# Durham (603)

## INFO LINES & SERVICES
**The UNH Alliance** 862-4522 6:30pm Mon

# Exeter (603)

## SPIRITUAL GROUPS
**United Church of Christ** 21 Front St., nr. Court St. (Exeter Cong. Church) 772-6221 10am Sun

# Fitzwilliam (603)

## ACCOMMODATIONS
**Hannah Davis House** 585-3344 gay-friendly • full brkfst • smokefree • $60-115

# Franconia (603)

## ACCOMMODATIONS
**Blanche's B&B** 351 Easton Valley Rd. 823-7061 gay-friendly • full brkfst • smokefree

**Bungay Jar B&B & Cottage** 823-7775/(800) 421-0701 gay-friendly • full brkfst • saunas • smokefree • wheelchair access • $75-95

**Foxglove, A Country Inn** 823-8840 gay-friendly • food served

**The Horse & Hound Inn** 205 Wells Rd. 823-5501 clsd April & Nov • gay-friendly • full brkfst • kids/pets ok • restaurant open for dinner except Tue • $13-18

**Raynor's Motor Lodge** Main St. (Rtes. 142 & 18) 823-9586 gay-friendly • swimming • non-smoking rms. avail. • $45-65

# Franklin (603)

## ACCOMMODATIONS
**The Englewood** 69 Cheney St. 934-1017 mostly women • full brkfst • smokefree • lesbian-owned/run

# Glen (603)

## ACCOMMODATIONS
**Will's Inn** Rte. 302 383-6757 gay-friendly • swimming • non-smoking rms avail. • limited wheelchair access

# Hart's Location (603)

## ACCOMMODATIONS
**The Notchland Inn** Rte. 302 374-6131/(800) 866-6131 gay-friendly • country inn on 400 acres • brkfst & dinner avail. • fireplaces • full bar • $135-260

# Hillsborough (603)

## ACCOMMODATIONS
**The Inn at Maplewood Farm** 464-4242 gay-friendly • full brkfst • $75-115

# Jackson (603)

## ACCOMMODATIONS
**Wildcat Inn & Tavern** Rte. 16A 383-4245 gay-friendly • landscaped gardens • tavern 3pm-midnight wknds • restaurant 6pm-9pm • $14-23

# Keene (603)

## ACCOMMODATIONS
**The Post and Beam B&B** Center St., Sullivan 847-3330 gay-friendly • full brkfst • wheelchair access • women-owned/run • $50-90

## BOOKSTORES & RETAIL SHOPS
**Oasis** 45 Central Square 352-5355 10am-9pm, 11am-6pm Sun • alternative spiritual books & supplies

# Lancaster (603)

## RESTAURANTS
**S&S Lancaster Restaurant** Rte. 3 788-2802 6am-9pm, til 10pm Th-Sat • American/Chinese • full bar

## Manchester (603)

### BARS & NIGHTCLUBS
**Club Merri-Mac** 201 Merrimack **623-9362** 2pm-1:30am • popular • lesbians/gay men • dancing/DJ • private club

**Front Runner/Manchester Civic Club** 22 Fir St. **623-6477** 3pm-1:30am • popular • lesbians/gay men • dancing/DJ • transgender-friendly • live shows • private club

**Sporters** 361 Pine St. **668-9014** 5pm-1am, from 3pm Sun • mostly gay men • neighborhood bar • dancing/DJ

### TRAVEL AGENTS
**Martinelli Travel** Appletree Mall, Londonderry **434-4989/(800) 324-4989** IGLTA

## Peterborough (603)

### INFO LINES & SERVICES
**Gender Talk North** 924-8828

## Portsmouth (603)

### BARS & NIGHTCLUBS
**Desert Hearts** 948 Rte. 1 Bypass **431-5400** from 8pm, from 6pm Sun, clsd Mon-Tue • mostly women • dancing/DJ • private club • wheelchair access

### TRAVEL AGENTS
**Worldwise Travel Co.** 10 Vaughan Mall, #14 **430-9060/(800) 874-9473** IGLTA

## Sugar Hill (603)

### RESTAURANTS
**Polly's Pancake Parlor** Rte.117 (exit 38 off 93 N.) **823-5575** 7am-3pm, til 7pm wknds

## NEW JERSEY

## Asbury Park (732)

### INFO LINES & SERVICES
**Gay/Lesbian Community Center** 626 Bangs Ave. **774-1809/775-4429** call for events

### BARS & NIGHTCLUBS
**Bond Street Bar** 208 Bond St. **776-9766** 4pm-midnight, til close Fri-Sat • mostly women • neighborhood bar

**Down the Street** 230 Cookman Ave. **988-2163** 2pm-2am (seasonal) • popular • mostly gay men • beach crowd • dancing/DJ • live shows • food served • videos • volleyball • wheelchair access

### RESTAURANTS
**Raspberry Cafe** 16 Main Ave. **988-0833** brkfst & lunch

**The Talking Bird** 224 Cookman **775-9708** lunch & dinner, til 4am Fri-Sat • $4-9

### SPIRITUAL GROUPS
**Trinity Episcopal Church** 503 Asbury Ave. **775-5084** 8am & 10am Sun • call for Integrity mtg. info

## Atlantic City (609)

### INFO LINES & SERVICES
**New Jersey Division of Travel & Tourism** (800) 537-7397

### ACCOMMODATIONS
**The Rose Cottage** 161 S. Westminster Ave. **345-8196** lesbians/gay men • near bars & casinos

**Surfside Resort Hotel** 18 S. Mt. Vernon Ave. **347-0808/(888) 277-7873** lesbians/gay men • small, upscale straight-friendly hotel • sundeck • also restaurant in summer

### BARS & NIGHTCLUBS
**Brass Rail Bar & Grill** (at 'Surfside Resort Hotel') **348-0192** 24hrs • popular • lesbians/gay men • women's night Fri • neighborhood bar • live shows • food served

**Ladies 2000 784-8341** scheduled parties for women by women • call for times & locations

**Reflections** 181 South Carolina Ave. **348-1115** 24hrs • lesbians/gay men • neighborhood bar • dancing/DJ • videos • wheelchair access

**Studio Six Video Dance Club** (upstairs at 'Brass Rail') **348-3310** 10pm-6am • popular • lesbians/gay men • dancing/DJ • live shows • videos

### RESTAURANTS
**White House Sub Shop** 2301 Arctic Ave. **345-1564** 10am-10pm, til 11pm Fri-Sat

### TRAVEL AGENTS
**Schreve Lazar Travel** (at 'Bally's Park Place Casino Hotel', Boardwalk & Park Place) **348-1189/(800) 322-8280**

## Bloomingdale (201)

### INFO LINES & SERVICES
**Gal-a-vanting** 838-5318 sponsors women's parties • call for details

## Boonton (201)

### BARS & NIGHTCLUBS
**Connexions** 202 Myrtle Ave. **263-4000** 8pm-close Wed-Sat • lesbians/gay men • ladies night Wed • dancing/DJ • food served

## Brick (908)

### TRAVEL AGENTS
**Uniglobe Monarch Travel** 291 Herbertsville Rd. **840-2233** IGLTA

## Cape May (609)

### ACCOMMODATIONS
**The Virginia Hotel** 25 Jackson St. **884-5700/(800) 732-4236** gay-friendly • also 'The Ebbitt Room' restaurant • seafood/cont'l • IGLTA

## Cherry Hill (609)

### SPIRITUAL GROUPS
**Unitarian Universalist Church** 2916 Chapel Ave. (school) **667-3618** 10:15am Sun

## Clark (908)

### TRAVEL AGENTS
**Ambassador World Travel** 118 Westfield Ave. #7 **388-9500** IGLTA

## Clifton (201)

### RESTAURANTS
**Rutt's Hut Clifton** 417 River Rd. **779-8615** til 11pm, til 1am Fri-Sat • hot dogs & onion rings

### TRAVEL AGENTS
**Travel Four** 1033 Rte. 46 E. #A101 **473-0066** IGLTA

## Denville (201)

### BOOKSTORES & RETAIL SHOPS
**Perrin & Treggett Booksellers** 3130 Rte. 10 W., Denville Commons **328-8811/(800) 770-8811** 10am-9pm, til 6pm Sat, noon-5pm Sun • large lesbigay section

## Edison (908)

### SPIRITUAL GROUPS
**New Jersey's Lesbian & Gay Havurah** 650-1010

## Fanwood (908)

### TRAVEL AGENTS
**Village Travel** 322-8700 IGLTA

## Florence (609)

### EROTICA
**Florence Book Store** Rte. 130 S., 4 mi S. of Rte. 206 **499-9853**

## Florham Park (201)

### TRAVEL AGENTS
**Florham Park Travel** 15 James St. **377-1300** IGLTA

## Garwood (908)

### TRAVEL AGENTS
**Unique Travel** 331 South Ave. **789-3303** IGLTA

## Hazlet (908)

### TRAVEL AGENTS
**Galaxsea Cruises/Travel** 3048 Rte. 35 (K-Mart shopping ctr.) **335-1000/(800) 331-7245** IGLTA

## Hoboken (201)

### BARS & NIGHTCLUBS
**Excalibur** 1000 Jefferson St. **795-1023** 9pm-3am, clsd Mon-Wed • popular • lesbians/gay men • dancing/DJ • live shows • wheelchair access

### RESTAURANTS
**Maxwell's** 1039 Washington St. **656-9632** 5pm-2am, til 3am Fri-Sat • mostly gay men • dancing/DJ • Italian/American • live shows • wheelchair access • $7-12 • unconfirmed

## Jersey City (201)

### BARS & NIGHTCLUBS
**Uncle Joe's** 154 1st St. **659-6999** 9pm-2am, til 3pm Fri-Sat, from 4pm Sun • mostly gay men • dancing/DJ • neighborhood bar • Jersey girls night Sun

### RESTAURANTS
**Plato's** 310 12th St. **653-2585** 5pm-11pm • full bar

### SPIRITUAL GROUPS
**Christ United Methodist Church** Tonnele Ave. & JFK Blvd. **332-8996** also support groups

## Lambertville (609)

### ACCOMMODATIONS
**York Street House B&B** 42 York St. **397-3007** gay-friendly • smokefree • IGLTA • lesbian-owned/run • $65-150

### EROTICA
**Joy's Books** 103 Springbrook Ave. **397-2907**

## Livingston (201)

### TRAVEL AGENTS
**Travel With Eileen** 31 Cornell Dr. **992-7238** IGLTA

## Long Branch (201)

### BARS & NIGHTCLUBS
**Pharaoh's Beach Club** 115 Ocean Ave. **933-2151** Mon, Wed & Sat only • on the boardwalk

## Madison (201)

### BOOKSTORES & RETAIL SHOPS
**Pandora Book Peddlers** 9 Waverly Pl. **822-8388** 10am-6pm, til 7:30pm Th, til 5pm Sat, clsd Sun-Mon • feminist bookstore & book club

## Maplewood (201)

### SPIRITUAL GROUPS
**Dignity Metro New Jersey** 550 Ridgewood Rd. (St. George's Episcopal Church) **857-4040** 8pm 1st Sun (mtg.) & 4pm 3rd Sun (service)

## Montclair (201)

### INFO LINES & SERVICES
**Crossroads Real Estate Referral Network (800) 442-9735** non-profit lesbigay realtor referrals

### BOOKSTORES & RETAIL SHOPS
**Cohen's** 635 Bloomfield Ave. **744-2399** 6am-8pm, til 2pm Sun • magazines • cafe

### EROTICA
**Dressing for Pleasure** 590 Valley Rd. **746-5466** lingerie • latex • leather

## Morris Plains (201)

### TRAVEL AGENTS
**Frankel Travel** 60 E. Hanover Ave. **455-1111/(800) 445-6433** IGLTA

## Morristown (201)

### INFO LINES & SERVICES
**GAAMC Gay/Lesbian Youth in NJ Helpline 285-1595** 7:30pm-10:30pm • mtgs. 1:30pm-4:30pm Sat • call for location

**Gay Activist Alliance in Morris County 285-1595** 7:30pm-10:30pm • mtgs./activities 8:30pm Mon at 21 Normandy Hts. Rd. • also 'Women's Network'

## New Brunswick (732)

### INFO LINES & SERVICES
**Bisexual Network of NJ** (at Pride Ctr.) 7:30pm Tue
**Latinos Unidos** (at Pride Center) **846-2232** 8pm Mon
**Pride Center of New Jersey** 211 Livingston Ave. **846-2232** hours vary • call first
**Rutgers Univ. Lesbian/Gay/Bisexual Hotline** 932-7886 (seasonal) call for details

### RESTAURANTS
**The Frog and the Peach** 29 Dennis St. **846-3216** 11:30am-11pm, til 1am Th-Sat • full bar • wheelchair access • $40-60
**Stage Left** 5 Livingston Ave. **828-4444** 5:30pm-2am, from 4:30pm Sun • popular • lesbians/gay men • some veggie • full bar • $10-12

### SPIRITUAL GROUPS
**Dignity New Brunswick** 109 Nichol Ave. (Friends Mtg. House) **254-7942** 7:30pm 2nd Sat (service) & 7:30pm 3rd Fri (mtg.)

**MCC Christ the Liberator** 40 Davidson Rd. (St. Michael's Chapel), Piscataway **846-8227** 5:30pm Sun

## New Foundland (201)

TRAVEL AGENTS
**Berkshire Travel** 64 Oak Ridge Rd. **208-1200** IGLTA

## Newark (201)

BARS & NIGHTCLUBS
**First Choice** 533 Ferry St. **465-1944** 8pm-2am, til 3am Th-Sat • lesbians/gay men • more women Sat • dancing/DJ • mostly African-American • ladies night Th • unconfirmed

**Murphy's Tavern** 59 Edison Pl. **622-9176** 8pm-2am • lesbians/gay men • dancing/DJ • mostly African-American • wheelchair access

PUBLICATIONS
**The Lavender Express** 235-0585 newsletter w/resource & events listings

SPIRITUAL GROUPS
**Oasis** 621-8151 Tue evenings • lesbigay ministry of the Episcopal Church • call for info

## North Bergen (201)

TRAVEL AGENTS
**LifeStyles T&E** 8-75th St. **861-5059** IGLTA

## Oak Ridge (201)

BARS & NIGHTCLUBS
**Yacht Club** 5190 Berkshire Valley Rd. (5 mi. off of Rte. 15) **697-9780** 7pm-3am, from 2pm Sun • popular • lesbians/gay men • dancing/DJ • Sun BBQ • wheelchair access

## Orange (908)

INFO LINES & SERVICES
**Intergroup AA** 668-1882

## Paramus (201)

BARS & NIGHTCLUBS
**The Dragon Supper Club** 650 From Rd. **986-0800** 9pm-3am Sun only

# The Pillars B&B
### Located in the Gay Capital of New Jersey

A restored Victorian Mansion on a secluded acre of trees and wild-flowers, in the Van Wyck Brooks Historic District, offering the G/L/B/T guest an experierience of gracious hospitality. Breakfasts feature Swedish home baking or cook your own vegetarian meals. Afternoon and evening wine or other beverages. Private baths, terry robes, and many other amenities for your comfort and convenience. Easy access to NYC, Jersey Shore, Women's bars, major interstate highways. Ideal for the business traveller. Member IGLTA. Call for rates. Reservations required.

922 Central Ave. Plainfield, New Jersey 07060
(800) 888-Pillars • (908)753-0922
Website: http://www.bestinns.net/usa/nj/rdpillars.html
Email: pillars2@juno.com

## Perth Amboy (908)

BARS & NIGHTCLUBS
**The Other Half** Convery Blvd. (Rte. 35) & Kennedy **826-8877** 9pm-2am, til 3am Fri-Sat • popular • mostly gay men • dancing/DJ • unconfirmed

## Plainfield (908)

ACCOMMODATIONS
▲ **The Pillars** 922 Central Ave. **753-0922/(888) PILLARS (745-5277)** gay-friendly • Georgian/Victorian mansion • smokefree • infants & kids over 12 ok • dogs ok (call first) • IGLTA

BARS & NIGHTCLUBS
**The Rusty Spigot** 308 Watchung Ave. **755-4000** noon-1am, til 2am Fri-Sat • gay-friendly • neighborhood bar

## Princeton (609)

TRAVEL AGENTS
**Edwards Travel Service** 8 S. Tulane St. **924-4443/(800) 669-9692**

## Ramsey (201)

TRAVEL AGENTS
**Liberty Travel** 69 Spring St. **934-3778** IGLTA

## Red Bank (908)

INFO LINES & SERVICES
**Monmouth Ocean Transgender Infoline** 219-9094 mtgs. • support

BOOKSTORES & RETAIL SHOPS
**Earth Spirit** 16 W. Front St. 842-3855 10am-6pm, til 8pm Fri, noon-5pm Sun • New Age center & bookstore • lesbigay sections

## Ringwood (201)

ACCOMMODATIONS
**Ensanmar** 2 Ellen Dr. **831-0898** women only • community retreat • support groups

## River Edge (201)

BARS & NIGHTCLUBS
**Feathers** 77 Kinder Kamack Rd. **342-6410** 9pm-2am, til 3am Sat • popular • mostly gay men • dancing/DJ • live shows • theme nights • unconfirmed

## Rocky Hill (609)

TRAVEL AGENTS
**Travel Registry** 127 Washington St. **921-6900/(800) 346-6901** IGLTA

## Rosemont (609)

RESTAURANTS
**The Cafe** 88 Kingwood-Stockton Rd. 397-4097 8am-3pm, dinner from 5pm Wed-Sat, clsd Mon • BYOB

## Sandy Hook

ENTERTAINMENT & RECREATION
**Sandy Hook Beach** Gateway Nat'l Recreation Area, parking lot 'G'

## Sayreville (908)

BARS & NIGHTCLUBS
**Colosseum** 7090 Rte. 9 (at Rte. 35 N.) **316-0670** 9pm-3am • lesbians/gay men • dancing/DJ • live shows
**Sauvage** 1 Victory Cir. **727-6619** 7pm-3am, from 4pm Sun • popular • mostly women • neighborhood bar • dancing/DJ • food served

## Somerdale (609)

BARS & NIGHTCLUBS
**Le Galaxy** Somerdale Rd. & White Horse Pike (Rte. 30) **435-0888** 8pm-close • lesbians/gay men • ladies night Tue

## Somerset (908)

BARS & NIGHTCLUBS
**The Den** 700 Hamilton St. **545-7329** 8pm-2am, from 7pm Sat, from 5pm Sun • popular • lesbians/gay men • dancing/DJ • country/western Sun & Tue • live shows • 18+ • wheelchair access

## South Orange (201)

TRAVEL AGENTS
**La Salle Travel Services** 70 Taylor Pl. **378-3400** IGLTA

## South Plainfield (908)

TRAVEL AGENTS
**Leisure Council** 754-1575
**Park Travel Agency** 2119 Park Ave. **756-3800** IGLTA

## Stockton (609)

ACCOMMODATIONS
**Woolverton Inn** 6 Wollverton Rd. **397-0802** gay-friendly • full brkfst • jacuzzi

## Teaneck (201)

INFO LINES & SERVICES
**First Tuesday** 61 Church St. (St. Paul's Lutheran Church) **779-1434** 7:30pm 1st Tue • lesbian social group

## Trenton (609)

BARS & NIGHTCLUBS
**Buddies Pub** 677 S. Broad St. **989-8566** 5pm-2am, from 6pm wknds • lesbians/gay men • dancing/DJ
**Center House Pub** 499 Center St. **599-9558** 4pm-2am, from 7pm wknds • lesbians/gay men • neighborhood bar • quiet conversation bar • garden patio

## Union City (201)

BARS & NIGHTCLUBS
**Nite Lite** 509 22nd St. **863-9515** 8pm-3am Wed-Sun • lesbians/gay men • dancing/DJ • live shows • gay-owned/run • unconfirmed

## Westfield (908)

TRAVEL AGENTS
**Turner World Travel** 560 Springfield Ave. **233-3900** IGLTA

## Williamstown (609)

TRAVEL AGENTS
**Friendly Travel** 309 Gordon Ave. **262-1111** IGLTA

## Woodbury (609)

INFO LINES & SERVICES
**AA Gay/Lesbian** (at 'Rainbow Place') **848-2455** 7pm Wed
**Rainbow Place** 1103 N. Broad **848-2455** 7pm-9pm Tue & 7:30pm-10pm Fri • info line • community center

TRAVEL AGENTS
**TM Group Travel Services** 875 Kings Hwy. #200 **853-1919** IGLTA

# NEW MEXICO

## Albuquerque (505)

INFO LINES & SERVICES
**AA Gay/Lesbian** 266-1900 call for times/locations • smokefree mtgs.
**Alternative Erotic Lifestyles** 345-6484 pansexual S/M group
**Bi's R Us** 836-5239 women's social network
**Common Bond Community Center** 4013 Silver St. SE 266-8041 6pm-9pm
**New Mexico Outdoors** 822-1093 active lesbigay outdoors group
**Sirens** 877-7245 women's motorcycle club • also sponsors Summer Solistice event
**UNM Women's Resource Center** 1160 Mesa Vista Hall NV 277-3716 8am-5pm, clsd wknds • some lesbian outreach

ACCOMMODATIONS
**Hacienda Antigua Retreat** 6708 Tierra Dr. NW 345-5399/(800) 484-2385 x9954 gay-friendly • full brkfst • hot tub • swimming • smokefree • kids 3+ yrs ok • gay-owned
▲ **Hateful Missy & Granny Butch's Boudoir & Manure Emporium** 29 Jara Millo Loop, Vequita 243-7063/(800) 397-2482 lesbians/gay men • full brkfst • hot tub • kitchen access
**Mountain View** 296-7277 mostly women • full brkfst wknds • smokefree • kids ok • wheelchair access • lesbian-owned/run
**Nuevo Dia** 11110 San Rafael Ave. NE 856-7910 lesbians/gay men • hot tub • kids ok
**The Rainbow Lodge** 115 Frost Rd., Sandia Park 281-7100 mtn. retreat • lesbians/gay men • panoramic views • full brkfst • smokefree • kids ok (call first) • pets ok
**Rio Grande House** 3100 Rio Grande Blvd. NW 345-0120 gay-friendly • landmark adobe residence close to Old Town • full brkfst • non-smoking rms avail. • older kids ok • pets ok (call first)
**Tara Cotta** 3118 Rio Grande Blvd. NW 344-9443 gay-friendly • hot tub • nudity ok • smokefree • small dogs ok • priv. patio • gay-owned/run • $70-85
**W.E. Mauger Estate** 701 Roma Ave. NW 242-8755 gay-friendly • intimate Queen Anne residence • full brkfst

**W.J. Marsh House** 301 Edith SE **247-1001/(800) 956-2774** gay-friendly • full brkfst • shared bath • women-owned/run • $60-120

**Wyndham Albuquerque Hotel 843-7000/(800) 227-1117** gay-friendly • swimming • also 'Rojo Bar & Grill'

## BARS & NIGHTCLUBS

**Albuquerque Mining Co. (AMC)** 7209 Central Ave. NE **255-4022** 3pm-2am, til midnight Sun • popular • mostly gay men • dancing/DJ Mon

**Albuquerque Social Club** 4021 Central Ave. NE (rear alley) **255-0887** noon-2am, til midnight Sun • popular • lesbians/gay men • dancing/DJ • private club

**Foxes Lounge** 8521 Central Ave. NE **255-3060** 10am-2am, noon-midnight Sun • mostly gay men • dancing/DJ • live shows • wheelchair access

**Legends West** 6132 4th St. NW **343-9793** 4pm-2am, from 6pm Sat, til midnight Sun, clsd Mon • lesbians/gay men • dancing/DJ

**The Pulse** 4100 Central SE **255-3334** 8pm-2am, til mid Sun • mostly gay men • dancing/DJ

**The Ranch** 8900 Central SE **275-1616** 11am-2am, til midnight Sun • mostly gay men • dancing/DJ • country/western • also 'Cuffs' leather bar inside • wheelchair access

## CAFES

**Cafe Intermezzo** 3513 Central NE **265-2556** 10am-11pm, til midnight Fri-Sat • sandwiches • salads • beer/wine

**Emma's Silvertone Cafe** 2201 Silver Ave. SE **255-8728** 8am-10pm, til midnight Fri-Sat, til 5pm Sun • women-only events 6pm Sun • plenty veggie • $8-10

## RESTAURANTS

**Chef du Jour** 119 San Pasquale SW **247-8998** 11am-2pm, clsd wknds • plenty veggie • wheelchair access • $4-9

**Double Rainbow** 3416 Central SE **255-6633** 6:30am-midnight • plenty veggie • wheelchair access • $4-8

**Frontier** 2400 Central SE **266-0550** 24hrs • good brkfst burritos

## ENTERTAINMENT & RECREATION

**Women in Movement** 899-3627 production company • Memorial Day festival

**(505) 861-3328**     **(800) 397-2482**

Rita Long

Butch Young

## HATEFUL MISSY AND GRANNY BUTCH'S ALL NEW BOUDOIR AND **MANURE** EMPORIUM

*A rather queer Bed & Breakfast*

▼

Relax and forget your worries on more than 12 acres of heaven in a splendid adobe farmhouse with views to die for and zillions of birds for you birdwatchers

A tasteful, yet irreverent Bed and Breakfast reminiscent of Miss Kitty's Saloon

WE'VE MOOOVED TO THE COUNTRY AN HOUR SOUTH OF ALBUQUERQUE WHERE THE GRAVY'S STILL LUMPY BUT THE BEDS AIN'T.

## BOOKSTORES & RETAIL SHOPS
**Full Circle Books** 2205 Silver SE 266-0022/(800) 951-0053 9am-8pm, til 5pm Sun, til 6pm Mon • feminist/lesbian

**In Crowd** 3106 Central SE 268-3750 10am-6pm, noon-4pm Sun • lesbigay art • clothing • accessories • wheelchair access

**Newsland Books** 2112 Central Ave. SE 242-0694 8am-9pm

**Page One** 11018 Montgomery NE 294-2026/(800) 521-4122 7am-11:30pm

**Sisters and Brothers Bookstore** 4011 Silver Ave. SE 266-7317/(800) 687-3480 (ORDERS ONLY) 10am-6pm, til 8pm Fri-Sat • lesbigay

## PUBLICATIONS
**Out! Magazine** 243-2540 lesbigay news-magazine

**Women's Voices** 875-0112 feminist newspaper

## TRAVEL AGENTS
**All World Travel** 1930 Juan Tabo NE #D 294-5031/(800) 725-0695

**American Express Travel** 6600 Indian School Blvd. 883-3677/(800) 219-1023 IGLTA

**North & South Travel & Tours** 215 Central Ave. NW 246-9100/(800) 585-8016 IGLTA

**The Travel Scene** 2424 Juan Tabo Blvd. NE 292-4343/(800) 658-5779

## SPIRITUAL GROUPS
**Dignity New Mexico** 1815 Los Lomas 880-9031 7pm 1st Sun

**Emmanuel MCC** 341 Dallas NE 268-0599 10am Sun

**First Unitarian Church** 3701 Carlisle NE 884-1801 9:30am & 11am Sun

**Jewish Gay/Lesbian Group** 275-9721

**MCC of Albuquerque** 2404 San Mateo Pl. NE 881-9088 10am Sun

## EROTICA
**The Leather Shoppe** 4217 Central Ave. NE 266-6690

**Pussycat III** 4012 Cental Ave. NE 268-1631

## Cloudcroft (505)

### BOOKSTORES & RETAIL SHOPS
**Off The Beaten Path** 100 Glorieta Ave. 682-7284 9am-6pm • eclectic gifts • original artwork • women-owned/operated

## Las Cruces (505)

### INFO LINES & SERVICES
**AA Gay/Lesbian** 527-1803

**Matrix** PO Box 992, Mesilla, 88046 local inquiries • newsletter

### BOOKSTORES & RETAIL SHOPS
**Spirit Winds Gifts** 2260 Locust St. 521-0222 7:30am-8pm, til 10pm Fri-Sat, 8:30am-5pm Sun

### TRAVEL AGENTS
**Uniglobe Above & Beyond Travel** 2225 E. Lohman #A 527-0200/(800) 578-5888 IGLTA

### SPIRITUAL GROUPS
**Holy Family Parish** 1701 E. Missouri (Lutheran Church) 522-7119 5:30pm Sun • inclusive Evangelical Anglican Church

**Koinonia** 521-1490 7:30pm Th • lesbigay group for people of all religious traditions

## Madrid (505)

### ACCOMMODATIONS
**Madrid Lodging** 14 Opera House Rd. 471-3450 gay-friendly • suite • hot tub • smokefree • $55-65

### BARS & NIGHTCLUBS
**Mineshaft Tavern** 2846 State Hwy. 14 473-0743 11am-2am • gay-friendly • live shows • also restaurant • some veggie

### CAFES
**Java Junction** 2855 State Hwy. 14 438-2772 8am-7pm • also B&B

### BOOKSTORES & RETAIL SHOPS
**Impatient Artifacts** 2875 State Hwy. 14 474-6878 10am-5pm, clsd Tue • folk art & rustic furniture

## Placitas (505)

### ACCOMMODATIONS
**El Peñasco** 771-8909 gay-friendly • historic adobe guesthouse • sleeps 1-4 • btwn. Albuquerque & Santa Fe • women-owned/run • $75-95

## Ruidoso (505)

### ACCOMMODATIONS
**Sierra Mesa Lodge** 336-4515 gay-friendly • full brkfst • smokefree

## Santa Fe (505)

### INFO LINES & SERVICES

**AA Gay/Lesbian** 1915 Rosina St. (Friendship Circle) **982-8932**

**Santa Fe Lesbian/Gay Hotline** 982-3301 recorded info

### ACCOMMODATIONS

**Arius Compound** 982-2621/(800) 735-8453 gay-friendly • 3 adobe casitas • kitchens • hot tub • patio • gay-owned/run • $80-135

**Casa Torreon** 1613 Calle Torreon 982-6815 gay-friendly • adobe guesthouse • kitchen • smokefree • kids ok • $85+

**Four Kachinas Inn** 512 Webber St. 982-2550/(800) 397-2564 clsd Jan • gay-friendly • smokefree • kids 10+ ok • courtyard • wheelchair access • $70-125

**Galisteo Inn** 466-4000 clsd Jan • gay-friendly • 23 mi. SE of Santa Fe • swimming • smokefree • older kids ok • horse boarding avail. • also restaurant • nouvelle Southwestern (Wed-Sun) • plenty veggie • wheelchair access

**Heart Seed B&B Retreat & Spa** 471-7026 gay-friendly • located on Turquoise Trail 25 mi. S of Santa Fe • full brkfst • hot tub • smokefree • sundeck • also day spa • $79-89

**Hummingbird Ranch** 471-2921 gay-friendly • 2-1/2 acre ranchette • women-owned/run • $75-125

**Inn of the Turquoise Bear** 342 E. Buena Vista St. **983-0798**/(800) 396-4104 lesbians/gay men • hot tub • smokefree • private/shared baths • gay-owned/run

**La Tienda Inn** 445-447 W. San Francisco St. **989-8259**/(800) 889-7611 gay-friendly • smokefree • wheelchair access • $100-165

**Marriott Residence Inn** 1698 Galisteo St. **988-7300**/(800) 331-3131 gay-friendly • swimming • non-smoking rms. avail. • wheelchair access

**Open Sky B&B** 471-3475/(800) 244-3475 gay-friendly • smokefree • kids ok (call first) • wheelchair access

▲ **Triangle Inn** 455-3375 lesbians/gay men • secluded rustic adobe compound • non-smoking casitas avail. • kids/pets ok • wheelchair access • lesbian-owned/run • $90-140

*The* **Triangle Inn**
*Santa Fe*

Southwest adobe compound
Individual casitas with kitchens
Hot Tub • Private Courtyards • Fireplaces
13 miles north of Santa Fe

P.O. Box 3235
Santa Fe, New Mexico 87501
505 • 455 • 3375

Karan Ford & Sarah Hryniewicz
Innkeepers

# The Ruby Slipper

**A Taos Bed & Breakfast**

## WHY OUR GUESTS KEEP COMING BACK:

Fabulous Breakfasts ★ Seven Beautiful Guestrooms ★ Fireplaces ★ Private Baths & Entrances ★ Secluded Hot Tub ★ Lovely Grounds ★ Ideal Location ★ Casual & Friendly ★ Great Conversation

**RAVE REVIEWS!**
**$79-104**

*The perfect balance of privacy and personal attention!*

## TAOS OFFERS:

Old World Charm ★ Awesome Skies Dramatic Sunsets ★ Majestic Mountains Historical Sites ★ Mountain Biking Spiritual Mecca ★ Pristine Air ★ Tons of Galleries ★ Great Eateries ★ Hot Air Ballooning ★ Tranquility ★ Horseback Riding ★ Festivals ★ Transformation Natural Hot Springs ★ Day Trips ★ Indian Pueblos ★ Whitewater Rafting ★ Skiing Music ★ Relaxation ★ Hiking ★ Healing

*"The Ruby Slipper creates an atmosphere of relaxation that's difficult to avoid. Even the most ardent Type-A personality would be hard pressed to ignore its calming effect."*
—THE ALBUQUERQUE JOURNAL

**Taos, New Mexico ★ 505-758-0613**

**The Water Street Inn** 427 W. Water St. 984-1193/(800) 646-6752 gay-friendly • historic adobe inn • jacuzzi • smokefree • kids/pets ok • wheelchair access • $110-170

## BARS & NIGHTCLUBS
**Drama Club** 125 N. Guadalupe 988-4374 4pm-close • lesbians/gay men • dancing/DJ • live shows

## CAFES
**Galisteo Corner Cafe** 201 Galisteo St. 984-1316 7am-7pm, til 9pm Fri-Sat • coffee shop • some lesbigay periodicals

## RESTAURANTS
**Cafe Pasqual's** 121 Don Gaspar 983-9340 7am-10:30pm • popular • Southwestern • some veggie • beer/wine • wheelchair access • $12-18

**Dave's Not Here** 1115 Hickock St. 983-7060 11am-10pm, clsd Sun • New Mexican • some veggie • beer/wine • women-owned/run

**Paul's** 72 Marcy St. 982-8738 dinner • modern int'l • some veggie • wheelchair access • $11-18

**SantaCafe** 231 Washington Ave. 984-1788 lunch & dinner • Southwestern/Asian • some veggie • full bar • $19-24

**Tecolote Cafe** 1203 Cerrillos Rd. 988-1362 7am-2pm, clsd Mon • popular • great brkfst • some veggie • $5-8

**Vanessie of Santa Fe** 434 W. San Francisco 982-9966 5:30pm-10:30pm (bar til 1am) • popular • lesbians/gay men • steak house • piano bar

## BOOKSTORES & RETAIL SHOPS
**The Ark** 133 Romero St. 988-3709 10am-8pm, til 5pm wknds • spiritual
**Downtown Subscription** 376 Garcia St. 983-3085 newsstand • coffee shop

# Taos (505)

## ACCOMMODATIONS
**Brooks Street Inn** 758-7525/(800) 758-1489 gay-friendly • full brkfst • smokefree • kids 5+ ok • $80-105

▲ **The Ruby Slipper B&B** 758-0613 gay-friendly • near Taos Plaza • full brkfst • smokefree • kids ok • wheelchair access • IGLTA • women-owned/run

# NEW YORK

## Adirondack Mtns. (518)

### INFO LINES & SERVICES
**Lesbigay Info** 359-7358 local contact

### ACCOMMODATIONS
**Amethyst B&B** 848-3529/(410) 252-5990 summer only • women only • full brkfst • swimming • smokefree

**The Doctor's Inn** 891-3464/(888) 518-3464 gay-friendly • full brkfst • private/shared baths • IGLTA

**King Hendrick Motel** 1602 Lake George Rd. (State Rte. 9), Lake George 792-0418 gay-friendly • swimming • cabins avail.

**Stony Water B&B** 873-9125/(800) 995-7295 gay-friendly • full brkfst • swimming • wheelchair access • lesbian-owned/run

## Albany

### INFO LINES & SERVICES
**Gay AA** (at Community Center) 7:30pm Sun • lesbian AA at 7:30pm Tue

**Lesbian/Gay Community Center** 332 Hudson Ave. 462-6138 7pm-10pm, til 11pm Fri-Sat, 10am-2pm Sun (cafe) • 24hr directory

**TGIC (Transgenderists Independence Club)** 436-4513 live 8pm-10pm Th • social group meets weekly

**Women's Building** 79 Central Ave. 465-1597 community center

### ACCOMMODATIONS
▲ **The State House** 393 State St. 465-8079 gay-friendly • smokefree • gay-owned/run

**The Turnλround Spa** 201 Washington St., Sharon Springs 284-2271 lesbians/gay men • small hotel & health spa • smokefree

### BARS & NIGHTCLUBS
**Cafe Hollywood** 275 Lark St. 472-9043 3pm-3am • gay-friendly • neighborhood bar • videos

**JD's Playhouse** 519 Central Ave. 446-1407 4pm-4am, clsd Mon • lesbians/gay men • neighborhood bar • dancing/DJ

## Spectacular Accommodation
### 19th-Century Elegance & Design
### Downtown Albany
### Overlooking Washington Park

# The State House
G U E S T   R E S I D E N C E

## Best Bed & Breakfast in the Capital Region
" Metroland Magazine"

A private guest residence in Albany's most exclusive historic residential neighborhood. Near exciting restaurants, night life, museums, theaters, shopping, and a variety of activities.

393 State Street Albany, NY 12210
Ph: 518-427-6063     Fax: 518-463-1316

**Longhorns** 90 Central Ave. **462-4862**
4pm-4am • mostly gay men •
country/western

**Oh Bar** 304 Lark St. **463-9004** 2pm-2am
• mostly gay men • neighborhood bar •
multi-racial • videos

**Power Company** 238 Washington Ave.
**465-2556** 2pm-2am, til 4am wknds •
mostly gay men • dancing/DJ • wheelchair access

**Waterworks Pub** 76 Central Ave. **465-
9079** 4pm-4am • popular • mostly gay
men • dancing/DJ • garden bar

## RESTAURANTS

**Cafe Lulu** 288 Lark St. **436-5660** 11am-
midnight, til 1am Fri-Sat •
Mediterranean • plenty veggie •
beer/wine • $5-9

**Debbie's Kitchen** 290 Lark St. **463-3829**
10am-9pm, 11am-6pm Sat, clsd Sun •
sandwiches • salads • $3-5

**El Loco Mexican Cafe** 465 Madison Ave.
**436-1855** clsd Mon • some veggie • full
bar

**Mother Earth** 217 Western Ave. **434-
0944** 11am-11pm • vegetarian • BYOB •
wheelchair access • $3-6

**The Unlimited Feast** 340 Hamilton St.
**463-6223** lunch Mon-Fri, dinner Wed-Sat
• some veggie • full bar • patio • wheelchair access • $14-20

**Yono's** 289 Hamilton St. **436-7747**
4:30pm-10pm, clsd Sun • Indonesian/
cont'l • some veggie • full bar

## ENTERTAINMENT & RECREATION

**Face the Music** WRPI 91.5 FM **276-6248**
4pm-6pm Sun • feminist radio

**Homo Radio** WRPI 91.5 FM **276-6248**
noon-2:30pm Sun

## BOOKSTORES & RETAIL SHOPS

**Romeo's** 299 Lark St. **434-4014** 11am-
9pm, noon-5pm Sun

**Video Central** 37 Central Ave. **463-4153**
10am-10pm • lesbigay books • magazines

## PUBLICATIONS

**Community** 462-6138 x37

## TRAVEL AGENTS

**Atlas Travel Center** 1545 Central Ave.
**464-0271** IGLTA

**Freedom Travel** 212 Clifton Country
Mall, Clifton Park **371-1866/(888) 718-
6423**

## SPIRITUAL GROUPS

**First United Presbyterian Church of
Troy** 1915 5th Ave., Troy **272-2771** 10am
Sun

**Grace & Holy Innocents Episcopal
Church** 498 Clinton Ave. **465-1112** 8am
& 9am Sun

**MCC of the Hudson Valley** 275 State St.
(Emmanuel Baptist Church) **785-7941**
1pm Sun • wheelchair access

## GYMS & HEALTH CLUBS

**Fitness for Her** 333 Delaware Ave.,
Delmar **478-0237** women-only • child
care avail. • wheelchair access • les-
bian-owned/run

## EROTICA

**Savage Leather & Gifts** 88 Central Ave.
**434-2324**

# Annandale-on-Hudson    (914)

## INFO LINES & SERVICES

**Bard BiGALA (Bisexual/Gay/Lesbian
Alliance)** Bard College **758-6822** (GENER-
AL SWITCHBOARD)/**758-7454** (DEAN OF
STUDENTS) active during school year

# Binghamton    (607)

## INFO LINES & SERVICES

**AA Gay/Lesbian** 183 Riverside Dr.
(Unitarian Church) **722-5983** 7pm Wed &
Sat

**Gay/Lesbian/Bi Resource Line** **729-
1921/(800) 287-7557** (LOCAL ONLY)
7:30pm-9:30pm Mon-Th

**Queer Student Union** 777-2202 call for
info

**Women's Center & Event Line** 724-3462

## BARS & NIGHTCLUBS

**Risky Business** 201 State St. **723-1507**
9pm-1am, from 5pm Th-Fri, til 3am Fri-
Sat • popular • mostly gay men • danc-
ing/DJ

**Squiggy's** 34 Chenango St. **722-2299**
5pm-1am, til 3am Fri-Sat, from 8pm Sun
• lesbians/gay men • Ladies' Night Mon
• dancing/DJ

## CAFES

**Java Joe's** 81 State St. **774-0966** 7:30am-
10pm, til midnight Fri-Sat, 10am-2pm
Sun • mostly women • sandwiches &
desserts • gallery • live shows • patio •
wheelchair access

## PUBLICATIONS

**Amethyst** 723-5790

**Hera c/o Women's Center** 770-9011 local feminist newspaper
**Lavender Life** 771-1986

### SPIRITUAL GROUPS
**Affirmation (United Methodist)** 83 Main St. (enter in back through parking lot) **775-3986** 7pm Sun

## Buffalo                                    (716)

### INFO LINES & SERVICES
**Gay/Lesbian Community Network** 239 Lexington Ave. **883-4750** live 7pm-10pm Fri

**Gay/Lesbian Youth Services** 190 Franklin St. **855-0221** 6:30pm-9pm, clsd Wed & wknds

**Lesbian/Gay/Bisexual Alliance** 362 Student Union, SUNY-Buffalo, Amherst 645-3063

### ACCOMMODATIONS
**Danner House B&B** 12549 Niagara River Pkwy., Niagara Falls OT **(905) 295-5166** lesbians/gay men • full brkfst • jacuzzi • smokefree • 10 min. from Buffalo

### BARS & NIGHTCLUBS
**Buddies** 31 Johnson Park **855-1313** 1pm-4am • lesbian/gay men • dancing/DJ • live shows • wheelchair access

**Cathode Ray** 26 Allen St. **884-3615** 1pm-4am • mostly gay men • neighborhood bar • videos • wheelchair access

**Club Marcella** 150 Theatre Pl. **847-6850** 10pm-4am, from 4pm Fri, clsd Mon • lesbians/gay men • dancing/DJ • live shows • wheelchair access

**Compton's After Dark** 1239 Niagara St. **885-3275** 4pm-4am • mostly women • dancing/DJ • live shows • sandwiches • some veggie • $4-7

**Lavender Door** 32 Tonawanda St. **874-1220** 6pm-4am, from 4pm Fri, clsd Mon • mostly women • neighborhood bar • wheelchair access

**Metroplex** 729 Main St. **856-5630** 10pm-4am, clsd Mon • lesbians/gay men • dancing/DJ • alternative • 18+

**Mickey's** 44 Allen St. **886-9367** 10am-4am • gay-friendly • neighborhood bar

**Stagedoor** 20 Allen St. **886-9323** 5pm-4am • mostly older gay men • neighborhood bar • karaoke • piano bar • patio

**The Underground** 274 Delaware Ave. **855-1040** 4pm-4am, from noon wknds • mostly gay men • more women Tue & Sun • dancing/DJ

### ENTERTAINMENT & RECREATION
**Dyke TV** Channel 18 10:30pm Tue • 'weekly, half hour TV show produced by lesbians for lesbians'

### BOOKSTORES & RETAIL SHOPS
**Rainbow Pride Gift Shop** 175 Hodge St. **881-6126** 5pm-9pm, from 1pm Sat, noon-5pm Sun, clsd Mon • lesbigay gifts • video rentals • gay-owned/run

**Talking Leaves** 3158 Main St. **837-8554** 10am-6pm, til 8pm Wed-Th, clsd Sun

**Village Green Bookstore** 765-A Elmwood Ave. **884-1200** 9am-11pm, til midnight Fri-Sat • wheelchair access

### TRAVEL AGENTS
**Destinations Unlimited** 130 Theater Pl. **855-1955**/**(800) 528-8877** IGLTA

**Earth Travelers** 683 Dick Rd. **685-2900** IGLTA

### SPIRITUAL GROUPS
**Dignity** 833-8995 call for events

### EROTICA
**Village Books & News** 3102 Delaware Ave., Kenmore **877-5027** 24hrs

## Canaseraga                           (607)

### ACCOMMODATIONS
**Fairwise Llama Farm** 1320 Rte. 70 **545-6247** lesbians/gay men • full brkfst • located btwn. Letchworth & Stony Brook Parks

## Catskill Mtns.

### ACCOMMODATIONS
**Bradstan Country Hotel** White Lake **(914) 583-4114** gay-friendly • also piano bar & cabaret • 9pm-1am Fri-Sun

**Greene Mountain View Inn** Tannersville **(518) 589-9886** gay-friendly • near Hunter Mtn. skiing & summer festivals

**Inn at Stone Ridge** Rte. 209, Stone Ridge **(914) 687-0736** gay-friendly • full brkfst • also fine dining • full bar • $12-25 • patio • $95-145

**Palenville House B&B** Palenville **(518) 678-5649** gay-friendly • full brkfst • hot tub • private/shared baths • smokefree

**The Pines Resort Hotel** S. Fallsburg **(800) 367-4637** gay-friendly • kids ok • 'Gay/Lesbian Weekend' in November • wheelchair access • $90

▲ **Point Lookout Mountain Inn** The
Mohican Trail, Rte. 23, E. Windham **(518)
734-3381** gay-friendly • close to Ski
Windham & Hunter Mtn. • hot tub •
non-smoking rms avail. • also 'Bella
Vista Restaurant' • Mediterranean/classic
American • $11-18 • also 'Rainbow Cafe
& Cliffside Deck' • women-owned/run •
wheelchair access • $60-125

**Red Bear Inn & Restaurant** West Kill
**(518) 989-6000/(888) 232-7466** (seasonal) lesbians/gay men • leather • smokefree • full bar • dancing/DJ

**River Run B&B** Fleischmanns **(914) 254-
4884** gay-friendly • Queen Anne
Victorian • full brkfst • IGLTA

**Stonewall Acres (914) 791-9474/(800)
336-4208** gay-friendly • guest farmhouse
• cottages • full brkfst • swimming

**RESTAURANTS**

**Catskill Rose** Rte. 212, Mt. Tremper
**(914) 688-7100** from 5pm Wed-Sun •
some veggie • full bar • patio • $13-19

**ENTERTAINMENT & RECREATION**

**Frog Hollow Farm** Old Post Rd., Esopus
**(914) 384-6424** riding school & camp

**Solstice Farm Stable** Stanfordville **(914)
868-1413** riding school & camp

**TRAVEL AGENTS**

**Hollowbrook Travel at Allsport** 17 Old
Main St., Fishkill **(914) 896-0227** IGLTA

## Cooperstown                    (607)

**ACCOMMODATIONS**

**Toad Hall B&B** 547-5774 gay-friendly •
full brkfst • smokefree • $90

**Tryon Inn** 124 Main St., Cherry Valley
**264-3790** gay-friendly • also restaurant •
country French • some veggie • gay-
owned/run $12-16

## Cuba                            (716)

**ACCOMMODATIONS**

**Rocking Duck Inn** 28 Genesee Pkwy.
**968-3335** gay-friendly • full brkfst • also
'Aunt Minnie's Tavern'

Anytime is the right time
for romance at

# POINT LOOKOUT MOUNTAIN INN

## Just Imagine...

- Candlelight dinners by a roaring fire
- Relaxing in our hot tub
- A lovely room with a breathtaking view of five states
- Helping yourself to our trademark "Raid the Refrigerator Breakfast"

Don't deny you and your love that weekend you've always wanted.

Join us at

## POINT LOOKOUT MOUNTAIN INN
on the Historic Mohican Trail
**518/734-3381**
Route 23, Box 33, East Windham, NY 12436
Only One Hour From Albany! • Mariana DiToro & Rosemary Jensen, Owners/Innkeepers

# Elmira (607)

## ACCOMMODATIONS
**Rufus Tanner House B&B** 60 Sagetown Rd., Pine City **732-0213** gay-friendly • full brkfst • hot tub • smokefree

## BARS & NIGHTCLUBS
**The David** 511 Railroad Ave. **733-2592** 4pm-1am, from 7pm wknds • popular • lesbians/gay men • dancing/DJ

# Fire Island (516)

*(see also Long Island)*

## INFO LINES & SERVICES
**AA Gay/Lesbian** (at the Fire House), Cherry Grove **654-1150**

## ACCOMMODATIONS
**Boatel** Pines/Dunes Yacht Club, Harbor Walk **597-6500** lesbian/gay men • swimming

**Cherry Grove Beach Hotel** Main & Ocean, Cherry Grove **597-6600** mostly gay men • swimming • nudity • non-smoking rm avail. • wheelchair access • IGLTA

**Dune Point Guesthouse 597-6261** lesbians/gay men • wheelchair access

**Holly House** Holly Walk nr. Bayview Walk, Cherry Grove **597-6911** seasonal • lesbian/gay men

**Island Properties** 37 Fire Island Blvd. **597-6900** weekly, monthly, & seasonal rentals • also properties for sale

**Sea Crest** Lewis Walk, Cherry Grove **597-6849** seasonal • lesbians/gay men

## BARS & NIGHTCLUBS
**Cherry's** Cherry Grove **597-6820** noon-4am • lesbians/gay men • piano bar

**Ice Palace** (at 'Cherry Grove Beach Hotel') **597-6600** hours vary • popular • lesbians/gay men • dancing/DJ • live shows

**The Island Club & Bistro** Fire Island Blvd. **597-6001** 6pm-4am • mostly gay men • dancing/DJ • live shows • food served • $15-28

**Pavillion** Fire Island Blvd. **597-6131** 4pm-6am • lesbians/gay men • popular T-dance & morning dancing • also 'Yacht Club' restaurant • opens at noon

## RESTAURANTS
**Michael's** Dock Walk, Cherry Grove **597-6555** 24hrs Sat

**Top of the Bay** Dock Walk at Bay Walk, Cherry Grove **597-6699** 7pm-midnight • popular • lesbians/gay men • $18-23

# Glens Falls (518)

## BARS & NIGHTCLUBS
**Club M** 70 South St. **798-9809** noon-4am • lesbians/gay men • dancing/DJ • wheelchair access

## TRAVEL AGENTS
**LaPoint's Hometown Travel** 94 Bay St. **793-3390** IGLTA

# Hartsdale (914)

## TRAVEL AGENTS
**Choice Travel** 267 S. Central Park Ave. **993-3300** IGLTA

# Highland (914)

## BARS & NIGHTCLUBS
**Prime Time** Rte. 9 W. **691-8550** 9pm-4am, clsd Mon-Wed • mostly gay men • dancing/DJ

## RESTAURANTS
**The Would Bar & Grill** 120 North Rd. **691-9883** lunch & dinner, clsd Sun • some veggie • full bar • patio • $16-22

# Hudson Valley (914)

*(see also Kingston, New Paltz, Poughkeepsie & Stone Ridge)*

## ACCOMMODATIONS
**Alexander Hamilton House** 49 Van Wyck St., Croton-on-Hudson **271-6737** gay-friendly • full brkfst • smokefree

## RESTAURANTS
**Cafe Pongo** 69 Broadway, Tivoli **757-4403** lunch, dinner & Sun brunch • gay night Fri • call for details

**Northern Spy Cafe** Rte. 213, High Falls **687-7298** dinner nightly & Sun brunch, clsd Tue • plenty veggie • full bar • wheelchair access • $11-18

**Quinn's Restaurant** 330 Main St., Beacon (Hudson River) **831-8065** great bread

## PUBLICATIONS
▲ **In The Life 227-7456** lesbigay newspaper w/quick reference guide

## TRAVEL AGENTS
**Virga's Travel Service 221-2455** IGLTA

# In·The·LIFE

THE TRI-STATE LESBIAN & GAY

**NEWSPAPER**

In Print or on the Web....
*"absolutely the best connection to the*
*Lesbian and Gay Community"*

PO Box 921 Wappingers Falls, NY 12590-0921 ▼ 1-914-227-7456 ▼ Fax: 1-914-226-5313

FOR ADVERTISING & SUBSCRIPTION INFORMATION CALL: 1-914-227-7456

http://www.inthelife.com

## SPIRITUAL GROUPS

**Trinity Episcopal Church** 7 S. Highland (Rte. 9), Ossining **941-0806** 7:30am & 10am Sun

## Ithaca (607)

### INFO LINES & SERVICES

**AA Gay/Lesbian** 201 E. Green St. (Mental Health Serv. Bldg.) **273-1541** 5:30pm Sun

**Ithaca Gay/Lesbian Activities Board (IGLAB)** 273-1505 (**COMMON GROUND BAR**) 3rd Tue • sponsors events including 'Finger Lake Gay/Lesbian Picnic'

**LesBiGayTrans Info Line** (Cornell University) **255-6482** noon-4pm Mon-Fri

**Women's Community Building** 100 W. Seneca **272-7622** 9am-5pm, evenings & wknds by appt.

### ACCOMMODATIONS

**Pleasant Grove B&B** 168 Pleasant Grove Rd. **387-5420/(800) 398-3963** gay-friendly • above Cayuga Lake • full brkfst • sundeck

**Sleeping Bear B&B** 208 Nelson Rd. **277-6220** (formerly 'Cricket & Liz's Log Home') • women only • full brkfst • hot tub • swimming • lesbian-owned/run

### BARS & NIGHTCLUBS

**Common Ground** 1230 Danby Rd. **273-1505** 4pm-1:30am, clsd Mon • popular • lesbians/gay men • dancing/DJ • also restaurant • some veggie • $5-8

### RESTAURANTS

**ABC Cafe** 308 Stewart Ave. **277-4770** lunch & dinner, wknd brunch, clsd Mon • beer/wine • vegetarian • $6-8

### BOOKSTORES & RETAIL SHOPS

**Borealis Bookstore** 111 N. Aurora St. **272-7752** 10am-9pm, noon-5pm Sun • independent alternative • lesbigay sections • wheelchair access

## Jamestown (716)

### BARS & NIGHTCLUBS

**Nite Spot** 201 Windsor 7pm-2am • lesbians/gay men • dancing/DJ • live shows • unconfirmed

**Sneakers** 100 Harrison **484-8816** 2pm-2am • lesbians/gay men • dancing/DJ • wheelchair access

### BOOKSTORES & RETAIL SHOPS

**Literary Tea** 23 E. 3rd St. #102 **664-1890** 11am-7pm, clsd Sun • bookstore • tea-room • B&B

## Kingston (914)

### RESTAURANTS

**Armadillo Bar & Grill** 97 Abeel St. **339-1550** lunch & dinner • full bar • patio

**Crossroads Restaurant** 33 Broadway **340-0151** 11:30am-10pm, kitchen til 9pm, clsd Mon • piano bar

### TRAVEL AGENTS

**Advanced Travel Network** 1132 Morton Blvd. **336-4655** IGLTA

## Lake Placid (518)

### RESTAURANTS

**Artists' Cafe** 1 Main St. **523-9493** 8am-10pm • steak & seafood • full bar • $9-15

**Dakota Cafe** 124 Main St. **523-2337** steak & seafood

## Long Island (516)

*(see also Fire Island)*

*Long Island is divided into 2 geographical areas:*

## Long Island—Nassau County

## Long Island—Suffolk County

## Long Island–Nassau (516)

### INFO LINES & SERVICES

**Pride for Youth Coffeehouse** 170 Fulton St., Farmingdale **679-9000** 7:30pm-11:30pm Fri

**Women's Alternative Community Center** 699 Woodfield Rd., W. Hempstead **483-2050** call for events & info

### BARS & NIGHTCLUBS

**Blanche** 47-2 Boundary Ave., South Farmingdale **694-6906** 4pm-4am • mostly gay men • neighborhood bar • live shows

**Chameleon** 40-20 Long Beach Rd., Long Beach **889-4083** 9pm-4am, clsd Mon-Wed • popular • lesbians/gay men • dancing/DJ • women's night Fri • unconfirmed

**Libations** 3547 Merrick Rd., Seaford **679-8820** 3pm-4am, from 5pm Mon • lesbians/gay men • neighborhood bar

**Silver Lining** 175 Cherry Ln., Floral Park **354-9641** 9pm-4am clsd Mon-Tue • lesbians/gay men • dancing/DJ • live shows • videos • wheelchair access • unconfirmed

### ENTERTAINMENT & RECREATION

**Jones Beach** Field #6

TRAVEL AGENTS
**Travel Masters of NY** 823 Willow Rd., Franklin Square **485-0707** IGLTA

SPIRITUAL GROUPS
**Dignity** 781-6225 8pm 2nd & 4th Sat

## Long Island–Suffolk (516)

INFO LINES & SERVICES
**EEGO (East End Gay Organization)** 324-3699

ACCOMMODATIONS
**132 North Main** 132 N. Main, East Hampton **324-2246** seasonal • mostly gay men • mini-resort • swimming • wheelchair access

**Centennial House** 13 Woods Ln., East Hampton **324-9414** gay-friendly • full brkfst • swimming • gay-owned/run

**Cozy Cabins Motel** 537-1160 seasonal • lesbians/gay men

**EconoLodge—MacArthur Airport** 3055 Rte. 454, Ronkonkoma **588-6800**/(800) **553-2666** gay-friendly • budget motel • non-smoking rms avail.

**EconoLodge—Smithtown/Hauppauge** 755 Rte. 347, Smithtown **724-9000**/(800) **553-2666** gay-friendly

**Gandalf House** 298-4769 gay-friendly

**Summit Motor Inn** 501 E. Main St., Bay Shore **666-6000**/(800) **869-6363** gay-friendly

**Sunset Beach** 749-2001 gay-friendly • food served • $115-245

BARS & NIGHTCLUBS
**Bedrock** 121 Woodfield Rd., W. Hempstead **486-9516** 8pm-3am, from 1pm Sun, clsd Mon • popular • mostly women • dancing/DJ • live shows

**Bunkhouse** 192 N. Main St., Montauk Hwy., Sayville **567-2865** 8pm-4am, from 5pm Sun • popular • mostly gay men • dancing/DJ • live shows

**Forever Green** 841 N. Broome Ave., Lindenhurst **226-9357** 8pm-4am, from 7pm Sun (DJ) • mostly women • neighborhood bar

**St. Mark's Place** 65-50 Jericho Trnpk., Commack **499-2244** 4pm-4am • lesbians/gay men • dancing/DJ • also restaurant • some veggie • wheelchair access • lesbian-owned • $4-14

**Swamp** 378 Montauk Hwy., Wainscott **537-3332** 6pm-4am, clsd Tue • call for winter hours • mostly gay men • dancing/DJ • also 'Annex' restaurant • cont'l/seafood (clsd Sun) • $16-20

**Thunders** 1017 E. Jericho Trnpk., Huntington Station **423-5241** 9pm-4am, clsd Mon • lesbians/gay men • dancing/DJ • piano bar Tue-Fri

RESTAURANTS
**Butchers Boys** 220 Montauk Hwy., Sayville **563-6679** 4pm-2am, clsd Tue • steakhouse • full bar • $9-17

ENTERTAINMENT & RECREATION
**Fowler Beach** Southampton

TRAVEL AGENTS
**Fantastic Tours & Travel** 6143 Jericho Trpk., Commack **462-6262** IGLTA

**Welcome Travel Agency** 340 Portion Rd., Lake Ronkonkoma **585-7070** IGLTA

**West Hills Travel/Empress Travel** 444 W. Jericho Trpk., Huntington **692-9800** IGLTA

SPIRITUAL GROUPS
**Dignity** 654-5367 2nd & last Sun

**Unitarian Universalist Fellowship** 109 Brown Rd., Huntington **427-9547** 10:30am Sun

## Middletown (914)

BARS & NIGHTCLUBS
**Legends** 343 E. Main St. **343-0098** 7pm-4am • lesbians/gay men • dancing/DJ

## Naples (716)

ACCOMMODATIONS
**Landmark Retreat B&B** 396-2383 gay-friendly • full brkfst • wheelchair access

## New Paltz (914)

ACCOMMODATIONS
**Ujjala's B&B** 2 Forest Glen **255-6360** gay-friendly • full brkfst • body therapy • sweat lodges

RESTAURANTS
**Locust Tree Restaurant** 215 Hugenot St. **255-7888** lunch & dinner, clsd Mon • cont'l • full bar • patio • $14-20

BOOKSTORES & RETAIL SHOPS
**The Painted Word** 36 Main St. **256-0825** 10am-10pm, til 6pm Sun-Mon • lesbigay • cafe • wheelchair access

TRAVEL AGENTS
**New Paltz Travel Center** 7 Cherry Hill Center **255-7706** IGLTA

## NEW YORK CITY

*New York City is divided into 8 geographical areas:*

**N.Y.C.—Overview**
**N.Y.C.—Soho, Greenwich & Chelsea**
**N.Y.C.—Midtown**
**N.Y.C.—Uptown**
**N.Y.C.—Brooklyn**
**N.Y.C.—Queens**
**N.Y.C.—Bronx**
**N.Y.C.—Staten Island**

### N.Y.C.—Overview

INFO LINES & SERVICES

**AA Gay/Lesbian Intergroup** (at Lesbian/Gay Community Ctr.) **647-1680** call for mtg. schedule

**African Ancestral Lesbians United for Societal Change** (at Lesbian/Gay Community Ctr.) 8pm Th

**Asians & Friends of NY** (at Lesbian/Gay Community Ctr.) 8pm 3rd Sat

**Bisexual Gay/Lesbian Transgender Youth of NY** (at Lesbian/Gay Community Ctr.) 1:30pm Sat

**Bisexual Network 459-4784** info on variety of social & political groups

**Bisexual Women of Color** (at Lesbian/Gay Community Ctr.) 6:30pm 1st & 3rd Fri

**Bisexual Women's Group** (at Lesbian/Gay Community Ctr.) 6:30pm 2nd & 4th Wed

**Butch/Femme Society** (at Lesbian/Gay Community Ctr.) 6:30pm 3rd Wed

**EDGE (Education in a Disabled Gay Environment) 929-7178** wheelchair access • TTY calls accepted

**Eulenspiegel Society 388-7022** 7:30pm Tue & Wed, $5 • pansexual S/M group • newsletter

**FLAB (Fat is a Lesbian Issue)** (at Lesbian/Gay Community Ctr.) 4:30pm 2nd Sun • fat-positive discussion group & dinner • allies welcome

SOME GIRLS JUST WANNA HAVE FUN
...OTHERS HAVE FUN

1 (888) 44 DINAH
GIRL BAR & CLUB SKIRTS

# New York City

*I*n the film *Mondo New York,* demi-monde denizen Joey Arias put it best: "New York is the clit of the world!"

Get ready for the most stimulating trip of your life! You've come to *the* city of world-famous tourist attractions: from the skyscrapers to the subway, New York is like no other place. Whether you pride yourself on your cultural sophistication, or lack thereof, you're going to find endless entertainment. There are plays, musicals, operas, museums, and gallery shows, performance art, street theater and street life...and that's just for starters.

To get the most out of your visit, do your homework before you come. Call for a calendar of events at the **Lesbian/Gay Community Center** which houses meeting spaces for every conceivable group of lesbigaytrans+ people.

New York's performance art is a must-see for any student of modern culture. The best bets for intelligent, cutting edge shows by women and queers are **W.O.W. (Women's One World) Café** and P.S. 122 on 1st Ave. at 9th St., where lesbian artist Holly Hughes got her start. For "twofers"—half-price tickets to Broadway and off-Broadway shows available the day of the show—stop by the TKTS booth on 47th St. at Broadway. For the latest reviews and hot off-off-Broadway theaters, check the queer-friendly Village Voice newspaper.

Of course, you can stimulate a lot more than your cultural sensibilities in New York. Gourmands cans experience oral orgasms ranging from a delicate quiver to a blinding throb every day. For instance, before that Broadway show, head to one of the many restaurants along 46th St. at 9th Ave. When in Brooklyn, brunch along 7th Ave.; you'll find plenty of lesbigay company on a Sunday morning.

Shopping, too, affords shivers of delight. Check out the fabulous thrift shops and the designer boutiques. Cruise Midtown on Madison Ave., E. 57th St., or 5th Ave. in the 50's, at Trump Tower or another major shopping mall, and touch clothing more expensive than your last car. Other recommended districts for blowing cash on hipster fashions and accessories include St. Mark's Place in the Village (8th St. between 1st and 2nd Aves.); Broadway from 8th to Canal St.; and any major intersection in Soho and the East Village.

To titillate your mind, peruse the shelves at **A Different Light** or **Oscar Wilde Memorial Bookshop**, or make an appointment to stop by the **Lesbian Herstory Archives** in Brooklyn. If you're in the mood for love, visit **Eve's Garden,** New York's women's erotic boutique; men are only allowed in if accompanied by a woman.

You could spend days at the big art museums in Uptown near Central Park, but budget some time for the galleries in SoHo (south of Houston—pronounced How-ston, not like the city in Texas—between Broadway and 6th Ave.). You can pick up a gallery map in the area.

For musical entertainment, make your pilgrimage to The Kitchen, legendary site of experimental and freestyle jazz, or CBGB's, legendary home of noisy music (the Ramones started American punk here in 1974).

Nightlife... we know you've been holding your breath! Run, don't walk to the **Clit Club**; Friday nights on W. 14th St. are the sexiest, hottest dyke nights in town. **Crazy Nanny's** really happens seven days a week, and several other women's bars are nearby. **Shescape** produces women's club nights at various locations, so call for their latest events. (New York is also home to plenty of one-nighters, so be sure to pick up a copy of **HX for Her** for up-to-the-minute club happenings.) Kinky dykes should get the latest schedule for the **Vault** partyspace in the Village. And no one should miss the Drag King scene in this gender-bending city.

If this isn't enough excitement, experience the City in June when New York hosts numerous Lesbian/Gay Pride-related cultural events, from their week-long Film Festival to the Pride March itself.

One last bit of advice: there's more to New York City than Manhattan. Brooklyn has long been home to lesbians escaping the extortionist rents of Manhattan. To taste dyke life in this borough, stop by **Rising Cafe** or Brooklyn's lesbigay bookstore, **Beyond Words**. If you'll be out on Long Island, stop by the **Women's Alternative Community Center** in W. Hempstead or **Bedrock** women's bar. In Suffolk County, **Forever Green** and **Thunders** are the bars of choice.

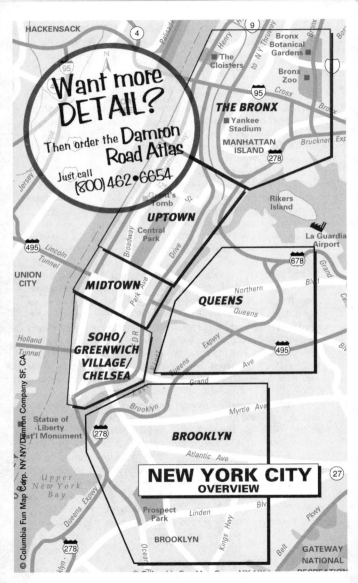

**Where the Girls Are:**
Upwardly mobile literary
types hang in the West
Village, hipster dykes cruise
the East Village, upper-
crusty lesbians have cocktails in Midtown, and
working-class dykes live in
Brooklyn.

**Lesbigay Pride:** Last
Sunday in June.

**Annual Events:**

February - Saint-at-Large
**White Party:** 674-8541.

March - Saint-at-Large **Black
Party:** 674-8541. Night of
a Thousand Gowns: 807-
8767. Imperial Court benefit for AmFAR.

May - **AIDS Walk-a-thon:**
807-9255. AIDS benefit.

June - **New York Int'l
Gay/Lesbian Film Festival:**
343-2707. Week-long fest.

September - **Wigstock:** 620-
7310. Outrageous
wig/drag/performance fes-
tival in Tompkins Square
Park in the East Village.

October - **All Saint's Party:**
674-8541.

November - **AIDS Dance-a-
thon:** 807-9255. AIDS benefit. New York Lesbian/Gay
Experimental Film/Video
Fest: 501-2309. Film,
videos, installations &
media performances.

December 31: Saint-at-Large
**New Year's Party:** 674-
8541.

**City Info:** 397-8222.

**Attractions:** Broadway.
Carnegie Hall. Central Park.
Ellis Island. Empire State
Building. Greenwich
Village. Lincoln Center.
Metropolitan Museum of
Art. Radio City Music Hall.
Rockefeller Center. Statue
of Liberty. The newly
bowlerized Times Square.
United Nations. Wall
Street. World Trade Center.

**Best View:** Coming over
any of the bridges into
New York or from the
Empire State Building or
the World Trade Center.

**Weather:** A spectrum of
extremes with pleasant
moments thrown in. Spring
and fall are the best times
to visit.

**Transit:** Wave an arm on
(almost) any streetcorner
for a taxi. Carey Airport
Shuttle: 718/632-0500.
Public transit: 718/330-
1234.

New York City

(212/718)

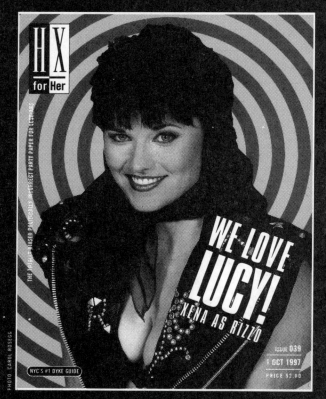

**Changing New York City Dyke-Life As You Know It!**

HX for Her

THE TRULY BIASED PREMIER INCORRECT PARTY PAPER FOR LESBIANS

PHOTO: CAROL ROSEGG

NYC'S #1 DYKE GUIDE

WE LOVE LUCY! XENA AS RIZZO

ISSUE 039
1 OCT 1997
PRICE $2.00

**OFFERING COMPLETE LISTINGS ON THE WHO, WHAT, WHERE, WHEN AND HOW OF THE NEW YORK SCENE**

FOR ADVERTISING AND SUBSCRIPTION INFORMATION
**CALL 212-352-3535**

# The
# Lesbian
## and Gay
# Community
### Services
# Center
*of* NEW YORK

**Serving more than 5,000 people every week**

| Call | Write | Visit |
|------|-------|-------|
| (212) | 208 West 13th Street | Any day |
| 620-7310 | NYC 10011-7799 | 9AM-11PM |

*website:* WWW.GAYCENTER.ORG

*Get on the mailing list for our free monthly calendar of events. Fill out this form and mail it to:*

**The Center, 208 West 13th St., NYC 10011-7799**

NAME

ADDRESS

CITY, STATE, ZIP

PHONE

**Gay/Lesbian National Hotline (888) 843-4564** 6pm-11pm

**Gay/Lesbian Switchboard of New York** 777-1800

**Hetrick-Martin Institute** 2 Astor Pl. **674-2400/674-8695 (TTY)** extensive services for lesbigay youth • also publishes 'You Are Not Alone' resource directory

**Just Couples** (at Lesbian/Gay Community Ctr.) 3:30pm 1st Sun

**Las Buenas Amigas** (at Lesbian/Gay Community Ctr.) 2pm 1st & 3rd Sun • Latina lesbian group

**Lesbian Herstory Archives (718) 768-3953** exists to gather & preserve records of lesbian lives & activities • located in Park Slope, Brooklyn • wheelchair access

**Lesbian Switchboard 741-2610** 6pm-10pm, clsd wknds

▲**Lesbian/Gay Community Services Center** 208 W. 13th St. **620-7310** 9am-11pm • wheelchair access

**Metropolitan Gender Network (718) 461-9050**

**NY CyberQueers** (at Lesbian/Gay Community Ctr.) 7pm 3rd Th • lesbigay & transgender 'computer pros'

**SAGE: Senior Action in a Gay Environment** (at Lesbian/Gay Community Ctr.) 741-2247

**SALGA (South Asian Lesbian/Gay Association)** (at Lesbian/Gay Community Ctr.) 3:30pm 2nd Sat

**Sirens Motorcycle Club** (at Lesbian/Gay Community Ctr.) 8pm 3rd Tue

**Support Group for Single Lesbians** (at Lesbian/Gay Community Ctr.) 6:30pm Tue & Fri

**Twenty Something** (at Lesbian/Gay Community Ctr.) 8pm 1st & 3rd Tue • social alternative to bars for lesbigays in late teens, 20s & early 30s

### ACCOMMODATIONS

**New York Reservation Center 977-3512** lesbians/gay men • IGLTA

### ENTERTAINMENT & RECREATION

**Dyke TV** Manhattan Channel 34 8pm Tue • 'weekly half-hour TV show produced by lesbians, for lesbians'

**Think It's Not When It Is (718) 949-5162** theater company promoting positive lesbigay images

### PUBLICATIONS

**Female FYI (888) 921-4206**

**Feminist Caucus of NAAFA 721-8259** fat women's newsletter

**Gayellow Pages 674-0120** annual guidebook • national & regional editions

**H/X Magazine/ H/X for Her 627-0747** complete weekly party paper

**LGNY 691-1100** newspaper

**Manhattan Spirit 268-0454**

**Next 627-0165** the dish on New York's nightlife

**Pucker Up/Black Dog Productions (718) 486-6966** pansexual erotica zine

**Twist (718) 381-8776** covers tri-state area & PA

### SPIRITUAL GROUPS

**Buddhist Lesbians/Gays: Maitri Dorje** (at Lesbian/Gay Community Ctr.) 6pm 2nd Tue

**Congregation Beth Simchat Torah** 57 Bethune St. **929-9498** 8:30pm Fri (8pm summers) • lesbigay synagogue • wheelchair access

**Dignity** 218 W. 11th St. (St. John's) **627-6488**

**Integrity NYC 691-7181**

**MCC of New York** 446 W. 36th St. **629-7440** 10am & 7pm Sun

**Meditation for Gays/Lesbians/Bisexuals** (at Lesbian/Gay Community Ctr.) 8pm 2nd & 4th Wed

**National Conference for Catholic Lesbians (718) 680-6107** national group • bi-annual conference • quarterly newsletter • for local NY chapter call (212) 663-2963

**Society of Friends (Quakers)** Earl Hall (Columbia University at 116th & Broadway) 777-8866 11am Sun

## N.Y.C. — Soho, Greenwich & Chelsea                    (212)

### ACCOMMODATIONS

**Abingdon B&B** 13 8th Ave. (at W. 12th) **243-5384** lesbians/gay men • smokefree

**Chelsea Inn** 46 W. 17th St. (at 5th & 6th Sts.) **645-8989** gay-friendly

**Chelsea Mews Guest House** 344 W. 15th St. (at 8th & 9th Aves.) **255-9174** mostly gay men

**Chelsea Pines Inn** 317 W. 14th St. (at 8th & 9th Aves.) **929-1023** lesbians/gay men • IGLTA

▲**Colonial House Inn** 318 W. 22nd St. (at 8th & 9th Aves.) **243-9669/(800) 689-3779** mostly gay men • IGLTA

*Your home away from home in...*
# New York City

Winner of *Out & About Magazine's*
1994-1997 *Editor's Choice Award*

Bed & Breakfast
All rooms equipped
with Phones, Cable TV
and A/C

Private / Shared Baths

Lounge; Roof Sundeck

Some w/Refrigerators
and Fireplaces

Rooms from $65.00

Conveniently located ...
Reservations suggested

# COLONIAL HOUSE INN
318  West 22nd Street, New York, N.Y. 10011
Tel: (212) 243-9669        Fax: (212) 633-1612
Email: houseinn@aol.com      (800) 689-3779
Website: www.colonialhouseinn.com

**Commerce Court: Greenwich Village Lodging** 36 Commerce St. **741-0126** gay-friendly • B&B in 1841 renovated brick row house

**East Village B&B 260-1865** women only • apt rental

**The Gramercy Park Hotel** 2 Lexington Ave. (at E. 21st St.) **475-4320/(800) 221-4083** gay-friendly

**Holiday Inn** 138 Lafayette St. **966-8898** gay-friendly

**Hotel Washington Square** 103 Waverly Pl. (at MacDougal St.) **777-9515/(800) 222-0418** gay-friendly

**Incentra Village House** 32 8th Ave. (at W. 12th St.) **206-0007** lesbians/gay men

**Soho Grand Hotel** 310 W. Broadway (at Canal St.) **965-3000/(800) 965-3000** gay-friendly • wheelchair access

## BARS & NIGHTCLUBS

**13 Bar & Lounge** 35 E. 13th St. (at University Pl.) **979-6677** gay-friendly

**Angels** 44 Walker St. (at Church St.) **391-0099** call for Women's Night info

**The Attic** 77 W. Houston St. (at W. Broadway) **388-1384** gay-friendly

**B.M.W. Bar** 199 7th Ave. (at 21st St.) **229-1807** 24hrs • gay-friendly • food served • beer/wine only

**The Bar** 68 2nd Ave. (at 4th St.) **674-9714** 3pm-4am • mostly gay men • neighborhood bar

**Bar d'O** 29 Bedford St. (at Downing St.) **627-1580** 7:30pm-3am • gay-friendly live shows • Ladies' Night Mon

**Barracuda** 275 W. 22nd St. (at 7th & 8th Aves.) **645-8613** 4pm-4am • popular • mostly gay men • live shows

**The Boiler Room** 86 E. 4th St. (at 2nd Ave.) **254-7536** 4pm-4am • popular • mostly gay men • neighborhood bar

**Boots & Saddle** 76 Christopher St. (at 7th Ave.) **929-9684** 8am-4am, noon-4pm Sun • mostly gay men • neighborhood bar

**Bowery Bar** 358 Bowery **475-2220** gay-friendly • neighborhood bar

**Bra Bar** 1st Ave. & E. 9th St. (at 'P.S. 122') **539-8882** mostly women • dancing/DJ

**The Break** 232 8th Ave. (at 22nd St.) **627-0072** 2pm-4am • mostly gay men

**Cherry** 87 7th Ave S. (Time West Cafe) **560-2290** 10:30pm-2am Sun • rooftop cocktail party

**Clit Club** 432 W. 14th St. (at 'Mother') **366-5680** 10pm Fri only • popular • mostly women • dancing/DJ • multi-racial • live shows • wheelchair access

**Crazy Nanny's** 21 7th Ave. S. (at Levoy) **929-8356/366-6312 (EVENT LINE)** 4pm-4am • mostly women • dancing/DJ after 10pm Th-Sat • live shows • also 'Strap' 2nd Sun • social club for leather/fetish-oriented lesbians

**Crow Bar** 339 E. 10th St. (at Ave. B) **420-0670** 9pm-4am • lesbians/gay men • live shows

**Cubbyhole** 281 W. 12th St. (at W. 4th St.) **243-9041** 4pm-3am • mostly women • neighborhood bar

**Dick's Bar** 192 2nd Ave. (at 12th St.) **475-2071** 2pm-4am • mostly gay men

**Diva Hut** 27th St. at 12th Ave. ('Kenny Scharf Room' at Tunnel) **946-4475/387-2043** from 11pm Fri • mostly women • transgender-friendly

**The Dugout** 185 Christopher St. (at Washington St.) **242-9113** 4pm-2am, from noon Fri-Sun • mostly gay men • neighborhood bar • sports bar

**Eighty Eights** 228 W. 10th St. (at Hudson) **924-0088** 4pm-4am • gay-friendly • piano bar • cabaret • Sun brunch

**Flamingo East** 219 2nd Ave. (at 13th St.) **533-2860** gay-friendly

**Flava Party** 340 Broadway (at 'Club Fahrenheit', enter on Leonard) **340-1017** 8pm-4am Wed only • mostly women • dancing/DJ • multi-racial • live shows • buffet

**Gloria Hole@Nowbar** 22 7th Ave. S (at Leroy St.) **802-9502** 10pm Th & Sun • transgendered & pals

**Hell** 59 Gansevoort St. (at Washington) **727-1666** lesbians/gay men

**Henrietta Hudson** 438 Hudson (at Morton) **243-9079** 3pm-4am • mostly women • neighborhood bar • wheelchair access

**Honey Pot** 232 E. 9th St. (at 'Cafe Tabac') (at 2nd & 3rd Aves.) **(917) 729-0614** 10pm-close Wed • mostly women

**Jackie 60** 432 W. 14th St. (at 'Mother') (at 9th Ave.) **677-6060** 10pm-4am Tue only • lesbians/gay men • dancing/DJ • live shows

**Keller's** 384 West St. **243-1907** 2pm-4am • mostly gay men • neighborhood bar • African-American

**LoverGirl NYC** 504 W. 16th St. (at 10th Ave.) **631-1000** 10pm-4:30am sat • mostly women • dancing/DJ • multi-racial • live shows

**Marie's Crisis** 59 Grove St. **243-9323** 5pm-3am • popular • lesbians/gay men • piano bar from 9:30pm

**Meow Mix** 269 E. Houston St. (at Ave. 'A') **254-1434** 8pm-4am, clsd Mon • popular • mostly women • dancing/DJ • live shows

**The Monster** 80 Grove St. (at W. 4th St.) **924-3557** 4pm-4am • mostly gay men • dancing/DJ

**The Oaks** 49 Grove St. (at Bleecker) **367-9390** 4pm-4am • mostly gay men • piano bar

**Opera** 539 W. 21st St. (at 10th Ave.) **229-1618** gay-friendly • alternative • live shows • wheelchair access

**The Playhouse** 526 Canal St. (at Washington St.) **358-5718** 9pm Wed-Sat • transgendered

**Pyramid** 101 Ave. 'A' (at 6th St.) **604-4588** gay-friendly

**Q Bar** 188 Ave. 'A' (at 12th St.) **777-6254** 11pm Wed • lesbians/gay men • live shows

**Roxy** 515 W. 18th St. (at 10th Ave.) **645-5156** rollerskating 8pm-2am Tue • dance floor Sat 11pm • popular • gay-friendly • alternative • live shows

**Rubyfruit Bar & Grill** 531 Hudson St. (at Charles St.) **929-3343** 3pm-4am • mostly women • food served

**Shedevil** 59 Gansevoort St. (Hell) (at Washington St.) **560-2290** 7pm-3am Tue • lesbians/gay men • dancing/DJ

**Shescape** **686-5665** women only • dance parties held at various locations throughout NYC area

**Squeeze Box** 511 Greenwich St. (at 'Don Hill's') (at Spring St. ) **334-1390** from 10pm Fri only • lesbians/gay men • dancing/DJ • live shows

**Stonewall Inn** 53 Christopher St. (at 7th Ave.) **463-0950** 4pm-4am • mostly gay men

**Velvet** 167 Ave. 'A' (at 10th & 11th) 10:30pm Sun 'Club Casanova' • lesbians/gay men • transgender-friendly • Drag King performances

**Wonder Bar** 505 E. 6th St. (at Ave. 'A') **777-9105** 8pm-4am • lesbians/gay men • neighborhood bar • videos

**WOW! Wednesdays** 248 W. 14th St. (at 7th Ave.) **631-1102** 6:30pm-3am Wed • mostly women • dancing/DJ • live shows

## CAFES

**Cafe Tabac** 232 E. 9th St. **674-7072** 6pm-3am • no meals • full bar

## RESTAURANTS

**Around the Clock** 9th St. (at 3rd Ave.) **598-0402**

**Benny's Burritos** 112 Greenwich Ave. **633-9210** 11:30am-midnight • cheap & huge

**Big Cup** 228 8th Ave. (at 22nd St.) **206-0059** mostly gay men

**Black Sheep** 344 W. 11th St. **242-1010** popular • mostly gay men • 6pm-11pm • fine dining w/nostalgic country cooking • $16-25

**Blue Ribbon** 97 Sullivan St. (at Spring St.) **274-0404** 4am-4am • chef hangout

**Brunetta's** 190 1st Ave. (at 11th St.) **228-4030** popular • lesbians/gay men • Italian • some veggie • $8-10

**Caffe Raffaella** 134 7th Ave. (at Charles St.) **929-7247**

**Casinis** 54 E. 1st St. (at 2nd Ave.) **777-1589** 6pm-midnight, til 2am wknds • French bistro

**Chelsea Bistro & Bar** 358 W. 23rd St. (at 9th Ave.) **727-2026** 5:30pm-11pm • trendy French • full bar

**Circa** 103 2nd Ave. (at E. 6th St.) **777-4120** lunch & dinner • popular • full bar • wheelchair access • women-owned/run

**Claire** 156 7th Ave. (at 19th St.) **255-1955** noon-11:30pm

**Cola's** 148 8th Ave. (at 17th St.) **633-8020** 4:30pm-11pm • popular • Italian • some veggie • $8-12

**Comfort Diner** 214 E. 4th St. (at 3rd Ave.) **867-4555**

**Community Bar & Grill** 216 7th Ave. (at 22nd St.) **242-7900** lunch & dinner • live shows

**Eighteenth & Eighth** 159 8th Ave. (at 18th St. (of course!)) **242-5000** boys, boys, boys

**Empire Diner** 210 10th Ave. (at 22nd St.) **243-2736** 24hrs • upscale diner

**First** 87 1st Ave. (at 6th St.) **674-3823** 5:30pm-3am, from 11am Sun • hip crowd

**Florent** 69 Gansevoort St. (at Washington) **989-5779** 9am-5am, 24hrs Fri-Sat • popular • French diner • $10-15

**Food Bar** 149 8th Ave. (at 17th St.) **243-2020** 3pm-midnight • popular • mostly gay men

**Garage** 99 7th Ave. S. (at Grove St.) **645-0600** plenty veggie • live jazz

**Global 33** 93 2nd Ave. (5th St.) **477-8427** 5pm-midnight • int'l tapas • full bar • $8-15

**Good Luck Cheng's** 206 W. 23rd St. (at 7th Ave.) **645-2999**

**La Nouvelle Justine** 206 W. 23rd St. **727-8642** popular • dominants & slaves serve it up in this SM-themed restaurant

**Life Cafe** 343 E. 10th St. (at Ave. 'B') **477-8791**

**Lips** 2 Bank St. **675-7710** dinner nightly, Sun brunch • full bar • 'the ultimate in drag dining'

**Lucky Cheng's** 24 1st Ave. (at 2nd St.) **473-0516** 6pm-midnight • popular • Chinese • full bar • live shows

**Lucky Dog Diner** 167 1st Ave. (at 10th St.) **260-4220**

**Mary's Restaurant** 42 Bedford St. (at 7th Ave.) **741-3387**

**Restivo** 209 7th Ave. (at 22nd St.) **366-4133** noon-midnight • gourmet • gay-owned/run

**Sacred Chow** 522 Hudson St. (at 10th St.) **337-0863** wheelchair access

**Sarong Sarong** 343 Bleecker St. (at 11th St.) **989-0888** opens 11am • popular • Malaysian • some veggie • full bar

**Sazerac House Bar & Grill** 533 Hudson (at Charles) **989-0313** noon-11pm • Cajun • full bar • $8-20

**Stingy Lulu's** 129 St. Marks Pl. (at Ave. 'A') **674-3545**

**Trattoria Pesce Pasta** 262 Bleecker St. **645-2993** noon-midnight

**Universal Grill** 44 Bedford St. (at 7th Ave.) **989-5621** lunch, dinner & Sun brunch • popular • lesbians/gay men

**The Viceroy** 160 8th Ave. (at 18th St.) **633-8484** noon-midnight • popular • full bar

**Windows on India** 344 E. 6th St. (at 1st Ave.) **477-5956** noon-midnight • best food in NYC's 'Little India'

## ENTERTAINMENT & RECREATION

**Girl Strike at Bowlmor Lanes** 110 University (at 12th & 13th) **686-5665/255-8188** 8:30pm-1:30am Sun • women only

**WOW Cafe Cabaret** 59 E. 4th St. **777-4280** Th-Sat • women's theater

## BOOKSTORES & RETAIL SHOPS

**A Different Light** 151 W. 19th St. (at 7th Ave.) **989-4850/(800) 343-4002** 10am-midnight • lesbigay bookstore

**Alternate Card & Gift Shop** 85 Christopher St. (at 7th Ave.) **645-8966** noon-11pm

**Bleecker Street Books** 350 Bleecker St. **675-2084** 10am-midnight

**Don't Panic** 98 Christopher St. (at Bleecker St.) **989-7888** 11am-9pm • lesbigay T-shirts & more

**Greetings** 45 Christopher St. **242-0424** 11am-10pm

**Oscar Wilde Memorial Bookshop** 15 Christopher St. (at 7th Ave.) **255-8097** 11:30am-9pm • lesbigay

**Rainbows & Triangles** 192 8th Ave. (at 19th St.) **627-2166** 11am-9pm • lesbigay

**Soho Books** 351 W. Broadway (at Grant) **226-3395** 10am-midnight

## TRAVEL AGENTS

**Easyway USA** 350 5th Ave. #6608 **629-0964** IGLTA

**The Greek Island Connection** 889 9th Ave. **581-4784** IGLTA

**Islander's Kennedy Travel** 183 W. 10th St. **242-3222/(800) 988-1181** also Queens location: 314 Jericho Trnpk., Floral Park (516) 352-4888 • IGLTA

**The People Travel Club** 156 5th Ave. #1025 **627-4004** IGLTA

**Rich Worldwide Travel** 500 5th Ave. #325 **997-1600** IGLTA

## SPIRITUAL GROUPS

**Church of St. Luke in the Fields (Episcopal)** 487 Hudson St. **924-0562** 10am Sun & 6:15pm wkdays

## GYMS & HEALTH CLUBS

**American Fitness Center** 128 8th Ave. **627-0065** popular • mostly gay men • day passes avail.

**Archives Gym** 666 Greenwich Ave. **366-3725** day passes avail.

**David Barton Gym** 552 6th Ave. **727-0004** lesbians/gay men • day passes avail.

**Health & Fitness** 22 W. 19th St. **929-6789** lesbians/gay men • day passes avail.

## SEX CLUBS

**The Vault** 28 10th Ave. (at 13th St.) **255-6758** 7pm-11pm 3rd Sun, doors close at 8:30pm • women only

## EROTICA

**Pleasure Chest** 156 7th Ave. S. (at Charles) **242-2158**

# N.Y.C.—Midtown (212)

## ACCOMMODATIONS

**Central Park South B&B** **586-0652** lesbians/gay men • wheelchair access

**Gershwin Hotel** 7 E. 27th St. (at 5th Ave.) **545-8000**

**Hotel Beverly** 125 E. 50th St. **753-2700/(800) 223-0945** gay-friendly • food served • IGLTA

**The Hotel Metro** 45 W. 35th St. (at 5th Ave.) **947-2500/(800) 356-3870** gay-friendly

**Park Central Hotel** 870 7th Ave. (at 56th St.) **247-8000/(800) 346-1359** gay-friendly • also restaurant • wheelchair access

**Travel Inn** 515 W. 42nd St. (at 10th Ave.) **695-7171** gay-friendly • IGLTA

## BARS & NIGHTCLUBS

**Cleo's Saloon** 656 9th Ave. (at 46th St.) **307-1503** 8am-4am • mostly gay men • neighborhood bar

**Clubhouse** 215 W. 28th St. (at 7th Ave.) **726-8820** lesbians/gay men • dancing/DJ • mostly African-American

**Danny's Skylight Room** 346 W. 46th St. (at 9th Ave.) **265-8133** gay-friendly • live shows • food served

**Don't Tell Mama** 343 W. 46th St. (at 9th Ave.) **757-0788** 4pm-4am • popular • gay-friendly • live shows

**Edelweiss** 578 11th Ave. (at 43rd St.) **629-1021** 5:30pm-4am • gay-friendly • dancing/DJ • live shows • fun mix of drag, transgender & everything else

**The Greenhorn Saloon** 818 10th Ave. (at 54th St.) **582-5665** 4pm-4am • mostly gay men • neighborhood bar • country/western • also 'Caroline's Oasis' from 8pm • dancing/DJ • transgender-friendly • live shows • patio

**Her/She Bar** Mid Block W. 27th St. (at 11th & 12th Ave.) **631-1093** 10:30pm-4:30am Fri • mostly women • dancing/DJ • $8 cover

**Julie's** 204 E. 58th St. (at 2nd Ave.) **688-1294** 5pm-4am • mostly women • professional • DJ Wed-Sun

**Octagon** 555 W. 33rd St. **947-0400** Fri only • mostly gay men • dancing/DJ • mostly African-American

**Rome** 290 8th Ave (at 24th St) **242-6969** mostly gay men • live shows

**She-Bang** (at 10th Ave.) **631-1102** 10pm-5am Sat • mostly women • dancing/DJ • live shows • call for location

**Sidebar** 366 8th Ave. (at 28th St.) **244-2668** mostly gay men • dancing/DJ • mostly African-American • live shows

**South Dakota** 405 3rd Ave. (at 29th St.) **684-8376** 3pm-4am • mostly gay men • neighborhood bar

**Twilo** 530 W. 27th St. (at 10th Ave.) **268-1600** 11pm-7am Fri-Sat • gay-friendly • dancing/DJ • live shows

**The Web** 40 E. 58th St. (at Park Ave.) **308-1546** 4pm-3am • mostly gay men • dancing/DJ • mostly Asian

## CAFES

**Cafe Un Deux Trois** 123 W. 44th St. **354-4148** noon-midnight • popular • bistro • $12-24

## RESTAURANTS

**Mangia e Bevi** 800 9th Ave. (at 53rd St.) **956-3976** noon-midnight • Italian

**Revolution** 611 9th Ave. (at 43rd St.) **489-8451** 5pm-midnight • trendy video dining

**Rice & Beans** 744 9th Ave. (at 50th St.) **265-4444** 11am-10pm • Latin/Brazilian • plenty veggie

**Townhouse Restaurant** 206 E. 58th (at 3rd Ave.) **826-6241** lunch & dinner, Sun brunch, late on wknds • popular • lesbians/gay men • eclectic & elegant • plenty veggie • live shows • $10-23

## TRAVEL AGENTS

**Empress Travel** 138 E. 34th St. **685-1800** IGLTA

**Kon Travel** 310 Madison Ave. (at 42nd St.) **286-9410** IGLTA

**Liberty Travel** 298 Madison Ave. (at 41st St.) **689-5600** IGLTA

**Pied Piper Travel** 330 W. 42nd St. #1804 **239-2412/(800) 874-7312** IGLTA

**RMC Travel** 424 Madison Ave. #705 (at 49th St.) **754-6560** IGLTA

**Roberta Sonnino Travel** 19 W. 34th St. (at 7th Ave.) **714-2540** IGLTA

**SPA Adventures** 325 W. 45th St. #910 (at 8th Ave.) **399-0700** IGLTA

**Stevens Travel Management** 432 Park Ave. S., 9th flr. (at 29th St.) **696-4300/(800) 275-7400** IGLTA

**Travel Innovations** 1501 Broadway #506 (at 43rd St.) **354-3100** IGLTA

### EROTICA

**Eve's Garden** 119 W. 57th St. #420 **757-8651** noon-7pm, clsd Sun • women's sexuality boutique

## N.Y.C. — Uptown                    (212)

### ACCOMMODATIONS

**Malibu Studios Hotel** 2688 Broadway **222-2954/(800) 647-2227** gay-friendly • $45-80+

### BARS & NIGHTCLUBS

**Brandy's Piano Bar** 235 E. 84th St. (at 2nd Ave.) **650-1944** 4pm-4am • mostly gay men • wheelchair access

**Bridge Bar** 309 E. 60th St. (at 2nd Ave.) **223-9104** 4pm-4am • mostly gay men

**Candle Bar** 309 Amsterdam (at 74th St.) **874-9155** 2pm-4am • popular • mostly gay men • neighborhood bar

**Columbia Dance** 116th St. at Broadway (Earl Hall) **854-1488** lesbians/gay men

**Oscar Wilde** 221 E. 58th St. (at 2nd Ave.) **486-7309** mostly gay men • professional

**Regents** 317 E. 53rd St. (at 2nd Ave.) **593-3091** noon-4am • mostly gay men • also restaurant • Italian • plenty veggie • $7-17

### RESTAURANTS

**Carnegie Delicatessen** 854 7th Ave. (at nr. 55th St.) **757-2245** 7am-4am • one of NYC's most famous delis

### TRAVEL AGENTS

**Deep Journeys Ltd.** 98 Riverside Dr. #5H **595-9573** IGLTA

**Discretion** 527 W. 143rd St. #44 **368-0717** IGLTA

## N.Y.C. — Brooklyn                    (718)

### BARS & NIGHTCLUBS

**Carry Nation** 363 5th Ave., Park Slope **788-0924** 4pm-3am • lesbians/gay men • neighborhood bar

**Celebrity's** 8705 3rd Ave., Bay Ridge **745-9652** 6pm-4am, from 4pm Sun, clsd Mon • lesbians/gay men • ladies night Tue

**One Hot Spot** 1 Front St. (under Brooklyn Bridge) **852-0139** 9pm-3am, from 6pm Th, clsd Sun-Tue • lesbians/gay men • dancing/DJ • multi-racial • live shows • wheelchair access

**Rising Cafe** 186 5th Ave. (at Sackett) **789-6340** call for hours

**The Roost** 309 7th Ave. (at 8th St.) **788-9793** noon-2am • gay-friendly • neighborhood bar

**Sanctuary** 444 7th Ave. (at 15th St.) **832-9800** 9pm-close • lesbians/gay men • neighborhood bar • dancing/DJ • theme nights

**Spectrum** 802 64th St. **238-8213** 9pm-4am Wed-Sun • popular • lesbians/gay men • dancing/DJ • live shows • unconfirmed

**Whatever Lounge** 71 Pineapple St., Brooklyn Hts. **246-1484** 4pm-4am • mostly gay men • ladies night Th • food served

**Wildflower** 9235 4th Ave. (at 93rd St.) **238-6566** Wed-Sun • lesbians/gay men • dancing/DJ • live shows

### CAFES

**Kokobar Cybercafe & Bookstore** 59 Lafayette Ave. (at Fulton) **243-9040** 7am-10pm, 10am-11pm Sat, til 10pm Sun • lesbians/gay men • wheelchair access

### RESTAURANTS

**200 Fifth** 200 5th Ave. (at Union & Berkeley) **638-0023/638-2925** from 4pm • eclectic • full bar • live shows

**Aunt Suzie** 247 5th Ave. (at Garfield Pl.) **788-2868** Italian

**Johnny Mack's** 1114 8th Ave. **832-7961** 4pm-11pm, til 1am Fri-Sat, noon-3:30pm Sat & Sun (brunch)

**Max & Moritz** 426-A 7th Ave. **499-5557** from 5:30pm • French/American

**Santa Fe Grill** 62 7th Ave. **636-0279** from 5:30pm • French/American

### ENTERTAINMENT & RECREATION

**Dyke TV** Channel 34/67 **343-9335** midnight 1st Fri • 'weekly half-hour TV show produced by lesbians, for lesbians'

### BOOKSTORES & RETAIL SHOPS

**Beyond Words** 186 5th Ave., Park Slope (at Sackett) **857-0010** hours vary • lesbigay • lesbigay-owned

### PUBLICATIONS

**Brooklyn Pride** **670-3337** newsletter

## TRAVEL AGENTS
**Avalon Travel** 9421 3rd Ave. (at 94th St.) **833-5500** IGLTA

**Deville Travel Service** 7818 3rd Ave. (at 78th St.) **680-2700**

**J. Bette Travel** 4809 Ave. 'N' #279 **241-3872** IGLTA

**Sea Rapture By M.A.B.** 225 Vandalia Ace. #14D **642-0740** IGLTA

## SPIRITUAL GROUPS
**Brooklyn Heights Synagogue** 117 Remsen St. **522-2070** 6:30pm Fri

**First Unitarian Church of Brooklyn** 50 Monroe Pl. **624-5466** 11am Sun

# N.Y.C.—Queens (718)

## INFO LINES & SERVICES
**Q-GLU (Queens Gay/Lesbians United)** **205-6605** 1st Tue

## BARS & NIGHTCLUBS
**Amnesia** 32-03 Broadway (at 32nd St.), Astoria **204-7010** gay-friendly • dancing/DJ

**The Boulevard** 137-65 Queens Blvd., Briarwood **739-2200** 8pm-4am • mostly gay men

**Krash** 34-48 Steinway St., Astoria **366-2934** lesbians/gay men • more women Sat • dancing/DJ • multi-racial

**Music Box** 40-08 74th St. (at Roosevelt Ave.), Jackson Hts. **429-9356** 4pm-4am • mostly gay men • multi-racial • leather

## TRAVEL AGENTS
**Riverdale Travel Service** 5705 Mosholu Ave., Riverdale **549-5950** IGLTA

# N.Y.C.—Bronx (212)

## INFO LINES & SERVICES
**BLUES (Bronx Lesbians United in Sisterhood)** 330-9196

**Bronx Lavender Community Center** 2432 Grand Concourse #504 (at 187th) **379-1093 x4**

## BARS & NIGHTCLUBS
**Sadie's Too** 5592 Broadway (at 231st St.) **548-9410** from 6pm • mostly gay men • neighborhood bar

**Up & Down Bar** 1306 Union Port Rd. (at Westchester Ave.) **822-9585** 9pm-4am Tue only

## ENTERTAINMENT & RECREATION
**Dyke TV** Channel 70 10pm Wed & Th • 'weekly half-hour TV show produced by lesbians, for lesbians'

# N.Y.C.—Staten Island (718)

## INFO LINES & SERVICES
**Lambda Associates of Staten Island** 876-8786

## BARS & NIGHTCLUBS
**The Amazon** 23 Sands St. (Bay St.), Stapleton **816-0713** 9pm-4am • lesbians/gay men • dancing/DJ • unconfirmed

**Visionz** 492 Bay St. **273-7354** from 8pm, from 6pm Sun w/T-dance • lesbians/gay men • dancing/DJ • also outdoor cafe • hot tub

## TRAVEL AGENTS
**Haggart Travel** 75 St. Marks Pl. **981-7015** IGLTA

# Niagara Falls (716)
*(see also Niagara Falls, Ontario)*

## ACCOMMODATIONS
**Old Niagara House B&B** 610 4th St. **285-9408** gay-friendly

## BARS & NIGHTCLUBS
**Club Alternate** 492 19th St. (Ferry) mostly gay men • dancing/DJ • inquire locally • unconfirmed

# Nyack (914)

## BARS & NIGHTCLUBS
**Barz** 327 Rte. 9 W. **353-4444** 5pm-4am, from 1pm Sun, clsd Mon • lesbians/gay men • dancing/DJ • wheelchair access

**Coven Cafe** 162 Main St. **358-9829** noon-midnight, til 2am Fri-Sat, clsd Mon • gay-friendly • also restaurant • cont'l w/Southern accent • wheelchair access • $8-20

## BOOKSTORES & RETAIL SHOPS
**New Spirit Books & Beyond** 128 Main St. **353-2126** noon-7pm, clsd Mon

# Ontario (315)

## TRAVEL AGENTS
**Catherine's Travel Service** 528 Haley Rd. **524-8733** IGLTA

## Orange County (914)

### Info Lines & Services
**Orange County Gay/Lesbian Alliance** 782-1525 7:30pm Tue

### Restaurants
**Folderol II** Rte. 284, Westtown 726-3822 lunch & dinner, 3pm-9pm Sun, clsd Mon • French/farmhouse • some veggie • wheelchair access • gay-owned/run • $13-23

## Oswego (315)

### Info Lines & Services
**SUNY Oswego Women's Center** 243 Hewitt Union, 2nd flr. 341-2967

### Travel Agents
**Tioga Travel** 189 Main St. 687-4144 IGLTA

## Plattsburg (518)

### Bars & Nightclubs
**Blair's Tavern** 30 Marion St. 561-9071 4pm-2am, from 6pm wknds • lesbians/gay men • dancing/DJ • ladies night Th

## Port Chester (914)

### Bars & Nightclubs
**Sandy's Old Homestead** 325 N. Main St. 939-0758 8am-4am • gay-friendly • food served • wheelchair access

## Poughkeepsie (914)

### Info Lines & Services
**Poughkeepsie GALA (Gay/Lesbian Association)** 431-6756 7:30pm Tue • call for events

### Bars & Nightclubs
**Congress** 411 Main St. 486-9068 3pm-4am, from 8pm Sun • lesbians/gay men • neighborhood bar • wheelchair access

## Rochester (716)

### Info Lines & Services
**AA Gay/Lesbian** 232-6720 (AA#) call for mtg. schedule
**Gay Alliance** 179 Atlantic Ave. 244-8640 1pm-9:30pm, til 6pm Fri, clsd wknds

### Bars & Nightclubs
**Anthony's 522** 522 E. Main St. 325-2060 noon-2am • lesbians/gay men • neighborhood bar

**Atlantis** 10-12 S. Washington St. 423-9748 call for events • mostly gay men • dancing/DJ

**Avenue Pub** 522 Monroe Ave. 244-4960 4pm-2am • popular • mostly gay men • neighborhood bar • dancing/DJ

**Club Marcella** 123 Liberty Pole Wy. 454-5963 clsd Mon-Tue • lesbians/gay men • dancing/DJ • live shows

**Club Quintana** 34 Glide St. 464-9446 9pm-1am Th only • lesbians/gay men • dancing/DJ • unconfirmed

**Common Grounds** 139 State St. 262-2650 11am-2am • lesbians/gay men • neighborhood bar

**Freakazoid** 169 N. Chestnut St. 987-0000 gay-friendly • dancing/DJ • alternative • also fetish club • call for events

**Muther's** 40 S.Union 325-6216 3pm-2am • lesbians/gay men • women's night 2nd & 3rd Th • T-Dance Sun • live shows • also restaurant • some veggie • patio • $5-18

**R Bar** 145 E. Main St. 232-7240 7pm-2am, clsd Sun • mostly women • neighborhood bar • food served • wheelchair access

**Tara Lounge** 153 Liberty Pole Wy. 232-4719 noon-2am • popular • lesbians/gay men • neighborhood bar • piano bar

### Cafes
**Little Theatre Cafe** 240 East Ave. 258-0412 6pm-10pm, from noon wknds, til midnight Fri-Sat • popular • soups • salads • live shows • wheelchair access • $5-10

### Restaurants
**Slice of Life Cafe** 742 South Ave. 271-8010 11:30am-8pm, 10am-2pm Sun, clsd Mon-Tue • vegetarian

**Triphammer Grill** 60 Browns Race 262-2700 lunch & dinner, clsd Sun-Mon (dinner) • patio • full bar • $10-22

### Bookstores & Retail Shops
**The Pride Connection** 728 South Ave. 242-7840 10am-9pm, noon-6pm Sun • lesbigay

**Silkwood Books** 633 Monroe Ave. 473-8110 11am-6pm, til 9pm Th-Fri, noon-5pm Sun, clsd Mon • women's/new age • wheelchair access

**Village Green Books** 766 Monroe Ave. 461-5380 6am-11pm • also 1954 W. Ridge Rd. location 723-1600

## PUBLICATIONS

**Empty Closet** 244-9030 lesbigay newspaper • resource listings

## TRAVEL AGENTS

**DePrez Travel** 145 Rue De Ville **442-8900** ask for Ray • IGLTA

**Park Ave. Travel** 25 Buckingham St. **256-3080** IGLTA

## SPIRITUAL GROUPS

**Calvary St. Andrew's Parish (Presbyterian)** 68 Ashland St. **325-4950** 10am Sun & noon Tue • 'More Light' congregation

**Community Christian Fellowship** 835 South Ave. (South Avenue Baptist Church) **234-9776** 5:30pm Sun • Evangelical lesbigays & friends

**Dignity/Integrity** 17 S. Fitzhugh (Church of St. Luke & St. Simon Cyrene) **262-2170** 5pm Sun

**Open Arms MCC** 175 Norris Dr. **271-8478** 10:30am Sun • wheelchair access

## EROTICA

**Dundalk News** 561 State St. **325-2248** 24hrs

**Rochester Custom Leathers** 274 N. Goodman St. **442-2323/(800) 836-9047** 11am-9pm • popular

# Saratoga Springs (518)

## BOOKSTORES & RETAIL SHOPS

**Nahani** 482 Broadway **587-4322** 10am-6pm, noon-5pm Sun • wheelchair access

# Schenectady (518)

## BARS & NIGHTCLUBS

**Blythewood** 50 N. Jay St. **382-9755** 9pm-4am • mostly gay men • neighborhood bar • wheelchair access

# Seneca Falls (315)

## ACCOMMODATIONS

**Guion House** 32 Cayuga St. **(315) 568-8129/631-8919** gay-friendly • full brkfst • smokefree

## RESTAURANTS

**Gene's Grille at the Gould** 108 Fall St. **568-4403** lunch & dinner • bistro • full bar • wheelchair access • $4-15

# Sharon Springs (518)

## RESTAURANTS

**Rockville Cafe & Bakery** Main St. **284-3015** 6:30am-2pm, clsd Mon

# Syracuse (315)

## INFO LINES & SERVICES

**AA Gay/Lesbian** 463-5011 **(AA#)** call for mtg. schedule

**Lesbian Discussion Group** call Women's Center for info

**Lesbian Social Group** call Women's Center for info

**Pride Community Center** 745 N. Salina St. **426-1650** 6pm-10pm Wed-Fri, from noon Sat

**Women's Information Center** 601 Allen St. **478-4636** 10am-4pm, clsd wknds • wheelchair access

## ACCOMMODATIONS

**John Milton Inn** Carrier Circle, Exit 35 **463-8555/(800) 352-1061** gay-friendly

## BARS & NIGHTCLUBS

**Armory Pub** 400 S. Clinton **471-9059** 8am-2am • mostly gay men • dancing/DJ • wheelchair access

**Mr. T's** 218 N. Franklin St. **471-9026** 3pm-2am, from noon Sun • popular • mostly gay men • neighborhood bar • dancing/DJ

**My Bar** 205 N. West St. **471-9279** 10am-2am, til 4am Fri-Sat • mostly women • dancing/DJ • food served (lunch, dinner & late night brkfst)

**Plato** 1203 Milton Ave. **468-9830** 4pm-2am, from 7pm Sat, from noon Sun, clsd Mon-Tue • mostly women • dancing/DJ

**Ryan's** 408-410 Pearl St. **471-9499** 8pm-2am, from noon Sun, clsd Mon-Wed • popular • mostly gay men • dancing/DJ • videos • wheelchair access

**Trexx** 319 N. Clinton St. **474-6408** 8pm-2am, til 4am Fri-Sat, clsd Mon-Tue • mostly gay men • dancing/DJ • live shows • wheelchair access

## CAFES

**Happy Endings** 317 S. Clinton St. **475-1853** 8am-11pm, 10am-2am Fri-Sat, 6pm-11pm Sun • lunch & coffeehouse • live shows • wheelchair access

## RESTAURANTS

**Tu Tu Venue** 731 James St. (enter on Willow St.) **475-8888** 4pm-1am, clsd Sun • popular • full bar • women-owned/run • $12-15

## BOOKSTORES & RETAIL SHOPS

**My Sister's Words** 304 N. McBride St. **428-0227** 10am-6pm, til 8pm Th-Fri, clsd Sun (except Dec) • women's • community bulletin board

## SPIRITUAL GROUPS

**Ray of Hope MCC** 326 Montgomery St. (YMCA) **471-6618** 6pm Sun • wheelchair access

## Utica (315)

### BARS & NIGHTCLUBS

**That Place** 216 Bleecker St. **724-1446** 8pm-2am, from 4pm Fri • popular • mostly gay men • dancing/DJ • leather • wheelchair access • unconfirmed

## White Plains (914)

### INFO LINES & SERVICES

**Lesbian Line 949-3203** 6pm-10pm

**The Loft** 200 Hamilton Ave. **948-4922** switchboard 1pm-4pm, 7pm-10pm • lesbigay community center • annual local gay cruise • also newsletter 948-2932

### BARS & NIGHTCLUBS

**Stutz** 202 Westchester Ave. **761-3100** 5pm-4am • popular • mostly gay men • dancing/DJ • live shows

### TRAVEL AGENTS

**Aquarius Travel** 25 Rockledge Ave. #603 **682-5663** IGLTA

## Woodstock (914)

### INFO LINES & SERVICES

**Wise Woman Center** 246-8081 women only • workshops • correspondence courses • newsletter

### ACCOMMODATIONS

**Woodstock Inn** 38 Tannery Brook Rd. **679-8211** gay-friendly • swimming hole • wheelchair access

### CAFES

**Tinker Street Cafe** 59 Tinker St. **679-2487** noon-4am • live music • patio

### BOOKSTORES & RETAIL SHOPS

**Golden Notebook** 29 Tinker St. **679-8000** 10:30am-7pm, til 9pm (summers) • lesbigay section • wheelchair access

## Yonkers (914)

### TRAVEL AGENTS

**Good Bye's Travel** 3 David Ln. #7Q **969-5763** nationwide service

# NORTH CAROLINA

## Asheville (704)

### INFO LINES & SERVICES

**CLOSER (Community Liaison for Support, Education & Reform)** 277-7815 call for info

**Lambda AA** All Souls Church, Biltmore Village **254-8539 (AA#)** 8pm Fri

**OutFit** 277-7815 1st & 3rd Sat • lesbigay youth support group

### ACCOMMODATIONS

**27 Blake Street** 27 Blake St. **252-7390** women only • Victorian home • $65

**Acorn Cottage B&B** 25 St. Dunstans Cir. **253-0609/(800) 699-0609** gay-friendly • full brkfst • smokefree

**Apple Wood Manor Inn** 62 Cumberland Cir. **254-2244** gay-friendly • full brkfst

**The Bird's Nest B&B** 41 Oak Park Rd. **252-2381** lesbians/gay men • comfortable, secluded & quiet B&B • located on the second flr. of a turn-of-the-century home • lesbian-owned/run • $85

▲ **Camp Pleiades 688-9201 (SUMMER)/(904) 241-3050 (WINTER)** open Memorial Day-Halloween • women only • mtn. retreat • cabins • swimming • all meals included • smokefree • private/shared baths • lesbian-owned/run • $45-85

**Emy's Nook 669-0507** women only • lesbian-owned/run • $45

**The Inn on Montford** 296 Montford Ave. **254-9569/(800) 254-9569** gay-friendly • full brkfst • English cottage • $115-160

**Mountain Laurel B&B** 139 Lee Dotson Rd., Fairview **628-9903** mostly women • full brkfst • 25 mi. from Asheville • lesbian-owned/run • $80

### BARS & NIGHTCLUBS

**The Barber Shop/Hairspray Cafe** 38 N. French Broad Ave. **258-2027** 7pm-2am • lesbians/gay men • dancing/DJ • live shows • private club • also 'Club Metropolis' from 10pm Th-Sat

**O. Henry's** 59 Haywood St. **254-1891** 1pm-2am, from 11am Sat • lesbians/gay men • neighborhood bar • dancing/DJ • private club

**Scandals** 11 Grove St. **252-2838** 10pm-3am, clsd Sun-Wed • lesbians/gay men • dancing/DJ • live shows • 18+ Th • wheelchair access • also 'Getaways' • quiet lounge • videos

## CAFES

**Laurey's** 67 Biltmore Ave. **252-1500** 10am-6pm, til 4pm Sat, clsd Sun • popular • bright cafe w/delicious salads & cookies • also dinners to-go • women-owned/run • wheelchair access

## RESTAURANTS

**Grove Street Cafe** 11 Grove St. **255-0010** 6pm-1am Wed-Sat (summer T-dance & BBQ 2pm-8pm Sun) • steaks/seafood • some veggie • full bar • patio • $10-15

**Laughing Seed Cafe** 40 Wall St. **252-3445** 11:30am-9pm, til 10pm Th-Sat, clsd Sun • vegetarian/vegan • beer/wine • patio • wheelchair access • $4-9

## BOOKSTORES & RETAIL SHOPS

**Downtown Books & News** 67 N. Lexington Ave. **253-8654** 8am-6pm, from 6am Sun • used books & new magazines

**The Goddess Store** 382 Montford Ave. **258-3102** noon-6pm, clsd Sun-Mon • lesbian/feminist gifts • divination tools • Wiccan items • call for class schedules • wheelchair access

**Jewels That Dance: Jewelry Design** 63 Haywood St. **254-5088**

**Malaprop's Bookstore & Cafe** 55 Haywood St. **254-6734**/**(800) 441-9829** 9am-8pm, til 10pm Fri-Sat, noon-6pm Sun • readings • performances

**Rainbow's End** 10 N. Spruce St. **285-0005** 10am-8pm • lesbigay

## PUBLICATIONS

**Community Connections** 251-2449 unconfirmed

## TRAVEL AGENTS

**Journeys** 8 Biltmore Ave. **232-0800**/**(800) 256-8235** IGLTA

**Kaleidoscope Travel** 120 Merrimon Ave. **253-7777**/**(800) 964-2001**

## SPIRITUAL GROUPS

**The Cathedral of All Souls** Biltmore Village **274-2681** 8am, 9am & 11am Sun, noon & 5:45pm Wed • wheelchair access

**MCC of Asheville** 1 Edwin Pl. (Unitarian Universalist Church) **232-0062** 6:30pm Sun • wheelchair access

# It's Always Women's Week At...

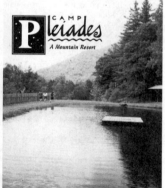

**Camp Pleiades,** a 67-acre mountain resort in western North Carolina. Swim in a stream-fed pond, hike wooded trails, enjoy evening campfires. Whitewater rafting, horseback riding, golf and galleries are nearby. Sleep in private or group cabins and share fabulous family style meals. Open Memorial Day through Labor Day and Fall Foliage. Call or write for 1998 season brochure.

**Nov. - April** 390 Garden Lane, Atlantic Beach, FL 32233  904/241-3050
**May - Sept.** Rt. 2 Box 250 Hughes Gap Road, Bakersville, NC 28705
704/688-9201  e-mail Starcamp@aol.com

**St. Joan of Arc Catholic Church** 919 Haywood Rd. **252-3151** 5pm Sat, 8:30am & 11:30am Sun

**Unitarian Universalist Church of Asheville** 1 Edwin Pl. **254-6001** 9am & 11am Sun (10am Sun summers) • wheelchair access

**WHISPER (Women's Holy Inspirational Performances, Events & Ritual)** **258-3102** weekly classes

EROTICA
**Octopus' Garden** 102 N. Lexington Ave. **254-4980**

## Bat Cave (704)

ACCOMMODATIONS
**Old Mill B&B** **625-4256** gay-friendly • full brkfst

## Blowing Rock (704)

ACCOMMODATIONS
**Stone Pillar B&B** 144 Pine St. **295-4141** gay-friendly • full brkfst • historic 1920s house • wheelchair access

## Cashiers (704)

ACCOMMODATIONS
**Jane's Aerie Cottage** **743-9002** popular • mostly women • cottage in great mtn. location

## Chapel Hill (919)

*(see also Raleigh/Durham)*

INFO LINES & SERVICES
**Orange County Women's Center** 210 Henderson **968-4610** 9am-7:30pm, til 5pm Fri, clsd wknds • wheelchair access

ACCOMMODATIONS
**Joan's Place** **942-5621** women only • shared baths • lesbian-owned/run • $45-48

RESTAURANTS
**Crooks Corner** 610 Franklin St. **929-7643** 6pm-10:30pm, Sun brunch • Southern • some veggie • full bar • wheelchair access • $20-25

**Weathervane Cafe** Eastgate Shopping Ctr. **929-9466** lunch & dinner, Sun brunch • some veggie • full bar • patio • wheelchair access • $10-20

BOOKSTORES & RETAIL SHOPS
**Internationalist Books** 405 W. Franklin St. **942-1740** 10am-8pm, til 6pm Sun • progressive/alternative • 'Movie Night' Fri

SPIRITUAL GROUPS
**Community Church (Unitarian Universalist)** 106 Purefoy Rd. **942-2050** 11am Sun

## Charlotte (704)

INFO LINES & SERVICES
**AA Gay/Lesbian** 3200 Park Rd. (St. Luke's Lutheran Church) **332-4387 (AA#)** 8pm Tue

**Gay/Lesbian Switchboard** **535-6277** 6:30pm-10:30pm

BARS & NIGHTCLUBS
**Brass Rail** 3707 Wilkinson Blvd. **399-8413** 5pm-2am, from 3pm Sun • popular • mostly gay men • neighborhood bar • leather • private club • wheelchair access

**Chaser's** 3217 The Plaza **339-0500** 5pm-2am, from 3pm Sun • lesbians/gay men • dancing/DJ • live shows • videos • private club • wheelchair access

**Have a Nice Day Cafe** 314 N. College St. **373-2233** lesbians/gay men • dancing/DJ • alternative • '70s retro club Mon

**Liaisons** 316 Rensselaer Ave. **376-1617** 5pm-1am • popular • lesbians/gay men • neighborhood bar • private club • women-owned/run

**Mythos** 300 N. College St. **375-8765/559-5959 (INFO LINE)** 10pm-3am, t. 4am wknds • popular • gay-friendly • more gay Wed-Th • dancing/DJ • alternative • live shows • private club • wheelchair access

**Oleen's Lounge** 1831 South Blvd. **373-9604** 8pm-2am, from 3pm Sun, clsd Mon-Wed • popular • lesbians/gay men • dancing/DJ • live shows • wheelchair access

**Scorpio's Lounge** 2301 Freedom Dr. **373-9124** 9pm-3:30am, clsd Mon & Th • lesbians/gay men • dancing/DJ • country/western Tue • live shows • karaoke • videos • private club • wheelchair acces

**Vintage** 4220 E. Independence Blvd. **536-7566** 10pm-close Th-Sat • lesbians/gay men • dancing/DJ • alternative • mostly African-American • live shows • 18+ • ladies night Th

## RESTAURANTS

**300 East** 300 East Blvd. **332-6507** 11am-11pm • some veggie • full bar • $8-15

**521 Cafe** 521 N. College **377-9100** lunch Tue-Fri, dinner nightly • Italian • some veggie • full bar • wheelchair access • $8-15

**Dikadees Front Porch** 4329 E. Independence Blvd. **537-3873** 11am-10pm, til 11pm Fri-Sat • some veggie • full bar • wheelchair access • $6 & up

**Dilworth Diner** 1608 East Blvd. **333-0137** 10:30am-9pm, til 11pm Fri-Sat, 11am-9pm Sun • beer/wine

**El Gringo Grill & Cantina** 3735 Monroe Rd. **347-4241** lunch Mon-Fri, dinner daily • Mexican • some veggie • full bar • wheelchair access

**Lupie's Cafe** 2718 Monroe Rd. **374-1232** 11am-11pm, from noon Sat, clsd Sun • homestyle • some veggie • $5-10

## BOOKSTORES & RETAIL SHOPS

**Paper Skyscraper** 330 East Blvd. **333-7130** 10am-7pm, til 9pm Fri, til 6pm Sat, noon-5pm Sun • books on art, contemporary fiction • gifts • wheelchair access

**Rising Moon Books & Beyond** 510 E. 35th St. **332-7473** noon-8pm, 1pm-5pm Sun, clsd Mon-Tue• lesbigay & multicultural books • wheelchair access

**Urban Evolution** 1329 East Blvd. **332-8644** 10am-9pm, 1pm-6pm Sun • clothing & more

**White Rabbit Books** 834 Central Ave. **377-4067** 11am-9pm, 1pm-6pm Sun • lesbigay • also magazines, T-shirts & gifts

## PUBLICATIONS

▲ **The Front Page** (919) 829-0181 lesbigay newspaper

**In Unison** (803) 771-0804 lesbigay newspaper

**Q Notes** 531-9988 lesbigay newspaper

## TRAVEL AGENTS

**Mann Travels** 9009-2 J. M. Keynes Dr. **547-1240**/(800) 849-2028 IGLTA

**Pink Fairy/Damron Atlas World Travel** 1409 East Blvd. #6-A **332-5545**/(800) 243-3477 IGLTA

## SPIRITUAL GROUPS

**Lutherans Concerned** 1900 The Plaza (Holy Trinity Church) **651-4328** 5pm 1st Sun • dinner & program

**MCC Charlotte** 4037 E. Independence Blvd. #300 **563-5810** 10:45am & 7:30pm Sun

## GYMS & HEALTH CLUBS

**Charlotte 24-Hour Fitness Center** 3900 E. Independence Blvd. **537-9060** 24hrs wkdays

## Durham

*(see Raleigh/Durham)*

## Elizabethtown                      (910)

### TRAVEL AGENTS

**North & South Travel** 118 W. Broad St. **862-8557**/(800) 585-8016

## Fayetteville                        (910)

### BARS & NIGHTCLUBS

**Choices** 4325 Bragg Blvd. **867-3878** clsd Mon-Tue • lesbians/gay men • dancing/DJ • piano bar • live shows • also restaurant

**Millennium** 2540 Gillespie St. **485-2037** 9pm-close, clsd Mon-Tue • mostly gay men • dancing/DJ • ladies night Fri • live shows • also sports bar • private club • wheelchair access

**Spektrum** 107 Swain St. **868-4279** 5pm-3am • lesbians/gay men • dancing/DJ • live shows • patio

### EROTICA

**Priscilla's** 3800 Sycamore Dairy Rd. **860-1776**

## Franklin                           (704)

### ACCOMMODATIONS

**Phoenix Nest (904)** 421-1984 gay-friendly • mtn. cabin • sleeps 4 • smokefree • $325

**Rainbow Acres (Honey's)** 369-5162/(800) 442-6400 (ASK FOR CAREN) women only • rental home • smokefree • fireplace • great views

## Greensboro                         (910)

### INFO LINES & SERVICES

**Gay/Lesbian Hotline** 855-8558 7pm-10pm Sun & Tue-Th

**Live & Let Live AA** 2200 N. Elm (St. Pius Catholic Church) **854-4278** 8pm Tue

### BARS & NIGHTCLUBS

**Babylon** 221 S. Elm St. **275-1006** popular • lesbians/gay men • dancing/DJ • alternative • private club • call for events

**The Palms** 413 N. Eugene St. **272-6307** 9pm-2:30am • mostly gay men • dancing/DJ • live shows • private club • unconfirmed

**Warehouse 29** 1011 Arnold St. **333-9333** 9pm-3am, clsd Mon-Tue • mostly gay men • dancing/DJ • live shows • private club

BOOKSTORES & RETAIL SHOPS
**White Rabbit Books** 1833 Spring Garden St. **272-7604** 11am-9pm, 1pm-6pm Sun • lesbigay • also magazines, T-shirts & gifts

TRAVEL AGENTS
**Carolina Travel** 2054 Carolina Circle Mall **621-9000/(800) 289-9009** IGLTA

SPIRITUAL GROUPS
**St. Mary's MCC** 6720 W. Friendly Ave. **297-4054** 7pm Sun

## Greenville (919)

BARS & NIGHTCLUBS
**Paddock Club** 1008-B Dickinson **758-0990** 8pm-2:30am, clsd Mon-Tue • lesbians/gay men • dancing/DJ • alternative • live shows • private club • wheelchair access

## Hickory (704)

BARS & NIGHTCLUBS
**Club Cabaret** 101 N. Center St. **322-8103** 9pm-3am, clsd Mon-Wed • lesbians/gay men • dancing/DJ • live shows • private club • wheelchair access

SPIRITUAL GROUPS
**MCC Hickory** 109 11th Ave. NW (Unitarian Church) **324-1960** 7pm Sun & 7:30pm Tue

## High Point (910)

TRAVEL AGENTS
**Travel Quest** 3030-A S. Main St. **434-3867** IGLTA

## Hot Springs (704)

ACCOMMODATIONS
**The Duckett House Inn** **622-7621** lesbians/gay men • full brkfst • Victorian farmhouse • creek swimming • also restaurant • vegetarian (reservations required)

## Jacksonville (910)

BARS & NIGHTCLUBS
**Cheers** 258 Marine Blvd. (Hwy. 17) **455-2063** 9pm-close Wed & Fri-Sat only • mostly gay men • live shows

EROTICA
**Priscilla's** 113-A Western Blvd. **355-0765**

## New Bern (919)

ACCOMMODATIONS
**Harmony House Inn** 215 Pollock St. **636-3810/(800) 636-3113** gay-friendly • full brkfst • kids ok • $70-130

## Outer Banks (919)

INFO LINES & SERVICES
**Outer Banks GLC** **441-7287** social group • also publishes newletter

ACCOMMODATIONS
**Advice 5¢ B&B** 111 Scarborough Ln., Duck **255-1050/(800) 238-4235** gay-friendly • smokefree • $80-160

## Raleigh/Durham (919)

*(see also Chapel Hill)*

INFO LINES & SERVICES
**AA Gay/Lesbian (Live & Let Live)** 1601 Hillsboro St. (YMCA), Raleigh **783-6144** 8pm

**Gay/Lesbian Helpline of Wake County** **821-0055** 7pm-10pm

**Outright—Triangle Lesbian/Gay Youth** **286-2396/(800) 879-2300** 6pm-9pm info & referrals, 2pm Sat mtg.

**Steps, Traditions & Promises AA** 2109 N. Duke (Christ Lutheran), Durham **286-9499** (AA#) 7:30pm Tue

ACCOMMODATIONS
**Oakwood Inn** 411 N. Bloodworth St., Raleigh **832-9712** gay-friendly • full brkfst

BARS & NIGHTCLUBS
**All About Eve** 711 Rigsbee Ave., Durham **688-3002** 8pm-10pm, from 9pm Fri-Sat, 1pm-8pm Sun • mostly women • dancing/DJ • private club • deck • volleyball court • wheelchair access

**Boxers** 5504 Chapel Hill Blvd., Durham **489-7678** from 5pm • mostly gay men • alternative • professional • videos

# The Front Page

## The Most Comprehensive Coverage of the Carolinas

**Local, National and World News • Opinion
AIDS/HIV Coverage • Features • Cartoons
Film, Music & Book Reviews • Calendar
Community Resources • *Carolina Pulse*
Horoscope • Ms. Behavior • Classifieds**

To Send News, Letters, or Calendar Items
and for Advertising Information:
Post Office Box 27928 • Raleigh, NC 27611
(919) 829-0181 • Fax: (919) 829-0830
E-mail: frntpage@aol.com

**Available Free Across the Carolinas
and by Subscription**

*Biweekly*
*26 issues per year*
$30 bulk rate
$52 first class mail
$2 sample copy

FREE Personals
With Voice
Mail

*Serving the Gay and Lesbian Community Since 1979*

**CC** 313 W. Hargett St., Raleigh **755-9599** 8pm-close, from 4pm Sun • mostly gay men • dancing/DJ • live shows • piano bar • 18+ • private club • wheelchair access

**Legends** 330 W. Hargett St., Raleigh **831-8888** 9pm-close • mostly gay men • more women Th • mixed crowd wknds • dancing/DJ • private club • patio • wheelchair access

**Power Company** 315 W. Main St. (enter rear), Durham **683-1151** 9pm-close • lesbians/gay men • dancing/DJ • live shows • private club • wheelchair access

## CAFES

**Black Dog Cafe** 208 E. Martin, Raleigh **828-1994** lunch & dinner, Sun brunch, clsd Mon-Tue • some veggie • full bar • wheelchair access • $6-17

## RESTAURANTS

**Irregardless Cafe** 901 W. Morgan St., Raleigh **833-8898** lunch & dinner, Sun brunch • plenty veggie • $9-15

**Magnolia Grill** 1002 9th St., Durham **286-3609** 6pm-9:30pm, clsd Sun • contemporary Southern • full bar • wheelchair access

**Main Street Cafe** 313 W. Main St., Durham **682-4315** 8am-6pm, til midnight Fri • NY deli • transgendered-friendly • live shows • beer/wine • wheelchair access

**Rathskeller** 2412 Hillsborough St., Raleigh **821-5342** 11am-11pm • some veggie • full bar • wheelchair access • $10-20

**Vertigo Diner** 426 S. McDowell St., Raleigh **832-4477** lunch Mon-Fri & dinner Wed-Sat, clsd Sun • full bar

## BOOKSTORES & RETAIL SHOPS

**Lady Slipper** (800) 634-6044 distributor of women's music & videos • also newsletter

**Reader's Corner** 3201 Hillsborough St., Raleigh **828-7024** 10am-9pm, til 6pm wknds, from 1pm Sun • used books

**Regulator Bookshop** 720 9th St., Durham **286-2700** 9am-8pm, til 5pm Sun

**White Rabbit Books** 309 W. Martin St., Raleigh **856-1429** 11am-9pm, 1pm-6pm Sun • lesbigay • also magazines, T-shirts & gifts • wheelchair access

## Lemon Tree Inn

912 Greenwood Road ❖ Spruce Pine, NC 28777
(704) 765-6161

*Just off the Blueridge Parkway, then north on Hwy. 226*
*Great for gemstone mining and peace in the mountains.*

42 units on seven wooded acres ❖ Very quiet
Suites ❖ Apartments ❖ Rooms
TV ❖ Telephone ❖ Air/Heat ❖ Continental Breakfast
Gay owned ❖ Open year-round ❖ Lesbians/gays/straights
Lounge (BYOB) ❖ 24 hr room service
Full service restaurant on-site
Nearby ski resorts (27 miles)
Offering low winter rates

❖ *Real hospitality for a real pleasing price* ❖

PUBLICATIONS
▲ **The Front Page 829-0181** lesbigay newspaper

TRAVEL AGENTS
**Rainbow Travel** 2801 Blue Ridge Rd. #103, Raleigh **571-9054/(800) 633-9350** IGLTA

SPIRITUAL GROUPS
**St. John's MCC** 805 Glenwood Ave., Raleigh **834-2611** 11am & 7:15pm Sun
**Unitarian Universalist Fellowship** 3313 Wade Ave., Raleigh **781-7635** 9:30am & 11:15am Sun

EROTICA
**Innovations** 517 Hillsborough St., Raleigh **833-4833** leather • fetishwear • piercings

## Spruce Pine                              (704)
ACCOMMODATIONS
▲ **The Lemon Tree Inn** 912 Greenwood Rd. **765-6161** gay-friendly • also restaurant on premises • gay-owned/run

## Spruce Ridge                             (704)
ACCOMMODATIONS
**Shepherd's Ridge 765-7809** open March-Nov • mostly women • cottage in the woods • sleeps 2-4 • smokefree • $55

## Wilmington                               (910)
INFO LINES & SERVICES
**GROW Switchboard** 341-11 S. College Rd. #182 **799-7111** 6pm-10pm

ACCOMMODATIONS
**Blue Heaven B&B** 517 Orange St. **772-9929/(800) 338-1748** gay-friendly • smokefree • women-owned/run • $60-125

**Ocean Princess Inn** 824 Ft. Fischer Blvd. S., S. Kure Beach **458-6712/(800) 762-4863** gay-friendly • swimming • smokefree • wheelchair access • $89-159

**The Taylor House Inn** 14 N. 7th St. **763-7581/(800) 382-9982** gay-friendly • 1905 house • full brkfst • smokefree • $85-180

BARS & NIGHTCLUBS
**Mickey Ratz** 115-117 S. Front St. **251-1289** 5pm-2:30am • lesbians/gay men • dancing/DJ • live shows • private club

## Winston-Salem                            (910)
INFO LINES & SERVICES
**Gay/Lesbian Hotline 855-8558** 7pm-10pm Sun, Tue-Th

BARS & NIGHTCLUBS
**Bourbon Street** 916 Burke St. **724-4644** 8pm-close, clsd Mon • lesbians/gay men • ladies' night Wed • dancing/DJ • live shows • private club • wheelchair access

**Club Odyssey/Retro Bar** 4019 Country Club Rd. **774-7071** popular • lesbians/gay men • dancing/DJ • live shows • 18+

**Satellite** 701 N. Trade St. **722-8877** from 5pm • lesbians/gay men • more women Th • dancing/DJ • live shows

SPIRITUAL GROUPS
**Holy Trinity Church** 2873 Robinhood Rd. **725-5355** 7pm Sun & 7pm Wed
**MCC of Winston-Salem 784-8009** 6pm Sun • call for directions

# NORTH DAKOTA

## Fargo                                     (701)
INFO LINES & SERVICES
**The 10% Society** , Moorhead MN **(218) 236-2200** confidential support group for lesbian/gay/bisexual students
**Hotline 235-7335** 24hrs • general info hotline • some lesbigay resources

RESTAURANTS
**Fargo's Fryn Pan** 302 Main St. **293-9952** 24hrs • popular • wheelchair access

EROTICA
**Adult Books & Cinema X** 417 NP Ave. **232-9768** 24hrs

## Grand Forks                              (701)
INFO LINES & SERVICES
**The UGLC (University Gay/Lesbian Community) 777-4321** educational & social group

## Minot                                     (701)
EROTICA
**Risque's** 1514 S. Broadway **838-2837**

# OHIO

## Akron (330)

### INFO LINES & SERVICES
**AA Intergroup** 1190 Inman St. (church) 253-8181 7:30pm Mon & 8pm Fri at 47 E. State St. (church)

### BARS & NIGHTCLUBS
**Adams Street Bar** 77 N. Adams St. 434-9794 4:30pm-2:30am, from 3pm Sat, from 9pm Sun • popular • mostly gay men • dancing/DJ

**Club 358** 358 S. Main 434-7788 5pm-2:30am • mostly gay men • wheelchair access

**Interbelt** 70 N. Howard St. 253-5700 9:30pm-2:30am, from 2pm Sun, clsd Tue & Th • mostly gay men • dancing/DJ • live shows • patio

**Roseto's** 627 S. Arlington St. 724-4228 6pm-1am • mostly women

**Tear-Ez** 360 S. Main 376-0011 11am-2:30am • mostly gay men • neighborhood bar • live shows • wheelchair access

### CAFES
**Cheryl's Daily Grind** 1662 Merriman Rd. 869-9980 7am-6pm, til 9pm Th, 8am-3pm Sun • lesbian-owned/run

### RESTAURANTS
**The Sandwich Board** 1667 W. Market St. 867-5442 11am-8pm, clsd Sun • plenty veggie

### PUBLICATIONS
**Exposé Magazine** 699-6131 covers Cleveland, Akron, Canton, Warren, Youngstown & Lorain

**Gay People's Chronicle** (216) 631-8646

### TRAVEL AGENTS
**Parkside Travel** 3310 Kent Rd. #6, Stow 688-3334/(800) 552-1647 IGLTA

**Travel Agents International** 2855 W. Market St. #115 836-6500/(800) 888-8360 IGLTA

### SPIRITUAL GROUPS
**Cascade Community Church** 1196 Inman St. 773-5298 2pm Sun

**New Hope Temple** 1215 Kenmore Blvd. 745-5757 10am Sun & 7pm Wed

## Amherst (216)

### INFO LINES & SERVICES
**Gay/Lesbian Info Center** 150 Foster Park Rd. ('Deca Realty Bldg.' lower level) 988-5326/(800) 447-7163 drop-in 6pm-9pm Wed

## Athens (614)

### BARS & NIGHTCLUBS
**Gina G's** 47 Main St., Chauncey 797-4291 9am-1am • gay-friendly • dancing/DJ • live shows • food served

## Canton (330)

### BARS & NIGHTCLUBS
**540 Club** 540 Walnut Ave. NE 456-8622 9pm-2:30am, clsd Sun-Mon • mostly gay men • dancing/DJ • wheelchair access

**Boardwalk** 1127 W. Tuscarawas 453-8000 5pm-2:30am • mostly gay men • dancing/DJ • wheelchair access

**La Casa Lounge** 508 Cleveland Ave. NW 453-7432 11am-2:30am • mostly gay men • neighborhood bar • wheelchair access

**Side Street Cafe** 2360 Mahoning St. NE 453-8055 3pm-1am, clsd Sun • mostly women • neighborhood bar • food served • wheelchair access

### PUBLICATIONS
**Exposé Magazine** 699-6131 covers Cleveland, Akron, Canton, Warren, Youngstown & Lorain

### EROTICA
**Tower Bookstore** 219 12th St. NE 455-1254

## Cincinnati (513)

### INFO LINES & SERVICES
**AA Gay/Lesbian** 320 Resor Ave. (church) 861-9966 8pm Mon, Wed & Fri

**Cincinnati Youth Group** 684-8405/(800) 347-8336 (OH ONLY) 24hr info • mtg. 6pm Sun at 103 William Howard (rear entrance)

**Gay/Lesbian Community Switchboard** 651-0070 6pm-11pm Sun-Fri, clsd holidays

**Ohio Lesbian Archives** 4039 Hamilton Ave. (above 'Crazy Ladies Books') 541-1917 Tue night & by appt. • Lesbian AA meets 6:30pm Mon

**PACT (People of All Colors Together)** 395-7228 social/support group • call for events

**Women Helping Women** 216 E. 9th St. 381-5610 (CRISIS LINE) 24hr hotline • crisis center • support groups • lesbian referrals

## ACCOMMODATIONS

**Prospect Hill B&B** 408 Boal St. 421-4408 gay-friendly • full brkfst • smoke-free • IGLTA • gay-owned/run • $89-149

## BARS & NIGHTCLUBS

**Bullfish's** 4023 Hamilton Ave. 541-9220 from 7pm, from 6pm Sun • mostly women • neighborhood bar

**Chasers** 2640 Glendora 861-3966 7pm-2:30am, clsd Mon • lesbians/gay men • dancing/DJ • live shows Th & Sun • free pizza Fri

**Colors** 4042 Hamilton Ave. 681-6969 5pm-2:30am • popular • mostly gay men • neighborhood bar • videos

**The Dock** 603 W. Pete Rose Wy. 241-5623 4pm-2:30am, from 8pm Mon • popular • lesbians/gay men • dancing/DJ • live shows • volleyball court • patio • wheelchair access

**Junkers Tavern** 4158 Langland 541-5470 7:30am-1am • gay-friendly • neighborhood bar

**Milton's** 301 Milton St. 784-9938 4pm-2:30am • gay-friendly • neighborhood bar

**Plum St. Pipeline** 241 W. Court 241-5678 4pm-2:30am • popular • mostly gay men • neighborhood bar • live shows • videos

**Shirley's** 2401 Vine St. 721-8483 8pm-2:30am, from 4pm Sun, clsd Mon • mostly women • dancing/DJ • wheelchair access

**Shooters** 927 Race St. 381-9900 4pm-2:30am • mostly gay men • dancing/DJ • country/western • dance lessons 8pm Tue & Th

**Simon Says** 428 Walnut 381-7577 11am-2:30am, from 1pm Sun • popular • mostly gay men • neighborhood bar • wheelchair access

**Spurs** 326 E. 8th St. 621-2668 4pm-2:30am • popular • mostly gay men • leather • wheelchair access

**The Subway** 609 Walnut St. 421-1294 6am-2:30am, from noon Sun • mostly gay men • neighborhood bar • dancing/DJ • live shows • food served

**Warehouse** 1313 Vine St. 684-9313 gay-friendly

## CAFES

**Kaldi's Cafe & Books** 1204 Main St. 241-3070 10am-1am • some veggie • full bar • live shows • wheelchair access

## RESTAURANTS

**Boca** 4034 Hamilton Ave. 542-2022

**Carol's Corner Cafe** 825 Main St. 651-2667 11am-1am (bar til 2:30am) • popular • some veggie • full bar • wheelchair access • $4-8

**The Diner on Sycamore** 1203 Sycamore 721-1212

**Mullane's** 723 Race St. 381-1331 11:30am-11pm, from 5pm Sat, clsd Sun • plenty veggie • beer/wine • wheelchair access • $5-12

## ENTERTAINMENT & RECREATION

**Alternating Currents** WAIF FM 88.3 333-9243/961-8900 3pm Sat • lesbigay public affairs radio program • also 'Everywomon' 1pm Sat

## BOOKSTORES & RETAIL SHOPS

**Crazy Ladies Bookstore** 4039 Hamilton Ave. 541-4198 11am-8pm, til 6pm Sat, noon-4pm Sun • women's

**Left-Handed Moon** 48 E. Court St. 784-1166 11:30am-7pm, clsd Sun • cards • gifts

**Pink Pyramid** 907 Race St. 621-7465 11am-10:30pm, til midnight Fri-Sat, clsd Sun • lesbigay bookstore & gifts

## PUBLICATIONS

**Dinah** local women's newsletter

## TRAVEL AGENTS

**Apache Travel** 5017 Cooper Rd. 793-5522 ask for Laura

**Provident Travel Corp.** 221 E. 4th St., 2800 Atrium II 621-4900 IGLTA

**Victoria Travel** 3330 Erie Ave. 871-1100/(800) 626-4932 ask for Dan • IGLTA

## SPIRITUAL GROUPS

**Dignity** 3690 Winding Wy. near Xavier Univ. 557-2111 7:30pm 1st & 3rd Sat

**Integrity Greater Cincinnati** 65 E. Hollister (Church of Our Savior) 242-7297 6:30pm 3rd Mon

**New Spirit MCC** 5501 Hamilton Ave. (church) 681-9090 7pm Sun & Wed

## Cleveland (216)

### INFO LINES & SERVICES

**AA Gay/Lesbian** 7801 Detroit Ave. (Comm Rm.) **241-7387** 8:30pm Fri

**Cleveland Lesbian/Gay Community Center** 1418 W. 29th St. **522-1999** noon-7pm, til 5pm Tue, clsd wknds

**Cleveland Lesbian/Gay Hotline** 781-6736 24hr recorded info

**GLOWS (Gay/Lesbian Older Wiser Seniors)** 331-6302 7:30pm 2nd Tue

**Women's Center of Greater Cleveland** 4828 Lorain Ave. **651-1450/651-4357(HELPLINE)** 9am-5pm, clsd wknds • lesbian group 7pm Fri

### ACCOMMODATIONS

**Clifford House** 1810 W. 28th St. **589-9432** gay-friendly • close to downtown • fireplaces

### BARS & NIGHTCLUBS

**Aunt Charlie's The Cage** 9506 Detroit Ave. **651-0727** 4pm-2:30am • mostly gay men • dancing/DJ • live shows • karaoke

**Barbary Lane** 2619 Noble Rd., Cleveland Hts. **382-2033** 4pm-1am, clsd Sun • lesbians/gay men • also restaurant

**Club Visions** 1229 W. 6th **566-0060** 4pm-2:30am, til 4am Fri, from 6pm Sat • popular • mostly gay men • dancing/DJ • live shows • wheelchair access

**Five Cent Decision (The Nickel)** 4365 State Rd. (Rte. 94) **661-1314** 4pm-2:30am • mostly women • neighborhood bar

**The Grid** 1281 W. 9th **623-0113** 4pm-2:30am • popular • lesbians/gay men • more women Sun • neighborhood bar • dancing/DJ

**The Hawk** 11217 Detroit Ave. **521-5443** 10am-2:30am, from noon Sun • lesbians/gay men • neighborhood bar • wheelchair access

**Legends** 11719 Detroit, Lakewood **226-1199** 11am-2:30am, from 7pm Sun • popular • mostly gay men • dancing/DJ • karaoke Mon & Wed

**Metronome** 1946 St. Clair Ave. **241-4663** 8:30pm-2:30am, 5pm-11pm Sun, clsd Mon-Tue & Th • mostly women • dancing/DJ • live shows • wheelchair access

**MJ's Place** 11633 Lorain Ave. **476-1970** 4pm-2:30am, clsd Sun • mostly gay men • women's night Th • neighborhood bar • karaoke • women very welcome

**Muggs** 3194 W. 25th St. **661-5365** noon-2:30am • lesbians/gay men • neighborhood bar • food served

**Ohio City Oasis** 2909 Detroit Ave. **574-2203** 8am-2:30am, from noon Sun • mostly gay men • leather • country/western Sun

**Paradise Inn** 4488 State Rd. (Rte. 94) **741-9819** 11am-2:30am • lesbians/gay men • neighborhood bar

**The Rec Room** 15320 Brookpark Rd. **433-1669** 6pm-1am • mostly women • dancing/DJ • food served • wheelchair access • women-owned/run

**Scarlet Rose's Lounge** 2071 Broadview Rd. **351-7511** 5pm-2am, noon-8pm Sun • mostly women • neighborhood bar

**Too's Attraxxions** 6757 W. 130th St., Parma Hts. **842-4669** 8pm-2:30am

**U4ia** 10630 Berea Rd. **631-7111** 9:30pm-3am Fri-Sun • popular • lesbians/gay men • dancing/DJ • live shows • wheelchair access

### CAFES

**Lonesome Dove Cafe** 3093 Mayfield Rd. **397-9100** 7am-6pm • some veggie • beer/wine • $5-7

**Patisserie Baroque** 1112 Kenilworth Ave. **861-1881** 8am-6pm, til 7pm Fri, from 10am Sat, clsd Sun-Mon • Euro-style pastry shop

**Red Star Cafe** 11604 Detroit Ave. **521-7827** 7am-11pm, til 1am Fri-Sat • lesbians/gay men • wheelchair access

### RESTAURANTS

**Billy's on Clifton** 11100 Clifton Blvd. **281-7722** 11am-9pm, clsd Mon • some veggie • $5-12

**Cafe Tandoor** 2096 S. Taylor Rd., Cleveland Hts. **371-8500/371-8569** lunch & dinner • Indian • plenty veggie

**Club Isabella** 2025 University Hospital Rd. **229-1177** lunch & dinner, dinner only Sat • Italian • full bar • live jazz nightly • $15-25

**Fulton Ave. Cafe** 1835 Fulton Ave. **522-1835** 4pm-2:30am, from 8pm wknds • full bar

**Harmony Bar & Grille** 3359 Fulton Ave. **398-5052** 11am-midnight, 4pm-1am wknds, clsd Mon • Eastern European & Italian

**Hecks** 2927 Bridge Ave. **861-5464** dinner from 5pm • reservations recommended

# Cleveland

*C* leveland is making a comeback, after the recession and several economic facelifts. Actually, only some districts, like the Flats, have had a beauty makeover. Other districts never lost the funky charm of this city that's home both to the Rock 'N Roll Hall of Fame and the Cleveland Symphony Orchestra.

Speaking of funky, flash back to the '60s with a trip down Coventry Road. University Circle is rumored to be another hangout of the avant garde, as is Murray Hill, known for its many galleries. While you're at it, make time for some serious art appreciation in the galleries of the world-famous Cleveland Museum of Art.

To touch base with the lesbian community, pick up a copy of the **Gay People's Chronicle** to find out more about the ever-changing bar/coffeehouse scene. For a wholesome meal, try the women-run **The Inn on Coventry.** After dinner, you'll discover that Cleveland has something many major US cities don't: 4 women's bars! So head out to dance at the **Metronome** or **The Rec Room.** For a more laid-back atmosphere, try **Scarlet Rose's Lounge** or **The Five Cent Decision** (known to locals as **The Nickel**).

---

## Cleveland (216)

**Where the Girls Are:** Dancing downtown near Public Square, hanging out on State Rd. below the intersection of Pearl and Broadview/Memphis.

**Annual Events:** February - Olympus Weekend circuit parties: 556-5525.

**City Info:** 621-4110.

**Attractions:** Cleveland Metroparks Zoo. Coventry Road district. Cuyahoga Valley National Recreation Area. The Flats.

**Transit:** Yellow-Zone Cab: 623-1500. AmeriCab: 881-1111.

**The Inn on Coventry** 2785 Euclid Heights Blvd., Cleveland Hts. **371-1811** 7am-9pm, 9am-3pm Sun • homestyle • some veggie • full bar • women-owned/run • $5-20

**Snickers** 1261 W. 76th St. **631-7555** noon-10pm, 4pm-11pm Sat • some veggie • full bar • wheelchair access • $7-16

### BOOKSTORES & RETAIL SHOPS

**Bank News** 4025 Clark **281-8777** 10:30am-8:30pm, clsd Sun

**Body Language** 3291 W. 115th St. **251-3330/(888) 429-7733** noon-9pm, til 5pm Sun • 'an educational store for adults in alternative lifestyles'

**Bookstore on W. 25th St.** 1921 W. 25th St. **566-8897** 10am-6pm, noon-5pm Sun • lesbigay section

**Borders Bookshop & Espresso Bar** 2101 Richmond Rd., Beachwood **292-2660** 9am-10pm, 11am-midnight Fri-Sat, 11am-9pm Sun • lesbigay section

**The Clifton Web** 11512 Clifton Rd. **961-1120** 10am-9pm, noon-5pm Sun • cards • gifts

**Daily Planet News** 1842 Coventry Rd. **321-9973** 6:30am-10pm • newspapers • magazines • gifts • wheelchair access

### PUBLICATIONS

**Exposé Magazine** (330) 699-6131 covers Cleveland, Akron, Canton, Warren, Youngstown & Lorain

**Gay People's Chronicle** 631-8646 lesbigay newspaper

**Valentine News** 676-0000

### TRAVEL AGENTS

**Cardinal Worldwide Travel** 4911 Grant Ave. **341-8333/(800) 535-8233** IGLTA

**Flite II** 23611 Chagrin Blvd., Beachwood **464-1762/(800) 544-3881**

**Green Road Travel** 2111 S. Green Rd., S. Euclid **381-8060**

**Playhouse Square Travel** 1160 Henna Bldg., 1422 Euclid Ave. #1160 **575-0813/(800) 575-0813** IGLTA

**Sun Lovers' Cruises & Travel** 3860 Rocky River Rd. **252-0900/(800) 323-1362** IGLTA

**The Travel Place** 22965 Lorain Rd., Fairview Park **734-1886** IGLTA

**Uncommon Destinations** 3121 Bridge Ave. **939-8099** IGLTA

### SPIRITUAL GROUPS

**Chevrei Tikva** 2728 Lankershire Rd., Cleveland Hts. **932-5551** 8pm 1st & 3rd Fri • lesbigay synagogue

**Emmanuel Christian Fellowship Church** 10034 Lorain Ave. **651-0129** 10:45am & 6:30pm Sun, 7:30pm Wed

**Integrity NE Ohio** 18001 Detroit (St. Peter's Church) **939-0405** 5pm 3rd Sun

**Presbyterians for Lesbian/Gay Concerns** 2780 Noble Rd., Cleveland Hts. **932-1458** 5:30pm 2nd Sat • potluck & mtg.

### EROTICA

**Laws Leather Shop** 11112 Clifton Blvd. **961-0544** hours vary, clsd Mon-Tue

---

## Columbus          (614)

**Where the Girls Are:** Downtown with the boys, north near the University area, or somewhere in-between.

**Lesbigay Pride:** June: 299-7764.

**Annual Events:**

September - Ohio Lesbian Festival: 267-3953.

**City Info:** 221-2489.

**Attractions:** Short North gallery area. Columbus Zoo. Columbus Museum of Modern Art. German Village district. Ohio State University. Wexner Center for the Arts.

**Weather:** Truly midwestern. Winters are cold; summers are hot.

**Transit:** Yellow Cab: 444-4444. Northway Taxicab: 299-8022/299-1191. Independent: 235-5551. Airport Express Shuttle: 476-3004. Central Ohio Transit Authority (COTA): 228-1776.

## Columbus (614)

### INFO LINES & SERVICES

**AA Gay/Lesbian** 253-8501 call for mtg. schedule

**Bi-Lines** 341-7015 call for events

**Dragon Leather Club** 258-7100 pansexual leather group

**Gay/Lesbian/Bi Alliance of OSU** 340 Ohio Union, 1739 N. High St. 292-6200 student group

**Nosotros** 292-6200 lesbigay Latina/o social group • call for time/location

**Ohio Division of Travel & Tourism** (800) 282-5393

**Sisters of Lavender** 93 W. Weisheimer (Unitarian Church) 575-9646 7:30pm Wed • lesbian support group

**Stonewall Union Hotline/Community Ctr.** 1160 N. High St. 299-7764 10am-7pm, 9am-5pm Fri, clsd wknds • wheelchair access

## *Columbus*

*T*he center of lesbian life in Columbus is Clintonville (affectionately known as "Clitville"), just north of the OSU campus. While you're in the neighborhood, stop by popular dyke hangouts like **Common Grounds, Moonspinners Cafe** or **Summit Station**, where you can also pick up the latest news as well as a calendar of events in the popular homegrown newsmagazine **Sovereignty** or **Gay People's Chronicle** and **Stonewall Journal.**

The Short North—the stretch of High Street just north of Downtown—is a funky, artsy neighborhood that hosts a Gallery Hop the first Saturday of every month. After the shops start closing around 10pm (or later), check out **Blazer's Pub,** or try the Short North Pole for fantastic ice cream concoctions. If you need to refuel, try the **Coffee Table;** we hear it's as popular with local dykes as with the cruisin' gay boys.

The night before the Gallery Hop is First Friday at **Wall Street,** the downtown lesbian dance club, and every gay girl for a hundred miles shows up. Stop by early to catch the free buffet.

Sports dykes, check out Berliner Park, any season, to watch women's softball, volleyball or basketball leagues. Even the non-athletic head to the **Far Side,** the **Grapevine,** or **Slammers** afterwards to celebrate the thrill of victory.

The best time of all is the Gay Pride March that always falls the same weekend in June as ComFest. This is the community festival at Goodale Park in Victorian Village which hosts a wide variety of merchants, food, information, and music.

*– By reader Ada Kardos. Updated by Damron editors.*

# D I N A H
# S H O R E
# W E E K E N D

## MARCH 26-29, 1998

## PALM SPRINGS

The Ultimate Hotel & Entertainment
Package at the All Inclusive

**DOUBLE TREE RESORT**

Book today to ensure availability.
For hotel and party ticket Info Call

## 310.281.7358

For Airline reservations call
1•800•433•1790 • Star#: S0237LG

Produced by JOANI WEIR PRODUCTIONS
POM POM PRODUCTIONS • KLUB BANSHEE

**WOW (Women's Outreach for Women)**
1950-H N. 4th St. **291-3639** 9am-5pm,
mtgs. 5pm-8pm • women's recovery center • wheelchair access

## ACCOMMODATIONS

**Columbus B&B** 763 S. 3rd St. **444-8888**
gay-friendly • referral service for German
Village district • $55-65

**Courtyard by Marriott** 35 W. Spring St.
**228-3200**/(800) 321-2211 gay-friendly •
wheelchair access

**The Gardener's House** 556 Frebis Ave.
**444-5445** lesbians/gay men only • spa •
smokefree • $38-48

**Summit Lodge Resort & Guesthouse**
**385-3521** popular • clothing optional
resort • mostly gay men • camping avail.
• hot tub • swimming • also restaurant •
wheelchair access

## BARS & NIGHTCLUBS

**Blazer's Pub** 1205 N. High St. **299-1800**
2pm-2:30am, 3pm-midnight Sun • les-
bians/gay men • neighborhood bar

**Clubhouse Cafe** 124 E. Main **228-5090**
4pm-midnight, from noon Sun, clsd Mon
• lesbians/gay men • desserts served

**Downtown Connection** 1126 N. High St.
**299-4880** 3pm-2:30am • mostly gay men
• sports bar

**The Far Side** 1662 W. Mound St. **276-
5817** 5pm-1am, til 2:30am Fri-Sat, from
1pm Sun • lesbians/gay men • neighborhood bar

**Garrett's Saloon** 1071 Parsons Ave. **449-
2351** 11am-2:30am • mostly gay men •
neighborhood bar

**Grapevine Cafe** 73 E. Gay St. **221-8463**
5pm-1am, clsd Mon • lesbians/gay men
• live shows • some veggie • full bar •
wheelchair access • $7-15

**Havana Video Lounge** 862 N. High **421-
9697** 5pm-2:30am • popular •
lesbians/gay men • live jazz Tue • videos
• wheelchair access

**Remo's** 1409 S. High St. **443-4224**
10am-2:30am, clsd Sun • lesbians/gay
men • neighborhood bar • food served •
pizza & subs • wheelchair access

**Slammers Pizza Pub** 202 E. Long St.
**469-7526** 11am-2:30am, from 2:30pm
wknds • lesbians/gay men • karaoke •
wheelchair access

**South Bend** 126 E. Moler St. **444-9606**
mostly gay men • neighborhood bar •
wheelchair access

# Sovereignty Magazine

### Celebrating
*The Lighter Side*
Of The
Gay/Lesbian Community

### Featuring:
Hundreds of Pictures
Of Many Who Are Out and Proud
Highlights of Events
Upcoming Events
Community Contributions
True Confessions of Drag Queens
And Much, Much More....

Subscriptions are $24 per year
or send $4 for 1 issue

### Send to:
Sovereignty Magazine
PO Box 259
Brice, OH 43109
or charge by phone
1-800-813-1976 (access code 05)
1-614-833-6848

### Now accepting:
Visa, Mastercard
Discover & American Express

**Summit Station** 2210 Summit St. **261-9634** 4pm-2:30am • mostly women • neighborhood bar • dancing/DJ

**Tabu** 349 Marconi Blvd. **464-2270** 3pm-2:30am, til 4am Fri-Sat • mostly gay men • neighborhood bar • food served

**Trends** 40 E. Long St. **461-0076** 5pm-2:30am • popular • mostly gay men • dancing/DJ • wheelchair access

**Union Station Video Cafe** 630 N. High St. **228-3740** 11am-2:30am, clsd Sun • lesbians/gay men • food served • plenty veggie • internet access • $6-10

**Union Station Video Cafe** 630 N. High St. **228-3546** 11am-2:30am • lesbians/gay men • also restaurant

**Wall Street** 144 N. Wall St. **464-2800** 6pm-2:30am, clsd Mon-Tue • popular • mostly women • dancing/DJ • live shows • wheelchair access

## CAFES

**The Coffee Table** 731 N. High St. **297-1177**

**Cup-O-Joe Cafe** 627 3rd St. **221-1563**

**King Ave. Coffeehouse** 247 King Ave. **294-8287** 11am-11pm, clsd Mon • popular • funky bohemian crowd • vegetarian • $3-7

**Kona Cafe** 53 Parsons Ave. **280-5662**

**Moonspinners Cafe** 2659 N. High St. **262-3133**

## RESTAURANTS

**Chinese Village** 2124 Lane St. **297-7979**

**Common Grounds** 2549 Indianola Ave. **263-7646** 9am-midnight, til 11pm Sun, from 4pm Mon

**Frank's Diner** 59 Spruce St. **621-2233** wheelchair access

**The Galaxy Cafe** 1099 W. 1st Ave., Grandview **299-5140** clsd Mon • Cuban/Southwestern • full bar • wheelchair access

**L'Antibes** 772 N. High St. (at Warren) **291-1666** dinner from 5pm, clsd Sun-Mon • French (vegetarian on request) • full bar • wheelchair access • from $16

**Lost Planet Pizza & Pasta** 680 N. High St. **228-6191** wheelchair access

**Out on Main** 122 E. Main **224-9520** 5pm-10pm, til 11pm Fri-Sat, from 11am Sun 'Gospel brunch' • live shows • full bar • wheelchair access

## BOOKSTORES & RETAIL SHOPS

**ACME Art Company** call for location **299-4003** 1pm-7pm Wed-Sat • alternative art space • call for hours • also 'Cafe Ashtray' Fri

**An Open Book** 761 N. High St. **291-0080** 11am-10pm, from 10am wknds, til 6pm Sun • lesbigay • wheelchair access

**The Book Loft of German Village** 631 S. 3rd St. **464-1774** 10am-midnight • lesbigay section

**Creative-A-Tee** 874 N. High St. **297-8844** noon-7pm, til 6pm Sat, clsd Sun

**Hausfrau Haven** 769 S. 3rd St. **443-3680** 10am-6:30pm, til 5pm Sun • cards • gifts • wine

**Kukala's Tanning & Tees** 636 N. High St. **228-8337** noon-7pm, til 6pm Sun • lesbigay gifts • leather • women-owned/run

**M.J. Originals** 745 N. High St. **291-2787** 11am-7pm, til 6pm Sat, 1pm-5pm Sun • jewelry • gifts

**Metro Video** 848 N. High St. **291-7962** lesbigay videos • large selection

**The Shadow Realm** 3347 N. High St. **262-1175** metaphysical & occult bookstore • sponsors the annual 'Witch's Ball' in Oct • wheelchair access

## PUBLICATIONS

▲ **Lesbian Health News** 481-7656 see ad in mail order section

▲ **Sovereignty** 833-6848 lesbigay newsmagazine

**The Stonewall Union Journal** 299-7764

## TRAVEL AGENTS

**First Discount Travel** 2134 Tremont Ctr. **488-9860** IGLTA

**Just Travel** 82 S. High St., Dublin **791-9500**/(800) 622-8660 ask for Paul • IGLTA

**Travelplex East** 760 Morrison Rd. #C, Gahanna **863-3600**/(800) 837-9909 IGLTA

## SPIRITUAL GROUPS

**Dignity Columbus** 203 King Ave. (Presbyterian Church) **451-6528** 7pm 3rd Fri

**Lutherans Concerned** 155 S. James Rd. **447-7018** 1pm 1st Sun

**New Creation MCC** 787 E. Broad St. **224-0314** 10:30am Sun

**Spirit of the Rivers** 1066 N. High St. **470-0816** 10:30am Sun • ecumenical service

**St. Paul's Episcopal Church** 787 E. Broad St. **221-1703** 5pm Sun • wheelchair access

## GYMS & HEALTH CLUBS
**Body Life Fitness** 384 Dublin Ave. **221-4766**

## EROTICA
**Bexley Video** 3839 April Ln. **235-2341**

**Diablo Body Piercing** 636 N. High St. **221-4887** clsd Tue

**I.M.R.U.** 235 N. Lazelle (above 'Eagle Bar') **228-9660** 11:30pm-2am Fri-Sat • leather

# Dayton (937)

## INFO LINES & SERVICES
**AA Gay/Lesbian** 20 W. 1st St. (church) **222-2211** 8pm Sat

**Dayton Lesbian/Gay Center & Hotline** 819 Salem Ave. **274-1776** 7pm-11pm (hotline) • center 6:30pm Wed • coffeehouse 8pm Fri

**Youth Quest 630-3333** lesbigay youth group 22 & under

## BARS & NIGHTCLUBS
**1470 West** 34 N. Jefferson St. **461-1470** 9pm-2:30am, til 4am Fri-Sat, clsd Mon-Wed • popular • lesbians/gay men • dancing/DJ • live shows • videos • wheelchair access

**Asylum** 605 S. Patterson Blvd. **228-8828** 9pm-close, clsd Sun-Mon • gay-friendly • dancing/DJ • alternative • 18+

**Down Under** 131 N. Ludlow St. **228-1050** 11am-2:30pm for lunch Mon-Fri, bar from 7pm Th-Sat • mostly women • dancing/DJ • wheelchair access

**Dugout** 619 Salem Ave. **274-2394** 10am-2:30am • lesbians/gay men • neighborhood bar • dancing/DJ • food served

**Jessie's Celebrity** 850 N. Main St. **461-2582** 3pm-2:30am • popular • mostly gay men • dancing/DJ • live shows • karaoke • food served • wheelchair access

**The Manhattan Nightclub** 1227 Wilmington **294-0713** 5pm-2:30am, clsd Sun • mostly gay men • dancing/DJ • country/western Tue • HiNRG Fri-Sat • wheelchair access

**Right Corner** 105 E. 3rd St. **228-1285** noon-2:30am • mostly gay men • neighborhood bar • wheelchair access

## CAFES
**Cold Beer & Cheeseburgers** 33 Jefferson St. **222-2337** 11am-11pm, noon-8pm Sun • full bar • wheelchair access

**Gloria Jean's Coffee Bean** 2727 Fairfield Commons (mall), Beavercreek **426-1672/(888) 437-5486** 9am-9pm, noon-6pm Sun • gay-owned/run

**Jefferson Rose Cafe** 8 Jefferson St. **226-9303** gay-owned/run

**Samuel Johnson Coffee House** 39 N. Main St. **228-1948** 9am-8pm, til 11pm Fri-Sat, til 7pm Sun, til 2:30pm Mon • wheelchair access

## RESTAURANTS
**The Spaghetti Warehouse** 36 W. 5th St. **461-3913** more gay Mon w/'Friends of the Italian Opera'

**What You Eat** 524 E. 5th St. **225-3855** 11am-9pm, til 10pm Fri-Sat, clsd Sun-Mon • vegetarian • beer/wine • $5-10

## BOOKSTORES & RETAIL SHOPS
**Books & Co.** 350 E. Stroop Rd. **298-6540** 9am-11pm

**Q Giftshop** 1966 N. Main St. **274-4400** noon-7pm, 1pm-5pm Sun • lesbigay

## PUBLICATIONS
**The Spectrum 278-5877**

## SPIRITUAL GROUPS
**Community Gospel Church** 546 Xenia Ave. **252-8855** 10am Sun & 7:30pm Wed

**MCC** 1630 E. 5th St. **228-4031** 10:30am & 6:30pm Sun

# Fremont (419)

## BARS & NIGHTCLUBS
**Saloon Bar** 531 W. State **334-9340** 2pm-2:30am, from 4pm wknds, clsd Mon • mostly gay men • neighborhood bar

# Glenford (614)

## ACCOMMODATIONS
**Springhill Farm Resort 659-2364** women only • cabins & restored barn on 30 acres • hot tub • swimming

# Kent (330)

## INFO LINES & SERVICES
**Kent Lesbian/Gay/Bisexual Union** KSU **672-2068**

## Cafes

**The Zephyr Cafe** 106 W. Main St. **678-4848** 8am-9pm, til 10pm wknds, clsd Mon • live shows • vegetarian • wheelchair access • women-owned/run • $3-7

# Lima (419)

## Bars & Nightclubs

**Somewhere In Time** 804 W. North St. **227-7288** 7pm-2:30am, from 8pm Fri-Sat • lesbians/gay men • dancing/DJ Fri-Sat • live shows

# Logan (614)

## Accommodations

**Glenlaurel—A Scottish Country Inn & Cottages** 15042 Mt. Olive Rd., Rockbridge **385-4070/(800) 809-7378** gay-friendly • full brkfst & dinner • smokefree • $140-240

**Spring Wood Hocking Hills Cabins** 15 mi. SE of Columbus **385-2042** lesbians/gay men • cabins • hot tub • smokefree • wheelchair access • $85-90

# Lorain (216)

## Info Lines & Services

**Gay/Lesbian Info Center** 150 Foster Park Rd. (Deca Realty Bldg. lower level), Amherst **988-5326/(800) 447-7163** drop-in 6pm-9pm Wed

## Bars & Nightclubs

**The Serpent** 2223 Broadway **246-9002** 8pm-2:30am, from 4pm Sun • mostly gay men • neighborhood bar • dancing/DJ • live shows • patio • wheelchair access

## Publications

**Exposé Magazine (330) 699-6131** serving Cleveland, Akron, Canton, Warren, Youngstown & Lorain

# Mentor (216)

## Info Lines & Services

**Hugs East 974-8909** 7pm-9pm Wed, phone 24hrs • lesbigay info & referrals for Ashtabula, Geauga & Lake counties

# Newark (614)

## Bars & Nightclubs

**Bulldog Lounge** 35 N. 3rd St. **345-9729** 7pm-2:30am • lesbians/gay men • neighborhood bar

# Oberlin (216)

## Info Lines & Services

**Oberlin Lesbian/Gay/Bisexual Union** 775-8179

# Oxford (513)

## Info Lines & Services

**Miami University Gay/Lesbian/Bisexual Alliance** 529-3823

# Portsmouth (614)

## Accommodations

**1835 House B&B** 353-1856 gay-friendly • swimming • smokefree

# Sandusky (419)

## Bars & Nightclubs

**Rainbow Bay** 306 W. Water St. **624-8118** 4pm-2:30am, from 1pm wknds • lesbians/gay men • dancing/DJ • live shows

## Bookstores & Retail Shops

**City News** 139 Columbus Ave. **626-1265** 7am-5:30pm

# Springfield (937)

## Bars & Nightclubs

**Chances** 1912 Edwards Ave. **324-0383** 8:30pm-2:30am, clsd Tue • gay-friendly • dancing/DJ • live shows • patio

# Toledo (419)

## Info Lines & Services

**AA Gay/Lesbian** 2272 Collingwood Blvd. **472-8242** 8pm Wed & Sun

**Pro Toledo Info Line 472-2364** 4pm-11pm

## Bars & Nightclubs

**Blu Jean Cafe** 3606 Sylvania Ave. **474-0690** 4pm-2:30am • popular • lesbians/gay men • more women Th • live shows • karaoke • food served • wheelchair access

**Bretz** 2012 Adams St. **243-1900** 4pm-2:30am, til 4am Fri-Sat, clsd Mon-Tue • popular • mostly gay men • dancing/DJ • alternative • live shows • videos

**Caesar's Show Bar** 133 N. Erie St. **241-5140** 8pm-2:30am, clsd Mon-Wed • lesbians/gay men • dancing/DJ • live shows • wheelchair access

**Hooterville Station** 119 N. Erie St. **241-9050** 5:30am-2:30am • mostly gay men • dancing/DJ • patio • wheelchair access

### CAFES

**Sufficient Grounds** 3160 Markway (Cricket West Mall) **537-1988** 7am-11pm, til midnight Fri-Sat, 8am-10pm Sun • live shows • wheelchair access • also 420 Madison 243-5282

### BOOKSTORES & RETAIL SHOPS

**Tallulah's** 6725 W. Central **843-7707** 11am-6pm, til 8pm Tue-Th, clsd Sun • feminist giftshop • wheelchair access
**Thackeray's** 3301 W. Central Ave. **537-9259** 9am-9pm, 10am-6pm Sun • wheelchair access

### TRAVEL AGENTS

**Great Ways Travel** 4625 W. Bancroft **536-8000**/(800) 729-9297 IGLTA

### SPIRITUAL GROUPS

**MCC Good Samaritan** 720 W. Delaware **244-2124** 9am & 11am Sun

### EROTICA

**Adult Pleasures** 4404 N. Detroit **476-4587** 24hrs

## Tremont (216)

### BARS & NIGHTCLUBS

**Hi & Dry Inn** 2207 W. 11th St. **621-6166** 5pm-2am • gay-friendly • neighborhood bar • food served • plenty veggie • patio • $5-10

## Warren (330)

### BARS & NIGHTCLUBS

**The Alley** 441 E. Market St. (enter rear) **394-9483** 2pm-2:30am • lesbians/gay men • dancing/DJ • live shows • wheelchair access
**The Crazy Duck** 121 Pine St. SE **394-3825** 4pm-2:30am • popular • lesbians/gay men • dancing/DJ • 18+ • wheelchair access

### PUBLICATIONS

**Exposé Magazine 699-6131** covers Cleveland, Akron, Canton, Warren, Youngstown & Lorain

## Wooster (330)

### ACCOMMODATIONS

**Kimbilio Farm** 6047 TR 501, Big Prairie **378-2481** women only • B&B • also cabin • swimming • 45 min. from Akron • wheelchair access (cabin only) • $50

## Yellow Springs (937)

### INFO LINES & SERVICES

**Gay/Lesbian Center** Antioch College 767-7331 x601

### RESTAURANTS

**Winds Cafe & Bakery** 215 Xenia Ave. **767-1144** call for hours • plenty veggie • full bar • wheelchair access • women-owned/run • $15-20

### BOOKSTORES & RETAIL SHOPS

**Epic Bookshop** 232 Xenia Ave. **767-7997** 10am-6pm, til 9pm Fri, noon-6pm Sun

## Youngstown (330)

### BARS & NIGHTCLUBS

**Phil's Place** 10 E. Laclede **782-6991** 4pm-2:30am • mostly women • neighborhood bar • patio • wheelchair access
**Sophies** 2 E. LaClede **782-8080** 5pm-2:30am • lesbians/gay men • neighborhood bar
**Troubadour** 2622 Market St. (enter back lot) **788-4379** 9pm-2:30am • lesbians/gay men • dancing/DJ • live shows • wheelchair access

### PUBLICATIONS

**Exposé Magazine 699-6131** covers Cleveland, Akron, Canton, Warren, Youngstown & Lorain

### TRAVEL AGENTS

**L.B. Burger Travel Service** 517 Bank One Building **744-5035**/(800) 625-5035 IGLTA

# OKLAHOMA

## El Reno (405)

### ACCOMMODATIONS

**The Good Life RV Resort** Exit 108 I-40, 1/4 mile S. **884-2994** gay-friendly • 32 acres • 100 campsites & 100 RV hookups • swimming

## Lawton (405)

### BARS & NIGHTCLUBS

**Triangles** 8-1/2 NW 2nd St. **351-0620** 8:30pm-2am, clsd Mon • lesbians/gay men • neighborhood bar • dancing/DJ • live shows • wheelchair access

## Norman (405)

### BARS & NIGHTCLUBS

**Club Underground** 1311 S. Jenkins **329-9665** 7pm-2am, clsd Mon-Tue • lesbians/gay men • more women Th • dancing/DJ • live shows • unconfirmed

## Oklahoma City (405)

### INFO LINES & SERVICES

**AA Live & Let Live** 3405 N. Villa **947-3834** noon, 5:30pm & 8pm

**Gay/Lesbian Outreach** 4400 N. Lincoln **425-0399/424-7711** counseling & support for youth

**Herland Sister Resources** 2312 NW 39th St. **521-9696** 10am-5pm Sat, from 1pm Sun • women's resource center • wheelchair access

**Oasis Resource Center** 2135 NW 39th St. **525-2437/524-6000** 7pm-10pm, til midnight Fri-Sat

**Oklahoma Traveler Information** (800) **652-6552**

### ACCOMMODATIONS

**America's Crossroads B&B** **495-1111** reservation service for private homes

**Appletree Suites** 6022 NW 23rd St. **495-3881** full-size apt. suites

**Arbors of MacArthur** 1601 N. MacArthur **495-1152** fully furnished & equipped 1- & 2-bdrm suites

**Habana Inn** 2200 NW 39th St. **528-2221** popular • lesbians/gay men • swimming • full bars & restaurant on premises • wheelchair access

**Walnut Gardens** 6700 NW 16th St. **787-5151** full-size apt. suites • fully furnished & equipped

### BARS & NIGHTCLUBS

**Angles** 2117 NW 39th St. **524-3431** 9pm-2am, clsd Mon-Wed • popular • lesbian/gay men • dancing/DJ • live shows • wheelchair access

**Bunkhouse** 2800 NW 39th St. **943-0843** 1pm-2am • popular • lesbians/gay men • dancing/DJ • country/western • leather • live shows • restaurant 5pm-10pm, til 4am Fri-Sat • southern home cooking • wheelchair access • $3-7

**Copa** (at 'Habana Inn') **525-0730** 9pm-2am • lesbians/gay men • dancing/DJ • live shows • wheelchair access

**Finish Line** (at 'Habana Inn') **525-0730** noon-2am • lesbians/gay men • dancing/DJ • country/western

**Hi-Lo Club** 1221 NW 50th St. **843-1722** noon-2am • lesbians/gay men • neighborhood bar • live shows

**K.A.'s** 2024 NW 11th **525-3734** 2pm-2am • mostly women • neighborhood bar • beer bar • Sun brunch

**The Park** 2125 NW 39th St. **528-4690** 5pm-2am, from 3pm Sun • popular • mostly gay men • dancing/DJ • patio • wheelchair access

**Tramps** 2201 NW 39th St. **528-9080** noon-2am, from 10am wknds • popular • mostly gay men • dancing/DJ • wheelchair access

**Wreck Room** 2127 NW 39th St. **525-7610** 9pm-close Fri-Sat • popular • lesbians/gay men • dancing/DJ • live shows • 18+ • juice bar

### CAFES

**Grateful Bean Cafe** 1039 Walker **236-3503** 8am-5pm, til midnight Fri, 10am-2pm Sun • live shows

---

## Oklahoma City (405)

**Annual Events:**

May - Herland Spring Retreat: 521-9696. Music, workshops, campfire.

September - Herland Fall Retreat: 521-9696.

**City Info:** 297-8912.

**Attractions:** Myriad Garden's Crystal Bridge. National Cowboy Hall of Fame. National Softball Hall of Fame.

**Transit:** Yellow Cab: 232-6161. Airport Express: 681-3311. Metro Transit: 235-7433.

# The
# Habana
# Inn

## Sunday thru Thursday
## from $32.95   1 or 2 persons (Holidays Excluded)

Cable TV*Showtime
Free Local Phones*200 Rooms

2200 N.W. 39th Expressway OKC
(405) 528 2221  Reservations only 1-800-988-2221

## All Located inside the Habana Inn

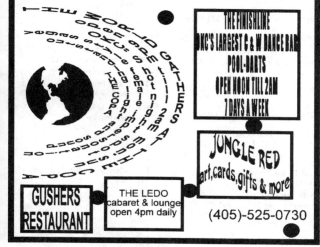

THE WORLD GATHERS AT THE COPA
open one OKC's hottest female hot night spot every
2am 1-W.39E
THE COPA

THE FINISHLINE
OKC'S LARGEST C & W DANCE BAR
POOL-DARTS
OPEN NOON TILL 2AM
7 DAYS A WEEK

JUNGLE RED
art, cards, gifts & more

GUSHERS RESTAURANT

THE LEDO
cabaret & lounge
open 4pm daily

(405)-525-0730

RESTAURANTS

**Bricktown Brewery Restaurant** 1 N. Oklahoma **232-2739** 10am-midnight, til 2am Fri-Sat • dancing/DJ

**Gusher's Restaurant** (at 'Habana Inn') **528-2221 x411** 11am-10:30pm, 7am-3:30am Fri-Sat • wheelchair access

**The Patio Cafe** 5100 N. Classen **842-7273** 7am-2pm

PUBLICATIONS

**Community News** 582-6397

**Gayly Oklahoman** 528-0800 lesbigay newspaper

**The Herland Voice** 521-9696 newsletter

TRAVEL AGENTS

**TLC Travel Professionals** 1015 S. Meridian **948-1740/(800) 852-1740** IGLTA

SPIRITUAL GROUPS

**Lighthouse MCC** 1148 N. MacArthur **942-2822** 10:30am Sun & 7pm Wed

**Oklahoma City Religious Society of Friends (Quakers)** 312 SE 25th St. **631-4174** 10am Sun

EROTICA

**Christie's Toy Box** 3126 N. May Ave. **946-4438**

**Jungle Red** (at 'Habana Inn') **524-5733** wheelchair access

**The Luv-Bead** 4310 N. Western **524-0202** piercing studio

**Ziggyz** 4005 N. Pennsylvania **521-9999**

## Stillwater                              (405)

INFO LINES & SERVICES

**Lesbigay Community Assoc. of OSU** **744-5252**

## Tulsa                                  (918)

INFO LINES & SERVICES

**BLGTA** 2839 E. 8th St. **583-9780** 6:30pm Sun

**The Lesbigay Pride Center/TOHR** 1307 E. 38th St. **743-4297** noon-6pm, clsd Sun • women's supper club Wed • wheelchair access

**TULSA (Tulsa Uniform/Leather Seekers Assoc.)** 838-1222

BARS & NIGHTCLUBS

**Bamboo Lounge** 7204 E. Pine **832-1269** 11am-2am • mostly gay men • neighborhood bar • wheelchair access

**Concessions** 3340 S. Peoria **744-0896** 9pm-2am, clsd Mon-Tue • popular • lesbians/gay men • dancing/DJ • live shows • wheelchair access

**Lola's** 2630 E. 15th **749-1563** 4pm-2am • lesbians/gay men • neighborhood bar • live shows

**New Age Renegade/The Rainbow Room** 1649 S. Main St. **585-3405** 2pm-2am • popular • lesbians/gay men • neighborhood bar • live shows • patio

**Silver Star Saloon** 1565 S. Sheridan **834-4234** 7pm-2am, clsd Mon-Tue • mostly women Sat • more women Sat • dancing/DJ • country/western • wheelchair access • unconfirmed

**T.N.T.** 2114 S. Memorial **660-0856** 3pm-2am • popular • mostly women • dancing/DJ

CAFES

**Java Dave's** 1326 E. 15th St. (Lincoln Plaza) **592-3317** 7am-11pm

RESTAURANTS

**Samson & Delilah** 10 E. 5th St. **585-2221** lunch & dinner • cont'l • plenty veggie

**Wild Fork** 1820 Utica Square **742-0712** 7am-10pm, clsd Sun • full bar • wheelchair access • women-owned/run • $10-20

BOOKSTORES & RETAIL SHOPS

**The Pride Store** 1307 E. 38th St., 2nd flr. **743-4297** noon-6pm, clsd Sun • lesbigay • wheelchair access

PUBLICATIONS

**Queer Times** 835-5050/(800) 598-7533

**Tulsa Family News** 583-1248

TRAVEL AGENTS

**TLC Travel Professionals** 6015 S. Sheridan **492-1852/(800) 290-6798** IGTA

SPIRITUAL GROUPS

**Dignity/Integrity** 5635 E. 71st St. (church) **298-4648** 5pm 2nd Sat

**Family of Faith MCC** 5451-E S. Mingo **622-1441** 11am Sun

EROTICA

**Body Piercing by Nicole** 2722 E. 15th **712-1122**

# OREGON

## Ashland (541)

### INFO LINES & SERVICES
**Womansource** 482-2026 feminist group • sponsors cultural activities like '1st Fri Coffeehouse' & annual Fall Gathering (wheelchair access) • also publishes 'Community News'

### ACCOMMODATIONS
**The Arden Forest Inn** 261 W. Hersey St. 488-1496/(800) 460-3912 gay-friendly • full brkfst • smokefree • kids okay • wheelchair access • gay-owned/run • $60-115

**Country Willows B&B Inn** 1313 Clay St. 488-1590/(800) 945-5697 gay-friendly • full brkfst • swimming • jacuzzi • smokefree • wheelchair access • IGLTA

**Dandelion Garden Cottage** 488-4463 women only • retreat

**Neil Creek House B&B** 341 Mowetza Dr. 482-6443/(800) 460-7860 gay-friendly • full brkfst • swimming • smokefree • $100-175

**Rogues Inn** 600 E. Main St. 482-4770/(800) 276-4837 gay-friendly • apts.

**The Royal Carter House** 514 Siskiyou Blvd. 482-5623/(800) 460-9053 gay-friendly • full brkfst • swimming

**Will's Reste** 482-4394 lesbians/gay men • spa

### CAFES
**Ashland Bakery/Cafe** 38 E. Main 482-2117 7am-9pm • plenty veggie • wheelchair access • $5-8

**Renaissance Chocolates** 240 E. Hersey #12 488-8344/(800) 587-7201 7am-5pm

### RESTAURANTS
**Geppetto's** 345 E. Main 482-1138 8am-midnight • Italian • full bar • wheelchair access • $8-13

### BOOKSTORES & RETAIL SHOPS
**Bloomsbury Books** 290 E. Main St. 488-0029 8am-10pm, from 9am Sat, 10am-9pm Sun

## Astoria (503)

### ACCOMMODATIONS
**Rosebriar Hotel** 636 14th St. 325-7427/(800) 487-0224 gay-friendly • upscale classic hotel • full brkfst • wheelchair access

## Beaverton (503)

### RESTAURANTS
**Swagat Indian Cuisine** 4325 SW 109th Ave. 626-3000 lunch & dinner • beer/wine

### TRAVEL AGENTS
**Morris Travel** 8285 SW Nimbus #140 626-4766 IGLTA

## Bend (541)

### INFO LINES & SERVICES
**Beyond the Closet** 317-8966 social/support

**Out & About** 388-2395 sponsors socials & potlucks • newsletter

### CAFES
**Cafe Paradiso** 945 NW Bond St. 385-5931 8am-11pm, til midnight wknds

**Royal Blend** 1075 NW Newport 383-0873 7am-6pm

### BOOKSTORES & RETAIL SHOPS
**Curiosity Shoppe & Juice Bar** 140 NW Minnesota 382-3408

### PUBLICATIONS
**Living Beyond the Closet** 317-8966

## Blue River (541)

### ACCOMMODATIONS
**River's Edge Inn** 91241 Blue River Rd. 822-3258/(800) 250-1821 gay-friendly • 40 mi. east of Eugene • full brkfst

## Burns (541)

### ACCOMMODATIONS
▲ **Bontemps Motel** 74 W. Monroe 573-2037/(800) 229-1394 gay-owned • non-smoking rms avail. • see ad pg. 386

## Corvallis (541)

### INFO LINES & SERVICES
**After 8 Club** 101 NW 23rd 752-8157 7pm 2nd Tue • lesbigay educational & support group

**Lesbian/Gay/Bisexual Student Alliance-OSU** 737-6360 7pm Mon at Women's Center

### BOOKSTORES & RETAIL SHOPS
**Downtown Book Bin** 2228 SW 3rd 752-0040 7am-8pm, 9:30am-6pm Sat, from noon Sun • also 'Monroe Ave. Book Bin' 2305 NW Monroe 753-8398 • more text books

**Grass Roots Bookstore** 227 SW 2nd St. 754-7668 9am-7pm, til 9pm Fri, til 5:30pm Sat, 11am-5pm Sun • wheelchair access • music section • espresso bar

## Days Creek (541)

ACCOMMODATIONS
**Owl Farm** 679-4655 (INFO LINE ONLY) women only • open women's land for retreat or residence • camping sites avail.

## Eugene (541)

INFO LINES & SERVICES
**Gay/Lesbian AA** 342-4113 (AA#) call for mtg. schedule
**Lesbian/Gay/Bisexual/Transgender Alliance-UO** 346-3360 9am-5pm • social 4pm-6pm Th • wheelchair access
**TLC (The Lesbian Connection)** 2360 Fillmore 683-2793 active lesbian social group
**Women's Center** University of Oregon 346-4095/346-3327 9am-6pm (office) • some lesbian outreach

ACCOMMODATIONS
**Campus Cottage B&B** 1136 E. 19th Ave. 342-5346 gay-friendly • full brkfst • women-owned

BARS & NIGHTCLUBS
**Club Arena** 959 Pearl St. 683-2360 7pm-2:30am • popular • lesbians/gay men • dancing/DJ • live shows • videos

RESTAURANTS
**Keystone Cafe** 395 W. 5th 342-2075 7am-3pm • popular brkfst • plenty veggie
**Pass the Pepper** 959 Pearl St. 683-2360 7am-9pm, clsd Sun • full bar til 2:30am • wheelchair access • $8-16

BOOKSTORES & RETAIL SHOPS
**Hungry Head Bookstore** 1212 Willamette 485-0888 10:30am-6pm, noon-5pm Sun • progressive/alternative titles
▲ **Mother Kali's Bookstore** 720 E. 13th Ave. 343-4864 9am-6pm, from 10am Sat • lesbigay/feminist & multi-racial sections • wheelchair access

damron online

www.damron.com

damronco@aol.com

**Peralandra Books & Music** 199 E. 5th Ave., Station Sq. **485-4848** 10am-6pm, clsd Sun • metaphysical titles

**Ruby Chasm** 152 W. 5th #4 344-4074 10am-6pm, noon-5pm Sun • goddess gifts • books • wheelchair access

## PUBLICATIONS

**View Magazine** 302-6523 'chronicle of gay & lesbian life'

**Womyn's Press** 302-8146 eclectic feminist newspaper since 1970

## TRAVEL AGENTS

**Classic World Travel** 656 Charnelton **343-1992** IGLTA

**Global Affair** 285 E. 5th Ave. **343-8595**/(800) 755-2753 IGLTA • women-owned/run

## SPIRITUAL GROUPS

**MCC** 23rd & Harris (1st Congregational Church) **345-5963** 4pm Sun

## EROTICA

**Exclusively Adult** 1166 S. 'A' St., Springfield **726-6969** 24hrs

## Grants Pass (541)

### ACCOMMODATIONS

**Whispering Pines B&B/Retreat** 9188 W. Evans Creek Rd., Rogue River **582-1757**/(800) 788-1757 popular • lesbians/gay men • full brkfst • swimming • hot tub • smokefree • shared bath • $55-$65

**Womanshare** 862-2807 women only • cabin • campground • hot tub

## La Pine (541)

### ACCOMMODATIONS

**Diamond Stone Guest Lodge & Gallery** 16693 Sprague Loop **536-6263**/(800) 600-6263 gay-friendly • full brkfst

## Lake Oswego (503)

### TRAVEL AGENTS

**Nova Travel** 27 S. State St. #230 **697-4460** IGLTA

# Mother Kali's Books
*Celebrating Women's Lives in all our Diversities*

SPECIAL ORDERS

CARDS

NEW BOOKS

BOOKS ON TAPE

MUSIC

USED BOOKS

LOCAL REFERRALS

**720 E. 13th Ave. (at Hilyard)**     **(541)343-4864**

**Kali @ EFN.Org**

FREE PARKING IN BASEMENT                    WCA

# OCEAN GARDENS INN

## A Haven by the Sea . . .

*Seven tastefully appointed oceanfront units overlooking the Pacific are nestled among flower and shrub gardens. From your room or the backyard hot tub, you can watch gray whales spout and the sun melt into the horizon.*
*The air here is different!*
*Come feel it!*
*Gift Certificates available.*
*AAA Approved*

*Your hosts,*
*Marilee Haase & Sandy Pfaff*

## LINCOLN CITY
### (541) 994-5007
### (800) 866-9925

## Lincoln City     (541)

ACCOMMODATIONS
▲ **Ocean Gardens Inn** 2735 NW Inlet **994-5007**/**(800) 866-9925** gay-friendly • spectacular views of the ocean • hot tub • smokefree • lesbian-owned/run • $65-150

RESTAURANTS
**Over the Waves** 2945 NW Jetty Ave. **994-3877** 8am-10pm, lounge open til 2am wknds • live shows • $12-18
**Road's End Dory Cove** Logan Rd. **994-5180** 11:30am-9pm • steak & seafood

## Medford     (541)

INFO LINES & SERVICES
**AA Gay/Lesbian** 773-4848 (AA#)

## Newport     (541)

ACCOMMODATIONS
**Cliff House B&B** 563-2506 gay-friendly • oceanfront • full brkfst • hot tub • smokefree
**Green Gables B&B** (at 'Green Gables Bookstore') 265-9141 gay-friendly • full brkfst • ocean view • jacuzzi • smokefree • lesbian-owned/run

RESTAURANTS
**Mo's Annex** 657 SW Bay Blvd. **265-7512** great chowder

BOOKSTORES & RETAIL SHOPS
**Green Gables Bookstore** 156 SW Coast St. **265-9141** 10am-5pm • women's • also used/children's books & women's music • also publishes 'Class' newsletter

## Pacific City     (503)

CAFES
**White Moon Cow Cafe** 35490 Brooten Rd. **965-5101** 9am-6pm • wheelchair access • also bookstore • lesbian-owned

## Portland     (503)

*(see also Vancouver, WA)*

INFO LINES & SERVICES
**50+ Portland** 281-4424/331-0415 3rd Sat • social group for lesbians 50+
**Asian/Pacific Islander Lesbian/Gay/Bisexual Info Hotline** 232-6408 educational/social/support group
**Bisexual Community Forum** 285-4848 7:30pm 2nd & 4th Wed • Utopia Coffeehouse at 3320 SE Belmont St.

Cascade AIDS Project 620 SW 5th Ave. #300 223-5907/(800) 777-2437 (PACIFIC NW ONLY) provides a variety of non-medical services

Gay Resource Center/Oregon AIDS Hotline 223-2437/(800) 777-2437 (PACIFIC NW ONLY) 10am-9pm, noon-3pm wknds

Lesbian Community Project 282-8090 multi-cultural political & social events

Live & Let Live Club 2940-A SE Belmont St. 238-6091 call for mtg. schedule

Love Makes a Family 228-3892 many groups • call for locations • also radio show on KKEY 1150 AM • 7am Wed

Northwest Gender Alliance 646-2802 3rd Tue & 2nd Sat • transgender support group • newsletter

Oregon Tourism Commission (800) 547-7842 call for a free catalog

ACCOMMODATIONS

Holladay House B&B 1735 NE Wasco St. 282-3172 gay-friendly • full brkfst

Hotel Vintage Plaza 422 SW Broadway 228-1212/(800) 243-0555 popular • gay-friendly • wheelchair access • $150-250

MacMaster House 1041 SW Vista Ave. 223-7362/(800) 774-9523 gay-friendly • historic mansion near the Rose Gardens

Sullivan's Gulch B&B 1744 NE Clackamas St. 331-1104 lesbians/gay men • IGLTA • $65-75

BARS & NIGHTCLUBS

Bar of the Gods 4801 SE Hawthorne 232-2037 5pm-2:30am, from 3pm summers • gay-friendly • beer/wine • wheelchair access

Boxx's 1035 SW Stark 226-4171 11:30am-2:30am • mostly gay men • videos • wheelchair access • also 'Brig' from 9pm • dancing/DJ

Brew Sisters Pub 53 NW 1st Ave. 274-9901 from 5pm, from noon Sat • mostly women • beer/wine • live shows • women-owned/run • wheelchair access

C.C. Slaughter's 1014 SW Stark St. 248-9135 11am-2:30am • popular • mostly gay men • dancing/DJ • country/western on Wed & Sun • videos • food served

Candlelight Room 2032 SW 5th 222-3378 10am-2:30am, from 11am wknds • gay-friendly • live shows • food served

Choices Pub 2845 SE Stark St. 236-4321 4pm-1am, til 2:30am wknds • mostly women • dancing/DJ • wheelchair access

Club Diva 2845 SE Stark St. (at 'Choices Pub') 227-1889 8pm-2am Sat only • mostly women • dancing/DJ

Code Blue 282-6979 mostly women • call for events & locations

Darcelle XV 208 NW 3rd Ave. 222-5338 5pm-2:30am, clsd Sun • gay-friendly • live shows • food served • wheelchair access

Eagle PDX 1300 W. Burnside 241-0105 4pm-2:30am • mostly gay men • leather

Egyptian Club 3701 SE Division 236-8689 noon-2:30am, Sun brunch • mostly women • dancing/DJ • live shows • also restaurant • pasta & more • some veggie • wheelchair access • $5-10

Embers Nightclub 110 NW Broadway 222-3082 11am-2:30am • popular • mostly gay men • dancing/DJ • live shows • wheelchair access

Evolution 333 SW Park 242-2899 10pm-4am, clsd Mon-Tue • popular • lesbians/gay men • dancing/DJ • 18+/all ages • live shows • no alcohol

Fox & Hound 217 NW 2nd Ave. 243-5530 7am-2am • mostly gay men • also restaurant • wheelchair access

Gail's Dirty Duck Tavern 439 NW 3rd 224-8446 3pm-2:30am, from noon wknds • mostly gay men • neighborhood bar • leather • wheelchair access

Hideaway Pub 4229 SE 82nd 788-2213 noon-2:30am, til midnight Sun • gay-friendly • neighborhood bar

Hobo's 120 NW 3rd Ave. 224-3285 from 4pm, from 2pm Sun • gay-friendly • live shows • also restaurant • some veggie • wheelchair access • $5-20

La Luna 215 SE 9th Ave. 241-5862 9pm-2am • gay-friendly • dancing/DJ • live shows • 18+

Melody Ballroom 615 SE Alder 232-2759 special events space • call for events

Panorama 341 SW 10th 221-7262 9pm-4am Fri-Sat only • popular • gay-friendly • dancing/DJ • beer/wine • wheelchair access

Silverado 1217 SW Stark St. 224-4493 9am-2:30am • popular • mostly gay men • dancing/DJ • live shows • also restaurant • wheelchair access

Starky's 2913 SE Stark St. (at 29th) 230-7980 11am-2am • popular • lesbians/gay men • neighborhood bar • also restaurant • some veggie • patio • $10-20

**Three Sisters Tavern** 1125 SW Stark St. 228-0486 1pm-2:30am, clsd Sun • mostly gay men • neighborhood bar • dancing/DJ

**Tiger Bar** 317 NW Broadway 222-7297 11am-2:30am • gay-friendly • Asian restaurant • wheelchair access

## CAFES

**Bread & Ink Cafe** 3610 SE Hawthorne Blvd. 239-4756 7am-9pm, 8am-10pm Sat, 9am-2pm & 5pm-9pm Sun • popular • beer/wine • wheelchair access

**Cafe Lena** 2239 SE Hawthorne Blvd. 238-7087 8am-midnight, clsd Mon • popular • live shows • wheelchair access

**Coffee Cow** 5204 NE Sacramento 282-9910 hours vary

**Coffee People** 533 NW 23rd St. 221-0235 6am-10pm, from 7am Sun • popular

**Cup & Saucer Cafe** 3566 SE Hawthorne Blvd. 236-6001 7am-9pm, til 6pm Sun-Mon • popular • full menu • smokefree

**Espress It!** 1026 SW Stark 227-2551 from 5pm • lesbians/gay men • coffeehouse/sandwiches • also gallery

**Marco's Cafe & Espresso Bar** 7910 SW 35th, Multnomah 245-0199 7am-9:30pm, from 8am wknds, til 2pm Sun

**Saucebox** 214 SW Broadway 241-3393 11:30am-2am, clsd Sun-Mon • lesbians/gay men • multi-ethnic menu • plenty veggie • full bar • $4-6

## RESTAURANTS

**Acapulco's Gold** 2610 NW Vaughn 220-0283 popular • hearty Mexican • full bar

**The Adobe Rose** 1634 SE Bybee Blvd. 235-9114 4pm-9pm, clsd Sun • New Mexican • some veggie • beer/wine • $5-7

**Assaggio** 7742 SE 13th 232-6151 5:30pm-9:30pm, clsd Sun-Mon • Italian • plenty veggie • beer/wine

**B.J.'s Brazilian Restaurant** 7019 SE Milwaukie Ave. 236-9629 lunch & dinner, clsd Sun

**Bastas Trattoria** 410 NW 21st 274-1572 lunch & dinner • northern Italian • some veggie • full bar • $7-12

**Bijou Cafe** 132 SW 3rd Ave. 222-3187 7am-3pm • popular • plenty veggie • $4-7

# Portland                    (503)

**Where the Girls Are:** Snacking granola while cycling (that's motorcycling) in the mountains, wearing boots and flannel. (Aw, hell, we don't know!)

**Lesbigay Pride:** July: 295-9788.

**Annual Events**

June - The Gathering: 482-2026. Annual pagan camp in the Oregon Woods

September - Northwest Women's Music Celebration. Participatory event for musicians, songwriters & singers, NOT performance-oriented.

October - Living in Leather: 614/899-4406. National conference for the leather, SM and fetish communities.

**City Info:** 244-5794 x5051.

**Attractions:** Microbreweries. Mt. Hood Festival of Jazz. Old Town. Pioneer Courthouse Square. Rose Festival. Washington Park.

**Best View:** International Rose Test Gardens at Washington Park.

**Weather:** The wet and sometimes chilly winter rains give Portland its lush landscape that bursts into beautiful colors in the spring and fall. Summer brings sunnier days. (Temperatures can be in the 50°s one day and the 90°s the next.)

**Transit:** Radio Cab: 227-1212.

# Portland

**S**prawling along the Columbia River at the foot of Mt. Hood, you'll find this city that's home to rainy days, roses, and the punk activist Riot Grrrls of 'zine & grunge fame. If you're searching for the proof that Portland is a lesbian-friendly city, look no further than the Portland Building. Atop the roof you'll find a statue of Portlandia, a city landmark and an amazon icon.

Nearby you can explore the Mount St. Helens National Volcanic Monument or the 5,000 acres of Macleay Park. And if you love jazz, head for the hills; the Mt. Hood Festival of Jazz brings the best of the jazz world to town every August.

Lesbian life here focuses on the outdoors and cocooning at home with small groups of friends. To get in touch, pick up a recent copy of the statewide newspaper **Just Out,** call the **Lesbian Community Project,** or contact **Sisterspirit,** a women's spirituality resource.

Portland's bar scene for women has exploded, with several new offerings. If you'd like to sample some of the local microbrews, stop by **Choices** or **Brew Sisters.** For a nourishing meal, hit **Old Wives Tales** or the **Egyptian Club** then pep up with java and art at **Espress It!** or the smokefree **Cup & Saucer Cafe** before heading to **Club Diva**.

Culturally minded visitors won't want to miss **In Other Words,** the only women's bookstore in town. They carry music along with a large selection of women's literature. **Powell's** is a new/used bookstore that's both legendary and huge, and we've heard that its lesbian/gay section is a good meeting place on weekend nights—there's even a little cafe. **It's My Pleasure** serves up erotica for women, and **In Her Image Gallery** shows women's art.

**Brasserie Montmartre** 626 SW Park **224-5552** lunch & dinner, Sun brunch • bistro • live jazz • full bar

**Cafe des Amis** 1987 NW Kearney **295-6487** 5:30pm-10pm, clsd Sun • French • full bar • wheelchair access • $12-24

**Caffe Fresco** 2387 NW Thurman **243-3247** 7am-4pm, til 2pm Sun • Italian

**Caribou Cafe & Bar** 503 W. Burnside **227-0245** noon-1am, from 5pm Sat, from 3pm Sun • diner • some veggie • full bar • wheelchair access • $4-9

**Esparza's Tex-Mex Cafe** 2725 SE Ankeny St. **234-7909** 11:30am-10pm, clsd Sun-Mon • popular

**Fish Grotto** 1035 SW Stark (at 'Boxx's' bar) **226-4171** 11:30am-10:30pm, from 4:30pm wknds • popular • some veggie • full bar • $8-24

**Genoa** 2832 SE Belmont **238-1464** by reservation only • clsd Sun • 7-course Italian dinner (prix-fixe) • beer/wine • $48

**Gypsy Cafe** 625 NW 21st **796-1859** 11am-2am Mon-Fri, 9am-2am wknds, brunch • some veggie

**Hamburger Mary's** 239 SW Broadway Dr. **223-0900** 7am-2am • popular • full bar • $7-11

**Hobo's** 120 NW 3rd Ave. **224-3285** from 4pm, from 2pm Sun • popular • live shows • wheelchair access

**Indigine** 3725 SE Division St. **238-1470** dinner Tue-Sun, 9am-2pm Sun brunch, clsd Mon

**L'Auberge** 2601 NW Vaughn St. **223-3302** 5:30pm-11pm, til midnight wknds • French • some veggie • full bar

**Majas Taqueria** 1000 SW Morrison **226-1946** 10am-11pm, til 10pm Mon-Wed, clsd Sun

**Old Wives Tales** 1300 E. Burnside St. **238-0470** 8am-9pm, til 10pm Fri-Sat • multi-ethnic vegetarian • beer/wine • wheelchair access • $7-14

**Papa Haydn** 701 NW 23rd Ave. **228-7317** bistro • some veggie • full bar

**Pizzacato** 505 NW 23rd **242-0023** 11am-9pm, til 10pm Fri-Sat • popular • plenty veggie

**Ron Paul Charcuterie** 1441 NE Broadway **284-5439** 8am-10pm, til midnight Fri-Sat, 9am-4pm Sun • fancy French deli plus • some veggie • beer/wine

**Santa Fe Taqueria** 831 NW 23rd **220-0406** 11am-10pm, til 11pm Fri-Sat • popular • Mexican • some veggie • full bar • patio

**Shakers Cafe** 1212 NW Glisan **221-0011** 7:30am-3:30pm, clsd Mon • homecooking • some veggie • beer/wine

**Starky's** 2913 SE Stark St. **230-7980** lesbians/gay men

**Vista Spring Cafe** 2440 SW Vista **222-2811** 11am-10pm, from noon wknds, til 9pm Sun • beer/wine

**Wildwood** 1221 NW 21st Ave. **248-9663** 11am-9pm • popular • full bar

**Zefiro** 500 NW 21st **226-3394** lunch & dinner, clsd Sun • Mediterranean/Southeast Asian • some veggie • full bar

## BOOKSTORES & RETAIL SHOPS

**Counter Media** 927 SW Oak 11am-7pm, noon-6pm Sun • alternative comics • vintage gay books/periodicals

**In Her Image Gallery** 3208 SE Hawthorne **231-3726** 10am-6pm, clsd Mon-Tue • wheelchair access

**In Other Words** 3734 SE Hawthorne Blvd. **232-6003** 10am-9pm, til 5pm Sun • women's books • music • wheelchair access

**The Jellybean** 721 SW 10th Ave. **222-5888** 10am-6pm, clsd Sun • cards • T-shirts • gifts • wheelchair access

**Laughing Horse Bookstore** 3652 SE Division **236-2893** 11am-7pm, clsd Sun • alternative/progressive • wheelchair access

**Looking Glass Bookstore** 318 SW Taylor **227-4760** 9am-6pm, from 10am Sat, clsd Sun

**Powell's Books** 1005 W. Burnside St. **228-4651**/**(800) 878-7323** 9am-11pm, til 9pm Sun • new & used books • cafe • wheelchair access

**Presents of Mind** 3633 SE Hawthorne **230-7740** 10am-7pm, til 6:30pm Sat, 11am-5:30pm Sun • jewelry • cards • unique toys • wheelchair access

**Twenty-Third Ave. Books** 1015 NW 23rd Ave. **224-5097** 9:30am-9pm, from 10am Sat, 11am-7pm Sun • general • lesbigay section • wheelchair access

## PUBLICATIONS

**Just Out** **236-1252** lesbigay newspaper w/extensive resource directory

## TRAVEL AGENTS

**Advantage Travel Service** 812 SW Washington St. #200 **225-0186** IGLTA

**Away To Travel** 7314 NE Fremont St. **281-1234** IGLTA • contact Joanne Ross

**Gulliver's Travels & Voyages** 514 NW 9th Ave. **221-0013/(800) 875-8009** IGLTA

**Hawthorne Travel Company** 1939 SE Hawthorne Blvd. **232-5944/(800) 232-5944** IGLTA

**In Touch Travel, NW** 121 SW Morrison #270 **223-1062/(800) 568-3246** IGLTA

**J&M Travel** 4370 NE Halsey #138 **249-0305/(800) 875-0305** IGLTA

**Joan Sher Travel Consultants at GK Travel** 10260 SW Greenburg Rd. #150 **244-0344/(800) 200-0344** IGLTA • ask for Joan

**Mikuni Travel Service** 1 SW Columbia St. #1010 **227-3639/(800) 248-0624** IGLTA

**Travel Agents International** 917 SW Washington St. **223-1100/(800) 357-3194** ask for Rip • IGLTA

**Ultimate Travels** 621 SW Morrison #435 **220-8866/(800) 446-4117** IGLTA

**Uniglobe Lane Travel** 1211 NW 23rd **223-6055/(800) 450-6055** IGLTA

**World Travel** 700 NE Multnomah #478 **231-1600** IGLTA

## SPIRITUAL GROUPS

**Congregation Neve Shalom** **246-8831** 8:15pm Fri & 9am Sat • conservative synagogue w/lesbigay outreach

**Dignity Portland** SW 13th at Clay (St. Stephen's Episcopal Church) **295-4868** 7:30pm Sat

**MCC Portland** 2400 NE Broadway **281-8868** 10:30am Sun & 7pm Wed • wheelchair access

**Pagan Info Line 650-7045** also publishes 'Open Ways' newsletter

**Sisterspirit 294-0645** celebration w/ women sharing spirituality • wheelchair access

**St. Stephen's Episcopal Church** 1432 SW 13th Ave. **223-6424** 7:45am & 10am Sun, 12:15pm Wed

## GYMS & HEALTH CLUBS

**Inner City Hot Springs** 2927 NE Everett St. **238-1065** gay-friendly • wellness center

**Princeton Athletic Club** 614 SW 11th Ave. **222-2639** gay-friendly

## EROTICA

**The Crimson Phoenix** 1876 SW 5th Ave. **228-0129** 'sexuality bookstore for lovers' • wheelchair access

**Fantasy for Adults** 3137 NE Sandy Blvd. **239-6969** 24hrs

**It's My Pleasure** 4258 SE Hawthorne **236-0505** sex toys & books for women

**Leatherworks** 2908 SE Belmont St. **234-2697**

**Spartacus Leather** 302 SW 12th Ave. **224-2604**

## Rockaway Beach          (503)

### ACCOMMODATIONS

**Bear & Penguin Inn** 421 N. Miller **355-8610** gay-friendly

## Roseburg          (541)

### INFO LINES & SERVICES

**Gay/Lesbian Switchboard 672-4126** 24hrs • publishes newsletter

### BARS & NIGHTCLUBS

**Roma Cocktail Lounge & Restaurant** 5096 Hwy. 99 S. **679-7100** 4pm-2am, kitchen til 10pm • Italian • live shows

## Salem          (503)

### RESTAURANTS

**Off Center Cafe** 1741 Center St. NE **363-9245** 7am-2:30pm, from 8am wknds, 6pm-9pm Th-Sat • popular brkfst • some veggie • wheelchair access • $7-12

### BOOKSTORES & RETAIL SHOPS

**Rosebud & Fish** 524 State St. **399-9960** 10am-7pm, noon-5pm Sun • alternative bookstore

### PUBLICATIONS

**Community News 363-0006** monthly

### SPIRITUAL GROUPS

**Dignity** 1020 Columbia St. (St. Vincent's Church) **363-0006** 7:30pm 2nd & 4th Sat

**Sweet Spirit MCC** Lancaster Dr. & Silverton Rd. (back room in Beauty College) **363-6618** 11am Sun

**Unitarian Universalist Congregation of Salem** 490 19th St. NE **364-0932** 9:30am & 11:15am Sun (10am only summers)

## Sheridan (503)

ACCOMMODATIONS
**Middle Creek Run** 25400 Harmony Rd.
**843-7606** gay-friendly • full brkfst • hot
tub • swimming

## Tigard (503)

TRAVEL AGENTS
**The Travel Shop** 10115 SW Nimbus Ctr.
#600 **684-8533/(800) 285-8835** ask for
Mark • IGLTA

## Tiller (541)

ACCOMMODATIONS
**Kalles Family RV Ranch** 233 Jackson
Creek Rd. **825-3271** lesbians/gay men •
camping sites • RV hookups • btwn.
Medford & Roseburg

## Wilsonville (503)

TRAVEL AGENTS
**Travel Network** 29756 Town Ctr. Loop W.
#C **570-0761** IGLTA

## Yachats (541)

ACCOMMODATIONS
**Morningstar Gallery & B&B** 95668 Hwy.
101 S. **547-4412** mostly women • full
brkfst • oceanfront • hot tub • smokefree
• $85-150
**Ocean Odyssey 547-3637/(800) 800-
1915** gay-friendly • vacation rental
homes in Yachats & Waldport • women-
owned/run • $75-125
**The Oregon House** 94288 Hwy. 101 **547-
3329** gay-friendly • smokefree • wheelchair access
**See Vue Motel** 95590 Hwy. 101 S. **547-
3227** gay-friendly

## PENNSYLVANIA

## Allentown (610)

*(see also Bethlehem)*

INFO LINES & SERVICES
**Your Turf 439-8755 (MCC)** 7pm Fri • lesbigay youth group • call for location

BARS & NIGHTCLUBS
**Candida's** 247 N. 12th St. **434-3071**
2am-2pm • lesbians/gay men • neighborhood bar • food served
**Moose Lounge/Stonewall** 28-30 N. 10th
St. **432-0706** 4pm-2am • popular • les-
bians/gay men • dancing/DJ • live shows
• videos • food served

SPIRITUAL GROUPS
**Grace Covenant Fellowship Church** 913
Hamilton St. **740-0247** 10:45am Sun

## Altoona (814)

INFO LINES & SERVICES
**Gay/Lesbian/Bisexual Info 944-3583**
8:30am-4:30pm, clsd wknds • ask for
Melanie

BARS & NIGHTCLUBS
**Escapade** 2523 Union Ave., Rte. 36 **946-
8195** 8pm-2am, from 6pm Sun • also
restaurant • gay-owned/run

## Ardmore (610)

TRAVEL AGENTS
**Swain Travel Services** 6 W. Lancaster
Ave. **896-9595/(800) 227-9246** IGLTA

## Beaver Falls

BARS & NIGHTCLUBS
**A.S.S. (Alternative Subway Stop)** 1204
7th Ave. (enter rear) 8pm-2am, clsd Sun
• mostly gay men • dancing/DJ • unconfirmed

## Bethlehem (610)

INFO LINES & SERVICES
**Lehigh Valley Lesbians** 424 Center St.
(Unitarian Church) **439-8755 (MCC)** 7pm
3rd Th

BARS & NIGHTCLUBS
**Diamonz** 1913 W. Broad St. **865-1028**
3pm-2am, from 2pm wknds • mostly
women • dancing/DJ • live shows • also
restaurant • fine dining (clsd Mon) •
some veggie • wheelchair access • $7-15

## SPIRITUAL GROUPS
**MCC of the Lehigh Valley** 424 Center St. (Unitarian Church) **439-8755** 6pm Sun

## Bridgeport (610)

### BARS & NIGHTCLUBS
**The Lark** 302 Dekalb St. (Rte. 202 N.) **275-8136** 8pm-2am, from 4pm Sun • mostly gay men • dancing/DJ • dinner served

## Bristol (215)

### EROTICA
**Bristol News World** 576 Bristol Pike (Rte. 13 N.) **785-4770** 24hrs

## Conshohoken (610)

### BARS & NIGHTCLUBS
**Rio** 225 Washington St. **941-9911** from 9pm Sun only • lesbians/gay men • dancing/DJ • patio

## East Stroudsburg (717)

### ACCOMMODATIONS
▲ **Rainbow Mtn. Resort & Restaurant** **223-8484** popular • lesbians/gay men • B&B w/ deluxe stes. • cabins (seasonal) • swimming • also restaurant • full bar • dancing/DJ Fri-Sat • piano bar • transgender-friendly • IGLTA

## Edinboro (814)

### INFO LINES & SERVICES
**Identity 732-2000** student group

## Emlenton (412)

### ACCOMMODATIONS
**Apple Alley** 214 River Ave. **867-9636**/(800) 547-8499 gay-friendly • riverfront • full brkfst • smokefree • $40-60

## Ephrata (717)

### TRAVEL AGENTS
**Zeller Travel** 4213 Oregon Pike **859-4710**/(800) 331-4359 IGLTA

## Erie (814)

### INFO LINES & SERVICES
**Erie Gay News 456-9833** excellent resource • newsletter
**Lambda Group AA** 7180 New Perry Hwy. (Unitarian Universalist Church) **452-2675** 8pm Sun • wheelchair access

Your all season gay resort in the Pocono Mountains

Charming Accomodations
Restaurant
Dance Club and Piano Bar
Olympic size Pool
85 private wooded acres

RAINBOW MOUNTAIN
R▾E▾S▾O▾R▾T

210 Mt Nebo Road
E. Stroudsburg, PA 18301

www.rainbowmountain.com

717 223-8484

**Trigon: Lesbian/Gay/Bisexual Coalition** 898-6164 student group

**Womynspace** 7180 New Perry Hwy. (Unitarian Universalist Church) **454-2713** 7:30pm 1st Sat • alcohol- & smokefree women's coffeehouse

### ACCOMMODATIONS

**Castle Great House** 231 W. 21st St. **454-6465** lesbians/gay men • smokefree • $50

### BARS & NIGHTCLUBS

**The Embers** 1711 State St. **454-9171** 8pm-2am, clsd Sun • mostly gay men • dancing/DJ • piano bar • food served

**Lizzy Bordon's Part II** 3412 W. 12th St. **833-4059** 9pm-2am, clsd Sun • popular • lesbians/gay men • dancing/DJ • patio • wheelchair access

### CAFES

**Coffeeright** 160 E. Front St. **451-6976** hours vary, clsd Sun • wheelchair access

**Cup-A-Ccinos Coffeehouse** 18 N. Park Row **456-1151** 7:30am-9pm, til midnight Th-Sat, from 9am Sat, clsd Sun • live shows • wheelchair access

### RESTAURANTS

**Aroma's Coffeehouse** 2174 W. 8th St. **456-5282** til 11pm, til midnight Fri-Sat, til 4pm Sun • occasional live shows

**Coqui's Gourmet Deli** 3443 W. Lake Rd. **835-2272** pizza/sandwiches

**La Bella Bistro** 556 W. 4th **454-3616** clsd Sun-Mon • BYOB • $9-20

**Pie in the Sky Cafe** 463 W. 8th St. **459-8638** 7:30am-2pm, dinner from 5pm Fri-Sat, clsd Sun • BYOB • wheelchair access

**Tapas** 17 W. 9th St. **454-8797** 7am-3pm, til 11pm Th, til 4am Fri-Sat, til 9pm Sun

### PUBLICATIONS

**Gay Peoples' Chronicle** (216) 631-8646

### SPIRITUAL GROUPS

**Temple Anshe Hesed** 930 Liberty St. **454-2426** 8pm Fri

**Unitarian Universalist Congregation of Erie** 7180 New Perry Hwy. **864-9300** 10:30am Sun

## Greensburg (412)

### BARS & NIGHTCLUBS

**RK's Safari Lounge** 108 W. Pittsburgh St. **837-6614** 9pm-2am, clsd Sun • popular • mostly gay men • dancing/DJ • patio • wheelchair access

## Harrisburg (717)

### INFO LINES & SERVICES

**Gay/Lesbian Switchboard** 234-0328 6pm-10pm

### BARS & NIGHTCLUBS

**B-tls** 891 Eisenhower Blvd. **939-1123** 8pm-2am, clsd Sun-Wed • mostly women • dancing/DJ • videos • pool table • food served • women-owned/run

**Neptune's Lounge** 268 North St. **233-3078** 4pm-2am, from 2pm Sun • popular • mostly gay men • neighborhood bar • dinner 5pm-9pm Tue-Th

**Stallions** 706 N. 3rd St. (enter rear) **233-4681** 4pm-2am • popular • mostly gay men • dancing/DJ • karaoke • also restaurant • dinner Th-Sat • wheelchair access

**Strawberry Cafe** 704 N. 3rd St. **234-4228** 2pm-2am, clsd Sun • mostly gay men • neighborhood bar • videos • wheelchair access

### RESTAURANTS

**Colonnade** 300 N. 2nd St. **234-8740** 7am-8:30pm, clsd Sun • seafood • full bar • wheelchair access • $8-15

**Paper Moon** 268 North St. **233-0581** 5pm-9pm, til 11pm wknds • lesbians/gay men • $5-10

### SPIRITUAL GROUPS

**MCC of the Spirit** 2873 Jefferson St. **236-7387** 10:30am & 7pm Sun

## Indiana (412)

### BOOKSTORES & RETAIL SHOPS

**Josephine's** 1176 Grant St. #2180 **465-4469** 11am-5pm, 10am-4pm Sat, clsd Sun • feminist

## Johnstown (814)

### BARS & NIGHTCLUBS

**Casanova** 5977 Somerset Pike (Rte. 985), Boswell **629-9911** 6pm-2am, from 5pm Sun

**Lucille's** 520 Washington St. **539-4448** 9pm-2am, clsd Sun-Mon • lesbians/gay men • dancing/DJ • live shows

## Kutztown (610)

### ACCOMMODATIONS

**Grim's Manor B&B** 10 Kern Rd. **683-7089** lesbians/gay men • 200 yr. old stone farmhouse on 5 acres • full brkfst • older kids ok • $65

# Lancaster (717)

### INFO LINES & SERVICES
**Gay/Lesbian Helpline** 397-0691 7pm-10pm Sun, Wed & Th
**Pink Triangle Coalition** 394-6260 also youth mtgs.

### ACCOMMODATIONS
**Maison Rouge B&B** 2236 Marietta Ave. 399-3033/(800) 309-3033 gay-friendly • full brkfst • smokefree • $95-125 .

### BARS & NIGHTCLUBS
**Sundown Lounge** 429 N. Mulberry St. 392-2737 8pm-2am, from 3pm Fri-Sat, clsd Sun • mostly women • dancing/DJ
**Tally Ho** 201 W. Orange 299-0661 6pm-2am, from 8pm Sun • popular • lesbians/gay men • dancing/DJ (11pm-2am Wed-Sun)

### RESTAURANTS
**Loft** (above 'Tally Ho' bar) 299-0661 lunch Mon-Fri, dinner Mon-Sat • French • $15-25

### BOOKSTORES & RETAIL SHOPS
**Borders Bookshop** 940 Plaza Blvd. 293-8022 til 11pm • lesbigay section

### SPIRITUAL GROUPS
**MCC Vision of Hope** 130 E. Main St., Mountville 285-9070 10am & 7pm Sun

# Malvern (610)

### ACCOMMODATIONS
**Pickering Bend B&B** 656 Church Rd. 933-0183 gay-friendly • built in 1790 • 2 stes. • kitchen • fireplaces • kids/pets ok • $90-115

# Manheim (717)

### BARS & NIGHTCLUBS
**Rooster's** 168 S. Main St. 665-6211 6pm-2am • mostly women

# Monroeville (412)

### EROTICA
**Monroeville News** 2735 Stroschein Rd. 372-5477 24hrs

# Montgomeryville (215)

### TRAVEL AGENTS
**Thomas Travel Service** 362-1711/(800) 666-3600/2988 IGLTA

## New Hope (215)

### INFO LINES & SERVICES
**AA Gay/Lesbian** 862-0327/574-6900 (AA#)

### ACCOMMODATIONS
**The Fox & Hound B&B** 246 West Bridge St. **862-5082/(800) 862-5082** gay-friendly • 1850s stone manor • $65-165

**The Lexington House** 6171 Upper York Rd. **794-0811** lesbians/gay men • 1749 country home • full brkfst • swimming • $125-160

**The Raven** 385 West Bridge St. **862-2081** popular • mostly gay men • swimming • also restaurant • cont'l

▲ **The Victorian Peacock B&B** 309 E. Dark Hollow Rd., Pipersville **766-1356** lesbians/gay men • swimming • spa • smokefree • women-owned/run • $95-135

**York Street House B&B** 42 York St., Lambertville NJ **(609) 397-3007** gay-friendly • smokefree • IGLTA • lesbian-owned/run • $65-150

### BARS & NIGHTCLUBS
**The Cartwheel** 427 York Rd. (US 202) **862-0880** 5pm-2am • popular • lesbians/gay men • dancing/DJ • live shows • piano bar • also restaurant • wheelchair access • $6-18

**Ladies 2000 (609)** 784-8341 scheduled parties for women by women • call for times & locations

**The Raven Bar & Restaurant** (at 'The Raven' accommodations) **862-2081** 11am-2am • lesbians/gay men

### RESTAURANTS
**Country Host** 463 Old York Rd. (Rte. 202) **862-5575** 7am-10pm • full bar • wheelchair access • $7-12

**Havana** 105 S. Main St. **862-9897** 11am-midnight, bar til 2am • some veggie • live shows • $9-16

**Karla's** 5 W. Mechanic St. **862-2612** lunch & dinner, late night brkfst Fri-Sat • Italian • some veggie • full bar • live shows • $15-25

**Mother's** 34 N. Main St. **862-5270** 9am-10pm • some veggie • $10-20

Bucks County a region rich in beauty, history, and recreation.

The Victorian Peacock

BED & BREAKFAST

The Victorian Peacock, a classic style three story mansion set on 5 country acres, which tastefully combines expertly crafted period details, tall windows, ornate wood working, and oak floors to reflect the warmth and the atmosphere of a more genteel time. Wraparound veranda, roaring fireplace, elegant suites lavishly decorated with antique furnishings, ceiling fans, oversized beds, fine linens, plush comforters, A/C, heated pool and spa.

Experience the magic of beautiful country-side with rolling hills, covered bridges, stone manors, woodlands with running creeks and historic towpath along the river.

309 E. Dark Hollow Rd. Pipersville PA 18947
215•766•1356
Lesbian Owned and Operated
*New Hope, the vacation alternative to P-town and Fire Island*

**Odette's** South River Rd. **862-3000**
11am-10pm, piano bar & cabaret til 1am
• some veggie • wheelchair access • $15-25

**Wildflowers** 8 W. Mechanic St. **862-2241**
(seasonal) noon-10pm, til 11pm Fri-Sat
• some veggie • BYOB • outdoor dining •
$8-15

## BOOKSTORES & RETAIL SHOPS

**Book Gallery** 19 W. Mechanic St. **862-5110** 11am-7pm (call for Feb-May hours)
• feminist/lesbian

**Ember'glo Gifts** 27 W. Mechanic St. **862-2929** 11am-6pm, wknds only (winters)

**Sappho's Garden** 95 S. Main St. **862-1326**

## TRAVEL AGENTS

**Lynn Travel Associates** 862-5015 IGLTA

## EROTICA

**Grownups** 2 E. Mechanic St. **862-9304**
11am-7pm, til 11pm Fri-Sat

**Le Chateau Exotique** 5 W. Bridge St.
**862-3810** fetishwear

## New Milford                    (717)

### ACCOMMODATIONS

**Oneida Camp & Lodge** 465-7011 (seasonal) mostly gay men • oldest gay-owned/operated campground dedicated to the lesbigay community • swimming • nudity

## Philadelphia                    (215)

### INFO LINES & SERVICES

**AA Gay/Lesbian** 574-6900 call for mtg. schedule

**BiUnity** 724-3663 group for bisexual men & women

**Female Trouble** 928-5090 social/educational woman-woman S/M group • 18+ • newsletter

**Gay/Lesbian Switchboard** 546-7100 7pm-10pm

**Gender Transgressors** 386-2790 info • referrals

**Penn Women's Center** 3643 Locust Walk 898-8611

**Philadelphia Convention & Visitors Bureau** 16th St. & JFK Blvd. 636-4400/(800) 225-5745 publishes 'Philadelphia Gay & Lesbian Travel News' • IGLTA

**Sisterspace of the Delaware Valley** 476-8856 sponsors 'Sisterspace Pocono Weekend' & other events • newsletter

**Unity** 1207 Chestnut St. 851-1912 9am-5:30pm Mon-Fri, clsd wknds • lesbigay/transgender support/social services

**William Way Gay/Lesbian/Bisexual/ Transgendered Commmunity Center** 1315 Spruce St. 732-2220 noon-9pm Mon-Th, special events Fri, clsd wknds • also 'Lesbigay Library & Archives of Philadelphia'

## Philadelphia          (215)

**Where the Girls Are:** Partying downtown near 12th St., south of Market.

**Annual Events:**

May 7-11 - **Pridefest Philadelphia:** 790-7820. Weekend of gay/lesbian film, performances, literature, sports, seminars, parties & more.

June 12-15 - **Womongathering:** 609/694-2037. Women's spirituality fest.

December 31 - **Mummer's Strut:** 732-3378. New Year's Eve party benefitting Pridefest.

**City Info:** 636-1666.

**Attractions:** Academy of Natural Sciences Museum (299-1000). Afro-American Historical and Cultural Museum. Betsy Ross's Home. Liberty Bell. National Museum Of American Jewish History. Philadelphia Museum of Art (763-8100).

**Best View:** Top of Center Square, 16th & Market.

**Weather:** Winter temperatures hover in the 20°s. Summers are humid with temperatures in the 80°s and 90°s.

**Transit:** United Cab: 238-9500. Quaker City Cab: 728-8000.

## ACCOMMODATIONS

**Abigail Adams B&B** 1208 Walnut St. **546-7336/(800) 887-1776** gay-friendly • smokefree • kids ok

**Antique Row B&B** 341 S. 12th St. **592-7802** gay-friendly • 1820s townhouse in heart of gay community • full brkfst

**Bag & Baggage B&B** 338 S. 19th St. **546-3807** gay-friendly • kids ok

**Doubletree Hotel** 237 S. Broad St. **893-1659/(800) 222-8733** gay-friendly • IGLTA

**Embassy Suites Center City** 1776 Ben Franklin Pkwy. **561-1776/(800) 362-2799** gay-friendly • IGLTA

**Gaskill House** 312 Gaskill St. **413-2887** gay-friendly • full brkfst • smokefree

**Glen Isle Farm** 30 mi. out of town, in Downingtown **(610) 269-9100/(800) 269-1730** gay-friendly • full brkfst • smokefree • older kids ok (call first)

**Latham Hotel** 135 S. 17th St. **563-7474/(800) 528-4261** gay-friendly

**Rittenhouse Hotel** 210 W. Rittenhouse Sq. **546-9000/(800) 635-1042** gay-friendly • food served

**Travelodge—Stadium** 2015 Penrose Ave. **755-6500/(800) 578-7878** gay-friendly • swimming • full bar • wheelchair access

## BARS & NIGHTCLUBS

**2-4 Club** 1221 St. James St. **735-5772** from midnight Mon-Th, call for wknd hours • mostly gay men • dancing/DJ • private club

# Philadelphia

*T*hough it's packed with sites of rich historical value, don't miss out on Philadelphia's multi-cultural present. To get a feel for this city, browse the Reading Terminal Market, a quaint old farmer's market preserved within the new Convention Center. Here, smalltime grocers and farmers of many cultures sell their fresh food.

A vital element in many of these cultures is the growing lesbian community. To connect with the scene, call the **Lesbian/Gay Switchboard**, check out **Sisters,** a women's dance bar, or call **Ladies 2000** to find out about their next women's party

And don't even think of leaving town before you visit **Giovanni's Room,** Philadelphia's legendary lesbian/gay bookstore. Here you can pick up the latest lesbian bestseller, love of your life or copy of the local publications: the **Philadelphia Gay News, Labyrinth** women's paper and **Pride Weekly** (formerly Au Courant).

**247 Bar** 247 S. 17th St. **545-9779** noon-2am • popular • mostly gay men • live shows • videos • also restaurant

**Bike Stop** 204 S. Quince St. **627-1662** 4pm-2am, from 1pm Sat, from 3pm Sun • popular • mostly gay men • 4 flrs. • dancing/DJ • alternative • leather (very leather-women-friendly) • home bar of 'Female Trouble' • live shows • also cafe • some veggie • S6-16

**Black Banana** 205 N. 3rd **925-4433** 10pm-3am, from midnight wkdays • gay-friendly • dancing/DJ • alternative • wheelchair access

**C.R. Bar** 6405 Market St., Upper Darby **(610) 734-1130** 8pm-2am, clsd Sun • mostly gay men • neighborhood bar

**Club Unique I** 1415 Locust St. **732-6047** 9pm-2:30am Sun only • mostly gay men • dancing/DJ • mostly African-American

**Club Unique II** 68 N. 12th St. **732-6047** 9pm-2:30am Wed-Fri only

**Deluxe** 305 S. 11th St. **829-9151** Wed-Sun • gay-friendly • dancing/DJ • drag & cabaret shows

**Fluid** 613 S. 4th St. **629-3686** from 9pm • gay-friendly • dancing/DJ

**Key West** 207 S. Juniper **545-1578** 4pm-2am, from 2pm Sun • lesbians/gay men • dancing/DJ • live shows • also restaurant • dinner Wed-Sat, Sun brunch • wheelchair access • $8-15

**The Khyber** 56 S. 2nd St. **238-5888** gay-friendly • Wed gay night • live shows • also restaurant

**Ladies 2000 (609)** 784-8341 scheduled parties for women by women • call for times & locations

**Milborn Social Club** (upstairs at 'C.R. Bar') **(610) 734-1130** from midnight Fri-Sat, 4pm-2am Sun • mostly gay men • dancing/DJ • private club

**Port Blue** 2552 E. Allegheny Ave., Port Richmond **425-4699** 4pm-2am, clsd Sun-Mon • gay-friendly • neighborhood bar

**Raffles** 243 S. Camac St. **545-6969** 4pm-2am • popular • lesbians/gay men • 3 bars • dancing/DJ • live shows • also restaurant • $8-16

**Rodz/Tyz/Bottoms** 1418 Rodman St. **546-1900** various bars & hours • lesbians/gay men • dancing/DJ • piano bar • also restaurant • some veggie • $10-12

**Shampoo** 417 N. 8th St. **922-7500** 9pm-2am, clsd Sun-Wed • more gay Fri

**Sisters** 1320 Chancellor St. **735-0735** 4pm-2am • mostly women • dancing/DJ • wheelchair access

**The Westbury** 261 S. 13th **546-5170** 10am-2am • mostly gay men • neighborhood bar • also restaurant • dinner til 10pm, til 11pm wknds • gourmet home-cooking • some veggie • wheelchair access • $9-14

**Woody's** 202 S. 13th St. **545-1893** 11am-2am • popular • mostly gay men • dancing/DJ • country/western • dance lessons • 18+ Wed • videos • food served • wheelchair access

CAFES

**10th Street Pour House** 262 S. 10th St. **922-5626** 7:30am-11pm, from 9am Sat, 10am-8pm Sun

**Cheap Art Cafe** 260 S. 12th St. **735-6650** 24hrs

**Millennium Coffee** 212 S. 12th St. **731-9798** open til midnight

**Rhino Coffee Roastery & Cafe** 212 South St. **923-2630** 7am-midnight, from 8:30am wknds

RESTAURANTS

**16th Street Bar & Grill** 264 S. 16th St. **735-3316** 11:30am-11pm, bar open til 2am • Mediterranean • some veggie • full bar • $10-20

**The Adobe Cafe** 4550 Mitchell St., Roxborough **483-3947** 4:30pm-10:30pm • live shows • $9-12

**Astral Plane** 1708 Lombard St. **546-6230** 5pm-11pm • some veggie • full bar • $10-20

**Backstage Bar & Restaurant** 614 S. 4th St. **627-9887** 4pm-2am, dinner from 6pm-10pm, Sun brunch • $10-20

**Cafe Nola** 328 South St. **627-2590** Creole • full bar

**Cafe on Quince** 202 S. Quince St. **592-1750** dinner & Sun brunch • women-owned/run

**Circa** 1518 Walnut St. **545-6800** lunch, dinner, Sun brunch • wheelchair access

**Diner on the Square** 1839 Spruce St. **735-5787** 24hrs • $7-10

**Harmony Vegetarian** 135 N. 9th St. **627-4520** 11am-10pm, til midnight Fri-Sat

**The Inn Philadelphia** 251 S. Camac St. **732-2339** 4:30pm-10pm, til 9pm Sun • cont'l • some veggie • full bar • $12-26

**Jack Rabbit Slims** 602 2nd St. **625-9533** 24hrs • call for gay events • wheelchair access

# Philadelphia's Fastest Growing Feminist Voice...

• information and analysis of current issues and events of relevance to women by women.

• profiles of community leaders and organizations.

• listing of events for women in the Philadelphia area including arts & entertainment, lectures, workshops, social gatherings, support groups & more.

• display ads offering products and services to women from businesses and professionals.

• for over 15 years, Philadelphia's only alternative publication from a woman's perspective.

subscriptions are $20 per year (10 issues)

for advertising information, write or call address below

Labyrinth

The Philadelphia Women's Newspaper by Westbury Publishing, Inc.

271 S. 15th St, Ste. 1706 • PO Box 58489 • Philadelphia, PA 19102 • 215-546-6686

**Judy's Cafe** 627 S. 3rd St. **928-1968** 5:30pm-midnight, Sun brunch from 10:30am • full bar • women-owned/run • $9-17

**Latimer's Deli** 255 S. 1st St. **545-9244** 9am-9pm, til 11pm Fri • Jewish deli

**Liberties** 705 N. 2nd St. **238-0660** lunch & dinner, Sun brunch • full bar • live jazz wknds • $10-16

**Makam's Kitchen** 2401 Lombard **546-8832** 10am-10pm • live shows

**Michael's** 239 Chestnut St. **829-9126** 5pm-9pm, til 10:30pm Fri-Sat, 11am-3pm Sun, clsd Mon • Italian

**Mont Serrat** 623 South St. **627-4224** noon-midnight • some veggie • full bar • $6-15

**My Thai** 2200 South St. **985-1878** 5pm-10pm, til 11pm Fri-Sat • $10-20

**Palladium/Gold Standard** 3601 Locust Walk **387-3463** dinner, bar til 12:30am • some veggie • wheelchair access • $10-25

**Philadelphia Tea Party** 1334 Walnut St. **732-8327** 11am-10pm, til midnight Fri-Sat, clsd Sun • $5-10

**Roosevelt's Pub** 2222 Walnut **636-9722** lunch & dinner • some veggie • full bar • $5-12

**Savoy Restaurant** 232 S. 11th St. **923-2348** 24hrs • popular afterhours • $5-7

**Shing Kee** 52 N. 9th St. **829-8983** lunch & dinner • BYOB • gay-owned/run

**Striped Bass** 1500 Walnut St. **732-4444** lunch, dinner & Sun brunch • upscale dining

**Waldorf Cafe** 20th & Lombard Sts. **985-1836** dinner • some veggie • full bar • wheelchair access • $12-18

**White Dog Cafe** 3420 Sansom St. **386-9224** lunch & dinner • full bar • $7-18

## ENTERTAINMENT & RECREATION

**Dyke TV** Channel 54 9pm & midnight Th • 'weekly half-hour TV show produced by lesbians, for lesbians'

**'Q Zine'** WXPN-FM 88.5 **898-6677** 8pm Sun • lesbigay radio

## BOOKSTORES & RETAIL SHOPS

**Afterwords** 218 S. 12th St. **735-2393** 10am-midnight

**Giovanni's Room** 345 S. 12th St. **923-2960** call for hours, open 7 days a week • popular • lesbigay/feminist bookstore

**Thrift for AIDS** 633 South St. **592-9014** noon-9pm

**Travelers Emporium** 210 S. 17th St. **546-2021** 10am-6pm, clsd Sun

## PUBLICATIONS

**Greater Philadelphia Women's Yellow Pages** (610) **446-4747**

▲ **Labyrinth** **546-6686** women's newspaper

**PGN (Philadelphia Gay News)** **625-8501**

**Pride Weekly** **790-1179**

**Tell-A-Woman** **564-5810**

## TRAVEL AGENTS

**Lambda Travel** **925-3011**/(800) **551-2240** ask for Scott • IGLTA

**Sigmund Travel** 262 S. 12th St. **735-0090**

**Travel Now** 202 S. 12th St. **985-0229**/(800) **581-4430** IGLTA

**Twin Travel** 1101 Spruce St. **923-2995**

**Will Travel** 118 S. Bellevue Ave., Longhorn **741-4492**/(800) **443-7460** IGLTA

## SPIRITUAL GROUPS

**Beth Ahavah** 8 Letitia St. **923-2003** 8pm 1st, 3rd & 5th Fri

**Christ Episcopal Church** 2nd above Market **922-1695** 9am & 11am Sun

**Dignity** 330 S. 13th St. (church) **546-2093** 7pm Sun

**Integrity** 1904 Walnut St. (church) **382-0794** 7pm 1st & 3rd Wed • pastoral counseling avail.

**MCC** 2125 Chestnut St. (First Unitarian Church) **563-6601** 7pm Sun

**Old First Reformed Church (United Church of Christ)** 4th & Race Sts. **922-4566**

## GYMS & HEALTH CLUBS

**12th St. Gym** 204 S. 12th St. **985-4092** 6am-11pm • gay-friendly

## EROTICA

**Condom Kingdom** 441 South St. **829-1668** safer sex materials • toys including bondage equip.

**Franny's Place at Both Ways** 201 S. 13th St. **985-2344** piercings • leather • coffee & bagels

**Infinite Body Piercing** 626 S. 4th St. **923-7335**

**The Pleasure Chest** 2039 Walnut **561-7480** clsd Sun-Mon

## Pittsburgh (412)

### INFO LINES & SERVICES

**AA Gay/Lesbian** 471-7472

**Asians & Friends Pittsburgh** 681-1556

**Gay/Lesbian Community Center Phoneline** 422-0114 6:30pm-9:30pm, 3pm-6pm Sat, clsd Sun

**ISMIR (International Sexual Minorities Information Resource)** 422-3060 monthly calendar of regional, national, int'l lesbigay events

**TransFamily** 758-3578 (ASK FOR JAN) 2nd Tue • call for location • support for transgendered people, their families & friends

**TransPitt** 224-6015 transgender social/support group

### ACCOMMODATIONS

**Brewers Hotel** 3315 Liberty Ave. 681-7991 gay-friendly • residential

**Camp Davis** 311 Red Brush Rd., Boyers 637-2402 May thru 2nd wknd in Oct • lesbians/gay men • adults 21+ only • pets on leash • call for events • 1 hr from Pittsburgh

**The Inn on the Mexican War Streets** 1606 Buena Vista St. 231-6544 lesbians/gay men • gay-owned/run

**The Priory** 614 Pressley 231-3338 gay-friendly • 24-rm Victorian • kids ok • wheelchair access

### BARS & NIGHTCLUBS

**Brewery Tavern** (at 'Brewers Hotel') 681-7991 10am-2am, from noon Sun • gay-friendly

**Donny's Place** 1226 Herron Ave. 682-9869 5pm-2am, from 3pm Sun • popular • lesbians/gay men • dancing/DJ • country/western • live shows • 18+ • food served

**The Frog's Pond** 223 Atwood St., Oakland 682-7707 lesbians/gay men • dancing/DJ • live shows • karaoke • also restaurant

**House of Tilden** 941 Liberty Ave., 2nd flr. 391-0804 10pm-3am • lesbians/gay men • dancing/DJ • private club • unconfirmed

**Icon** 333 4th Ave. 261-0881 from 9pm Tue, from 5pm Wed-Fri, from 8pm Sat, clsd Mon • lesbians/gay men • dancing/DJ

**Images** 965 Liberty Ave. 391-9990 5pm-2am, from 9pm Sun • mostly gay men • karaoke • videos

**Metropol** 1650 Smallman St. 261-4512 8pm-2am, clsd Mon-Tue • popular • gay-friendly • more gay Th • dancing/DJ • alternative • live shows • food served • wheelchair access

**New York, New York** 5801 Ellsworth Ave. 661-5600 4pm-2am, from 11am Sun • popular • mostly gay men • piano bar Wed & Fri • karaoke Sun • also restaurant • some veggie • wheelchair access • $9-15

**Pegasus Lounge** 818 Liberty Ave. 281-2131 4pm-2am, from 8pm Sat, clsd Sun • popular • mostly gay men • dancing/DJ • live shows

**Pittsburgh Eagle** 1740 Eckert St. 766-7222 8pm-2am, clsd Sun • mostly gay men • dancing/DJ • leather • wheelchair access

**Real Luck Cafe** 1519 Penn Ave. 566-8988 3pm-2am • lesbians/gay men • neighborhood bar • food served • cafe menu • some veggie • wheelchair access • $5

**Rusty Rail** 704 Thompson Ave., McKees Rocks 331-9011 4pm-2am, clsd Sun • lesbians/gay men • country/western • karaoke • food served

### CAFES

**Common Grounds Coffeehouse** 5888 Ellsworth Ave. 362-1190 10am-11pm, til 2am Fri-Sat, til 10pm Sun • lesbian-owned/run • wheelchair access

### RESTAURANTS

**Rosebud** 1650 Smallman St. 261-2221 lunch & dinner, clsd Mon • live shows • wheelchair access • $8-15

### BOOKSTORES & RETAIL SHOPS

**The Bookstall** 3604 5th Ave. 683-2644 9:30am-5:30pm, til 4:30pm Sat, clsd Sun • general • wheelchair access

**Slacker** 1321 E. Carson St. 381-3911 noon-10pm, til 7pm Sun • magazines • clothing • leather • piercings • wheelchair access

**St. Elmo's Books & Music** 2214 E. Carson St. 431-9100 9:30am-9:30pm, til 5pm Sun • progressive

### PUBLICATIONS

**Out** 243-3350

### TRAVEL AGENTS

**Alternative Travels** 900 Penn Ave. 263-2930/(800) 333-9500 IGLTA

**Bon Ami Travel Service** 309 1st St., Apollo 478-2000/(800) 426-6264 IGLTA

**Cruises & Tours McKnight** 7440 McKnight Rd., 202 Ross Park Ctr. **366-7678/(800) 992-7678** ask for Frank • IGLTA

**Forum Travel Ltd.** 4608 Winthrop St. **681-4099** IGLTA

**Holiday Travel** 5832 Library Rd., Bethel Park **835-8747**

**Morgan Delfosse Travel** 856-3084/(800) 538-2617

**Travel Systems, Ltd.** Station Sq. **321-8511** IGLTA

## SPIRITUAL GROUPS

**Bet Tikvah** 682-2604 7:30pm 1st Fri • lesbigay shabbat

**First Unitarian Church** Moorewood Ave. at Ellsworth **621-8008** 11am Sun (10am summers) • also 'Three Rivers Unitarian Universalists for Lesbigay Concerns' • 343-2523 • potluck last Fri

**Integrity Pittsburgh** 315 Shady Ave., Verona **734-8409** 7:30pm 2nd Wed (call for summer schedule)

**MCC of Pittsburgh** 4836 Ellsworth Ave. **683-2994** 7pm Sun

## EROTICA

**Boulevard Videos & Magazines** 346 Blvd. of the Allies **261-9119** 24hrs • leather • toys

**Golden Triangle News** 816 Liberty Ave. **765-3790** 24hrs

**Iron City Ink Tattoo/Hellion House Body Piercing** 1814 Penn Ave. **683-9888** clsd Sun

## Poconos (717)

### ACCOMMODATIONS

▲ **Blueberry Ridge** 629-5036 women only • full brkfst • hot tub • smokefree • kids ok • holiday packages • $55-70

▲ **Rainbow Mtn. Resort** 223-8484 popular • lesbians/gay men • atop Pocono mtn. on 85 acres (see ad under East Stroudsburg)

▲ **Stoney Ridge** 629-5036 lesbians/gay men • secluded log home • kitchen • kids/pets ok • $250wknd/$550 week

# STONEY RIDGE

**ENJOY THE CHARMING COMFORT OF THIS CEDAR LOG HOME POCONO GETAWAY**

**FOR RESERVATION INFORMATION CALL: PAT OR GRETA**

**717-629-5036**

"OPEN YEAR ROUND"

# *Blueberry Ridge*

PAT OR GRETA

**717-629-6036**

*In the Pocono Mts. Tannersville, PA*

*Women's Guest House*

"OPEN YEAR ROUND"

## Quakerstown (215)

EROTICA
**Adult World** 80 S. West End Blvd. (Rte. 309) **538-1522**

## Reading (610)

BARS & NIGHTCLUBS
**Nostalgia** 1101 N. 9th St. **372-5557** 9am-11pm, til 2am Fri-Sat • mostly women • neighborhood bar

**Rainbows** 935 South St. (below Adams Apple) **373-7929** 8pm-2am Fri-Sat only • mostly women • dancing/DJ

**Red Star** 11 S. 10th St. **375-4116** 5pm-2am, clsd Mon-Tue • popular • mostly gay men • dancing/DJ • leather • live shows • food served

**Scarab** 724 Franklin **375-7878** 9pm-2am, clsd Sun • popular • lesbians/gay men • dancing/DJ

## Scranton (717)

BARS & NIGHTCLUBS
**Silhouette Lounge** 523 Linden St. **344-4259** 10am-2am, clsd Sun • mostly gay men • neighborhood bar • leather

CAFES
**Prufrock's** 342 Adams Ave. **963-0849** 11am-6pm, clsd Sun • alternative cafe • gallery • live shows

## State College (814)

INFO LINES & SERVICES
**Gay/Lesbian/Bisexual/Transgender Switchboard** 237-1950 info • peer counseling

**Women's Resource Center** 140 W. Nittany Ave. **234-5050 (24HR HOTLINE)/234-5222** 9am-7pm, clsd wknds

BARS & NIGHTCLUBS
**Chumley's** 108 W. College **238-4446** 5pm-2am, from 6pm Sun • popular • lesbians/gay men • wheelchair access

**Players** 112 W. College Ave. **234-1031** 8pm-2am • gay-friendly • more gay Sun • dancing/DJ • videos

## Warminster (215)

TRAVEL AGENTS
**Danca Travel** 531 N. York Rd. **443-5030/(800) 443-5039** IGLTA

## Wayne (610)

TRAVEL AGENTS
**L'Arc en Ciel** 964-7888 IGLTA

## Wilkes-Barre

INFO LINES & SERVICES
**Coming Home (AA)** 97 S. Franklin Blvd. (Pres. Church) noon Th

BARS & NIGHTCLUBS
**Rumors Lounge** 315 Fox Ridge Plaza **825-7300** 5pm-2am, from 8pm Mon-Tue • popular • lesbians/gay men • dancing/DJ • also restaurant • wheelchair access

**Selections** 45 Public Sq., Wilkes-Barre Ctr. **829-4444** 9pm-2am, clsd Sun • popular • lesbians/gay men • dancing/DJ • also restaurant • wheelchair access • $5-15

**The Vaudvilla (The Vaude)** 465 Main St., Kingston **287-9250** 4pm-2am, clsd Sun • popular • lesbians/gay men • dancing/DJ • live shows • videos

## Williamsport (717)

INFO LINES & SERVICES
**Gay/Lesbian Switchboard of North Central PA** 327-1411 6pm-3am • open 365 days

BARS & NIGHTCLUBS
**Peachie's Court** 320 Court St. **326-3611** 3pm-2am, clsd Sun • lesbians/gay men • neighborhood bar

**The Rainbow Room** 761 W. 4th St. **320-0230** 4pm-2am, clsd Sun • popular • lesbians/gay men • dancing/DJ • live shows • videos • food served • unconfirmed

## York (717)

INFO LINES & SERVICES
**York Area Lambda** 846-9636 lesbigay social/educational group • newsletter
**York Lesbian Alliance** 848-9142

BOOKSTORES & RETAIL SHOPS
**Her Story Bookstore** 2 W. Market St., Hallam **757-4270** 11am-7pm, 9am-5pm Sat, noon-5pm Sun • women's books • music • videos • gifts • gourmet coffee • women-owned/run

EROTICA
**Cupid's Connection Adult Boutique** 244 N. George St. **846-5029**

# RHODE ISLAND

## Cranston (401)

TRAVEL AGENTS
**Anywhere Travel** 1326 Plainfield St. **943-3300/352-8947** ask for Joe

## Little Compton (401)

RESTAURANTS
**Commons Restaurant** Town Center **635-4388** brkfst & lunch

## Narragansett (401)

RESTAURANTS
**Aunt Carrie's** Point Judith **783-7930** fresh seafood

## Newport (401)

ACCOMMODATIONS
**Brinley Victorian Inn** 23 Brinley St. **849-7645** gay-friendly • New England smoke-free • $79-149

**Hydrangea House Inn** 16 Bellevue Ave. **846-4435/(800) 945-4667** popular • lesbians/gay men • full brkfst • near beach

**The Melville House Inn** 39 Clark St. **847-0640/(800) 711-7184** lesbians/gay men • full brkfst • $65-145

**The Prospect Hill Guest House** 32 Prospect Hill St. **847-7405** lesbians/gay men • smokefree • $75-145

BARS & NIGHTCLUBS
**David's** 28 Prospect Hill St. **847-9698** 5pm-1am, from 2pm wknds • popular • lesbians/gay men • neighborhood bar • dancing/DJ • T-dance Sun • patio

RESTAURANTS
**Restaurant Bouchard** 505 Thames St. **846-0123** dinner, clsd Tue

**Whitehorse Tavern** corner of Marlborough & Farewell **849-3600** classic

## Providence (401)

INFO LINES & SERVICES
**AA Gay/Lesbian** Wayland & Lloyd (church) **438-8860** 7pm Fri

**Enforcers RI** PO Box 5770, 02903 leather/SM/fetish group for men & women

**Gay/Lesbian Helpline of Rhode Island** **751-3322** 7pm-10pm

**Gay/Lesbian/Bisexual/Transgender Alliance** **863-3062** student group

**Sarah Doyle Women's Center** 185 Meeting St. (Brown University) **863-2189** referrals • also lesbian collective group

**Triangle Center** 645 Elmwood Ave. **861-4590**

BARS & NIGHTCLUBS
**Club 171** 171 Chestnut St. **272-0177** 7pm-midnight, til 1am Fri-Sat • mostly gay men • dancing/DJ

**Club In Town** 95 Eddy St. **751-0020** noon-1am, til 2am Fri-Sat • popular • mostly gay men • piano bar • videos

**Devilles** 10 Davol Sq. (Simmons Bldg.) **751-7166** 4pm-1am, til 2am Fri-Sat, clsd Mon • popular • mostly women • neighborhood bar • dancing/DJ Wed-Sat • wheelchair access

**Gerardo's** 1 Franklin Sq. **274-5560** 4pm-1am, til 2am Fri-Sat • lesbians/gay men • dancing/DJ • live shows • wheelchair access

**Mirabar** 35 Richmond St. **331-6761** 3pm-1am • mostly gay men • dancing/DJ • piano bar • wheelchair access

**New Galaxy** 202 Washington St. **831-9206** noon-1am • mostly gay men • dancing/DJ • live shows • videos • wheelchair access

**The Providence Eagle** 200 Union St. **421-1447** 6pm-1am, til 2am Fri-Sat • mostly gay men • leather • wheelchair access

**Union Street Station** 69 Union St. **331-2291** noon-1am, til 2am Fri-Sat • mostly gay men • dancing/DJ • live shows • wheelchair access

**Wheels** 125 Washington **272-6950** noon-1am, til 2am Fri-Sat • lesbians/gay men • live shows • videos • wheelchair access

CAFES
**Coffee Cafe** 257 S. Main St. **421-0787** 7am-4pm, from 8am Sat, 10am-3pm Sun • patio • gay-owned/run

RESTAURANTS
**Al Forno** 577 South Main St. **273-9760** dinner • popular • Little Rhody's best dining experience • $13-24

**Applause** 960 Hope St. **274-6055** wait staff are all singers

**Camille's** 71 Bradford St. **751-4812** lunch & dinner • full bar

**Down City Diner** 151 Weybosset St. **331-9217** lunch & dinner • popular Sun brunch (very gay) • full bar • wheelchair access

**Julian's** 318 Broadway **861-1770** 7am-3pm, clsd Mon

**Lucy's** 441 Atwells Ave. **273-1189** lunch & dinner, Sun brunch, clsd Mon • full bar • patio • wheelchair access • lesbian-owned • $7-14

**Rue de l'Espoir** 99 Hope St. **751-8890** lunch & dinner, clsd Mon • full bar • women-owned/run • $12-20

**Turchetta's** 312 Wickenden St. **861-1800** dinner only, clsd Mon • Italian • plenty veggie • wheelchair access • gay-owned/run • $7-14

### BOOKSTORES & RETAIL SHOPS
**Books on the Square** 471 Angell St. **331-9097** 9am-9pm, til 10pm Fri-Sat • some lesbigay titles

**Esta's on Thayer St.** 257 Thayer St. **831-2651** videos • pride items • Tarot readings

### PUBLICATIONS
**Options 831-4519** extensive resource listings

### TRAVEL AGENTS
**Travel Concepts** 45 Seekonk St. **453-6000/(800) 983-6900** ask for Roger • IGLTA

### SPIRITUAL GROUPS
**Bell St. Chapel (Unitarian)** 5 Bell St. **831-3794** 10am Sun

**Dignity 273-4297** 2pm 2nd & 4th Sun • also 'Defenders' (leather/levi service org.) chapter

**Integrity** 474 Fruit Hill Ave. (St. James Church) **353-2079** 4:30pm 2nd Sun

**Morning Star MCC** 231 Main St., Cherry Valley MA **553-4320/(508) 892-4320** 11am Sun & 7pm Wed

**R.I. & S.E. Mass. Gay Jewish Group (508) 992-7927**

**St. Peter's & Andrew's Episcopal Church** 25 Pomona Ave. **272-9649** 8am & 10am Sun, 7pm Wed (healing service)

## Smithfield (401)

### BARS & NIGHTCLUBS
**The Loft** 325 Farnum Pike **231-3320** 11am-1am, from 10am wknds & summers • lesbians/gay men • swimming • also restaurant • Sun brunch • wheelchair access

## Warwick (401)

### BOOKSTORES & RETAIL SHOPS
**Barnes & Noble** 1441 Bald Hill Rd. **828-7900** 9am-11pm, 11am-7pm Sun • lesbi-gay section

### TRAVEL AGENTS
**Global Excellence—The Travel Agency** 155 Jefferson Blvd. **732-8080/(800) 339-3600**

## Westerly (401)

### ACCOMMODATIONS
**The Villa** 190 Shore Rd. **596-1054/(800) 722-9240** gay-friendly • near beach • swimming • smokefree •$75-225

## Woonsocket (401)

### BARS & NIGHTCLUBS
**Kings & Queens** 285 Front St. **762-9538** 7pm-1am, til 2am Fri-Sat • lesbians/gay men • neighborhood bar • dancing/DJ

## South Carolina

### Charleston (803)

#### Info Lines & Services
**Acceptance Group (Gay AA)** St. Stephen's Episcopal (Anson St.) 762-2433/747-8774 (AA#) 8pm Tue & 6:30pm Sat

**LGLA (Lowcountry Gay/Lesbian Alliance)** Infoline 720-8088

#### Accommodations
**1854 B&B** 34 Montagu St. 723-4789 lesbians/gay men • Italianate antebellum dwelling in historic Charleston

**65 Radcliff Street** 65 Radcliff St. 577-6183 lesbians/gay men

**Charleston Beach B&B** 588-9443 lesbians/gay men • unobstructed views of the Atlantic Ocean • full brkfst • swimming • nudity • 8-person spa • $45-100

▲ **Charleston Columns** 8 Vanderhorst St. 722-7341 lesbians/gay men • antebellum lodging in historic district • smokefree • $75-135

**Crabapple Cottage** 300-F Medway Rd., Goose Creek 797-6855 gay-friendly • swimming • lesbian-owned/run

#### Bars & Nightclubs
**The Arcade** 5 Liberty St. 722-5656 9:30pm-close, clsd Mon-Wed • popular • mostly gay men • dancing/DJ • alternative • live shows • karaoke • wheelchair access

**Deja Vu II** 445 Savannah Hwy. 556-5588 5pm-3am • mostly women • dancing/DJ • live shows • food served • private club • wheelchair access • unconfirmed

**Dudley's** 346 King St. 723-2784 4pm-3am, from 2pm Sun • popular • mostly gay men • neighborhood bar • live shows • private club

#### Cafes
**Bear E. Patch** 801 Folly Rd. 762-6555 7am-8pm • patio • wheelchair access

#### Restaurants
**Blossom Cafe** 171 E. Bay St. 722-9200 11:30am-midnight, til 1am wknds

**Cafe Suzanne** 4 Center St. 588-2101 5:30pm-9:30pm, Sun brunch, clsd Mon • live jazz • $10-15

*In Charleston's Historic District*

Southern
Charm
at...

# Charleston Columns

A beautiful, intimate and hospitable antebellum lodging. A short walk to the city's fine restaurants, tourist attractions, great shopping and exciting nightlife.

**(803) 722-7341**
E-mail: chs65@aol.com
**8 Vanderhorst Street, Charleston, SC 29403**

**Mickey's** 137 Market St. **723-7121** 24hrs • popular

**St. Johns Island Cafe** 3406 Maybank Hwy., St. Johns Island **559-9090** brkfst & lunch Mon-Sat, dinner Wed-Sat • popular • Southern homecooking • beer/wine • $6-11

**Vickery's of Beaufain Street** 15 Beaufain St. **577-5300** 11am-3am • popular • Cuban influence • some veggie • $6-15

### PUBLICATIONS

▲ **The Front Page** (919) 829-0181

**In Unison** 771-0804 statewide lesbigay newspaper

**Q Notes** (704) 531-9988

### SPIRITUAL GROUPS

**MCC Charleston** 2010 Hawthorne Dr. #10 **760-6114** 11am Sun • wheelchair access

## Columbia                    (803)

### INFO LINES & SERVICES

**AA Gay/Lesbian** 254-5301 call for mtg. schedule

**South Carolina Division of Tourism** 734-0235

**South Carolina Pride Center** 1108 Woodrow St. **771-7713** 24hr message, live 6pm-10pm, from 2pm Sat, clsd Sun

### BARS & NIGHTCLUBS

**Candy Shop** 1903 Two Notch Rd. mostly gay men • dancing/DJ • mostly African-American • private club • unconfirmed

**Capital Club** 1002 Gervais St. **256-6464** 5pm-2am • mostly gay men • neighborhood bar • professional • private club • wheelchair access

**Metropolis** 1801 Landing 799-8727 10pm-close, from 9pm Fri-Sun, clsd Mon • lesbians/gay men • dancing/DJ • live shows • private club

**Pipeline** 1109 Assembly **771-0121** 9pm-6am, clsd Sun-Tue • lesbians/gay men • neighborhood bar • live shows • private club • unconfirmed

**Traxx** 416 Lincoln St. **256-1084** mostly women • dancing/DJ • live bands • private club • wheelchair access

### RESTAURANTS

**Alley Cafe** 911 Lady St. **771-2778** lunch Tue-Fri, dinner Tue-Sat • full bar

### BOOKSTORES & RETAIL SHOPS

**Intermezzo** 2015 Devine St. **799-2276** 10am-midnight • general bookstore

**Stardust Books** 2000 Blossom St. **771-0633** 10:30am-6pm, clsd Sun-Mon • spiritual

### PUBLICATIONS

**In Unison** 771-0804 statewide lesbigay newspaper

### TRAVEL AGENTS

**B&A Travel Service** 2728 Devine St. **256-0547**/(800) 968-7658 IGLTA

**Travel Professionals International** 1931 Bull St. #B 765-1212 IGLTA

### SPIRITUAL GROUPS

**MCC Columbia** 1111 Belleview **256-2154** 11am Sun

### EROTICA

**Chaser's** 3128 Two Notch Rd. **754-6672** 24hrs

## Florence                    (803)

### BARS & NIGHTCLUBS

**City Limits** 3027 E. Palmetto St. **317-1764** Wed-Sat • mostly gay men • dancing/DJ • live shows

**Rascal's Deli & Lounge** 526 S. Irby St. **665-2555** til 5pm, 7pm-2am Sat, 3pm-2am Sun • lesbians/gay men • live shows • private club

### BOOKSTORES & RETAIL SHOPS

**Books-a-Million** 1945 W. Palmetto St. **679-5376**

## Greenville                    (864)

### BARS & NIGHTCLUBS

**The Castle** 8 Le Grand Blvd. **235-9949** 19:30pm-4am, clsd Mon-Wed • popular • lesbians/gay men • dancing/DJ • live shows • videos • private club • wheelchair access

**New Attitude** 706 W. Washington St. **233-1387** 10pm-close wknds • lesbians/gay men • dancing/DJ • mostly African-American • unconfirmed

**South Ramp** 404 Airport Rd. **242-0102** 7pm-midnight Wed-Th, til 2am Fri-Sat, 3pm-midnight Sun, clsd Mon-Tue • lesbians/gay men • dancing/DJ • country/western • wheelchair access

### SPIRITUAL GROUPS

**MCC** 314 Lloyd St. **233-0919** 11am & 6pm Sun

## Hilton Head (803)

BARS & NIGHTCLUBS
**Moon Jammers** 11 Heritage Plaza, Pope Ave. **842-9195** 8pm-2am • lesbians/gay men • neighborhood bar • dancing/DJ • alternative • live shows • private club • wheelchair access

## Moncks Corner (803)

TRAVEL AGENTS
**Russell Travel Services** 219 Hwy. 52 N. #R **761-6888** IGLTA

## Myrtle Beach (803)

BARS & NIGHTCLUBS
**Illusions** 1012 S. Kings Hwy. **448-0421** 9pm-close • lesbians/gay men • women's night Th • dancing/DJ • live shows • unconfirmed

**Time Out** 520 8th Ave. N. **448-1180** 6pm-close, til 2am Sat • popular • mostly gay men • neighborhood bar • dancing/DJ • private club • wheelchair access

## Rock Hill (803)

BARS & NIGHTCLUBS
**Hideaway** 405 Baskins Rd. **328-6630** 8pm-close, clsd Mon-Wed • lesbians/gay men • neighborhood bar • private club • unconfirmed

## Santee (803)

TRAVEL AGENTS
**All Around Travel Network** 1568 Village Square Blvd. **854-2475/(800) 395-4255** IGLTA

## Spartanburg (864)

BARS & NIGHTCLUBS
**Cheyenne Cattlemen's Club** 995 Asheville Hwy. **573-7304** 8pm-2am, til 4am Fri, from 3pm Sun • mostly gay men • dancing/DJ • live shows • live bands • private club

**Cove Lounge & Club** 9112 Greenville Hwy. **576-2683** from 8pm, from 3pm Sun • lesbians/gay men • dancing/DJ • private club

## SOUTH DAKOTA

### Pierre

INFO LINES & SERVICES
**South Dakota Dept. of Tourism (800) 952-3625 (IN-STATE ONLY)/(800) 732-5682 (OUT-OF-STATE ONLY)**

### Rapid City (605)

INFO LINES & SERVICES
**FACES** 625-1/2 Main St. #3 **343-5577** drop-in 7pm-10pm Tue, 1:30pm-5pm wknds

**Gay/Lesbian Talk Line** 394-8080 6pm-10pm, clsd Sun

ACCOMMODATIONS
**Camp Michael B&B** 13051 Bogus Jim Rd. **342-5590** lesbians/gay men • peaceful getaway in the woods of the Black Hills • full brkfst

PUBLICATIONS
**Faces of South Dakota** 343-5577

EROTICA
**Heritage Bookstore** 912 Main St. **394-9877**

### Sioux Falls (605)

INFO LINES & SERVICES
**The Sioux Empire Gay & Lesbian Coalition** 333-0603 24hrs

ACCOMMODATIONS
**Camp America** 425-9085 gay-friendly • 35 mi. west of Sioux Falls • camping • RV hook up • women-owned/run • $10-16

BARS & NIGHTCLUBS
**Touchez** 323 S. Phillips Ave. (enter rear) **335-9874** 8pm-2am • popular • lesbians/gay men • dancing/DJ • food served

SPIRITUAL GROUPS
**St. Francis & St. Clare MCC** 1129 E. 9th St. **332-3966** 5:30pm Sun, 7pm summers

EROTICA
**Studio One Book Store** 311 N. Dakota Ave. **332-9316** 24hrs

## TENNESSEE

### Chattanooga (423)

INFO LINES & SERVICES
**Lambda Youth** 517-4601 youth group for ages 13-18

BARS & NIGHTCLUBS
**Alan Gold's** 1100 McCallie Ave. **629-8080** 4:30pm-3am • popular • lesbians/gay men • dancing/DJ • live shows • food served • wheelchair access
**Chuck's II** 27-1/2 W. Main **265-5405** 6pm-1am, til 3am Fri-Sat • lesbians/gay men • neighborhood bar • dancing/DJ • country/western • patio

EROTICA
**Condoms & Etc.** 27 W. Main St. **266-3668**

### Cleveland (423)

BARS & NIGHTCLUBS
**D's Place** 1685 Clingin Ridge Dr. **614-4185** 5pm-midnight, clsd Sun • lesbians/gay men • dancing/DJ • neighborhood bar

### Gatlinburg (423)

ACCOMMODATIONS
**Little Bell Cabin** 573-8572 gay-friendly • cabin • lesbian-owned/run • $85

BOOKSTORES & RETAIL SHOPS
**Blue Moon Signs** 813 Glades Rd. **436-8733** unique gifts designed & handcrafted by women • custom redwood signs • wood turnings

### Haley (615)

RESTAURANTS
**Our House** 389-6616/(800) 876-6616 clsd Mon • popular • fine dining • some veggie • by reservation only • wheelchair access • $10-20

### Jackson (901)

BARS & NIGHTCLUBS
**The Other Side** 3883 Hwy. 45 N. **668-3749** 5pm-close, from 7pm Sat, clsd Mon • lesbians/gay men • live shows

### Jamestown (615)

ACCOMMODATIONS
**Laurel Creek Campground** 879-7696 clsd Nov-April • gay-friendly • camping • rentals • RV hookups • hiking • swimming

### Johnson City (423)

BARS & NIGHTCLUBS
**New Beginnings** 2910 N. Bristol Hwy. **282-4446** 9pm-2am, 8pm-3am Fri-Sat, clsd Mon • popular • lesbians/gay men • dancing/DJ • live shows • also restaurant • wheelchair access
**Queen of Clubs** 1408 E. Main St. **928-2616** lesbians/gay men • neighborhood bar • dancing/DJ • alternative • multiracial • live shows • 18+ • beer & set-ups only • wheelchair access

SPIRITUAL GROUPS
**MCC of the Tri-Cities** Coast Valley Unitarian Church **283-7554** 7pm Sun

### Knoxville (423)

INFO LINES & SERVICES
**AA Gay/Lesbian** 3219 Kingston Pike (Tenn. Valley Unitarian Church) **522-9667** 7pm Mon & Fri
**Gay/Lesbian Helpline** 521-6546 (MCC#) 7pm-11pm

BARS & NIGHTCLUBS
**Carousel II** 1501 White Ave. **522-6966** 9pm-3am • popular • lesbians/gay men • dancing/DJ • live shows • unconfirmed
**Electric Ballroom** 1213 Western Ave. **525-6724** 9pm-3am Sun & Tue-Th, from 6pm Fri-Sat, clsd Mon • mostly gay men • dancing/DJ • live shows • food served • wheelchair access • unconfirmed

BOOKSTORES & RETAIL SHOPS
**Davis Kidd Bookstore** The Commons, 113 N. Peters Rd. **690-0136** 9:30am-10pm, 10am-6pm Sun • general • wheelchair access
**Violets & Rainbows** 2426 Mineral Springs **687-5552** noon-9pm, 10am-6pm Sat, clsd Sun • lesbigay • wheelchair access

TRAVEL AGENTS
**Bryan Travel** 5614 Kingston Pike, Melrose Place **588-8166/(800) 234-8166** IGLTA

## SPIRITUAL GROUPS

**MCC Knoxville** 934 N. Weisgarber Rd. (United Church of Christ) **521-6546** 6pm Sun

# Memphis (901)

## INFO LINES & SERVICES

**Gay/Lesbian Switchboard** 324-4297 7:30pm-11pm

**Memphis Lambda Center (AA)** 1488 Madison **276-7379** 8pm nightly • meeting place for 12-Step groups

## ACCOMMODATIONS

**Talbot Heirs Guesthouse** 99 S. 2nd St. **527-9772/(800) 955-3956** gay-friendly • funky decor • smokefree • kids ok • $150-250

## BARS & NIGHTCLUBS

**501 Club** 111 N. Claybrook **274-8655** noon-3am, til 6am Fri-Sat • mostly gay men • dancing/DJ • live shows • food served • wheelchair access

**Amnesia** 2866 Poplar **454-1366** 8pm-3am, clsd Mon-Tue • popular • lesbians/gay men • dancing/DJ • alternative • swimming • patio • dinner nightly • wheelchair access • unconfirmed

**Autumn Street Pub** 1349 Autumn St. **274-8010** 1pm-3am, clsd Mon-Tue • lesbians/gay men • neighborhood bar • dancing/DJ • food served • patio • wheelchair access

**Backstreet** 2018 Court Ave. **276-5522** 8pm-3am, til 6am wknds • lesbians/gay men • more women Sun afternoon & Tue • dancing/DJ • beer & set-ups only • wheelchair access

**Crossroads** 1278 Jefferson **725-8156** noon-3am • lesbians/gay men • neighborhood bar • beer & set-ups only

**David's** 1474 Madison **278-4313** 3pm-3am, from noon Sat • mostly gay men • neighborhood bar • beer & set-ups only

## Memphis

**M**any people around the world know Memphis as the city of two musical phenomena—the blues and the King. The blues were born when W.C. Handy immortalized "Beale Street", and, as for the King, Elvis lived and died here. From everywhere on earth, people come to visit his home and pay their respects at Graceland (800/238-2000).

Despite the stereotype of Southern cities as homophobic, Memphis has a strong lesbian community. There's **Meristem Women's Bookstore** and **Secrets** women's bar. Memphis also has a number of mixed bars & clubs like the popular **Amnesia** and **Backstreet.**

For the complete rundown of local groups and events, check out the latest edition of **Triangle Journal News** or call the **Gay/Lesbian Switchboard.**

**Madison Flame** 1588 Madison **278-9839** 5pm-3am • lesbians/gay men • neighborhood bar • dancing/DJ Th-Sat • country/western Th

**One More** 2117 Peabody Ave. **278-8015** 10am-3am, from noon Sun • gay-friendly • neighborhood bar • multi-racial • food served

**Secrets** 1528 Madison **278-9321** 5pm-3am • mostly women • dancing/DJ • live shows • beer & set-ups only • wheelchair access

**Sunshine Lounge** 1379 Lamar **272-9843** 7am-midnight, til 3am Fri-Sat • gay-friendly • neighborhood bar • beer & set-ups only • wheelchair access

CAFES

**Coffee Cellar** 3573 Southern 320-7853 7am-midnight, 8am-8pm Sat • patio • wheelchair access

**Java Cabana** 2170 Young Ave. 272-7210 1pm-11pm Sun & Tue-Th, til midnight Fri-Sat, clsd Mon • coffeehouse • also 'Viva Memphis Wedding Chapel' & art gallery

**P&H Cafe** 1532 Madison 726-0906 11am-3am, from 5pm Sat, clsd Sun • beer/wine • wheelchair access

RESTAURANTS

**Alternative Restaurant** 553 S. Cooper 725-7922 11am-8pm, til midnight Fri-Sat, clsd Sun • homecooking • BYOB • gay-owned/run

**Automatic Slim's Tonga Club** 83 S. 2nd St. 525-7948 lunch & dinner Mon-Fri, dinner til 11pm Fri-Sat, clsd Sun • Caribbean & Southwestern • plenty veggie • full bar • wheelchair access

**Cafe Society** 212 N. Evergreen Ave. **722-2177** lunch & dinner, til 11pm Fri-Sat • full bar • wheelchair access

**John Will's Barbecue Pit** 5101 Sanderland Dr. **761-5101** 11am-9:30pm, til 10:30pm wknds • full bar

**Maxwell's** 948 S. Cooper St. **725-1009** 11am-3am, 5pm-3am wknds • Mediterranean • full bar • wheelchair access

**Saigon Le** 51 N. Cleveland **276-5326** 11am-9pm, clsd Sun • pan-Asian

BOOKSTORES & RETAIL SHOPS

**Davis Kidd Booksellers** 397 Perkins Rd. Ext. **683-9801** 9:30am-10pm, 10am-6pm Sun • general • lesbigay titles

**Meristem Women's Bookstore** 930 S. Cooper **276-0282** 10am-6pm • wheelchair access

PUBLICATIONS

**Triangle Journal News** 454-1411 lesbigay newspaper • extensive resource listings

SPIRITUAL GROUPS

**First Congregational Church** 246 S. Watkins **278-6786** 9am & 10:30am Sun, 6pm Wed

**Holy Trinity Community Church** 1559 Madison **726-9443** 11am & 7pm Sun, 7pm Wed

**Integrity** 102 N. Second St. (Calvary Episcopal Church) **525-6602** 6pm 3rd Tue

**Safe Harbor MCC** 2117 Union Ave. (Union Ave. UMC) **458-0501** 11am & 7pm Sun

---

## Memphis    (901)

**Where the Girls Are:** On Madison Ave., of course, just east of US-240.

**City Info:** 543-5333.

**Attractions:** Graceland, home and grave site of Elvis. Beale Street. Mud Island. Overton Square.

**Best View:** A cruise on any of the boats that ply the Mississippi River.

**Weather:** Suth'n. H-O-T and humid in the summer, cold (30°s-40°s) in the winter, and a relatively nice (but still humid) spring and fall.

**Transit:** Yellow Cab: 526-2121.

## Nashville (615)

### INFO LINES & SERVICES

**AA Gay/Lesbian** 831-1050 call for mtg. schedule

**Center for Lesbian/Gay Community Services** 703 Berry Rd. **297-0008** 6pm-9pm

**Nashville Women's Alliance** call 'Center' for times & locations

### ACCOMMODATIONS

**IDA** 904 Vikkers Hollow Rd., Dowelltown **597-4409** lesbians/gay men • camping avail. May-Sept • private community 'commune' located in the hills • 1hr SE of Nashville

**Savage House** 165 8th Ave. N. **244-2229** gay-friendly • 1840s Victorian townhouse • full brkfst

### BARS & NIGHTCLUBS

**176 Underground** 176 2nd Ave. N. **742-8909** 9pm-3am • gay-friendly • dancing/DJ • alternative

**Chez Collette** 300 Hermitage Ave. **256-9134** 4pm-3am • mostly women • neighborhood bar • women-owned/run

**Chute Complex** 2535 Franklin Rd. **297-4571** 5pm-3am • 5 bars • popular • mostly gay men • dancing/DJ • country/western • leather • live shows • also restaurant • wheelchair access

**Connection Complex** 901 Cowan St. **742-1166** popular • lesbians/gay men • dancing/DJ • live shows • gift shop • also restaurant • from 6pm Wed-Sun • some veggie • $5-15

**Gas Lite** 167-1/2 8th Ave. N. **254-1278** 4:30pm-1am, til 3am Fri-Sat, from 3pm wknds • lesbians/gay men • food served

**KC's Club 909** 909 Church St. **251-1613** 6pm-3am, clsd Tue • mostly women • dancing/DJ • live shows • also a deli • wheelchair access

## *Nashville*

*T*here's only one "Country Music Capital of the World," and that's Nashville. And there's no better place on earth to enjoy country and western music than at the Grand Ole Opry (889-6611). Be sure to plan ahead and get a performance schedule.

Many of the greats of country music have homes in Nashville, and there are plenty of bus tours to show you exactly where your favorite stars live. The Country Music Hall of Fame and Museum (255-5333) is also a favorite stop for diehard fans.

After you've sat still listening to great music so long you can't stand it, get up and dance. Nashville has three women's bars—**Chez Collette, KC's Club 909** and **Ralph's.** Keep your star-gazing eyes open while you're cloggin' away on the floor; you never know who you might see! For more sedate activities, pick up a copy of **Query** at the **Center for Lesbian/Gay Community Services.**

If you're driving east, you'll pass through Knoxville—a small city with a quaint old town section and the main University of Tennessee. Call the **Gay/Lesbian Helpline** about local events.

**Ralph's** 515 2nd Ave. S. **256-9682** 5pm-midnight, til 3am Fri-Sat • mostly women • wheelchair access • women-owned/run

**The Triangle** 1401 4th Ave. S. **242-8131** 8am-3am, from noon Sun • lesbians/gay men • neighborhood bar • food served • wheelchair access

**Victor Victoria's** 111 8th Ave. N. **244-7256** 11am-3am, from noon-3am Sun • mostly gay men • dancing/DJ • live shows • wheelchair access

RESTAURANTS

**Garden Allegro** 1805 Church St. **327-3834** 8am-9pm, from 10am wknds • plenty veggie • juice bar • $4-7

**The Mad Platter** 1239 6th Ave. N. **242-2563** lunch, dinner by reservation only, clsd Sun-Mon • Californian • some veggie • wheelchair access • $20-30

**Towne House Tea Room** 165 8th Ave. N. **254-1277** buffet lunch wkdays • $5-10

**World's End** 1713 Church St. **329-3480** 4pm-1am, clsd Mon • American • full bar • $8-15

ENTERTAINMENT & RECREATION

**Gay Cable Network** Channel 19 9pm Tue & 10pm Sat

BOOKSTORES & RETAIL SHOPS

**Davis-Kidd Booksellers** 4007 Hillsboro Rd. **385-2645** 9:30am-10pm • general • lesbigay section

**Outloud Books & Gifts** 1805-C Church St. **340-0034** til 10pm • lesbigay

**Tower Books** 2404 West End Ave. **327-8085** 9am-midnight • large lesbigay section

PUBLICATIONS

**ETC. Magazine (404) 888-0063** bar & entertainment guide for Southeast

**Query** 259-4135 lesbigay newspaper

TRAVEL AGENTS

**International Travel** 4004 Hillsboro Rd. #214-B **385-1222** IGLTA

**Pride Travel** 1123 Murfreesboro Rd. **360-8445** IGLTA

SPIRITUAL GROUPS

**MCC** 1502 Edge Hill Ave. **874-9636** 7pm Sun

# Newport (423)

ACCOMMODATIONS

**Christopher Place** 1500 Pinnacles Wy. **623-6555/(800) 595-9441** gay-friendly • full brkfst • smokefree • IGLTA • wheelchair access

# Saltillo (901)

ACCOMMODATIONS

**Parker House** 1956 Tutwiller Ave. **278-5844** lesbians/gay men • Southern country house • full brkfst • swimming • by reservation only • 2 hours from Memphis

# Shelbyville (615)

CAFES

**Pope's Cafe** on the Square **684-7933** brkfst & lunch, clsd Sun

# Nashville (615)

**Where the Girls Are:** Just north of I-65/40 along 2nd Ave. S. or Hermitage Ave.

**City Info:** 259-4700.

**Attractions:** Country Music Hall of Fame and Museum. Grand Ole Opry.

**Best View:** Try a walking tour of the city.

**Weather:** See Memphis.

**Transit:** Yellow Cab: 256-0101. Music City Taxi: 889-0038. Gray Line Airport Shuttle: 275-1180. MTA: 862-5950.

# **Texas**

## Abilene (915)

### Bars & Nightclubs
**Just Friends** 201 S. 14th St. **672-9318**
7pm-midnight, til 1am Fri, til 2am Sat,
clsd Mon • lesbians/gay men • dancing/DJ • live shows • wheelchair access

### Spiritual Groups
**Exodus MCC** 672-7922 10:45am & 6pm
Sun • call for location

## Amarillo (806)

### Info Lines & Services
**Amarillo Lesbian/Gay Alliance Info
Line** 373-5725 7:30pm 1st Tue • 'Queer
Dinner Club' meets twice monthly

### Bars & Nightclubs
**Classifieds** 519 E. 10th St. **374-2435**
noon-2am, clsd Mon • lesbians/gay men
• dancing/DJ • live shows • wheelchair
access
**The Ritz** 323 W. 10th Ave. **372-9382**
2pm-2am • lesbians/gay men • dancing/DJ • country/western • live shows
**Sassy's** 309 W. 6th St. **374-3029** 5pm-
2am • lesbians/gay men • dancing/DJ •
alternative

### Cafes
**B&E Coffeehouse** 3806 W. 6th **351-0084**
3pm-midnight, clsd Sun • beer/wine

### Restaurants
**Italian Delight** 2710 W. 10th **372-5444**
lunch & dinner, clsd Sun • some veggie •
beer/wine • wheelchair access • $5-10

### Spiritual Groups
**Amarillo Unitarian Universalist
Fellowship** 4901 Cornell **355-9351** 10am
Sun • call for winter hours
**MCC of Amarillo** 2123 S. Polk St. **372-
4557** 10:30am Sun & 7pm Wed

## Arlington (817)

*(see also Fort Worth)*

### Info Lines & Services
**Tarrant County Lesbian/Gay Alliance**
1219 6th Ave., Fort Worth **877-5544** info
line • newsletter
**Women's Fellowship** (at Trinity MCC)
**265-5454** monthly social/support group
• call for info

### Bars & Nightclubs
**Arlington 651** 1851 W. Division **275-9651**
4pm-2am • popular • mostly gay men •
dancing/DJ • live shows • karaoke •
wheelchair access

### Travel Agents
**Gateway Travel & Tours** 1902 W.
Pioneer Pkwy. #100 **548-7222** IGLTA

### Spiritual Groups
**Trinity MCC** 609 Truman **265-5454**
10:45am Sun

## Austin (512)

### Info Lines & Services
**ALLGO (Austin Latino/a Lesbian/Gay
Organization)** 472-2001 6:30pm 3rd Th
**Cornerstone Community Center** 1117
Red River St. **708-1515**
**Hotline** 472-4357 24hrs • info • crisis
counseling
**Texas Tourist Division** 462-9191/(800)
888-8TEX

### Accommodations
**Carrington's Bluff** 1900 David St. **479-
0638/(800) 871-8908** gay-friendly • full
brkfst • wheelchair access
**Driskill Hotel** 604 Brazos St. **474-
5911/(800) 252-9367** gay-friendly • food
served • wheelchair access
**Governor's Inn** 611 W. 22nd St. **477-
0711/(800) 871-8908** gay-friendly • full
brkfst • wheelchair access
**Lazy Oak Inn** 211 W. Live Oak **447-
8873/(800) 871-8908** gay-friendly •
wheelchair access
**Omni Hotel** 700 San Jacinto **476-
3700/(800) 843-6664** gay-friendly •
rooftop pool • health club • wheelchair
access
**Park Lane Guest House** 221 Park Ln.
**447-7460** lesbians/gay men • kitchen •
kids ok • pets ok (call first) • $75-85 •
also cottage • wheelchair access • $110
($15/extra person) • women-owned/run
**Summit House B&B** 1204 Summit St.
**445-5304** gay-friendly • full brkfst •
reservation required

### Bars & Nightclubs
**Area 52** 404 Colorado **474-4849** 10pm-
close, clsd Mon-Tue • popular • lesbians/gay men • dancing/DJ • alternative
• 18+ • wheelchair access

# *Austin*

**U**ntil recently, Austin was the best kept secret in Texas. A refreshing bastion of left-wing, non-confrontational radicalism, in many ways this most collegiate of cities seems to belong anywhere but the Lone Star State. Better known as the home of the South By Southwest (SXSW) music festival, it's hard to believe Austin is actually the state capital and the seat of the Texas legislature.

When harried urbanites in Dallas and Houston want a quick getaway, many head to the natural beauty of the Texas Hill Country. Just outside of the Capital City local boys and girls entertain themselves in the naturally cool (68° year round) waters of Barton Springs. The liberal attitudes at Hippie Hollow, site of the lesbigay First and Last Splash Festivals, has long been a favorite of the clothing-optional crowd.

In town, entertainment centers around the Mardi Gras atmosphere of 6th Street downtown, where live and recorded music offerings run the gamut from hard-core punk to tear-jerkin' country & western. Most of the bars are mixed, female and male, straight and gay; Austin's lesbian scene currently has only one full time women's bar, **Sister's Edge.** Club kids of all stripes dance, dance, dance at the progressive **Area 52.**

The popular bookstore, **Book Woman,** is a great resource for connecting with like-minded women of every hue. The store regularly schedules seminars, book signings and discussion groups; check in for details on all the women's events around town. Austin Women's Rugby Club matches are also popular, as are Spring and Summer softball and volleyball leagues. Try Fans of Women's Sports for the latest schedules and contacts.

Happily, Austin's lesbigay newsweekly, the **Texas Triangle,** which was in danger of closing down a few years ago, is still going strong. It's also still the best source for checking out all the current goings-on.

*– By reader Deirdre S. Green. Updated by Damron editors.*

**Blue Flamingo** 617 Red River 469-0014 noon-2am • gay-friendly • neighborhood bar • live shows • strong coffee served

**'Bout Time** 960 N. IH-35 832-5339 2pm-2am • popular • lesbians/gay men • neighborhood bar • transgender-friendly • live shows • volleyball court • wheelchair access

**Casino El Camino** 517 E. 6th St. 469-9330 4pm-2am • gay-friendly • neighborhood bar • psychedelic punk jazz lounge • great burgers

**The Edge** 213 W. 4th 480-8686 2pm-4am • lesbians/gay men • neighborhood bar • dancing/DJ • wheelchair access

**The Forum** 408 Congress Ave. 476-2900 2pm-2am • popular • also 'Cuff' leather bar

**Rainbow Cattle Company** 305 W. 5th St. 472-5288 2pm-2am • mostly gay men • dancing/DJ • country/western • food served

**Sister's Edge** 113 San Jacinto Blvd. 457-8010 2pm-2am • mostly women • dancing/DJ • patio • wheelchair access

### CAFES

**High Life Cafe** 407 E. 7th St. 474-5338 9am-midnight, til 1am Fri-Sat • bistro fare

**Joe's Bakery & Coffeeshop** 2305 E. 7th St. 472-0017 10am-4pm, 7am-3pm wknds • Tex-Mex

**Soma** 212 W. 4th St. 474-7662 7am-midnight • til 4am Fri-Sat • espresso bar • some veggie

### RESTAURANTS

**Bitter End Bistro & Brewery** 311 Colorado St. 478-2337 wood-baked pizza

**Castle Hill Cafe** 1101 W. 5th St. 476-0728 lunch & dinner, clsd Sun • $11-16

**Eastside Cafe** 2113 Manor Rd. 476-5858 lunch & dinner • some veggie • beer/wine • wheelchair access • $8-15

**Katz's** 618 W. 6th St. 472-2037 24hrs • NY-style deli • full bar • wheelchair access • $8-15

**Momma's Diner** 314 Congress Ave. 469-9369 24hrs • great homecooking • full bar

**Romeo's** 1500 Barton Springs Rd. 476-1090 Italian • some veggie • beer/wine • wheelchair access • $10-14

**Suzi's Chinese Kitchen** 1152 S. Lamar 441-8400 lunch & dinner

**Threadgill's** 6416 N. Lamar 451-5440 11am-10pm • great chicken-fried steak

**West Lynn Cafe** 1110 W. Lynn 482-0950 vegetarian • beer/wine • $5-10

## Austin                    (512)

**Where the Girls Are:** Downtown along Red River St., or 4th/5th St. near Lavaca, or at the music clubs and cafes downtown and around the University.

**Annual Events:**

August 22-Sept 4 - **Austin G/L Int'l Film Festival** (10th year): 472-3240.

May 3-4 & Labor Day - **Splash Days**. Weekend of parties in clothing-optional Hippie Hollow.

**City Info:** Texas Tourist Division: 800/888-8839. Greater Austin Chamber of Commerce: 478-9383.

**Attractions:** Aqua Festival. Elisabet Ney Museum. George Washington Carver Museum. Hamilton Pool. Laguna Gloria Art Museum. McKinney Falls State Park. Mount Bonnell. Museo del Barrio de Austin. Zilker Park.

**Best View:** State Capitol.

**Weather:** Summers are real scorchers (high 90°s—low 100°s) and last forever. Spring, fall and winter are welcome reliefs.

**Transit:** Yellow-Checker: 472-1111. Various hotels have their own shuttles. Austin Transit: 474-1200.

**Xena** 10201 Jollyville Rd. **345-9944** 11am-10:30pm, til 11pm Fri-Sat • extensive wine list • full bar

### ENTERTAINMENT & RECREATION
**Word of Mouth Women's Theatre** 837-9806

### BOOKSTORES & RETAIL SHOPS
**Book Woman** 918 W. 12th. St. **472-2785** 10am-9pm, noon-6pm Sun • cards • jewelry • music • wheelchair access • women-owned/run

**Celebration!** 108 W. 43rd **453-6207** 10am-6:30pm, clsd Sun • women's earth magic store • women-owned/run

**Congress Avenue Booksellers** 716 Congress Ave. **478-1157** 7:45am-6pm, 10am-3pm wknds • lesbigay section

**Lobo** 3204-A Guadalupe **454-5406** 10am-10pm • lesbigay • wheelchair access

**N8** 1014-B N. Lamar **478-3446** 10am-9pm, noon-6pm Sun • designer/club clothes • wheelchair access

### PUBLICATIONS
**Exposure** 479-7000 gay boy party paper

**Texas Triangle** 459-1717 lesbigay newspaper includes arts calendar & statewide resource list

### TRAVEL AGENTS
**Capital of Texas Travel** 3006 Medical Arts St. **478-2468/(800) 880-0068** IGLTA

**Creative Travel Center** 8650 Spicewood Springs Rd. #210 **331-9560** IGLTA

**West Austin Travel** 2737 Exposition Blvd. **482-8197/(800) 541-8583** IGLTA

### SPIRITUAL GROUPS
**First Unitarian Church** 4700 Grover Ave. **452-6168** 9:30am & 11:15am Sun • wheelchair access

**MCC Austin** 4700 Grover Ave. (Unitarian church) **708-8002** 7pm Sat

**Mishpachat Am Echad** 451-7018 lesbigay Jewish social group

### EROTICA
**Forbidden Fruit** 512 Neches **478-8358**

## Beaumont (409)

### INFO LINES & SERVICES
**Lambda AA** 6300 College **835-1508** 8pm Mon, Tue, Th & Sat

### BARS & NIGHTCLUBS
**Copa** 304 Orleans St. **832-4206** 9pm-2am • popular • lesbians/gay men • dancing/DJ • live shows • wheelchair access • unconfirmed

**Sundowner** 497 Crockett St. **833-3989** 4pm-2am • lesbians/gay men • dancing/DJ • live shows • beer/wine • BYOB

### RESTAURANTS
**Carlo's** 2570 Calder **833-0108** 11am-10:30pm, til 11pm Fri-Sat, clsd Sun-Mon • Italian/Greek • live shows

### SPIRITUAL GROUPS
**Spindletop Unitarian Church** 1575 Spindletop Rd. **833-6883** 10:25am Sun

## College Station (409)

### INFO LINES & SERVICES
**Gayline** Texas A&M Gay/Lesbian/Bisexual Student Services **847-0321**

**Lambda AA** Bryan 361-7976 (AA#) call for mtg. schedule

### BARS & NIGHTCLUBS
**The Club** 308 N. Bryan Ave., Bryan **823-6767** 9pm-2am, clsd Sun-Mon • popular • lesbians/gay men • dancing/DJ • 18+ • live shows

**Dudley's Draw** 311 University **846-3030** 11am-1am • gay-friendly • neighborhood bar • wheelchair access

### CAFES
**Copasetic Cafe** 108 College Main **260-3323** 7am-2am

## Corpus Christi (512)

### INFO LINES & SERVICES
**Lambda AA** 1315 Craig (MCC Corpus Christi) **882-8255** 7pm Th & 8pm Fri

### ACCOMMODATIONS
**The Anthony's By The Sea** 732 Pearl St., Rockport **729-6100/(800) 460-2557** gay-friendly • quiet retreat • full brkfst • swimming • hot tub • gay-owned/run • $60-80

**Christy Estates Suites** 3942 Holly St. **854-1091** gay-friendly • 1- & 2-bdrm suites • hot tubs & spas • non-smoking rms avail. • wheelchair access

**The Sea Horse Inn** 749-5221 lesbians/gay men • Euro-style inn on dunes of Mustang Island & Port Aransas • swimming

### BARS & NIGHTCLUBS
**Club Zodiac** 4125 Gollihar **853-5080** 3pm-2am, from noon Sun • mostly women • dancing/DJ • live shows • women-owned/run

**The Hidden Door** 802 S. Staples St. **882-5002** 3pm-2am, from noon Sun • mostly gay men • leather • wheelchair access

**Mingles** 512 S. Staples **884-8022** 8pm-2am, clsd Mon-Wed • mostly women • dancing/DJ • unconfirmed

**UBU** 511 Starr **882-9693** 9pm-2am Wed-Sun • gay-friendly • dancing/DJ • live shows • wheelchair access

### SPIRITUAL GROUPS

**MCC of Corpus Christi** 1315 Craig St. **882-8255** 11am & 7pm Sun • wheelchair access

## Dallas (214)

### INFO LINES & SERVICES

**Crossdressers/TV Helpline** 264-7103

**First Class Limousine Service** 5117 Vandelia St. **559-4733**/(800) 546-6112

**Gay/Lesbian Community Center** 2701 Reagan St. **528-9254** hours vary • call first • also credit union • wheelchair access

**Gay/Lesbian Information Line** 520-8781 24hr recorded info

**Lambda AA** 2727 Oaklawn **522-6259** call for mtg. schedule

**Lesbian Friendship Connection** 521-5342 x269 monthly social/discussion groups

**Umoja Hermanas** 943-8750 group for lesbian & bisexual women of color

### ACCOMMODATIONS

**The Courtyard on the Trail** 8045 Forest Trail **553-1900**/(800) 484-6260 x0465 gay-friendly • full brkfst • swimming • smokefree • gay-owned/run • $95-125

▲ **The Inn on Fairmount** 3701 Fairmount **522-2800** lesbians/gay men • hot tub • gay-owned/run • $85-125

**Melrose Hotel** 3015 Oaklawn Dr. **521-5151**/(800) 635-7673 gay-friendly • historic hotel in Oak Lawn district • swimming • non-smoking rms avail. • popular piano bar & lounge

### BARS & NIGHTCLUBS

**Anchor Inn** 4024 Cedar Springs **526-4098** 4pm-2am • mostly gay men • live shows • also 'Numbers' 521-7861 from 7am

## *The Inn on Fairmount*

### In the Heart of Gay & Lesbian Dallas

❖ Continental Breakfast
❖ Evening Wine & Cheese
❖ Close to Bars & Restaurants
❖ Direct Dial Telephones

❖ Private Baths
❖ Jacuzzi
❖ Color TV's
❖ Visa, MC Accepted

**3701 Fairmount, Dallas, TX 75219**
**(214) 522-2800 FAX 522-2898**

*The ambiance of an inn, the luxury of a fine hotel.*

# Dallas

**D**espite Dallas's conservative reputation as the buckle of the Bible Belt, this city has mellowed a great deal since the economic meltdown of the late 1980s. Two openly gay men have been elected to the City Council and sexual orientation is included in the city's anti-discrimination policy.

Dallas is a relatively young city, but wealthy residents have created a legacy of art museums, historical sites and entertainment districts that will keep you busy. The Arts District in downtown is home to the Dallas Museum of Art (DMA) and a fabulous collection of modern masters, pre-Columbian artifacts, and the Reeves collection of Impressionist art and decorative pieces. The 6th Floor Museum, where Oswald allegedly perched while assassinating JFK, is a fascinating exploration of the facts and conspiracy theories. Old City Park recreates a pioneer village with original dwellings, period re-enactments, and exhibits. The West End, home of Planet Hollywood, the West End Marketplace and the Dallas World Aquarium offers a concentration of shops, restaurants and diversions in one spot.

East of downtown is Deep Ellum, one of Dallas' earliest African-American communities (Ellum is the way early residents pronounced Elm). Today it's live music central, with a variety of clubs offering a host of local and national bands, 7 nights a week. Just about anything goes here, as long as it's left of center. Every segment of the population is represented in an ever-growing collection of off-beat bars, restaurants, shops, and tattoo parlors.

Further east is Fair Park, site of the State Fair of Texas every fall. Anytime of the year you can enjoy a wonderful day here touring the African-American Museum, the Science Place and its IMAX theatre, Dallas Aquarium and Horticulture Center. The surrounding neighborhood is the current artists' habitué of choice with studios, showrooms, and gathering places along State and Parry streets.

The lesbian and gay community of Dallas is thriving, concentrated in Oak Lawn, just north of downtown. Most of the business-

es along the Cedar Springs Strip (Cedar Springs Rd. between Oak Lawn Ave. and Douglas) are gay-owned, and all are lesbigay-friendly. Same sex couples populate the sidewalks and restaurant tables day and night. Parking can be next to impossible on weekend nights, though, and take care if you decide to park on darkened side streets.

The local women's community is less visible than the gay men's, but you will find three full time women's bars—**Buddies II, Jugs** and **Sue Ellen's**—and several active women's organizations. The community's churches and sports groups are also popular meeting places for singles. Lesbian couples are concentrated in the suburbs of Oak Cliff or in Casa Linda, near White Rock Lake.

*- By reader Deirdre S. Green. Updated by Damron editors.*

## Dallas (214)

**Where the Girls Are:** Oak Lawn in central Dallas is the gay and lesbian stomping grounds, mostly on Cedar Springs Ave.

**Lesbigay Pride:** September: 521-0638.

**Annual Events:**

February - Black Gay/Lesbian Conference: 964-7820.

June 14 - Razzle Dazzle Dallas: 407-3553. Dance party & carnival benefitting PWAs.

September - Oak Lawn Arts Festival: 407-3553.

**City Info:** 800/752-9222.

**Attractions:** Dallas Arboretum & Botanical Garden. Dallas Museum of Art. Dallas Theatre Center/ Frank Lloyd Wright. Texas State Fair & State Fair Park.

**Best View:** Hyatt Regency Tower.

**Weather:** Can be unpredictable. Hot summers (90°s—100°s) with possible severe rain storms. Winter temperatures hover in the 20°s through 40°s range.

**Transit:** Yellow Cab: 426-6262.

**Bamboleo's** 5027 Lemmon St. **520-1124** 9pm-2am, clsd Mon-Th • lesbians/gay men • dancing/DJ • Latino/a clientele • wheelchair access

**Buddies II** 4025 Maple Ave. **526-0887** 11am-2am, from noon Sun • mostly women • country/western wknds • live shows

**Hideaway Club** 4144 Buena Vista **559-2966** 8am-2am, from noon Sun • mostly gay men • professional • piano bar • patio

**J.R.'s** 3923 Cedar Springs Rd. **528-1004** 11am-2am • popular • mostly gay men • grill til 4pm • wheelchair access

**Jugs** 3810 Congress **521-3474** noon-2am • mostly women • dancing/DJ • multi-racial • live shows • wheelchair access • women-owned/run

**Round-Up Saloon** 3912-14 Cedar Springs Rd. **522-9611** 8pm-2am, clsd Mon-Tue • mostly gay men • dancing/DJ • country/western • wheelchair access

**Santa Fe** 3851 Cedar Springs Rd. **521-7079** noon-2am • lesbians/gay men • neighborhood bar

**Side 2 Bar** 4006 Cedar Springs Rd. **528-2026** 10am-2am • lesbians/gay men • neighborhood bar • wheelchair access

**Spankee's Club** 6750 Shady Brook Ln. **739-4760** 4pm-2am, from 8am wknds • gay-friendly • dancing/DJ • wheelchair access

**Sue Ellen's** 3903 Cedar Springs Rd. **559-0707** 3pm-2am, from noon wknds • popular • mostly women • dancing/DJ • live shows/bands • Sun BBQ • patio • wheelchair access

**Village Station** 3911 Cedar Springs Rd. **526-7171** 9pm-3am, from 5pm Sun • popular • mostly gay men • dancing/DJ • videos • Sun T-dance • also 'Rose Room' cabaret

## CAFES

**Dream Cafe** 2800 Routh St. **954-0486** 7am-10pm, til 11pm Fri-Sat • popular • plenty veggie • wheelchair access • $7-12

**Oak Cliff Coffee House** 408 N. Bishop **943-4550** 7am-10pm • deli • salads • gay-owned/run

## RESTAURANTS

**Ali Baba Cafe** 1905 Greenville Ave. **823-8235** lunch & dinner, Sun lunch only, clsd Mon • Middle Eastern

**Black-Eyed Pea** 3857 Cedar Springs Rd. **521-4580** 11am-10:30pm • Southern homecooking • some veggie • wheelchair access • $5-10

**Blue Mesa Grill** 5100 Beltline Rd., Addison **934-0165** 11am-10pm, from 10am Sun • great fajitas • full bar

**Bombay Cricket Club** 2508 Maple Ave. **871-1333** lunch & dinner • Indian

**The Bronx Restaurant & Bar** 3835 Cedar Springs Rd. **521-5821** lunch & dinner, Sun brunch, clsd Mon • some veggie • wheelchair access • gay-owned/run • $8-15

**Cafe Society** 4514 Travis St. **528-6543** 11am-11pm, 10am-midnight Fri-Sat, til 10pm Sun • women-owned/run

**Cremona Bistro & Cafe** 3136 Routh St. **871-1115** 11am-10:30pm • Italian • full bar

**Fresh Start Market & Deli** 4108 Oak Lawn **528-5535** 8am-8pm, 9am-6pm Sat, 11am-6pm Sun • organic • plenty veggie • wheelchair access • gay-owned/run

**Highland Park Cafeteria** 4611 Cole St. **526-3801**

**Hunky's** 4000 Cedar Springs Rd. **522-1212** 11am-10pm • popular • grill • beer/wine • patio • wheelchair access • gay-owned/run • $5-10

**Mansion on Turtle Creek** 2821 Turtle Creek Blvd. **526-2121** lunch, dinner Sun brunch • Southwestern • $26-48

**Monica Aca Y Alla** 2914 Main St. **748-7140** popular • Tex-Mex • full bar • live shows Fri-Sat • transgender-friendly • wheelchair access

**The Natura Cafe** 2909 McKinney Ave. **855-5483** lunch & dinner • healthy • full bar

**Spasso Pizza & Pasta Co.** 4000 Cedar Springs **521-1141** 11am-midnight, til 1am Fri-Sat • some veggie • full bar • wheelchair access • gay-owned/run

**Sushi on McKinney** 4502 McKinney Ave. **521-0969** lunch & dinner, til 11pm Fri-Sat • full bar • wheelchair access

**Thai Soon** 2018 Greenville Ave. **821-7666** lunch & dinner, til midnight Fri-Sat

**Vitto's** 316 W. 7th St. **946-1212** lunch & dinner, til 11pm Fri-Sat • Italian • beer/wine • wheelchair access • gay-owned/run

**Ziziki's** 4514 Travis St., #122 in Travis Walk **521-2233** 11am-11pm, til midnight Fri-Sat, clsd Sun • Greek • full bar • wheelchair access

## ENTERTAINMENT & RECREATION
**Center Stage Cabaret** 4411 Lemmon Ave. #201 **528-6767**

## BOOKSTORES & RETAIL SHOPS
**Crossroads Market** 3930 Cedar Springs Rd. **521-8919** 10am-10pm,11am-9pm Sun • lesbigay bookstore • wheelchair access

**Off the Street** 4001-B Cedar Springs **521-9051** 10am-9pm, noon-6pm Sun • lesbigay gifts

**Tapelenders** 3926 Cedar Springs Rd. **528-6344** 9am-midnight • lesbigay gifts • video rental • gay-owned/run

## PUBLICATIONS
**Dallas Voice** 754-8710 lesbigay newspaper

**TWT (This Week in Texas)** 521-0622 great statewide resource listings

**The Underground Station** PO Box 224571 **283-1047** covers central Sunbelt region

## TRAVEL AGENTS
**Alternative International Travel** 7616 LBJ Fwy. #524 **980-4540** IGLTA

**P.S. Travel (Exclusive Travel Designs)** 3131 Turtle Creek #620 **526-8866** IGLTA

**Planet Travel** 3102 Maple Ave. #450 **965-0800** IGLTA

**Plaza Travel** 15851 Dallas Pkwy. #190 **980-1191** IGLTA

**Pleasure Travel/Cruise Again Too** 4837 Cedar Springs Rd. #216 **526-1126/(800) 583-3913** IGLTA

**Strong Travel** 8201 Preston Rd. #160 **361-0027/(800) 747-5670** IGLTA

**The Travel Bureau** 8150 Brookriver #S-101 **905-3995** IGLTA

**Travel Emporium** 3408 Oak Lawn Ave. **520-7678/(800) 999-3644** IGLTA

**Travel Friends** 8080 N. Central Expwy. #320 **891-8833/(800) 862-8833** IGLTA

**Travel Professionals International** 700 E. Park Blvd. #102, Plano **(972) 881-5517/(800) 349-2670** IGLTA

**Travel With Us** 6116 N. Central Expwy. #175 **987-2563/(800) 856-2563** IGLTA

**White Heron Travel** 4849 Greenville Ave. #173 **692-0446** ask for Mark Lee • IGLTA

## SPIRITUAL GROUPS
**Cathedral of Hope MCC** 5910 Cedar Springs Rd. **351-1901** 9am, 11am & 6:30pm Sun, 6:30pm Wed & Sat • wheelchair access

TREAT YOURSELF TO A GOOD TIME

...YOU KNOW YOU DESERVE IT

1 (888) 44 DINAH
GIRL BAR & CLUB SKIRTS

**Congregation Beth El Binah** (972) 497-1591 lesbigay Jewish congregation

**Dignity Dallas** 6525 Inwood Rd. (St. Thomas the Apostle Episcopal Church) 521-5342 x832 6pm Sun • wheelchair access

**First Unitarian Church of Dallas** 4015 Normandy 528-3990 9am & 11am Sun (10am Sun summers)

**Holy Trinity Community Church** 4402 Roseland 827-5088 11am Sun

**Honesty Texas (Baptist)** (Cathedral of Hope MCC) 521-5342 x233 7:30pm 1st Tue

**St. Thomas the Apostle Episcopal Church** 6525 Inwood Rd. 352-0410 8am & 10am Sun

**White Rock Community Church** 722 Tennison Memorial Rd. 320-0043 9:30am & 11am Sun

GYMS & HEALTH CLUBS

**Centrum Sports Club** 3102 Oak Lawn 522-4100 gay-friendly • swimming

EROTICA

**Alternatives** 1720 W. Mockingbird Ln. 630-7071

**Leather by Boots** 2525 Wycliff #124 528-3865

**Shades of Grey Leather** 3928 Cedar Springs Rd. 521-4739 wheelchair access

## Denison                                  (903)

BARS & NIGHTCLUBS

**Goodtime Lounge** 2520 N. Hwy. 91 N. 463-9944 6pm-2am, from 2pm Sun • lesbians/gay men • more women Wed • private club • unconfirmed

## Denton                                   (817)

BARS & NIGHTCLUBS

**Bedo's** 1215 E. University Dr. 566-9910 8pm-midnight, from 6pm Fri, til 1am Sat, from 5pm Sun • lesbians/gay men • dancing/DJ • live shows • private club • wheelchair access • women-owned/run • unconfirmed

SPIRITUAL GROUPS

**Harvest MCC** 5900 S. Stemmons 321-2332 10:30am Sun

# GAY/LESBIAN/BISEXUAL/ TRANSGENDER/HIV-POSITIVE

**Have you been hurt, beaten, intimidated, threatened, discriminated against, or verbally or physically abused?**

## REPORT THE VIOLENCE, GET SUPPORT

LΛMBDA GLBT Community Ser▼ices

# Anti-Violence Project

24-hours, confidential

# 915-562-GAYS

**800-259-1536 outside El Paso**

*Since 1991, we've been making El Paso proud!*

# El Paso (915)

## INFO LINES & SERVICES

▲ **GLBT Community Center** 910 N. Mesa (enter rear) 562-4297

**Lambda Line/Lambda Services** 562-4297 24hrs • info

**Youth OUTreach** (contact Lambda Line) 562-4297

## BARS & NIGHTCLUBS

**The Old Plantation** 301-309 S. Ochoa St. 533-6055 8pm-2am, til 4am Th-Sat, clsd Mon-Wed • popular • lesbians/gay men • dancing/DJ • live shows • videos • wheelchair access

**San Antonio Mining Co.** 800 E. San Antonio Ave. 533-9516 3pm-2am • popular • lesbians/gay men • dancing/DJ • videos • wheelchair access

**U-Got-It** 216 S. Ochoa 533-9510 8pm-2am, clsd Sun-Tue • mostly gay men • dancing/DJ • alternative • live shows • wheelchair access • unconfirmed

**The Whatever Lounge** 701 E. Paisano St. 533-0215 3pm-2am • mostly gay men • dancing/DJ • Latino/a clientele • beer/wine • BYOB • wheelchair access

## RESTAURANTS

**The Little Diner** 7209 7th St., Canutillo 877-2176 true Texas fare

## PUBLICATIONS

**Lambda News** 562-4297

## TRAVEL AGENTS

**P.S. Travel** 8838-C Viscount Blvd. 598-6188 IGLTA

## SPIRITUAL GROUPS

**MCC of El Paso** 9828 E. Montana (Plaza del Sol) 591-4155 10am Sun (worship) & 7pm Fri (fellowship)

# Fort Worth (817)

## INFO LINES & SERVICES

**Lambda AA** 921-2871/332-3533 (AA#) call for mtg. schedule

**Second Tuesday** 877-5544 lesbian social group • unconfirmed

**Tarrant County Lesbian/Gay Alliance** 1219 6th Ave. 877-5544 info line • newsletter

## ACCOMMODATIONS

**Two Pearls B&B** 804 S. Alamo St., Weatherford 596-9316 lesbians/gay men • modernized 1898 home • full brkfst • women-owned/run

## BARS & NIGHTCLUBS

**651Club Fort Worth** 651 S. Jennings Ave. 332-0745 noon-2am • mostly gay men • more women Fri-Sat • dancing/DJ • country/western • wheelchair access

**The Corral Club & Patio Bar** 621 Hemphill St. 335-0196 11am-2am, from noon Sun • mostly gay men • dancing/DJ • videos • patio • wheelchair access

**D.J.'s** 1308 St. Louis St. 927-7321 7pm-2am, til 3am Fri-Sat, clsd Mon-Tue • popular • lesbians/gay men • dancing/DJ • live shows • also restaurant

## CAFES

**Metro Cafe & Market** 500 W. 7th St. (Nations Bank Plaza) 877-5282 7am-8pm, 9am-3pm Sat, clsd Sun • beer/wine • patio • wheelchair access • women owned/run

**Paris Coffee Shop** 704 W. Magnolia 335-2041

## PUBLICATIONS

**Alliance News** 1219 6th Ave. 877-5544

## TRAVEL AGENTS

**Country Day Travel** 6022 Southwest Blvd. 731-8551 IGLTA

**Fantastic Voyages** 9001 Willoughby Ct. 568-8611 IGLTA

**Good Times Travel Services** 577-0041 IGLTA

## SPIRITUAL GROUPS

**Agape MCC** 4516 SE Loop 820 535-5002 9am & 11am Sun • wheelchair access

**First Jefferson Unitarian Universalist** 1959 Sandy Ln. 451-1505 11am Sun • lesbigay group 7pm 1st Th • wheelchair access

# Galveston (409)

## INFO LINES & SERVICES

**Lambda AA** 23rd & Ursula (ACCT office) 684-2140 8pm Tue & Th & 7pm Sun

## ACCOMMODATIONS

**Galveston Island Women's Guesthouse** 763-2450 women only • smokefree • near beach • sundeck

## BARS & NIGHTCLUBS

**Evolution** 2214 Ships Mechanic Rd. 763-4212 4pm-2am, til 4am Fri-Sat • popular • lesbians/gay men • dancing/DJ • videos

**Kon Tiki Club** 312 23rd St. **763-6264**
4pm-2am, from 2pm wknds • popular •
lesbians/gay men • dancing/DJ • live
shows
**Longfellows** 2405 Post Office Rd. **763-8800** 2pm-2am, from noon wknds •
mostly gay men • neighborhood bar •
live shows
**Robert's Lafitte** 2501 'Q' Ave. **765-9092**
10am-2am, from noon Sun • mostly gay
men • live shows • wheelchair access

## Granbury (817)

### ACCOMMODATIONS

**Pearl Street Inn B&B** 319 W. Pearl St.
**579-7465** gay-friendly • full brkfst • hot
tub

## Groesbeck (817)

### ACCOMMODATIONS

**Rainbow Ranch** 729-5847/**(888) 875-7596** gay-friendly • camping • RV hookup • on Lake Limestone halfway btwn.
Houston & Dallas

## Gun Barrel City (903)

### ACCOMMODATIONS

**Triple B Cottages** 451-5105
lesbians/gay men • 78 mi. from Dallas on
Cedar Creek Lake

### BARS & NIGHTCLUBS

**231 Club** 602 S. Gun Barrel ( Hwy. 198)
**887-2061** 4pm-midnight, til 1am Sat,
from 10am wknds • gay-friendly • neighborhood bar • food served • wheelchair
access

## *Houston*

**W**ith mild winters and blazing summers, Houston is the hottest
lesbian spot in the Southwest. From the Astrodome to San
Jacinto, Houston welcomes sports fans, historians, and shoppers. This
thriving urban center even has bars bigger than your hometown (the
**Ranch**) where you can dance the night away.

Shop the emporiums devoted to women, from **Inklings** alternative bookstore and **Crossroads Market** with their hip coffee bar
and periodicals, to **Lucia's**. Fine and casual dining among beautiful
women takes place all over the cruisy Montrose (where lesbians are
said to shop and party) and Heights neighborhoods. Try elegant **Baba
Yega's** and **Java Java**. Take some time to admire the mansions of the
Montrose and the elegant Victorian homes of the Heights.

For a change of scenery, check out the babes on Galveston
Island beach, about a one hour drive south. While you're there,
refresh yourself and dance at **Evolution**, a popular lesbigay bar.

After you've seen and done all this city has to offer, collapse in
your jacuzzi suite at the historic **Lovett Inn** and kick back with a
copy of the **Houston Voice**.

*– By reader Esperanza Lavender Jazz Paz.*
*Updated by Damron editors.*

# Houston (713)

## INFO LINES & SERVICES

**Gay/Lesbian Hispanics Unidos** 813-3769 7pm 2nd Wed

**Gay/Lesbian Switchboard** 529-3211 7pm-10pm, clsd wknds

**Houston Area Women's Center/Hotline** 1010 Waugh Dr. **528-2121** 9am-9pm, til noon Sat, clsd Sun • wheelchair access

**Lambda AA Center** 1201 W. Clay **521-1243** noon-11pm, til 1am Fri-Sat • wheelchair access

**LOAFF (Lesbians Over Age Fifty)** 1505 Nevada (Houston Mission Church) **869-1482** 2pm 3rd Sun • call for info

## ACCOMMODATIONS

**Angel Arbor** 848 Heights Blvd. **868-4654/(800) 722-8788** gay-friendly • full brkfst • no kids/pets • close to downtown • $85-125

**The Lovett Inn** 501 Lovett Blvd., Montrose **522-5224/(800) 779-5224** gay-friendly • historic home of former Houston mayor & Federal Court judge • swimming • IGLTA

**Patrician B&B Inn** 1200 Southmore Blvd. **523-1114/(800) 553-5797** gay-friendly • 1919 three-story mansion • full brkfst • $79-109

**Rainbow's Inn** Groves **(409) 962-1497** lesbians/gay men • rental home on Lake Sam Rayburn • 2-1/2 hrs from Houston

## BARS & NIGHTCLUBS

**Backyard Bar & Grill** 10200 S. Main **660-6285** 5pm-2am, from noon wknds • gay-friendly • more gay wknds • volleyball courts • food served • dinner theater Fri-Sun • call for events • wheelchair access

**The Berryhill II** 12726 North Fwy. **873-8810** 6pm-2am • lesbians/gay men • neighborhood bar • dancing/DJ • live shows • wheelchair access • women-owned/run

**Chances** 1100 Westheimer **523-7217** 10am-2am • lesbians/gay men • dancing/DJ • live shows • wheelchair access

**Cousins** 817 Fairview **528-9204** 7am-2am, from11am Sat • lesbians/gay men • neighborhood bar • live shows • wheelchair access

**Gentry** 2303 Richmond **520-1861** 2pm-2am • popular • mostly gay men • neighborhood bar • live shows • wheelchair access

**Heaven** 800 Pacific **521-9123** 9pm-2am Wed-Sat, from 7pm Sun, clsd Mon-Tue • popular • mostly gay men • dancing/DJ • 18+ Wed & Sat • live shows Th • videos

**Incognito** 2524 McKinney **237-9431** 9pm-2am, from 6pm Sun, clsd Mon-Tue • lesbians/gay men • mostly African-American • live shows

**Inergy** 5750 Chimney Rock **666-7310** 8pm-2am, clsd Tue & Th • popular • lesbians/gay men • dancing/DJ • multiracial • live shows

# Houston (713)

**Where the Girls Are:** Strolling the Montrose district near the intersection of Montrose and Westheimer or out on Buffalo Speedway at the Plaza.

**Lesbigay Pride:** 529-6979.

**City Info:** 800/231-7799.

**Attractions:** Allen's Landing & Old Market Square. Astrodome. Astroworld/ Waterworld. Bayou Bend Collection. Galleria Mall. LBJ Space Center.

**Best View:** Spindletop, the revolving cocktail lounge on top of the Hyatt Regency.

**Weather:** Humid all year round— you're not that far from the Gulf of Mexico. Mild winters, although there are a few days when the temperatures drop into the 30's. Winter also brings occasional rainy days. Summers are very hot.

**Transit:** Yellow Cab: 236-1111.

**J.R.'s** 808 Pacific **521-2519** 11am-2am, from noon Sun • popular • mostly gay men • more women Fri • live shows • videos • wheelchair access

**Jo's Outpost** 1419 Richmond **520-8446** 11am-2am • mostly gay men • neighborhood bar

**Q Cafe** 2205 Richmond Ave. **524-9696** 4pm-2am • gay-friendly • martini & cigar bar • plenty veggie • wheelchair access

**The Ranch** 9200 Buffalo Speedwy. **666-3464** 4pm-2am, clsd Mon • 3 bars • popular • mostly women • dancing/DJ • country/western • volleyball court • wheelchair access

**Zimm's European Bar** 4321 Montrose **521-2002** 3pm-11pm, til 2am Fri-Sat • gay-friendly • lounge & cigars

### CAFES

**Diedrich Coffee** 4005 Montrose **526-1319**

**Java Java Cafe** 911 W. 11th **880-5282** til midnight Fri-Sat • popular

**Toopes Coffeehouse** 1830 W. Alabama **522-7662** 6am-11pm, from 7am wknds • cafe • some veggie • beer/wine • patio • wheelchair access • lesbian-owned/run

### RESTAURANTS

**A Moveable Feast** 2202 W. Alabama **528-3585** 9am-10pm • plenty veggie • also health food store • wheelchair access • $7-12

**Baba Yega's** 4704 Grant **522-0042** 11am-10pm • popular • plenty veggie • full bar • patio • $5-10

**Barnaby's Cafe** 604 Fairview **522-0106** 11am-10pm, til 11pm Fri-Sat • popular • beer/wine • wheelchair access

**Black-Eyed Pea** 2048 W. Grey **523-0200** 11am-10pm • popular • Southern • wheelchair access • $5-10

**Brasil** 2604 Dunlavy **528-1993** 9am-2am • bistro • plenty veggie • beer/wine

**Cafe Annie** 1728 Post Oak Blvd. **840-1111** lunch & dinner

**Captain Benny's Half Shell** 8506 S. Main **666-5469** lunch & dinner, clsd Sun • beer/wine

**Chapultepec** 813 Richmond **522-2365** 24hrs • Mexican • some veggie • beer/wine • $8-15

**Charlie's** 1100 Westheimer **522-3332** 24hrs • lesbians/gay men • full bar • wheelchair access • $5-10

**House of Pies** 3112 Kirby **528-3816** 24hrs • popular • wheelchair access • $5-10

**Magnolia Bar & Grill** 6000 Richmond Ave. **781-6207** Cajun • full bar • wheelchair access

**Ming's Cafe** 2703 Montrose **529-7888**

**Ninfa's** 2704 Navigation **228-1175** 11am-10pm • popular • Mexican • some veggie • full bar • $7-12

**Ninos** 2817 W. Dallas **522-5120** lunch & dinner, dinner only Sat, clsd Sun • Italian • some veggie • full bar • $10-20

**Pot Pie Pizzeria** 1525 Westheimer **528-4350** 11am-11pm, til 10pm Sun • Italian • some veggie • beer/wine • $5-10

**Spanish Flower** 4701 N. Main **869-1706** 24hrs, til 10pm Tues • Mexican • some veggie • beer/wine • $7-12

### ENTERTAINMENT & RECREATION

**'After Hours'** KPFT-FM 90.1 **526-4000** midnight-4am Sat • lesbigay radio • also 'Lesbian/Gay Voices' 6pm Fri

### BOOKSTORES & RETAIL SHOPS

**Basic Brothers** 1232 Westheimer **522-1626** 10am-9pm, noon-6pm Sun • lesbigay gifts • wheelchair access

**Crossroads Market Bookstore/Cafe** 1111 Westheimer **942-0147** 7am-11pm, til midnight Fri-Sat • lesbigay • wheelchair access

**Hyde Park Gallery** 711 Hyde Park **526-2744** from noon, clsd Tue-Wed • lesbigay art gallery

**Inklings: An Alternative Bookstore** 1846 Richmond Ave. **521-3369/(800) 931-3369** 10:30am-6:30pm, noon-5pm Sun, clsd Mon • lesbigay/feminist • jewelry • music • videos

**Lobo—Houston** 3939-S Montrose Blvd. **522-5156** 10am-10pm • lesbigay books • videos • wheelchair access

**Lucia's Garden** 2942 Virginia **523-6494** 10am-6pm, til 7pm Tue & Th, clsd Sun • spiritual herb center

### PUBLICATIONS

**Houston Voice** 529-8490/(800) 729-8490 lesbigay newspaper

**OutSmart** 520-7237 lesbigay newsmagazine

**TWT (This Week in Texas)** 527-9111 statewide

**The Wand** PO Box 980601, 77098

## TRAVEL AGENTS

**Advance Travel** 10700 NW Fwy. #160 **682-2002/(800) 292-0500** popular • IGLTA

**Carol's Travel** 2036 East T. C. Jester #C **862-9888/(800) 862-9909** IGLTA

**DCA Travel** 1535 W. Loop S. #115 **629-5377/(800) 321-9539**

**Future Travel** 16850 Diana Ln. **480-1988** IGLTA

**Golden Globetrotters** 12600 Bissonnet #A4 **495-2822** IGLTA

**In Touch Travel** 1814 Powderhorn, Katy **(281) 347-3596**

**The Travel Partnership** 1411-A Bonnie Brae **526-4471** IGLTA

**Uniglobe Destinations In Travel** 2727 Allen Pkwy. #PL-02 **520-7526/(800) 520-7560** IGLTA

**Uniglobe First Choice Travel** 2236 W. Holcombe **667-0580/(800) 856-1835** IGLTA

**Uniglobe Universal Travel** 14455 Memorial Dr. **497-1668** IGLTA

**Voyages & Expeditions** 8323 Southwest Fwy. #470 **776-3438/(800) 818-2877** IGLTA

**Woodlake Travel** 1704 Post Oak Rd. **942-0664/(800) 245-6180** IGLTA

## SPIRITUAL GROUPS

**Dignity Houston** 1307 Yale #8 **880-2872** 7:30pm Sat & 5:30pm Sun

**Integrity** 6265 S. Main (Autry House) **432-0414** 7pm 2nd & 4th Mon

**MCC of the Resurrection** 1919 Decatur St. **861-9149** 9am & 11am Sun

**Mishpachat Alizim** **748-7079** worship & social/support group

## GYMS & HEALTH CLUBS

**Fitness Exchange** 4040 Milan **524-9932** popular • gay-friendly

**YMCA Downtown** 1600 Louisiana St. **659-8501** 5am-10pm, 8am-6pm Sat, from 10am Sun • gay-friendly • swimming

## EROTICA

**Leather by Boots** 807 Fairview **526-2668**

**Leather Forever** 711 Fairview **526-6940**

## Humble                                    (281)

## TRAVEL AGENTS

**After Five Travel & Cruises** 2602 Killdeer Ln. **441-1369** IGLTA

## Laredo                                    (210)

## BARS & NIGHTCLUBS

**Discovery** 2019 Farragut **722-9032** 6pm-2am, clsd Mon-Tue • lesbians/gay men • dancing/DJ • Latina/o clientele • live shows • beer/wine

## Longview                                  (903)

## BARS & NIGHTCLUBS

**Decisions** 2103 E. Marshall **757-4884** 3pm-2am • lesbians/gay men • more women Fri • dancing/DJ • live shows • patio • wheelchair access

**Lifestyles** 446 Eastman Rd. **758-8082** 11am-2am • lesbians/gay men • dancing/DJ • patio

## CAFES

**Brother's Coffee Bar & Gallery** 302-A Spur 63 **758-3707** 9am-midnight, from 4pm Sun

## SPIRITUAL GROUPS

**Church With A Vision MCC** 420 E. Cotton St. **753-1501** 10am Sun • wheelchair access

## Lubbock                                   (806)

## INFO LINES & SERVICES

**AA Lambda** (at MCC) **828-3316** 8pm Fri

**LLGA (Lubbock Lesbian/Gay Alliance)** **766-7184** 7:30pm 2nd Wed • call for location

## BARS & NIGHTCLUBS

**The Captain Hollywood** 2401 Main St. **744-4222** 8pm-2am • lesbians/gay men • dancing/DJ • country/western • wheelchair access

## SPIRITUAL GROUPS

**MCC** 4501 University Ave. **792-5562** 11am & 6pm Sun, 7:30pm Wed • wheelchair access

## Odessa/Midland                            (915)

## BARS & NIGHTCLUBS

**Fictxions** 409 N. Hancock **580-5449** 9:30pm-2am, clsd Mon • lesbians/gay men • dancing/DJ • live shows • wheelchair access

**Miss Lillie's Nitespot** 8401 Andrews Hwy. **366-6799** 8pm-2am, clsd Mon • popular • lesbians/gay men • dancing/DJ • live shows • videos • wheelchair access

SAN ANTONIO · TEXAS

*The Painted Lady*

# INN ON BROADWAY

Visit one of the
4 most charming cities
in the country.
And stay at one of the
most elegant gay
guesthouses in Texas.

WALKING DISTANCE TO
THE RIVER WALK AND CLUBS
▸
LUXURIOUS SUITES
AND GUESTROOMS WITH
4-STAR AMENTIES
▸
VCR'S WITH OVER
200 MOVIES TO CHOOSE FROM
▸
PHONES WITH PRIVATE
LINES/ANSWERING MACHINES
▸
MICROWAVES, REFRIGERATORS
COFFEE MAKERS

Call for reservations or more information
## 210-220-1092

FAX 210-299-4185
E-MAIL TRVL2SA@AOL.COM

### SPIRITUAL GROUPS

**Holy Trinity Community Church** 412 E. Gist, Midland **570-4822** 11am Sun

## Rio Grande Valley (210)

### BARS & NIGHTCLUBS

**Colors** 703 N. Ed Carey, Harlingen **440-8663** 8pm-2am, til 3am Fri-Sat, clsd Mon-Wed • lesbians/gay men • dancing/DJ • live shows • wheelchair access

**P.B.D.'s** 2908 Ware Rd., McAllen **682-8019** 8pm-2am • mostly gay men • neighborhood bar • wheelchair access

**Tenth Avenue** 1820 N. 10th St., McAllen **682-7131** 8pm-2am, clsd Mon-Tue • lesbians/gay men • dancing/DJ • Latina/o clientele • live shows • wheelchair access

## S. Padre Island ⋅ (956)

### ACCOMMODATIONS

**Upper Deck—A Guesthouse** 120 E. Atol **761-5953** mostly gay men • swimming • nudity

## San Angelo (915)

### BARS & NIGHTCLUBS

**Silent Partners** 3320 Sherwood Wy. **949-9041** 6pm-2am, clsd Mon • mostly women • dancing/DJ • country/western Wed • live shows • women-owned/run

## San Antonio (210)

### INFO LINES & SERVICES

**Gay/Lesbian Community Center** 923 E. Mistletoe **732-4300** 1pm-8pm, til 10pm Fri (movie night) • wheelchair access

**The Happy Foundation** 411 Bonham **227-6451** lesbigay archives

**Lambda Club AA** 8546 Broadway #255 **824-2027** 8:15pm daily

**San Antonio Gay/Lesbian Switchboard** **733-7300**

### ACCOMMODATIONS

**Adams House B&B** 231 Adams St. **224-4791/(800) 666-4810** gay-friendly • full brkfst • also carriage house & guesthouse avail.

**Adelynne Summit Haus I & II** 427 W. Summit Ave. **736-6272/(800) 972-7266** gay-friendly • full brkfst

**Arbor House at La Villita** 540 S. St. Mary's St. **472-2005/(888) 272-6700** gay-friendly • IGLTA • gay-owned/run • $95-175

**Desert Hearts Cowgirl Club** 796-7446 women only • 2-bdrm cabin on 30 acres • dinner served • kitchen • swimming • horseback riding • $168-238 (for 2) • lesbian-owned/run

**Elmira Motor Inn** 1123 E. Elmira 222-9463/(800) 584-0800 gay-friendly

**The Garden Cottage** (800) 235-7215 gay-friendly • private

▲ **The Painted Lady Inn on Broadway** 620 Broadway 220-1092 popular • lesbians/gay men • private art deco suites • $58-138

**San Antonio B&B** 510 E. Guenther 222-1828 gay-friendly • full brkfst • hot tub

## BARS & NIGHTCLUBS

**2015 Place** 2015 San Pedro **733-3365** 2pm-2am • mostly gay men • neighborhood bar • live shows • patio

**8th St. Restaurant & Bar** 416 8th St. 271-3227 4:30pm-midnight, til 2am Fri-Sat • gay-friendly • bar has lesbian following • patio

**The Annex** 330 San Pedro Ave. **223-6957** 4pm-2am • mostly gay men • neighborhood bar • patio • wheelchair access

**The Bonham Exchange** 411 Bonham St. 271-3811 4pm-2am, from 8pm wknds, til 4am Fri-Sat • popular • gay-friendly • dancing/DJ • alternative • videos • 18+ on Wed • patio

## San Antonio

*A*lthough its moment of glory was more than 150 years ago, the Alamo has become a mythological symbol that still greatly influences San Antonians of today. The Alamo was a mission in which a handful of Texans—including Davy Crockett and Jim Bowie—kept a Mexican army of thousands at bay for almost two weeks.

San Antonians are fiercely proud of this heritage, and maintain a rough-n-ready attitude. This is just as true of the dykes in San Antonio as anyone else.

You'll find most of them at **Chances** or **Nexus** acting like cowgirls, or at **Textures** feminist bookstore catching up on the latest. If you can rope one of your very own, why not take her away for the weekend to the **Desert Hearts Cowgirl Club**'s ranch accommodations.

Though there's no gay ghetto in this spread-out city, there are some lesbian-friendly businesses clustered along various streets, including the 5000 blocks of S. Flores and McCullough, the 1400-1900 blocks of N. Main, and scattered along Broadway and San Pedro.

For sight-seeing, there's always The Alamo, and the two-and-a-half mile Texas Star Trail walking tour that starts and ends there. The architecture in old San Antonio is quaint and beautiful—stop by the **Bonham Exchange** for a taste. Better yet, there's the view from the deck of **The Painted Lady Inn on Broadway** bed & breakfast.

**Cameo** 1123 E. Commerce **226-7055** 10pm-4am Fri-Sat • gay-friendly • dancing/DJ • beer/wine • underground mini-rave

**Chances** 115 General Krueger **348-7202** 2pm-2am • mostly women • dancing/DJ • live shows

**Eagle Mountain Saloon** 1902 McCullough Ave. **733-1516** 4pm-2am • mostly gay men • dancing/DJ • country/western • wheelchair access

**Lorraine's** 7834 South Presa (at Military) **532-8911** 6pm-2am • gay-friendly • dancing/DJ

**Mick's Hideaway** 5307 McCullough **828-4222** 3pm-2am • lesbians/gay men • neighborhood bar • patio • wheelchair access

**New Ponderosa** 5007 S. Flores **924-6322** 6pm-2am, from 3pm wknds • lesbians/gay men • dancing/DJ • Latina/o clientele • live shows

**Nexus SA (San Antonio)** 8021 Pinebrook **341-2818** 6pm-2am, from 7pm Fri-Sat • mostly women • dancing/DJ • country/western • wheelchair access • women-owned/run

**Red Hot & Blues** 450 Soledad **227-0484** 4pm-2am • gay-friendly • dancing/DJ • videos • live shows • on the river walk • wheelchair access

**The Saint** 1430 N. Main **225-7330** 9pm-2am Fri, til 4am Sat only • mostly gay men • dancing/DJ • alternative • 18+ • live shows

**Silver Dollar Saloon** 1418 N. Main Ave. **227-2623** 2pm-2am • mostly gay men • dancing/DJ • country/western • videos • 2-story patio bar • 'Trash Disco' Sun • wheelchair access

**Sparks** 8011 Webbles St. **653-9941** 3pm-2am • mostly gay men • live shows • videos

**Woody's** 826 San Pedro **271-9663** 2pm-2am • mostly gay men • videos

### CAFES

**Candlelight Coffeehouse** 3011 N. St. Mary's **738-0099** 11am-midnight, clsd Mon

**Freedom Coffee House & Deli** 2407 N. St. Mary's **737-3363** noon-midnight • live music

### RESTAURANTS

**Giovanni's Pizza & Italian Restaurant** 1410 Guadalupe **212-6626** 10am-7pm, clsd Sun • some veggie • $7-12

**Madhatter's Tea** 3606 Ave. 'B' **821-6555** 11am-midnight, from 9am wknds • BYOB • patio • wheelchair access

**North St. Mary's Brewing Co. Pub & Deli** 2734 N. St. Mary's **737-6255** 7pm-2am • live shows

### ENTERTAINMENT & RECREATION

**Dyke TV** 'weekly half-hour TV show produced by lesbians, for lesbians' • call (212) 343-9335 for more info

### BOOKSTORES & RETAIL SHOPS

**On Main** 2514 N. Main **737-2323** 10am-6pm, clsd Sun • gifts

---

## San Antonio  (210)

**Where the Girls Are:** Coupled up in the suburbs or carousing downtown.

**Annual Events:** Late April - Fiesta San Antonio.

**City Info:** 270-8748 or 800/447-3372.

**Attractions:** The Alamo. Cowboy Museum & Gallery. Fiesta Texas Theme Park. La Villita. King William Historic District.

**Best View:** From the deck of The Painted Lady Inn on Broadway.

**Weather:** 90°s/60°s in the summer; 60°s/40°s in the winter.

**Transit:** Yellow Cab: 226-4242.

**Q Bookstore** 2803 N. St. Mary's **734-4299** noon-9pm, clsd Mon • lesbigay
**Textures Bookstore** 5309 McCullough **805-8398** 10am-6pm • feminist
**Zebra'z** 1216 E. Euclid Ave. **472-2800** 9am-9pm, til 11pm wknds • lesbigay

PUBLICATIONS
**Bar Talk** 533-8215
**The Marquise** 545-3511
**WomanSpace** 828-5472

TRAVEL AGENTS
**Advantage Plus Travel** 800 NW Loop 410 #306-S **366-1955/(800) 460-3755** IGLTA
**B&B Travel Connections** 800 NW Loop 410 #306-S **979-7811/(800) 362-6560** IGLTA
**First Class Travel/CTN** 2313 NW Military #101 **341-6363** IGLTA

SPIRITUAL GROUPS
**Dignity** St. Anne's St. & Ashby Pl. (St. Anne's Convent) **558-3287** 5:15pm Sun
**MCC of San Antonio** 611 E. Myrtle **472-3597** 10:30am & 7pm Sun, 7pm Wed
**Re-Formed Congregation of the Goddess** 828-4601 Dianic Wiccan group • unconfirmed
**River City Living MCC** 202 Holland **822-1121** 11am Sun

EROTICA
**FleshWorks/Skins & Needles** 110 Jefferson **472-0313**
**Minx** 1621 N. Main Ave. #2 **225-2639** piercing studio

## Sherman (903)

BARS & NIGHTCLUBS
**Good Time Lounge** 2520 Hwy. 91 N. **463-9944** 7pm-2am • lesbians/gay men

TRAVEL AGENTS
**About Travel** 5637 Texoma Pkwy. **893-6888/(800) 783-6481**

## Temple (254)

BARS & NIGHTCLUBS
**Bill's Hard Tymes** 313 S. 1st St. **778-9604** 9pm-2am, clsd Mon • mostly gay men • military clientele

## Texarkana (501)

BARS & NIGHTCLUBS
**The Gig** 201 East St. (Hwy. 71 S.) **773-6900** 7pm-2am, clsd Mon • lesbians/gay men • dancing/DJ • private club • live shows

## Tyler (903)

BARS & NIGHTCLUBS
**Outlaws** Hwy. 110 (4 miles S. of Loop 323) **509-2248** gay-friendly • dancing/DJ • 18+

SPIRITUAL GROUPS
**St. Gabriel's Community Church** 13904 Country Rd. 193 **581-6923** 10:30am Sun • newsletter • wheelchair access

## Victoria (512)

ACCOMMODATIONS
**Friendly Oaks B&B** 210 E. Juan Linn St. **575-0000** gay-friendly • full brkfst • wheelchair access

## Waco (254)

INFO LINES & SERVICES
**Gay/Lesbian Alliance of Central Texas** 752-7727/(800) 735-1122 (IN-STATE ONLY) info • newsletter • pride shop

BARS & NIGHTCLUBS
**David's Place** 507 Jefferson **753-9189** 7pm-2am • lesbians/gay men • dancing/DJ • live shows • wheelchair access

SPIRITUAL GROUPS
**Central Texas MCC From the Heart** 1601 Clay Ave. **752-5331** 10:45am Sun & 7:30pm Wed
**Unitarian Universalist Fellowship of Waco** 4209 N. 27th St. **754-0599** 10:45am Sun
**Unity Church of the Living Christ** 400 S. 1st, Hewitt **666-9102** 11am Sun

## Wichita Falls (817)

BARS & NIGHTCLUBS
**Rascals** 811 Indiana **723-1629** noon-2am • lesbians/gay men • dancing/DJ • live shows • BYOB

SPIRITUAL GROUPS
**MCC** 1407 26th St. **322-4100** 11am Sun & 7pm Wed

# UTAH

## Bicknell (801)

TOUR OPERATORS
**CowPie Adventures** Boulder Mtn. 297-2140 camping trips

## Capitol Reef (801)

ACCOMMODATIONS
**Capitol Reef Inn & Cafe** 360 W. Main St., Torrey 425-3271 gay-friendly • great vegetarian menu
**Sky Ridge B&B Inn** 425-3222 gay-friendly • full brkfst • hot tubs • near Capitol Reef Nat'l Park • smokefree • woman-owned/run • $82-120

## Escalante (801)

ACCOMMODATIONS
**Rainbow Country B&B & Tours** 826-4567/(800) 252-8824 gay-friendly • full brkfst • hot tub • smokefree • gay-owned/run • $39-65

## La Sal (801)

ACCOMMODATIONS
**Mt. Peale Resort B&B** 686-2284 gay-friendly • hot tub

## Logan (801)

INFO LINES & SERVICES
**Cache Valley Lesbian/Gay Youth Group** Faith & Fellowship Center 753-3135 8pm Th • ask for Courtney

SPIRITUAL GROUPS
**MCC Bridgerland** 1315 E. 700 N. (Faith & Fellowship Center) 750-5026 11am Sun

## Ogden (801)

INFO LINES & SERVICES
**Ogden Women's Group** 625-1660 lesbian social/support group • call for events

BARS & NIGHTCLUBS
**Brass Rail** 103 27th St. 399-1543 3pm-1am • lesbians/gay men • women's night Fri • dancing/DJ • private club

SPIRITUAL GROUPS
**MCC Ogden** 210 W. 22nd St. 394-0204 11am Sun

**Unitarian Universalist Society of Ogden** 2261 Adams Ave. (YCC) 394-3338 10:30am Sun

## Park City (801)

ACCOMMODATIONS
**The Old Miners Lodge** 645-8068/(800) 648-8068 gay-friendly • full brkfst • hot tub • smokefree • $95-245
**Resort Property Management** (800) 243-2932 IGLTA

RESTAURANTS
**Zoom Roadhouse Grill** 660 Main St. 649-9108 lunch & dinner

TOUR OPERATORS
**Sportours Travel** 655-0500 IGLTA

## Salt Lake City (801)

INFO LINES & SERVICES
**AA Gay/Lesbian** 539-8800 call for mtg. schedule
**Bisexual Group** Stonewall Center 539-8800 call for info
**Community Real Estate Referrals** (800) 346-5592 gay realtor at your service • no rentals
**S/M Social & Support Group** Stonewall Center 539-8800 7pm Th • pansexual • call for info
**U of U Women's Resource Center** 581-8030 info • lesbian support group
**Utah Gay/Lesbian Youth Group** Utah Stonewall Center 539-8800 drop-in 5pm-7pm • mtg. 7pm Wed
**Utah Stonewall Center** 770 S. 300 W. 539-8800 1pm-9pm, til 6pm Sat, clsd Sun • referrals • many mtgs.

ACCOMMODATIONS
**Aardvark B&B** 533-0927 gay-friendly • call for reservations & info • non-profit • benefits helpline • full brkfst • smokefree • kids/pets ok • wheelchair access
**Anton Boxrud B&B** 57 S. 600 E. 363-8035/(800) 524-5511 gay-friendly • full brkfst
**Peery Hotel** 110 W. Broadway 521-4300/(800) 331-0073 popular • gay-friendly • also restaurant • full bar • wheelchair access • $79-149
**Saltair B&B/Alpine Cottages** 164 S. 900 E. 533-8184/(800) 733-8184 popular • gay-friendly • full brkfst • also cottages from 1870s • smokefree • $55-139

## Bars & Nightclubs

**Bricks Tavern** 579 W. 200 S. **328-0255**
9:30pm-2am • popular • mostly gay men
• very women-friendly • dancing/DJ • 18+

**Kings** 108 S. 500 W. **521-5464** 4pm-2am,
from noon Fri-Sun • lesbians/gay men •
dancing/DJ • private club • wheelchair
access

**Paper Moon** 3424 S. State St. **466-8517**
4pm-1am, 1pm-midnight Sun • mostly
women • dancing/DJ • private club •
wheelchair access

**Radio City** 147 S. State St. **532-9327**
11am-1am • mostly gay men • beer only
• wheelchair access

**The Sun** 702 W. 200 S. **531-0833** noon-
2am • popular • lesbians/gay men •
dancing/DJ • Sun brunch • country/west-
ern • patio • wheelchair access

**The Trapp** 102 S. 600 W. **531-8727**
11am-1am • lesbians/gay men • danc-
ing/DJ • country/western • private club •
wheelchair access

**The Vortex** 32 Exchange Pl. **521-9292**
9:30pm-2am • gay-friendly • dancing/DJ
• alternative • patio

## Cafes

**Bill & Nadas Cafe** 479 S. 600 E. **359-
6984** 24hrs

**Caffe Med** 2020 S. State **487-6589**
6:30am-6:30pm

**Coffee Garden** 898 E. 900 S. **355-3425**
7am-10pm • wheelchair access

## Restaurants

**Baci Trattoria** 134 W. Pierport Ave. **328-
1333** lunch & dinner • some veggie • full
bar • wheelchair access • $6-25

**Capitol Cafe** 54 W. 200 S. **532-7000**
11am-10pm, til 11pm Fri-Sat, from 4pm
Sun • full bar • wheelchair access

**Idle Isle** 24 S. Main St., Brigham City
**734-2468** 11am-8pm, til 9pm Fri-Sat,
clsd Sun

**Lambs Restaurant** 169 S. Main St. **364-
7166** 7am-9pm

**Market St. Grill** 50 Market St. **322-4668**
lunch, dinner, Sun brunch • seafood &
steak • full bar • wheelchair access •
$15-30

**Rio Grande Cafe** 270 S. Rio Grande **364-
3302** lunch & dinner • popular •
Mexican • some veggie • full bar • $4-8

**Santa Fe** 2100 Emigration Canyon **582-
5888** lunch & dinner, Sun brunch • some
veggie • $10-12

## Entertainment & Recreation

**Concerning Gays & Lesbians** KRCL 91
FM **363-1818** 12:30pm-1pm Wed

## Bookstores & Retail Shops

**A Woman's Place Bookstore** 1400
Foothill Dr. #236 **583-6431** 10am-9pm, til
6pm Sat, noon-5pm Sun • wheelchair
access • women-owned/run

**Cahoots** 878 E. 900 S. **538-0606** 10am-
7pm, noon-5pm Sun • wheelchair access

**Gypsy Moon Emporium** 1011 E. 900 S.
**521-9100** 11am-6pm, clsd Sun • metaphysical

## Publications

**Labrys** **486-6473** women's newsletter w/
community directory

**The Pillar** **265-0066** lesbigay newspaper

## Travel Agents

**Olympus Tours & Travel** 311 S. State St.
#110 **521-5232**/(800) 338-9661

**Travel Zone/Cruise Zone** 757 E. South
Temple **531-1606**/(800) 531-1608 IGLTA

## Spiritual Groups

**Restoration Church (Mormon)**
Stonewall Center **(800) 677-7252**
11:30am Sun

**Sacred Light of Christ MCC** 823 S. 600
E. **595-0052** 11am Sun

**South Valley Unitarian Universalist
Society** 6876 S. 2000 E. **944-9723**
10:30am Sun

## Erotica

**All For Love** 3072 South Main St. **487-
8358** leather/SM boutique

**Blue Boutique** 2106 S. 1100 E. **485-2072**

**Mischievous** 559 S. 300 W. **530-3100**

**Video One** 484 S. 900 W. **539-0300** also
cult & art films

# Springdale (801)

## Accommodations

**Red Rock Inn** 998 Zion Park Blvd. **772-
3836** gay-friendly • full brkfst • smokefree • wheelchair access • lesbian-
owned/run • $65-135

# VERMONT

## Andover (802)

ACCOMMODATIONS

**The Inn At High View** East Hill Rd. 875-2724 gay-friendly • full brkfst • swimming • smokefree • IGLTA • $80-135

## Arlington (802)

ACCOMMODATIONS

**Candlelight Motel** 375-6647/(800) 348-5294 gay-friendly • swimming • IGLTA • $40-80

**Hill Farm Inn** 375-2269/(800) 882-2545 gay-friendly • full brkfst • dinner avail. • $70-125

RESTAURANTS

**Arlington Inn** Rte. 7A 375-6532/(800) 443-9442 clsd Sun-Mon • cont'l

## Belmont (802)

ACCOMMODATIONS

**Alice's Place** 259-2596 gay-friendly • full brkfst • women-owned

## Brattleboro (802)

ACCOMMODATIONS

**Mapleton Farm B&B** 257-5252 gay-friendly • full brkfst • smokefree • kids 10+ ok • small pets by arr.

BARS & NIGHTCLUBS

**Rainbow Cattle Company** Rte. 5, Dummerston 254-9830 8pm-2am, from 5pm Sun • lesbians/gay men • dancing/DJ • country/western

RESTAURANTS

**Common Ground** 25 Elliott St. 257-0855 lunch & dinner, clsd Tue • vegetarian/local fish • plenty veggie • beer/wine • $6-13

**Peter Haven's** 32 Elliott St. 257-3333 6pm-10pm, clsd Sun-Mon • cont'l

BOOKSTORES & RETAIL SHOPS

**Everyone's Books** 23 Elliott St. 254-8160 10am-6pm, til 8pm Fri, 11am-4pm Sun • wheelchair access

## Burlington (802)

INFO LINES & SERVICES

**AA Gay/Lesbian** St. Paul's Church on Cherry St. 658-4221 7pm Th

**Outright Vermont** 865-9677/(800) 452-3428 support/education for lesbigay youth • also hotline

**Univ. of VT Gay/Lesbian/Bisexual Alliance** 656-0699 7pm Mon

**Vermont Gay Social Alternatives** 865-3734 social events • newsletter

ACCOMMODATIONS

**Allyn House B&B** 57 Main St., Essex Jct. 878-9408 gay-friendly • full brkfst • smokefree • $55-65

**The Black Bear Inn** Bolton Valley 434-2126/(800) 395-6335 gay-friendly • full brkfst • swimming • hot tub • $69-139

**Grünberg House B&B** Waterbury 244-7726/(800) 800-7760 gay-friendly • full brkfst • jacuzzi • sauna • smokefree • kids ok • $55-140

**Hartwell House B&B** 170 Ferguson Ave. 658-9242 gay-friendly • swimming • shared bath • woman-owned/run

**Howden Cottage B&B** 32 N. Champlain St. 864-7198 lesbians/gay men • smokefree • kids by arr.

BARS & NIGHTCLUBS

**135 Pearl** 135 Pearl St. 863-2343 noon-2am • lesbians/gay men • dancing/DJ • 18+ Fri • smokefree juice bar downstairs • wheelchair access

RESTAURANTS

**Alfredo's** 79 Mechanics Ln. 864-0854 4:30pm-10pm, from 3pm Sun • Italian • some veggie • full bar • wheelchair access • $6-12

**Daily Planet** 15 Center St. 862-9647 11:30am-10:30pm • plenty veggie • full bar til 1am • $6-15

**Silver Palace** 1216 Williston Rd. 864-0125 11:30am-9:30pm • Chinese • some veggie • full bar • $10-15

BOOKSTORES & RETAIL SHOPS

**Chassman & Bem Booksellers** 81 Church St. Market Place 862-4332 9am-9pm, til 5pm Sun • wheelchair access

PUBLICATIONS

**Out in the Mountains** PO Box 177, 05402

TRAVEL AGENTS

**American-International Travel Services** 864-9827 IGLTA

**Travel Network** 1860 Williston Rd., South Burlington 863-4300/(800) 203-2929 IGLTA

SPIRITUAL GROUPS
**Dignity Vermont** 655-6706
**First Unitarian Universalist Society** 152 Pearl St. **862-5630** ask about 'Interweave' (G/L/B/T/S Group)

## Essex Junction (802)

RESTAURANTS
**Loretta's** 44 Park St. **879-7777** lunch Tue-Fri, dinner Tue-Sat, clsd Sun-Mon • Italian • plenty veggie • take-out avail. • women-owned/run

## Hartland Four Corners (802)

ACCOMMODATIONS
**Twin Gables** 463-3070 gay-friendly • near outdoor recreation • smokefree • kids ok • $50-65

## Hyde Park (802)

ACCOMMODATIONS
**Arcadia House** 888-9147 lesbians/gay men • swimming • smokefree

## Killington (802)

ACCOMMODATIONS
**Cortina Inn** Rte. 4 773-3333/(800) 451-6108 gay-friendly • hot tub • swimming • smokefree • kids/pets ok • food served • also tavern • wheelchair access • $89-139

## Ludlow (802)

RESTAURANTS
**Michael's Seafood & Steak** Rte. 103 **228-5622** 5pm-9:30pm • full bar

## Lyndonville (802)

RESTAURANTS
**Miss Lyndonville Diner** Rte. 5 626-9890 6am-8pm

## Manchester (802)

CAFES
**The Black Swan** Rte. 7A S. 362-3807 dinner from 5:30pm, clsd Tue-Wed • cont'l/game
**Little Rooster Cafe** Rte. 7A S. 362-3496 7am-2pm, clsd Wed

## Manchester Center (802)

RESTAURANTS
**Chanticleer** Rte. 7A N. 362-1616 clsd Mon-Tue

BOOKSTORES & RETAIL SHOPS
**Northshire Bookstore** Main St. **362-2200** 10am-5:30pm, til 9pm Fri, til 7pm Sat, clsd Sun

## Manchester Village (802)

RESTAURANTS
**Bistro Henry** Rtes. 11 & 30 362-4982

## Marlboro (802)

RESTAURANTS
**Skyline Restaurant** Rte. 9, Hogback Mountain **464-5535** 7:30am-9pm, clsd Tue-Th (winters) • wheelchair access

## Montgomery Center (802)

ACCOMMODATIONS
**Phineas Swann B&B** 326-4306 gay-friendly • full brkfst • smokefree • kids ok • dinner avail.

## Montpelier (802)

RESTAURANTS
**Julio's** 44 Main St. **229-9348** lunch & dinner, from 4pm wknds • Mexican
**Sarducci's** 3 Main St. 223-0229 11:30am-10pm • Italian • some veggie • full bar • wheelchair access • $8-15
**Wayside Restaurant** Rte. 302 223-6611 6:30am-9:30pm • wheelchair access

BOOKSTORES & RETAIL SHOPS
**Phoenix Rising** 104 Main St., 2nd flr. **229-0522** 10am-5pm, 11am-3pm wknds • jewelry • gifts

## Shaftsbury (802)

ACCOMMODATIONS
**Country Cousin B&B** 375-6985/(800) 479-6985 lesbians/gay men • full brkfst • smokefree • IGLTA • $70-85

## St. Johnsbury (802)

INFO LINES & SERVICES
**Game Ends** 748-5849 social activities group
**Umbrella Women's Center** 1 Prospect Ave. **748-8645** lesbian support & resources

## ACCOMMODATIONS

▲ **Greenhope Farm** 533-7772 mostly women • full brkfst • smokefree • horseback-riding • near skiing • $65-85

▲ **Highlands Inn** PO Box 118-WT, Bethlehem NH, 03574 **(603) 869-3978** women only • hot tub • kids/pets ok • wheelchair access (see ad page 3)

## Stowe (802)

### ACCOMMODATIONS

**Buccaneer Country Lodge** 3214 Mountain Rd. 253-4772/**(800) 543-1293** gay-friendly • full kitchen suites • full brkfst • swimming • smokefree

**Fitch Hill Inn** 888-3834/**(800) 639-2903** gay-friendly • full brkfst • dinner by arr. • swimming • hot tub • older kids ok • $75-150

## Waterbury (802)

### EROTICA

**Video Exchange** 21 Stowe St. 244-7004 clsd Sun

## Woodstock (802)

### ACCOMMODATIONS

**The Ardmore Inn** 23 Pleasant St. 457-9652/**(800) 497-9652** gay-friendly • full brkfst • $85-150

**Country Garden Inn B&B** 37 Main St., Quechee 295-3023 gay-friendly • full brkfst • swimming

**Maitland-Swan House** 457-5181/**(800) 959-1404** gay-friendly • early-19th century home • full brkfst • smokefree • unconfirmed

**Rosewood Inn** 457-4485/**(203) 829-1499** gay-friendly • full brkfst • smokefree • kids ok

**South View B&B** 484-7934 gay-friendly • classic Vermont log home • smokefree

## Worchester (802)

### INFO LINES & SERVICES

**Women of the Woods** 229-0109 lesbian social group

# Greenhope Farm
### BED & BREAKFAST

• 140 private acres of nature trails.

• Horseback riding on our own gentle horses.

• Cross country ski from our door.

• Cozy rooms and secluded campsites.

*RFD Box 2260*
*East Hardwick, VT 05836*
*(802) 533-7772*

## VIRGINIA

### Alexandria (703)

TRAVEL AGENTS
**Destinations** 1800 Diagonal Rd. Plaza D **684-8824** IGLTA
**Empress Travel** 4533 Duke St. **823-0060** IGLTA
**Just Vacations** 501 King St. **838-0040**

SPIRITUAL GROUPS
**Church of the Resurrection (Episcopal)** 2280 N. Beauregard St. **998-0888** 8am & 10am Sun, 10am Wed
**Mt. Vernon Unitarian Church** 1909 Windmill Ln. **765-5950** 10am Sun

### Arlington (703)

*(see also Washington, DC)*

INFO LINES & SERVICES
**Arlington Gay/Lesbian Alliance** 522-7660 monthly mtgs.

ACCOMMODATIONS
**Best Western Arlington Hotel** 2480 S. Glebe Rd. **979-4400** gay-friendly • IGLTA

CAFES
**Java Shack** 2507 N. Franklin Rd. **527-9556** 7am-10pm, til midnight Fri, from 8am wknds • lesbians/gay men

PUBLICATIONS
**Woman's Monthly 527-4881** covers DC & VA community events

SPIRITUAL GROUPS
**Clarendon Presbyterian Church** 1305 N. Jackson St. **527-9513** 10am Sun

### Bedford (540)

TRAVEL AGENTS
**G.W. Travel & Tours** 109 N. Bridge St. **586-0231** IGLTA

### Cape Charles (757)

ACCOMMODATIONS
**Sea Gate B&B** 9 Tazewell Ave. **331-2206** gay-friendly • full brkfst • afternoon tea • near beach on quiet, tree-lined street
**Wilson-Lee House** 403 Tazewell Ave. **331-1954** gay-friendly • full brkfst • IGLTA

### Charlottesville (804)

INFO LINES & SERVICES
**Gay AA** (at Church House, Thomas Jefferson Unitarian Church, Rugby Rd.) **293-8227** 7pm Mon
**Gay/Lesbian Information Service** 296-8783 also contact for 'Piedmont Triangle Society' • active social group
**Women's Center** 14th & University (UVA) **982-2361** 8:30am-5pm, clsd wknds

ACCOMMODATIONS
**Intouch Women's Center** 589-6542 women only • campground • recreational area • wheelchair access
**The Mark Addy** 56 Rodes Farm Dr., Nellysford **361-1101**/(800) 278-2154 gay-friendly • full brkfst • swimming • smokefree • wheelchair access • gay-owned/run
**Thousand Acres B&B** 574-8807 women only • 1 hr. S. of Charlottesville on a private river

BARS & NIGHTCLUBS
**Club 216** 216 W. Water St. (enter rear) **296-8783** 9pm-2am, til 4am Fri-Sat, clsd Sun-Wed • lesbians/gay men • dancing/DJ • live shows • private club • wheelchair access

RESTAURANTS
**Bistro 151** Valley Green Center, Nellysford **361-1463** lunch & dinner, clsd Mon • full bar til midnight, til 2am wknds
**Eastern Standard/Escafe** 102 Old Preston Ave. (W. end downtown mall) **295-8668** 5pm-midnight, til 2am Th-Sat, clsd Sun-Mon • lesbians/gay men • Asian/Mediterrean • some veggie • full bar • live shows • gay-owned/run • $8-16

SPIRITUAL GROUPS
**Lesbian & Gay Chavurah** 295-8884/982-2361 lesbigay Jewish study group
**MCC** 717 Rugby Rd. (Thomas Jefferson Memorial Church) **979-5206** 6pm Sun

### Culpepper (703)

TRAVEL AGENTS
**Culpepper Travel** 763 Madison Rd. #208-B **825-1258**/(800) 542-4881 IGLTA

## Falls Church (703)

RESTAURANTS
**The Courtyard** 6108 Arlington Blvd. **533-2828** lunch & dinner • Sun jazz brunch

SPIRITUAL GROUPS
**MCC of Northern VA** 2709 Hunter Mill Rd. (Fairfax Unitarian Church), Oakton **532-0992** 6pm Sun

## Fredericksburg (540)

RESTAURANTS
**Merrimans** 715 Caroline St. **371-7723** lunch & dinner, lounge til 2am, clsd Mon • popular • lesbians/gay men • fresh natural homemade cuisine • plenty veggie • full bar • dancing/DJ • $7-18

## Herndon (703)

TRAVEL AGENTS
**Alexis Travel USA** 1037 Sterling Rd. #201 **318-8998** IGLTA

## Lexington (540)

ACCOMMODATIONS
**Longdale Inn** 6209 Longdale Furnace Rd., Clifton Forge **862-0892/(800) 862-0386** gay-friendly • full brkfst • smokefree • $75-120

## Lynchburg (804)

INFO LINES & SERVICES
**Gay/Lesbian Helpline** 847-5242 live 7pm-10pm Tue

## New Market (540)

ACCOMMODATIONS
**A Touch of Country B&B** 9329 Congress St. **740-8030** gay-friendly • full brkfst • smokefree

## Newport News (757)

BOOKSTORES & RETAIL SHOPS
**Out of the Dark** 530 Randolph Rd. **596-6220** 10am-6pm, til 8pm Fri-Sat, clsd Sun-Mon • Wiccan/pagan

EROTICA
**Mr. D's Leather & Novelties** 9902-A Warwick Blvd. **599-4070**

## Norfolk (757)

INFO LINES & SERVICES
**Hampton Roads Gay/Lesbian Info Line** 622-5617 24hr recorded info

BARS & NIGHTCLUBS
**Charlotte's Web** 6425 Tidewater Dr. (Roland Park Shopping Ctr.) **853-5021** 10am-2am • mostly women • dancing/DJ • Sun brunch • wheelchair access
**Club Rumours** 4107 Colley Ave. **440-7780** 11am-2am, clsd Mon-Wed • lesbians/gay men • dancing/DJ • more women Wed & Fri
**The Garage** 731 Granby St. **623-0303** 8am-2am, from 10am Sun • popular • mostly gay men • neighborhood bar • food served • wheelchair access • $3-9
**Hershee Bar** 6117 Sewells Pt. Rd. **853-9842** 4pm-2am, from noon wknds • mostly women • dancing/DJ • live shows • food served • some veggie • $2-7
**Late Show** 114 E. 11th St. **623-3854** midnight til dawn • popular • lesbians/gay men • dancing/DJ • food served • private club
**Ms. P** 6401 Tidewater Dr. **853-9717** 8pm-2am, clsd Mon-Wed • mostly women • dancing/DJ
**Nutty Buddy's** 143 E. Little Creek Rd. **588-6474** 4pm-2am, Sun brunch • popular • lesbians/gay men • dancing/DJ • karaoke • also restaurant • some veggie • live shows • wheelchair access • $10-15

RESTAURANTS
**Broadway Diner** 119 W. Charlotte St. **627-4491** 7am-7pm, til 2pm Sun • fresh fast food
**Charlie's Cafe** 1800 Granby St. **625-0824** 7am-8pm, til 3pm wknds • some veggie • beer/wine • $3-7
**Uncle Louie's** 132 E. Little Creek Rd. **480-1225** 8am-11pm, til midnight Fri-Sat, til 10pm Sun, bar til 2am, deli 9am-8pm • Jewish fine dining • live shows • karaoke • wheelchair access • $5-15
**White House Cafe/Private Eyes** 249 York St. **533-9290** 11am-2am • grand buffet Sun • some veggie • full bar • dancing/DJ • live shows • wheelchair access • $5-15

BOOKSTORES & RETAIL SHOPS
**Lambda Rising** 9229 Granby St. **480-6969** 10am-midnight • lesbigay • wheelchair access

**Phoenix Rising East** 808 Spotswood Ave. **622-3701/(800) 719-1690** 11am-9pm, til 10pm Fri-Sat, til 7pm Sun • lesbigay

**Two of a Kind** 6123 Sewells Pt. Rd. **857-0223** 11am-9pm, til 11pm Wed-Th, til 2am Fri-Sat, 2pm-7pm Sun • lesbigay • wheelchair access

PUBLICATIONS
**Our Own Community Press** 625-0700 lesbigay newspaper

TRAVEL AGENTS
**Moore Travel** 7516 Granby St. **583-2362** IGLTA

SPIRITUAL GROUPS
**All God's Children Community Church** 9229 Granby St. **480-0911** 10:30am Sun & 7:30 pm Wed

**Dignity** 600 Tabbot Hall Rd. **625-5337** 6:30pm Sun

**New Life MCC** 4035 E. Ocean Ave. **362-3056** 10:30am Sun

EROTICA
**Ghent Video & Newsstand** 1911 Colonial Ave. **627-1277**

**Leather & Lace** 149 E. Little Creek Rd. 583-4334

## Richmond (804)

INFO LINES & SERVICES
**AA Gay/Lesbian** 355-1212 call for mtg. schedule

**Gay Info Line** 967-9311

**Richmond Lesbian Feminist** 796-9988 community entertainment & educational group

**Richmond Organization for Sexual Minority Youth** 353-2077 3pm-8pm Mon & Wed

**Virginia Division of Tourism** (800) 847-4882

**Virginians for Justice** 643-4816 statewide lesbigay organization

ACCOMMODATIONS
**Bellmont Manor B&B Inn** 6600 Belmont Rd., Chesterfield **745-0106/(800) 809-9041 x69** gay-friendly • full brkfst • smokefree • wheelchair access • gay-owned/run

BARS & NIGHTCLUBS
**Babe's of Carytown** 3166 W. Cary St. **355-9330** 11am-1am, til 2am Fri-Sat, from 8pm Sat, 9am-5pm Sun • mostly women • dancing/DJ • food served • homecooking • some veggie • wheelchair access • women-owned/run • $4-7

**Broadway Cafe & Bar** 1624 W. Broad St. **355-9931** 5:30pm-2am, from 6pm wknds • wheelchair access • $7-10

**Cafine's Cafe/Boom** 401 E. Grace St. **775-2233** lunch & dinner, til 2am Th-Sat, clsd Sun-Mon • gay-friendly • dancing/DJ

**Casablanca Lounge & Restaurant** 6 E. Grace St. **648-2040** 11am-2am, from 3pm Sat • mostly gay men • karaoke • videos • lunch served • some veggie • wheelchair access • $5-8

## Norfolk (757)

**Annual Events:**

May - Virginia Women's Music Festival: 589-6542.

September - Wild Western Women's Weekend.

**City Info:** 800/368-3097.

**Attractions:** Douglas MacArthur Memorial. Norfolk Navy Base. St. Paul's Episcopal Church. The Chrysler Museum. Waterside Festival Marketplace.

**Transit:** Yellow Cab: 622-3232. Norfolk Airport Shuttle: 857-1231. Tidewater Regional Transit: 627-9297.

**Club Colors** 536 N. Harrison St. **353-9776** 10pm-3am Fri-Sat • lesbians/gay men • ladies night Fri • dancing/DJ • multi-racial • food served • wheelchair access

**Fielden's** 2033 W. Broad St. **359-1963** midnight-6am, clsd Mon-Wed • popular • mostly gay men • dancing/DJ • BYOB • private club • wheelchair access

### BOOKSTORES & RETAIL SHOPS

**Carytown Books** 2930 W. Cary St. **359-4831** 9am-7pm, til 5pm Sun • lesbigay section • wheelchair access

**Phoenix Rising** 19 N. Belmont Ave. **355-7939**/(800) 719-1690 11am-7pm • lesbigay bookstore • wheelchair access

### TRAVEL AGENTS

**Covington International Travel** 4401 Dominion Blvd., Glen Allen **747-7077**/(800) 922-9238 IGLTA

**Latitudes** 3 N. 19th St. **644-7047** IGLTA

**The Travel Store** 5203 S. Laburnum Ave. **222-2100** IGLTA

### SPIRITUAL GROUPS

**MCC Richmond** 2501 Park Ave. **353-9477** 9am, 10:45am & 6:30pm Sun

## Roanoke (540)

### INFO LINES & SERVICES

**The Roanoke Valley Supper Club** 772-5702 social group • regional info

### BARS & NIGHTCLUBS

**The Alternative Complex (Edge)** 3348 Salem Trnpk. **344-4445** 9pm-close Fri-Sun • food served • live shows • unconfirmed

**Backstreet Cafe** 356 Salem Ave. **345-1542** 7pm-2am, til midnight Sun • lesbians/gay men • neighborhood bar • food served

**Club 1919** 434 Church Ave. SW **343-9443**/343-1919 9pm-3am, clsd Sun-Tue • mostly gay men • dancing/DJ • also 'Magnolia's' • lunch served Mon-Fri • also 'Commonbond' • women's night Sat • live shows

**The Park** 615 Salem Ave. **342-0946** 9pm-close, clsd Mon-Tue & Th • popular • lesbians/gay men • dancing/DJ • live shows • videos • private club • wheelchair access

## *The Ruby Rose Inn*

*Bed & Breakfast*
*in the beautiful Shenandoah Valley*

Canoe, kayak, tube, the Shenandoah River
Swim, picnic, fish, at Lake Arrowhead
Explore Luray Caverns. Golf all day
Hike the Massenutten or Blue Ridge Mtns.
All rooms w/pvt baths, A/C, Cottage w/jacuzzi,fpl
Full breakfasts daily.
Candlelight dinner available off season
We always accomodate dietary restrictions
Perfect for small committment parties.
Lesbian owned
Info: 1-540-778-4680
Rosemary & Deb, Innkeepers

RESTAURANTS
**The Le Grande Dame** 3348 Salem Trnpk. (at 'The Edge') **344-4445** 6pm-1am • lesbians/gay men • dinner & dancing • call for events • unconfirmed

BOOKSTORES & RETAIL SHOPS
**Out Word Connections** 114 Kirk Ave. SW **985-6886** noon-8pm, til 9pm Fri-Sat • lesbigay bookstore

PUBLICATIONS
**Blue Ridge Lambda Press** 890-6612 covers western VA
**Buddies/Shout!** 989-1579 entertainment • personals

SPIRITUAL GROUPS
**MCC of the Blue Ridge** 2015 Grandin Rd. SW (Unitarian Church) **344-4444** 3pm Sun
**Unitarian Universalist Church** 2015 Grandin Rd. SW **342-8888** 11am Sun (10am summers)

## Shenandoah Valley (540)

INFO LINES & SERVICES
**SVGLA (Shenandoah Valley Gay/Lesbian Assoc.)** 574-4636 24hr touchtone info • weekly mtgs. • also dances and potlucks

ACCOMMODATIONS
▲ **The Ruby Rose Inn** 778-4680 mostly women • full brkfst • jacuzzi • smokefree • women-owned/run • $90-135
**Ruffner House** Ruffner House Ln., Luray 743-7855 gay-friendly • full brkfst • hot tub • swimming • smokefree • gay-owned/run • $80-150

## Virginia Beach (757)

BARS & NIGHTCLUBS
**Ambush** 2838 Virginia Beach Blvd. **498-4301** 4pm-2am • mostly gay men • neighborhood bar

PUBLICATIONS
**Lambda Directory** 486-3546

TRAVEL AGENTS
**Travel Merchants** 2232 Virginia Beach Blvd. #112 **463-9790**

## Williamsburg (757)

TRAVEL AGENTS
**American Dream Vacations** 800 Penniman Rd. **220-9427** IGLTA

# WASHINGTON

## Bellevue (206)

*(see also Seattle)*

SPIRITUAL GROUPS
**East Shore Unitarian Church** 12700 SE 32nd St. **747-3780** 9:15am & 11:15am Sun (10am summers) • wheelchair access

## Bellingham (360)

INFO LINES & SERVICES
**Lesbian/Gay/Bisexual Alliance** Western Washington University **650-6120** social/political group

BARS & NIGHTCLUBS
**Rumors** 1119 Railroad Ave. **671-1849** noon-2am • lesbians/gay men • dancing/DJ • multi-racial • beer/wine

CAFES
**Tony's Coffee** 1101 Harris Ave., Fairhaven **738-4710** 7am-10pm • plenty veggie • patio • wheelchair access

BOOKSTORES & RETAIL SHOPS
**Rainbow Bridge** 304 W. Champion St. **715-3684** 10am-10pm, noon-6pm Mon • lesbigay bookstore • gifts • women-owned/run
**Village Books** 1210 11th St. **671-2626** 9am-10pm, til 8pm Sun

EROTICA
**Great Northern Bookstore** 1308 Railroad Ave. **733-1650**
**Kalamalka Studio** 2518 Meridian **733-3832** tattoos • piercings

## Bremerton (360)

INFO LINES & SERVICES
**West Sound Family** 792-3960 lesbigay social/support group

ACCOMMODATIONS
**Tricia's Place** 813-9008 cabin • RV hookup • near outdoor recreation

BARS & NIGHTCLUBS
**Brewski's** 2810 Kitsap Wy. (enter off Wycuff St.) **479-9100** 11am-2am • gay-friendly • neighborhood bar • food served • wheelchair access

BOOKSTORES & RETAIL SHOPS
**Footnotes** 1790 NE Riddell Rd. **377-5949** lesbigay

**DAMRON
ROAD ATLAS**
Features over 150
full-color maps of
North America
and Europe
with detailed
listings of the
latest lesbigay
destinations.
For credit card
orders or a free
brochure of
Damron Guides
call
(800) 462-6654

### Chelan (509)

ACCOMMODATIONS
**Whaley Mansion** 415 3rd St. **682-5735/(800) 729-2408** gay-friendly • full brkfst • smokefree • $85-135

### Ellensburg (509)

INFO LINES & SERVICES
**Central Gay/Lesbian Alliance (CWU) 963-1391** contact Sally Thelen for more info

### Everett (206)

INFO LINES & SERVICES
**AA Gay/Lesbian** 2324 Lombard (church basement) **252-2525** 7pm Mon

BARS & NIGHTCLUBS
**Everett Underground** 1212 California Ave. **339-0807** 3pm-2am • lesbians/gay men • dancing/DJ • multi-racial • live shows • karaoke • food served • wheelchair access

BOOKSTORES & RETAIL SHOPS
**Orion at Twilight/Highlights** 2934-B Colby Ave. **303-8624** 11am-7pm, clsd Sun • metaphysical store • also publishes pagan newsletter

### Gig Harbor (206)

ENTERTAINMENT & RECREATION
**Blue Heron Sailing 851-5259** women-owned/run

### Kent (253)

BARS & NIGHTCLUBS
**Sappho's** 226 1st Ave. S. **813-2776** 3pm-2am, from 11am Sat, from 1pm Sun, clsd Tue • lesbians/gay men • neighborhood bar • dancing/DJ • karaoke • also restaurant

### Kirkland (206)

BOOKSTORES & RETAIL SHOPS
**Magazine City** 12063 124th Ave. NE **820-9264**

## La Conner (360)

ACCOMMODATIONS

**The Heron** 117 Maple Ave. **466-4626** gay-friendly • full brkfst • hot tub • smokefree • pets ok • wheelchair access
**The White Swan Guesthouse** 1388 Moore Rd., Mt. Vernon **445-6805** gay-friendly • 1890s farmhouse • also cabin avail. • smokefree • $75-135

## Lynnwood (206)

EROTICA

**Lynnwood Tattoo** 15315 Hwy. 99 #7 **742-8467**

## Mt. Vernon (360)

RESTAURANTS

**Deli Next Door** 210 S. 1st St. **336-3886** 9am-7pm, til 4pm Sun • healthy American • plenty veggie • wheelchair access • $4-6

BOOKSTORES & RETAIL SHOPS

**Scott's Bookstore** 121 Freeway Dr. **336-6181**

## Ocean Park (360)

ACCOMMODATIONS

**Shakti Cove** 665-4000 lesbians/gay men • cottages • $60-70

## Olympia (360)

INFO LINES & SERVICES

**Free at Last AA** 11th & Washington (United Church) **352-7344** 7pm Th
**Lesbian/Gay/Bisexual Support Services** **943-4662** 24hrs
**Queer Alliance** Evergreen State College **866-6000 x6544** social/support group

BARS & NIGHTCLUBS

**Thekla** 116 E. 5th Ave. **352-1855** 6pm-2am • gay-friendly • dancing/DJ • live shows • wheelchair access

BOOKSTORES & RETAIL SHOPS

**Bulldog News** 116 E. 4th Ave. **357-6397** 7am-9pm

SPIRITUAL GROUPS

**Eternal Light MCC** 219 'B' St. **352-8157**

## Pasco (509)

BARS & NIGHTCLUBS

**Out and About** 327 W. Lewis **545-4817** 5pm-2am • lesbians/gay men • dancing/DJ • wheelchair access

## Port Angeles (360)

ACCOMMODATIONS

**Maple Rose Inn** 112 Reservoir Rd. **457-7673/(800) 570-2007** gay-friendly • full brkfst • hot tub • smokefree • decks • $79 & up

## Port Townsend (360)

ACCOMMODATIONS

**Gaia's Getaway** 4343 Haines St. **385-1194** lesbians/gay men • large studio apt. in small village on Olympic peninsula • smokefree • $60
**The James House** 1238 Washington St. **385-1238** gay-friendly • smokefree • near tennis, golf & kayaking • $75-165
**Ravenscroft Inn** 533 Quincy St. **385-2784** gay-friendly • seaport inn w/views of Puget Sound • gourmet brkfst • smokefree • $67-165

## Pullman (509)

INFO LINES & SERVICES

**Washington State U. LesBiGay Group** **335-6388**

## San Juan Islands (360 )

ACCOMMODATIONS

**Blue Rose B&B** 1811 9th St., Anacortes **293-5175/(888) 293-5175** gay-friendly • full brkfst • $80-95
**The Gallery Suite B&B** 302 1st St., Langley **221-2978** gay-friendly • condo rental on the water • art gallery/B&B • smokefree • wheelchair access • $110
**The Inn at Swifts Bay** **468-3636** popular • gay-friendly • full brkfst • Tudor-style B&B on San Juan Islands • spa • fireplace • smokefree • IGLTA
**The Sea Haven II** 3766 S. Bells Rd., Langley **730-3766** gay-friendly • cottage on Whidbey Island w/view of Cascade Mtns. • women-owned/run • unconfirmed
**The Whidbey Inn** 106 1st St., Langley **221-7115** gay-friendly • full brkfst • located on bluff over Saratoga Passage Waterway & Mtns. • smokefree • $110-160
**WindSong B&B Inn** **376-2500/(800) 669-3948** gay-friendly • full brkfst • hot tub • smokefree • $115-140

## Seattle (206)

### INFO LINES & SERVICES

**Aradia Women's Health Center** 1300 Spring St. **323-9388** 10am-6pm, clsd Sun

**Capitol Hill Alano** 1222 E. Pine St. **587-2838 (AA#)/322-9590 (CLUB)** noon, 5:30pm & 8pm

**Counseling Service for Sexual Minorities** 1820 E. Pine **323-0220** noon-9pm, til 6pm Fri, clsd wknds

**FTM Outreach Phoneline** Ingersoll Gender Center **329-6651** 6pm-8pm Wed • live one-on-one info/support for FTMs, by FTMs

**Lambert House** 1818 15th Ave. **322-2735** 4pm-10pm, til midnight Fri-Sat, from noon Sat • drop-in center for sexual minority youth

**Lesbian Resource Center** 1808 Bellevue Ave. #204 **322-3953** 2pm-7pm, clsd wknds

**Partners Task Force for Gay/Lesbian Couples 935-1206**

**Seattle Bisexual Women's Network 517-7767** active social/support organization

**The TEN (The Eastside Network) 450-4890** social/support group for Seattle's East Side

### ACCOMMODATIONS

**B.D. Williams House** 1505 4th Ave. N. **285-0810/(800) 880-0810** gay-friendly • 1905 Queen Anne mini-mansion

**Bacon Mansion/Broadway Guesthouse** 959 Broadway **329-1864/(800) 240-1864** gay-friendly • Edwardian-style Tudor • IGLTA

▲ **Bed & Breakfast on Broadway** 722 Broadway Ave. E. **329-8933/(888) 329-8933** gay-friendly • full brkfst

**Capitol Hill Inn** 1713 Belmont Ave. **323-1955** gay-friendly • full brkfst

**Chambered Nautilus B&B** 5005 22nd Ave. NE **522-2536/(800) 545-8459** gay-friendly • full brkfst

**The Country Inn** 685 NW Juniper St., Issaquah **392-1010** gay-friendly • private estate • full brkfst • hot tub

▲ **Gaslight Inn** 1727 15th Ave. **325-3654** popular • gay-friendly • swimming • smokefree • IGLTA • $68-158

**Hill House B&B** 1113 E. John St. **720-7161/(800) 720-7161** popular • lesbians/gay men • full brkfst

**HAVE YOU HEARD?**

...ABOUT THE SIZZLING ALL-WOMEN VACATION FEATURING THE BEST PARTIES AND ENTERTAINMENT WITH 15,000 WOMEN FROM ACROSS THE PLANET!

...OF COURSE YOU HAVE

**1 (888) 44 DINAH**
**GIRL BAR & CLUB SKIRTS**

## Bed and Breakfast on Broadway

*Relax in elegant, quiet & intimate setting. Gleaming chandeliers, antiques, oriental rugs, paintings by NW artists and Russel Lyons grace this restored 1901 NW style home. Spacious rooms w/ private baths. Non-smoking. AMEX, MC, VISA.*

Toll Free 1-(888) 329-8933

722 Broadway Ave. East, Seattle, WA 98102

Don Fabian & Russel Lyons (206) 329-8933

# GASLIGHT INN

*A Seattle Tradition*

Private Baths
Continental Breakfast
Sundeck
Seasonal Heated Pool

*for longer stays, ask about the*
HOWELL STREET SUITES

6 Full Suites & 1 Studio      Off-Street Parking
Color Remote TV, Phone      Fax Available

1727 15th Ave. ❦ Seattle, WA 98112 ❦ 206/325-3654

# Seattle

**S**eattle's lush natural beauty—breathtaking views of Puget Sound and the Cascade Mountains—is actually more incredible than most let on. In addition, Seattle has small-town friendliness, as well as an international reputation for sophisticated cafe culture and cyber-cool.

The Space Needle is located in the Seattle Center, a complex that includes an opera house, Arena Coliseum and the Pacific Science Center. If the line isn't too long, take the Monorail from downtown. (Be sure to sit on the righthand side and keep your face pressed to the window. This scenic ride is almost over before it begins.) Another landmark is the quaint/touristy Pike Place Market (where all those commercials that feature mounds of fish are filmed).

For the perfect day trip, ferry over to the Olympic Peninsula and enjoy the fresh wilderness, or cruise by "Dykiki" a waterfront park on Lake Washington. Or sign up for an outdoors trip with one of the women-owned tour operators: **Adventure Associates** has trips listed in our *Tour Operators* section in the back of this book.

For shopping, the Broadway Market in queer Capitol Hill is a multi-cultural shopping center. **The Pink Zone** lesbian-owned body art shop is here, and we're told the girl-watching is best from the Market's espresso bar. If you're not a caffeine junkie, check out the **Gravity Bar** at the Market, where you can get almost any fruit or vegetable in liquid, shake or sandwich form.

Speaking of coffee, Seattle's hazy days have nurtured a *haute* coffee culture here—so be careful to order your java correctly, or ask questions if you're unsure. The natives respect frank ignorance more than confused pretense. Lattes—one-third espresso, two-thirds hot foamy milk—are the standard, and come iced or hot. Don't do dairy? Order a soy latte instead.

Of course, where to drink in Seattle is just as important as what to drink. For strong coffee served by strong women, stop in at **Cafe Vivace** on Denny. If, however, you want a hip cafe with comfy chairs, then muse away those hours in a wingback at **Cafe Paradiso.**

**Beyond the Closet** is the local lesbigay bookstore where you can get a copy of the **Seattle Gay News**. Seattle's main women's bar, **Wildrose Tavern,** is popular with the 30+ crowd, while 20-somethings head for the **Easy** or to the alterna-queer **Re-bar** on Thursdays. Country gals line-dance at **Timberline.**

For sex toys, check out **Toys in Babeland** women's erotica. Pick up your safer sex supplies at the non-profit **Rubber Tree.**

If you enjoy island life, ferry over to one of the San Juan Islands for a relaxing stay at one of the lesbian-friendly guesthouses. Or head up north to Vancouver, British Columbia, Seattle's beautiful Canadian cousin.

## Seattle (206)

**Where the Girls Are:** Living in the Capitol Hill District, south of Lake Union, and working in the Broadway Market, Pike Place Market, or somewhere in between.

**Entertainment:** Chicken Soup Brigade: 328-8979. Monthly gay bingo. Harvard Exit: 323-8986. Repertory film theater. Seattle's Gay Men's Chorus: 323-0750. Tacky Tourists: 233-8842. Sponsors annual Queen City Cruise, The Bump & other fabulous social events/fundraisers. Team Seattle: 322-7769. A 35-team gay network.

**Lesbigay Pride:** Freedom Day Committee: 346-0189. Last Sunday in June.

**Annual Events:**

September - AIDSwalk: 329-6923, 4th Sunday. Bumbershoot: 622-5123.

**City Info:** 461-5800.

**Attractions:** International District. Pike Place Market. Pioneer Square. Seattle Art Museum. Space Needle. Woodland Park Zoo.

**Best View:** Top of the Space Needle.

**Weather:** Winter's average temperature is 50° while summer temperatures can climb up into the 90°s. Be prepared for rain at any time during the year.

**Transit:** Farwest: 622-1717. Broadway Cab: 622-4800. Airport Shuttle Express: 622-1424. Metropolitan Transit: 553-3000.

▲ **Landes House B&B** 712 11th Ave. E. **329-8781/(888) 329-8781** lesbians/gay men • two 1906 houses joined by deck • hot tub • near Broadway

**Moonlight Bay B&B** 10710 SW Cowen Rd., Vashon Island **567-4333** lesbians/gay men

**Pioneer Square Hotel** 77 Yesler Wy. **340-1234/(800) 800-5514** gay-friendly

**Scandia House** 2028 34th Ave. S. **722-6216** gay-friendly

**The Shafer-Baillie Mansion** 907 14th Ave. E. **322-4654** gay-friendly • $79-115

**Wild Lily Ranch B&B** (360) 793-2103 lesbians/gay men • on Skykomish River • swimming • nudity • IGLTA

## BARS & NIGHTCLUBS

**C.C. Attle's** 1501 E. Madison **726-0565** 6am-2am • popular • mostly gay men • neighborhood bar • videos • also 'Cadillac Grill Diner' • 323-4017 • 7am-4am, 24hrs wknds • some veggie • wheelchair access

**Changes** 2103 N. 45th St. **545-8363** noon-2am • mostly gay men • neighborhood bar • beer/wine • wheelchair access

**The Cuff** 1533 13th Ave. **323-1525** 2pm-2am • popular • mostly gay men • leather • uniform bar • wheelchair access

**Double Header** 407 2nd Ave. **624-8439** 10am-1am • mostly gay men • neighborhood bar • 'one of the oldest gay bars in the US'

**The Easy** 916 E. Pike **323-8343** 11am-2am • mostly women • dancing/DJ • live shows • food served • wheelchair access

**Elite Tavern** 622 Broadway Ave. E. **324-4470** 10am-2am • lesbians/gay men • neighborhood bar • beer/wine • wheelchair access

**Elite Two** 1658 E. Olive Wy. **322-7334** noon-2am • lesbians/gay men • neighborhood bar • beer/wine

**Hana Restaurant & Lounge** 1914 8th Ave. **340-1536** noon-2am • mostly gay men • piano bar • Japanese food • wheelchair access

**HopScotch** 332 15th Ave. E. **322-4191** 11am-11pm, from 8am Sat, from 3pm Sun • gay-friendly • 100+ single malt scotches • food served

*Landes*

*House*

**BED & BREAKFAST**

712 11th Ave. East     Seattle, WA 98102

**(206) 329-8781**

**Kid Mohair** 1207 Pine St. **625-4444** 7pm-2am, clsd Mon • gay-friendly • women's night Wed • dancing/DJ • live shows • gay-friendly

**Mr. Paddywhacks** 722 E. Pike St. **322-4024**

**Neighbors Restaurant & Lounge** 1509 Broadway (entrance on alley) **324-5358** 3pm-2am, til 4am Fri-Sat, clsd Mon • popular • mostly gay men • dancing/DJ • live shows • wheelchair access

**Nitelite Cafe & Lounge** 1920 2nd Ave. **448-4852** noon-2am, from 10am wknds, restaurant 7am-11pm • gay-friendly • wheelchair access

**Oz Lounge** 1501 E. Olive Wy. **720-9963**

**R Place** 619 E. Pine **322-8828** 2pm-2am • mostly gay men • neighborhood bar • videos • 3 stories • wheelchair access

**Re-bar** 1114 Howell **233-9873** 9pm-2am • popular • gay-friendly • dancing/DJ • 'Queer Disco' Th • live shows

**Rendezvous** 2320 2nd Ave. **441-5823** gay-friendly • neighborhood bar

**Romper Room** 106 1st Ave. N. **284-5003** 4pm-2am, til 3am wknds • gay-friendly • dancing/DJ

**Safari Sportsbar & Grille** 1518 11th Ave. **328-4250** 11am-2am • lesbians/gay men • dancing/DJ • wheelchair access

**The Seattle Eagle** 314 E. Pike St. **621-7591** 2pm-2am • mostly gay men • leather • patio • wheelchair access

**Showbox** 1426 1st Ave. **628-3151** gay-friendly

**Six-Eleven Tavern** 611 2nd Ave. **340-9795** mostly gay men • neighborhood bar • beer/wine

**Tacky Tavern** 1706 Bellevue **720-8187** mostly gay men • neighborhood bar

**Thumpers** 1500 E. Madison St. **328-3800** 11am-2am • popular • mostly gay men • food served • more women in dining room • wheelchair access • $7-15

**Timberline Tavern** 2015 Boren Ave. **622-6220** 6pm-2am, from 4pm Sun, clsd Mon • lesbians/gay men • dancing/DJ • country/western • dance lessons 7:30pm Tue-Fri • beer/wine

**The Vogue** 2018 1st Ave. **443-0673** 9pm-2am • gay-friendly • dancing/DJ • live shows

**Wildrose Tavern & Restaurant** 1021 E. Pike St. **324-9210** 11am-midnight, til 2am Fri-Sat • mostly women • live shows • food served • some veggie • wheelchair access • $4-6

## CAFES

**Addis Cafe** 61224 E. Jefferson **325-7805** 8am-midnight • popular • Ethiopian • $3-7

**Beyond the Edge Cafe** 703 E. Pike St. **325-6829** 10am-11pm, til 5pm Sun • live shows

**Cafe Paradiso** 1005 E. Pike **322-6960** 6am-1am, til 4am Fri-Sat • popular

**Cafe Septieme** 214 Broadway Ave. E. **860-8858** 9am-midnight • popular • lesbians/gay men

**Cafe Vivace** 901 E. Denny Wy. #100 **860-5869** 6am-11pm • popular • very cute girls

## RESTAURANTS

**Al Boccalino** 1 Yesler Wy. **622-7688** 5pm-10pm • classy southern Italian

**Black Cat Cafe** 4110 Roosevelt Wy. NE **547-3887** 10:30am-8:30pm, clsd Mon • funky atmosphere • vegetarian • wheelchair access • under $5

**Campagne** 86 Pine St. **728-2800** 5:30pm-10pm • reservations recommended

**Dahlia Lounge** 1904 4th Ave. **682-4142** lunch & dinner • some veggie • full bar • $9-20

**Frontier Restaurant & Bar** 2203 1st Ave. **441-3377** 10am-2am • best cheap food in town • full bar • wheelchair access

**Giorgina's Pizza** 131 15th Ave. E. **329-8118** 11am-10pm, from 4pm Sat, clsd Sun

**Gravity Bar** 415 E. Broadway **325-7186** 9am-10pm • vegetarian/juice bar • also downtown location 448-8826 • wheelchair access

**Hamburger Mary's** 1525 E. Olive Wy. **324-8112**

**Jack's Bistro** 405 15th Ave. E. **324-9625** lunch & dinner, clsd Mon • some veggie • full bar • wheelchair access • $10-12

**Kokeb** 9261 12th Ave. **322-0485** lunch & dinner • Ethiopian • some veggie • full bar • $5-10

**Mae's Phinney Ridge Cafe** 6410 Phinney Ridge N. **782-1222** 7am-3pm • brkfst menu • some veggie • wheelchair access

**Plaza Mexico** 4116 University Wy. NE **633-4054** 11am-10pm • full bar

**Queen City Grill** 2201 1st Ave. **443-0975** noon-11pm, from 5pm wknds • popular • fresh seafood • some veggie • wheelchair access

**Sunlight Cafe** 6403 Roosevelt Wy. NE **522-9060** 7am-9pm • vegetarian • beer/wine • wheelchair access • $3-9

**Szmania's** 3321 W. McGraw St. **284-7305** lunch & dinner, clsd Mon

**Wild Ginger Asian Restaurant & Satay Bar** 1400 Western Ave. **623-4450** 5pm-midnight

## ENTERTAINMENT & RECREATION

**Dyke TV** 'weekly half-hour TV show produced by lesbians, for lesbians' • call (212) 343-9335 for more info

**Lesbian & Gay History Walking Tour** 1122 E. Pike St. #797 **233-8955** seasonal • call for info & reservations

**Parachutes over Snohomish (800) 338-5867 (JUMP)** train & jump the same day

## BOOKSTORES & RETAIL SHOPS

**Bailey/Coy Books** 414 Broadway Ave. E. **323-8842** 10am-10pm, til 11pm Fri-Sat, 11am-8pm Sun • wheelchair access

**Beyond the Closet Bookstore** 518 E. Pike **322-4609** 10am-10pm, til 11pm Fri-Sat • lesbigay

**Broadway Market** 401 E. Broadway popular • mall full of queer & hip stores

**Edge of the Circle** 701 E. Pike **726-1999** 10am-8pm • alternative spirituality store

**Fremont Place Book Company** 621 N. 35th **547-5970** 11am-6:30pm, til 8pm Fri-Sat • progressive bookstore

**Left Bank Books** 92 Pike St. **622-0195** worker-owned collective • some lesbigay titles

**Metropolis** 7220 Greenwood Ave. N. **782-7002** 10am-7pm • cards & gifts

**Pistil Books & News** 1013 E. Pike St. **325-5401** 10am-10pm, til midnight Fri-Sat, til 8pm Sun

**Red & Black Books** 432 15th Ave. E. **322-7323** 10am-8pm

**Sunshine Thrift Shops** 1605 12th Ave. #25 **324-9774** 11am-7pm, clsd Mon • non-profit for AIDS organizations

## PUBLICATIONS

**Gay Ink Magazine** 382-2644

**Lesbian Resource Center Community News (LRC)** 233-8631

**Seattle Sounds** 242-5240 alternative paper w/gay section

**SGN (Seattle Gay News)** 1605 12th Ave. #31 **324-4297** lesbigay newspaper

**The Stranger** 323-7101 queer-positive alternative weekly

**Women's Yellow Pages of NW Washington** 726-9687

## TRAVEL AGENTS

**All-Around Travel** 4701 42nd Ave. SW **938-3030/(800) 426-4505** IGLTA

**Business Travel NW** 100 S. King #300 **682-2915** IGLTA

**Capitol Hill Travel** 401 Broadway E. #204 (in the 'Broadway Market') **726-8996/(800) 726-8996** IGLTA

**Europe Express** 4040 Lake Washington Blvd. #101, Kirkland **(800) 927-3876** IGLTA

**It's Your World Travel** 1411 E. Olive Wy. **328-0616/(800) 955-6077** IGLTA

**Passport Travel** 6720 NE Bothell Wy. **365-6755/(800) 373-6160** IGLTA

**Progressive Travels** 224 W. Galer #C **285-1987/(800) 245-2229** IGLTA

**Royalty Travel** 1200 5th Ave., IBM Plaza Level West **623-7474** IGLTA

**Sunshine Travel** 519 N. 85th St. **784-8141** IGLTA

**Travel Solutions** 4009 Gilman Ave. W. **281-7202/(800) 727-1616** IGLTA

**Woodside Travel** 3130 E. Madison St. #102 **325-1266** IGLTA

## SPIRITUAL GROUPS

**Affirmation (Mormon)** 720-1768 monthly potluck • also newsletter

**Congregation Tikvah Chadashah** 20th Ave. E. & E. Prospect (Prospect Cong. Church) **329-2590** 8:15pm 2nd & 4th Fri • shabbat services

**Dignity Seattle** 723 18th Ave. E. (St. Joseph's Church) **325-7314** 7:30pm Sun • Catholic

**Grace Gospel Chapel** 2052 NW 64th St., Ballard **784-8495** 10am Sun & 7pm Wed

**Integrity Puget Sound** 1245 10th Ave. E. (Chapel of St. Mark's) **525-4668** 7pm Sun

**MCC** 704 E. 19th (Russian Center) **325-2421** 11am Sun

## GYMS & HEALTH CLUBS

**BQ Workout** (in the 'Broadway Market') **860-3070** gay-friendly • day passes avail.

**World Gym** 825 Pike St. **583-0640**

## EROTICA

**The Crypt** 1310 E. Union St. **325-3882**

**Fantasy Unlimited** 102 Pike St. **682-0167**

**Onyx Leather** 328-1965 by appt. only

**The Pink Zone** 401 Broadway E. (in the 'Broadway Market') **325-0050** tattoos • piercings

**The Rubber Tree** 4426 Burke Ave. N. **633-4750** 10am-7pm, clsd Sun • non-profit safer sex supplies • referrals

Toys in Babeland 711 E. Pike 328-2914
women's sex toy store

## Seaview (360)

### ACCOMMODATIONS
Sou'wester Lodge Beach Access Rd.
(38th Place) 642-2542 gay-friendly •
inexpensive suites, cabins w/kitchens &
vintage trailers • smokefree • $39-109

## Spokane (509)

### INFO LINES & SERVICES
AA Gay/Lesbian 224 S. Howard
(upstairs) 624-1442 6:30pm Mon
Lesbian/Gay Community Services
Hotline 489-2266 24hrs
Rainbow Regional Community Center
224 S. Howard St. 458-2741

### ACCOMMODATIONS
Sun Flower Cottage 4114 N. Wall St.
326-7707 lesbians/gay men • full brkfst •
smokefree

### BARS & NIGHTCLUBS
Dempsey's Brass Rail 909 W. 1st St.
747-5362 3pm-2am • popular • les-
bians/gay men • dancing/DJ • also
restaurant • wheelchair access • $5-12
Hour Place 415 W. Sprague 838-6947
noon-2am • lesbians/gay men • danc-
ing/DJ • also restaurant • some veggie •
wheelchair access • $5-8
Pumps II W. 4 Main St. 747-8940 3pm-
2am, from noon wknds • lesbians/gay
men • dancing/DJ • live shows • food
served

### BOOKSTORES & RETAIL SHOPS
Auntie's Bookstore & Cafe W. 402 Main
St. 838-0206 9am-9pm, 11am-6pm Sun •
wheelchair access
Boo Radley's 232 N. Howard 456-7479
10am-7pm, 11am-6pm Sun • gift shop
Rings & Things 714 W. Main St. 624-
8949 gay gifts

### PUBLICATIONS
Stonewall News Spokane 456-8011

### TRAVEL AGENTS
Edwards LaLone Travel S. 5
Washington 747-3000/(800) 288-3788
IGLTA

### SPIRITUAL GROUPS
Emmanuel MCC 307 W. 4th Ave. 838-
0085 10:30am Sun

## Tacoma (206)

### INFO LINES & SERVICES
AA Gay/Lesbian 209 S. 'J' St. (church)
474-8897 7:30pm Mon & Fri • 7:30pm
Tue (301 N. 'K' St.)
Oasis 596-2860 lesbigay youth group
run by Health Dept.
Tacoma Lesbian Concern 752-6724
social events • resource list

### ACCOMMODATIONS
Chinaberry Hill 302 Tacoma Ave. N. 272-
1282 gay-friendly • very romantic • full
brkfst • hot tub • kids ok • smokefree •
$95-125

### BARS & NIGHTCLUBS
24th Street Tavern 2409 Pacific Ave.
572-3748 noon-2am • lesbians/gay men
• dancing/DJ • transgender-friendly • live
shows • beer/wine • wheelchair access
733 Restaurant & Lounge 733
Commerce St. 305-9872 6pm-2am • les-
bians/gay men • dancing/DJ • transgender-friendly • live shows
The Gold Ball Grill & Spirits 2708 6th
Ave. 305-9861/627-0430 8am-2am • les-
bians/gay men • neighborhood bar •
dancing/DJ • transgender-friendly •
karaoke • beer garden • gambling
Spout & Toad 1111 Center St. 272-1412
6am-2am • gay-friendly • also restaurant

### PUBLICATIONS
South End News 927-4130/292-1099
Tacoma's Own 756-0520

### SPIRITUAL GROUPS
New Heart MCC 2150 S. Cushman 272-
2382 11am Sun & 7pm Wed

## Vancouver (360)

*(see also Portland, OR)*

### BARS & NIGHTCLUBS
North Bank Tavern 106 W. 6th St. 695-
3862 noon-2am • lesbians/gay men •
beer/wine • food served • wheelchair
access

### TRAVEL AGENTS
First Discount Travel 11700 NE 95th St.
#110 896-6200/(800) 848-1926 ask for
Carl • IGLTA

### SPIRITUAL GROUPS
MCC of the Gentle Shepherd 4505 E.
18th St. (church) 695-1480 6pm Sun •
wheelchair access

## WEST VIRGINIA

### Beckley (304)

EROTICA
**Blue Moon Video** 3427 Robert C. Byrd Dr. **255-1200** clsd Sun

### Berkeley Springs (304)

EROTICA
**Action Books & Video** Rte. 522 S. **258-2529**

### Bluefield (304)

BARS & NIGHTCLUBS
**The Shamrock** 326 Princeton Ave. **327-9570** Fri-Sat only • lesbians/gay men • dancing/DJ

### Charleston (304)

INFO LINES & SERVICES
**COGLES (Community Oriented Gay/Lesbian Events/Services)** 1517 Jackson St. **345-0491**
**West Virginia Lesbian/Gay Coalition** **343-7305**
**West Virginia Tourism Division** (800) **225-5982**

BARS & NIGHTCLUBS
**Broadway** 210 Broad St. **343-2162** 4pm-3am, from 1pm wknds • mostly gay men • dancing/DJ • private club • wheelchair access
**Grand Palace** 617 Brooks St. **342-9532** noon-2:30am • mostly gay men • dancing/DJ • live shows • videos • private club
**Tap Room** 1022 Quarrier St. (enter rear) **342-9563** 5pm-midnight, later wknds • mostly gay men • neighborhood bar • private club

RESTAURANTS
**Lee Street Deli** 1109 Lee St. E. **343-3354** 11am-3pm, bar til 1am

PUBLICATIONS
**Graffiti** 1505 Lee St. **342-4412** alternative entertainment guide • mostly non-gay

### Huntington (304)

BARS & NIGHTCLUBS
**Driftwood Lounge** 1121 7th Ave. **696-9858** 5pm-3am • lesbians/gay men • dancing/DJ • videos • wheelchair access • also 'Beehive' upstairs • open wknds • lesbians/gay men • live shows
**Polo Club** 733 7th Ave. (enter rear) **522-3146** 3pm-3:30am • lesbians/gay men • more women Tue • dancing/DJ • live shows • private club • wheelchair access
**The Stonewall** 820 7th Ave. (enter rear) **528-9317** 5pm-3:30am • popular • lesbians/gay men • more women Wed-Th • dancing/DJ

RESTAURANTS
**Calamity Cafe** 1555 3rd Ave. **525-4171** 11am-10pm, til 3am wknds • live shows • Southern/Western • plenty veggie • full bar • wheelchair access • $10-15

EROTICA
**Bookmark Video** 1119 4th Ave. **525-6861**
**House of Video** 1109 4th Ave. **525-2194**

### Lost River (304)

ACCOMMODATIONS
**The Guesthouse** Settlers Valley Wy. **897-5707** lesbians/gay men • full brkfst • swimming • steam & spa • smokefree • $108-116

### Martinsburg (304)

EROTICA
**Variety Books & Video** 255 N. Queen St. **263-4334** 24hrs

### Morgantown (304)

INFO LINES & SERVICES
**Gay/Lesbian Switchboard** **292-4292**

BARS & NIGHTCLUBS
**Class Act** 335 High St. (enter rear) **292-2010** 8pm-3am, clsd Mon • lesbians/gay men • dancing/DJ • live shows • private club

TRAVEL AGENTS
**Suncrest Travel** 428 Oakland St. **599-2056**/(800) 627-8669 IGLTA

EROTICA
**Select Books & Videos** 237 Walnut St. **292-7714** 24hrs

## Stonewall Jackson Lake (304)

ACCOMMODATIONS
**FriendSheep Farm** 462-7075 mostly women • secluded retreat • campsites • smokefree

## Upper Tract (304)

ACCOMMODATIONS
**Wildernest Inn** 257-9076 gay-friendly • full brkfst • smokefree • $65-85

## Wheeling (304)

BARS & NIGHTCLUBS
**Tricks** 1429 Market St. (behind 'Market St. News') 232-1267 9pm-2am, til 3am Fri, clsd Mon-Tue • lesbians/gay men • dancing/DJ • live shows

EROTICA
**Market St. News** 1437 Market St. 232-2414 24hrs

# WISCONSIN

## Appleton (414)

BARS & NIGHTCLUBS
**Diversions** 1413 Green Valley, Neenah 725-3374 7pm-2am, from 3pm Sun, clsd Mon • lesbians/gay men • dancing/DJ • live shows

**Rascals Bar & Grill** 702 E. Wisconsin Ave. 954-9262 5pm-2am, from noon Sun • lesbians/gay men • more women Fri • food served • patio

## Aztalan (414)

BARS & NIGHTCLUBS
**Crossroads Bar** W. 6642 Hwy. 'B', Lake Mills 648-8457 1pm-2am, clsd Mon • gay-friendly

## Baileys Harbor (414)

ACCOMMODATIONS
**Blacksmith Inn B&B** 839-9222 gay-friendly

## Beloit (608)

BOOKSTORES & RETAIL SHOPS
**A Different World** 414 E. Grand Ave. 365-1000 10am-8:30pm, til 5pm Mon, clsd Sun • women's & children's books

## Eagle River (715)

ACCOMMODATIONS
**Edgewater Inn** 5054 Hwy. 70 W. 479-4011 gay-friendly • non-smoking rms avail. • kids ok

## Eau Claire (715)

ACCOMMODATIONS
**Back of the Moon** F-3625 Country Rd. N., Augusta 286-2409 women only • B&B retreat • smokefree

BARS & NIGHTCLUBS
**Scooters** 411 Galloway (behind adult bookstore) 835-9959 5pm-2am, from 3pm wknds • lesbians/gay men • dancing/DJ • live shows • wheelchair access

**The Trading Company** 304 Eau Claire St. 838-9494 9pm-2:30am, clsd Sun-Mon • mostly gay men • dancing./DJ • live shows

**Wolf's Den** 302 E. Madison 832-9237 6pm-2:30am • mostly gay men • neighborhood bar

## Geneva Lakes (414)

ACCOMMODATIONS
**Allyn Mansion Inn** 511 East Walworth Ave., Delavan 728-9090 gay-friendly • full brkfst • smokefree • gay-owned

**Eleven Gables Inn on the Lake** 493 Wrigley Dr., Lake Geneva 248-8393/(800) 362-0395 gay-friendly • full brkfst wknds • smokefree • wheelchair access • $109-179

RESTAURANTS
**C.J. Wiz's** 126 'B' E. (Geneva Sq. Mall) 248-1949 unconfirmed

## Green Bay (414)

INFO LINES & SERVICES
**Gay AA** 494-9904 call for mtg. schedule

BARS & NIGHTCLUBS
**Brandy's II** 1126 Main St. 437-3917 11am-2am • mostly gay men • neighborhood bar

**Java's/Za's** 1106 Main St. 435-5476 8pm-2:30am • lesbians/gay men • dancing/DJ • videos • 18+ Sun

**Napalese Lounge** 515 S. Broadway 432-9646 3pm-2am • mostly gay men • wheelchair access

**Sass** 840 S. Broadway 437-7277 5pm-2am, from noon Sun (winters) • lesbians/gay men • dancing/DJ

PUBLICATIONS
**Quest** PO Box 1961, 54301

SPIRITUAL GROUPS
**Angel of Hope MCC** 614 Forest St. **432-0830** 11am Sun

## Hayward (715)

ACCOMMODATIONS
**The Lake House** 5793 Division on the Lake, Stone Lake **865-6803** gay-friendly • full brkfst • swimming • smokefree • kids ok by arr. • wheelchair access • lesbian-owned/run •$55-75

## Hazel Green (608)

ACCOMMODATIONS
**Percival's Country Inn** 1030 S. Percival St. (Hwy. 80) **854-2881/484-5306 CODE 3344** queen suites • full brkfst • jacuzzi • smokefree • wheelchair access

## Hazelhurst (715)

BARS & NIGHTCLUBS
**Willow Haven Resort/Supper Club** 4877 Haven Dr. **453-3807** gay-friendly • cabin rentals • full bar • $8-16

## Hixton (715)

ACCOMMODATIONS
**Inn at Pine Ridge** 984-2272 women only • full vegetarian brunch • hot tub • sauna • lesbian-owned/run • $40-80

## Kenosha (414)

*(see also Racine)*

BARS & NIGHTCLUBS
**Club 94** 9001 120th Ave. **857-9958** 7pm-2am, from 3pm Sun, clsd Mon • popular • lesbians/gay men • dancing/DJ • live shows • videos

## La Crosse (608)

INFO LINES & SERVICES
**Gay/Lesbian Support Group** 126 N. 17th St. **784-7600** 7:30pm Sun

ACCOMMODATIONS
**Chela's B&B and Forest Camping Retreat** Gays Mills **735-4829** women only • camping on 35 acres of women's land • also 2 rms. avail. • full brkfst • sauna • kids/pets ok • lesbian-owned/run • $10 camping/ $50 room

**Trillium B&B** 625-4492 gay-friendly • also cottages (sleep 5) • 35 mi. from La Crosse • full brkfst

BARS & NIGHTCLUBS
**Cavalier** 114 N. 5th **782-9061** 2pm-2am • gay-friendly • gay evenings only • wheelchair access
**Rainbow's End** 417 Jay St. **782-9802** 11am-2am, from 6pm Sat, clsd Sun • lesbians/gay men • neighborhood bar

BOOKSTORES & RETAIL SHOPS
**Rainbow Revolution** 122 5th Ave. S. **796-0383** 10am-5:30pm, til 5pm Sat, clsd Sun • alternative • wheelchair access
**Red Oaks Books** 323 Pearl St. **782-3424** 9am-8pm, til 9pm Fri, 10am-5pm wknds • lesbigay section

PUBLICATIONS
**Leaping La Crosse** 783-0069 newsletter

## Laona (715)

ACCOMMODATIONS
**Laona Hostel** 5397 Beech St. **674-2615** gay-friendly • dorm-style/youth hostel rms

## Madison (608)

INFO LINES & SERVICES
**Apple Island** 849 E. Washington **258-9777** women's space • sponsors social events
**Campus Women's Center** 710 University Rm. 202 (UW) **262-8093** support programs
**Gay Line** 255-4297 9am-9pm, clsd wknds
**Lesbian Line** 255-0743 9am-9pm, clsd wknds
**LesBiGay Campus Center** 510 Memorial Union **265-3344** drop-in 9am-4pm • social events • general info
**The United** 14 West Mifflin St. #103 **255-8582** 9am-9pm, clsd wknds • drop-in center • library • newsletter • AA group meets 6pm Sat
**Wisconsin Division of Tourism** (800) 432-8747

ACCOMMODATIONS
**Prairie Garden B&B** W. 13172 Hwy. 188, Lodi **592-5187/(800) 380-8427** lesbians/gay men • 30 min. from Madison • full brkfst • smokefree • kids/pets by arr. • $55-115

## BARS & NIGHTCLUBS

**Cardinal** 418 E. Wilson St. **251-0080** 8pm-2am, clsd Mon • gay-friendly • more gay Th • dancing/DJ

**Flamingo** 636 State **257-3330** 8pm-2am • gay-friendly • college crowd • lunch served 11am-2pm

**Geraldine's** 3052 E. Washington Ave. **241-9335** 4pm-2am • lesbians/gay men • dancing/DJ

**Green Bush** 914 Regent St. **257-2874** 4pm-2am • gay-friendly • food served

**Manoeuvres** 150 S. Blair (at the 'Wilson Hotel') **258-9918** 4pm-2am, clsd Mon • mostly gay men • dancing/DJ • videos

**Shamrock** 117 W. Main St. **255-5029** 2pm-2am, from 11am Fri-Sat, from 5pm Sun • lesbians/gay men • dancing/DJ • also grill • wheelchair access • $2-4

## RESTAURANTS

**Monty's Blue Plate Diner** 2089 Atwood Ave. **244-8505** 7am-10pm, til 9pm Sun-Tue, from 7:30am wknds • some veggie • beer/wine • wheelchair access • $5

**Wild Iris** 1225 Regent St. **257-4747** 11:45am-10pm, from 9am wknds • Italian/Cajun • some veggie • beer/wine • $8-12

## ENTERTAINMENT & RECREATION

**Dyke TV** Channel 4 8:30pm Mon • 'weekly half-hour TV show produced by lesbians, for lesbians'

**Nothing to Hide** cable Ch. 4 **241-2500** 8:30pm Wed • lesbigay TV show

## BOOKSTORES & RETAIL SHOPS

**A Room of One's Own** 317 W. Johnson St. **257-7888** 9:30am-8pm, 10am-6pm Tue, Wed & Sat, noon-5pm Sun • women's books • music

**Borders Book Shop** 3416 University Ave. **232-2600** 9am-11pm, til 8pm Sun • les-bigay section • also espresso bar

**Going Places** 2860 University Ave. **233-1920** travel-oriented books

**Mimosa** 212 N. Henry **256-5432** 9:30am-6pm, noon-5pm Sun • self-help books

**Pic-A-Book** 506 State St. **256-1125** 9am-8pm, til 5pm Sun

# Outdoor Trips...for women.

### Adventures for all seasons!

**Snowshoeing, kayaking, backpacking...and more.
Day excursions to two week trips.**

We'll take you fly fishing and biking in warm weather, cross country skiing and winter camping when the snow is falling and many more activities for every season in between.

Camping or lodge accommodations available.

Call or write for a brochure.

## Pathways and Passages

P.O. Box 158   Montello, WI 53949   (608) 297-7440

**We Are Family** 524 E. Wilson (at the 'Wilson Hotel') 258-9006 noon-9pm, from 8am Sat • pride gifts • espresso

PUBLICATIONS
**Of a Like Mind** 257-5858 women's newsletter of goddess spirituality

TRAVEL AGENTS
▲ **Pathways & Passages** 297-7440
**Dan's Travel** The Gateway, 600 Williamson St. 251-1110/(800) 476-0305 IGLTA

SPIRITUAL GROUPS
**Integrity/Dignity** 1001 University Ave. (St. Francis Episcopal) 836-8886 7:30pm 2nd & 4th Sun (Sept-May)
**James Reeb Unitarian Universalist Church** 2146 E. Johnson St. 242-8887 10am Sun (summers) • call for winter hours

EROTICA
**Piercing Lounge** 520 University Ave. #120 284-0870
**Red Letter News** 2528 E. Washington 241-9958 24hrs

## Maiden Rock (715)

ACCOMMODATIONS
**Eagle Cove B&B** 448-4302/(800) 467-0279 gay-friendly • hot tub • smokefree • pets ok • wheelchair access • $50-100

## Mauston (608)

ACCOMMODATIONS
**CK's Outback** W 5627 Clark Rd. 847-5247 women only • B&B • camping

## Milton (608)

ACCOMMODATIONS
**Chase on the Hill B&B** 11624 State Rd. 26 868-6646 gay-friendly • full brkfst

## Milwaukee (414)

INFO LINES & SERVICES
**AA Galano Club** 2408 N. Farwell Ave. 276-6936 call after 5pm for mtg. schedule
**AA Gay/Lesbian** 771-9119
**Black Gay Conciousness Raising** 933-2136 7:30pm 3rd Mon • call for info
**Gay Information & Services** 444-7331 24hr referral service
**Gay People's Union Hotline** 562-7010 7pm-10pm

## Milwaukee (414)

**Where the Girls Are:** In East Milwaukee south of downtown, spread out from Lake Michigan to S. Layton Blvd.

**Annual Events:** June - Pagan Spirit Gathering: 608/924-2216. Summer solstice celebration in Mt. Horeb.

**City Info:** 800/231-0903.

**Attractions:** Annunciation Greek Orthodox Church. Breweries. Grand Avenue. Mitchell Park Horticultural Conservatory. Summerfest. Pabst Theatre.

**Best View:** 41st story of First Wisconsin Center. Call 765-5733 to arrange a visit to the top floor observatory.

**Weather:** Summer temperatures can get up into 90°s. Spring and fall are pleasantly moderate but too short. Winter brings snows, cold temperatures and even colder wind chills.

**Transit:** Yellow Cab: 271-6630. Milwaukee Transit: 344-6711.

# Milwaukee

*M*ilwaukee holds a place of honor in the collective dyke cultural memory as the home of TV's Laverne & Shirley, a cute couple if we ever saw one. (You didn't really think that big "L" on Laverne's chest was a monogram, did you?)

You'll find plenty of breweries in this historically German-American city...and plenty of lesbians, too. The bars here are relaxed: **B's Bar** is a country/western dance bar with more women on weekends, **Fannie's** is a beer-garden with a dancefloor, while **Kathy's Nut Hut** and **Station 2** are more intimate bars. **Club 219** is a mixed lesbian/gay bar with dancing, shows and a multi-racial clientele. **AfterWords** is the lesbigay bookstore, and it's got an espresso bar to boot!

Women of color can hook up with others via the social group, **Imani** or **PACT**. For other groups, scan one of the local papers, or call the **Gay Information & Services Line.**

Just an hour-and-a-half west of Milwaukee is Madison—home of the University of Wisconsin, and, from what we hear, a hotbed of academic & cultural feminism. That includes dyke separatism and feminist spirituality, as well as anti-violence and anti-pornography activism. If that branch of feminism interests you, call the **Campus Women's Center,** the **Lesbigay Center** or **Apple Island** for current events. Stop by **A Room of One's Own** for a copy of the local publication **Of A Like Mind**, an excellent resource for pagan women's networking.

Gay Youth Milwaukee 265-8500/(888) 429-8336 (OUTSIDE MILWAUKEE)
Gemini Gender Group 297-9328 2nd Sat • transgender support • call for location
Imani 521-4565 social/support group for Black lesbians
Lesbian Alliance 264-2600
PACT (People of All Colors Together) 871-3048 3rd Sun • newsletter
SAGE Milwaukee 271-0378 for older lesbigays • call after 4pm
Ujima 272-3009 African-American social/support group

## ACCOMMODATIONS

Park East Hotel 916 E. State St. 276-8800/(800) 328-7275 gay-friendly • smokefree • also restaurant • some veggie • wheelchair access • $10-15

## BARS & NIGHTCLUBS

10% Club 4322 Fond du Lac 447-0910 3pm-2am, from 4pm wknds • lesbians/gay men • neighborhood bar
1100 Club 1100 S. 1st St. 647-9950 7am-2am • mostly gay men • dancing/DJ • food served • $4-15
The B's Bar 1579 S. 2nd St. 672-5580 3pm-2am, from noon wknds • lesbians/gay men • more women wknds
Club 219 219 S. 2nd St. 271-3732 5pm-2am • lesbians/gay men • dancing/DJ • multi-racial • live shows
Emeralds 801 E. Hadley 265-7325 1:30pm-2am • mostly gay men
Fannie's 200 E. Washington St. 643-9633 7pm-2am, from 4pm Sun • popular • mostly women • wheelchair access
Grubb's Pub & Le Grill 807 S. 2nd St. 384-8330 9pm-3:30am • lesbians/gay men

# DINAH SHORE
## PALM SPRINGS WEEKEND
### MARCH 26-29, 1998

The Ultimate Hotel & Entertainment Package at the All Inclusive
**DOUBLE TREE RESORT**
Book today to ensure availability. For hotel and party ticket Info Call
**310.281.7358**

For Airline reservations call
1•800•433•1790

Produced by JOANI WEIR PRODUCTIONS • POM POM PRODUCTIONS • KLUB BANSHEE

**Henry's Pub at Coffee Trader** 2625 N. Downer Ave. **332-9690** noon-2am • lesbians/gay men • full menu • wheelchair access

**Just Us** 807 S. 5th St. **383-2233** 5pm-2am, from 4pm Fri, from 6pm Sat • lesbians/gay men • dancing/DJ • transgender-friendly

**Kathy's Nut Hut** 1500 W. Scott **647-2673** 2pm-2am, from noon wknds • mostly women • neighborhood bar • also grill menu • use caution in the neighborhood

**La Cage (Dance, Dance, Dance)** 801 S. 2nd St. **383-8330** 9pm-2am • popular • mostly gay men • more women wknds • dancing/DJ • live shows • food served • wheelchair access

**M&M Club** 124 N. Water St. **347-1962** 11am-2am • mostly gay men • more women wknds • live shows • food served • some veggie • wheelchair access • $5-10

**Mama Roux** 1875 N. Humboldt **347-0344** 3pm-2am • lesbians/gay men • Jamaican/Cajun menu • wheelchair access

**The Nomad** 1401 E. Brady St. **224-8111** noon-2am • gay-friendly • sponsors 'Women's Music Week'

**Renez Coz Corner II** 3500 W. Park Hill Ave. **933-7363** 8pm-2am, clsd Mon • lesbians/gay men • dancing/DJ • multiracial

**South Water Street Dock** 354 E. National **225-9676** 3pm-2am • mostly gay men • wheelchair access

**Station 2** 1534 W. Grant **383-5755** 6pm-midnight, til 2:30am Fri-Sat, clsd Tue • mostly women • neighborhood bar

**Walker's Point Marble Arcade** 1101 S. 2nd St. **647-9430** 3pm-2am • lesbians/gay men • bowling alley • live shows • food served • wheelchair access

**Zippers** 819 S. 2nd St. **645-8330** 3pm-2am, 2pm-2:30am wknds • mostly gay men

## CAFES

**Cafe Knickerbocker** 1030 E. Juneau Ave. **272-0011** 6:30am-10pm, til 11pm wknds • popular • some veggie • full bar • wheelchair access • $8-15

**Cafe Melange** 720 N. 3rd St. **291-9889** 6am-2am, from 11am wknds • wheelchair access • $10 & up

**Walkers Point Cafe** 1106 S. 1st St. **384-7999** 10am-4am

## RESTAURANTS

**La Perla** 734 S. 5th St. **645-9888** 10:30am-10pm, til 11:30pm Fri-Sat • Mexican • $7-14

**Wild Thyme Cafe** 231 E. Buffalo **276-3144** lunch & brunch

## BOOKSTORES & RETAIL SHOPS

**AfterWords Bookstore & Espresso Bar** 2710 N. Murray **963-9089** 10am-10pm, til 11pm Fri-Sat, noon-6pm Sun • lesbigay • wheelchair access

**Designing Men** 1200 S. 1st St. **389-1200** noon-7pm, from 3pm Mon-Tue, til 10pm Fri-Sat, til 6pm Sun

**Peoples' Books** 3512 N. Oakland Ave. **962-0575** 10am-7pm, til 6pm Sat, noon-5pm Sun

**Schwartz Bookstore** 209 E. Wisconsin Ave. **274-6400** 9:30am-5:30pm, clsd Sun

**Yellow Jacket** 2225 N. Humboldt Ave. **372-4744** noon-7pm, til 5pm Sun • vintage clothes

## PUBLICATIONS

**In Step** 278-7840

**Q Voice** 278-7524

**Wisconsin Light** 372-2773

**Women's Yellow Pages of Greater Milwaukee** 789-1346

## TRAVEL AGENTS

**American Express Travel Service** 330 E. Silver Spring Dr. **332-3157x227** IGLTA

**Horizon Travel** N81 W15028 Appleton Ave., Menomonee Falls **255-0704/(800) 562-0219** IGLTA

**Landmark Enterprises** 735 N. Water St. **276-6355** IGLTA

**Travel Consultants** 2222 N. Mayfair, Wauwatosa **453-8300/(800) 486-0975** IGLTA

**Travel Experience** 501 E. Otjen **744-6020/(800) 707-3767** IGLTA

**Trio Travel** 2812 W. Forest Home Ave. **384-8746/(800) 417-4159** IGLTA

## SPIRITUAL GROUPS

**Dignity** 2506 Wauwatosa Ave. (St. Pius X Church) **444-7177** 6pm Sun

**First Unitarian Society** 1342 N. Astor **273-5257** 9:30am Sun

**Integrity** 914 E. Knapp **276-6277**

**Lutherans Concerned** 372-9663 call for info

**Milwaukee MCC** 924 E. Juneau (Astor Hotel) **332-9995** 11am & 7pm Sun

**St. James Episcopal Church** 833 W. Wisconsin Ave. **271-1340** 10:30am Sun • call for wkday service schedule

EROTICA
**Booked Solid** 7035 W. Greenfield Ave., West Allis **774-7210**
**Popular News** 225 N. Water St. **278-0636** toys • B&D videos

## Mineral Point (608)

ACCOMMODATIONS
**The Cothren House** 320 Tower St. **987-2612** gay-friendly • full brkfst • gay-owned/run

RESTAURANTS
**Chesterfield Inn** 20 Commerce St. **987-3682** seasonal • Cornish/American • some veggie • full bar • $10-16

## Oshkosh (414)

*(see also Appleton)*

EROTICA
**Pure Pleasure** 1212 Oshkosh Ave. **235-9727**

## Racine (414)

BARS & NIGHTCLUBS
**JoDee's International** 2139 Racine St. (S. Hwy. 32) **634-9804** 7pm-2am • lesbians/gay men • dancing/DJ • live shows • courtyard
**What About Me?** 600 6th St. **632-0171** 7pm-2am, from 3pm Tue & Fri, clsd Mon • lesbians/gay men • neighborhood bar

EROTICA
**Racine News & Video** 316 Main St. **634-9827**

## Sheboygan (414)

BARS & NIGHTCLUBS
**The Blue Lite** 1029 N. 8th St. **457-1636** 2pm-2am, til 2:30am Fri-Sat • mostly gay men • neighborhood bar

## Stevens Point (715)

INFO LINES & SERVICES
**Women's Resource Center** 1209 Fremont (University of Wisconsin Nelson Hall) **346-4242 x4851** 10am-4pm, clsd wknds • some lesbian outreach

BARS & NIGHTCLUBS
**Platwood Club** 701 Hwy. 10 W. **341-8862** 9pm-close Th-Sat • lesbians/gay men • dancing/DJ • wheelchair access

## Sturgeon Bay (414)

ACCOMMODATIONS
**Chadwick Inn B&B** 25 N. 8th Ave. **743-2771** gay-friendly
**The Chanticleer B&B** 4072 Cherry Rd. **746-0334** gay-friendly • swimming • smokefree • kids ok • wheelchair access • $115-175

## Superior (715)

BARS & NIGHTCLUBS
**JT's Bar & Grill** 1506 N. 3rd St. **394-2580** 4pm-2am, from 1pm wknds • popular • lesbians/gay men • dancing/DJ • wheelchair access
**The Main Club** 1217 Tower Ave. **392-1756** 3pm-2am, til 2:30am Fri-Sat • mostly gay men • dancing/DJ • wheelchair access
**Molly & Oscar's** 405 Tower Ave. **394-7423** 3pm-2am, til 2:30am Fri-Sat • gay-friendly • neighborhood bar
**Trio** 820 Tower Ave. **392-5373** 1pm-2am • mostly women • neighborhood bar • wheelchair access

## Wascott (715)

ACCOMMODATIONS
**Wilderness Way** 466-2635 women only • resort property • cabins • camping • RV sites • swimming • camping $12-16 • cottages $48-68

## Wausau (715)

BARS & NIGHTCLUBS
**Oz** 320 Washington **842-3225** 7pm-2am, from 5pm Th-Fri, from 4pm Sun • lesbians/gay men • dancing/DJ • wheelchair access

## Winter (715)

ACCOMMODATIONS
**Flambeau Forest Resort** 332-5236 gay-friendly • wheelchair access

## WYOMING

### Cheyenne (307)

INFO LINES & SERVICES
**United Gay/Lesbians of Wyoming** 632-5362 info • referrals • also newsletter

EROTICA
**Cupid's** 511 W. 17th **635-3837**

### Etna (307)

BOOKSTORES & RETAIL SHOPS
**Blue Fox Studio & Gallery** 107452 Hwy. 89 **883-3310** open 7 days • hours vary • pottery & jewelry studio • local travel info

### Jackson (208)

ACCOMMODATIONS
**Bar H Ranch** (208) 354-2906/(800) 244-1444 seasonal • lesbians/gay men • also women-only horseback riding trips in Grand Tetons (see 'WomanTours' or 'Bar H Ranch' under Tour Operators section) • lesbian-owned/run

**Fish Creek Lodging** (208) 652-7566 lesbians/gay men • rental log cabin • kids ok • women-owned/run

**Nowlin Creek Inn** 733-0882 gay-friendly • B&B • log cabin • full brkfst • hot tub • $95-225

**Redmond Guest House** 110 Redmond St., Jackson Hole 733-4003 seasonal • lesbians/gay men• apt. rental • smoke-free • kids/pets ok • lesbian-owned/run • $110

**Spring Creek Resort** 1800 Spirit Dance Rd. 733-8833/(800) 443-6139 popular • gay-friendly • swimming • non-smoking rms. avail. • food served • wheelchair access

**Three Peaks Inn** 53 S. Hwy. 33, Driggs ID (208) 354-8912 gay-friendly • full brkfst • kids ok • women-owned/run

BOOKSTORES & RETAIL SHOPS
**Valley Books** 125 N. Cache 733-4533

### Riverton (307)

RESTAURANTS
**Country Cove** 301 E. Main **856-9813** 7am-3pm, 5pm-9pm • seafood • plenty veggie • wheelchair access • women-owned/run • $7-10

### Thermopolis (307)

ACCOMMODATIONS
**Out West B&B** 1344 Broadway **864-2700** gay-friendly • near world's largest natural hot spring • full brkfst • smokefree • kids ok • gift shop • gay-owned/run

By now, you've probably heard about DYKE TV's **bi-weekly television show,** but did you know we now air in nearly **60 cities nation-wide** and have the potential to reach **6 million house-holds** all over the USA?

Plus...we offer **free video production workshops** for lesbians who'd like to begin producing their own work. We also create **educational videos** alone and with other community organizations. We also maintain an extensive **video archive library** with hours of dyke herstory on tape!

If you want **more info,** and your very own **DYKE TV sticker** or **button,** mail us your name and address. Or, visit our Web site at **www.dyketv.org** or call **(212) 343-9335**

Check our listing under "Info Lines & Services" in your city or town in the Damron Women's Traveller!

**What time is DYKE TV on?**

For more info on **DYKE TV**—and a sticker or button—mail this to us!

Name: _____

Address: _____

City: _____ State: _____ ZIP: _____

(check one) ◯ sticker ◯ button

Send to: DYKE TV, P.O. Box 55, Prince St. Station, New York, NY 10012

# Canada
# Caribbean
# Mexico
# Costa Rica
# Europe

**Note:** *In most countries other than the USA and Canada,* **listings are alphabetical by city** *rather than by state, province or region.*

# Looking for Dorothy?

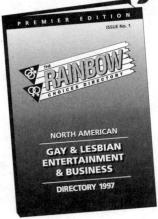

## Find her in the Rainbow!

The Rainbow Choices Directory is your lesbian and gay entertainment & business source which will reach more than a quarter of a million lesbian and gay shoppers. Don't miss out on this exciting opportunity!

### Book your ad today!
# (416) 762-1320
### Fax (416) 762-3600

THE RAINBOW CHOICES DIRECTORY IS A WHOLLY OWNED DIVISION OF RAINBOW DIRECTORY INC.

## PROUDLY GAY OWNED AND OPERATED

## ALBERTA

### Calgary (403)

#### INFO LINES & SERVICES

**Front Runners AA** 777-1212 8:30pm Mon-Th, 7:30pm Fri-Sat • call for location

**Gay/Lesbian Center & Info Line** 223 12th Ave. SW #206 234-8973/9752 7pm-10pm • women's drop-in 7pm Sun • many groups including 'Of Color' & 'Queer Youth'

**Illusions Social Club** 236-7072 transgender club

#### ACCOMMODATIONS

**Black Orchid Manor B&B** 1401 2nd St. NW 276-2471 lesbians/gay men • leather-friendly

**The Foxwood B&B** 1725 12th St. SW 244-6693 lesbians/gay men • full brkfst • $50-75

**Westways Guest House** 216 25th Ave. SW 229-1758 lesbians/gay men • full brkfst • hot tub • smokefree • $45-88

#### BARS & NIGHTCLUBS

**Arena** 310 17th Ave. SW 244-8537 9pm-3am, clsd Sun-Wed • gay-friendly • dancing/DJ

**The Backlot** 209 10th Ave. SW 265-5211 2pm-2am, from 4pm (winters) • lesbians/gay men • martini lounge • wheelchair access

**Diva's Martini Bar** 1154 Kensington Cres. NW 270-3739 7am-2am • gay-friendly • live jazz

**Loading Dock/Detour** 318 17th Ave. SW 244-8537 3pm-3am • mostly gay men • neighborhood bar • dancing/DJ

**Midnight Cafe/Bar** 840 14th Ave. SW (at the 'Best Western Hotel') 229-9322 7am-3am • gay-friendly • food served

**Money Penny's** 111 15th Ave. SW 263-7411 11am-2am • lesbians/gay men • neighborhood bar • food served • patio • wheelchair access

**Rooks** 112 16th Ave. NW 277-1922 11am-2am • mostly women • dancing/DJ

**The Warehouse** 731 10th Ave. SW (alley entrance) 264-0535 9pm-3am, clsd Sun & Tue • gay-friendly • dancing/DJ • private club

#### CAFES

**Cafe Beano** 1613 9th St. SW 229-1232 7am-midnight • some veggie • wheelchair access

**Grabbajabba** 1610 10th St. SW 244-7750 7am-11pm • lesbians/gay men • cafe • some veggie • wheelchair access • $2-7

**Max Beanie's Coffee Bar** 1410 4th St. SW 237-6185 9am-10pm, clsd Sun • wheelchair access

#### RESTAURANTS

**Andrews Pizza** 719 Edmonton Trail NE 230-4202 11am-1am • more gay wknights • full bar • wheelchair access

**Folks Like Us** 110 10th St. NW 270-2241 11am-8pm, til 6pm Sat, til 4:30pm Mon, clsd Sun • lesbians/gay men • bistro menu • plenty veggie • beer/wine • lesbian-owned/run • $4-7

**The Koop Cafe** 211-B 12th Ave. SW 269-4616 11am-1am

**Victoria's** 306 17th Ave. SW 244-9991 lunch, dinner, wknd brunch • homecooking • some veggie • full bar • wheelchair access • $6-10

**Wicked Wedge Pizza** 618 17th Ave. SW 228-1024

#### BOOKSTORES & RETAIL SHOPS

**A Woman's Place** 1412 Centre St. S. 263-5256 10am-6pm, clsd Sun • women's bookstore • large lesbigay section • wheelchair access

**Books 'n Books** 738-A 17th Ave. SW 228-3337 10am-6pm, til 10pm Th-Fri • wheelchair access

**Daily Globe** 1004 17th Ave. SW 244-2060 periodicals

**With the Times** 2212-A 4th St. SW 244-8020 8:30am-11pm

#### PUBLICATIONS

**Outword!** 1412 Centre St. S.

**Perceptions** (306) 244-1930 covers the Canadian prairies

**QC** 630-2061 lesbigay newsmagazine for Alberta

#### TRAVEL AGENTS

**Fletcher/Scott Travel** 803 8th Ave. SW 232-1180/(800) 567-2467 (IN CANADA ONLY) IGLTA

**Leisure Life Vacations** 333 11th Ave. SW #1100 287-9730

**Let's Talk Travel Worldwide Ltd.** 4428 16th Ave. NW 247-0600 IGLTA

**Stonewall Connections** 3545 32nd Ave. NE #320 250-3061/(800) 360-8773

**Uniglobe Swift Travel** 932 17th Ave. SW #220 244-7887

EROTICA

**After Dark** 1314 1st St. SW **264-7399**

**Angelheart Tattoo Studio** 6130 1A St. SW #52 **259-5662** noon-6pm, clsd Sun-Mon

**B&B Leatherworks** 6802 Ogden Rd. SE **236-7072** clsd Sun-Mon • drag/fetish items

**Tad's Bookstore** 1217-A 9th Ave. SE **237-8237** wheelchair access

## Edmonton (403)

INFO LINES & SERVICES

**AA Gay/Lesbian** 424-5900

**Gay Line** 486-9661 voicemail for local groups & services

**Gay/Lesbian Community Centre** 10112 124th St. **488-3234** 7pm-10pm Mon-Fri • also youth group

**Gay/Lesbian Info Line** 988-4018 24hr recorded info & event listing

**Northern Chaps** 486-9661 x2 9pm 1st & 3rd Fri at 'Boots' • mixed SM group

**Womonspace** 9930 106th St. (basement) 482-1794 mtgs. • social events

ACCOMMODATIONS

**Northern Lights B&B** 8216 151st St. **483-1572** lesbians/gay men • full brkfst • swimming • $45-60

BARS & NIGHTCLUBS

**The Bar at the Crockery** 4005 Calgary Trail N. **435-4877** 7pm-2am • mostly women

**Boots 'N Saddle/Garage Cafe** 10242 106th St. **423-5014** 3pm-2am, cafe from noon • mostly gay men • private club • wheelchair access

**Rebar** 10551 Whyte Ave. **433-3600** 8pm-3am • gay-friendly • dancing/DJ • wheelchair access

**The Roost** 10345 104th St. **426-3150** 8pm-3am • mostly gay men • dancing/DJ • live bands

CAFES

**Boystown Cafe** 10116 124th St. **488-6636** 11am-midnight • lesbians/gay men • beer/wine • wheelchair access • also 'Buddys' bar (upstairs)

RESTAURANTS

**Cafe de Ville** 10116 124th St. **488-6636** lunch, dinner & Sun brunch • cont'l

**Jazzberry's** 9965 82nd Ave. **433-2039**

**Vi's by the River** 9712 111th St. **482-6402** 11am-1am • full bar

BOOKSTORES & RETAIL SHOPS

**Audrey's Books** 10702 Jasper Ave. **423-3487** 9am-9pm, 9:30am-5:30pm Sat, noon-5pm Sun

**Divine Decadence** 10441 82nd Ave. **439-2977** 10am-9pm • hip fashions • accessories

**The Front Page** 10846 Jasper Ave. **426-1206** 8am-6pm • periodicals

**Greenwood's Bookshoppe** 10355 82nd Ave. **439-2005** 9:30am-9pm, til 5:30pm Sat, clsd Sun

**Orlando Books** 10640 Whyte Ave. **432-7633** 10am-6pm, til 9pm Th-Fri, noon-4pm Sun • women's • lesbigay section • wheelchair access

**Varscona Books** 10309 Whyte Ave. **439-4195** 10am-6pm, til 9pm Th, clsd Sun

SPIRITUAL GROUPS

**Lambda Christian Church** 11148 84th Ave. **474-0753** 7pm Sun

**MCC Edmonton** 10086 MacDonald Dr. **429-2321** 7:15pm Sun • also 'Wayward Daughters' women's group 431-2128

## Grand Prairie (403)

INFO LINES & SERVICES

**Peace Gay/Lesbian Association** 539-3325 7:30pm-9:30pm, clsd Sun-Mon

BARS & NIGHTCLUBS

**Touché** 8502 112th St. #201 **538-9998** 9pm-3am, from 2pm Sun • lesbians/gay men • neighborhood bar • dancing/DJ • private club

## Lethbridge (403)

INFO LINES & SERVICES

**GALA (Gay/Lesbian Association of Lethbridge)** 329-4666 7pm-10pm Wed • social group

**Lighthouse Social Club** 380-4257 monthly dances & weekly events for lesbians/gays • unconfirmed

## Millet (403)

ACCOMMODATIONS

**Labyrinth Lake Lodge** 878-3301 mostly women • retreat space • swimming

## Red Deer (403)

INFO LINES & SERVICES

**Gay/Lesbian Association of Central Alberta** 340-2198 7pm-9pm Wed

### BARS & NIGHTCLUBS
**The Other Place** Bay #3-4, 5579 47th St. **342-6440** 4pm-3am, til 11pm Sun • lesbians/gay men • dancing/DJ • wheelchair access

### TRAVEL AGENTS
**546780 Alberta Ltd.** 126 Rupert Cres. **341-4184** IGLTA

## Rocky Mtn. House (403)

### ACCOMMODATIONS
**Country Cabin B&B 845-4834** gay-friendly • cabins • hot tub • swimming • pets ok

## BRITISH COLUMBIA

## Birken (604)

### ACCOMMODATIONS
**Birkenhead Resort** Pemberton **452-3255** gay-friendly • cabins • campsites • hot tub • swimming • $54-76

## Courtenay (250)

### INFO LINES & SERVICES
**Women's Resource Centre** 3205 S. Island Hwy. **338-1133** 10am-4am, clsd Fri-Sun

## Cranbrook (250)

### INFO LINES & SERVICES
**Cranbrook Women's Resource Centre** 20-A 12th Ave N. **426-2912** 9am-4pm, from noon Th, til 1pm Fri, clsd wknds

## Duncan (250)

### INFO LINES & SERVICES
**Island Gay/Lesbian Society of Duncan** 748-7689

## Fort Nelson (250)

### INFO LINES & SERVICES
**Women's Resource Centre** 5004 52nd Ave. W. **774-3069** 8:30am-noon & 1pm-4pm, clsd wknds

## Gokten (250)

### INFO LINES & SERVICES
**Golden Women's Resource Centre** **344-5317** 9am-4pm, 11am-3pm Fri, clsd wknds

## Kelowna (250)

### INFO LINES & SERVICES
**Kelowna Women's Resource Centre** 347 Leon #107 **762-2355** 9am-4pm, til 7pm Wed, clsd Fri-Sun

**Okanagan Rainbow Coalition** 436 Bernard Ave., 2nd flr. **860-8555** 7pm-10pm, clsd Sun • sponsors dances & coffeehouse • women's group Wed

### ACCOMMODATIONS
**The Flags B&B** 2295 McKinley Rd., RR 1 Site 10 C2 **868-2416** seasonal • lesbians/gay men • mini-resort • full brkfst • hot tub • swimming • nudity • $40-65

### CAFES
**Bean Scene** 274 Bernard Ave. **763-1814** 7am-10pm, 9am-9pm Sun • patio • wheelchair access

### RESTAURANTS
**Greek House** 3159 Woodsdale Rd. **766-0090** 11am-10pm, from 4pm wknds • cont'l

## Nanaimo (250)

### ACCOMMODATIONS
**Dorchester Hotel** 70 Church St. **754-6835** gay-friendly

### BARS & NIGHTCLUBS
**Neighbours** 70 Church St. (in hotel) **716-0505** 6pm-1am • lesbians/gay men • videos

### CAFES
**Olde Firehall Coffee Roastery** 34 Nichol St. #2 **754-7733** 9am-midnight, til 1am Fri-Sat • cafe • vegetarian • $5

### RESTAURANTS
**Flo's Diner** 187 Commercial St. **753-2148** 7am-7pm • gay-owned/run

### BOOKSTORES & RETAIL SHOPS
**A Different Drummer** 70 Church St. #B2 **753-0030** 10am-5:30pm, noon-5pm Sun • cards • gifts • wheelchair access

### PUBLICATIONS
**The Point** 729-7123

## Nelson (250)

### INFO LINES & SERVICES
**Nelson Women's Centre** 507 Hall St. **352-9916** noon-4pm Tues-Wed, Fri
**West Kootaney Gay/Lesbian Line** **354-4297** social group

## ACCOMMODATIONS

**Hestia's 229-5325** women only • quiet retreat • all meals (vegetarian) • swimming • pets ok (call first) • $75-95

## Port Renfrew (250)

### ACCOMMODATIONS

**Wild Women Retreat 382-6686/ 748-1579** 3-bdrm rental home • $40-60

## Prince George (250)

### INFO LINES & SERVICES

**GALA North 562-6253** 24hr recorded info • social group
**Teen Crisis Line 564-8336** 4pm-11pm

### ACCOMMODATIONS

**Hawthorne B&B** 829 P.G. Pulp Mill Rd. **563-8299** gay-friendly • full brkfst • hot tub • $60-70

### CAFES

**The Isle Pierre Pie Co.** 409 George St. **564-1300** 9am-11pm

## Prince Rupert (250)

### INFO LINES & SERVICES

**Prince Rupert Gay Info Line 627-8900**

## Qualicum Beach (250)

### ACCOMMODATIONS

**Bahari B&B** 5101 Island Hwy. W. **752-9278** gay-friendly • full brkfst • hot tub • apt rental • $60-150

## Quesnel (250)

### INFO LINES & SERVICES

**Women's Resource Centre** 690 Mclean St. **992-8472** 9am-4pm, clsd wknds

## Salt Spring Island (250)

### ACCOMMODATIONS

**The Blue Ewe** 1207 Beddis Rd. **537-9344** lesbians/gay men • full brkfst • hot tub w/ocean view • nudity ok
**Green Rose by the Water** Ganges **537-9927** gay-friendly • apt rental
**Saltspring Driftwood Bed & Brunch** 1982 N. End Rd. **537-4137** gay-friendly • miniature farm for art & animal lovers • kids/pets ok
**Summerhill Guesthouse** 209 Chu-An Dr. **537-2727** lesbians/gay men • on the water • full brkfst • $75-95

**Sunnyside Up B&B** 120 Andrew Pl. **653-4889** lesbians/gay men • panoramic views • full brkfst • hot tub • deck • $85

### BARS & NIGHTCLUBS

**Moby's Pub** 124 Upper Ganges **537-5559** 10am-1am • gay-friendly • neighborhood bar

### RESTAURANTS

**Pomadori** 375 Baker Rd. **537-2247** dinner only

## Tofino (250)

### ACCOMMODATIONS

**BriMar B&B** 1375 Thornberg Cres. **725-3410/(800) 714-9373** gay-friendly • full brkfst • smokefree • $60-120
**Gemini Place Suite/B&B** 1108 Abraham Dr. **725-4427** gay-friendly
**West Wind Guest House & Cottage** 1321 Pacific Rim Hwy. **725-2224** lesbians/gay men • 5 min. from beach • hot tub • $105-125

### RESTAURANTS

**Blue Heron** 634 Campbell St. **725-4266** 7am-midnight • full bar
**Crab Bar** 601 Campbell St. **725-4266** dinner only • beer/wine

## Vancouver (604)

### INFO LINES & SERVICES

**AA Gay/Lesbian 434-3933/434-2553 (TDD)**
**The Gay/Lesbian Library** 1170 Bute St. (at 'G/L Centre') **684-5309** 7:30pm-9:30pm, from 4:30pm Mon, 3pm-6pm Wed • lending library
**Vancouver Gay/Lesbian Centre** 1170 Bute St. **684-6869** 11am-5pm, 7pm-10pm
**Vancouver Lesbian Centre** 876 Commercial Dr. **254-8458** 11am-6pm, noon-5pm Sat, clsd Sun-Wed
**Women & Sobriety** 261 E. 12th Ave. **434-3933** 8pm Sun

### ACCOMMODATIONS

**The Albion Guest House** 592 W. 19th Ave. **873-2287** lesbians/gay men • full brkfst • hot tub • $60-155
**Brighton House B&B** 2826 Trinity St. **253-7175** gay-friendly • 1906 character home • mtn. & water views • full brkfst • $115-135CAN • kids 12+ ok
**The Buchan Hotel** 1906 Haro St. **685-5354/(800) 668-6654** gay-friendly • $45-130

# Vancouver (604)

**Lesbigay Info:** Vancouver Gay/Lesbian Centre: 684-6869. 1170 Bute St. Vancouver Lesbian Centre: 254-8458.

**Where the Girls Are:** In the West End, between Stanley Park and Gastown, or exploring the beautiful scenery elsewhere.

**Lesbigay AA:** 434-3933/ 434-2553 (TDD).

**Lesbigay Pride:** August: 737-7433.

**Annual Events:**

January - New Year's Day Polar Bear Swim.

May - Vancouver International Marathon.

June - Dragon Boat Festival. Du Maurier Jazz Festival.

July - Folk Music Festival.

September - International Film Festival.

**City Info:** Vancouver Travel Info Centre: 683-2000.

**Attractions:** Stanley Park. Gastown. Chinatown. Capilano Suspension Bridge. Wreck Beach (great gay beach).

**Best View:** Biking in Stanley Park, or on a ferry between peninsulas and islands. Atop one of the surrounding mountains.

**Weather:** It's cold and wet in the winter (32-45°), but it's absolutely gorgeous in the summer (52-75°)!

**Transit:** Yellow Cab: 681-1111. Vancouver Airporter: 244-9888. A Visitors' Map of all bus lines is available through the tourist office listed above. B.C. Transit: 521-0400.

---

**The Chelsea Cottage B&B** 2143 W. 46th Ave. **266-2681** gay-friendly

**Colibri B&B** 1101 Thurlow St. **689-5100** lesbians/gay men • full brkfst • gay-owned/run • $55-150

**Columbia Cottage** 205 W. 14th Ave. **874-5327** gay-friendly • 1920s Tudor • full brkfst • IGLTA • $80-155

**Dufferin Hotel** 900 Seymour St. **683-4251** gay-friendly • food served • $70+ • also 3 bars • lesbians/gay men

**French Quarter B&B** 2051 W. 19th Ave. **737-0973** gay-friendly • cottages • full brkfst • swimming • gym • smokefree • French spoken

**Heather Cottage** 5425 Trafalgar St. **261-1442** lesbians/gay men • $70-125

**Heritage House Hotel** 455 Abbott St. **685-7777** lesbians/gay men • also 3 bars • live shows • $55-75

**The Johnson Heritage House B&B** 2278 W. 34th Ave. **266-4175** gay-friendly • full brkfst • shared bath • smokefree • $60-145

**The Manor Guest House** 345 W. 13th Ave. **876-8494** gay-friendly • full brkfst • apt avail. • $65-175

**Mountain B&B** 258 E. Balmoral Rd. **987-2725** gay-friendly • full brkfst

**Nelson House B&B** 977 Broughton St. **684-9793** lesbians/gay men • full brkfst • jacuzzi en suite • IGLTA • $78-155

**'O' Canada House** 1114 Barclay St. **688-0555** gay-friendly • beautifully restored 1897 Victorian home • full brkfst • snacks avail. • $150-195 • gay-owned/run

**Penny Farthing Inn** 2855 W. 6th Ave. **739-9002** gay-friendly • 1912 heritage house in Kitsilano • $75-165

**Pillow 'n Porridge Guest House** 2859 Manitoba St. **879-8977** gay-friendly • kitchenettes • kids ok • women-owned • wheelchair access • $115-140

**River Run Cottages** 4551 River Rd. W., Ladner **946-7778** gay-friendly • on the Fraser River • wheelchair access

## *Vancouver*

Just three hours north of Seattle is Vancouver, one of the most beautiful cities in the world. To enjoy the greenery, visit Stanley Park, the largest city park in North America. Also worth a visit is historic Gastown, where Vancouver began in the 1860s, now a lively area with boutiques, antique shops, and a vast array of restaurants.

Dyke dancing machines should check out the women's nights at the city's many mixed bars—start out Friday at the **Lotus Club** women's night. Sundays are hot at **Celebrities, Denman Station,** and on alternate Sundays, try the **Riley Cafe** or **Fly Girl.**

For bookstores, try **Women in Print,** or the lesbian/gay bookstore, **Little Sisters.** While you're at one, pick up a copy of **Kinesis,** the women's newsmagazine, **Xtra! West,** the local gay paper, or the aptly named **Lezzie Smut.** Speaking of smut, check out **Womyn's Ware** for all your erotica needs—including women's dungeon parties; call the store for info on the next **Muffs & Cuffs** event.

Vegetarians will fare well at **La Quena** co-op, or fast food veggie **O-Tooz.** Vancouver has tons of lesbian-friendly services, so inquire at the **Vancouver Gay/Lesbian Community Centre** to find the perfect activity. And ask about their annual Lesbian Pride Week!

**Rural Roots** 4939 Ross Rd., Mt. Lehman **856-2380** mostly gay men • 1 hr. from Vancouver • full brkfst • hot tub • smokefree • wheelchair access • $35-65
**Sunshine Hills B&B** 11200 Bond Blvd., North Delta **596-6496** gay-friendly • full brkfst • shared bath • $55-60
▲ **The West End Guest House** 1362 Haro St. **681-2889** gay-friendly • 1906 historic Victorian • full brkfst • some veggie • $99-190

### BARS & NIGHTCLUBS
**Celebrities** 1022 Davie St. **689-3180** 9pm-2am, til midnight Sun • mostly gay men • women's night Sun • dancing/DJ • live shows

**Charlie's Lounge** (at 'Heritage House Hotel') **685-7777** 11am-1:30am • lesbians/gay men • 'Fabulous 40' Sat for women 40+

**Chuck's Pub** (at 'Heritage House Hotel') **685-7777** 11am-1:30am • lesbians/gay men • dancing/DJ • live shows

**Denman Station** 860 Denman 669-3448
7pm-2am, til midnight Sun • mostly gay
men • more women Sun • neighborhood bar • dancing/DJ • live shows •
karaoke • videos

**Fly Girl/Jet Boy** 669-1753/(800) 567-
1662 popular monthly dance • call for
info

**Limelight Cabaret** 23 W. Cordova
688-5351 lesbians/gay men • men-only
Sat • theme nights

**Lotus Club** (at 'Heritage House Hotel')
685-7777 lesbians/gay men • women's
night Fri • dancing/DJ

**Muffs & Cuffs** 254-2543 women only •
dungeon play parties • call for dates &
locations

**Numbers** 1042 Davie 685-4077 8pm-
2am, til midnight Sun • mostly gay men
• dancing/DJ • live shows • videos

**The Odyssey** 1251 Howe St. 689-5256
9pm-2am • popular • mostly gay men •
dancing/DJ

**Royal Pub** 1025 Granville St. (at 'Royal
Hotel') 685-5335 11am-11pm • mostly
gay men • neighborhood bar • live
bands Wed-Sat

## CAFES

**The Edge** 1148 Davie St. 688-3395
7am-4am, til 2am Sun

**Harry's** 1716 Charles St. 253-1789 9am-
11pm, 10am-6pm wknds • deli • wheelchair access

**Homer's** 1249 Howe St. 689-2444 3pm-
3am • coffee & billards • beer/wine

**The Second Cup** 1184 Denman
669-2068 7am-11pm • pastries • wheelchair access

**Spuntino's** 1103 Davie St. 685-9658
24hrs • patio

## RESTAURANTS

**Cafe S'il Vous Plaît** 500 Robson St.
688-7216 lunch & dinner til 10pm, til
11pm Sat, clsd Sun • homecooking •
plenty veggie • wheelchair access • $3-6

**Canton Village** 1043 Davie St. 669-2638
lunch & dinner • free delivery after 5pm

**Chianti's** 1850 W. 4th St. 738-8411 lunch
& dinner

**Cincin** 1154 Robson 688-7338 dinner
only wknds • Italian/Mediterranean •
full bar

**Catering to discerning
travellers of all persuasions.
Located in Vancouver's most
enlightened neighbourhood,
the West End. Close to clubs,
restaurants, shopping,
beaches and Stanley Park.**

**Vancouver's Pink Victorian**

*The* **West End Guest House**
1362 Haro St. Vancouver, BC, V6E 1G2 tel: (604) 681-2889, fax: (604) 688-8812

**Delilah's** 1739 Comox St. **687-3424** 5:30pm-midnight • some veggie • full bar • wheelchair access • $18-29

**Hamburger Mary's** 1202 Davie St. **687-1293** 8am-3am, til 4am Fri-Sat • some veggie • full bar • $5-10

**Henry's Landing** 2607 Ware St. **854-3679** lunch & dinner

**India Gate** 616 Robson St. **684-4617**

**Isadora's** 1540 Old Bridge St., Granville Island **681-8816** 8am-10pm • plenty veggie • beer/wine • cooperatively run

**La Quena** 1111 Commercial Dr. **251-6626** 11am-11pm • vegetarian • wheelchair access • $3-5

**Lola's at the Century House** 432 Richards St. **684-5652** great menu & atmosphere • full bar

**Luxy Bistro** 1235 Davie St. **681-9976** 9am-11pm • some veggie • full bar • wheelchair access

**Mario's** 33555 S. Fraser Wy. **852-6919** lunch & dinner • Italian

**Martini's** 151 W. Broadway **873-0021** 11am-2am • great pizza • full bar

**Milestone's** 1145 Robson St. **682-4477** great brunch • full bar

**Naam** 2724 W. 4th St. **738-7151** 24hrs • vegetarian

**O-Tooz** 1068 Davie St. **689-0208** 7am-midnight • lowfat vegetarian fast food

**The Oasis** 1240 Thurlow St. (upstairs) **685-1724** dinner, Sat & Sun brunch • int'l cuisine • piano bar • patio

**Riley Cafe** 1661 Granville St. **684-3666** 11:30am-10pm • BBQ • some veggie • full bar • also 'Riley T' • alternative lesbigay social night 1st & 3rd Sun • wheelchair access • $5-12

**Squire's** 1030 Denman **688-6264** noon-10pm, from 10am wknds • vegetarian • full bar • $6-10

## ENTERTAINMENT & RECREATION

**Lotus Land Tours** 1251 Cardero St., Ste. 1251 **684-4922** day paddle trips • no experience necessary (price includes pick-up and meal)

**Rockwood Adventures** 1330 Fulton Ave., W. Vancouver **926-7705** rain forest walks for all levels w/ free hotel pick up

**Sunset Beach**

**Wreck Beach** below UBC

## BOOKSTORES & RETAIL SHOPS

**D&R Clothing** 1112 Davie St. **687-0937** 11am-6:30pm, til 9pm Fri, til 8pm Sat, noon-6pm Sun • clubwear & underwear

**Little Sister's** 1238 Davie St. **669-1753/(800) 567-1662 (IN CANADA ONLY)** 10am-11pm • lesbigay

**Return to Sender** 1076 Davie St. **683-6363** 11am-8pm • cards • gifts • wheelchair access • also 990 Denman St. 688-9959

**Spartacus Books** 311 W. Hastings **688-6138** 10am-8:30pm, noon-6pm wknds • progressive

**State of Mind** 1100 Davie St. **682-7116** designer queer clothes

**Women in Print** 3566 W. 4th Ave. **732-4128** 10am-6pm, noon-5pm Sun • women's • wheelchair access • women-owned/run

## PUBLICATIONS

**Angles** 688-0265

**Diversity Magazine** 937-7447 pansexual fetish/fantasy zine

**Kinesis** 255-5499 women's news-magazine

**Lezzie Smut** 252-6299 lesbian erotica for all North America

▲ **Rainbow Choices Directory** (416) 762-1320/(888) 241-3569 lesbigay entertainment & business directory for Canada

**Xtra! West** 684-9696 lesbigay newspaper

## TRAVEL AGENTS

**English Bay Travel** 1267 Davie St. **687-8785** IGLTA

**Progressive Travel** 1120 Davie St. **687-3837/(800) 910-1120** IGLTA

**Super Natural Adventures** 626 West Pender St., main flr. **683-5101** hiking & helicopter-hiking trips in Western & Northern Canada

**Travel Destinations** 505-1200 Burrard St. **685-8636** IGLTA

## SPIRITUAL GROUPS

**Dignity/Integrity** 432-1230

**MCC** 3214 W. 10th (St. James) **739-7959** 7:15pm Sun

## EROTICA

**Love's Touch** 1069 Davie St. **681-7024**

**Mack's Leathers** 1043 Granville **688-6225**

**Next Body Piercing** 1068 Granville St. **684-6398** hours vary

**Womyns' Ware** 896 Commercial Dr. **254-2543/(888) WYM-WARE (ORDERS ONLY)** hours vary, clsd Mon • toys • fetishwear • lesbian-owned/run

# altitude 98

**THE 6TH ANNUAL
GAY & LESBIAN
SKI WEEK**

**WHISTLER RESORT
B.C., CANADA**

**FEBRUARY 1–8, 1998**

**VANCOUVER STAY
JANUARY 31, 1998**

**INFORMATION**
**1-888-altitude (258-4883)**

**WEBSITE**
**www.outontheslopes.com**

**E-MAIL**
**altitude@outontheslopes.com**

**OUT ON THE SLOPES PRODUCTIONS**
101 - 1184 Denman Street, #190
Vancouver, B.C., V6G 2M9, Canada
Tel. (604) 688-5079 • Fax (604) 688-5033

## Vernon (250)

INFO LINES & SERVICES
**NOGO (North Okanagan Gay Org.)** 558-6198/542-4842 social group
**Rural Lesbian Association** 542-7531

ACCOMMODATIONS
**Rainbows End** 542-4842 lesbians/gay men • full brkfst • hot tub • some shared baths • smokefree • pets ok • wheelchair access

## Victoria (250)

INFO LINES & SERVICES
**Gay/Lesbian AA** 383-7744
**LGB Alliance at Univ. of Victoria** 472-4393
**Women's Creative Network** 1910 Store St. **382-7768** women's private social club • mtgs. • dances • events

ACCOMMODATIONS
**The Back Hills** 4470 Leefield **478-9648** women only • 30 min. from Victoria in the Metchosin Hills • full brkfst • near outdoor recreation • smokefree • pets ok • $50
**Big House B&B for Women** 1601 Ross St. **598-9858** women only • $40-70
**Claddagh House B&B** 1761 Lee Ave. 370-2816 gay-friendly • brkfst • $55-85
**Hospitality Exchange** 385-4945
**Oak Bay Guest House** 1052 Newport Ave. 598-3812 gay-friendly • near beaches
**The Weekender B&B** 10 Eberts St. **389-1688** April-Oct (wknds only Nov-March) • lesbians/gay men • seaside • smokefree • $75-105

BARS & NIGHTCLUBS
**BJ's Lounge** 642 Johnson (enter on Broad) **388-0505** noon-1am • lesbians/gay men • lunch daily
**Rumours** 1325 Government St. (basement) **385-0566** 9pm-2am, til midnight Sun • lesbians/gay men • dancing/DJ

CAFES
**Fiddleheads** 1284 Gladstone Ave, Fernwood Village **386-1199**

RESTAURANTS
**The Water Club Restaurant & Winebar** 703 Douglas St. **388-4200** 11am-11pm

BOOKSTORES & RETAIL SHOPS
**Bolen Books** 1644 Hillside Ave. #111 (shopping ctr.) 595-4232 8:30am-10pm

**Everywoman's Books** 635 Johnson St. **388-9411** 10:30am-5:30pm, clsd Sun

## Whistler (604)

ACCOMMODATIONS
**The Whistler Retreat B&B** 8561 Drifter Wy. **938-9245** lesbians/gay men • brkfst • outdoor hot tub • sauna • $65-110

RESTAURANTS
**Anasazi** 2021 Karen Cres. **932-3000** dinner only • Southwestern • full bar
**Boston Pizza** 2011 Innsbruck Dr. **932-7070** 11am-11pm • full bar
**La Rua** 4557 Blackcomb Blvd. **932-5011** Italian/cont'l
**Monks Grill** base of Blackcomb **932-9677** lunch & dinner • grill menu • bar
**Old Mole Cantina** base of gondola **932-3888** 11:30am-11pm • full bar • wheelchair access

## Winfield (250)

ACCOMMODATIONS
**Willow Lane** 11571 Turtle Bay Ct. **766-4807** lesbians/gay men • full brkfst • near outdoor recreation

# MANITOBA

## Brandon (204)

INFO LINES & SERVICES
**Gays/Lesbians of Western Manitoba** 727-4297 7pm-9pm Fri

## Winnipeg (204)

INFO LINES & SERVICES
**Gay/Lesbian Resource Center** 1-222 Osborne St. S. **284-5208** 1pm-4:30pm (office), 7:30pm-10pm (info line), clsd wknds • info in French Wed
**New Freedom AA Group** 300 Hugo (St. Michael & All Angels) **942-0126** 8:30pm Th & 3:30pm Sun
**Women's Centre** 786-9788 drop-in resource center
**Women's Resource Centre** 1088 Pembina Hwy. **477-1123** 9am-noon & 1pm-4:30pm, clsd wknds

ACCOMMODATIONS
**Masson's B&B** 181 Masson St. **237-9230** gay-friendly • full brkfst • hot tub • gay-owned/run

**Winged Ox Guest House** 82 Spence St.
**783-7408** gay-friendly • full brkfst •
some veggie • smokefree • kids ok •
$35-50

### BARS & NIGHTCLUBS

**Club 200** 190 Garry St. **943-6045** 4pm-
2am, clsd Sun • lesbians/gay men •
dancing/DJ • live shows • dinner served
• some veggie • $7-11

**Gio's** 272 Sherbrooke St. **786-1236** 9pm-
2am, clsd Sun • mostly gay men • danc-
ing/DJ • live shows • private club

**Happenings** 274 Sherbrooke St.
(upstairs) **774-3576** 9pm-2am, til 3am
Sat, clsd Sun • lesbians/gay men •
dancing/DJ • live shows • private club

**Ms. Purdy's Women's Club** 226 Main St.
**989-2344** 8pm-2am, clsd Sun-Mon •
women only • men welcome Fri • danc-
ing/DJ • live shows • private club •
women-owned/run

### CAFES

**Winona's Coffee & Ice** 775-2588

### RESTAURANTS

**Times Change Blues Cafe** 234 Main
**957-0982** from 8pm, clsd Mon-Wed •
some veggie • live shows • under $6

### BOOKSTORES & RETAIL SHOPS

**Dominion News** 263 Portage Ave. **942-
6563** 8am-9pm, noon-6pm Sun • some
gay periodicals

**The Lavender Rose Booksellers** 574
Broadway Ave. **779-4969** noon-6pm, til
9pm Th-Fri, from 10am Sat, noon-5pm
Sun, clsd Mon • women's/lesbigay

**McNally Robinson** 1120 Grant Ave.
#4000 **453-2644** 9am-10pm, til 11pm Fri,
10am-6pm Sun • some gay titles •
wheelchair access

**Mondragon Bookstore & Cafe** 91
Albert St. **946-5241** 9am-midnight, clsd
Sun-Mon • veggie/vegan • smokefree

### PUBLICATIONS

**Perceptions** (306) 244-1930 covers the
Canadian prairies

**Swerve** 942-4599 lesbigay newspaper

### TRAVEL AGENTS

**Out 'N About Travel** 100 Osbourne St.
S. # 207 **477-6799** IGLTA

### SPIRITUAL GROUPS

**Affirm (United Church)** 452-2853

**Dignity** 287-8583 7:30pm 1st & 3rd Th

**MCC** 396 Broadway (St. Stephen's
United Church) **661-2219** 7:30pm Sun

**EROTICA**

**Unique Boutique** 615 Portage Ave. **775-
5435** 10am-midnight, til 10pm wknds

## NEW BRUNSWICK

### Fredericton (506)

INFO LINES & SERVICES

**Fredericton Gay Line** 457-2156
6:30pm-8:30pm Tue & Th

BARS & NIGHTCLUBS

**Kurt's Dance Warehouse/Phoenix
Rising** 377 King St., 3rd flr. **453-0740**
8pm-1am • lesbians/gay men • danc-
ing/DJ • wheelchair access

SPIRITUAL GROUPS

**New Hope MCC** 749 Charlotte St.
(Unitarian Fellowship House) **455-4622**
7pm Sun

### Moncton (506)

BARS & NIGHTCLUBS

**Triangles** 234 St. George St. **857-8779**
clsd Mon • lesbians/gay men • dancing

TRAVEL AGENTS

**Time Lines Travel** 210 Park St. **382-
7171** IGLTA

### Sackville (506)

ACCOMMODATIONS

**Georgian House** RR #3 **536-1481** seasonal • gay-friendly • 1840 home in
quiet country setting • $45-50

### St. John (506)

ACCOMMODATIONS

**Mahogany Manor** 220 Germain St. **636-
8000** gay-friendly • smokefree • wheelchair access • $55-65

BARS & NIGHTCLUBS

**Bogarts** 9 Sydney St. **652-2004** 8pm-
2am, clsd Sun-Tue winters •
lesbians/gay men • dancing/DJ

## NEWFOUNDLAND

### Corner Brook (709)

INFO LINES & SERVICES
**Women's Resource Centre** 639-8522

### St. John's (709)

INFO LINES & SERVICES
**Gay/Lesbian Info Line** 753-4297 7pm-10pm Tue & Th
**Women's Centre** 83 Military Rd. 753-0220 9am-5pm, clsd wknds

ACCOMMODATIONS
**Banberry House B&B** 116 Military Rd. 579-8006 gay-friendly • full brkfst

BARS & NIGHTCLUBS
**Schroders Piano Bar** 10 Bates Hill 753-0807 4pm-1am, til 2am Fri-Sat, til midnight Sun • gay-friendly • also 'Zapata's' restaurant downstairs • Mexican • some veggie
**Zone 216** 216 Duckworth St. 754-2492 8pm-2am, til midnight Sun • lesbians/gay men • dancing/DJ • wheelchair access

### Stevenville (709)

INFO LINES & SERVICES
**Bay St. George Women's Centre** 54 St. Clare Ave. 643-4444

## NOVA SCOTIA

### Bear River (902)

ACCOMMODATIONS
**Lovett Lodge Inn** 1820 Main St. 467-3917/(800) 565-0000 (CANADA ONLY) seasonal • full brkfst • smokefree • kids ok • $40-44

### Bridgetown (902)

ACCOMMODATIONS
**Pumpkin Ecological Wimmin's Farm** RR 5 665-5041 women only • rustic cabins • camping • swimming • workshops • drug/smoke/alcohol-free • girl kids ok • work exch. avail. • $45-65/$8 camping

### Cheticamp (902)

ACCOMMODATIONS
**Seashell Cabins** 125 Cheticamp Island Beach Rd. 224-3569 seasonal • gay-friendly • housekeeping units on the ocean • lesbian-owned/run

### Halifax (902)

INFO LINES & SERVICES
**Gay/Lesbian/Bisexual Line** 423-7129 7pm-10pm Th-Sat • also gay AA info
**Lesbigay Youth Project** 492-0444/(800) 566-2437

ACCOMMODATIONS
**Bob's B&B** 2715 Windsor St. 454-4374 gay-friendly • full brkfst • hot tub
**Centre Town Guest House** 2016 Oxford St. 422-2380 lesbians/gay men • hot tub • smokefree • French spoken • $40-75
**Fresh Start B&B** 2720 Gottingen St. 453-6616/(888) 453-6616 gay-friendly • full brkfst • $45-70
**Peggy's Cove** (401) 461-4533 seasonal • rental home • $500 wk

BARS & NIGHTCLUBS
**Reflections Cabaret** 5184 Sackville St. 422-2957 4pm-3:30am • lesbians/gay men • dancing/DJ • live shows • wheelchair access

CAFES
**The Daily Grind** 5686 Spring Garden Rd. 429-6397 7am-11pm • newsstand

RESTAURANTS
**Le Bistro** 1333 South Park 423-8428 lunch & dinner • some veggie • full bar • wheelchair access • $7-13

**Satisfaction Feast** 1581 Grafton St. **422-3540** 8am-10pm, from 4pm Sun • veggie • patio • wheelchair access • $5-12

**Soho** 1582 Granville St. **423-3049** 11:30am-10pm

**Sweet Basil** 1866 Upper Water St. **425-2133** lunch & dinner • full bar

### ENTERTAINMENT & RECREATION
**Queer News** CKDU (97.5FM) **494-6479** call for details

### BOOKSTORES & RETAIL SHOPS
**Atlantic News** 5560 Morris St. **429-5468** 8am-10pm • periodicals

**Entitlement Book Sellers** Lord Nelson Arcade **420-0565** 9:30am-10pm, noon-6pm Sun

**Frog Hollow Books** 5640 Spring Garden Rd., 2nd flr. **429-3318**

**Inside Out Books** 1574 Argyle St. #2 **425-1538** noon-8pm, 1pm-5pm Sun • lesbigay

**The Open Closet & Gifts** 1574 Argyle St. #4 **422-4220** noon-6pm

**Schooner Used Books** 5378 Inglis St. **423-8419** 9:30pm-6pm, til 9pm Fri, til 5:30pm Sat, clsd Sun • large selection of women's titles

**Smithbooks** 5201 Duke St. (Scotia Sq.) **423-6438** 9:30am-6pm, til 9pm Th-Fri

**Trident Booksellers & Cafe** 1570 Argyle St. **423-7100** 8:30am-9pm

### PUBLICATIONS
**Wayves** 429-2661

### SPIRITUAL GROUPS
**Safe Harbour MCC** 5500 Inglis St. (church) **453-9249** 7:30pm Sun

## Lunenburg (902)

### ACCOMMODATIONS
**Brook House** 3 Old Blue Rocks Rd. **634-3826** gay-friendly • seasonal • $45-65

## Sydney (902)

### INFO LINES & SERVICES
**Women's Unlimited Feminist Association** 564-5926 unconfirmed

## Yarmouth (902)

### ACCOMMODATIONS
**Murray Manor B&B** 225 Main St. **742-9625** gay-friendly • full brkfst

## ONTARIO

## Bancroft (613)

### ACCOMMODATIONS
**Greenview Guesthouse** 332-3922 women only • country retreat • full brkfst & dinner • plenty veggie • hot tub • sauna

## Brighton (613)

### ACCOMMODATIONS
**Butler Creek B&B** 475-1248 gay-friendly
**Main Street B&B** 96 Main St. **475-0351** gay-friendly • full brkfst • swimming

### BOOKSTORES & RETAIL SHOPS
**Lighthouse Books** 17 Prince Edward St. **475-1269** 9:30am-5:30pm, clsd Sun-Mon

## Cambridge (519)

### BARS & NIGHTCLUBS
**Robin's Nest** 26 Hobston St. (in Farmers Bldg., Galt St. entrance) **621-2688** seasonal • mostly women • country/western

### ENTERTAINMENT & RECREATION
**Out & About** CKWR (98.7 FM) **623-5717**

## Dutton (519)

### ACCOMMODATIONS
**Victorian Court B&B** 235 Main St. **762-2244** lesbians/gay men • smokefree • wheelchair access • $45-75

## Fort Erie (905)

### ACCOMMODATIONS
**Whistle Stop Guesthouse** 871-1265 women only • full brkfst • $65

## Grand Valley (519)

### ACCOMMODATIONS
**Manfred's Meadow Guest House** 925-5306 lesbians/gay men • all meals included • swimming • sauna • spa • smokefree • $78-99

## Guelph (519)

### INFO LINES & SERVICES
**Gay Line** 836-4550

### BOOKSTORES & RETAIL SHOPS
**Bookshelf Cafe** 41 Quebec St. **821-3311** 9am-9pm, til 10pm Fri-Sat, 10:30am-3pm Sun (bar noon-1am) • also cinema & restaurant • some veggie • $5-10

## Hamilton (905)

### ACCOMMODATIONS

**The Cedars Tent & Trailer Park** 1039 5th Concession Rd. RR2, Waterdown **659-3655** lesbians/gay men • private campground • swimming • also social club • dancing/DJ • karaoke • wknd restaurant • some veggie

### BARS & NIGHTCLUBS

**Cafe 121** 121 Hughson St. N. **546-5258** noon-1am • lesbians/gay men • dancing/DJ • also restaurant • some veggie • $3-10

**The Embassy Club** 54 King St. E. **522-7783** 11am-3am Fri-Sat only • mostly gay men • neighborhood bar • dancing/DJ

**Windsor Bar & Grill** 31 John St. N. **308-9939** 11am-2am • lesbian/gay men • dancing/DJ

### BOOKSTORES & RETAIL SHOPS

**The Gomorrah's** 158 James St. S. (lowel level) **526-1074** noon-6pm, til 8pm Fri, from 10am Sat, til 4pm Sun • lesbigay

**The Women's Bookstop** 333 Main St. W. **525-2970** 10:30am-7pm, til 5pm Sat, clsd Sun • wheelchair access

## Jasper (613)

### ACCOMMODATIONS

**Starr Easton Hall 283-7497** gay-friendly • B&B-inn • full brkfst • also restaurant • int'l fine dining • some veggie • full bar • live shows • wheelchair access • $60-80

## Kingston (613)

### INFO LINES & SERVICES

**Lesbian/Gay/Bisexual Phoneline & Directory 531-8981** 7pm-9pm, clsd Fri-Sun

### BARS & NIGHTCLUBS

**Club 477** 477 Princess St. **547-2923** 8pm-1am, til 3am Fri-Sat • popular • lesbians/gay men • dancing/DJ • alternative

### CAFES

**Chinese Laundry Cafe** 291 Princess St. **542-2282** 10am-1am • cafe food & desserts • some veggie • $4-8

### BOOKSTORES & RETAIL SHOPS

**WomenSource 544-7141/(800) 385-7337** women's books

## Kitchener (519)

### BARS & NIGHTCLUBS

**Club Renaissance** 24 Charles St. N. **570-2406** 9pm-3am, clsd Mon-Tue • lesbians/gay men • dancing/DJ • food served • live shows

### TRAVEL AGENTS

**TCB Travel** 600 Doon Village Rd. **748-0850** ask for Linda

**Uptown Travel** 104 King St. S. **886-3320/(800) 667-0803** IGLTA

### SPIRITUAL GROUPS

**Brethren/Mennonite Council for Lesbigay Concerns** PO Box 43031 **579-3394** Christian support/social network • ask for Gloria

## London

### INFO LINES & SERVICES

**AA Gay/Lesbian** 649 Colborne (at 'Halo Club') • 7pm Mon & Wed • also at Bishop Cronin Church (downstairs) • 8pm Fri • mostly women

**Gay Line 433-3551** 7pm-10pm Mon

**UW Out 432-3078** 7:30pm-10pm Mon • lesbigay student group

### BARS & NIGHTCLUBS

**Halo Club (Gay/Lesbian Community Center)** 649 Colborne St. **433-3762** 7pm-midnight, 9pm-2am wknds • lesbians/gay men • last Fri women only • dancing/DJ • live shows • private club • wheelchair access • also monthly newsletter

**The Junction/Track 722** 722 York St. **438-2625** 24hrs • mostly gay men • food served • live shows • wheelchair access

**The Partner's** 186 Dundas St. **679-1255** 2pm-2am • lesbians/gay men • food served • patio • wheelchair access

**Sinnz** 347 Clarence St. **432-0622** 5pm-3am • lesbians/gay men • dancing/DJ • patio • wheelchair access

### CAFES

**Blackfriars Cafe** 46 Blackfriars **667-4930** 10am-10pm • popular • lesbians/gay men • plenty veggie • full bar • $4-10

### RESTAURANTS

**The Green Tomato** 172 King St. **660-1170** lunch & dinner

### BOOKSTORES & RETAIL SHOPS
**Adonis** 722 York St., 2nd flr. **438-2848** 11am-9pm, til midnight Fri • lesbigay
**Mystic Book Shop** 616 Dundas St. **673-5440** 11am-6pm, clsd Sun • spiritual
**Womansline Books** 573 Richmond St. **679-3416** 10am-5:30pm, til 6pm Fri, clsd Sun • lesbian/feminist

### PUBLICATIONS
**Girl Cult** 48 Craig St. **434-0961** literary porn zine

### SPIRITUAL GROUPS
**Dignity London** (2nd flr. of 'Halo Club') **686-7709** (EVENINGS) 7:30pm 2nd Mon
**Holy Fellowship MCC** 442 Williams St. **645-0744** 7:20pm Sun

## Maynooth (613)

### ACCOMMODATIONS
**Wildewood Guesthouse** 338-3134 lesbians/gay men • all meals included • hot tub • swimming • kids ok by arr. • wheelchair access • $130-150

## Niagara Falls (905)
*(see also Niagara Falls & Buffalo, NY)*

### ACCOMMODATIONS
**Danner House B&B** 12549 Niagara River Pkwy. **295-5166** lesbians/gay men • full brkfst • jacuzzi • smokefree • $85
**Fairbanks House** 4965 River Rd. **371-3716** lesbians/gay men • full brkfst

## Niagara-on-the-Lake (905)

### ACCOMMODATIONS
**The Saltbox B&B** 223 Gate St., Box 773 **468-5423** gay-friendly

## North Bay (705)

### INFO LINES & SERVICES
**Gay/Lesbian/Bisexual North Bay Area** 495-4545 7pm-9pm Mon • social & support group • newsletter

## Oshawa (905)

### INFO LINES & SERVICES
**Proud & Out Durham** 571-7263

### BARS & NIGHTCLUBS
**Club 717** 717 Wilson Rd. S. #7 **434-4297** 9pm-3am, clsd Mon-Wed • mostly gay men • also referral service

## Ottawa (613)
*(see also Hull, Province of Québec)*

### INFO LINES & SERVICES
**237-XTRA** 237-9872 touch-tone lesbigay info
**Gayline/Télégai** 238-1717 7pm-10pm • bilingual helpline
**Pink Triangle Services** 71 Bank St. (above McD's) **563-4818** many groups & services
**Women's Place** 755 Somerset St. W. **231-5144** 9am-4pm, clsd wknds • drop-in center

### ACCOMMODATIONS
**Gabrielle's Guesthouse** 40 Gilmour St. **237-0829** women only • smokefree • reservations required
**Rideau View Inn** 177 Frank St. **236-9309/(800) 268-2082** gay-friendly • full brkfst • smokefree • $58-85

### BARS & NIGHTCLUBS
**Centretown Pub** 340 Somerset St. W. **594-0233** 2pm-1am • lesbians/gay men • dancing/DJ • food served • videos • leather bar upstairs • piano bar downstairs • Th-Sat
**Coral Reef Club** 30 Nicholas **234-5118** Fri-Sat only • lesbians/gay men • more women Fri • dancing/DJ • unconfirmed
**Frankie's on Frank** 303 Frank St., 3rd flr. **233-9195** clsd Sun-Wed • lesbians/gay men • more women Sat • dancing/DJ • live shows
**Icon** 366 Lisgar St. **235-4005** 8pm-3am, clsd Sun-Wed • lesbians/gay men • neighborhood bar • dancing/DJ
**The Lookout** 41 York, 2nd flr. **789-1624** noon-2am • lesbians/gay men • food served • balcony • wheelchair access
**Market Station Bar & Bistro** 15 George St. (downstairs) **562-3540** 2pm-1am, brunch from 11am Sun • gay-friendly • dancing/DJ

### CAFES
**Blue Moon Cafe** 311 Bank **230-1239** 10am-midnight • lesbians/gay men • French • veggie on request • $5-15

### RESTAURANTS
**Alfonsetti's** 5830 Hazeldern, Stittsville **831-3008** noon-11pm, from 5pm Sat, clsd Sun • Italian • veggie • $12-22
**Cafe Antonio's** 327 Somerset St. W. **235-0319** lunch & dinner

**The Cafe News** 284 Elgin **567-6397**
noon-midnight • some veggie • full bar
• wheelchair access • $6-18

**Fairouz** 343 Somerset St. W. **233-1536**
Lebanese

**Manfred's** 2280 Carling Ave. **829-5715**
lunch & dinner • cont'l • some veggie •
full bar • $10-16

### BOOKSTORES & RETAIL SHOPS

**After Stonewall** 105 4th Ave., 2nd flr.
**567-2221** 10am-6pm, til 9pm Fri, noon-
4pm Sun • lesbigay bookstore

**Food for Thought Books** 103 Clarence
St. **562-4599** 10am-10pm

**Mags & Fags** 254 Elgin St. **233-9651**
gay periodicals

**Mother Tongue Books/Femmes de
Parole** 1067 Bank St. **730-2346** 9am-
6pm, til 9pm Th-Fri, clsd Sun

**Octopus Books** 116 3rd Ave. **233-2589**
10am-6pm, til 9pm Th-Fri, clsd Sun-Mon
• progressive

**Wilde's** 367 Bank St. **234-5512** noon-
9pm • lesbigay • wheelchair access

### PUBLICATIONS

**Capital Xtra!** 303-177 Nepean St. **237-
7133** lesbigay newspaper

▲ **Rainbow Choices Directory** (416) **762-
1320/(888) 241-3569** lesbigay entertainment & business directory for Canada

### SPIRITUAL GROUPS

**Dignity Ottawa Dignité** 386 Bank St.
**746-7279**

## Peterborough                    (705)

### INFO LINES & SERVICES

**Rainbow Community/Trent Lesbigay
Collective** 290 Rubidge St. **876-
1845/743-5414** 7:30pm-9:30pm Mon

### ACCOMMODATIONS

**Windmere 652-6290/(800) 465-6327**
gay-friendly • full brkfst • sauna

### BARS & NIGHTCLUBS

**Friends Bistro** 452 George St. **876-0368**
lesbians/gay men • clsd Mon

### EROTICA

**Forbidden Pleasures** 91 George St. N.
**742-3800**

## Picton                          (613)

### ACCOMMODATIONS

**Hadden-Holme B&B** 75 W. Mary St.
**476-7555** gay-friendly

### BARS & NIGHTCLUBS

**Neighbours on 49** RR2, Hwy. 49 **476-
8428** 11am-11pm • gay-friendly • 2nd
Sat of the month private gay dance
9pm-2am

## Port Sydney                     (705)

### ACCOMMODATIONS

**Divine Lake Resort & Cottages** 385-
1212/(800) 263-6600 lesbians/gay men
• resort • brkfst & dinner included •
some veggie • swimming • nudity •
wheelchair access • IGLTA • US$72-96

## Sault Ste. Marie                (705)

### BARS & NIGHTCLUBS

**The Warehouse** 196 James St. **759-1903**
4pm-2:30am • lesbians/gay men • danc-
ing/DJ • live shows • afterhours •
unconfirmed

## Stratford                       (519)

### ACCOMMODATIONS

**Burnside Guest Home** 139 William St.
**271-7076** gay-friendly • on Lake Victoria •
full brkfst • hot tub • smokefree • $40-70

**The Maples of Stratford** 220 Church
St. **273-0810** gay-friendly • smokefree •
$50-90

### BARS & NIGHTCLUBS

**Old English Parlour** 101 Wellington St.
**271-2772** 11:30am-1am, brunch from
10am Sun • gay-friendly • some veggie •
wheelchair access • $10-16

### RESTAURANTS

**Down the Street** 30 Ontario St. **273-
5886** noon-11pm • Mediterranean/
Mexican • full bar • live shows • $10-12

### BOOKSTORES & RETAIL SHOPS

**Fanfare Books** 92 Ontario St. **273-1010**
9:30am-8pm, til 5:30pm Mon, til 5pm Sun

## Sudbury                         (705)

### ACCOMMODATIONS

**Rainbow Guest House** 43 Lorne St.
**688-0561** gay-friendly

### BARS & NIGHTCLUBS

**D-Bar** 83 Cedar St. **670-1189** 8pm-1am
• lesbians/gay men • dancing/DJ • shows

## Thunder Bay                     (807)

### INFO LINES & SERVICES

**Northern Women's Centre** 184 Camelot
St. **345-7802** 9:30am-5pm, clsd wknds

## ACCOMMODATIONS

**Pine Brook Lodge B&B** 683-6114
gay-friendly • food served

## BARS & NIGHTCLUBS

**Harbour 16** 16 S. Cumberland St.
**346-9118** gay-friendly • more gay wknds
• dancing/DJ

## BOOKSTORES & RETAIL SHOPS

**Northern Women's Bookstore** 65 Court
St. S. **344-7979** 11am-6pm, clsd Sun-
Mon • wheelchair access
**Rainbow Books** 264 Bay St. 345-6272
11am-10pm, noon-6pm Sun

## Toronto (416)

### INFO LINES & SERVICES

**519 Church St. Community Centre** 519
Church St. 392-6874 9:30am-10:30pm,
noon-5pm wknds • location for numerous events • wheelchair access
**925-XTRA** 925-9872 touch-tone lesbigay visitors' info
**AA Gay/Lesbian** 487-5591 call for mtgs

**Canadian Lesbian/Gay Archives** 86
Temperance St. **777-2755** 7:30pm-10pm
Tue-Th
**Flashline** 462-7540 DJ Denise Benson's
women's event line
**Lesbigay Youth Line** 962-9688/(800)
**268-9688** 7pm-10pm, clsd Sun
**Toronto Area Gay/Lesbian Phone Line**
964-6600 7pm-10pm Mon-Sat • counseling
**Toronto Convention & Visitors
Association** (800) 363-1990
**Transsexual Transition Support Group**
519 Church St. **925-9872 x2121** 7pm-
10pm 2nd & 4th Fri • for all members of
the gender community & their signifi-
cant others
**Two-Spirited People of the First
Nations** 2 Carlton St. #1006 944-9300
lesbigay Native group
**Women's Centre** 49 St. George St. (Univ.
of Toronto) 978-8201 pro-lesbian center
• call for times

### ACCOMMODATIONS

**Acorn House B&B** 255 Donlands Ave.
463-8274 mostly gay men

# DINAH SHORE
## PALM SPRINGS WEEKEND
### MARCH 26-29, 1998

The Ultimate Hotel & Entertainment
Package at the All Inclusive
**DOUBLE TREE RESORT**
Book today to ensure availability.
For hotel and party ticket Info Call

**310.281.7358**

For Airline reservations call
1•800•433•1790

Produced by JOANI WEIR PRODUCTIONS • POM POM PRODUCTIONS • KLUB BANSHEE

**Allenby B&B** 223 Strathmore Blvd. **461-7095** gay-friendly

**Amblecote B&B** 109 Walmer Rd. **927-1713** gay-friendly • smokefree • IGLTA • $55-70

**Catnaps Guesthouse** 246 Sherbourne St. **968-2323/(800) 205-3694** lesbians/gay men • $45-65

**Dundonald House** 35 Dundonald St. **961-9888/(800) 260-7227** lesbians/gay men • full brkfst • hot tub

**Hotel Selby** 592 Sherbourne St. **921-3142/(800) 387-4788** lesbians/gay men • swimming • IGLTA • $50-110

**Huntley House** 65 Huntley St. **923-6950** gay-friendly

**Mike's on Mutual** 333 Mutual St. **944-2611** mostly gay men • B&B-private home • smokefree • $55-65

**Seaton Pretty** 327 Seaton St. **972-1485** gay-friendly • full brkfst

**Ten Cawthra Square B&B** 10 Cawthra Sq. **966-3074/(800) 259-5474** lesbians/gay men • fireplaces • smokefree • pets ok

**Toronto B&B** 588-8800/927-0354 gay-friendly • contact for various B&Bs

**The Toronto Townhouse** 56-D West Ave. **469-8230** lesbians/gay men • smokefree • $55-125

**Winchester Guesthouse** 35 Winchester St. **929-7949** lesbians/gay men

### BARS & NIGHTCLUBS

**Bar 501** 501 Church **944-3163** 11am-1am • lesbians/gay men • neighborhood bar

**Barn** 83 Granby **977-4684** 9pm-1am, til 4am Fri-Sat • popular • mostly gay men • dancing/DJ • leather • also 'Stables' 977-4702

## *Toronto*

*T*oronto, the capital city of Ontario, is the cultural and financial center of eastern Canada. Not far from Buffalo and Niagara Falls, Toronto has a European ambiance. Restaurants and shops from Asia, India, Europe, and elsewhere attract natives and tourists alike to the exotic Kensington Market (buy your fresh groceries here), Toronto's Chinatown, and the funky shops and artsy cafés on Queen Street West.

For intrepid shoppers, Toronto has a lot to offer. **Out in the Street** carries lesbigay accessories. Big, beautiful femmes can check out **Take a Walk on the Wild Side** for larger-size finery. The **Omega Centre** is the place for metaphysical literature and supplies. Toronto is also well-known for its repertory film scene, so try not to miss the two-week Lesbian Gay Film Fest in the spring, or the global film Festival of Festivals in September. In April, Toronto has *two* weeks of leather pride, topped by the Ms. & Mr. Leather Toronto contest.

Any other time of year, you'll find the women hanging out at **Tango** or **Rose Cafe**—unless it's Friday night, when they might be at **Shag Sundays.** To find out about the latest women's nights, check out the weekly **Xtra!**, available at the **Toronto Women's Bookstore**, and other queer-friendly establishments.

**Big Giant at Government** 132 Queens Quay E. **869-0045** 10pm-4am Fri only • lesbians/gay men • dancing/DJ

**The Black Eagle** 459 Church St. (upstairs) **413-1219** 4pm-1am, from 2pm Sat, brunch from noon Sun • mostly gay men • leather • theme nights

**Bulldog Cafe** 457 Church St. **923-3469** noon-2am • lesbians/gay men • neighborhood bar • also restaurant • home-cooking • $8-12

**Carrington's** 5 St. Joseph St. **944-0559** 11am-2am • mostly gay men • sports bar & dance club

**Catch 22** 379 Adelaide St. W. **703-1583** 9pm-3am, clsd Sun-Tue • gay-friendly • dancing/DJ

**Circus** 488 Yonge St. **963-4348** gay-friendly • Sun women's night • dancing/DJ

**Crews/Tango** 508 Church St. **972-1662** noon-3am • mostly gay men • 'Tango' from 7pm Tue-Sat • mostly women • dancing/DJ

**El Convento Rico** 750 College St. **588-7800** 8pm-4am Wed-Sun, clsd Mon-Tue • mostly gay men • dancing/DJ • Latin/salsa music • mostly Latino-American • live shows

**Industry 'Slam'** 901 King St. W. **260-2660** 10pm-8am Sat only • gay-friendly • dancing/DJ • patio • wheelchair access

**Phoenix 'Grand'** 410 Sherbourne St. **323-1251** gay-friendly • gay night Th • dancing/DJ

**The Playground** 11-A St. Joseph St. **923-2595** 12:30am-4am, from 11pm Fri-Sat, clsd Mon • lesbians/gay men • dancing/DJ

**Queen's Head Pub** 263 Gerrard St. E. **929-9525** 4pm-1am • gay-friendly • neighborhood bar • food served • patio • wheelchair access

**Rose Cafe** 547 Parliament **928-1495** 5pm-1am, from 8pm winters • mostly women • dancing/DJ • live shows • food served • some veggie • women-owned/run • $5-10

**Shag Sundays** 923 Dundas St. W. (black brick bldg.) **603-2702** Sun only • mostly women • dancing/DJ

**Studio 619** 619 Yonge St., 2nd flr. **922-3068** 11am-1am • mostly gay men • dancing/DJ

**Trax V** 529 Yonge St. **963-5196** 11am-1am • popular • mostly gay men • dancing/DJ • piano bar • live shows • wheelchair access

**Whiskey Saigon** 250 Richmond **593-4646** 10pm-2am, clsd Mon-Wed • gay-friendly • dancing/DJ • live shows • rooftop patio

**Woody's** 467 Church St. **972-0887** noon-2am • popular • mostly gay men • neighborhood bar • wheelchair access

## Toronto (416)

**Lesbigay Info:** 519 Church St. Community Centre: 392-6874. Gay/Lesbian Phone Line: 964-6600, 7pm-10pm Mon-Sat. Xtra! Gay/Lesbian Info Line: 925-9872 (touchtone info).

**Where the Girls Are:** On Parliament St. or elsewhere in 'The Ghetto'—south of Bloor St. W., between University Ave. and Parliament St.

**Lesbigay AA:** AA Gay/Lesbian: 487-5591.

**Lesbigay Pride:** July: 214-0232.

**City Info:** 800/363-1990.

**Attractions:** Eaton Square. CN Tower. Nation Phillips Square. Royal Ontario Museum.

**Best View:** The top of the World's Tallest Building, of course: the CN Tower. Or try a sightseeing air tour or a three-masted sailing ship tour.

**Weather:** Summers are hot (upper 80°s–90°s) and humid. Spring is gorgeous. Fall brings cool, crisp days. Winters are cold and snowy, just as you'd imagined they would be in Canada!

**Transit:** Co-op Taxi: 504-2667. Grey Coach: 393-7911. Transit Information: 393-4636.

## CAFES

**Cafe Diplomatico** 594 College **534-4637** 8am-1am • popular • brkfst • in the center of Little Italy

**The Second Cup** 548 Church St. **964-2457** 24hrs • popular • coffee/desserts

**Threshold Cyber Cafe** 527 Bloor St. W. **588-0881**

## RESTAURANTS

**Avalon** 270 Adelaide St. W. **979-9918** intimate dining

**The Babylon** 553 Church St. **923-2626** 11am-4pm

**Bistro 422** 422 College St. **963-9416** 4pm-midnight

**Byzantium** 499 Church St. **922-3859** 5:30pm-1am • eastern Mediterranean • full bar

**Cafe Jambalaya** 501 Yonge St. **922-5262** Cajun, Caribbean & vegetarian

**Cafe Volo** 587 Yonge St. **928-0008** 11am-10pm, bar til 1am • some veggie • $9-13

**The Courtyard** (at 'Hotel Selby') **921-0665** open May-Sept • full bar • patio

**Hughie's Burgers Fries & Pies** 777 Bay St. **977-2242** full bar • patio

**Il Fornello** 1560 Yonge St. **920-8291** Italian • plenty veggie • also 486 Bloor W. • **588-9358** • also 576 Danforth Ave. **466-2931**

**La Hacienda** 640 Queen W. **703-3377** lunch & dinner • Mexican • sleazy, loud & fun

**The Living Well** 692 Yonge St. **922-6790** noon-1am, til 3am Fri-Sat • plenty veggie • full bar • $8-12

**The Mango** 580 Church St. **922-6525** 11am-1am • popular • lesbians/gay men • full bar • patio

**Pints** 518 Church St. **921-8142** 11:30am-1am • plenty veggie • neighborhood bar • $6-8

**PJ Mellon's** 489 Church St. **966-3241** 11am-11pm • Thai/cont'l • some veggie • wheelchair access • $7-12

**Rivoli Cafe** 332 Queen S. W. **597-0794** 11:30am-11pm, bar til 1am • int'l • some veggie • $8-12

**Splendido** 88 Harbord St. **929-7788** great decor & gnocchi

**Superior Restaurant** 253 Yonge St. **214-0416** 11:30am-midnight • full bar • wheelchair access

**Trattoria Al Forno** 459 Church St. **944-8852** 11am-10pm, from 5pm wknds

**Zelda's** 76 Wellesley St. E. **922-2526**

**ZiZi Trattoria** 456 Bloor St. W. **533-5117**

## BOOKSTORES & RETAIL SHOPS

**A Different Booklist** 746 Bathurst St. **538-0889** 10am-10pm • multi-cultural

**Ex Libris** 467 Church St., 2nd flr. **975-0580** 11am-9pm, til 6pm Wed, from 10am Sat, from noon Sun • new/used lesbigay books

**Glad Day Bookshop** 598-A Yonge St. **961-4161** 10am-9pm, noon-8pm Sun • lesbigay

**The Omega Centre** 29 Yorkville Ave. **975-9086**/**(888) 663-6377** (IN CANADA) 10am-9pm, til 5pm wknds • metaphysical books & supplies

**Out in the Street** 551 Church St. **967-2759**/**(800) 263-5747** hours vary • lesbigay accessories

**Take a Walk on the Wide Side** 161 Gerrard St. E. **921-6112** 10am-7pm, til 11pm Sat • drag emporium

**This Ain't The Rosedale Library** 483 Church St. **929-9912** 10am-7pm

**Toronto Women's Bookstore** 73 Harbord St. **922-8744** 10:30am-6pm, til 7pm Fri, noon-5pm Sun

**Volumes** 74 Front St. E. **366-9522** large selection of int'l periodicals

## PUBLICATIONS

**Fab 599-9273** glossy nat'l lesbigay magazine

**Icon** 960-9607/**(888) 444-4266**

**The Pink Pages** 864-9132 annual lesbigay directory

▲ **Rainbow Choices Directory** 762-1320/**(888) 241-3569** countrywide

**Siren** 778-9027

**Sorority Magazine** 324-2225 lesbian publication for Canada & US

**Xtra!** 925-6665 lesbigay newspaper

## TRAVEL AGENTS

**La Fabula Travel & Tours** 551 Church St. **920-3229**/**(800) 667-2475** IGLTA

**Latitudes Travel** 506 Danforth Ave. **463-2402**/**(800) 558-5179** IGLTA

**Livent** 165 Avenue Rd. #600 **324-5427**/**(800) 555-3559**

**Talk of the Town Travel** 565 Sherbourne St. **960-1393** IGLTA

**Travel Clinic** 506 Church St. #200 **962-2422**/**(800) 387-1240** IGLTA

## SPIRITUAL GROUPS

**Christos MCC** 353 Sherbourne St. (St. Luke's United Church) **925-7924** 7pm Sun

**Congregation Keshet Shalom** 925-9872 x2073/925-1408

**Dignity Toronto Dignité** 11 Earl St. 925-9872 x2011 6:30pm 2nd & 4th Sat

**Integrity Toronto** 925-9872 x2050/(905) 273-9860

**MCC Toronto** 115 Simpson Ave. 406-6228 9am, 11am & 7pm Sun

## GYMS & HEALTH CLUBS

**The Bloor Valley Club** 555 Sherbourne St. 961-4695 gay-friendly • swimming

**Celestina** 462-1491 women's steambath • call for info • women-owned/run

## EROTICA

**Allure** 357-1/2 Yonge St. 597-3953

**Come As You Are** 701 Queen St. W. 504-7934 11am-7pm, til 9pm Th-Fri, til 6pm Sat, noon-5pm Sun • co-op owned sex store

**Doc's Leathers** 726 Queen W. 504-8888 call for appt • fetish clothes • toys • fantasy equipment

**Good For Her** 181 Harbord St. 588-0900 11am-7pm, til 6pm Sat, noon-5pm Sun (women only), clsd Mon-Tue • women's sexuality products

**North Bound Leather** 19 St. Nicholas St. 972-1037 toys • clothing • wheelchair access

**Passage Body Piercing** 473 Church St. 929-7330 also tattoos • scarification

**Priape** 465 Church St. 586-9914/(800) 461-6969 toys • leather

**Studio Auroboros** 580 Yonge St. 962-7499 body ornaments • piercings

## Trenton                                    (613)

### INFO LINES & SERVICES

**S.E.A.L.** 475-1121 info line • newsletter

### ACCOMMODATIONS

**Devonshire House B&B** 394-4572 gay-friendly • Italianate-style red brick farmhouse ca. 1875 • full brkfst • $38-48

## Whitby                                     (905)

### BARS & NIGHTCLUBS

**The Bar** 110 Dundas St. W. 666-3121 8pm-3am, clsd Mon-Wed • lesbians/gay men • dancing/DJ

## Windsor                                    (519)

### INFO LINES & SERVICES

**Lesbian/Gay/Bisexual Phone Line** 973-4951 8pm-10pm Th-Fri

### BARS & NIGHTCLUBS

**Club Happy Tap Tavern** 1056 Wyandotte St. E. 256-8998 2pm-1am, from 8pm Sun • lesbians/gay men • more women Sun • dancing/DJ • live shows

**Limelight** 1880 Wyandotte St. E. 252-0887 4pm-2am, from 11am wknds • lesbians/gay men • neighborhood bar • food served

### SPIRITUAL GROUPS

**MCC Windsor** 977-6897 7pm Sun • call for location

# PRINCE EDWARD ISLAND

## Charlottetown                             (902)

### INFO LINES & SERVICES

**Women's Network** 368-5040

### ACCOMMODATIONS

**Charlottetown Hotel** 894-7371 gay-friendly • swimming • also restaurant • cont'l • lounge clsd Sun • $10-25

**Rainbow Lodge** Station Main, Vernon Bridge 651-2202/(800) 268-7005 gay-friendly • full brkfst • 15 min. outside of town • $80

### BARS & NIGHTCLUBS

**Baba's Lounge** 81 University Ave. 892-7377 noon-2am, from 5pm Sun • gay-friendly • also restaurant • Canadian/Lebanese • some veggie

### BOOKSTORES & RETAIL SHOPS

**Book Mark** 172 Queen St. (in mall) 566-4888 8:30am-9pm • will order lesbian titles

### PUBLICATIONS

**Gynergy Books/Ragweed Press** 566-5750 feminist press • lesbian-owned

## Summerside                                (902)

### INFO LINES & SERVICES

**East Prince Women's Info Centre** 75 Central St. 436-9856 9am-4pm, clsd wknds

# PROVINCE OF QUEBEC

## Chicoutimi (418)

### BARS & NIGHTCLUBS
**Bar Rosco** 70 W. rue Racine 545-9744
3pm-3am • mostly gay men • unconfirmed

## Drummondville (819)

### INFO LINES & SERVICES
**Maison des Femmes (Women's Resource)** 102 rue St-George 477-5957
some lesbian info

### ACCOMMODATIONS
**Motel Alouette** 1975 Boul. Mercure 478-4166 gay-friendly

## Hull (613)

*(see also Ottawa, Ontario)*

### ACCOMMODATIONS
**Le Jardin des Trembles** 29 rue des Chardonnerets 595-8761 women only • $45-55

### BARS & NIGHTCLUBS
**Le Pub de Promenade** 175 Promenade de Portage 771-8810 11am-3am • popular • lesbians/gay men • neighborhood bar • dancing/DJ

## Joliette (514)

### ACCOMMODATIONS
**L'Oasis des Pins** 381 boul. Brassard, St. Paul de Joliette 754-3819 gay-friendly • swimming • camping April-Sept • restaurant open year-round

## Mont Tremblant (819)

### ACCOMMODATIONS
**Versant Ouest B&B** 110 Chemin Labelle 425-6615/(800) 425-6615 lesbians/gay men • country home near skiing • full brkfst • $60-95

## Montréal (514)

### INFO LINES & SERVICES
**AA Gay/Lesbian** 4024 Hingston Ave. (church) 376-9230 7pm Tue & 7:30pm Th
**Gay Line/Gai Ecoute** 866-5090/(888) 505-1010 7pm-11pm
**Gay/Lesbian Community Centre of Montréal** 2035 Amherst St. 528-8424 9am-9pm, clsd wknds
**in•fo** 252-4429 (AKA-4GAY) 24 hour info
**Women's Centre of Montréal** 3585 St-Urbain 842-4780 9am-5pm, til 9pm Tue, clsd wknds • wheelchair access

### ACCOMMODATIONS
**Angelica B&B** 1215 Ste-Elisabeth 844-5048 gay-friendly • full brkfst • $55-120
**Au Bon Vivant Guest House** 1648 Amherst 525-7744 popular • lesbians/gay men • IGLTA • $49-79
**Au Stade** 254-1250 also 'Cachet Accommodations Network' reservation service
**Auberge de la Fontaine** 1301 Rachel St. est 597-0166/(800) 597-0597 gay-friendly • kids ok • wheelchair access • $99-185
**Auberge Encore** 53 rue Milton 524-2493 lesbians/gay men
**Auberge L'Un et L'Autre** 1641 Amherst 597-0878 lesbians/gay men • also restaurant & full bar
**Le Chasseur B&B** 1567 rue St-André 521-2238/(800) 451-2238 mostly gay men • 1920s European townhouse • summer terrace • #39-99
**Chateau Cherrier** 550 Cherrier St. 844-0055/(800) 816-0055 lesbians/gay men • full gourmet brkfst • $50-75
**Les Dauphins** 1281 Beaudry St. 525-1459 gay-friendly
**La Douillette** 7235 de Lorimier St. 376-2183 women only • full brkfst • $40-60
**Ginger Bread House** 1628 St-Christophe 597-2804 mostly gay men • IGLTA
**Hébergement Touristique du Plateau Mont-Royal** 1301 rue Rachel est 597-0166/(800) 597-0597 gay-friendly • B&B network/reservation service
**Home Suite Hom** 523-4642/(800) 429-4983 home exchange
**Hotel Américain** 1042 St-Denis 849-0616 gay-friendly • kitchen • private/shared bath • 33-65
**Hotel de la Couronne** 1029 St-Denis 845-0901 gay-friendly

# Montréal

*M*ontréal is the world's second-largest French-speaking city, and arguably Canada's most cosmopolitan city. There is much to see and do here. You'll discover the Place Ville-Marie, an immense underground shopping promenade. Theatre, dance and music companies as well as a celebrated symphony orchestra thrive in this historic city. Pay a visit to the Latin Quarter and Old Montréal. If you're in town at the end of August, don't miss the World Film Festival. Enjoy the cycling paths along the river banks.

Montréal also has a strong women's community, with several women's guesthouses, a lesbian/gay bookstore and a variety of women's services through the **Women's Centre.** Montréal is home to many women's bars: **Cabaret Sapho, O' Side, Sisters,** and the women-only **Exit.** You can't help but have a wonderful time here.

Just remember that the people of Québec are proud of their French heritage and language. Brush up on your French, or at least learn some of the polite basics: *s'il vous plaît* (please), *merci* (thank you), *pardon* (excuse me), and the all-important question, *Parlez-vous anglais?* (Do you speak English?).

**Hotel du Parc** 3625 Parc Ave. **288-6666** gay-friendly

**Hotel Kent** 1216 rue St-Hubert **845-9835** gay-friendly • $30-65

**Hotel Le St-Andre** 1285 rue St-Andre **849-7070** gay-friendly

**Hotel Lord Berri** 1199 rue Berri **845-9236** gay-friendly • also restaurant • Italian/cont'l • wheelchair access

**Hotel Manoir des Alpes** 1245 rue St-André **845-9803** gay-friendly

**Hotel Pierre** 169 Sherbrooke est **288-8519** gay-friendly • kitchen • $30-65

**Hotel Vogue** 1425 rue de la Montagne **285-5555**/(800) 465-6654 popular • gay-friendly • full service upscale hotel • also restaurant • wheelchair access

**Lesbian/Gay Hospitality Exchange International** 523-1559 membership accommodations exchange

**Lindsey's B&B** 3974 Laval Ave. **843-4869** popular • women only • full brkfst • $55-80

**Le Pension Vallieres** 6562 de Lorimier St. **729-9552** women only • full brkfst • $60-75

**Roy d'Carreau Guest House** 1637 Amherst **524-2493** gay-friendly • smoke-free • $50-95

**Ruta Baggage** 1345 Ste-Rose **598-1586** gay-friendly • full brkfst

**Turquoise B&B** 1576 rue Alexandre de Sève **523-9943** gay-friendly • shared baths • $50-60

## BARS & NIGHTCLUBS

**L' Adonis** 1681 Ste-Catherine est **521-1355** 7pm-3am • usually men only • dancing/DJ • live shows • women allowed Mon-Tue

**Bistro 4** 4040 St-Laurent (Duluth) **844-6246** 9am-midnight, til 2am wknds • lesbians/gay men • food served • cafe

**Cabaret Sapho** 2015 Frontenac St. **523-0292** 8pm-3am • mostly women • shows

**Cafe Fetiche** 1426 Beaudry **523-3013** noon-3am, clsd Sun-Wed • mostly gay men • fetish night Fri • ladies night Sat

**Le Campus** 1111 Ste-Catherine est, 2nd flr. **526-9867** 7pm-3am • mostly gay men • live shows

**Citibar** 1603 Ontario est **525-4251** 11am-3am • lesbians/gay men • neighborhood bar

**Club Bolo** 960 rue Amherst **849-4777** mostly gay men • country/western

**Club Date** 1218 Ste-Catherine est **521-1242** 3pm-3am • gay-friendly • neighborhood bar

**L' Exit** 4297 St-Denis • 2pm-2am • women only • neighborhood bar • beer only

**Foufounes Electriques** 87 Ste-Catherine est **844-5539** gay-friendly • dancing/DJ • live bands • patio

**Groove Society** 1288 Amherst **284-1999** gay-friendly • dancing/DJ • live bands • open bar for women before midnight

**K.O.X.** 1450 Ste-Catherine est **523-0064** 3pm-3am • popular • lesbians/gay men • dancing/DJ • live shows

**Le Lounge** 1333 Ste-Catherine est **522-1333** popular • lesbians/gay men • dancing/DJ • live shows

**Max** 1166 Ste-Catherine est **598-5244** 3pm-3am • popular • mostly gay men • dancing/DJ

**Meteor** 1661 Ste-Catherine est **523-1481** 11am-3am • lesbians/gay men • dancing/DJ • food served

**O' Side** 4075-B St-Denis **849-7126** 1pm-3am • women only • neighborhood bar • also restaurant

**Playground** 1296 rue Amherst **284-2266** 2am-10am Sun • mostly gay men

**Pub du Village** 1366 Ste-Catherine est **524-1960** 9am-3am • popular • lesbians/gay men • food served

## Montréal (514)

**Lesbigay Info:** Centre Communitaire des Gais et Lesbiennes: 528-8424. Women's Centre of Montréal: 842-4780, 9am-5pm. Gay Info Line: 990-1414 (English), 521-1508 (French).

**Where the Girls Are:** In the popular Plateau Mont-Royal neighborhood, or in the bohemian area on Ste-Catherine est.

**Entertainment:** Info Gay Events Hotline: 252-4429.

**Lesbigay AA:** 376-9230.

**Lesbigay Pride:** July: 285-4011.

**Annual Events:**

June - Festival International de Jazz de Montréal: 871-1881. One of the five largest in the world.

August - Montréal World Film Festival: 848-9933. World-class.

October - Black & Blue Party: 875-7026. AIDS benefit dance & circuit party.

**City Info:** Province of Québec Visitors Bureau: 800/363-7777.

**Attractions:** Latin Quarter. Montréal Museum of Fine Arts. Old Montréal & Old Port. Olympic Park. Underground City. Les Halles de la Gare.

**Best View:** From a caleche ride (horse-drawn carriage), or from the patio of the old hunting lodge atop Mont Royal (the mountain in Parc du Mont-Royal).

**Weather:** It's north of New England so winters are for real. Beautiful spring and fall colors. Summers get hot and humid.

**Transit:** Diamond Cab: 273-6331.

**Sisters** 1456 Ste-Catherine est • 10pm-3am Fri-Sat only • popular • mostly women • dancing/DJ • live shows

**Sky** 1474 Ste-Catherine est **529-6969** 10pm-3am • popular • lesbians/gay men • more women Th • dancing/DJ • alternative

**Le St-Sulpice** 1680 St-Denis **844-9458** noon-3am • gay-friendly • dancing/DJ

**Taverne Plateau** 71 Ste-Catherine est **843-6276** 9am-midnight • gay-friendly

## CAFES

**Cafe Titannic** 445 St-Pierre **849-0894** 7am-5pm, clsd wknds • popular • salad & soup

## RESTAURANTS

**L' Ambiance (Salon de thé)** 1874 Notre-Dame ouest **939-2609** 10am-5pm, 11am-3pm Sun brunch • mostly women

**L' Amoricain** 1550 Fullum **523-2551**

**L' Anecdote I** 801 Rachel est **526-7967** 8am-10pm • burgers • some veggie

**Après le Jour** 901 Rachel est **527-4141** cont'l/seafood

**Bacci** 4205 St-Denis **844-3929** 11am-3am • full bar

**Bazou** 2004 Hôtel de Ville **526-4940**

**Callipyge** 1493 Amherst **522-6144** 5pm-11pm, clsd Mon-Tue • Québécois cuisine • popular Sun brunch

**La Campagnola** 1229 rue de la Montagne **866-3234** popular • Italian • great eggplant! • some veggie • beer/wine • $12-20

**Cantarelli** 2181 Ste-Catherine est **521-1817** Italian

**Chablis** 1639 St-Hubert **523-0053** Spanish/French • some veggie • full bar • patio

**Commensal** 400 Sherbrooke est (St-Denis) • vegetarian

**Le Crystal** 1140 Ste-Catherine est **525-9831** 7pm-5am • popular • Greek/American

**Da Salossi** 3441 St-Denis **843-8995** Italian • some veggie • beer/wine

**L' Exception** 1200 St-Hubert **282-1282** vegetarian

**L' Express** 3927 St-Denis **845-5333** 8am-3am • popular • French bistro • full bar • great pâté

**Paganini** 1819 Ste-Catherine • 11:30am-midnight • popular • fine Italian • some veggie

**La Paryse** 302 Ontario est **842-2040** 11am-11pm • lesbians/gay men • burgers • sandwiches

**Piccolo Diavolo** 1336 Ste-Catherine est **526-1336**

**Pizzédélic** 1329 Ste-Catherine est **526-6011** noon-midnight • pizzeria • some veggie • also 3509 boul. St-Laurent **282-6784** • also 370 Laurier ouest **948-6290**

**Saloon Cafe** 1333 Ste-Catherine est **522-1333** 11am-1am, til 3am Fri-Sat • popular • burgers • 'Le Lounge' upstairs

**L' Un & L'Autre** 1641 rue Amherst **597-0878** 11am-1am, from 5pm wknds • bistro • full bar

## ENTERTAINMENT & RECREATION

**Cinema du Parc** 3575 Parc **287-7272** repertory film theatre

## BOOKSTORES & RETAIL SHOPS

**L' Androgyne** 3636 boul. St-Laurent **842-4765** 9am-6pm, til 9pm Th-Fri • popular • lesbigay bookstore • wheelchair access

## PUBLICATIONS

**Fugues/Gazelle/Village** 848-1854 glossy lesbigay bar/entertainment guide

**Le Guide Gai du Québec/Insiders Guide to Gay Quebec** 523-9463 annual guide book

**Homo Sapiens** 987-3000

▲ **Rainbow Choices Directory** (416) 762-1320/(888) 241-3569 lesbigay business directory for Canada

## TRAVEL AGENTS

**M.A.P. Travel** 410 St-Nicholas #118 **287-7446/(800) 661-6627** IGLTA

**Voyages Alternative** 42 Pine Ave. W. #2 **845-7769** IGLTA

## GYMS & HEALTH CLUBS

**Body Tech** 1010 Ste-Catherine est **849-7000**

**Physotech** 1657 Amherst **527-7587** lesbians/gay men

## MEN'S CLUBS

**Colonial Bath** 3963 Colonial **285-0132** usually men only • women only Tue

## EROTICA

**Cuir Plus** 1321 Ste-Catherine est **521-7587** leather • sex toys • wheelchair access

**Priape** 1311 Ste-Catherine est **521-8451** toys & more

## Prevost (514)

### BARS & NIGHTCLUBS

**Le Secret** 3029 boul. Labelle (at 'Hotel Up North', Rte. 117 N.) **224-7350** 9pm-3am • lesbians/gay men • dancing • shows

## Québec (418)

### ACCOMMODATIONS

**727 Guest House** 727 rue d'Aiguillon, Québec **648-5686** lesbians/gay men

**Apartments B&B** 35 rue des Ramparts **655-7685** gay-friendly • restored monastery w/apts. avail. • full brkfst

**L' Auberge Du Quarter** 170 Grande Allée ouest **525-9726** gay-friendly • buffet brkfst

**Auberge Montmorency Inn** 6810 boul. Ste-Anne, L'Ange-Gardien **822-0568** gay-friendly • $55-100

**Le Coureur des Bois Guest House** 15 rue Ste-Ursule **692-1117/(800) 269-6414** lesbians/gay men

**Hotel la Maison Doyon** 109 rue Ste-Anne **694-1720** gay-friendly • $40-80

### BARS & NIGHTCLUBS

**L' Amour Sorcier** 789 Côte Ste-Geneviève **523-3395** 11:30am-3am • popular • lesbians/gay men • neighborhood bar • videos • terrace

**La Ballon Rouge** 811 rue St-Jean **647-9227** 9pm-3am • popular • mostly gay men • dancing/DJ

**Bar L' Eveil** 710 rue Bouvier #120 **628-0610** 11am-3am, clsd Mon-Tue • lesbians/gay men • neighborhood bar

**Fausse Alarme** 161 rue St-Jean **529-0277** 3pm-3am, from 11am summers • mostly gay men • neighborhood bar

**Pub du Carré** 945 rue d'Aiguillon **692-9952** 8am-midnight, clsd Sun • mostly gay men • neighborhood bar • beer only

**Taverne Le Draque** 815 rue St-Augustin **649-7212** 8am-3am • popular • mostly gay men • neighborhood bar • shows • beer/wine • wheelchair access

### CAFES

**Cartoon Cafe** 269 rue St-Jean **648-8967** hours vary • mostly women • women-owned/run

### RESTAURANTS

**Burger Club** 469 rue St-Jean **647-4049** lesbians/gay men • 9am-9pm • lesbian-owned/run

**Le Commensal** 860 rue St-Jean **647-3733** vegetarian

**Le Hobbit** 700 rue St-Jean **647-2677** from 8am • some veggie

**Kookening Kafe** 565 rue St-Jean **521-2121** 11am-midnight, til 1am Th-Sat

**La Playa** 780 rue St-Jean **522-3989** 'West Coast cuisine' • heated terrace

**Poisson d'Avril** 115 St-André **692-1010** French for 'April Fools'

**Restaurant Diana** 849 rue St-Jean **524-5794** 8am-1am, 24hrs Fri-Sat • popular

**Zorba Grec** 854 St-Jean **525-5509** 8am-5pm • Greek • wheelchair access

### BOOKSTORES & RETAIL SHOPS

**L' Accro Librairie** 845 rue St-Jean **522-9920** 11am-6pm, til 9pm Th-Fri • lesbigay

## Rimouski (418)

### INFO LINES & SERVICES

**Maison des Femmes de Rimouski** 78 Ste-Marie #2 **723-0333** 9am-noon & 3pm-7pm, clsd wknds • women's resource center

## Rouyn-Noranda (819)

### BARS & NIGHTCLUBS

**Station D** 82 Perreault ouest **797-8696** lesbians/gay men

## Sherbrooke (819)

### BARS & NIGHTCLUBS

**Complex 13-17** 13-15-17 Bowen sud **569-5580** 11am-3am • 3 bars • lesbians/gay men • dancing/DJ • lesbian bar downstairs

**Les Dames de Coeur** 54 rue King est **821-2217** 4pm-2am, clsd Mon-Tue • lesbians/gay men

### RESTAURANTS

**Au Pot au Vin** 40 rue King est **562-8882** lunch & dinner

## St-Donat (819)

### ACCOMMODATIONS

**Havre du Parc Auberge** 2788 Rte. 125 N. **424-7686** gay-friendly • quiet lakeside inn • food served

## St-Hyacinthe (514)

### BARS & NIGHTCLUBS

**Bistrot Mondor** 1400 Cascades ouest **773-1695** 8am-3am • mostly women • neighborhood bar

## Trois Rivières (819)

INFO LINES & SERVICES
**Gay Ami** 373-0771/693-1884 (FOR WOMEN) lesbigay social contacts

ACCOMMODATIONS
**Le Gîté Du Huard** 42 rue St-Louis 375-8771 gay-friendly

BARS & NIGHTCLUBS
**L' Intrigue** 1528 Notre-Dame 693-1979 gay-friendly
**La Maison Blanche #3** 767 St-Maurice 379-4233 9pm-3am • lesbians/gay men • dancing/DJ • live shows
**Le Lien** 1572 rue Royal 370-6492 1pm-3am • gay-friendly • neighborhood bar

## Verdun (514)

INFO LINES & SERVICES
**Centre des Femmes de Verdun** 4255 rue Wellington 767-0384 9am-noon & 1pm-4pm, clsd wknds • general women's center • limited lesbian info

# SASKATCHEWAN

## Ravenscrag (306)

ACCOMMODATIONS
**Spring Valley Guest Ranch** 295-4124 popular • gay-friendly • 1913 character home • cabin • tipis • also restaurant • country-style • $35-55

## Regina (306)

INFO LINES & SERVICES
**Circle of Pride AA Group** 585-3238 7:30pm Fri
**Pink Triangle Community Services** 24031 Broad St. 525-6046 8:30pm-11pm Tue & Fri
**Regina Women's Community Centre** 2505 11th Ave. #306 522-2777 9am-4:30pm, clsd wknds

BARS & NIGHTCLUBS
**Oscar's** 1422 Scarth St. 522-7343 8:30pm-2am • lesbians/gay men • shows

SPIRITUAL GROUPS
**Dignity Regina** 569-3666 6:30pm 3rd Sun
**Koinonia** 3913 Hillsdale Ave. 525-8542 7pm 2nd & 4th Sun • interfaith worship

## Saskatoon (306)

INFO LINES & SERVICES
**Gay/Lesbian AA** 665-5626
**Gay/Lesbian Line** 665-1224 noon-4:30pm & 7:30pm-10:30pm, til 5:30pm Sat

ACCOMMODATIONS
**Brighton House** 1308 5th Ave. N. 664-3278 gay-friendly • hot tub • smokefree • kids ok • wheelchair access • lesbian-owned • $35-55

BARS & NIGHTCLUBS
**Diva's** 220 3rd Ave. S. #110 (alley entrance) 665-0100 8pm-2am, clsd Mon • lesbians/gay men • dancing • private club

CAFES
**Cafe Browse** 269-B 3rd Ave. S. 664-2665 10am-10pm, from noon wknds • full bar

RESTAURANTS
**The Epicurean Cafe** 340 3rd Ave. N. 244-8880 11am-2am, from 4pm Sat, clsd Sun • full bar

BOOKSTORES & RETAIL SHOPS
**Out of the Closet** 241 2nd Ave S., 3rd flr. 665-1224 lesbigay materials • boutique run by the info line

PUBLICATIONS
**Perceptions** 244-1930 covers the Canadian prairies

TRAVEL AGENTS
**Jubilee Travel** 108-3120 8th St. E. 665-6945 IGLTA

SPIRITUAL GROUPS
**Affirm (United Church)** 653-1475 1st Sun

# YUKON

## Whitehorse (403)

INFO LINES & SERVICES
**Gay/Lesbian Alliance of the Yukon Territory** PO Box 5604, Y1A 5H4 667-7857
**Victoria Faulkner Women's Centre** 207-D Elliott 667-2693 11am-2pm, clsd wknds

## DOMINICAN REPUBLIC

### Puerto Plata (787)

#### ACCOMMODATIONS

**Purple Paradise** Cabarete 571-0637
women only • swimming • $55

### Santo Domingo (787)

#### ACCOMMODATIONS

**Hotel David** Arzobispo Novel 308, Zona
Colonial 688-8538 gay-friendly

#### BARS & NIGHTCLUBS

**Le Pousse Cafe** 107 19 de Marzo • popular • lesbians/gay men • dancing/DJ
**Pariguayso** Calle Padre Billini #412
682-2735 lesbians/gay men
**The Penthouse** Calle Saibo & 20th St.
(difficult to find) • clsd Sun-Wed • popular • lesbians/gay men • dancing/DJ

#### CAFES

**Industrias Taveras** Bonao 682-2735
cheese market on the way to the beaches of Puerto Plata • 40 mi. N. of Santo
Domingo on W. side of Autopista Duarte

#### RESTAURANTS

**Cafe Coco** Calle Sanchez 153 687-9624
noon-10pm • English • full bar • shows

## DUTCH WEST INDIES/ARUBA

### Oranjestad (297)

#### BARS & NIGHTCLUBS

**Cafe the Paddock** 94 L.G. Smith Blvd.
83-23-34 gay-friendly • neighborhood
bar
**The Cellar** 2 Klipstraat 82-64-90 3pm-
5am • popular • gay-friendly • neighborhood bar • also 'The Penthouse' from
11pm • lesbians/gay men • dancing/DJ •
alternative
**Jewel Box Revue** La Cabana Resort &
Casino 87-90-00 gay-friendly • shows
**Jimmy's** Waterweg & Middenweg 82-25-
50 afterhours • popular • gay-friendly •
neighborhood bar • food served
**Paradiso** 16 Wilhelminastraat

#### CAFES

**Grand Cafe Cobra** 60 L.G. Smith Blvd.
(Marisol Bldg.) 83-31-03

#### ENTERTAINMENT & RECREATION

**Sonesta Island** European (topless) side

## FRENCH WEST INDIES

### St. Barthelemy (596)

#### ACCOMMODATIONS

**Hostellerie des 3 Forces** Vitet
27-61-25/(800) 932-3222 gay-friendly •
mountaintop metaphysical retreat •
swimming • food • IGLTA • $120-170
**Hotel Normandie** 27-62-37 gay-friendly
**Hotel Saint-Barth Isle De France** 27-
61-81 gay-friendly • luxurious hotel
includes French cuisine • $300-800
**St. Bart's Beach Hotel** Grand Cul de
Sac 27-60-70 gay-friendly
**Village St. Jean** 27-61-39/(800) 633-
7411 gay-friendly

#### BARS & NIGHTCLUBS

**American Bar** Gustavia • gay-friendly •
food served
**Le Sélect** Gustavia 27-86-87 gay-friendly • more gay after 11pm

#### RESTAURANTS

**Eddie's Ghetto** Gustavia • Creole
**Newborn Restaurant** Anse de Caye 27-
67-07 French Creole

#### ENTERTAINMENT & RECREATION

**Anse Gouverneur St. Jean Beach** nudity
**Anse Grande Saline Beach** nudity •
gay section on the right side of Saline
**L'Orient Beach** gay beach

### St. Martin (590)

#### ACCOMMODATIONS

**Holland House** Philipsburg 52-25-72
gay-friendly • on the beach • $79-195
**Meridien L'Habitation** Anse Marcel
87-67-00/(800) 543-4300 gay-friendly •
great beach • $160-450
**Orient Bay** Mont Vernon 873-
1110/(800) 223-5695 gay-friendly • studio & apt units • $105-185

#### BARS & NIGHTCLUBS

**The Greenhouse** Bobby's Marina,
Philipsburg 52-29-41 gay-friendly •
dancing/DJ • food served
**Pink Mango** at 'Laguna Beach Hotel',
Nettle Bay 87-59-99 6pm-3am • popular
• lesbians/gay men • dancing/DJ

#### RESTAURANTS

**Le Pressoir** 87-76-62 $18-20
**Rainbow** Grand Case Beach 87-55-80
lunch & dinner • $23-27

## JAMAICA

### Montego Bay (809)

ACCOMMODATIONS
**Half Moon Club** 954-2211/(800) 237-3237 gay-friendly • $145-500

### Ocho Rios (312)

ACCOMMODATIONS
**Seagrape Villas** (312) 693-6884/(800) 637-3608

## PUERTO RICO

### Aguada (787)

ACCOMMODATIONS
**San Max** 868-2931 lesbians/gay men • guesthouse & studio apt on the beach • weekly rentals

BARS & NIGHTCLUBS
**Johnny's Bar** Carretera 115 gay-friendly • inquire at 'San Max' accommodations for directions

### Bayamón (787)

BARS & NIGHTCLUBS
**Gilligan's** Betances D-18 Hnas. Davila **786-5065** gay-friendly • live shows • private club
**Yabba Dabba Pub** Rd. 110 • open daily

### Cabo Rojo (787)

BARS & NIGHTCLUBS
**Village Pub Cafe** 851-6783 gay-friendly • inquire locally

### Caguas

BARS & NIGHTCLUBS
**Villa Camito Country Club** off old Hwy. 3 (turn right at 'Cafe de los Pisos') • from 6pm Sat • popular • lesbians/gay men • food served • live shows • unconfirmed

### Coamo (787)

ACCOMMODATIONS
**Parador Baños de Coamo** 825-2186/825-2239 gay-friendly • resort • mineral baths • also restaurant • full bar • kids ok • public baths

### Isabela

BARS & NIGHTCLUBS
**Paradise Cocktail Lounge** Hacia La Playa de Jobos, Carr. 466, at km.06.3 • 9pm-close, clsd Mon-Tue • mostly gay men • unconfirmed
**Villa Ricomar** 8 Calle Paz, Carretera 459, Barrio Jobos • from 9pm Fri-Sat, from 6pm Sun, clsd Mon-Fri • lesbians/gay men • dancing/DJ • live shows

### Mayaguez

BARS & NIGHTCLUBS
**Roma** Calle de Diego 151 • clsd Mon-Wed • lesbians/gay men • dancing/DJ • private club • unconfirmed

### Ponce

BARS & NIGHTCLUBS
**The Cave** Barrio Teneria #115 • mostly gay men • dancing/DJ • live shows

### San German

BARS & NIGHTCLUBS
**Norman's Bar** Carretera 318, Barrio Maresúa • 6pm-1am • lesbians/gay men • dancing/DJ • salsa & merengue
**The World** Rd. 360 km. 1 **264-2002** 10pm-7am, clsd Sun-Tue & Th • gay-friendly • dancing/DJ

### San Juan (787)

INFO LINES & SERVICES
**GEMA Hotline** 723-4538 lesbian alternative to the bar scene
**Madres Lesbianas** 722-4838 lesbian mothers group
**Telefino Gay** 722-4838/(800) 981-9179

ACCOMMODATIONS
**Atlantic Beach Hotel** 1 Calle Vendig, Condado **721-6900/(888) 611-6900** popular • lesbians/gay men • swimming • also restaurant • full bar • IGLTA
**Casa del Caribe Guest House** 57 Caribe St., Condado **722-7139** gay-friendly • $35-50
**Casita Bonita By The Sea** 3 Calle Histella **728-1241** lesbians/gay men • $70-80
**Condado Inn** 6 Condado Ave. **724-7145** lesbians/gay men • guesthouse • terrace restaurant & lounge • near beach

**El Canario Inn** 1317 Ashford Ave., Condado **722-3861**/**(800) 533-2649** gay-friendly

**El San Juan Hotel & Casino** 6063 Isla Verde Ave. **791-1000**/**(800) 468-2818** gay-friendly • great restaurant • swimming

**Embassy Guest House** 1126 Seaview, Condado **725-8284** across the street from beach

**Glorimar Guesthouse** 111 University Ave., Rio Piedras **759-7304**/**724-7440** gay-friendly • rms & apts

**Gran Hotel El Convento** 100 Christo St., Old San Juan **723-9020**/**(800) 468-2779** popular • gay-friendly • swimming

**Hotel Iberia** 1464 Wilson Ave., Condado **722-5380** lesbians/gay men • European-style hotel • also restaurant • gay-owned/run

**L' Habitation Beach Guesthouse** 1957 Calle Italia, Ocean Park **727-2499** lesbians/gay men • on the beach • IGLTA • $45-85

**Marriott Resort & Casino** 1309 Ashford Ave. **722-7200** gay-friendly • food served • swimming

**Numero Uno on the Beach** 1 Calle Santa Ana, Ocean Park **726-5010** gay-friendly • swimming • full bar & grill • wheelchair access

▲ **Ocean Walk Guest House** 1 Atlantic Pl., Ocean Park **728-0855**/**(800) 468-0615** gay-friendly • Spanish-style home on the beach near Condado • swimming • IGLTA

## BARS & NIGHTCLUBS

**Boccacio** Muñoz Rivera, Hato Rey (across from Fire Dept. on dead end street) • popular • lesbians/gay men • dancing/DJ • live shows

**Choices** 70 Eñasco, Hato Rey • open wknds • gay-friendly • dancing/DJ • unconfirmed

**Cups** Calle San Mateo #1708, Santurce **268-3570** clsd Mon • mostly women

**Eros** 1257 Ponce de Leon, Santurce **722-1131** 9pm-4am, clsd Mon-Tue • popular • lesbians/gay men • dancing/DJ • live shows • videos

**Junior's Bar** 602 Calle Condado, Santurce • 6pm-2am • lesbians/gay men • dancing/DJ • live shows

**La Laguna Night Club** 53 Calle Barranquitas, Condado • from 10pm • popular • mostly gay men • dancing/DJ • live shows • private club

**Music People** Jose de Diego, Santurce (next to 'Tia Maria's') • lesbians/gay men • dancing/DJ • live shows

## San Juan (787)

**Lesbigay AA:** 8pm Th, 150 Calle Del Parque, Santurce.

**Lesbigay Pride:** June. 261-2590.

**City Info:** 800/223-6530.

**Attractions:** El Morro (Fort). Plaza San José. Casa Blanca. City Wall. San Juan Gate. La Fortaleza. El Arsenal. Catedral de San Juan. Casa del Ayuntamiento (City Hall). Antiguo Casino. Museo de Arte e Historia. Museo Pablo Casals. El Yunque Rainforest. Camuy Caves. Beaches.

**Best View:** From El Morro or alternatively, one of the harbor cruises that depart from Pier 2 in Old San Juan.

**Weather:** Tropical sunshine year-round, with temperatures that average in the mid-80°s from November to May. Expect more rain on the northern coast.

**Tia Maria's** Jose de Diego, Stop 22, Ponce de Leon, Santurce • popular • gay-friendly • liquor shop & bar

### CAFES

**Cafe Amadeus** Calle San Sebastian **722-8635** popular • noon-midnight, clsd Mon

**Cafe Berlin** 407 Calle San Francisco, Old San Juan **722-5205** popular • espresso bar

**Cafe Matisse** 1351 Ashford Ave., Condado **723-7910** popular • live shows

### RESTAURANTS

**Al Dente** Calle Recinto Sur, Old San Juan **723-7303** Italian • $10-15

**Cafe Restaurant La Nueva Union** Carretera 2 & Hwy. 22 (btwn. Arecibo & Hatillo) **878-2353** great traditional fare • 35 mi. W. of San Juan towards the Rincon beaches

**Golden Unicorn** 2415 Calle Laurel **728-4066** 11am-11pm • Chinese

**La Bombonera** 259 San Francisco St., Old San Juan **722-0658** popular

**Panache** 1127 Calle Seaview **725-8284**

**The Parrott Club** 363 Calle Fortaleza, Old San Juan **725-7370** Nuevo Latino bistro & bar • $15-25

**Sam's Patio** 102 San Sebastian, Old San Juan

**Villa Appia** 1350 Ashford Ave., Condado **725-8711** Italian

### PUBLICATIONS

**Puerto Rico Breeze 282-7184** lesbigay newspaper

### EROTICA

**Condom World** 353 Calle San Francisco, Old San Juan **722-5348**

## Vieques Island            (809)

### ACCOMMODATIONS

**La Finca Caribe 741-0495** gay-friendly • guesthouse & cottage • smokefree • $50-650

**Villas of Vieques Island 741-0023/(800) 772-3050** gay-friendly • villa rentals • easy access to San Juan

### ENTERTAINMENT & RECREATION

**Camp Garcia** South Shore, Vieques • best beach • must have ID to enter

OCEAN WALK GUEST HOUSE

The Meeting of Europe & the Caribbean

Charming ambiance of Spanish decor in a lush, tranquil, romantic tropical setting, yet walking distance to female nightlife. Safe & secure economy singles to garden studio apartments. A perfect environment for females and their friends.
Laid-back casual atmosphere.
Directly on the beach.

Oceanfront Bar & Patio Grill
Swimming Pool
Three Sundecks
Continental Breakfast Included

**Atlantic Place #1
San Juan, PR 00911
(787) 728-0855
& 726-0445
1-800-468-0615
(Fax (787) 728-6434**

## US Virgin Islands Oceanfront Resort.

### This *is* Gay/Lesbian Paradise!

**Spectacular View**

**Beach Snorkeling**

**Oceanfront Pool**

**Friendly & Relaxed**

**Rooms/Suites w/Kitchens**

## 800-524-2018

## TOBAGO

### ACCOMMODATIONS

**Grafton Beach Resort** 639-0191 gay-friendly • food served • swimming • $160-250

**Kariwak Village** Crown Point 639-8442 gay-friendly • cottages • swimming • $50-90

### RESTAURANTS

**Rouselles** Bacolet St. 639-4738 West Indian • $12-15

### Store Bay Beach (868)

### RESTAURANTS

**Miss Jeans** E. side of the island nr. the airport 639-0211 great crab legs

## VIRGIN ISLANDS

### St. Croix (809)

### ACCOMMODATIONS

**King Christian Hotel** 59 Kings Wharf, Christiansted 773-2285 gay-friendly • swimming • also restaurant

▲ **On The Beach Resort** 127 Smithfield Rd., Frederiksted 772-1205/(800) 524-2018 beachfront resort • swimming • also restaurant • full bar

**Prince Street Inn** 402 Prince St., Frederiksted 772-9550 gay-friendly • apts • near beach

### BARS & NIGHTCLUBS

**The Last Hurrah** King St., Frederiksted 772-5225 gay-friendly

### RESTAURANTS

**Cafe Madeleine** Teague Bay 773-8141 Italian/cont'l • $20-25

**Craig & Sally's** Charlotte Amalie • Caribbean delights

### St. John (809)

### ACCOMMODATIONS

**Gallows Point Suite Resort** Cruz Bay 776-6434 gay-friendly • beachfront resort • all suites • swimming • kitchens • also restaurant • full bar

**Maho Bay & Harmony** V.I. National Park 776-6240/(800) 392-9004 gay-friendly • camping & environmentally aware resort

**Oscar's Guest House** Estate Pastory #27 776-6193/(800) 854-1843 gay-friendly • near outdoor recreation

**Sunset Pointe** 773-8100 rental residences

### RESTAURANTS

**Asolare** Rte. 20, Cruz Bay 779-4747 Asian • $20-25

**Barracuda Bistro** Wharfside Village 779-4966 diner fare • $5-10

**Le Chateau de Borbeaux** Junction 10, Centerline Rd. 779-4078 great view • $20-25

### TRAVEL AGENTS

**Sail Ananda** Cruz Bay 776-6922 private charters

## St. Thomas                              (809)

### ACCOMMODATIONS

**Blackbeard's Castle** 776-1234/(800) 344-5771 popular • gay-friendly • swimming • also restaurant • $110-190

**Danish Chalet Guest House** 774-5764/(800) 635-1531 gay-friendly • overlooking harbor • spa • deck • limited wheelchair access • $60-95

**Hotel 1829** Government Hill 776-1829/(800) 524-2002 gay-friendly • swimming • full bar

**Pavilions & Pools Hotel** 6400 Estate Smith Bay 775-6110/(800) 524-2001 gay-friendly • 1-bdrm villas each w/own private swimming pool • wheelchair access

### CAFES

**Lemon Grass Cafe** 777-1877

### RESTAURANTS

**Blackbeard's Castle** 776-1234

**Fiddle Leaf Restaurant** Government Hill • dinner only, clsd Sun • popular

**Romano's** eastern shore 775-3633 popular • Italian • $16-28

### ENTERTAINMENT & RECREATION

**Morning Star Beach** popular gay beach

### TRAVEL AGENTS

**Journeys by the Sea** 6501 Redhook Plaza, #201 (787) 775-3660/(800) 825-3632 yacht vacation • day sails • IGLTA

## Tortola                                 (809)

### ACCOMMODATIONS

**Fort Recovery Estate Village** 495-4354/(800) 367-8455 gay-friendly • swimming • kids ok • in British Virgin Islands

## MEXICO

## Acapulco                                (52-74)

### ACCOMMODATIONS

**Acapulco Las Palmas** 155 Ave. Las Conchas 87-08-43 lesbians/gay men • private villas • food service • swimming

**Casa Condesa** 125 Bella Vista 84-1616 mostly gay men

**Casa Le Mar** Lomas Del Mar 32-B 84-1022 mostly gay men • full brkfst • swimming • maid & cook avail.

**Fiesta American Condesa** Costera Miguel Aleman 84-2355/(800) 223-2332 gay-friendly • popular • swimming • $135-155

**Las Brisas** 84-1580/(800) 223-6800 popular • gay-friendly • luxury resort • rms w/private pools

**Royale De Acapulco & Beach Club** Calle Caracol 70, Fraccion Amiento Farallón 84-3707 gay-friendly • swimming • food served

**Villa Costa Azul** 555 Fdo. Magallanes 84-5462 lesbians/gay men • swimming • IGLTA

### BARS & NIGHTCLUBS

**Demas** Privada Piedra Picuda #17 (behind 'Carlos & Charlie's') • from 10pm • popular • lesbians/gay men • dancing/DJ

**La Melinche** Picuda 216 (behind Plaza Condesa) • mostly gay men • live shows

**Open House** back of Plaza Condesa (upstairs) 84-7285 mostly gay men • live shows

**Relax** Calle Lomas de Mar 7 84-0421 9pm-5am, clsd Mon-Wed • mostly gay men • dancing/DJ • live shows

### RESTAURANTS

**Beto's Beach Restaurant** Condesa Beach • lesbians/gay men

**Jovitos** Costera (across from the Fiesta Americana Condesa) • traditional fare • plenty veggie

**Kookaburra** Carretera Escénica (at Marina Las Brisas) 84-1448 popular • int'l • $20-25

**La Guera de Condesa** Condesa Beach

**La Tortuga** Calle Lomas del Mar 5-A • noon-2am • full bar

**Le Bistroquet** Andrea Doria #5, Fracc. Costa Azul 84-6860 popular • lesbians/gay men • turn off the costera at the Oceanic Park

**Su Casa/La Margarita** Ave. Anahuac 110 **84-4350** traditional cuisine • great views

## Aguascalientes

### BARS & NIGHTCLUBS

**Merendero Kikos** Calle Arturo J. Pani 132 • open til 11pm • gay-friendly • food served

### RESTAURANTS

**Restaurant Mitla** Calle Madero 220
**Restaurant San Francisco** Plaza Principal

## Cabo San Lucas          (52-114)

### ACCOMMODATIONS

**Hotel Hacienda Beach Resort** Playa el Medano **3-01-22/(800) 733-2226** gay-friendly • $145-350

### BARS & NIGHTCLUBS

**The Rainbow Bar & Grill** Blvd. de la Marina **#39-C 3-14-55** popular • lesbians/gay men • dancing/DJ • patio

### RESTAURANTS

**Casa Rafael's** Playa el Medano **3-07-39** elegant • $19-42
**Da Giorgio** on the corridor **3-29-88** romantic Italian • $7-20
**Damiana** Blvd. Mijares 8, San Jose del Cabo **3-04-99** seafood • $11-26
**Mi Casa** Ave. Cabo San Lucas **3-19-33** great chicken mole • $8-16

## Cancun          (52-98)

### ACCOMMODATIONS

**Camino Real** Paseo Kukulcan **85-2300/(800) 722-6466** gay-friendly • swimming
**Caribbean Reef Club** Puerto Morelos **(800) 322-6286** popular • gay-friendly • swimming • food served
**Playa Del Sol** Ave. Yaxchilan 31 **84-3690** gay-friendly • $60-95
**Villa Catarina** Calle Privada, Playa del Carmen • **73-0970** gay-friendly • $35-65

### BARS & NIGHTCLUBS

**Caramba** Ave. Tulum 87 **84-0032** 10pm-close • gay-friendly • dancing/DJ
**Picante Bar** Avenida Tulum 20 (east of Ave. Uxmal) • 9:30pm-4am • popular • mostly gay men
**Ta' Qüeno** Ave. Yaxachilián 15 • 9pm-4am • mostly gay men • dancing/DJ • live shows

### ENTERTAINMENT & RECREATION

**Chichén Itza** the must-see Mayan ruin 125 mi. from Cancun

### GYMS & HEALTH CLUBS

**Shape** Calle Conoco (1 blk from San Yaxchen) • gay-friendly

## Ciudad Juárez          (52-16)

### ACCOMMODATIONS

**Hotel de Luxe 15-0202** gay-friendly • restaurant & bar • inexpensive
**Plaza Continental** Ave. S. Lerdo de Tejada 112 **12-2610** gay-friendly • also restaurant

### BARS & NIGHTCLUBS

**Club La Madelon** Calle Santos Degollado 771 N. • lesbians/gay men • popular wknds • dancing/DJ • live shows
**Nebraska** Mariscal #251 Centro • til midnight • popular • lesbians/gay men
**Ritz** 1/2 block N. & 1/2 block E. of Hotel de Luxe **14-2291** open til 2am • mostly gay men • neighborhood bar

### RESTAURANTS

**El Coyote Invalido** Ave. Lerdo Sur, 24hrs

## Cozumel          (52-98)

### ACCOMMODATIONS

**La Perla Beach & Diving Resort** Playa Paraiso **72-0188/(800) 852-6404** gay-friendly • swimming
**Sol Cabañas del Caribe** beachfront **72-0017/0072/(800) 336-3542** gay-friendly • food served

### RESTAURANTS

**La Cosa Nostra** 15 Ave. Sur, 548 (btwn. 5 & 7) **212-75** Italian • also room rental avail. • lesbian-owned/run

## Cuernavaca          (52-73)

### ACCOMMODATIONS

**Casa Aurora B&B** Calle Arista 12 (antes 303) **18-6394** gay-friendly • Spanish classes can be arranged • $18-24
**Hotel Narajeva** Sonora 1000 Col. Vista Hermosa • gay-friendly
**Nido de Amor 18-0631** gay-friendly • suites in private home

### BARS & NIGHTCLUBS

**Shadee** Avenida Adolfo Lopez Mateos **12-4367** 9pm-4am • popular • mostly gay men • food served • live shows

## Durango (52-16)

### BARS & NIGHTCLUBS
**Bar Country** 122 Constitución Norte • lesbians/gay men • food served
**Buhós Restaurant & Bar** 615 • 5 de Febero **12-5811** gay-friendly
**Eduardos** 805 • 20 de Noviembre Pte. • lesbians/gay men

## Ensenada (52-68)

### BARS & NIGHTCLUBS
**Club Ibis** Blvd. Costero & Ave. Sagines • Fri-Sat only • gay-friendly • dancing/DJ
**Coyote Club** Blvd. Costero #4/5 & Diamante **47-3691** 9pm-3am clsd Mon-Tue • popular • lesbians/gay men • dancing/DJ • patio
**Ola Verde** Calle Segunda 459-A • popular late night • lesbians/gay men • food

### RESTAURANTS
**Mariscos California** Calle Ruiz & Segunda • 9am-9pm, clsd Mon • seafood

## Guadalajara (52-36)

### ACCOMMODATIONS
**Hotel Calinda Roma** Ave. Juárez 170 **(800) 228-5151** gay-friendly • food served
**Travel Recreation International** 1875 Ave. Libertad, Local-C, Sec Juárez **26-3398** gay-friendly • IGLTA

### BARS & NIGHTCLUBS
**Candilejas** 961 Ave. Niños Héroes (nr. 'Hotel Carlton') • 8pm-4am, clsd Mon • gay-friendly • dancing/DJ • live shows
**La Malinche** 1230 Alvaro Obregón St. & Calle 50, Libertad District • 8pm-3am • popular late night • mostly gay men • dancing/DJ • live shows • food served
**Monica's Disco Bar** 1713 Alvaro Obregón St., Libertad District **43-9544** 9pm-3am, clsd Mon • popular • dancing/DJ • live shows
**SOS Club** 1413 Ave. La Paz, Hidalgo District • 11pm-3am, clsd Mon • lesbians/gay men • dancing/DJ • live shows • popular lesbian hangout

### RESTAURANTS
**Brasserie** 1171 Prisciliano Sanchez St., downtown Juárez District
**Sanborn's** Juárez Ave. &16 de Septiembre st.
**Sanborn's Vallarta** 1600 Vallarta Ave., downtown Juárez District

## Guanajuato (52-47)

### ACCOMMODATIONS
**Castillo Santa Cecilia** Camino a La Valenciana **32-0477** excellent food
**Hotel Museo Posada Sante Fe** downtown **32-0084** gay-friendly

### BARS & NIGHTCLUBS
**El Incendio** Calle Cantarranas 15 **32-1372** gay-friendly

## Jalapa

### BARS & NIGHTCLUBS
**La Mansion** take a cab towards Bandarilla (20 min. NW of town) • Fri-Sat only • lesbians/gay men • live shows

## La Paz (52-11)

### ACCOMMODATIONS
**Casa La Paceña** Calle Bravo 106 **25-2748/(707) 869-2374 (OFF-SEASON)** open Nov-June • gay-friendly
**Gran Baja** gay-friendly • near harbor Mariano Abasolo
**Hotel Perla** 1570 Ave., Alvaro Obregón **22-0777 x131** gay-friendly

### BARS & NIGHTCLUBS
**Bar Intimo** Calle 16 de Septiembre • lesbians/gay men

## Manzanillo (52-33)

### ACCOMMODATIONS
**Las Hadas** Santiago Peninsula **34-1950/(800) 722-6466** gay-friendly • great resort & location • $180-400
**La Leyanda Villas** Club de Yates 12 **33-0281/(800) 232-8482** gay-friendly • private tropical setting
**Pepe's** **33-0616/(415) 346-4734** gay-friendly • food served

## Matamoros

### BARS & NIGHTCLUBS
**Montezuma Lounge** St. 6 Gonzalez • gay-friendly
**Mr. Lee Disco** Ave. de las Rosas, Col. Jardin • gay-friendly • dancing/DJ

## Mazatlan (52-69)

### BARS & NIGHTCLUBS
**Pepe Toro** Ave. de las Garzas 18, Zona Dorado **14-4167** 8pm-4am • lesbians/gay men • dancing • lunch daily

**Valentino's** Ave. Camarón Sabalo • gay-friendly • dancing/DJ

### CAFES
**Panama Restaurant Pasteleria** Ave. del las Garzas & Cammarron Sabalo • lesbians/gay men

### RESTAURANTS
**Restaurante Rocamar** Ave. del Mar, Zona Costera **81-6008** popular

**Señor Frogs** Ave. del Mar, Zona Costera • dancing/DJ • upscale seafood

## Merida                    (52-99)

### ACCOMMODATIONS
**Casa Exilio B&B** Calle 68, N. 495 (btwn. 57 & 59) **28-2505** gay-friendly

**Gran Hotel** Parque Hidalgo, Calle 60 #496 **24-7622** gay-friendly • food served

### BARS & NIGHTCLUBS
**Ciudad Maya** Calle 84 #506 **24-3313** lesbians/gay men

**Kabuki's** Calle 60 & 53 • lesbians/gay men • dancing/DJ • many bars in the area come & go—follow the crowd

**Romanticos Piano Bar** Calle 60 #461 9pm-3am • lesbians/gay men • shows

### CAFES
**Cafe Express** Calle 60 (across from Hidalgo Park)

### RESTAURANTS
**La Bella Epoca** Calle 69 #447 ('Hotel de Parque') **28-1928** 6pm-1am • Yucatan

## Mexicali

### BARS & NIGHTCLUBS
**Copacabana** Ave. Tuxtla Gutierrez & Baja California St. • mostly women • neighborhood bar

**El Taurino** Calle Zuazua 480 & Ave. José Maria Morelos • lesbians/gay men

**Los Panchos** Ave. Juárez 33 • popular • lesbians/gay men • oldest gay bar in Mexicali

**Shaflarelo's Bar** Ave. de la Reforma & Calle Mexico • open late • gay-friendly • live shows

**Tare** Calle Uxmal & Ave. Jalisco • mostly gay men

## México City              (52-5)

### INFO LINES & SERVICES
**Calamo Gay Center** 118 Culiacán, 3rd flr. • support & social group

**Casa de la Sal** A.C. Córdoba 76, Roma Sur **207-8042**

**Gay/Lesbian AA** 123 Culiacán Atlas, Colonia Hipodromo Condessa • 8pm Mon-Sat, 6pm Sun

**Voz Humana A.C.** 530-2873/2592

### ACCOMMODATIONS
**Aristos** Paseo de la Reforma #276 **211-0112/(800) 527-4786** gay-friendly • swimming

**Hotel Casa Blanca** Lafragua #7 **566-3211/(800) 448-8355** gay-friendly • swimming • food served

**Hotel Krystal Rosa** Liverpool #155 **221-3460/(800) 231-9860** gay-friendly • swimming • food served

**Hotel Michelangelo** Calle Rio Amazonas 78 **566-9877** gay-friendly • kitchen • $40

**Marco Polo** 27 Amberes, Pink Zone **207-1893/(800) 223-0888** gay-friendly • upscale hotel

**Westin Galeria Plaza** Hamburgo #195 **211-0014/(800) 228-3000** gay-friendly • swimming • food served

### BARS & NIGHTCLUBS
**Alquimia** Arriaga 31 • clsd Sun-Mon • mostly gay men • drag bar

**Anyway/Exacto** Monterrey 47 **533-1691** lesbians/gay men • live shows • food served • 3 flrs including women's bar

**Butterfly Disco** Calle Izazaga 9 & Ave. Lazaro Cárdenas Sur • 9pm-4am, clsd Mon • popular • lesbians/gay men • live shows

**Caztzi** Calle Carlos Arellano 4, Ciudad Satélite • lesbians/gay men • dancing/DJ • live shows

**Dolce Vita** Orizaba 146, Colonia Roma **585-7406** gay-friendly • popular • dancing/DJ

**Dreams** Reforma Norte 76 • clsd Sun-Mon • mostly gay men • dancing/DJ

**El Don** 79 Tonalá St. • 9pm-4am • lesbians/gay men • dancing/DJ • live shows

**El Taller** Ave. Florencia 37-A • lesbians/gay men • dancing/DJ • live shows

**Enigma** Calle Morelia 111 • more women Th

**Privata** Ave. Universidad 1901 Col. Copilco **661-5939** mostly gay men • dancing/DJ

**Tom's Leather Bar** Ave. Insurgentes Sur 357 • mostly gay men • leather

## RESTAURANTS

**El Almacen** Florencia 37 **207-6956** Mediterranean • full bar

**El Hábito** 13 Madrid St., Coyoacan District • avante-garde theater

**La Fonda San Francisco** Calle Velázquez de Leon 126 **546-4060** noon-1am • lesbians/gay men • live shows

**La Opera** Calle 5 de Mayo 10 • 1pm-midnight, clsd Sun • mostly gay men

**Vip's Hamburgo** 126 Calle Hamburgo, Zona Rosa • also at Paseo de la Reforma & Florencia (near Independence Angel Statue) • also Niza & Hamburgo

## BOOKSTORES & RETAIL SHOPS

**El Angel Azul** 64 Londres A & B • periodicals • clothing

**Sueños Salvajes** 177 E. Zapata, Col. Portales

## PUBLICATIONS

**Ser Gay 534-3804** covers all Mexico nightlife, limited resources

## TRAVEL AGENTS

**Stag Travel & Tours** 525-4658 IGLTA

# Monterey

## BARS & NIGHTCLUBS

**Charaos** Calle Isaac Garza Oriente & Zaragoza • open late, clsd Sun • gay-friendly • dancing/DJ

**Fridas** Calle Padre Mier Poniente • lesbians/gay men • live shows

**Obelisco** Ave. Juán Ignacio Ramón 333 Pte., 3rd flr. • 10pm-2am, clsd Sun-Tue • popular • lesbians/gay men • dancing/DJ • live shows

**Vongole** Blvd. Pedrera 300 **336-0335** 10pm-3am, clsd Sun-Tue • mostly gay men • dancing/DJ • live shows • unconfirmed

## BOOKSTORES & RETAIL SHOPS

**Revisteria Johnny** Calle Aramberri 807 Poniente

# Morelia (52-43)

## ACCOMMODATIONS

**CasaCamelinas B&B** 14-0963/(415) 661-5745 mostly women • 3-1/2 hours from Mexico City

## BARS & NIGHTCLUBS

**Los Ebines** Ave. Madero Pte. & Guadalajara 5039 • gay-friendly • dancing/DJ • live shows

---

**No Que No** Ave. Campestre & Rincón de los Compadres • 10pm-3am, clsd Mon • mostly gay men • dancing/DJ • live shows

## CAFES

**Cafe Bizare** 90 Ignacio Zaragoza (at 'Posada dela Soledad Hotel') **12-1818**

**Cafe Catedral** Portal Hidalgo 23

## RESTAURANTS

**Las Mercedes** Calle Leon Guzmán 47 **12-6113** popular

# Oaxaca (52-95)

## ACCOMMODATIONS

**Mission de los Angeles Hotel** 15-1500/1000/(800) 221-6509 gay-friendly • food served • swimming

**Stouffer Presidente** 300 Ave. 5 de Mayo (800) 468-3571 gay-friendly • 4-star hotel • food served • swimming

## BARS & NIGHTCLUBS

**Bar Jardin** Portal de Flores **16-2092** lesbians/gay men • food served

**Coronita** Bustamante & Xochitc • gay-friendly

**La Cascada** Bustamante, N. of Periferico • popular • mostly gay men • food served

## RESTAURANTS

**El Asador Vasco** Portal de Flores (upstairs) **16-9719** great views

# Pátzcuaro (52-45)

## ACCOMMODATIONS

**Hotel Posada San Rafael** Plaza Vasco de Quiroga **42-0770** gay-friendly • food served

## RESTAURANTS

**Doña Pala** Calle Quiroga

# Puebla

## BARS & NIGHTCLUBS

**Keops Disco** Calle 14 Poniente 101, Cholula • 10pm-3am Fri-Sat only • popular • lesbians/gay men • dancing/DJ • live shows

**La Cigarra** 5 Poniente & 7 Sur, Centro • popular • lesbians/gay men

**La Fuente** Hermanos Serdán 343 • gay-friendly • dancing/DJ

# Holly's Mexico

## A SPECIAL PLACE FOR EVERYONE
### South of the Border

Holly's Casa

# Walk To The Beach!
▼
## Kayaking, Surfing
## Relaxing!
#### Located 35 mi. from Puerto Vallarta

**Website: www.hollysplace.com**
e-mail: Hollys@oakweb.com

business calls
530-544-7040

reservations
800-745-7041

## Puerto Vallarta (52-32)

### ACCOMMODATIONS

**Casa de los Arcos** 22-5990/(800) 424-3434 x277 lesbians/gay men • private villa

**Casa dos Comales** Calle Aldama 274 23-2042 gay-friendly • $75-125

**Casa Panoramica B&B** 22-3656/(800) 745-7805 gay-friendly • overlooking Bandares Bay & old downtown Puerto Vallarta • full brkfst • swimming • IGLTA

▲ **Holly's Mexico** (800) 745-7041 mostly women • vacation rental • ocean view • $75

**Jungle Nancy Villa** (800) 936-3646 gay-friendly • lesbian-owned/run

**Paco Paco Descanso del Sol** 583 Pino Suarez 23-2077/(800) 936-3646 popular

**Red Parrot B&B** (514) 581-8376/(800) 821-1619 lesbians/gay men

**Vallarta Cora** 174 Pilitas 23-2815 gay-friendly • apts • swimming

**Villa Felíz** 22-0798/(800) 424-3434 x277 lesbians/gay men • full brkfst

### BARS & NIGHTCLUBS

**Blue Chairs (Tito's)** southern Los Muertos Beach • lesbians/gay men • food served

**Club Paco Paco** Ignacio L. Vallarta 278 22-1899 3pm-4am • popular • lesbians/gay men • dancing/DJ

**Los Balcones** 182 Juárez & Libertad, upstairs 24671 10pm-3am • mostly gay men • dancing/DJ

**Mario's** 264 Ignacio L. Vallarta 24-060 10am-3am • lesbians/gay men

**Paco's Ranch** Calle Venustiano Caranza 239 • 3pm-6am • popular • lesbians/gay men • dancing/DJ • live shows

**Paco's Sunset Bar** 583 Pino Suarez 23-2077 noon-10pm • popular • lesbians/gay men • swimming • also restaurant

**Zotano** 101 Morelos by Plaza Rio 30303 lesbians/gay men • dancing/DJ

### CAFES

**Adobe Cafe** 252 Basilio Badillo • Southwestern

**Cafe des Artistes** popular

**Cafe Sierra** Insurgentes 109 22-2748 9am-11pm • lesbians/gay men • full bar

**Le Bistro Jazz Cafe** Isla Ria Cuale #16-A • popular • expensive & touristy

**The Net House** Ignacio Vallarta 232 2-5764 cybercafe

**Rosa's Espresso** Olasa Altas 399

### RESTAURANTS

**Bombo's** 327 Corona • gourmet int'l

**Cuiza** Isla Rio Cuale, West Bridge 22-5646 lesbians/gay men

**La Palapa** Los Muertos Beach (nr. pier)

**Memo's Casa de los Hotcakes** 289 Basilio Badillo • popular

**Papaya 3** 169 Abasolo • natural food/sandwiches

**Santos** Francisca Rodriguez 136 22-5670 clsd Mon • lesbians/gay men • full bar

**Sego's** 625 Aguiles Serdán • popular • steaks/Mexican

### BOOKSTORES & RETAIL SHOPS

**Azul Siempre Azul** Ignacio Vallarta 228

**La Tienda** Rodolfo Gomez 122 • also Basilio Badillo 276 location

**Safari Accents** 244 Olas Altas

**Studio Rustico** Basilo Badillo 300 • gay-owned/run

### TRAVEL AGENTS

**Amadeus Tours** 23-2815

**Doin' It Right Travel** (415) 621-3576/(800) 936-3646 Puerto Vallarta gay travel specialist • IGLTA

## Queretaro

### BARS & NIGHTCLUBS

**La Iguana** Ave. Universidad 308 (at 'Hotel Maria Teresa') • gay-friendly • dancing/DJ • live shows

## San Jose del Cabo

### ACCOMMODATIONS

**Palmilla** Apartado Postal 52, 23400 (714) 833-3025/(800) 637-2226 gay-friendly • beach-front suites

## San Luis Potosí (52-48)

### BARS & NIGHTCLUBS

**Sheik** Calle Prolongación Zacatecas 347 12-7457 10pm-4am Fri-Sat • lesbians/gay men • dancing/DJ • live shows

## San Miguel De Allende (52-46)

### ACCOMMODATIONS

**Aristos San Miguel De Allende** 30 Calle Ancha de Santonio 52-0149/(800) 223-0880 gay-friendly • full-service hotel

**Casa de Sierra Nevada** 35 Calle Hospicio **52-0415/(800) 223-6510** gay-friendly

### BARS & NIGHTCLUBS
**El Ring** 25 Calle Hidalgo • 10pm-4am Fri-Sat • gay-friendly • dancing/DJ

## Tampico

### BARS & NIGHTCLUBS
**Bilbao** W. of Calle Francisco I. Madero Oriente & A. Serdan Sur • lesbians/gay men

**Tropicana Bar** Calle de General López de Lara Sur • lesbians/gay men

## Tepic                    (52-32)

### CAFES
**Cafe La Parroquia** Calle Amado Nerro 18 (upstairs) **12-6772**

### RESTAURANTS
**Wendy's** Ave. México, Norte 178 • (not burgers)

## Tijuana                   (52-66)

### INFO LINES & SERVICES
**Gay/Lesbian Info Line 88-0267**

### ACCOMMODATIONS
**Fiesta Americana Hotel** 4558 Blvd. Agua Caliente **81-7000/(800) 343-7821** gay-friendly • expensive rates

**La Villa De Zaragoza** 1120 Ave. Madero **85-1832** gay-friendly

**Plaza De Oro Hotel** 2nd St. & Ave. 'D' **85-1437** gay-friendly

**Valla Playas 89-1052/(619) 236-0984** gay-friendly • expensive rates

### BARS & NIGHTCLUBS
**Caramba** Ave. Revolución • gay-friendy • dancing/DJ • near 'Mike's Disco'

**El Taurino Bar** 198 Niños Héroes Ave. (btwn. 1st St. & Coahuila) **85-2478** 10am-3am, til 6am wknds • popular • lesbians/gay men • live shows

**Elilio's Cafeteria Musical** 1810-11 Calle Tercera (3rd St.) • nr. 'C' St. • from dusk til 3am • lesbians/gay men

**Extasis** Larroque 213 • lesbians/gay men • dancing/DJ

**Los Equipales** 2024 7th St. (opposite Jai Alai Palace) **88-3006** from 9pm, clsd Mon-Tue • popular • lesbians/gay men • dancing/DJ • live shows

**Mike's** 1220 Revolución Ave. & 6th St. **85-3534** 9pm-6am Mon-Tue only • popular • lesbians/gay men • dancing/DJ • live shows

**Noa Noa** Calle Primera & 154 'D' Miguel F. Martinez Ave. **81-7901** from 9pm, clsd Mon • popular • lesbians/gay men • dancing/DJ • live shows

**Terraza 9** Calle 5 & Ave. Revolución **85-3534** 8pm-2am • lesbians/gay men

**Villa Garcia** 751 Plaza Santa Cecilia • lesbians/gay men

### PUBLICATIONS
**Frontera Gay 88-0267**

## Toluca

### BARS & NIGHTCLUBS
**Bar El Conde** 201-E Passaje Curi Norte • gay-friendly • food served

**Bar El Jardin** 100-D Ave. Hildalgo Ote. • gay-friendly

**Cafe del Rey** Portal 20 de Noviembre • gay-friendly • food served

**Vip's Toluca** Paseo Tollocán & Blvd. Isidoro Fabela • lesbians/gay men

## Tuxtla Gutierrez

### BARS & NIGHTCLUBS
**Sandy's Bar** Calle 9 Sur & 8 Poniente (inquire in 'Via Fontana') • gay-friendly • transgender-friendly

## Veracruz                  (52-29)

### ACCOMMODATIONS
**Hotel Imperial** Plaza de Armas **32-8788** gay-friendly • food served • expensive

### BARS & NIGHTCLUBS
**Deeper** Calle Icazo 1005 (Victoria & Revillagigedo) **35-0265** lesbians/gay men • dancing/DJ

**Hippopotamos** Fracc. Costa Verde • 9pm-6am, clsd Mon-Wed • gay-friendly • dancing/DJ • live shows

**Sotano's Bar** Calle 1 & Olmedo **37-0444** 10pm-5am, clsd Sun-Wed • mostly gay men • dancing/DJ

## Villahermosa               (52-93)

### ACCOMMODATIONS
**Hotel Don Carlos** Ave. Madero 418, Centro **12-2499** gay-friendly • food served

**Hyatt Villahermosa** 106 Juarez Ave. **13-4444/(800) 233-1234** gay-friendly

BARS & NIGHTCLUBS
**Yardas** 1318 Ave. 27 de Febrero **13-4362**
• lesbians/gay men

## Zacatecas                          (52-49)

ACCOMMODATIONS
**Quinta Real Zacatecas** Ave. Rayon 434
22-9104/(800) 878-4484 • 5-star hotel

BARS & NIGHTCLUBS
**La Toma** Calle Juárez 116 • clsd Sun-
Tue • gay-friendly • dancing/DJ

CAFES
**Cafe Acropolis** Ave. Hidalgo

## Zihuatanejo

BARS & NIGHTCLUBS
**La Cambina del Captain** Calle Vincente
Guerrero & Nicolas Bravo, 2nd flr.
**La Casita** Camino escenico a Playa 'La
Ropa' (across from 'Kontiki' restaurant)
**Roca Rock** Calle 5 de Mayo • gay-friend-
ly • dancing/DJ

RESTAURANTS
**Splash** Calle Ejido & Calle Vincente
Guerrero • popular • lesbians/gay men

## COSTA RICA

## Arenal                          (506)

ACCOMMODATIONS
**Arenal Lodge** 228-3189 gay-friendly •
volcano views • $95

ENTERTAINMENT & RECREATION
**The Arenal Volcano** hourly eruptions
**Tabacon Hot Springs** La Fortuna
222-1072 10am-10pm • $13

## Manuel Antonio                  (506)

ACCOMMODATIONS
**El Parador** 777-1437/(800) 451-4398
gay-friendly • large resort • swimming
**El Parque** 777-0096 gay-friendly • food
served • $55-75
▲ **Hotel Casa Blanca** 777-0253
lesbians/gay men • walking distance to
gay beach • swimming • $40-80
**Makanda by the Sea** 777-0442 gay-
friendly • private oasis • swimming •
$85-125
**Si Como No** 777-1250/(800) 237-8207
popular • gay-friendly • swimming •
$85-210

# Casa

# Blanca

**Gay owned, gay managed guest house for
exclusively gay/lesbian guests!
Located within walking distance to the beach,
overlooking the Pacific and National Park!**

## Contact us for more information:

Hotel Casa Blanca de Manuel Antonio S.A.
Apdo. 194, Entrada "La Mariposa"
6350 Quepos-MI.Ant., Costa Rica, Central America
Phone and Fax: (+506) 777-0253

**Internet: cblanca@sol.racsa.co.cr
http://bertha.pomona.claremont.edu/cblanca/**

### BARS & NIGHTCLUBS

**Arco Iris** behind iron bridge at the waterfront, Quepos • gay-friendly

**Kamuk Pub** at 'Katuk Hotel' (downtown), Quepos • til 4am • gay-friendly • live shows

**Vela Bar** 1st Beach **777-0413** gay-friendly • food served

### RESTAURANTS

**El Barba Roja** Quepos • popular • great sunset location

**El Gran Escape** Quepos • clsd Tue • Tex-Mex

**Karola's** Quepos • clsd Wed • great brkfst w/a view

**Mar y Sombra** 1st Beach • local flavor

**The Plinio** (at the 'Hotel Plinio') **777-0055** Italian

**Tico Rico** paved road to national park, Quepos • lunch & dinner includes use of pool bar

### TRAVEL AGENTS

**Costa Rica Connection** (805) 543-8823/(800) 345-7422

## Puntarenas                    (506)

### ACCOMMODATIONS

**Casa Yemaya** 661-0956 women only • travel planning avail. • Spanish classes • lesbian-owned/run • $15-35

### BARS & NIGHTCLUBS

**La Deriva** • gay-friendly

## San Jose                      (800)

### ACCOMMODATIONS

**Amstel Amon** (800) 575-1253 gay-friendly • modern hotel • quiet location • food served

**Cariari Hotel & Country Club** (800) 227-4274 gay-friendly • luxury resort w/great golfing • swimming

**Colours—The Guest Residence** El Triangulo, Blvd. Rohrmoser **32-35-04**/(800) 934-5622/(305) 532-9341 lesbians/gay men • premier full-service accommodations w/tours & reservation services throughout Costa Rica • swimming • IGLTA • $70-109

**Don Carlos B&B** 221-6707 popular • gay-friendly • $50-60

**Hotel L'Ambiance** 949 Calle 27 **23-15-98** gay-friendly • also restaurant & bar • courtyard • IGLTA • $90

**Joluva Guesthouse** Calle 3 B, Aves. 9 & 11 #936 **223-7961**/(800) 298-2418 lesbians/gay men • $18-45

### BARS & NIGHTCLUBS

**Antros** Ave. 14 (btwn. Calles 7 & 9) • gay-friendly

**Cantabrico** Ave. 6 (btwn. Calles Central & 2nd) • lesbians/gay men

**De Ja Vu** Calle 2 (btwn. Aves. 14 & 16) • 8pm-close, from 9pm Fri-Sat, clsd Mon-Th • popular • lesbians/gay men • dancing/DJ • live shows • take taxi to avoid bad area

**El Churro Español** Calle 11 (btwn. Aves. 8 & 10) • lesbians/gay men

**La Avispa** Calle 1 #834 (btwn. Aves. 8 & 10—pink house) • clsd Mon & Th • mostly women Wed • popular T-dance Sun

**La Esmeralda** Ave. Segunda (btwn. Calles 5 & 7) • gay-friendly • food served • live shows

**La Taberna** Calle 1 (btwn. Aves. 7 & 9—no sign) • 6pm-midnight • mostly gay men • on 1st & 2nd flrs.

**Monte Carlo** Ave. 4 & Calle 2 (on corner) • gay-friendly

### CAFES

**Cafe de Teatro National** National Theatre **223-4488** lunch

### RESTAURANTS

**La Cocina de Lena** El Pueblo area • 5 min. from downtown • Costa Rican • $12

**La Perla** Calle Central Ave. 2 (on corner)

**La Piazetta** Paseo Colon • Italian • $18

**Machu Pichu** off Paseo Colon • just outside downtown area • Peruvian seafood • $18

**Nimbe** Escazu (suburb) 281-1739

**Vishnu Vegetarian Restaurant** Ave. 1 (btwn. Calles 3 & 1) • popular • $5

# FRANCE

## Paris (33-1)

Arrondisements (city districts) are listed after street addresses. 1er=1st arrondisement, 2e= 2nd arrondisement, etc.

Note: When phoning Paris from the US, dial the country code + the city code + the last 8 digits of the phone number.

### ACCOMMODATIONS

**Le 55 Guest House** 55 ave. Reille (14e) 01 45 89 91 82

**A Flat in Paris** 01 40 61 99 11

**Agora** 7 rue de la Cossonnerie (1er) 01 42 33 46 02

**Castille** 33 rue Cambon (1er) 01 44 58 44 58/(800) 448-8355 gay-friendly • ultra luxe hotel • $385-470

**Crillon** 10 place de la Concorde (8e) 01 47 23 78 33/(800) 888-4747 gay-friendly • ultra luxe hotel • $510-820

**Du Vieux Paris** 9 rue Gite-le-Coeur (6e) 01 43 54 41 66 gay friendly • historic bldg. • in-room minibar

**The Grand** 2 rue Scribe (9e) 01 40 07 32 32/(800) 327-0200 gay-friendly • ultra luxe hotel • $340-500

**L' Hôtel** 13 rue des Beaux-Arts (6e) 01 44 41 99 00 gay-friendly • small upscale hotel • $190-560

**Hôtel Beaubourg** 11 rue Simon le Franc (4e) 01 42 74 34 24 gay-friendly • $160-200

**Hôtel de la Bretonnerie** 22 rue St-Croix-de-la-Bretonnerie (4e) 01 48 87 77 63 gay-friendly • historic full service hotel • $125-155

**Hôtel de Saintonge** 16 rue de Saintonge (3e) 01 42 77 91 13 gay-friendly

**Hôtel des Nations** 54 rue Monge (5e) 01 43 26 45 24 gay-friendly • small independent hotel in the Latin Quarter

**Hôtel Les Iris** 80 rue de la Folie Regnault (11e) 01 43 57 73 30 gay-friendly

**Hôtel Moderne du Temple** 3 rue d'Aix (10e) 01 42 08 09 04 gay-friendly • economy class hotel in the middle of Paris

**Hôtel Muguet** 11 rue Chevert (7e) 01 47 05 05 93 gay-friendly • recently renovated • $92-102

**Hôtel Place des Vosges** 12 rue de Birague (4e) 01 42 72 60 46 gay-friendly • basic budget hotel • $60-98

**Hôtel Saint-Louis Marais** 1 rue Charles V (4e) 01 48 87 87 04 gay-friendly • small hotel • $120-140

**Insightful Travelers** 57 Rutland Sq., Boston MA (617) 859-0720 (US) gay-friendly • short-term apt rentals

**Libertel Croix-de-Malte** 5 rue de Malte (11e) 01 48 05 09 36/(800) 949-7562 gay-friendly • $94-107

**Libertel Grand Turenne** 6 rue de Turenne (4e) 01 42 78 43 25/(800) 949-7562 gay-friendly • $156-168

**Louxor** 4 rue Taylor (10e) 01 42 08 23 91 gay-friendly

**Paris Séjour Réservation** 645 N. Michigan Ave. #638, Chicago IL (312) 587-7707 (US) gay-friendly • short-term apt rentals

**The Ritz** 15 place Vendôme (1er) 01 42 60 38 30/(800) 223-6800 gay-friendly • ultra luxe hotel • $500-830

**Le Saint-Hubert** 27 rue Traversière (12e) 01 43 43 39 16 gay-friendly

### BARS & NIGHTCLUBS

**Amnesia Cafe** 42 rue Vieille du Temple (4e) 01 42 72 16 94 10am-2am • gay-friendly

**Le Bar du Palmier** 16 rue des Lombards (4e) 01 42 78 53 53 gay-friendly • food served

**Cafe Chantant Karaoke** 12 rue de Plâtre (4e) 01 48 87 51 04 lesbians/gay men • karaoke

**La Champmeslé** 4 rue Chabannais (2e) 01 42 96 85 20 6pm-6am • lesbians/gay men • live shows • women-only room

**Club 18** 18 rue de Beaujolais (1er) 01 42 97 52 13 lesbians/gay men • dancing/DJ • live shows

**Le Day Off** 10 rue de l'Isly (8e) 01 45 22 87 90 gay-friendly • neighborhood bar • food served

**DJ Cafe** 87 rue St-Honoré (1er) 01 40 26 31 92 gay-friendly • piano bar

**Le Duplex** 25 rue Michel-le-Comte (3e) 01 42 72 80 86 8pm-2am • lesbians/gay men • neighborhood bar

**L' Ego Club** 50 rue de la Chaussée d'Antin (9e) 01 42 85 20 38 10pm-close, from 7pm Sun, clsd Mon-Wed • mostly women • dancing/DJ • karaoke • women-only Th & Sun

## Paris

It's hard not to wax poetic about Paris. The most romantic city in the world, Paris has all the characteristics of a capricious lover. Beautiful and witty, dignified and grand, flirtatious and coy, Paris' admirers will tell you she's worthy of life-long devotion. It's hardly surprising, then, that so many artists and thinkers have made Paris their home. Whether it's the museums, the couture, the cafes, the history, the churches, the people... Paris seduces at every turn.

During the day, enjoy the incredible sights of Paris. Drop in at **Les Mots à la Bouche**, the lebigay bookstore, or, if you like your reading material a little spicier, try **La Scarabée d'Or**. At night, stop by one of the women's bars, like **El Scandalo** or **Unity Bar** for a drink. Then head for a lesbian-friendly restaurant; we hear **L'Accent** is particularly charming. Then head for **L'Enfer,** a dance club popular with *les parisiennes.*

## Paris (33-1)

**Lesbigay Info:** Centre Gai et Lesbien de Paris, 01 43 57 21 47, 3 rue Keller (11e). Canal Miel, 01 43 79 61 91 (lesbian info line). Ecoute Gaie, 01 44 93 01 02 (helpline), 6pm-10pm Mon-Fri.

**Lesbigay Pride:** Europride, 27 rue de Faubourg Montmartre, 9e, 01 47 70 01 50.

**City Info:** 01 49 52 53 54, 127 Ave. des Champs-Elysées (8e).

**Attractions:** Louvre. Eiffel Tower. Arc de Triomphe. Notre Dame. Sacré Coeur. Quartier Latin. Centre Pompidou. Musée d'Orsay. Catacombes. Bois de Boulogne. Père Lachaise cemetery: final resting place of Oscar Wilde, Colette, Gertrude Stein, Edith Piaf, Sarah Bernhardt, and Jim Morrison.

**Best View:** Eiffel Tower (of course!) and Sacré Coeur.

**Weather:** Paris really is beautiful in the springtime. Chilly in the winter, the temperatures reach the 70's during the summer.

**Transit:** Alpha Taxis: 01 45 85 85 85. Taxis Bleues: 01 49 36 10 10. Taxis-Radio Etoile: 01 41 27 27 27.

L' Ekivok 40 rue des Blancs Manteaux (4e) 01 42 71 03 29 11pm-close • lesbians/gay men • dancing/DJ • theme nights

L' Enfer 34 rue du Départ (14e) 01 42 79 94 94 midnight-6am Fri-Sat • mostly women • dancing/DJ

Entr'acte 25 blvd. Poissonnière (2e) 01 40 26 01 93 mostly women • dancing/DJ

Gayn's Bar 98 Quai de la Loire (19e) 01 40 03 01 40 9pm-close • gay-friendly • food served

Kit-Kat/Le Privilège 3 Cité Bergère (9e) 01 42 46 50 98 lesbians/gay men • dancing/DJ

Marginal 2 rue Lamandé (17e) 01 45 22 34 82 gay-friendly • neighborhood bar

Michou 80 rue des Martyrs 01 46 06 16 04 gay-friendly • drag shows

Monster's 135 rue St-Martin (4e) 01 42 72 72 72 gay-friendly

Le New Week 1 ave. de Clichy (18e) 01 43 87 17 88 gay-friendly • dancing/DJ

Objectif Lune 19 rue de la Roquette (11e) 01 48 06 46 05 gay-friendly

Open Bar 17 rue des Archives (4e) 01 42 74 62 60 gay-friendly • videos

Le Piano Zinc 49 rue des Blancs Manteaux (4e) 01 42 74 32 42 6pm-2am, clsd Tue • popular • lesbians/gay men • cabaret • smokefree

Queen 102 ave. des Champs-Elysées (8e) 01 43 43 28 48 midnight-6am • mostly gay men • dancing/DJ

El Scandalo 21 rue Keller (11e) 01 47 00 24 59 8pm-2am, clsd Mon-Tue • mostly women • neighborhood bar

Le Tropic Cafe 66 rue des Lombards (1er) 01 40 13 92 62 lesbians/gay men

Unity Bar 176-178 rue St-Martin (3e) 01 42 72 70 59 3pm-2am • mostly women • neighborhood bar

### CAFES

Bistrot Internet 40 blvd. Haussmann (9e) 01 42 82 30 33 10am-7pm • internet cafe

Cafe Beaubourg 100 rue St-Martin (4e) 01 48 87 63 96 next to Centre Pompidou

Cafe Orbita 14 rue Quatre-Septembre (2e) 01 43 25 76 77 10am-10pm • internet cafe

Cox's Cafe 15 rue des Archives (4e) 01 42 72 08 00 lesbians/gay men • internet cafe

The Léwis Cafe 23 rue de Pontieu (8e) 01 42 25 30 35 live shows

### RESTAURANTS

L' Accent 93 rue de Javel (15e) 01 45 79 20 26 clsd Sun • mostly women • Southern French

L' Amazonial 3 rue St-Opportune (1er) 01 42 33 53 13 lunch, dinner & Sun brunch • lesbians/gay men • Brazilian/int'l

Aquarius 54 rue St-Croix-de-la-Bretonnerie 01 48 87 48 71 vegetarian • $20

Au Coeur Couronne 6 rue de la Ferronerie (1er) 01 45 08 11 15 7am-2am

Au Diable des Lombards 64 rue des Lombards (1er) 01 42 33 81 84 brunch daily • American

Au Feu Follet 5 rue Raymond-Losserand (14e) 01 43 22 65 72 from 7:15pm, clsd Sun • mostly women

Au Pied de Cochon 6 rue Coquillière (1er) 01 45 08 48 90 open late • brasserie

Au Rendez-Vous des Camionneurs 72 Quai des Ofèvres (1er) 01 45 08 48 90 lesbians/gay men • traditional French

L' Auberge de la Reine Blanche 30 rue St-Louis en l'île (4th) 01 46 33 07 87 noon-11:30pm • lesbians/gay men • homestyle

Aux Trois Petits Cochons 31 rue Tiquetonne (2e) 01 42 33 39 69 clsd Mon

Le Bleu-Marine 28 rue Leopold-Bellan (2e) 01 42 36 92 44 seafood

La Canaille 4 rue Crillon (4e) 01 42 78 04 71 French

Caviar & Co. 5 rue de Reuilly (12e) 01 43 56 13 98 fish/caviar

La Chaise au Plafond 10 rue du Trésor (4e) 01 42 76 03 22 popular • bistro

Le Chat Pacha 28 rue Beautreillis 01 44 59 83 59 Egyptian

Chez Chareyre 7 rue de l'Echiquier (10e) 01 47 70 65 77 traditional French

Chez Tsou 16 rue des Archives (4e) 01 42 78 11 47 Chinese

Dave 39 rue Saint-Roch (1er) 01 42 61 49 48 popular • Chinese • gay-owned

Le Divin 41 rue St-Croix-de-la-Bretonnerie (4e) 01 42 77 10 20 clsd Mon • French

Fond de Cour 3 rue St-Croix-de-la-Bretonnerie (4e) 01 42 74 71 52 lunch, dinner & Sun brunch • French

The Foufounes 40 rue Vieille du Temple (4e) 01 42 78 86 12 lesbians/gay men • traditional French

**Le Gai Moulin** 4 rue Saint-Merri (4e) **01 42 77 60 60** lesbians/gay men • lunch & dinner, dinner only wknds • French/int'l

**La Gay Rite** 61 rue Quincampoix (4e) **01 40 27 90 52** fish/caviar • $18

**Jo Goldenberg** 7 rue des Rosiers (4e) **01 48 87 20 16** Jewish/Eastern European • popular Sun brunch • $15

**Le Loup Blanc** 42 rue Tiquetonne (2e) **01 40 13 08 35** popular • French

**The Macrobiotheque** 17 rue de Savoie (6e) **01 43 25 04 96** vegetarian

**La Madame Sans Gene** 19 rue de Picardie (3e) **01 42 71 31 71** inexpensive traditional French

**La Maison** 1 rue de la Bucherie (5e) **01 43 29 73 57** contemporary French • terrace dining • gay-owned/run

**Nini Peau d'Chien** 24 rue des Taillandiers (11e) **01 47 00 45 35** traditional French • popular wknds

**Le Petit Cabanon** 7 rue Ste-Apolline (3e) **01 48 87 66 53** mostly women • traditional French

**Les Planches Doudeauville** 36 rue Doudeauville (18e) **01 42 54 12 56** lesbians/gay men

**La Poule au Pot** 9 rue Vauvilliers (1er) **01 42 36 32 96** 7pm-6am, clsd Mon • bistro

**Ravi** 50 rue Verneuil **01 42 61 17 28** Indian • $55

**Reconfort** 37 rue de Poitou (4e) **01 42 76 06 36** popular • fish/caviar • $35

**Restaurant le Petit Prince** 12 rue de Lanneau (5e) **01 43 54 77 26** dinner, clsd Tue

**La Route du Château** 36 rue Raymond-Losserand (14e) **01 43 20 09 59** lesbians/gay men • French

**La Taverne de l'Est** 72 blvd. de Strasbourg (10e) **01 42 03 60 64** French • live shows

**Le Web Bar** 32 rue de Picardie (3e) **01 42 72 66 55** open late • internet cafe

**Xavier** 89 blvd. de Courcelles (8e) **01 43 80 78 22** lesbians/gay men • light fare

### ENTERTAINMENT & RECREATION

**'Tata Beach'** nr. Tuileries, across from Musée d'Orsay • sunbathing

### BOOKSTORES & RETAIL SHOPS

**La Librairie Fourmi Ailée** 19 rue du Fouarre (5e) • lesbian/feminist

**Les Mots à la Bouche** 6 rue Sainte-Croix-de-la-Bretonnerie (4e) **01 42 78 88 30** 11am-11pm, til midnight Fri-Sat, 2pm-6pm Sun • lesbigay bookstore • English titles

**La Scarabée d'Or** 61 rue Monsieur-le-Prince (6e) **01 46 34 63 61** 10am-7pm, clsd Sun • wide variety of pansexual erotic writing & art involving women

**The Village Voice** 6 rue Princesse (6e) **01 46 33 36 47** 10am-8pm, from 2pm Mon, clsd Sun • English language

### PUBLICATIONS

**3 Keller** **01 43 57 21 47** magazine of the Paris Gay/Lesbian Center

**Têtu** **01 48 03 84 30** stylish & intelligent lesbigay monthly

### TRAVEL AGENTS

**French Touch** 13 rue Stephenson (18e) **01 41 10 38 37**

**So Now You Know Someone in Paris** **01 40 29 06 76** concierge/guide service

### SPIRITUAL GROUPS

**Beit Haverim** **01 44 84 08 54** 8pm-10pm 1st & 3rd Wed • lesbigay Jewish social group

**David & Jonathan** 92-B rue de Picpus (12e) **01 43 42 09 49** 6pm-8pm Fri • interdenominational lesbigay Christian group

### GYMS & HEALTH CLUBS

**Les Bain du Marias** 31-33 rue des Blancs Manteaux (4e) **01 44 61 02 02** day spa • call for women's days

**Gymnasse Club** 147b rue St. Honoré **01 40 20 03 03** gay-friendly • day passes avail. • many locations throughout city

### EROTICA

**Démonia** 10 cité Joly (11e) • 11am-7pm • women's BDSM shop

## **UNITED KINGDOM**

### London (44-171)

#### INFO LINES & SERVICES

**Audre Lorde Clinic** 377-7312/(44-181) 846-1576/7 Wed & Fri • lesbian health clinic • call for appt. & location

**Black Lesbian/Gay Centre** 5/5A Westminster Bridge Rd., Rm. 113 **620-3885** 11am-7:30pm Tue & Th • helpline 7pm-10pm Th • 837-5364

**London Lesbian Line** 251-6911 2pm-10pm Mon & Fri & 7pm-10pm Tue-Th

**London Lesbian/Gay Switchboard** 837-7324 24hr

**Outlinks Lesbian/Gay/Bi Youth Project** 378-8732 4pm-6pm Tue & Th

#### ACCOMMODATIONS

**160 Regents Park Road** 160 Regents Park Rd., Primrose Hill **586-5266** lesbians/gay men • full brkfst • private/shared baths

**Bailey's Hotel** 140 Gloucester Rd. 737-6000 gay-friendly

**Comfort Hotel** 22-32 Cromwell Rd. 373-3300 gay-friendly

**George Hotel** Templeton Pl. 370-2285 gay-friendly

**Guy's** 38 Baldry Gardens (44-181) 679-7269 gay-friendly

**Holland Park Hotel** 6 Ladbroke Ter. 792-0216 gay-friendly

**Hotel Halifax** 65 Philbeach Gardens 373-4153 gay-friendly

**Manor House Hotel** 53 Manor Park (44-181) 318-5590 gay-friendly

**The New York Hotel** 32 Philbeach Gardens, Earl's Court 244-6884 lesbians/gay men • private/shared baths • non-smoking rms avail. • wheelchair access

**Number Seven Guesthouse** 7 Josephine Ave. (44-181) 674-1880 lesbians/gay men

**The Philbeach Hotel** 30-31 Philbeach Gardens 373-1244 gay-friendly

**Redcliffe Hotel** 268 Fulham Rd. 351-2467 gay-friendly

**Reeves Hotel** 48 Shepherd's Bush Green (44-181) 740-1158 gay-friendly

**Russell Lodge** 20 Little Russell St. 430-2489 gay-friendly

#### BARS & NIGHTCLUBS

*Note: 'Pub hrs' usually means 11am-11pm weekdays, and Sundays noon-3pm and 7pm-10:30pm.*

**The Angel** 65 Graham St. **608-2656** noon-midnight, til 11:30pm Sun • lesbians/gay men • women's night Tue • also restaurant

**Attic Bar** 13-14 Maiden Ln. (upstairs at the 'Peacock') **836-8260** 5:30pm-11:30pm • gay-friendly

**Bar Code** 3/4 Archer St. **734-3342** mostly gay men • pub hours

**The Beautiful Thing/ Marlow's** 443 New Cross Rd. (44-181) 691-9090 open late • 3 flrs. • lesbians/gay men • women only Wed • neighborhood bar • dancing/DJ • live shows • also restaurant

**Benjy's** 562-A Mile End Rd. **980-6427** 9pm-1am Sun only • popular • gay-friendly • dancing/DJ

**The Blah Bar** 305-A North End Rd. **385-9359** mostly gay men • dancing/DJ

**The Blarney Stone** 48A High St., Acton (44-181) 992-1568 lesbians/gay men • neighborhood bar • Irish pub • karaoke • private club

**The Box** Seven Dials, Monmouth St. 240-5828 pub hours, from noon Sun • lesbians/gay men • dancing/DJ • food served • women's night Sun

**Cafe Amsterdam** 142-148 W. Cromwell Rd., W. Kensington 602-8611 til midnight, til 2am wknds • lesbians/gay men • also restaurant • cabaret wknds

**Cafe Au-Reole** 233 Earls Ct. Rd. **912-1409** til midnight • lesbians/gay men

**Compton's of Soho** 53 Old Compton St. **437-4445** pub hours, 7pm-10:30pm Sun • popular • mostly gay men

**The Dome** 178 Junction Rd. • lesbians/gay men • 'Club Kali' 3rd Fri & 'Shakti' 4th Fri • dancing/DJ • multi-racial clientele

**Drill Hall** 16 Chenies St. **631-1353** 6pm-11pm • women only Mon • dancing/DJ

**Due South** 35 Stoke Newington High St. 249-7623 lesbians/gay men • women only Th • dancing/DJ • live shows

**Duke of Clarence** 140 Rotherfield St. 226-6526 lesbians/gay men • women only Wed • dancing/DJ • food served • live shows

**Duke of Clarence/ Clarries** 57 Portland Rd. **(44-181) 655-4184** open late • lesbians/gay men • neighborhood bar • dancing/DJ • cabaret

**The Empire** Little Turnstile **405-6791** gay-friendly

**FF** 63-B Clerkenwell Rd. (Turnmills) **250-3406** 9pm-6am Sun only • lesbians/gay men • dancing/DJ • wild techno

**Fridge Bar** 1 Town Hall Parade, Brixton Hill **326-5100** pub hours, from 5am Sun • also dance club

**George Music Bar** 114 Twickenham Rd., Isleworth **(44-181) 560-1456** lesbians/gay men • neighborhood bar • also restaurant • live shows

**Glass Bar** 190 Euston Rd. • women only

**The Gloucester** 1 King William Walk **(44-181) 858-2666** pub hours • gay-friendly • neighborhood bar • food served • live shows

**The Green House/ Prohibition Bar** 2-A Sunny Hill Rd., Streatham **677-7562** lesbians/gay men • dancing/DJ • live shows • also restaurant

**The Greyhound** 11 High St., Guildford • 7pm-11pm • lesbians/gay men • disco wknds • live shows

**H2O** 130 Balls Pond Rd., Islington **(44-181) 452-1330** fetish parties for men & women • theme nights • call for events

**Jacque of Clubs/ Diamonds** 47 Ossory Rd. (off Old Kent Rd.) **252-0007** 9pm-4am • women only Sat • dancing/DJ

**The Joiner's Arms** 116-118 Hackney Rd. • lesbians/gay men • neighborhood bar • live shows

**King William IV** 77 Hampstead High St. **435-5747** pub hours • lesbians/gay men • neighborhood bar • food served

**Klub Kruzin'** 269 West End Ln., West Hampstead **431-2211** pub hours • lesbians/gay men • neighborhood bar • live shows

**Leisure Lounge** 121 Holborn **738-2336** popular • 10pm-5am Fri 'Popstarz' • lesbians/gay men • dancing/DJ

**The Naughty Parrot** 78 E. Dulwich Grove **(44-181) 693-2975** pub hours • lesbians/gay men • hip cabaret

**The Oak** 79 Green Lanes **354-2791** til midnight, til 2am wknds • lesbians/gay men • women only Wed • dancing/DJ • live shows • also cafe

**Oasis/ Club en Femme** 388 Green Lanes, Haringay • 9pm-3am 1st Fri only • lesbians/gay men • dancing/DJ • glamour/drag night

**The Paradise Bar/ Je Suis Music** 460 New Cross Rd. • popular • 8pm-late Sun only • lesbians/gay men • dancing/DJ

**The Popstarz Bar** 2 George Ct., Adelphi **839-4012** pub hours • lesbians/gay men • neighborhood bar

**Queen's Arms** 63 Courthill Rd., Lewisham **(44-181) 318-7305** lesbians/gay men • neighborhood bar • live shows • upscale

**Raw** 120 Romford Rd. **(44-181) 534-1955** 9pm-2am Sat only • lesbians/gay men • dancing/DJ • food served • live shows

**Reflections** 8 Bridge Rd., Stratford **(44-181) 519-1296** open late • lesbians/gay men • dancing/DJ • cabaret

**Renegade Ranch** Great Russell St. (at 'Central Club Hotel') • 8pm-midnight Fri only • lesbians/gay men • dancing/DJ • country/western

**The Roebuck** 25 Rennell St. **(44-181) 852-1705** pub hours • lesbians/gay men • neighborhood bar • dancing/DJ • live shows • also restaurant

**Royal George** Valance Rd. **247-4150** pub hours • lesbians/gay men • neighborhood bar • cabaret

**Royal Oak** 73 Columbia Rd. **739-8204** pub hours, brkfst from 8am Sun • lesbians/gay men • women only Fri • neighborhood bar • food served • live shows

**Royal Vauxhall Tavern** 372 Kennington Ln. **582-0833** mostly gay men • women only Fri • neighborhood bar • dancing/DJ

**The Ship & Whale** 2 Gulliver St., Rotherhithe **394-3536** open late wknds • lesbians/gay men • neighborhood bar • dancing/DJ • live shows

**The Spiral Staircase** 138 Shoreditch High St. **613-1351** 8pm-2am, til 4am wknds • lesbians/gay men • neighborhood bar • dancing/DJ • karaoke • live shows

**Stepney's Nightclub/ Club Travestie** 373 Commercial Rd. (enter on Aylward St., off Jubilee St.) **(44-181) 788-4154** lesbians/gay men • dancing/DJ • live shows • 2nd & 4th Sat TV/TS night

**SubStation** 1A Dean St. 287-9608 mostly women last Sun only • 7pm-1am • 'Betty's' • dancing/DJ • neighborhood bar

**The Substation South** 9 Brighton Ter. 737-2095 popular • mostly gay men • dancing/DJ • leather • strict fetish dress code • private club

**The Tap** 2 Markhouse, Walthamstow 223-0767 5pm-11pm, from noon wknds • lesbians/gay men • neighborhood bar • dancing/DJ • karaoke • cabaret

**Tiffany's/ Way Out Club** 28 Minories (44-181) 363-0948 9pm-3am Sat only • transsexuals & their friends • dancing/DJ • live shows

**The Tube** Falconberg Court (next to the 'Astoria') 738-2336 open late • mostly gay men • dancing/DJ • theme nights

**The Village Soho** 81 Wardour St. 434-2124 mostly gay men • women only Fri at 'Girls on Top'

**The White Swan** 556 Commercial Rd. 780-9870 open late • lesbians/gay men • dancing/DJ • karaoke • live shows • food served

**The Woodman/ Dorothy's** 119 Stratford High St. (44-181) 519-8765 7pm-midnight, noon-10:30pm Sun • lesbians/gay men • dancing/DJ • live shows

**Woolwich Infant** 9 Plumstead Rd. (44-181) 854-3712 pub hours • lesbians/gay men • women only Mon • neighborhood bar • dancing/DJ • live shows

**Wow Bar** 15 Golden Square, Piccadilly • 8pm-11pm • women only Sat • also internet cafe

**The Yard** 57 Rupert St. 437-2652 noon-3pm, 6pm-11pm, clsd Sun • lesbians/gay men • 'Her/She Bar' Fri

## CAFES

**Cafe Joy** 69 Endell St. 419-1295 Caribbean

**First Out** 52 St. Giles High St. 240-8042 11am-11pm, noon-10:30pm Sun • lesbians/gay men • cont'l • smokefree upstairs • women's night Fri

**Freedom Cafe & Bar** 60-66 Wardour St. 734-0071 9am-11pm • trendy scene cafe

**Kulcha Kafe** Wild Ct. 831-6946 mostly women

**Old Compton Cafe** 34 Old Compton St. 439-3309 24hrs

# DINAH SHORE WEEKEND

**MARCH 26-29, 1998**

## PALM SPRINGS

The Ultimate Hotel & Entertainment Package at the All Inclusive

**DOUBLE TREE RESORT**

Book today to ensure availability. For hotel and party ticket Info Call

## 310.281.7358

For Airline reservations call
1•800•433•1790

Produced by JOANI WEIR PRODUCTIONS
POM POM PRODUCTIONS • KLUB BANSHEE

## London

**L**ondon is an amalgam of the most staid and traditional elements of English society and the most innovative in youth culture. Visitors can easily spend several weeks on only the best known tourist attractions and still miss the spirit of London. Like New York, London is really a collection of smaller towns and neighborhoods, each with a distinct feel.

While you're our taking in the sights, stop by **Silver Moon Women's Bookstore**. Though London has only one full-time women's pub, the **Glass Bar,** some of the men's clubs open their doors to lesbians one night a week. Fridays find the ladies in command at **Village Soho, Royal Vauxhall Tavern** and **Royal Oak**. If you're not up for a pub crawl, drop by **Kulcha Kafe**.

## London (171/181)

**Lesbigay Info:** 837-6768 (24hrs).
**Lesbigay AA:** 837-3337.
**City Info:** 824-8844.
**Attractions:** Buckingham Palace. Madame Tussaud's Wax Museum. Tate Gallery. St. Paul's Cathedral. Tower of London. Westminster Abbey. Victoria & Albert Museum. Dickens House. Kew Gardens. London Zoo. National Gallery. Shakespeare Globe Theatre. Big Ben.
**Best View:** From Tower Bridge (Tower Hill Tube).

**Weather:** London is warmer and less rainy than you may have heard. Summer temperatures reach the 70°s and the average annual rainfall is about half of that of Atlanta, GA, or Hartford, CT.
**Transit:** Freedom Cars: 734-1313. Ladycabs: 272-3019. Q Cars: 622-0333.

**Silver Screen Cafe & Bar** 233 Earl's Court Rd. **370-5700** 4pm-midnight, from 1pm wknds

## Restaurants

**Amazonas** 75 Westbourne Grove **243-0090** dinner only, lunch Sat • Brazilian/South American

**Balans** 60 Old Compton St. **437-5212** 9am-1am, til midnight Sun

**Creole Garden** 85 Battersea Rise 924-4454

**Eden du Carib** 74 Kingsgate Rd. 624-0024 Caribbean

**Fileric** 12 Queenstown Rd. **720-4844** French

**The Green Room** 62 Lavender Hill **223-4618** from 7pm, noon-4pm Sat • vegetarian/vegan • live jazz Fri

**Il Pinguino** 62 Brixton Rd. **735-3822** Italian

**Le Gourmet** 312 Kings Rd. **352-4483** transgender-friendly

**Mildred's** 58 Greek St. **494-1634** noon-11pm, clsd Sun • plenty veggie

**Nusa Dua** 11-12 Dean St. **437-3559** Indonesian

**Rossana's** 17 Strutton Ground **233-1701** cont'l/English

**Roy's** 234 Old Brompton Rd. **373-9995**

**Steph's** 39 Dean St. **734-5976** lunch & dinner, dinner only Sat, clsd Sun

**The Stockpot** 18 Old Compton St. **287-1066** 11:30am-11:30pm

**Wilde About Oscar** (at the 'Philbeach Hotel') **835-1858** eclectic

## Entertainment & Recreation

**Oval House Theater** Kennington 582-7680

## Bookstores & Retail Shops

**American Retro** 35 Old Compton St. **734-3477** 10:15am-7pm • gifts

**Gay's the Word** 66 Marchmont St. **278-7654** 10am-6pm, til 7pm Th, from 2pm Sun • lesbigay

**Silver Moon Women's Bookshop** 64-68 Charing Cross Rd. **836-7906**

**The Women's Book Shop** 45-46 Poland St. **437-1019**

## Publications

**Attitude** 987-5090

**Diva** 482-2576 lesbian magazine

**The Pink Paper** 296-6000 lesbigay newspaper

**THUD** 831-4666 lesbigay newsmagazine w/extensive resource & club listings

## Travel Agents

**Earth Travel** 49 Frith St. **734-3426**

**GinMar Travel** 10 Warnham, Sidmouth St. **278-7448** IGLTA

**Now Voyager** 7-11 Kensington High St. 938-3390

**Travel Designs** Suite #1, 3rd flr. Queen's House, 1 Leicester Pl. **432-3221**

## Spiritual Groups

**Jewish Gay/Lesbian Group** (44-181) 848-7319

**Jewish Gay/Lesbian Helpine** 706-3123

**MCC London** 2-A Sistova Rd., Balham (44-181) 675-6761 6pm Sun

## Gyms & Health Clubs

**Paris Gymnasium** Arch 73, Goding St., Vauxhall **735-8989** gay-friendly

**Soho Athletic Club** 10 Macklin St. **242-1290** gay-friendly

## Erotica

**London Piercing Clinic** 55 Portland Rd. 278-7654

**Metal Morphosis** 10-11 Moor St. **434-4554** piercing studio

**Paradiso Bodyworks** 41 Old Compton St. **287-2487** fetishwear

**Sh! Women's Erotic Emporium** 43 Coronet St. **613-5458** clsd Sun • also mail order

**Zipper Store** 283 Camden High St. **284-0537** fetishwear

## GERMANY

### Berlin (49-30)

#### INFO LINES & SERVICES

**AHA (Lesbian/Gay Center & Cafe)** Mehringdamm 61 **692-3600** 3pm-11pm Sun

**Lesbenberatung Lesbian Line 215-2000**

**Movin' Queer Berlin** Liegnitzer Str. 5 **618-6955** information & concierge services for lesbigay visitors

#### ACCOMMODATIONS

**Albatros Hotel Berlin** Rudolstädter Str. 42 **89 78 30** gay-friendly • food served

**Arco Hotel** Geisbergstr. 30 **218-2128** gay-friendly

**Bol's Hotel** Fuggerstr. 33 **217-7028** gay-friendly

**Charlottenburger Hof** Stuttgarter Platz 14 **32 90 70** gay-friendly • food served

**Hotel Kronprinz Berlin** Kronprinzendamm 1 **89 60 30** gay-friendly

**Hotel-Pension Zum Schild** Lietzenburger Str. 62 **885-9250** gay-friendly • centrally located

**Pension Niebuhr** Niebuhrstr. 74 **324-9595** gay-friendly

**Transit** Hagelberger Str. 53-54 **785-5051** gay-friendly

#### BARS & NIGHTCLUBS

**Action** Lietzenburger Str. 77 **882-5151** 5pm-close • lesbians/gay men • patio

**Bar Bizarr Club** Nostitzstr. 30 **449-2262** from 9pm • gay-friendly • leather • transgender-friendly • theme nights

**Bierhimmel** Oranienstr. 183 **615-3122** 3pm-3am • gay-friendly

**Boudoir** Brunnenstr. 192 **282-4067** 10pm-close Fri-Sat only • gay-friendly

**Cafe Anal** Muskauer Str. 15 **618-7064** 8pm-close, from 6pm wknds • popular • lesbians/gay men • transgender-friendly • leather night Mon

**K.O.B.** Potsdamer Str. 157 **215-2060** 10pm-close • women only • dancing/DJ

**Kumpelnest 3000** Lützowstr. 23 **261-6918** 5pm-5am, til 8am Fri-Sat • gay-friendly

**Na Und** Prenzlauer Allee 193 • 24hrs • gay-friendly

**Oh-Ase** Rathausstr. 5 **242-3030** 10am-2am, from 2pm Sun • popular • lesbians/gay men

**Pour Elle** Kalckreuthstr. 10 **218-7533** 9pm-5am Mon & Wed, from 6pm summers • mostly women

**Quincy Cocktail Bar** Yorckstr. 81 **785-7661** gay-friendly

**Romeo** Greifenhagener Str. 16 **447-6789** 11pm-8am • gay-friendly

## Berlin (49-30)

**Lesbigay Info:** AHA (Lesbian & Gay Center & Cafe), 692-3600, Mehringdamm 61, 3pm-11pm Sun. Mann-O-Meter (Gay Center), 216-8008, Motzstr. 5, 3pm-11pm, til 9pm Sun. Lesbenberatung (lesbian line): 215-2000.

**Entertainment:** Schwules Museum (Gay Museum), 881-1590, at AHA Center.

**Lesbigay AA:** 781-6262. Meets at Mann-O-Meter.

**Annual Events:** Berlin Film Festival.

**City Info:** Bahnhof Zoo: 313-9063. Hauptbahnhof: 279-5209.

**Attractions:** Memorial Church. Charlottenburg Palace. Zoologischer Garten.

**Weather:** Berlin is on the same parallel as Newfoundland, so if you're visiting in the winter, prepare for snow and bitter cold. Summer is balmy while spring and fall are beautiful, if sometimes rainy.

**Transit:** Würfelfunk Berlin: 21 01 01.

**Roses** Oranienstr. 187 **615-6570** 9:30pm-5am • popular • lesbians/gay men

**Shambala** Greifenhagener Str. 16 **447-6226** 6pm-3am • gay-friendly • cafe menu

**Vagabund** Knesebeckstr. 77 **881-1506** 5pm-close • gay-friendly • professional

**Whistle Stop** Knaackstr. 94 **442-7847** 6pm-close • mostly women

## CAFES

**Begine** Potsdamer Str. 139 **215-4325** 6pm-1am • women only • cultural center

**Cafe Berio** Maaßenstr. 7 **216-1946** 8am-1am

**Extra Dry** Pariser Str. 3 **885-2206** 11am-11pm • women only • alcohol- & chem-free space

**Kapelle** Zionskirchplatz 22-24 **449-2262** from 10am • cocktail bar after 8pm

## RESTAURANTS

**Abendmahl** Muskauer Str. 9 **612-5170** 6pm-1am • vegetarian & seafood

**Anderes Ufer** Hauptstr. 157 **784-1578** 11am-2am • popular

**Arc** Fasanenstr. 81-A, S-Bahn Bogen 559 **313-2625** 11am-2am • lesbians/gay men • also 'Club Banana' • mostly gay men

**Da Neben** Motzstr. 5 **217-0633** from 10am, from noon Sat, from 3pm Sun • full bar

**Flax** Chodowieckystr. 41 **441-9856** Sun brunch from 10am

**Guf** Nordufer 4 **453-2732** 6pm-3am, food served til 12:30am, clsd Mon

## Berlin

*I*n the past century, Berlin has seen just about everything: the outrageous art and cabaret of the Weimar era; the ravages of world war; ideological standoffs that physically divided families, lovers, and the city itself; and more recently, a largely peaceful revolution that brought Germany and the world together. Through it all, the Berliners have retained their own brand of cheeky humor—*Berliner Schnauze*, it's called—and a fierce loyalty to their city. While Berlin's museums and monuments are world-class, the city's real charm is in its cafes and counter-cultural milieu.

You may find the women's scene in Berlin more political than other places, but as a result you'll find a lot of support for women's culture and arts here, too. Check in at **Lilith Frauenbuchladen**, the well-stocked women's bookstore. Afterwards, stop by **Begine**, the women's cafe and cultural center or **Extra-Dry**, a chem-free cafe space. If you're a girl who just wants to have fun, visit **Fishbelly** for women's erotic toys and fashions. Later, check out one of the women's bars—**Pour Elle** or **Whistle Stop**—or shake your bootie at **K.O.B.**

**Jim's** Eberswalder Str. 32 **440-6379** full bar
**La Kantina** Kantstr. 146 **312-3135** full bar
**Rheingold Bistro** Rheinstr. 66 **859-2300**
7am-6pm, 8am-1pm Sat, clsd Sun
**Schall & Rauch Wirtshaus** Gleimstr. 23
**448-0770** open daily, brkfst from 10am
**SO 36** Oranienstr. 190 **615-2601** les-
bians/gay men • dancing/DJ • live shows
• theme nights
**Storch** Wartburgstr. 54 **784-2059**

## BOOKSTORES & RETAIL SHOPS
**Lilith Frauenbuchladen** Knesebeckstr.
86-87 **312-3102** 10am-6pm, til 4pm Sat,
clsd Sun • women's bookstore

## PUBLICATIONS
**Siegessäule** 235 **5390** monthly lesbigay
city magazine

## TRAVEL AGENTS
**Milu Reisen** Motzstr. 23 **217-6488**
**Over the Rainbow** Tempelhofer Damm
1-7 **6951-2652**
**Travel X** Pestalozzistr. 72 **324-9592**
women's & men's tour specialists
**Vedema-Reisen** Prenzlauer Allee 61
**421-0060**
**WBT** Anklamer Str. 38 **448-3845**

## SPIRITUAL GROUPS
**Yachad Berlin (33-221)** 19446 live 4pm-
6pm & 8pm-10pm Th-Fri, clsd wknds •
lesbigay Jewish group • call for info

## GYMS & HEALTH CLUBS
**Apollo** Borodinstr. 16 **467-4231** gay-
friendly • also Hauptstr. 150 location
**784-8203**
**Jump** Togostr. 76 **451-4712** gay-friendly
**Manuel's Sportstudio** Joachim-Friedrich-
Str. 37-38 **892-2080** gay-friendly
**Swiss Training** Alboinstr. 36-42 **754-1591**

## EROTICA
**Fishbelly** Grünewaldstr. 71-A **788-3015**
fetish fashions & toys for women
**Hautnah** Uhlandstr. 170 **882-3434**
leather • fetishwear

# THE NETHERLANDS
## Amsterdam                        (31-20)

### INFO LINES & SERVICES
**Gay/Lesbian Switchboard** 623-6565
10am-10pm, English spoken
**NVIH-COC** Rozenstraat 14 **623-1192**
1pm-6pm, clsd Sun-Tue, queer center

### ACCOMMODATIONS
**Aadam Wilhelmina Hotel**
Koninginneweg 169 **662-5467** gay-
friendly • charming • recently renovated
**Aero Hotel** Kerkstraat 49 **662-7728** gay-
friendly
**Amsterdam House** Amstel 176-A **626-
2577/(800) 618-1008 (IN US)** apts &
houseboat rentals
**Centre Apartments** Heintje Hoekssteeg
27 **627-2503**
**Chico's Guesthouse** St. Willibrordus-
straat 77 **675-4241** gay-friendly
**Drake's Guesthouse** Damrak 61 **638-
2367** gay-friendly
**Freeland Hotel** Marnixstraat 386 **622-
7511** gay-friendly
**Grand Hotel Krasnapolsky** Dam 9 **554-
9111** gay-friendly • full-service hotel
**Hotel Brian** Singel 69 **624-4661** gay-
friendly
**Hotel Golden Bear** Kerkstraat 37 **624-
4785** gay-friendly
**Hotel Monopole** Amstel 60 **624-6271**
gay-friendly
**Hotel New York** Herengracht 13 **624-
3066** mostly gay men
**Hotel Orfeo** Leidsekruistraat 14 **623-
1347** mostly gay men
**Hotel Sander** Jacob Obrechtstraat 69
**662-7574** gay-friendly • also 24hr bar
**Hotel Unique** Kerkstraat 37 **624-4785**
lesbians/gay men
**ITC Hotel** Prinsengracht 1051 **623-0230**
gay-friendly
**Johanna's B&B** Van Hogendorpplein 62
**684-8596** women only
**Liliane's Home** Sarphatistraat 119 **627-
4006** women only
**Rainbow Palace Hotel** Raadhuisstraat
33 **625-4317** mostly gay men
**Rubens B&B** Rubensstraat 38 bv **662-
9187** gay-friendly • smokefree
**Tulip Inn** Spuistraat 288-292 **420-4545**
gay-friendly
**Waterfront Hotel** Singel 458 **625-5774**
gay-friendly
**Westend Hotel** Kerkstraat 42 **624-8074**

# Amsterdam

The day that Amsterdam is known as the *Lesbian* and Gay Capital of Europe, there will be a lot of happy women. While even the soberest of gay visitors acts like a kid in a candy store when faced with the city's dazzling array of gay opportunity, the lesbian visitor may be disappointed with the somewhat limited, and hardly progressive, lesbian scene. (Be warned: the closest thing to a 'lesbian darkroom' here is when a bulb blows during a ballroom dancing session!)

Fortunately, lesbians are welcome at most of the gay establishments—though when it comes to leather bars or sex parties, it's often a boys-only club. One thing lesbians can share, though, is the largely tolerant atmosphere pervading this city in which same-sex couples can generally feel safe walking around hand in hand.

Despite today's apolitical climate, however, Amsterdam does have a colorful lesbian past and its fair share of characters. Way back in 1792, the jealous, murderous Bartha Schuurman was hung from the gallows for knifing her girlfriend's lover to death. In the 1970s, lesbian activists—in between scrawling pro-dyke grafitti—did manage to squat a few places and start some women's collectives. In fact, many current women's establishments—from bars to bookshops—emerged in that era when Dutch dykes got mad and rad. Don't forget legendary Dutch singer Mathilde Santing (often spotted at **Saarein**, the women-only bar) or the leather-clad 'Queen of the Zeedijk', Bet van Beeren, who was roaring up and down the Red Light District picking up babes long before today's Dykes on Bikes had their training wheels. To make some history of your own, stop by the women-only party at **COC** on Saturday night, or mix it up with lipstick femmes and cute baby dykes at the women-owned mixed bar **Vive la Vie**, or have your cocktails mixed at **Getto** on Tuesdays. (The Pink Pussycats are just purrfect!)

If the lesbian scene leaves you a little disappointed—the city of Amsterdam won't. Although there are many stark reminders of Nazi occupation during WWII—the old Jewish ghetto, the sobering Anne Frank House, and the Homomonument memorial to persecuted gays and lesbians—you couldn't wish for a more beautiful and romantic setting. Indulge your artisitic sensibilities at one of the 200 art galleries or museums rich in the work of old Dutch masters or modern-day artists Appel and Corneille—there's even one museum devoted entirely to the work of Van Gogh. And for those with a more *refined* kind of culture, there's always a tour of the Heineken brewery!

—By Pip, publisher of Trout. *Updated by Damron editors.*

## BARS & NIGHTCLUBS

**Amstel Taveerne** Amstel 54 **623-4254**

**April** Reguliersdwarsstraat 37 **625-9572** 4pm-1am, til 3am Fri-Sat

**Argos** Warmoesstraat 95 **623-4254**

**Cafe de Steeg** Halvemaansteeg 10 **620-0171**

**Camp Cafe** Kerkstraat 45 **622-1506** 11am-1am • full bar

**Casa Maria** Warmoesstraat 60 **627-6848**

**COC** Rozenstraat 14 **623-4079** women only Sat 10pm-3am • lesbians/gay men Fri & Sun

**The Cuckoo's Nest** Nieuwezijds Kolk 6 **627-1752**

**The Eagle Amsterdam** Warmoesstraat 90 **623-6758**

**Entre-Nous** Halvemaansteeg 14 **623-1700** 9pm-3am • lesbians/gay men

**Exit** Reguliersdwarsstraat 42 **625-8788** 11pm-4am • mostly gay men

**Fetish Faction** Haarlemmerstraat 124C **697-8094**

**Gaiety** Amstel 14 **624-4271**

**Getto** Warmoesstraat 51 **421-5151** noon-1am, til midnight Sun • mostly gay men • cocktail lounge • food served

**Havana** Reguliersdwarsstraat 17 **620-6788** 4pm-1am, til 2am Fri-Sat

**It** Amstelstraat 24 **625-0111** popular • gay Sat • dancing/DJ

**Mazzo** Rozengracht 114 **626-7500** gay-friendly • dancing/DJ

**Meia Meia** Kerkstraat 63 **623-4129**

**Mix Cafe** Amstel 50 8pm-3am

**Monica Bar** Lanfe Niezel 15 women only • Fri-Sat only

**Le Montmartre** Halvemaansteeg 17 **624-9216**

**Reality** Reguliersdwarsstraat 129 **639-3012**

**Roxy** Singel 465 **620-0354** Wed-Sun 11pm-5am • gay-friendly • gay Wed • dancing/DJ • 'Pussy Lounge' for women only every 3rd Sun 6pm-11pm

**Shako** Gravelandseveer 2 **639-3012**

**De Trut** inquire locally **612-3524**

**Vandenberg** Lindengracht 95 mostly women • cafe • pool table

**Vive-la-Vie** Amstelstraat 7 **624-0114** 3pm-2am, til 3am Fri-Sat • mostly women

**The Web** St. Jacobsstraat 6 **623-6758**

**Why Not** Nieuwe Zijds Voorburgwal 28

## CAFES

**Coffeeshop Downtown** Reguliersdwarsstraat 31

**Coffeeshop the Otherside** Reguliersdwarsstraat 6, gay smoking coffeeshop

**Dampkring** Handboogstraat at Heiligeweg • smoking coffeeshop • great fresh O.J.

**Global Chillage** Kerkstraat 51 smoking coffeeshop • publisher's choice

**De Rokerij** Lange Leided Warsstraat 41 smoking coffeeshop • full bar

**Saarein** Elandsstraat 119 **623-4901** 3pm-1am, til 2am Fri-Sat, clsd Mon • women only • brown cafe

# Amsterdam (31-20)

**Lesbigay Info:** Gay & Lesbian Switchboard: 623-6565. COC: 623-2683 (men) & 626-8300 (women).

**Annual Events:**

April - 30: Queen's Birthday.

June - Holland Festival.

July - last week: **Zomerfestijn.** International performing arts festival.

August 1-8 – Gay Games 1998. 20/427-1998. Tollfree USA: (888) 429-4263. http://www.gaygames.nl

**City Info:** VVV: 06/340 340 66 or visit their office directly opposite the Centraal Station.

**Attractions:** Homomonument. Anne Frank House. Red Light District. Van Gogh Museum. Royal Palace. Rijksmuseum.

**Weather:** Temperatures hover around freezing in the winter and rise to the mid-60°s in the summer. Rain is possible year-round.

**Taxis:** 677-7777. Can also be found at taxi stands on the main squares.

**Tops** Prinsengracht 480  smoking internet cafe

**Het Wonder** Huidenstraat 13 **639-1032** 2pm-midnight, til 1am Fri-Sat, clsd Mon

## Restaurants

**Ambrosia** Frederik Hendrikstraat 111-115 **684-9115** 6pm-11pm • organic

**Bojo** Lange Leidsedwarsstraat 51  til 6am • popular • Indonesian

**De Bolhoed** Prinsengracht 60-62 **626-1803** healthy cuisine • plenty veggie

**Dia de Sol** Reguliersdwarsstraat 23 **623-4259** til midnight • tapas

**Egg Cream** St. Jacobstraat 19 **623-0575** 11am-8pm • vegetarian

**Eten & Drinken** Warmoesstraat 7 **624-5173** gay-owned

**Françoise** Kerkstraat 176 **624-0145** 9am-6pm • mostly women

**Gary's Late Nite** Reguliersdwarsstraat 53 **420-2406** popular • fresh muffins

**Golden Temple** Utrechtsestraat 126 **626-8560** 5pm-10pm, noon-3pm Tue & Sat • Indian-influenced vegetarian & vegan • smokefree

**Granada** Leidsekruisstraat 13 **625-1073** Spanish

**Greenwoods** Singel 103  English-style brkfst & tea snacks

**Izmir** Kerkstraat 66  noon-midnight • Turkish

**Klaver Koning** Koningsstraat 29 **626-1085** 5:30pm-11pm, clsd Sun-Mon

**Het Land Van Walem** Keizersgracht 449 **625-3455** lesbian-owned • patio

**Malvesijn** Prinsengracht 598 **638-0899** 10am-1am • terrace

**Mankind** Weteringstraat 60 **638-4755**

**Maoz** Regulierbreestraat 45 **624-9290** 6pm-2am • falafel

**Le Monde** Rembrandtsplein 6 **626-9922** from 8am • terrace dining

**Oibibio** Prins Hendrikkade 20-21 **553-9328** 5:30pm-11pm • plenty veggie

**Restaurant Gerard** Gelderse kade 23 **638-4338** French

**Rose's Cantina** Reguliersdwarsstraat 38 popular • Tex-Mex

**'t Schooiertje** Lijnbaansgracht 190 **638-4035** 9am-11pm, clsd Fri • full bar

**Shitzen** Kerkstraat 108 **622-8627** clsd Mon • macrobiotic Japanese

**'t Sluisje** Torensteeg 1 **624-0813** from 5pm, clsd Wed • live shows

**La Strada** N.Z. Voorburgwal 93 **625-0276** lesbian-owned

**'t Swarte Schaep** Korte Leidsedwarsstraat 24 **622-3021** noon-11pm

**Tom Yam** Staalstraat 22 **622-9533** Thai • gay-owned

**Vegetarisch Eethuis Sisters** Nes 12 **626-3970** 5pm-11:30pm

**De Vliegende Schotel** Nieuwe Leliestraat 162 **625-2041** 5pm-11pm • vegetarian

**De Vrolijke Abrikoos** Weteringschans 76 **624-4672** 5pm-11:30pm • eclectic organic cuisine • plenty veggie • patio

**De Waaghals** Frans Halsstraat 29 **679-9609** 5pm-11pm • plenty veggie

**Warung Swietie** 1e Sweelinckstraat 1 popular • Surinamese/Javanese

## Bookstores & Retail Shops

**The American Book Center** Kalverstraat 185 **625-5537**

**Boekhandel Vrolijk** Paleisstraat 135 **623-5142** 10am-6pm, from 1pm Mon, til 9pm Th, til 5pm Sat, clsd Sun • lesbigay

**Clubwear-House** Herengracht 265 **622-8766** noon-6pm, clsd Sun

**Conscious Dreams** Kerkstraat 117 **626-6907** 'psychedelicatessen'

**Laundry Industry** Spui & Rokin  black trendy & formal clothing

**Xantippe** Prinsengracht 290 **679-9609** women's bookstore • English titles

## Publications

**Gay News Amsterdam** 623-3850

**Trout** 420-6775 queer-oriented alternative culture guide & calendar

## Erotica

**Black Body** Lijnbaansgracht 292 **626-2553**

**Female & Partners** Spuistraat 100 **620-9152** fashions & toys for women

**G-Force** Oudezijds Armsteeg 7 **420-1664**

**Hellen's Place** Overtoom 497 **689-5501** til 1am, til 2am wknds • women's erotic cafe & SM club • pansexual crowd

**De Leertent** Sarphatistraat 61 **627-8090**

**Mail & Female** Prinsengracht 489 **623-3916** erotic fashions & toys for women

**Mr. B** Warmoesstraat 89 **422-0003**

**Robin & Rik Leermakers** Runstraat 30 **627-8924**

# SPAIN

## Barcelona (34-3)

### INFO LINES & SERVICES

**Casal Lambda** Ample 5 **412-7272** 5pm-9pm, til 11pm Sat, clsd Sun • also newsletter

**Telefono Rosa (93) 900-601-601 (IN SPAIN)** 6pm-10pm

### ACCOMMODATIONS

**Barcelona Plaza Hotel** Plaza España 6-8 **426-2600** gay-friendly • full brkfst • swimming • jacuzzi • also restaurant & piano bar

**California Hotel** Calle Raurich 14 **317-7766** gay-friendly

**Gran Hotel Catalonia** Balmes 142-146 **415-9090** gay-friendly • full brkfst • food served • wheelchair access

**Hotel Albeniz** Aragón 591-593 **265-2626** gay-friendly • full brkfst • food served • wheelchair access

**Hotel Duques de Bergara** Bergara 11 **301-5151** gay-friendly • full brkfst • food served

**Hotel Mikado** Po Bonanova 58 **211-4166** gay-friendly • full brkfst • food served

**Hotel Roma** Avda. de Romo 31 **410-6633** gay-friendly • food served

**Regencia Colon Hotel** Calle Sagristans 13-17 **318-9858** gay-friendly • private/shared baths

### BARS & NIGHTCLUBS

**Arena** Balmes 32 • 10pm-5pm • popular • mostly gay men • dancing/DJ • videos

**Bahia** Calle Séneca 12 • 10pm-3:30am • mostly women

**Cafe de la Calle** Carrer Vic 11 **218-3863** 6pm-3am • lesbians/gay men

**Cafe de Lola** Calle Paris 173 • 6:30pm-3am • lesbians/gay men

**Cheek to Cheek** Muntaner 326 • lesbians/ gay men

**Daniel's** Plaza Cardona 7-8 **209-9978** mostly women • neighborhood bar

**Dietrich** Concell de Cent 255 • lesbians/gay men

**Distrito Distinto** Ava. Meridiana 104 • til 5am wknds • gay men • dancing/DJ

**Distrito Maritimo** Moll de la Fusta • gay-friendly

**EA3** Raurich 23 • lesbians/gay men

**Este Bar** Consell de Cent 257 **323-6406** popular • lesbians/gay men

**Free Girl** Calle M. Cubí 4 • mostly women • dancing/DJ

**Heyday** Bruniquer 59-61 • midnight-5pm, 6:30pm-3am Sun, clsd Mon-Wed • mostly gay men • dancing/DJ

**La Illa** Reig I Benet 3 • mostly women

**La Luna** Avda. Diagonal 323 • 9pm-3am, til 4am wknds • gay men • dancing/DJ

**Martin's** Passeig de Gràcia 130 **218-7167** midnight-close • mostly gay men • dancing/DJ • videos

**Member's** Séneca 3 **237-1204** 10pm-2:30am, til 3am Fri-Sat • mostly women

**Metro** Sepúlveda 185 **323-5227** mostly gay men • dancing/DJ

**Padam Padam** Raurich 9 **302-5062** 7pm-2am, clsd Sun • lesbians/gay men

**Punto BCN** Muntaner 63-65 **453-6123** 6pm-2am, til 3am wknds • gay men

**Satanassa** Aribau 27 • 10pm-2:30am, til 3:30am • mostly gay men

**Taller** Méjico 7-9 • 10pm-5am, til close Fri-Sat • mostly gay men • dancing/DJ

**Tatu** Cayo Celio 7 **425-3350** 10pm-4:30am, from 7pm Sun • mostly gay men • dancing/DJ • live shows

**Topxi** Valencia 358 **425-3350** 10pm-5am • mostly gay men • live shows

### CAFES

**Cafe dell'Opera** Rambla 76 **317-7585** light fare • $5

**Il Caffa di Francesco** Passeig de Gràcia 66 **488-2590**

### RESTAURANTS

**7 Portes** Passeig Isabel II 14 **319-3033** Catalan • $35

**Aire** Enrique Granados 48 **451-8462** lunch & dinner • Spanish

**Botafumeiro** Mayor de Gràcia 81 **218-4230** Galician seafood specialities • $55

**Cafe Miranda** Casanova 30 **453-5249** dinner • lesbians/gay men • $20

**Cafe Textil** Montcada 12 **317-7480** $10

**Los Caracoles** Escudellers 14 **302-3185** seafood • $20

**Egipte** Jerusalem 3 **317-7480** Catalan

**L' Elx al Moll** Moll d'Espanya **255-8117** seafood • $30

**La Nostra Illa** Reig I Benet 3 • mostly women • sandwiches • $5

**Tragaluz** Passeig de la Concepció 5 **487-0621** dinner • int'l gourmet • $30

## BOOKSTORES & RETAIL SHOPS

**Antinous** Josep Anselm Clavé 6 **301-9070** books • gifts • also cafe

**Cómplices** Cervantes 2 **301-9070** lesbigay bookstore • Spanish & English

## PUBLICATIONS

**Barcelona Rosa** 237-6809 bi-monthly cultural/political newspaper

**Info Gai** 318-1665 free bi-monthly newspaper in Catalan

## TRAVEL AGENTS

**Gay Friends Holidays/Magic Travel** Benet Marcade 9-11 238-0356 IGLTA

## EROTICA

**Condonería** Plaça Sant Josep Oriol **301-5745** clsd Sun

# Madrid (34-1)

## INFO LINES & SERVICES

**CFLM (Colectivo de Lesbianas Feministas de Madrid)** Barquillo 44, 2n. izq. **319-3689** lesbian-feminist group

**COGAM (Colectivo de Gays y Lesbianas de Madrid)** Espiritu Santo 37 **522-4517** lesbigay center • groups • library

**Gai Inform** 523-0070 5pm-9pm • helpline

**Transexualia** Apdo. de Correos 8584, 28080 • transsexual support

## ACCOMMODATIONS

**Hostal Hispano** Hortaleza 38, 2° 531-4871 gay-friendly

**Mónaco Hotel Residencia** Barbieri 5 522-4630 gay-friendly

**Suecia Hotel** Marqués de Casa Riera 4 531-6900 gay-friendly • jacuzzis

## BARS & NIGHTCLUBS

**Ambient** San Mateo 21 • 9pm-3am, clsd Mon • mostly women • dancing/DJ • food served

**Angels of Xenon** Calle Atocha 38 • midnight-7am Fri-Sat • gay-friendly • more gay Sat • also cafe

**La Bohemia** plaza Chueca • mostly women • neighborhood bar

**Escape** Gravina 13 • mostly women • neighborhood bar

**La Fusa** Sierpes 8 • noon-midnight • gay-friendly • neighborhood bar

**Goa After Club** Mesonero Romanos 13 • from 6am, Fri-Sat • lesbians/gay men • dancing/DJ

**Heaven** Calle Veneras 2 548-2022

**Lucas** San Lucas 11 • lesbians/gay men • neighborhood bar

**La Lupe** Torrecilla del Leal 12 • lesbians/gay men • neighborhood bar

**Medea** Cabeza 33 • mostly women • dancing/DJ

**Mito** Plaza Chueca • lesbians/gay men • neighborhood bar

**El Mojito** Calle Olmo 6 • 9pm-2:30am, til 3:30am Fri-Sat • gay-friendly • neighborhood bar • more gay Sun afternoon

**Ras** Barbieri 7 522-4317 9:30pm-4am, til 4:30am Fri-Sat, clsd Sun • popular • gay-friendly • very gay crowd

**Refugio** Dr. Cortezo 1 369-4038 midnight-6am, til 8am Fri-Sat, clsd Mon • popular • gay-friendly • dancing/DJ

**Rick's** Infantas 26 531-9186 10pm-5am • popular • gay-friendly

**La Rosa** Calle Tetuán 27 531-0185 11pm-4:30am, til 6am wknds • gay-friendly • dancing/DJ • also 'Stop' 9am-2pm wknds • afterhours club

**Sachas** Plaza Chueca 8 • lesbians/gay men • dancing/DJ

**Shangay Tea Dance** popular • Sun only • check local papers for location

**Truco** Gravina 10 • lesbians/gay men • neighborhood bar

## CAFES

**Cafe Acuarela** Calle Gravina 10 532-8735 3:30pm-2:30am

**Cafe Galdós** Pérez Galdós 1 532-1286 8am-2am • live shows

**Cafe la Troje** Pelayo 26 • full bar

**Corazón Negro** Colmenares 5 • full bar

## RESTAURANTS

**A Brasileira** Pelayo 49 308-3625 Brazilian • $15

**Casa Santa Cruz** Calle de la Bolsa 12 521-8623 Spanish • $40

**Casa Vallejo** San Lorenzo 9 308-6158 creative homestyle • $20

**Chez Pomme** Pelayo 4 532-1646 lunch & dinner • vegetarian

**La Dolce Vita** Cardenal Cisneros 58 445-0436 lunch & dinner • Italian

**La Galette** Conde de Arenal 11 676-0641 macrobiotic • $15

**Gula Gula** Infante 5 420-2919 lunch & dinner, clsd Mon • salad bar

**Marsot** Pelayo 6 531-0726 lunch & dinner, clsd Sun

**Momo** Augusto Figueroa 41 532-7162 $12

**Posada de la Villa** Cava Baja 9 **266-1860** Spanish • $50

**Restaurante Rochi** Pelayo 19 **521-8310** lunch & dinner • Spanish

**El Restaurante Vegetariano** Marqués de Santa Ana 34 **532-0927** lunch & dinner, clsd Mon • vegetarian

**Taberna de Antonio Sánchez** Mesón de Paredes 13 **539-7826** tapas • $20

**Taberna el Almendro** El Almendro 13 **365-4552** tapas • $10

### BOOKSTORES & RETAIL SHOPS

**Berkana Bookstore** Calle Gravina 11 **532-1393** lesbigay

### PUBLICATIONS

**Entiendes...?** Apdo. de Correos 3277, 28080 • bimonthly gay info & culture

**Shangay** **308-4539** free gay paper

### TRAVEL AGENTS

**CCJ Travel Plus** Calle Quintana 20, #3-B **542-6009**

**Fiesta Tours** **551-5294** personalized city itineraries

### SPIRITUAL GROUPS

**Cohesión** Apdo. de Correos 51057, 28080 • lesbigay Christians

### EROTICA

**Condoms & Co** Colón 3

**XXX** San Marcos 8

## Sitges (34-3)

### ACCOMMODATIONS

**Apartments Bonaventura** San Buenaventura 7 **894-9762** gay-friendly • studio apts

**El Roca** Cami cal Antoniet **894-0043** popular • gay-friendly • camping sites

**Hostal Madison** Sant Bartomeu 9 **894-6147** popular • gay-friendly

**Hotel Calipolis** Paseo Maritimo **894-1500** gay-friendly • upscale hotel

**Hotel Montserrat** Esplater 27 **894-0300** popular • gay-friendly

**Hotel Renaixenca** Isla de Cuba 13 **894-8375** gay-friendly • full brkfst

**Hotel Romàntic** Sant Isidre 33 **894-8375** popular • gay-friendly • full brkfst • private/shared baths • also full bar

**Madison Bahia Hotel** Parelladas 31-33 **894-0012** popular • gay-friendly

**Mirador Apartments** Isla de Cuba 21 **894-2412** gay-friendly • studio apts

**Pensión Esplater** Espalter 11 **894-0300** popular • gay-friendly • balconies

**San Sebastian Playa** Port Alegre 53 **894-8676** gay-friendly • swimming

**El Xalet** Esplater 27 **894-0300** popular • gay-friendly • food served

### BARS & NIGHTCLUBS

**Alfred** Santa Bárbara 10 • gay-friendly

**Bourbon's** Sant Bonaventura 10 **894-3347** 10:30pm-3am, til 3:30am • mostly gay men • dancing/DJ

**El Candil** Carreta 9 • seasonal • 10pm-3am, til 3:30am Fri-Sat • mostly gay men • dancing/DJ • food served from 7pm

**Phillip's Frankfurt Miraplay** Puerta Alegre 11 (by San Sebastian beach) • seasonal • 10:30-3am • gay-friendly • neighborhood bar • terrace

### CAFES

**Cafe Goya** San Francisco 42 • 9am-1am, clsd Wed off-season

**Elsa Coffee Shop** Parelladas 86 • seasonal • 9am-6:30pm • int'l brkfst all day

**Picnic** Passeig del Mar **811-0040** 9:30am-3am • call for winter hours • terrace

### RESTAURANTS

**Casa Hidalgo** Passeig del Mar **894-3895** seafood

**Oliver's** Isla de Cuba 39 **894-3516** Spanish

**El Trull** Mossén Félix Clará 3 **894-4705** French

# Camping & RV Spots

# Tour Operators & 1998 Tours
Cruises
Luxury Tours
Great Outdoors
Spiritual & Health Vacations
Custom Tours
Thematic Tours
Various Tour Operators

# 1998 Calendar of
Events
Leather Events
Conferences & Retreats
Women's Festivals & Gatherings
Spiritual Gatherings
Kids' Stuff

# Mail Order

# USA

## ALASKA

### Fairbanks (907)

**Billie's Backpackers Hostel** 2895 Mack Rd. **457-2034** gay-friendly • hostel & campsites • kids ok • food served • women-run • $15-20

## ARIZONA

### Sedona (520)

**Mustang B&B** 4257 Mustang Dr., Cottonwood **646-5929** lesbians/gay men • full brkfst • 25 min. from Sedona • smokefree • 1 RV hookup • movie theater • $45-65

## ARKANSAS

### Eureka Springs (501)

**Greenwood Hollow Ridge B&B** 253-5283 exclusively lesbigay • on 5 quiet acres • full brkfst • near outdoor recreation • shared/private baths • kitchens • pets ok • RV hookups • lesbian-owned/run • $45-65

## CALIFORNIA

### Clearlake (707)

**Edgewater Resort** 6420 Soda Bay Rd., Kelseyville **279-0208** gay-friendly • cabin • camping • $25-65

### Garberville (707)

**Giant Redwoods RV & Camp** 943-3198 gay-friendly • campsites • RV • located off the Avenue of the Giants on the Eel River • shared baths • kids/pets ok • $20-25

### Placerville (209)

**Rancho Cicada Retreat** 245-4841 mostly gay men • secluded riverside retreat in the Sierra foothills w/two-person tents & cabin • swimming • nudity • gay-owned/run • $100-200 (lower during wk)

### Russian River (707)

**Faerie Ring Campground** 16747 Armstrong Woods Rd., Guerneville **869-2746** gay-friendly • on 14 acres • RV spaces • near outdoor recreation • pets ok • $20-25

**Fife's Resort** 16467 River Rd., Guerneville **869-0656/(800) 734-3371** lesbians/gay men • cabins • campsites • also restaurant • some veggie • full bar • $10-20 • IGLTA • $50-215

**Redwood Grove RV Park & Campground** 16140 Neely Rd., Guerneville **869-3670** gay-friendly

**Riverbend Campground & RV Park** 11820 River Rd., Forestville **887-7662** gay-friendly • kids ok • wheelchair access

**Schoolhouse Canyon Park** 12600 River Rd. **869-2311** gay-friendly • campsites • RV • private beach • kids/pets ok

**The Willows** 15905 River Rd., Guerneville **869-2824/(800) 953-2828** lesbians/gay men • old-fashioned country lodge & campground • smokefree • $49-119

### Sacramento (916)

**Verona Village River Resort** 6985 Garden Hwy., Nicolaus **656-1320** lesbians/gay men • RV space • full bar • restaurant • store • marina

## COLORADO

### Fort Collins (970)

**Never Summer Nordic** 482-9411 lesbians/gay men • camping in yurts (portable Mongolian round houses) in Colorado Rockies • sleep 8-12 • mountain-biking & skiing

## FLORIDA

### Crescent City (904)

**Crescent City Campground** 698-2020/(800) 634-3968 gay-friendly • tenting sites • RV hookups • swimming • laundry • showers • $15 day, $90 week, $230 month

### Miami Beach/South Beach (305)

**Something Special** 7762 NW 14th Ct. (private home) 696-8826 noon-9pm, 2pm-7pm Sun • women only • vegetarian • plenty veggie • also tent space

### West Palm Beach (561)

**The Whimsey** 686-1354 resources & archives • political clearinghouse • also camping/RV space & apt • wheelchair access

## GEORGIA

### Dahlonega (706)

**Swiftwaters** 864-3229 seasonal • women only • on scenic river • full brkfst • hot tub • smokefree • deck • women-owned/run • $69-95 (B&B)/ $40-50 (cabins)/ $10 (camping)

## HAWAII

### Hawaii (Big Island) (808)

**Wood Valley B&B Inn** 928-8212 mostly women • plantation home B&B • tent sites • full veggie brkfst • sauna • smokefree • nudity • women-owned/run • $35-55

**Kalani Oceanside Eco-Resort** 965-7828/(800) 800-6886 gay-friendly • coastal retreat • conference center & campground w/in Hawaii's largest conservation area • full brkfst • swimming • food served • IGLTA

## MAINE

### Camden (207)

**The Old Massachusetts Homestead Campground** 789-5135/(800) 213-8142 open May-Nov • gay-friendly • cabins • tentsites • RV hookups • swimming

### Sebago Lake (207)

**Maine-ly For You** 583-6980 gay-friendly • cottages • campsites

## MASSACHUSETTS

### Martha's Vineyard (508)

**Webb's Camping Area** 693-0233 open May-Sept • gay-friendly • women-owned/run

## MICHIGAN

### Owendale (517)

**Windover Resort** 3596 Blakely Rd. 375-2586 women only • campsites • swimming • $20/yr membership fee • $13-18 camping fee

### Saugatuck (616)

**Camp It** 543-4335 seasonal • lesbians/gay men • campsites • RV hookups

## MINNESOTA

### Duluth (612)

**Rainbow Island** 473-7889 women only • camping • cabin • also workshops

### Kenyon (507)

**Dancing Winds Farm** 6863 Country 12 Blvd. 789-6606 lesbians/gay men • B&B on working dairy farm • tentsites • full brkfst • work exchange avail. • women-owned/run

## MISSISSIPPI

### Ovett (601)

**Camp Sister Spirit** 344-2005 mostly women • 120 acres of camping & RV sites • cabins • $10-20

## MISSOURI

### Noel (417)

**Sycamore Landing** 475-6460 open May-Sept • campsites • canoe rental

## MONTANA

### Boulder (406)

**Boulder Hot Springs Hotel & Retreat** 225-4339 gay-friendly • spiritual/recovery retreat • camping avail. • swimming • spas • food served • smokefree • call for info

### Ronan (406)

**North Crow Vacation Ranch** 2360 North Crow Rd. 676-5169 seasonal • lesbians/gay men • cabin • tipis • camping • 80 mi. S. of Glacier Park • hot tub • nudity • $10-20

## NORTH CAROLINA

### Asheville (704)

▲ **Camp Pleiades** 688-9201 (SUMMER)/(904) 241-3050 (WINTER) open Memorial Day-Halloween • women only • mtn. retreat • cabins • swimming • all meals included • smokefree • private/shared baths • lesbian-owned/run • $45-85

## OHIO

### Columbus (614)

**Summit Lodge Resort & Guesthouse** 385-3521 popular • clothing optional resort • mostly gay men • camping avail. • hot tub • swimming • also restaurant • wheelchair access

## OKLAHOMA

### El Reno (405)

**The Good Life RV Resort** Exit 108 I-40, 1/4 mile S. 884-2994 gay-friendly • 32 acres • 100 campsites & 100 RV hookups • swimming

## OREGON

### Days Creek (541)

**Owl Farm** 679-4655 (INFO LINE ONLY) women only • open women's land for retreat or residence • camping sites avail.

### Grants Pass (541)

**Womanshare** 862-2807 women only • cabin • campground • hot tub

### Tiller (541)

**Kalles Family RV Ranch** 233 Jackson Creek Rd. 825-3271 lesbians/gay men • camping sites • RV hookups • btwn. Medford & Roseburg

## PENNSYLVANIA

### New Milford (717)

**Oneida Camp & Lodge** 465-7011 (seasonal) mostly gay men • oldest gay-owned/operated campground dedicated to the lesbigay community • swimming • nudity

### Pittsburgh (412)

**Camp Davis** 311 Red Brush Rd., Boyers 637-2402 May thru 2nd wknd in Oct • cabins & campsites • lesbians/gay men • adults 21+ only • pets on leash • call for events • 1 hr from Pittsburgh

## SOUTH DAKOTA

### Sioux Falls (605)

**Camp America** 425-9085 gay-friendly • 35 mi. west of Sioux Falls • camping • RV hook up • women-owned/run • $10-16

## TENNESSEE

### Jamestown (615)

**Laurel Creek Campground** 879-7696 clsd Nov-April • gay-friendly • camping • rentals • RV hookups • hiking • swimming

### Nashville (615)

**IDA** 904 Vikkers Hollow Rd., Dowelltown 597-4409 lesbians/gay men • camping avail. May-Sept • private community 'commune' located in the hills • 1hr SE of Nashville

## TEXAS

### Groesbeck (817)

Rainbow Ranch 729-5847/(888) 875-7596 gay-friendly • camping • RV hook-up • on Lake Limestone halfway btwn. Houston & Dallas

## VIRGINIA

### Charlottesville (804)

Intouch Women's Center 589-6542 women only • campground • recreational area • wheelchair access

## WASHINGTON

### Bremerton (253)

Tricia's Place 813-9008 cabin • RV hookup • near outdoor recreation

## WEST VIRGINIA

### Stonewall Jackson Lake (304)

FriendSheep Farm 462-7075 mostly women • secluded retreat • campsites • smokefree

## WISCONSIN

### La Crosse (608)

Chela's B&B and Forest Camping Retreat Gays Mills 735-4829 women only • camping on 35 acres of women's land • also 2 rms. avail. • full brkfst • sauna • kids/pets ok • lesbian-owned/run • $10 camping/ $50 room

### Mauston (608)

CK's Outback W 5627 Clark Rd. 847-5247 women only • B&B • camping

### Wascott (715)

Wilderness Way 466-2635 women only • resort property • cabins • camping • RV sites • swimming • camping $12-16 • cottages $48-68

## CANADA

## BRITISH COLUMBIA

### Birken (604)

Birkenhead Resort Pemberton 452-3255 gay-friendly • cabins • campsites • hot tub • swimming • $54-76

## NOVA SCOTIA

### Bridgetown (902)

Pumpkin Ecological Wimmin's Farm RR 5 665-5041 women only • rustic cabins • camping • swimming • workshops • drug-, smoke- & alcohol-free • girl kids ok • work exch. avail. • $45-65/$8 camping

## ONTARIO

### Hamilton (905)

The Cedars Tent & Trailer Park 1039 5th Concession Rd. RR2, Waterdown 659-3655 lesbians/gay men • private campground • swimming • also social club • dancing/DJ • karaoke • wknd restaurant • some veggie

## PROVINCE OF QUEBEC

### Joliette (514)

L'Oasis des Pins 381 boul. Brassard, St. Paul de Joliette 754-3819 gay-friendly • swimming • camping April-Sept • restaurant open year-round

## SASKATCHEWAN

### Ravenscrag (306)

Spring Valley Guest Ranch 295-4124 popular • gay-friendly • 1913 character home • cabin • tipis • also restaurant • country-style • $35-55

## CARIBBEAN

## VIRGIN ISLANDS

### St. John (809)

Maho Bay & Harmony V.I. National Park 776-6240/(800) 392-9004 gay-friendly • camping & environmentally aware resort

## CRUISES

*Gay/Lesbian*

**Ocean Voyager (305) 379-5722/(800) 435-2531** 1717 N. Bayshore Dr. #4041, Miami, FL 33132 • Cruise Consultants, LTD • **IGLTA** member

> December—27, 1997-January 3—Western Caribbean
> February—21-March 3—Southern Caribbean, Total Solar Eclipse
> March—8-15—Western Caribbean
> April—4—South America Cruise
> May—23—Eastern Caribbean
> July—24—Alaska Inside Passage
> July—25—Russia/Scandinavia
> October—6—Hawaii
> October—30—FantasyFest: Key West, Bahamas
> November—21—Costa Rica

*Straight/Gay*

**Amazon Tours & Cruises (305) 227-2266/(800) 423-2791** 8700 W. Flagler #190, Miami, FL 33174 • weekly cruises, includes upper Amazon • **IGLTA** member

**Cruise Holidays of Beverly Hills (310) 652-8521** 224 S. Robertson, Los Angeles, CA 90211

**Holidays at Sea (707) 573-8300/(800) 444-8300** 1208 4th St., Santa Rosa, CA 95404 • **IGLTA** member

**Sea Safaris Sailing (941) 619-7183/(800) 497-2508** 3630 County Line Rd., Lakeland, FL 33811 • some women-only charter sail trips and cruises to the Keys

**Voyages & Expeditions (713) 776-3438/(800) 818-2877** 8323 Southwest Freeway #470, Houston, TX 77074 • group and individual deluxe cruises • **IGLTA** member

## LUXURY TOURS

*Gay/Lesbian*

**David's Trips & Tours (714) 723-0699/(888) 723-0699** 310 Dahlia Pl. Ste. A, Corona del Mar, CA 92625-2821 • luxury tours to Eastern Europe, South Africa and more • **IGLTA** member

## GREAT OUTDOORS

*Women Only*

**Adventures for Women (201) 930-0557** PO Box 515, Montvale, NJ 07645 • hiking, canoeing and cross-country skiing in the Adirondacks and beyond

**Alaska Women of the Wilderness Foundation (907) 688-2226/(800) 770-2226 (ALASKA ONLY)** PO Box 773556, Eagle River, AK 99577 • year-round wilderness and spiritual empowerment programs for women and girls

**Artemis Sailing Charters (208) 354-8804/(800) 247-1444** PO Box 931, Driggs, ID 83422 • sailing adventures worldwide

**Blue Moon Explorations (360) 856-5622/(800) 966-8806** PO Box 2568, Bellingham, WA 98227 • sea kayaking, rafting, ski trips in Pacific Northwest and Hawaii

    January—25-February 1—Kayak Magdalena Bay
    February—18-27—Kayak, hike, snorkel Hawaii
    March—22-28—Baja: Sea of Cortez whale migration
    April—4-11—Baja: Full Moon Sea of Cortez
    May—25-29—San Juan Islands Wildflowers & Kayaking
    June—29-July 3—San Juan Islands Kayaking
    August—10-14—British Columbia Inside Passage
    August—24-28—British Columbia West Coast
    September—21-25—San Juan Islands Kayaking
    October—5-9—Fall Colors Kayaking & Hiking

▲ **Common Earth Wilderness Trips (415) 455-0646** PO Box 1191, Fairfax, CA 94978 • non-profit women-owned • sliding scale • multicultural • cross-country skiing, backpacking and kayaking in California, the Southwest, and Alaska

**Call of the Wild Wilderness Trips (510) 849-9292** 2519 Cedar St., Berkeley, CA 94708 • hiking and wilderness trips for all levels in Western US

**Cloud Canyon Backpacking (805) 969-0982** 411 Lemon Grove Lane, Santa Barbara, CA 93108 • seasonal wilderness backpacking in Utah and the Sierra Nevadas

    March—TBA—New Zealand
    April—10-12—Southern California
    May—30-June 6—Slickrock Journey
    June—21-27—Escalante River Treks
    August—26-September 5—Alaska
    September—28-October 6—"Going Deeper"

COMMON EARTH
WILDERNESS TRIPS FOR WOMEN

*We are a women owned and operated non-profit, specializing in quality, memorable back packing and kayaking treks in California, the Southwest and Alaska!*

**MULTICULTURAL · SLIDING-SCALE
EXPERT GUIDES · CUSTOMIZED TRIPS**

P.O. BOX 1191 • FAIRFAX, CA 94978
(415) 455-0646

**Equinox (907) 274-9087** 618 W. 14th Ave., Anchorage, AK 99501 • rafting, canoeing, sea-kayaking and backpacking in Alaska's best wilderness

May—28-June 3—Granite and Glaciers: Tracy Arm Kayaking—co-ed
June—4-15—Colville River Canoeing
June—8-16—Trekking to the Caribou, Arctic Refuge
June—14-19—Kenai Fjords Kayaking—co-ed
June—17-26—Caribou Migration Rafting
June—28-July 7—Canning River: Wilderness paddling to Arctic Ocean
July—4-11—Glacier Bay Sea Kayaking
July—8-15—Denali Backpack & Paddle
July—12-17—Humpback Whales by Kayak
July—19-26—Copper River Rafting
July—25-30—Kenai Fjords Kayaking
August—4-11—Hidden Valleys of the Arctic Trek
August—6-13—Brooks Range Canoeing—co-ed
August—13-21—Arctic Divide Trek
August—14-23—Noatak Canoeing Odyssey—co-ed
August—25-September 3—Sheenjek River Rafting—co-ed
August—25-31—Caribou Migration Photography

**Mangrove Mistress (305) 294-4213** Murray Marine, 5710 U.S. 1, Key West, FL 33040 • snorkeling • nature exploring • sunset cruises • ceremonies

**Mountain Mama (505) 351-4312** PO Box 181, Cebolla, NM 87518 • horseback riding and camping in New Mexico

**OceanWomyn Kayaking (206) 325-3970** 620 11th Ave. E., Seattle, WA 98102 • guided sea kayaking adventures

**Outdoor Vacations for Women Over 40 (508) 448-3331** PO Box 200, Groton, MA 01450

January—24-31—California Dreamer, San Francisco, CA
February—21-28—Cross-Country Ski Methow Valley, WA
March—5-20—Auckland, New Zealand
March—6-13—Hike Joshua Tree & Anza Borrego, Palm Springs, CA
April—5-11—Hike & Raft Appalachian Mts., Atlanta, GA
April—15-25—Barging & Biking in Amsterdam, Holland
May—12-23—Walking Tours of Tuscany & Florence, Italy
May—19-30—Walking Tours of Tuscany & Florence, Italy
June—7-14—Yellowstone, MT & Grand Tetons, WY
June—19-27—Walking Tour in County Kerry, Ireland

**Pangaea Expeditions (406) 721-7719** PO Box 5753, Missoula, MT 59806 • river rafting in Montana • call for complete calendar

**Raven-Retreat (207) 546-2456/(800) 841-4586** PO Box 12, Millbridge, ME 04658 • hiking, biking, kayaking and more in Maine coastal mountain wilderness

**Sea Sense (860) 444-1404/(800) 332-1404** 25 Thames St., New London, CT 06320 • world-wide custom sailing courses

**Sheri Griffith River Expeditions (801) 259-8229/(800) 332-2439** PO Box 1324, Moab, UT 84532 • women-only river journeys

June—18-23—Majestic Canyons of the Green River
July—15-18—Cataract Canyon on the Colorado River
August—11-15—Cataract Canyon on the Colorado River
August—27-29—Westwater Canyon on the Colorado River

**Tethys Offshore Sailing for Women (360) 678-6253** 1874 Driftwood Way, Coupeville, WA 98239 • join Capt. Nancy Erley for a segment in her circumnavigation of the world

**Wild Women Expeditions (705) 866-1260** PO Box 145, Stn. B, Sudbury, ON P3E 4N5 • Canada's outdoor adventure company for women • wilderness canoe trips in Ontario's near-North • get-aways at 200-acre waterfront property

**Woman Tours (800) 247-1444** PO Box 931, Driggs, ID 83422 • bicycle tours for women

　　Feb—7-22—New Zealand
　　March—14-May 6—Trans-America Inn to Inn Tour, for women 50+
　　March—16-May 8—Cross Country Camping
　　May—23-30—Zion/Bryce: Bike & Hike
　　June—6-13—Yellowstone/Grand Tetons
　　June—6-11—Yellowstone/Grand Tetons
　　August—29-September 4—Canandian Rockies: Banff Jasper
　　September—5-13—Canadian Rockies: Hot Springs & Lakes
　　September—20-28—Bryce/Escalante/Capitol Reef
　　October—10-18—Mississippi: Natchez Trace
　　October 26-30—California: Sonoma/Napa Valley Vineyards to Waves

**Women in Motion (760) 754-6747/(888) 469-6636** PO Box 4533, Oceanside, CA 92052 • active vacations for women, with women, by women

**Women in the Wilderness (612) 227-2284** 566 Ottawa Ave., St. Paul, MN 55107 • adventure travel, outdoor skills and nature study

**Women on a Roll (310) 578-8888** PO Box 10965, Marina del Rey, CA 90295

　　February—26-March 1—Women's Winter Retreat, Mammoth Lakes, CA
　　July—4—Whitewater Rafting on American River, Middle Fork
　　November—14-23—Costa Rica

**Woodswomen (612) 822-3809/(800) 279-0555** 25 W. Diamond Lake Rd., Minneapolis, MN 55419 • non-profit tour operator • outdoor adventures • domestic and international • call for more complete calendar

　　December—28, 1997-January 1—Dogsledding in the Northland
　　February—13-28—New Zealand Bicycle Tour
　　March—7-13—Vacation in Cozumel
　　April—2-9—Josua Tree Rock Climbing
　　May—23-28—Navajo Land Trek, Utah
　　June—11-22—Exploring the Galapagos Islands
　　July—25-30—Kenai Fjords Sea Kayaking
　　August—19-22—Lake Superior Island Kayaking
　　September—20-26—Grand Canyon Backpacking
　　October—14-November 1—Trekking in the Himalayas, Nepal

### Women on the Water—SEE MANGROVE MISTRESS

**Women's EcoScapes (408) 479-0473** PO Box 1408, Santa Cruz, CA 95061 • coral reef ecology • snorkeling, kayaking, sailing • well-dolphin whale encounters • Key West, California, Hawaii

**Women's Outdoor Challenges (603) 763-5400** 40 Winn Hill Rd., Sunapee, NH 03782 • outdoor adventure programs for women of all ages

*Mostly Women*

▲ **Adventure Associates (206) 932-8352** PO Box 16304, Seattle, WA 98116 • co-ed and women-only outdoor adventures • **IGLTA** member

January—TBA—Cross-Country Ski, British Columbia
January—TBA—Cross-Country Ski, Yellowstone
January—TBA—Costa Rica Adventure
January—TBA—Safari East Africa
February—TBA—Cross-Country Ski North Cascades, WA
February—TBA—Trek Copper Canyon, Mexico
February—TBA—Sea Kayak Baja
March—TBA—Sea Kayaking Baja
March—TBA—Trek Nepal/Himalayas
May—TBA—Women's Challenge Personal Discovery Retreat
June—TBA—Whale Watch Sea Kayak Weekend
June—TBA—Women's Solstice Ocean Retreat
June—TBA—Raft Deschutes River, OR
June—TBA—East Africa Safari
July—TBA—Sea Kayak San Juan Islands, WA
July—TBA—Fly Fish the Tetons, ID
July—TBA—Backpack Wilderness Coast, WA
July—TBA—Lodge-based Hiking No. Cascades, WA
July—TBA—Llama Trek Olympic Mountains, WA
July—TBA—Mt. Rainier Women's Wilderness Retreat
July—TBA—Climb Mt. Baker, WA (Snow School)
August—TBA—Wilderness Gourmet/Basecamp Hiking, Cascades, WA
August—TBA—Sea Kayak San Juan Islands, WA
August—TBA—Backpack Tetons
August—TBA—Sail the Northern Aegean, Greece
August—TBA—Multi-Sport San Juan Islands, WA
August—TBA—Lodge-based Hiking Olympic Mts.
September—TBA—Bali/Lombok with Thalia Zepato
October—TBA—Trek Nepal Himalayas
Nov/Dec—TBA—Explore New Zealand
Nov/Dec—TBA—Cruise Galapagos/ Explore Ecuador
Nov/Dec—TBA—Costa Rica Tropical New Year's
Nov/Dec—TBA—Cross-Country Ski New Year's, Cascades, WA

**Bar H Ranch (208) 354-2906** PO Box 297, Driggs, ID 83422 • guesthouse and summer horseback trips in Wyoming's Tetons • near Jackson Hole, WY

▲ **Mariah Wilderness Expeditions (510) 233-2303/(800) 462-7424** PO Box 248, Port Richmond, CA 94807 • woman-owned • whitewater rafting in California and Central America • call for catalogs

March—28-April 4—Sea kayaking in Sea of Cortez
April—4-11—Belize & Guatemala Adventure Cruise
July—25-August 7—Colorado River in the Grand Canyon
November—7-17—Costa Rica

*Gay/Lesbian*

**Alaska Fantastic Fishing Charters (800) 478-7777** PO Box 2807, Homer, AK 99603 • deluxe cabin cruiser for big-game fishing (halibut)

**Lizard Head Expeditions (303) 831-7090/(888) 540-2737** 1280 Humboldt St. #32, Denver, CO 80218 • tours in central Rocky Mountains and Utah canyon country emphasizing mountaineering, canyoneering and other wilderness skills (women-only tours avail.) • **IGLTA** member

# ADVENTURE ASSOCIATES

PO BOX 16304 · SEATTLE WA 98116

## (206) 932-8352

**WOMEN TRAVELERS - EXPLORE YOUR WORLD**

Journey to Bali / Lombok • Kayak Baja
Safari East Africa • Sail Greek Isles • Trek Nepal
Explore New Zealand • Cruise Galapagos / Ecuador
and many other exotic, far-away places!
Pacific Northwest trips include rafting, seakayaking,
lodge-based hiking, backpacking, fly fishing,
llama trekking, x-skiing, and so much more!

*No Experience Needed • Small Groups • Free Brochure*

**Since 1987 - the best in women's adventures !**

## OUTDOOR ADVENTURES FOR WOMEN

# MARIAH

**WILDERNESS EXPEDITIONS**

AN UNFORGETTABLE
OUTDOOR EXPERIENCE

P.O. BOX 248, POINT RICHMOND, CA 94807
510-233-2303 · **800-4-MARIAH** · fax 510-233-0956

email: **rafting@mariahwe.com**
**www.mariahwe.com**

Join one of the oldest and most
successful women-owned wilderness companies in the U.S.

*Whitewater rafting...... Class
II-IV, Western States
Tropical Costa Rica...an Active Adventure
Baja Sea Kayaking...beautiful wilderness
Belize & Guatemala Eco-Cruise*

There Are a Number of Things to Know About Lesbian Travel...Fortunately, You Have Only One Number to Remember:

## 1-800-448-8550

## C r u i s e s
## T o u r s
## R e s o r t s

No matter where you want to go, how you want to get there or where you want to stay, The International Gay Travel Association's worldwide network of over 1000 gay & lesbian community-based travel agents will professionally guide you with the latest information on all the hot, new travel opportunities. For an IGTA travel agent or IGTA accommodations worldwide call today!

International Gay & Lesbian Travel Association

**IGLTA**

Opening Doors To Gay & Lesbian Travel & Adventure

Home Page: http://www.rainbow-mall.com/igta

**Maui Surfing School (808) 875-0625** PO Box 424, Puunene, HI 96784 • **IGLTA** member

**Alyson Adventures (617) 247-8170/(800) 825-9766** PO Box 181223, Boston, MA 02118 • **IGLTA** member
January—31-February 7—An Octopus's Garden—dive into Caribbean paradise
February—19-March 6—Boomerang—tour Australia
April—8-15—Natchez Trace—biking in the Old South
June—12-19—Mistral—biking in France
June—20-27—Edelweiss—biking in France
July—18-25—Butch Cassidy Days—multiple activities in the Tetons
July—26-August 2—The Grand—climbing the Grand Teton
September—12-19—Big Loire, Little Loire—biking in France
September—18-25—Valley of the Kings—biking in France
September—TBA—Provence Cycling Trips
October—TBA—Loire Valley Cycling Trips

**OutWest Adventures (406) 543-0262/(800) 743-0458** PO Box 8451, Missoula, MT 59807 • specializing in active Western vacations

**Rainbow Kayak Adventures (808) 965-9011** PO Box 983, Pahoa, HI 96778 • hiking, camping, kayaking, scuba and more

**Rainbow Tours (808) 328-8406** 87-3202 Guava Road, Kona Paradise, Captain Cook, HI 96704 • kayaking and snorkeling off black sand beaches of Kona Coast

**Undersea Expeditions (619) 270-2900/(800) 669-0310** PO Box 9455, Pacific Beach, CA 92169 • warm water diving and scuba trips worldwide • **IGLTA** member
February—Belize
March—Curacao
April—Kauai, Hawaii
August-September—Red Sea, Egypt
November—Belize
January, 1999—Cocos Island, Costa Rica

---

*Straight/Gay*

**Ahwahnee Whitewater Expeditions (209) 533-1401** PO Box 1161, Columbia, CA 95310 • women-only, co-ed and charter rafting

**Alta Expeditions (970) 882-2467/(888) 637-2582** 20839 Country Rd. 'W', Lewis, CO 81327 • wilderness experience with an archaeological emphasis including hiking, biking and van tours

**Artemis Wilderness Tours (512) 708-0756** PO Box 1574, El Prado, NM 87529 • whitewater boating and rafting in New Mexico and Colorado • cross-country skiing • kayaking • also women-only trips

**Cow Pie Adventures (801) 297-2140/(888) 4-COWPIE** PO BOX 6, Magna, UT 84044 • back country adventures in southern Utah

**Great Canadian Ecoventures (604) 730-0704/(800) 667-9453** 865 Hollywood, Box 545, Qualicum Beach, BC V9K 1T, Canada • wildlife photography tours

**Lotus Land Tours (604) 684-4922** 1251 Cardero St., Ste. 1251, Vancouver, BC V6G 2H9, Canada • day paddle trips, no experience necessary (price includes pick-up and meal)

**McNamara Ranch (719) 748-3466** 4620 County Rd. 100, Florissant, CO 80816 • horseback tours for 2-3

**Natural Habitat Adventures (303) 449-3711/(800) 543-8917** 2945 Center Green Ct., Boulder, CO 80301 • up-close encounters world-wide with wildlife in their natural habitats

**Outland Adventures (206) 932-7012** PO Box 16343, Seattle, WA 98116 • ecologically sensitive cultural tours with snorkeling and biking in Central America, Canada, Alaska and Washington State

**Paddling South & Saddling South (707) 942-4550/(800) 398-6200** 4510 Silverado Trail, Calistoga, CA 94515 • horseback, mountain biking, and sea kayak trips in Mexico (call for complete calendar)

> February—1-8—Sierra Ridge Ride-biking
> February—15-21—Traditional Plant Uses-hiking
> February—28-March 8—Wheels & Whales-biking
> March—1-7—Ranch Gardens & Swimmin' Holes-hiking
> March—21-29—Swimmin' Hole Ride-biking
> April—12-18—Sugar Cane Candy Village

**Passage to Utah (801) 582-1896** PO Box 520883, Salt Lake City, UT 84152 • custom trips in the West including hiking, horseback riding and river riding

**Pathways 'The Walking Folk' (770) 339-3640/(800) 707-9255** 867 John Court, Lawrenceville, GA 30245 • walking tours of the Southeast

**Progressive Travels (206) 285-1987/(800) 245-2229** 224 W. Galer Ste. C, Seattle, WA 98119 • classic walking and biking tours of Europe, North America, and Asia • **IGLTA** member

**Puffin Family Charters (907) 278-3346/(800) 978-3346** PO Box 90743, Anchorage, AK 99509

**Rainbow Country Tours/B&B (800) 252-8824** PO Box 333, Escalante, UT 84726 • gay-friendly hiking in Utah with custom tours available

**Rockwood Adventures (604) 926-7705** 1330 Fulton Ave., West Vancouver, Canada BC V7T 1N8, Canada • rain forest walks for all levels with free hotel pick up

**Super Natural Adventures (604) 683-5101** 626 West Pender St., Main Fl., Vancouver, BC V6B 1V9, Canada • hiking and helicopter-hiking trips in Northern and Western Canada

**Water Sport People (305) 296-4546** 511 Greene St., Key West, FL 33040 • scuba-diving instruction and group charters

**Women Sail Alaska (907) 463-3372/(888) 272-4525** PO Box 20348, Juneau, AK 99802 • experience the pristine beauty of southeast AK with lesbian guides

## SPIRITUAL & HEALTH VACATIONS

*Women Only*

**Her Wild Song (207) 721-9005** PO Box 515, Brunswick, ME 04011 • spiritually aware wilderness journeys for women

**Venus Adventures (207) 766-5655** PO Box 167-X, Peaks Island, ME 04108 • goddess-oriented tours for women to sacred sites in England and Ireland

**Wilderness Rites (415) 457-3691** 20 Spring Grove Ave., San Rafael, CA 94901 • vision quests for women

**Women's Mysteries Tours (303) 399-1646** sacred adventures • healing journeys

*Mostly Women*

**Hawk, I'm Your Sister** (505) 984-2268 PO Box 9109-WT, Santa Fe, NM 87504 •
women's wilderness canoe trips and writing retreats in the Americas and Russia
>   May—16-23—Writing Retreat
>   June—11-18—Revisioning Personal Power
>   June—26-July 2—Being a Healer in the 21st Century
>   August—24-September 11—Armu River, Russian Far East
>   October—3-16—Lake Titicaca, Bolivia & Machu Picchu, Peru

*Gay/Lesbian*

**Destination Discovery** (707) 963-0543/(800) 954-5543 PO Drawer 659, Rutherford,
CA 94573 • wellness vacations for lesbigay community including exclusive trips
for HIV+ gay men • **IGLTA** member

# CUSTOM TOURS

*Women Only*

**Activities** (714) 675-6200/(800) 876-8708 3328 Via Lido, Newport Beach, CA 92663
• custom-designed private women's tours and meetings in unique locations

**Tropical Tune-ups** (808) 882-7355/(800) 587-0405 PO Box 4488, Waikoloa, HI 96738
• customized retreats for 2 or more women • beachfront locations

*Gay/Lesbian*

**L'Arc en Ciel Voyages** (610) 964-7888/(800) 965-LARC (5272) PO Box 234, Wayne, PA
19087-0254 • custom-designed tour programs for the gay/lesbian community
>   December—27, 1997-January 1—New Years Eve on Top of the World, Iceland
>   January—16-24—Swiss Skiing Adventure
>   March—TBA—Ladies Week in Acapulco
>   November—TBA—Ladies Week in Acapulco

# THEMATIC TOURS

*Women Only*

**Asian Pacific Adventures** (213) 935-3156/(800) 825-1680 826 S. Sierra Bonita Ave.,
Los Angeles, CA 90036 • women's tours to Asia, India, Nepal and more
>   February—16-March 7—Focus on Women—India & Nepal
>   May—17-June 7—Scenic Southwest China Bike
>   May—17-30—Best of China Bike
>   June—29-July 13—Bali Through an Artist's Eye
>   August—9-21—Borneo: Sabah & Sarawak Headhunters, Hornbills & Orangutans
>   November—1-14—Best of China Bike
>   November—1-22—Scenic Southwest China Bike
>   November—TBA—Fertility Tour to Bhutan

**Canyon Calling** (520) 282-0916/(800) 664-8922 215 Disney Ln., Sedona, AZ 86336 •
7-day tours of the Southwest May-October each year

**Cetlacic** (617) 492-3531 apdo, Postal 1-201, CP 62000, Cuernavaca, Morelos, MEX-
ICO • alternative language school • learn about Mexico through the lens of
women's experience
>   January—5-17—Women and Social Change in Mexico
>   June—TBA—Lesbian Movement in Mexico

# CLUB *LeBon*

*All-inclusive, deluxe vacations for women at secluded, private resorts are the trademark of Club Le Bon. Twenty-five years experience in the travel industry, has led us to specialize in upscale Caribbean hide-aways with pristine beaches and beautiful views. Our groups are large enough to mingle, but small enough for an intimate rendezvue with your special someone, plan to join us soon.*

## Monarch Butterfly Tour & Spa
Dec 28 -Jan. 3, 1998  $839  Central Mexico

## "Kool Kids" Gay & Lesbian Family Vacation
June 21-28, 1997 $899/adult, $425 kids 2-12yrs
Bring the kids to a fun tropical paradise!

---

### New Years 2000 - Paradise Awaits
$200 Deposit will hold your space at this new, deluxe, 36 room  Hotel on the coast of Mexico.

---

*Call for brochure and current schedule!*

Call for a Brochure
**1-800-836-8687**
**908-826-1577**
P.O. Box 444
Woodbridge, NJ 07095
CLBUSA@aol.com

**Club Skirts**  Club Skirts/Girl Bar/Dinah Shore Women's Weekend parties • Dinah Shore hotline: 888-44-DINAH • also Club Skirts Labor Day in Monterey • Monterey hotline: 415-337-4962

**Joani Weir Productions & Klub Banshee** (310) 281-7358 all-inclusive hotel and entertainment package for women during Dinah Shore Weekend • special events throughout the year

**Merlyn's Journeys** (209) 736-9330/(800) 509-9330 PO Box 277, Altaville, CA 95221 • relaxing and adventurous getaways for women

**Robin Tyler Tours** (818) 893-4075 15842 Chase St., North Hills, CA 91343 • produces 'West Coast Women's Music & Comedy Festival' • cruises to China
   July—30-August 9—Women's Tour of Gay Games in Amsterdam

**Travel Pals** (805) 963-8339/(800) 324-9661 315 Mellifont Ave., Santa Barbara, CA 93103 • creative travel for small groups
   March—29-April 5—Mother/Daughter Baja Adventure
   May—1-10—Siena, Italy
   May—12-23—Ireland Walking Tour
   September—18-27—Siena, Italy

**RVing Women** (602) 983-4678/(888) 557-8464 Dept. MV, PO Box 1840, Apache Jct., AZ 85217 • RV club for women • call for events

### Mostly Women

▲ **Club Le Bon** (908) 826-1577/(800) 836-8687 PO Box 444, Woodbridge, NJ 07095 • tours for lesbians and for gay/lesbian parents and their kids

**Lost Coast Llama Caravans** 77321 Usal Rd., Whitehorn, CA 95489 • women-led pack trips

### Gay/Lesbian

**A Friend in New York** (201) 656-7282 260 7th St., Hoboken, NJ 07030 • personalized excursions tailored to your budget and schedule

**'Alley-Gator' Houseboat** (904) 775-7423 2161 Saragossa Ave., De Land, FL 32724 • houseboat tour on St. Johns River

**Cruisin' the Castro** (415) 550-8110 375 Lexington St., San Francisco, CA 94110 • guided walking tour of the Castro • **IGLTA member**

**Doin' It Right In Puerto Vallarta** (415) 621-3584 150 Franklin St. #208, San Francisco, CA 94102 • your gay Puerto Vallarta specialist • **IGLTA member**

**Fiesta Tours** (415) 986-1134/(888) 229-8687 323 Geary St. #619, San Francisco, CA 94102 • tours to Latin America for New Year's and Carnival in Rio • **IGLTA member**

**Gay Hawaiian Excursions** (808) 667-7466/(800) 311-4460 • **IGLTA** member

**Gay Insider Tours of New York** (201) 798-1558 193-195 Ogden Ave. #2D, Jersey City, NJ 07307 • **IGLTA member**

**GAYVentures** (305) 541-6141/(800) 940-7757 2009 SW 9th St., Miami, FL 33135 • Puerto Rico tours • **IGLTA member**

**New England Vacation Tours** (802) 464-2076/(800) 742-7669 PO Box 571 - Rte. 100, West Dover, VT 05356 • gay/lesbian tours (including fall foliage) conducted by a mainstream tour operator

**P.A.T.H. Adventure Tours of Australia** (011) 61-8-8271 4068 17, Rose Terrace, Wayville, S.A 5034, Australia

*Irresistible Escapes for The Lesbian Traveler, Her Family, and Friends*

*Let Babs Daitch make all your travel arrangements as she has for thousands of other women travelers.*

**ALASKA • MEXICO • HAWAII • CARIBBEAN**

## Babs Bringing the World a Little Bit Closer in 1998

*Alaskan Native Journeys plus Dykes and Dogs—Iditarod Winter Adventure,* Alaska • *Dykes at Disney World,* Orlando • *Matrimony and Magic,* Maui • *Lucy & Ethel's Big Apple Caper,* New York • *Much, much more!*

For Information: Contact **"Thanks, Babs"**
Toll Free 888-WOW-BABS
Fax 510-843-1266 E-mail ThanksBabs@aol.com
Website www.thanksbabs.com
and at AOL Keyword Thanksbabs

**Travel by Philip (501) 227-7690** PO Box 250119, Little Rock, AR 72225-5119 • specializes in gay motorcoach tours • **IGLTA** member

**Travel Keys Tours (916) 452-5200** PO Box 162266, Sacramento, CA 95816-2266 • antique tours and tours of dungeons and castles in Europe • **IGLTA** member

**Victorian Home Walks (415) 252-9485** 2226 15th St., San Francisco, CA 94114 • historical walking tour of San Francisco's Victorian homes • **IGLTA** member

**Way To Go Costa Rica (800) 835-1223** 2801 Blue Ridge Rd., Raleigh, NC 27607 • **IGLTA** member

*Straight/Gay*

**Connections Tours (305) 673-3153/(800) 688-8463 (OUT-TIME)** 169 Lincoln Rd., Ste. 302, Miami Beach, FL 33139 • local arrangements in Florida • **IGLTA** member

**Earth Walks (505) 988-4157** PO Box 8534, Santa Fe, NM 87504 • guided tour of American Southwest and Mexico

**Santa Cruz Tours (408) 439-8687** PO Box 3508, Santa Cruz, CA 95063 • nature sightseeing and winery tours

**Skunk Train California Western (707) 459-5248** 299 E. Commercial St., Willits, CA • scenic train trips

**Tall Ship Adventures (303) 755-7983/(800) 662-0090** 1389 S. Havana St., Aurora, CO 80012 • **IGLTA** member

# VARIOUS

*Women Only*

**Remote Possibilities (808) 875-7438/(800) 511-3121** 122 Central Ave., Wailuku, HI 96793
- June—21-28—Maui Women's Week
- July—5-11—Alaska Adventure Cruise
- September—12-18—French Wine Tasting Cruise
- October—4-11—Maui Women's Week

▲ **Thanks, Babs! (415) 552-1791/(888) 969-2227** 3938 19th St., San Francisco, CA 94114 • the vacation expert for women • **IGLTA** member
- January—29-February 1—Sapphos in Snow—Aspen,CO
- February—6-9—Girlz in the Snow—Copper Mt., CO
- February—12-17—Valentines in Vallarta, MX
- February—TBA—Mardi Gras in Sydney, Australia
- March—5-12—Dykes & Dogs Iditarod Winterfest—Anchorage, AK
- March—TBA—Lucy & Ethel's Big Apple Caper, New York City
- April—11-18—Swashbuckling Sisters, British Virgin Islands
- May—TBA—Australian Aboriginal & Red Desert Camp-Out
- June—4-8—Gay Day in Orlando—Disney, Sea World & Universal Studios
- June—27-July 7—Femmes Fatales—San Francisco
- July—TBA—Mademoiselles in Montreal
- July—31-August 9—Dykes on Dikes, Gay Games in Amsterdam
- August—TBA—Denali Rail & Inside Passage—Anchorage, AK
- August—28-30—Monterey Women's Labor Day Weekend
- September—9-13—WomenFest, Key West
- October—28-November 4—Halloween in Hawaii—Maui, HI
- November—11-18—Mayan Mistresses—Cozumel, MX
- December—TBA—Bells Are Ringing—Hawaii
- December—20-27—Femmes Fatales in Frisco for the Holidays

*Mostly Women*

▲ **Skylink** (707) 585-8355/(800) 225-5759 3577 Moorland, Santa Rosa, CA 95407 • low-cost tours worldwide for women in couples or single • air-included
> January—16-21—Sundance Film Fest & Ski Holiday—Utah
> February—22-March 2—Mardi Gras—Sydney, Australia
> March—TBA—Treasures of Italy
> March—26-30—Dinah Shore Women's Week—Palm Springs, CA
> April—4-11—Belize
> May—22-25—White Sulphur Springs Spa & Resort—St. Helena, CA
> June—13-20—Greek Cruise
> July—12-27—Kenya Photo Safari, Uganda Gorilla Trekking
> August—1-9—Gay Games—Amsterdam
> August—9-19—Irish Escapade
> August—28-29—Whitewater River Rafting
> September—TBA—Golfing Gals—Northern CA
> October—TBA—Women's Week—Provincetown, MA
> November—TBA—Golf/Theme Parks—Orlando, FL

*Gay/Lesbian*

**Above All Travel** (602) 946-9968 worldwide lesbian/gay cruises and tours

**All About Destinations** (602) 277-2703/(800) 375-2703 Gallery 3 Plaza, 3819 N. 3rd St., Phoenix, AZ 85012-2074 • **IGLTA** member
> February—9-13—Whale Watching, La Paz, Mexico

**All Continents Travel** (310) 645-7527/(800) 995-7997 5250 W. Century Bl. #626, Los Angeles, CA 90045 • **IGLTA** member

# WHERE IN THE WORLD DO YOU WANT TO GO?

## Galapagos? Cancun? Paris? Mom's?

Call for our brochure:
## 800-225-5759

Visit our website:
**www.skylinktravel.com**

A full service travel agency
▼
Custom travel arrangements
▼
Women-only escorted tours
▼
Gay-friendly destinations

## SKYLINK
TRAVEL SERVICES

DE SALVIO

MEMBER IGLTA, BACW

# Our Family
### Abroad℠

# Global travel
## for gay men and women

**Congenial companionship . . .**

*It makes the difference between
an ordinary trip and a great vacation.*

**Our Family Abroad**
will show you the most exciting
destinations around the world
in a totally gay-sensitive,
gay-friendly, yet
uniquely discreet
environment.

For our free
full-color brochure
or for reservations,
please contact your
travel professional
or call:

**800 / 999 5500**
in the U.S. and Canada

**212 / 459 1800**
outside the U.S. and Canada

**212 / 581 3756**
by fax

**www.familyabroad.com**

*Member*

**Blue Ridge Travel (704) 669-8681/(800) 948-3430** 102 Cherry St., Black Mountain, NC 28801 • lesbigay tours and cruises

**Different Strokes Tours (212) 262-3860/(800) 688-3301** 1841 Broadway Ste. 1207, New York, NY 10023 • gay cultural safaris to worldwide destinations • **IGLTA** member

▲ **Our Family Abroad (212) 459-1800/(800) 999-5500** 40 W. 57th St., New York, NY 10019 • all-inclusive package and guided motorcoach tours in Europe, Asia, Africa and South America • **IGLTA** member

   January—16-26—Ancient Egypt
   January—19-28—Caribbean Explorer
   January—25-February 9—India
   January—31-February 7—Yucatan & Mexico City
   February—13-23—Ancient Egypt
   February—14-March 2—Kenya & Tanzania
   February—15-March 2—South East Asia
   February—23-March 1—Caribbean Explorer
   July—31-August 9—Gay Games in Amsterdam

**Friends of Dorothy (415) 864-1600** 290 Roosevelt Way, #2, San Francisco, CA 94114 • **IGLTA** member

**Holigays Worldwide Travel (617) 321-7277/(888) 321-7277** 14 Darthmouth St., Malden, MA 02148 • **IGLTA** member

**Parkside Travel (216) 688-3334/(800) 552-1647** 3310 Kent Rd. Ste. 6, Stowe, OH 44224 • also Gay Travel Cub membership and discounts

**Sundance Travel (714) 752-5456 x277/(800) 424-3434 x277** 19800 MacArthur Blvd. #100, Irvine, CA 92612 • **IGLTA** member

*Straight/Gay*

**10,000 Waves (406) 549-6670** PO Box 7924, Missoula, MT 59807

**Atlas Travel Service (310) 670-3574/(800) 952-0120** 8923 S. Sepulveda Blvd., Los Angeles, CA 90045 • **IGLTA** member

**Florida Network Tours, Inc. (954) 458-4004** 621 W. Hallandale Beach Blvd., Hallandale, FL 33009 • **IGLTA** member

**Global Express (206) 467-0467/(800) 682-1988** 1904 3rd Ave., Ste. 900, Seattle, WA 98101 • cruises and tours • **IGLTA** member

**Kenny Tours, Ltd. (410) 643-9200** 106 Market Ct., Stevensville, MD 21666-2162 • **IGLTA** member

**Tal Tours (516) 825-0966/(800) 825-9399** 11 Sunrise Plaza #302, Valley Stream, NY 11580 • **IGLTA** member

## January

**16-18: Gay/Lesbian Weekend** *Catskill Mtns., NY*
two nights of entertainment & gay events • meals included • gay/lesbian • $269 • **(800) 367-4637**

**23-24: Women's Travel Expo** *San Francisco, CA*
2 days of seminars, events & speakers covering business & adventure travel • mostly women • $10-15 • **(510) 528-8425** • c/o *Maiden Voyages Magazine*, 109 Minna St. #240, San Francisco, CA 94105 • **WEB:** http://maiden-voyages.com

**24-31: Aspen Gay Ski Week** *Aspen, CO*
gay/lesbian • 2000+ attendees • **(970) 925-9249** • c/o *Aspen Gay/Lesbian Community*, Box 3143, Aspen, CO 81612

## February

**1-8: Whistler Gay Ski Week: Altitude '98** *Whistler, BC*
6th Annual Gay/Lesbian Ski Week • popular destination 75 mi. north of Vancouver • gay/lesbian • **(604) 688-5079/(888) 258-4883** • c/o *Out On The Slopes Productions*, 101-1184 Denman St. #190, Vancouver, BC, Canada V6G 2M9 • **EMAIL:** altitude@outontheslopes.com • **WEB:** www.outontheslopes.com

**5-8: Girlz 'n the Snow** *Copper Mountain, CO*
benefit for National Center for Lesbian Rights • women only • **(303) 402-7476** • c/o *Circles Magazine*, 1705 Fourteenth St. #326, Boulder, CO 80302 • **EMAIL:** circles@indra.com

**6-8: Aspen Women's Ski Weekend** *Aspen, CO*
proceeds go to the Susan G. Komen Breast Cancer Foundation • mostly women • 2000+ attendees • **(800) 525-6200** • c/o *Aspen Skiing Company*, PO Box 1248, Aspen, CO 81612

**6-9: Gay Ski East '98: The Winter Games** *Lake Placid, NY*
gay/lesbian • 200+ attendees • **(813) 734-1111** • c/o *Eclectic Excursions*, 2045 Hunters Glen Dr. Ste. 502, Duneden, FL 34698 • **EMAIL:** gayskieast@compuserve.com

**15: Desert AIDS Walk** *Palm Springs, CA*
gay/lesbian • **(760) 325-9255** • c/o *Desert AIDS Project*, 750 S. Vella Rd., Palm Springs, CA 92264

**24: Mardi Gras** *New Orleans, LA*
North America's rowdiest block party • mixed gay/straight • **(504) 566-5011** • c/o *New Orleans Convention & Visitors Bureau*, 1520 Sugarbowl Dr., New Orleans, LA 70112

## March

**13-21: Winterfest** *Lake Tahoe, NV*
AIDS benefit ski weekend • **(800) 754-1888** • c/o *Ski Connections*, 10356 Airport Rd. Hangar 1, Truckee, CA 96161

**23-29: Nabisco Dinah Shore Golf Tournament** *Palm Springs, CA*
see Club Skirts or Joani Weir Productions under Tour Operators for party & accomodation info • mostly women • **(619) 324-4546**

**26-29: Dinah Shore Women's Weekend** *Palm Springs, CA*
huge gathering of lesbians for pool parties, dancing and yes, some golf-watching • women only • **(888) 44-DINAH**

## April

**TBA: AIDS Dance-a-thon L.A.** *Los Angeles, CA*
AIDS benefit at Universal Studios • mixed gay/straight • $75+ pledges • **(213) 466-9255** • c/o *AIDS Walk LA*, PO Box 933005, Los Angeles, CA 90093

**TBA: AIDS Dance-a-thon San Francisco** *San Francisco, CA*
AIDS benefit dance at Moscone Center • mixed gay/straight • 7000+ attendees • **(415) 392-9255** • c/o *Mobilization Against AIDS*, PO Box 193920, San Francisco, CA 94119

**TBA: London Lesbian Film Festival** *London, ON*
mostly women • **(519) 432-6378** • c/o *London Lesbian Film Fest*, PO Box 46014, 956 Dundas St. E., London, ON, Canada N5W 3A1

*this is one* Pride Celebration *well worth* coming Out for!

Join Us for the World's Largest
Lesbian, Gay, Bisexual, Transgender
Pride Celebration!

June 27th & 28th, 1998

*san francisco*
c a l i f o r n i a    USA

*For Special Rates on Air, Hotel and Car Rental Call:*

 damron**atlas**
WORLD**TRAVEL**

*toll free* 1.888.907.9771
http://www.damronatlas.com

TBA: **We're Funny That Way** *Toronto, ON*
comedians from around the world perform at Canada's International Gay/Lesbian Comedy Festival • gay/lesbian • **(416) 964-3473** • c/o *WFTW Productions*, 50 Alexander St., Ste. 201, Toronto, ON, Canada M4Y 1B6

## May

1-3: **Russian River Women's Wknd** *Guerneville, CA*
2 hrs north of San Francisco • mostly women • **(707) 869-4522**/**(800) 253-8800**

1-3: **Splash Weekend** *Houston, TX*
celebrate Black Lesbian/Gay Pride • gay/lesbian • **(202) 843-6786** • c/o *Nat'l Black Gay/Lesbian Leadership Forum*, 1436 'U' St. NW #200, Washington, DC 20009

15-17 (also in June, Sept., and Oct.): **Paradise** *Greenfield, NH*
summer camp for grown-ups • also June 19-21, Sept. 11-13, Oct. 9-11 • women only • 70+ attendees • $100 • **(603) 532-7104** • c/o *Paradise*, 23 Thayer Rd., Rindge, NH 03461

22-June 7: **Spoleto Festival** *Charleston, SC*
one of the continent's premier avant-garde culture festivals, in late May • **(803) 722-2764** • c/o *Spoleto Festival USA*, PO Box 157, Charleston, SC 29402-0157

23: **Wigswood** *Atlanta, GA*
annual festival of peace, love & wigs • wig watchers welcome • **(404) 874-6782** • c/o *Act Up Atlanta*, 828 W. Peachtree St. NW, Ste. 206-A, Atlanta, GA 30308-1146

Memorial Day Wknd: **Black Lesbian/Gay Pride Weekend** *Washington, DC*
gay/lesbian • **(202) 843-6786** • c/o *Nat'l Black Gay/Lesbian Leadership Forum*, 1436 'U' St. NW #200, Washington, DC 20009

TBA: **AIDS Walk-a-thon** *New York, NY*
AIDS benefit • mixed gay/straight • **(212) 807-9255** • c/o *Gay Men's Health Crisis*, PO Box 10, Old Chelsea Stn., New York, NY 10113-0010

TBA: **Wild Women's Weekend** *Clearlake, CA*
parties • BBQ • tournaments • women only • $25+ • camping/RV • **(707) 279-0208** • c/o *Edgewater Resort*, 6420 Soda Bay Rd., Kelseyville, CA 95451

## June

6: **Gay Day at Disneyworld** *Orlando, FL*
**(888) 429-3527** • c/o *Good Time Gay Productions*, 450 W. 62nd St., Miami Beach, FL 33140

17-27: **San Francisco Int'l Lesbian/Gay Film Festival** *San Francisco, CA*
get your tickets early for a slew of films about us • 53,000+ attendees • **(415) 703-8650** • c/o *Frameline*, 346 9th St., San Francisco, CA 94103

18-21: **Washington DC AIDS Ride 3** *Washington, DC*
gay/lesbian • **(800) 825-1000**/**(202) 293-7433** • c/o *Washington DC AIDS Ride*, 1215 Connecticut Ave. NW, 3rd flr., Washington, DC 20036

20-Aug 16: **Pony Express Tour 1998** *Cross-country, USA*
women motorcyclists ride cross-country for Breast Cancer Research • women only • **(716) 768-6054** • c/o *Women's Motorcyclist Foundation*, 7 Lent Ave., LeRoy, NY 14482 • **EMAIL:** WMFGINSUE@aol.com

21-28: **Maui Women's Week** *Maui, HI*
7-day resort in Maui • tennis, golf, sailing, windsurfing, kayaking • women only • **(800) 511-3121** • c/o *Remote Possibilities*, 122 Central Ave., Wailuku, Maui, HI 96793 • **WEB:** http://www.remotepo.com

27-28: **San Francisco LGBT Pride Parade & Celebration** *San Francisco, CA*
**(415) 864-3733** • c/o *SFLGBTPCC*, 1390 Market St. #1225, San Francisco, CA 94102

TBA: **California AIDS Ride** *San Francisco, CA*
AIDS benefit bike ride from San Francisco to L.A. benefits Jeffrey Goodman Special Care Clinic • mixed gay/straight • **(800) 825-1000** • c/o *Pallotta TeamWorks*, 1525 Crossroads of the World, Los Angeles, CA 90028

TBA: **Lesbigaytrans Pride**                                *Everywhere, USA*
celebrate yourself and attend one – or many – of the hundreds of Gay Pride parades &
festivities happening in cities around the continent •

TBA: **New York Int'l Gay/Lesbian Film Festival**              *New York, NY*
week-long fest in early June • **(212) 254-7228** • c/o *The New Festival*, 47 Great Jones St.,
New York, NY 10012

# July

3-5: **At the Beach Weekend**                                 *Malibu, CA*
gay/lesbian • **(202) 843-6786** • c/o *Nat'l Black Gay/Lesbian Leadership Forum*, 1436 'U' St.
NW #200, Washington, DC 20009

3-5: **July 4th Kickback**                                *Kent's Store, VA*
watergames • women only • 80 attendees • $75 • **(804) 589-6542** • c/o *Intouch*, Rte. 2,
Box 1096, Kent's Store, VA 23084

16-26: **Philadelphia Gay/Lesbian Film Festival**           *Philadelphia, PA*
gay/lesbian • **(215) 790-1510/(800) 333-8521 EX. 33** • c/o *TLA Video*, 1520 Locust St.,
Philadelphia, PA 19102 • **EMAIL:** sales@tlavideo.com

24-26: **Hotter Than July Weekend**                            *Detroit, MI*
gay/lesbian • **(202) 843-6786** • c/o *Nat'l Black Gay/Lesbian Leadership Forum*, 1436 'U' St.
NW #200, Washington, DC 20009

26: **Zoo Party**                                           *San Diego, CA*
pride party at the zoo, 4pm-11pm, sells out quickly! • mostly men • 4000+ attendees •
$40/50 • **(619) 220-2137** • c/o *Powerhouse Productions*, 8586 Miramar Pl., San Diego, CA
92121 • **EMAIL:** bhardt@connectnet.com

TBA: **Crape Myrtle Festival**                 *Raleigh-Durham, Chapel Hill, NC*
week-long festival to raise money for AIDS & lesbigay concerns • movies • tournaments
• raffle • gala Saturday • mixed gay/straight • 1500 attendees • **(919) 967-3606/(800)
494-8497** • c/o *Crape Myrtle Festival, Inc.*, PO Box 9054, Chapel Hill, NC 27515 • **WEB:**
www.datalounge.com\cmf

# August

1-8, 1998: **Gay Games 1998**                        *Amsterdam, The Netherlands*
support lesbian and gay athletes as they compete in Amsterdam • gay/lesbian • **(31-20)
427-1998** • c/o *Stichting Gay/Lesbian Games*, PO Box 2837, 1000 CV Amsterdam, The
Netherlands • **WEB:** http://www.dds.nl/~gaygames

11-16: **National Gay Softball World Series**                  *Atlanta, GA*
gay/lesbian • **(412) 362-1247** • c/o *NAGAAA*, 1014 King Ave., Pittsburgh, PA 15206

28-Sept. 10: **Austin Gay/Lesbian International Film Festival**      *Austin, TX*
gay/lesbian • **(512) 476-2454** • c/o *AGLIFF*, PO Box 'L', Austin, TX 78713

28-30: **Club Skirts Monterey Bay Women's Wknd**            *Monterey, CA*
3 huge dance parties • golf tournament benefitting the Human Rights Campaign • live
comedy night • celebrity guests • book early! • mostly women • **(415) 337-4962** • c/o
*MT Productions*, 584 Castro St., San Francisco, CA 94114

28-30: **In the Life Weekend**                                *Atlanta, GA*
gay/lesbian • **(202) 843-6786** • c/o *Nat'l Black Gay/Lesbian Leadership Forum*, 1436 'U' St.
NW #200, Washington, DC 20009

TBA: **Camp Camp**                                         *Kezar Falls, ME*
summer camp for gay/lesbian adults • $800 • **(888) 924-8380** • c/o *Camp Camp*, 21
Palmer Square E., Princeton, NJ 08542 • **EMAIL:** billcole@worldnet.att.net

Labor Day Wknd: **Festival of Babes**                      *San Francisco, CA*
annual women's soccer tournament and celebration • mostly women • **(510) 428-
1489/(510) 848-4684** • c/o *GirlJock*, PO Box 882723, San Francisco, CA 94188

TBA: **gayday@wonderland**                                                      *Toronto, ON*
fundraiser for AIDS Committee of Toronto • gay/lesbian • **(416) 340-2437** • c/o *AIDS Committee*, 399 Church St., Toronto, ON, Canada M5B 2J6

TBA: **Halsted St. Fair**                                                      *Chicago, IL*
gay/lesbian • **(312) 883-0500**

TBA: **Wigstock**                                                      *New York, NY*
outrageous wig/drag/performance festival in Tompkins Square Park in the East Village • gay/lesbian • **(212) 620-7310**

## September

18-20: **Boston/New York AIDS Ride 4**                                                      *Boston, MA*
AIDS benefit bike ride from Boston to New York • mixed gay/straight • **(800) 825-1000** • c/o *Pallotta TeamWorks*, 1525 Crossroads of the World, Los Angeles, CA 90028

18-20: **Wild Western Women's Weekend**                                                      *Kent's Store, VA*
live country/western music & dancing • women only • 200 attendees • $85 • **(804) 589-6542** • c/o *Intouch*, Rte. 2, Box 1096, Kent's Store, VA 23084

25-27: **Russian River Women's Wknd**                                                      *Guerneville, CA*
mostly women • **(707) 869-4112/(800) 253-8800**

27: **AIDS Walk Toronto**                                                      *Toronto, ON*
gay/lesbian • **(416) 340-2437** • c/o *AIDS Committee of Toronto*, 399 Church St., Toronto, ON, Canada M5B 2J6

TBA: **AIDS Walk L.A.**                                                      *Los Angeles, CA*
mixed gay/straight • **(213) 466-9255** • c/o *AIDS Walk LA*, PO Box 933005, Los Angeles, CA 90093

TBA: **Cruise with Pride**                                                      *San Juan, PR*
Pride Foundation fundraiser in the Greek Islands, 6 days • gay/lesbian • 50+ cabins attendees • **(800) 340-0221** • c/o *Cruiseworld*, 901 Fairview Ave. N. #A150, Seattle, WA 98126

TBA: **'For Women Only' Golf Tournament**                                                      *Boston, MA*
tournament to raise money for Breast Cancer Assoc. • terrific prizes! • women only • 100+ attendees • **(617) 437-9757/(888) 562-2874** • c/o *Carol Nashe Group*, 134 St. Botolph St., Boston, MA 02115

TBA: **Gay Day at Paramount Kings Island**                                                      *Cincinnati, OH*
gay/lesbian • **(513) 651-0040** • c/o *Gay & Lesbian Community Center*, 214 E. 9th St., 5th flr., Cincinnati, OH 45202

TBA: **Gay Night at Knott's Berry Farm**                                                      *Orange County, CA*
amusement park rides, dancing & gay comedy • **(805) 222-7788** • c/o *Odyssey Adventures*, PO Box 923094, Sylmar, CA 91392

TBA: **Wild Women's Weekend**                                                      *Clearlake, CA*
parties • BBQ • tournaments • not for the mild mannered! • women only • $25+camping/RV • **(707) 279-0208** • c/o *Edgewater Resort*, 6420 Soda Bay Rd., Kelseyville, CA 95451

TBA: **Womyn's Wildlife Weekend**                                                      *Maui, HI*
camping • music • comedy • tournaments • women only • **(808) 573-3515** • c/o *WWW*, PO Box 1368, Paia, HI 96779

## October

3: **Castro St. Fair**                                                      *San Francisco, CA*
arts & community groups street fair, co-founded by Harvey Milk • $free • **(415) 467-3354**

4: **AIDS Walk**                                                      *Islip, NY*
gay/lesbian • **(516) 385-2451** • c/o *Long Island Association for AIDS Care*, PO Box 2859, Huntington Stn., NY 11746

# Holly Folly

The Annual Gay and Lesbian Holiday Festival

## FIRST WEEKEND IN DECEMBER
## PROVINCETOWN

*"Don we now our gay apparel..."*

## GAY HOLIDAY CHEER

### red & green parties

*Fabulous Feasts*

## Sensational Shopping

## Festive Accommodations

## Mr. & Ms. Santas

## Carolers & Snowwomen

**FOR MORE INFORMATION CALL 1-800-933-1963
or E-mail: Hollyfolly@provincetown.com
Web: www.provincetown.com/hollyfolly**

**4-11: Maui Women's Week** *Maui, HI*
7-day resort in Maui • tennis, golf, sailing, windsurfing, kayaking • women only • **(800) 511-3121** • c/o *Remote Possibilities*, 122 Central Ave., Wailuku, Maui, HI 96793 • **WEB:** http://www.remotepo.com

**11: National Coming Out Day** *Everytown, USA*
gay/lesbian • **(800) 866-6263** • c/o *National Coming Out Day*, PO Box 34640, Washington, DC 20043-4640

**15-25: Reel Affirmations Film Festival D.C.** *Washington, DC*
lesbian/gay films • gay/lesbian • **(202) 986-1119**

**18: Philadelphia AIDS Walk** *Philadelphia, PA*
gay/lesbian • **(215) 731-9255** • c/o *AIDSFUND*, 1227 Locust St., Philadelphia, PA

**TBA: Gay Night at Disneyland** *Anaheim, CA*
gay/lesbian • $32-37 • **(805) 222-7788** • c/o *Odyssey Adventures*, PO Box 923094, Sylmar, CA 91392

**TBA: Pride Film Festival Tampa** *Tampa, FL*
gay/lesbian • **(813) 837-4485** • 1222 Dale Mabry Ste. 602, Tampa, FL 33629

**TBA: Provincetown Women's Week** *Provincetown, MA*
very popular – make your reservations early! • mostly women • **(800) 637-8696/(508) 487-2313** • c/o *Provincetown Business Guild*, PO Box 421, Provincetown, MA 02657

## November

**TBA: AIDS Dance-a-thon** *New York, NY*
AIDS benefit • mixed gay/straight • 6000+ attendees • $75+ pledges • **(212) 807-9255** • c/o *Gay Men's Health Crisis*, PO Box 10, Old Chelsea Stn., New York, NY 10113-0010

**TBA: Film Festival** *Chicago, IL*
gay/lesbian • **(773) 384-5533** • c/o *Chicago Filmmakers*, 1543 W. Division, Chicago, IL 60622 • **WEB:** www.chicagofilmmakers.org/reeling

**TBA: Mix '98: New York Lesbian/Gay Experimental Film/Video Fest** *New York, NY*
film, videos, installations & media performances • write for info • **(212) 571-4242** • 11 John St. #801, New York, NY 10038 • **EMAIL:** echonyc.com

**TBA: Santa Barbara Lesbian/Gay Film Festival** *Santa Barbara, CA*
gay/lesbian • **(805) 963-3636** • c/o *Gay/Lesbian Resource Center*, 126 E. Haley Ste. A-17, Santa Barbara, CA 93101

## December

**4-6: Holly Folly** *Provincetown, MA*
gay & lesbian weekend holiday festival • parties • holiday concert • open houses • proceeds to Provincetown AIDS Support Group and Helping Our Women • **(800) 533-1983** • PO Box 573, Provincetown, MA 02657 • **EMAIL:** hollyfolly@provincetown.com

**31: Mummer's Strut** *Philadelphia, PA*
New Year's Eve party benefitting Pridefest • mixed gay/straight • $40-50 • **(215) 732-3378** • c/o *Pridefest*, 200 S. Broad St., Philadelphia, PA 19102

## LEATHER CONTESTS & GATHERINGS

### January

**16-19: Mid-Atlantic Leather Weekend** *Washington, DC*
gay/lesbian • **(202) 347-6025** • c/o *Centaurs MC c/o DC Eagle*, 639 New York Ave. NW, Washington, DC 20001

**16-19: Portland Uniform Weekend** *Portland, OR*
gay/lesbian • **(503) 228-6935** • c/o *In Uniform The Magazine*, PO Box 3226, Portland, OR 97208

### February

**12-14: Pantheon of Leather** *New Orleans, LA*
annual SM community service awards, at the Radisson Hotel (800) 824-3359 • mixed gay/straight • **(213) 656-5073** • c/o *The Leather Journal*, 7985 Santa Monica Blvc. 109-368, W. Hollywood, CA 90046

### April

**3-5: Rubbout 7** *Vancouver, BC*
annual pansexual rubber weekend • mostly men • 60-100 attendees • **(604) 253-1258** • PO Box 2253, Vancouver, BC, Canada V6B 3W2

### June

**TBA: Southeast Leatherfest** *Atlanta, GA*
gay/lesbian • **(888) 285-1955** • c/o *Southeast Leatherfest*, PO Box 78974, Atlanta, GA 30357 • **EMAIL:** kyle@crl.com

### July

**17-19: International Ms. Leather Contest** *Atlanta, GA*
contest • workshops • parties • mostly women • **(402) 451-7987** • c/o *Bare Images*, 4332 Browne St., Omaha, NE 68111 • **EMAIL:** imsl@synergy.net • **WEB:** www.leatheronlin/imsl

### September

**27: Folsom St. Fair** *San Francisco, CA*
huge SM/leather street fair, topping a week of kinky events • gay/lesbian • hundreds of thousands of local & visiting kinky men & women attendees • **(415) 861-3247** • c/o *SMMILE*, 1072 Folsom St. #272, San Francisco, CA 94103

**TBA: Central Valley Leatherfest** *Fresno, CA*
gay/lesbian • **(209) 224-2368** • c/o *Knights of Malta, Yosemite Chapter*, PO Box 4162, Fresno, CA 93744

**TBA: Power Surge** *Seattle, WA*
biannual leatherwomen's SM conference • women only • **(206) 233-8429** • c/o *Seattle Madness*, Broadway Sta., PO Box 23352, Seattle, WA 98102

### October

**10-12: Living in Leather** *Portland, OR*
national conference for the leather, SM and fetish communities • gay/lesbian • 600+ attendees • $115-175 • **(614) 899-4406** • c/o *National Leather Association*, 584 Castro St., Ste. 444, San Francisco, CA 94114-2500

## CONFERENCES & RETREATS

### February

13-15: **Black Gay/Lesbian Conference**                    *Washington, DC*
gay/lesbian • **(202) 843-6786** • c/o *Nat'l Black Gay/Lesbian Leadership Forum*, 1436 'U' St. NW #200, Washington, DC 20009

21-23: **Outwrite**                    *Boston, MA*
annual national lesbian/gay writers & publishers conference • gay/lesbian • 1500+ attendees • $55-65 • **(617) 426-4469** • c/o *Bromfield St. Educational Foundation*, 25 West St., Boston, MA 02111

### April

3-5: **Readers/Writers Conference**                    *San Francisco, CA*
4th annual weekend of workshops & roundtables with queer writer & readers, at the Women's Building • **(415) 431-0891**

### May

29: **Lambda Literary Awards**                    *Chicago, IL*
the 'Lammies' are the Oscars of lesbigay writing & publishing • gay/lesbian • **(202) 462-7924** • c/o *Lambda Book Report*, PO Box 73910, Washington, DC 20056

### July

TBA: **Dyke Art Retreat Encampment (DARE)**                    *Gaston, OR*
send SASE for info • group & individual art projects • mostly women • **(503) 985-9549** • c/o *Art Springs*, 40789 SW Hummingbird Ln., Gaston, OR 97119

TBA: **Lesbian/Gay Health Conference**                    *Atlanta, GA*
health and AIDS/HIV issues facing our communities • **(202) 939-7880** • c/o *Nat'l L/G Health Assoc.*, 1407 'S' St. NW, Washington, DC 20009

### October

10-12: **National Latino/a Lesbian/Gay Conference**                    *Chicago, IL*
gay/lesbian • **(202) 466-8240** • c/o *LLEGO*, 1612 'K' St. NW #500, Washington, DC 20006 • **EMAIL:** aquilgbt@llego.org

### November

TBA: **Creating Change Conference**                    *TBA, USA*
for lesbians, gays, bisexuals, transgendered people & queers into social activism • gay/lesbian • 1500+ attendees • **(202) 332-6483 x3329** • c/o *National Gay/Lesbian Task Force*, 2320 17th St. NW, Washington, DC 20009

## WOMEN'S FESTIVALS & GATHERINGS

### March

6-8: **Lesbian Pride Weekend**                    *Denver, CO*
a weekend of parties, events & street festivals in Denver • mostly women • **(303) 778-7900** • c/o *Out Front Colorado*, 244 Washington St., Denver, CO 80203

Easter Wknd: **Gulf Coast Womyn's Festival at Camp SisterSpirit**        *New Orleans, LA*
support a celebration of womyn's land in the South! • 2 1/2 hours from New Orleans, LA • entertainment & politics • mostly women • **(601) 344-1411** • c/o *Camp SisterSpirit*, PO Box 12, Ovett, MS 39464

### May

20-25: **Campfest Memorial Day Wknd**                    *Oxford, PA*
'The Comfortable Womyn's Festival' • women only • 1400+ attendees • $200 • **(609) 694-2037/(301) 598-9035 (TTY)** • PO Box 559, Franklinville, NJ 08322 • **EMAIL:** campfest@aol.com

A Night of Comedy

Tea Dance by the Sea

Cocktail & Pool Parties

Wine Tasting Dinners

Street Fair • Picnics

Wet T-Shirt Contest

Women's Reef Adventure

Author's Book Signings

Titty Tea • Scuba Trips

Annual Film Festival

Sunset Cruises

Golf Tournament

Kayak Tour

*Hoping to see you in Key West*

# 1998

# WOMEN FEST

## SEPT 9th-15th

American Eagle
American Airlines®
1-800-433-1790
Star File # SO187AG

**Coors LIGHT.**
*The Silver Bullet.*

THE FLORIDA KEYS & KEY WEST
*come as you are*

ATLANTIC SHORES
1-800-526-3559

**O u t**
MAGAZINE

**UNIGLOBE.**
Travel Express
1-800-507-9955

For more information, send a SASE to
201 Coppitt Road #106A • Key West, FL 33040
or e-mail: jacq5645@aol.com

*(WOMENFEST is always the Wednesday
following Labor Day)*

**22-24: Wiminfest** *Albuquerque, NM*
music, comedy, art, recreation & dances • mostly women • (800) 499-5688/(505) 899-3627 • c/o Women in Movement in New Mexico (WIMINM), PO Box 80204, Albuquerque, NM 87198

**28-31: National Women's Music Festival** *Bloomington, IN*
mostly women • (317) 927-9355 • PO Box 1427-WT, Indianapolis, IN 46206

**28-31: Virginia Women's Music Festival** *Kent's Store, VA*
women only • 600 attendees • $85 • (804) 589-6542 • c/o Intouch, Rte. 2, Box 1096, Kent's Store, VA 23084 • EMAIL: http://www.erols.com/wnzday

Memorial Wknd: **Women Outdoors National Gathering** *Peterborough, NH*
camping • hiking • workshops • women only • 140+ attendees • $120-175 • (860) 688-7637 • c/o Women Outdoors, Inc., 55 Talbot Ave., Medford, MA 02155 • EMAIL: wome-nout@aol.com

**TBA: Herland Spring Retreat** *Oklahoma City, OK*
music, workshops, campfire events & potluck • boys under 10 only • $15-60 sliding scale registration • mostly women • (405) 521-9696 • c/o Herland, 2312 NW 39th, Oklahoma City, OK 73112

**TBA: Hopland Women's Festival** *Hopland, CA*
women only • (415) 641-5212 • c/o HWF, PO Box 416, Hopland, CA 95449

**TBA: Maryland Womyn's Gathering** *Maryland Line, MD*
crafts • music • camping • women only • (410) 435-3111 • c/o In Gaia's Lap, PO Box 39, Maryland Line, MD 21105

## June

**11-14: Womongathering** *Pocono Mtns, PA*
women's spirituality fest • women only • 300+ attendees • $200 • (609) 694-2037/(301) 598-9035 (TTY) • PO Box 559, Franklinville, NJ 08322

## August

**29-Sept. 1: Northeast Women's Musical Retreat** *Branford, CT*
mostly women • (860) 293-8026 • c/o NEWMR, PO Box 550, Branford, CT 06405 • EMAIL: newmr97@aol.com

**7-9: West Kootenay Women's Festival** *Nelson, BC*
music • art • entertainment • Canada's oldest women's festival • women only • 200-300 attendees • $45-65 • (250) 352-9916 • c/o W. Kootenay Women's Assoc., 420 Mill St., Nelson, BC, Canada V1L 4B8

**11-16: Michigan Womyn's Music Festival** *Walhalla, MI*
music, performances, videos, movies and more • self-help, creative, spiritual, political and other workshops • childcare • ASL interpreting • differently-abled resources • women only • (616) 757-4766/(616) 898-3707 • PO Box 22, Walhalla, MI 49458

**29-30: Women Celebrating Our Diversity** *Luisa, VA*
usually last wknd in Aug • camping • ASL interpreting • mostly women • (540) 894-5126 • c/o Twin Oaks Community, 138 Twin Oaks Rd., Luisa, VA 23093

**TBA: Sister Subverter** *Minneapolis, MN*
radical women's gathering • trans-women-friendly • women only • (612) 822-2951 • c/o Sister Subverter, 3926 Stevens Ave., Minneapolis, MN 55409

**TBA: Sisterspace Poconos Wknd** *Poconos, PA*
mostly women • (215) 476-8856/(215) 747-7565 • c/o Sisterspace of the Delaware Valley, 542-A South 48th St., Philadelphia, PA 19143

## September

**4-6: The Fall Gathering** *Ashland, OR*
annual women's camp near Oregon mountain lake • women only • 150+ attendees • $60-90 • (503) 482-2026 • c/o Womansource, PO Box 335, Ashland, OR 97520

9-15: **WomenFest** *Key West, FL*
concerts, dances, theater, fair, film festival, seminars and more • mostly women • **(305) 296-4238** • 201 Coppitt Rd. #106A, Key West, FL 33040

11-13: **Womyn's Musical & Spiritual Awareness Festival** *Lava Hot Springs, ID*
camping on the Portneuf River • workshops • entertainment • women only • **(800) 757-1233/(208) 776-5800** • c/o *Aura Soma Lava*, PO Box 129, Lava Hot Springs, ID 83246

12: **Ohio Lesbian Festival** *Colombus, OH*
women only • 2000 attendees • **(614) 267-3953** • c/o *LBA*, PO Box 82086, Colombus, OH 43202

TBA: **Iowa Women's Music Festival** *Iowa City, IA*
mostly women • **(319) 335-1486** • c/o *Prairie Voices Collective*, 130 N. Madison, Iowa City, IA 52242

TBA: **Northern Lights Womyn's Music Festival** *McGregor, MN*
day-long festival in Minnesota wilderness • mostly women • 600-1000 attendees • **(218) 722-4903** • c/o *Aurora Northland Lesbian Center*, 32 E. 1st St. Ste. 104, Duluth, MN 55802

TBA: **Northwest Women's Music Celebration** *Portland, OR*
participatory event for musicians, songwriters & singers, NOT performance-oriented • mostly women • PO Box 66842, Portland, OR 97290

## October

TBA: **SistahFest** *Malibu, CA*
women only • **(202) 843-6786** • c/o *Nat'l Black Gay/Lesbian Leadership Forum*, 1436 'U' St. NW #200, Washington, DC 20009

## November

6-8: **Fat Women's Gathering** *Bay Area, CA*
women only • **(510) 836-1153** • c/o *NAAFA Feminist Caucus*, PO Box 29614, Oakland, CA 94614

# SPIRITUAL GATHERINGS

## February

13-15: **Pantheocon** *Oakland, CA*
pagan convention • mixed gay/straight • **(510) 653-3244** • c/o *Ancient Ways*, 4075 Telegraph Ave, Oakland, CA 94609

## April

3-5: **Moonsisters Drum Camp** *Sausalito, CA*
women only • 150 attendees • $215 • **(510) 547-8386** • c/o *Moonsisters Drum Camp*, PO Box 20918, Oakland, CA 94620 • **EMAIL:** moonsistah@aol.com

## May

15-17: **A Gathering of Priestesses** *Bagley, WI*
women's spirituality conference • mostly women • **(608) 257-5858** • c/o *Of a Like Mind*, Box 6677, Madison, WI 53716

## June

14-21: **Pagan Spirit Gathering** *Mt. Horeb, WI*
summer solstice celebration in Wisconsin, primitive camping, workshops, rituals • mixed gay/straight • **(608) 924-2216** • c/o *Circle Sanctuary*, PO Box 219, Mt. Horeb, WI 53572

TBA: **Ancient Ways Festival** *Harbin Hot Springs, CA*
annual 4-day mixed gender/orientation spring festival in May or June of pan-pagan rituals, workshops and music w/ lesbian/gay campsite • mixed gay/straight • **(510) 653-3244** • c/o *Ancient Ways*, 4075 Telegraph Ave., Oakland, CA 94609

TBA: **Northern California Women's Goddess Festival**     *Occidental, CA*
workshops • music • solstice ritual • at Ocean Song, a private nature reserve • women only • $150 • **(707) 829-9820** • c/o *Black Kat Productions*, 8031 Mill Station Rd., Sebastopol, CA 95472 • **EMAIL:** kat@monitor.net

TBA: **Sappho Lesbian Witchcamp**     *Vancouver, BC*
week-long gathering • women only • 35-40 attendees • $425 • **(604) 253-7189** • c/o *Sappho*, PO Box 21510, 1850 Commercial Dr., Vancouver, BC, Canada V5N 4A0

## July

TBA: **BC Witchcamp**     *Vancouver, BC*
week-long Wiccan intensive • mixed gay/straight • 100+ attendees • $550 • **(604) 253-7195/(604) 253-7189** • c/o *BC Witchcamp*, PO Box 21510, 1850 Commercial Dr., Vancouver, BC, Canada V5N 4A0

## August

28-30: **International Goddess Festival**     *Santa Cruz, CA*
celebration of goddess culture & Beltane • workshops, rituals, dances, music • mostly women • **(510) 444-7724** • c/o *Women's Spirituality Forum*, PO Box 11363, Oakland, CA 94611

TBA: **Elderflower Womenspirit Festival**     *Mendocino, CA*
in the Mendocino Woodlands • earth-centered spirituality retreat • reasonably priced, volunteer-run • women only • **(415) 263-5719/(916) 658-0697** • PO Box 7153, Redwood City, CA 94063

## October

2-4: **Moonsisters Drum Camp**     *Sausalito, CA*
women only • 150 attendees • $215 • **(510) 547-8386** • c/o *Moonsisters Drum Camp*, PO Box 20918, Oakland, CA 94620 • **EMAIL:** moonsistah@aol.com

31: **Halloween Spiral Dance**     *Oakland, CA*
annual ritual to celebrate turning of seasons & the crone • mostly women • **(510) 444-7724** • c/o *Women's Spirituality Forum*, PO Box 11363, , Oakland, CA 94611

TBA: **Int'l Conference on Spirituality for Gays/Lesbians**     *San Francisco, CA*
gay/lesbian • 500+ attendees • **(415) 281-9377** • c/o *Q Spirit*, 3739 Balboa St., 211, San Francisco, CA 94121 • **EMAIL:** QSpirit1@aol.com

TBA: **Witches Ball**     *Columbus, OH*
weekend pagan celebration of Samhain • mixed gay/straight • **(614) 421-7557** • c/o *Salem West*, 1209 High St., Columbus, OH 43201

# KIDS' STUFF

## August

16-29: **Mountain Meadow Summer Camp**     *Philadelphia, PA*
a kids' community with a feminist conscience • girls & boys entering grades 4-9 • **(215) 848-7566** • c/o *Mountain Meadow*, 35 W. Mount Airy Ave., Philadelphia, PA 19119

TBA: **Camp Lavender Hill**     *Sierra Nevadas, CA*
one-week summer camp for kids with lesbigay parents • swimming • hiking • theater and more • kids 7-17 • 30+ attendees • $400 • **(707) 544-8150** • c/o *Camp Lavender Hill*, PO Box 11335, Santa Rosa, CA

## BOOKS & MAGAZINES

**A Different Light Bookstores** (800) 343-4002 • books • cards • calendars • videos • catalog

**Bookwoman Books** PO Box 67, Media, PA 19149 • (601) 566-2990 • books • videos • posters • free catalog

**Brigit Books** (813) 522-5775 • lesbian & feminist titles • catalog

**Dykes to Watch Out For** c/o Alison Bechdel, PO box 215, Dept. LC, Jonesville, VT 05466 • send a stamp for catalog

**Heartland Books** PO Box 1105-N, East Corinth, VT 05040 • (800) 535-3755 • lesbian & feminist titles carefully selected by lesbians who love reading • free catalog

**Lamma's** (800) 955-2662 • women's books • music • jewelry • much more

▲ **Lesbian Health News** PO Box 12121, Columbus, OH 43212 • (614) 481-7656 • see ad in mail order section

**Magus Books** 1316 SE 4th St., Minneapolis, MN 55414 • (612) 379-7669 • noon-8pm, til 5pm wknds • alternative spirituality books • also mail order

**Naiad Press, Inc.** PO Box 10543, Tallahassee, FL 32302 • (904) 539-5965/ (800) 533-1973 • lesbian books & videos

**Spinsters Ink** 32 E. 1st St. #330, Duluth, MN 55802 • (218) 727-3222/(800) 301-6860 (orders only) • feminist fiction and non-fiction publishers • catalog

**Third Side Press** 2250 W. Farragut, Chicago, IL 60625 • (800) 471-3029 • lesbian press • fiction • erotica • health • free catalog

**Thunder Road Books** PO Box 1203, Secaucus, NJ 07096 • (888) 846-3773 • lesbian mail order • discounted books • CDs • videos • call for free flyer • send $2 for catalog

**Womankind Books** 5 Kivy St., Huntington Stn., New York, NY 11746 • (516) 427-1289/(800) 648-5333 • over 5,000 books & videos • free catalog

# NLGJA ▲ We are lesbian & gay journalists dedicated to accurate & fair journalism. We are resources to our colleagues. We are dedicated to opposing newsroom bias. We support equal treatment of all employees in health & job benefits. We invite our gay, lesbian, bisexual & heterosexual colleagues to learn more about our organization.

**NLGJA** 1718 M St. NW #245, Washington DC 20036
**voice** 202.588.9888 **fax** 202.588.1818 **web** www.nlgja.org

## Womyn to Womyn

**LESBIAN/BI Correspondence Club Magazine** with 60+ pages containing over 300 very "diversified" Members, photo section, poetry, articles, recipes, book reviews, directory listings of wimmins resources/shops/merchandise/health/travel/support groups & much more including our own "Dear W toW" advice column. CONFIDENTIAL using CODE numbers & mail forwarding. Send U.S. $4.00 chk/mo OR $4.50 IMO for a "discreetly" mailed 60+ page Issue of WtoW magazine & info. to:

**WtoW, 110 Cummings Lane, Rison, AR 71665 (870) 325-7006**

## Lesbian Health News

a bimonthly newsletter
health, news & views
personal & professional articles welcome

PO Box 12121
Columbus, OH 43212
614.481.7656

subscription:
$12-$25 year
$2 sample copy

free to incarcerated & institutionalized women

*Jewelry by*
**Poncé**

*Serving our community since 1983*

UNCONDITIONAL 30-DAY GUARANTEE
Specializing in: Commitment Rings • Custom
Designs • White & Yellow 14K & 18K
Leather Pride • Exotic Body Jewelry •
Pendants • Earrings • Watches • Inlay Stone
Rings (onyx, lapis) • Chains • Bracelets • Silver

*for info/free brochure call:*
**1-800-969-RING**

Visit our store in Laguna Beach, CA or our
Web site at www.jewelrybyponce.com/1
**WHOLESALE INQUIRIES WELCOME**

**Women in the Wilderness** 566 Ottawa Ave., St. Paul, MN 55107 • (612) 227-2284 • books, etc. for outdoorswomen and armchair adventurers

**Women Serving Women** PO Box 644, Seagoville, TX 75159 • (972) 287-5029 • lesbians galore! • lesbian books • pride products • travel consultants • free catalog

▲ **Womyn to Womyn** 110 Cummings Ln., Rison, AR 71665 • (870) 325-7006 • nat'l magazine w/ correspondence club for lesbian/bi-women (see ad in back mail order section)

## JEWELRY

**Bande Designs** 7102 Castor Ave., Philadelphia, PA 19149 • womyn's jewelry • send $1 for catalog

▲ **Jewelry by Ponce** 219 N. Broadway #331, Laguna Beach, CA • (714) 494-1399/(800) 969-7464 • specializing in commitment rings • free brochure

**Lavana Shurtliff Jewelry** (517) 773-3801 • flame-worked glass jewelry • catalog

**Lielin West Jewelers** PO Box 733, Benicia, CA 94510 • (707) 745-9000 • women's imagery in precious metals

**Lizzie Brown/Pleiades** PO Box 389, Brimfield, MA 01010 • (413) 245-9484 • woman-identified jewelry

**Sappho Studios** PO Box 48365, Watauga, TX 76148 • jewelry • gifts • cards • free catalog • see display ad

**Sumiche** PO Box 428, Waterville, OR 97489 • (541) 896-9841 • custom jewelry • commitment rings

## CLOTHING

**Banshee Designs** 923 SE 37th Ave., Portland, OR 97214 • 'garments for goddesses of every size' • adult sizes to 8X • send SASE with 55¢ postage for catalog

**Different Voices** (800) 824-3915 • gifts • T-shirts • pridewear • free catalog

**Dirt Roads and Damsels** 1457 Nelson St., Lakewood, CO 80215 • (303) 232-8298 • women-owned fly fishing & apparel company

**GLADrags** PO Box 722334, San Diego, CA 92172 • (619) 578-2155/ (888) GLADS4U • tasteful casualwear for the community • catalog

**Herspective** PO Box 8977, Emeryville, CA 94662 • (510) 653-2523 • t-shirts • gifts • catalog